SO-BFD-964

"*On Hallowed Ground* is an extraordinarily powerful, true story and a fresh Korean War history. Drawing on official records, letters, and written and oral recollections, it places readers in the middle of wrenching crosscurrents of emotion as American soldiers fight one of the crucial last battles of a stalemated war."
—Gen. Gordon R. Sullivan, USA (Ret.), chief of staff, U.S. Army, 1991–95, president, Association of the U.S. Army

"Bill McWilliams's stirring story will ensure that these brave soldiers of the Forgotten War will not be forgotten by the soldiers of today's generation."
—Gen. Carl E. Vuono, USA (Ret.), chief of staff, U.S. Army, 1987–91

"Well researched and well written, this book describes an inspiring chapter in American military history."
—Gen. John Wickham, USA (Ret.), commander-in-chief, UNC and ROK-US Combined forces in Korea, 1979–82, chief of staff, U.S. Army, 1983–87

"With its realistic accounts of brutal hand-to-hand fighting, devastating artillery and mortar barrages, day and night counterattacks, and small victories and defeats, this book offers invaluable lessons of small unit combat, which at the end of the day is where battles are won and lost."
—Gen. Art Brown, USA (Ret.), vice chief of staff, U.S. Army, 1987–89

"Bill McWilliams brilliantly reveals the extraordinary courage of those who fought the final, bitter, bloody, costly days of the Korean War while capturing important lessons about war, national and military policies, and the effects of those policies on battlefield decisions. Those lessons of a half century ago are just as applicable today."
—Gen. Jack I. Gregory, USAF (Ret.), chief of staff, Combined Forces Command, Korea, 1985–86, commander-in-chief, Pacific Air Forces, 1986–88

"As an airman, my perspective of combat was always above the mud and mire. *On Hallowed Ground* relates the true value of the soldier and gun to our overall military power. These stirring accounts bring back those final and bitter days of the war and the sacrifices made by those valiant riflemen."
—Lt. Gen. Walter D. Druen, Jr., USAF (Ret.), fighter pilot in Korea, 1952–53

An Association of the U.S. Army Book

ON HALLOWED GROUND

The Last Battle for Pork Chop Hill

BILL McWILLIAMS

Berkley Caliber Books, New York

Most Berkley Books are available at special quantity discounts for bulk purchases for sales promotions, premiums, fund-raising, or educational use. Special books, or book excerpts, can also be created to fit specific needs.

For details, write: Special Markets, The Berkley Publishing Group, 375 Hudson Street, New York, New York 10014.

A Berkley Caliber Book
Published by The Berkley Publishing Group
A division of Penguin Group (USA) Inc.
375 Hudson Street
New York, NY 10014

Copyright © 2004 by Bill McWilliams
Cover design by Erica Tricario
Cover photo © by Bettman/CORBIS

This book, or parts thereof, may not be reproduced in any form without permission. The scanning, uploading, and distribution of this book via the Internet or via any other means without the permission of the publisher is illegal and punishable by law. Please purchase only authorized electronic editions, and do not participate in or encourage electronic piracy of copyrighted materials. Your support of the author's rights is appreciated.

Naval Institute Press hardcover edition: 2004
Berkley Caliber trade paperback edition: October 2004

ISBN: 0-425-19926-6

Visit our website at www.penguin.com

This book has been cataloged by the Library of Congress

10 9 8 7 6 5 4 3 2 1

TO THE AMERICAN SOLDIER

If victory is long in coming, the men's weapons will grow dull and their ardor dampened. . . . In all history, there is no instance of a country having benefited from prolonged warfare.

Sun Tzu, *The Art of War*

The soldier above all other people, prays for peace, for he must bear the scars and deepest wounds of war.

Douglas MacArthur

CONTENTS

FOREWORD

In his work *On Hallowed Ground: The Last Battle for Pork Chop Hill,* Bill McWilliams brings readers another, extraordinarily powerful history and true story from the Korean War. Evoking all the crosscurrents of emotion from a frustrating, bitter, bloody, and stalemated conflict, he takes us onto outpost Pork Chop in July 1953, into the trenches and bunkers, alongside the men of the 7th Infantry Division's 17th and 32nd Infantry Regiments, and their supporting units, as they withstand repeated assaults by units of the Chinese Communist Forces' 23rd Army three weeks before the armistice.

Meticulously researched and told in the words of people who lived the events, the book resurrects long-dormant memories and searing images from a war not well understood—memories of events almost lost in history's shadows and the GIs' battlefield-borne cliché, "the forgotten war."

Filled with individual soldiers' accounts of small victories and defeats, tragedy, brutality, fear, horror, courage, devotion, and valor, in the fury and chaos of war, the book tells of a crucial battle and its many never-before-told stories—the recollections and writings of authentic and unsung heroes and their determined, five-day struggle to hold outpost Pork Chop at all costs. For those who have never fought in war or witnessed firsthand war's devastation as seen and felt by the GIs, noncommissioned officers, and junior officers, this book contains powerful examples of the responsibilities soldiers of the Korean War carried on the battlefield. The descriptions of battles in which they fought, and men's reactions to war, are vivid and starkly realistic.

Through official, then-secret command reports and command guidance, written and oral recollections, intelligence summaries and debriefings, battle records boards, and personal letters, the war and the battle for Pork Chop come alive. We learn how and why decisions were made, orders given, plans prepared, units moved—and then committed to the battle in repeated attempts to defend against and drive off Pork Chop, a brave, doggedly determined enemy. We see and hear the riflemen, machine gunners, squad leaders, platoon sergeants, battalion commanders, and division commanders act and speak in the furious seesaw struggle for the small, one-company-sized outpost.

From the privates, corporals, sergeants, lieutenants, and on up the chain of command to the commander-in-chief in Washington, D.C., we learn of brave, courageous, and fallible men, an increasingly controversial war, heavy casualties, contentious truce-negotiation issues, and their effects on battlefield decisions as well as the length and conduct of the war.

Generally chronological in structure, the narrative summarizes the early phases of the conflict: the North Koreans' surprise assault across the thirty-eighth parallel and their drive to push the unprepared Americans and South Koreans off the peninsula, the strategic surprise at Inchon, breakout from the Pusan Perimeter, the push to the Yalu River, and the Chinese Communists' massive intervention and the UN's fighting withdrawal southward. Then comes the turnaround, changed strategy, and counteroffensives of the UN's once badly mauled ground forces, the start of truce negotiations, the transition to stalemated battlefields, and the Communist Chinese Forces' final five months of bloody thrusts at the 7th Division and Pork Chop Hill.

As the story unfolds, we learn of the key issues which dragged out the truce negotiations, ultimately brought increasing constraints on field commanders, and virtually ended UN offensive operations on the ground. We see clearly how the transition to a military policy of "active defense" and the intense desire to hold down casualties stifled battlefield initiative, eventually yielded a struggle that became a throwback to World War I trench and bunker warfare, and, ironically, in the final months of the war resulted in far greater casualties.

Words like "defense in depth," "outposts," "outpost lines of resistance" (OPLR), and "main lines of resistance" (MLR) come alive. We learn of stunning surprises in Chinese and American infantry assaults; night and day counterattacks through withering artillery, mortar, automatic weapons, and small-arms fire; outguards and listening posts (LPs); brutal hand-to-hand fighting in the trenches and bunkers; ambush and reconnaissance patrols; artillery and mortar forward observers and their observation posts (OPs), fire missions, fire-control centers, fire "on position," time-on-target and "flash-fires"; combat engineers and their dangerous missions supporting the other combat arms, combat support, and combat service support units; tanks and armored personnel carriers (APCs) in the defense; and medics as they treat the wounded and dying and evacuate them from Pork Chop Hill to aid stations and hospitals.

We are with senior commanders and their key staff members during the battle when they ride to the outpost on APCs to assess the situation first-hand, learn the troops' resupply needs, and make decisions to relieve and replace battle-weary, casualty-depleted units—or take personal command of the outpost's defense. We are at command conferences when key decisions are made, and we are there when soldiers assist the wounded and carry the dead from the field. We also see the sharp contrasts between life and death on the line and the "garrison life" evident in units south of the main line of resistance.

In letters we read the innermost thoughts of young officers carrying the heavy responsibilities of life and death on the battlefield, and in the battle and war's aftermath the aching, poignant, lifetime effects on wives and families of men killed, wounded, and missing in action. The experiences and writings of Lt. Richard T. Shea, Jr., and Lt. Richard G. Inman, and the courage and loving devotion of their wives and families, bring balance and poignant reality to lives of service, which tragically all too often require the ultimate sacrifice.

These were America's citizen and professional soldiers of the 7th Infantry Division, draftees and volunteers, and their allies serving with the division: Republic of Korea soldiers integrated into American units; the Colombian and Ethiopian Battalions attached to the 7th; and Korean Service Corps Regiments, the thousands of Korean men who toiled and risked their lives, laboring unarmed to move supplies and ammunition, repair roads, build fortifications, retrieve the bodies of the dead, and rebuild Pork Chop's defenses, thus freeing more of soldiers' time for training, fighting, and surviving.

The American soldiers were fighting a protracted war which had diminishing support at home in the United States. At the same time, on the ground, most soldiers understood some type of peace was in the offing, and each could reasonably ask, would he be the last to die? Despite these conditions, American soldiers on Pork Chop time and time again responded to the orders of their junior officers and noncommissioned officers in the finest traditions of our military service.

In spite of the stalemated, unresolved conflict on the Korean peninsula, and America's half-century standing guard with the Republic of Korea against the totalitarian regime to the north, it's clear the United States, South Korea, and our UN allies during that war brought enormous gains to the noble causes of freedom and democracy in Northeast Asia. Since the war, the Republic of Korea has become a contributing and respected member of the family of nations and has accomplished astounding economic growth. *On Hallowed Ground* marks our collective achievements and stands as a memorable tribute to those who fought and gave their lives in the Korean War—a celebration of all that is good and right about the American soldier, and all Americans who lend their sons and daughters in defense of our nation, democracy, and free peoples everywhere.

Robert W. Sennewald
General U.S. Army (Ret.)
Former commander-in-chief,
United Nations Command and
the Combined Forces Command
(1982–1984)

ACKNOWLEDGMENTS

Researching history has a way of leading writers from one wonderful story to another. While researching *A Return to Glory,* a history and true story of the United States Military Academy, its cadets, graduates, and their honor code during the Korean War, I learned that two 1952 graduates had been killed in action two days apart in the last month of the war. Both were in the 17th Infantry Regiment. They were Lt. Richard T. Shea, Jr., of Ports-mouth, Virginia, and Lt. Richard G. Inman from Vincennes, Indiana. Additional work revealed they both were on Pork Chop Hill, in the same infantry battalion (the 1st of the 17th), in the same battle, and the full story of the battle had never been told in book form. Both men received posthumous awards for valor and heroism, Lieutenant Shea the Medal of Honor, Lieutenant Inman the Silver Star.

Though I researched and wrote a condensed version of the "Last Battle for Pork Chop Hill," and included it in *A Return to Glory* to shed more light on the roles of West Point graduates in the Korean War, the power and significance of the story continued to haunt and intrigue me. Plainly said, I could not let go of what I had encountered. Subsequently, I elected to broaden and deepen research into the July battle, and expand the condensed story into a book, emphasizing soldiers' stories, while, to the degree possible, attempting to answer the numerous questions such an event would raise.

The journey to Pork Chop Hill was not easy, but it certainly was far less difficult and painful than the roads taken by the men who fought there. It was from interviews, letters, written recollections, and e-mails by men who fought on "the Chop," as some called it, as well as artillerymen, forward observers, radio operators, former commanders, and medics, that I received the greatest inspiration and continuing drive to provide readers a complete account of the battle, an account that comes as close to the truth as a half-century's passage will allow.

To find all the pieces, and recreate the mosaic of July 1953's Pork Chop, enthusiastic support, kindness, courtesy, time, and energy came from numerous sources. Underlying the written recollections and interviews of eyewitnesses and participants in the battle was ground-breaking work by several authors and military writers, some of whom are no longer living. To them I owe a debt of everlasting gratitude.

First is the late Col. William R. Kintner, a 1940 Military Academy graduate who served in World War II and in Korea as the commander of the 3rd Battalion, 17th Infantry Regiment, in a period just prior to the battle. In March 1955, the *Army Combat Forces Journal* published an article titled "Pork Chop," written by Colonel Kintner. MacPherson Conner, a former platoon leader in Easy Company, 32d Infantry Regiment, provided me a copy of the article, which is a condensed account of the battle. The article became the foundation on which additional extensive research was based. The genesis of this project owes much to the life and service of Colonel Kintner.

Famed military historian Samuel L. A. Marshall wrote and published his classic work *Pork Chop Hill* shortly after interviewing participants in the 16–18 April battle for the outpost, then reconstructed and analyzed the engagement. His presence among the men of the 7th Infantry who fought the second battle; his thoughtful, technical, and human study of the event; and the writing which flowed from his research were invaluable in helping me understand the bitter July struggle. His work also established bases for comparisons between the March, April, and July battles and introduced me to the Ethiopian Battalion.

Author Clay Blair's marvelous history, *The Forgotten War,* provided an outstanding account of the first eighteen months of the war and a clear understanding of the more than two years of truce negotiations. I am deeply indebted to Blair and his monumental work, which painted a clear picture of the Korean War down to the battalion level.

Joseph E. Gonsalves, a former member of Easy Company, 17th Infantry Regiment, authored the *Battle at the 38th Parallel: Surviving the Peace Talks in Panmunjom* (2001). This excellent work, a history of Easy Company in the Korean War, helped me more fully understand the American soldier and the infantry companies of that era. His book was full of data, written recollections, personal letters, and other information offering an entirely different perspective of the war than found in other sources. In addition, Joe Gonsalves repeatedly volunteered his time, energy, research sources, advice, and counsel in helping me find specific research materials and Pork Chop Hill veterans to interview. I will never be able to adequately thank Joe for his kind, considerate, and enthusiastic support.

Robert M. Euwer, author, former forward observer and member of the 15th Anti-Aircraft Artillery Battalion in the 7th Division, and tireless worker for the Korean War Memorial in Washington, D.C., wrote and published *No Longer Forgotten: The Korean War and Its Memorial.* He has been equally tireless in urging publication of this book. Not only did Bob's book contain valuable material to help tell the story of Pork Chop Hill, but he graciously gave me permission to use selected maps, photographs, and other material not available elsewhere. Without his warm encouragement and assistance, this project could not have been completed.

Dale W. Cain, Sr., wrote *Korea: The Longest War,* which was published in 1997, in South Korea only, by the Ministry of Patriots and Veterans Affairs in the Republic of Korea. Dale, a wonderful gentleman and former member of Able Company of the 17th Regiment, graciously gave me a copy and permission to use material from the work. A small part of his story as a young soldier in Korea is in this work, along with a number of participants' accounts from his book, but his story, and kindness and consideration in answering my many questions, were crucial factors in my finally determining I should press ahead with this project.

James A. Brettell, Richard W. White, David L. Bills, and James R. Goudy provided comprehensive written recollections, photographs, and extensive interviews to capture the marvelous story of the 13th (Combat) Engineer Battalion's role in the final battle for Pork Chop. John W. Phillips, James N. Butcher, and Raymond Clark sent written recollections, some of which they had published over the years, and a large number of names of living Pork Chop veterans for possible interviews. Ronald K. Freedman, a former artillery forward observer, through his interview and written recollections, provided excellent material and connected me with Raymond Barry, an artillery liaison officer who miraculously survived critical, life-threatening wounds the final day of the battle.

Juan Raigoza, former artillery liaison officer to the Ethiopian Battalion, gave extraordinary insight into the battalion's officers and men as a fighting unit, as well as the lives their soldiers led, and the battalion's artillery targeting procedures. Joseph S. Kimmitt, Bill Roemer, Kenneth Swift, Robert J. Schaefer, Earl C. Acuff, Walter B. Russell, and Robert C. Hollander provided various pieces to the puzzle, including artillery and infantry operations, training, and coordination; division battle records boards; and signal communications. Walt Russell and James Butcher gave new insights into the April battle for Pork Chop and events not previously recorded. In addition, Bob Schaefer provided outstanding color photographs of Pork Chop and the area in which the 7th Division was fighting.

Kevin G. Quinn, in the midst of research for a book he is writing, took time out while in the National Archives to search for and retrieve invaluable nominating documents and related materials regarding the awards of four Distinguished Service Crosses to men who fought on Pork Chop Hill. The documents' contents were filled with facts, details, and eyewitness testimony, permitting me to corroborate other information important to the work while bringing the story to life.

Institutional contributors to this project were numerous, and without them the manuscript would have been impossible to complete. All were kind, thoughtful, courteous, and responsive. The National Archives' Rebecca Lentz Collier, Ruth Beamon, Kenneth D. Schlessinger, David A. Giordano, and Lee A. Gladwin found, retrieved, copied, and mailed numerous important command reports, other documents, and candidate photographs to help tell the story. The U.S. Army Military History Institute, Diane Jacob in the Virginia Military Institute Archives, the United States Military Academy Library Archives and Special Collections Division, the Idaho State Historical Society, and the Boise Public Library also provided documents, newspaper clippings, and magazine articles and pointed me toward other sources to research.

Next and for always, this story was given life by those who lived it or were close to the people who "had gone before." I will never forget as long as I live the magnificent men of Pork Chop Hill—and their wives and families. They were kind, thoughtful, and considerate in sharing their time and their sometimes terribly difficult, emotional recollections in telephone or personal interviews, letters, faxes, e-mails, and photographs. More than fifty men agreed to interviews, and every single one provided recollections and information that brought substance, enthusiasm, and excitement to the work and breathed life into the story. They were—and are—courageous, devoted soldiers and never-to-be-forgotten men who gave their all in Korea.

Their names are listed in the bibliography in the section titled "Interviews with the Author."

I particularly want to acknowledge three beautiful ladies and some magnificent, former soldiers and one airman of the Korean War who shared memories that often were bittersweet, if not terribly painful. All were inspirations. Joyce E. Himka, the former Joyce Riemann Shea; the late Barbara Colby, formerly Barbara Kipp Inman; and Mary Jo Inman Vermillion, sister of Richard G. Inman, told of husbands and a brother who gave "their last full measure of devotion" on the hills of Korea. Robert Inman, Richard's brother, also shared poignant, loving memories of times joyful and sad. William J. "Pat" Ryan, West Point class of 1951, told of his experiences while serving in the Air Force in three wars, including an important mission "near Old Baldy" the night of 3 July 1953.

David R. Hughes, former company commander, King Company, 7th Cavalry Regiment, 1st Cavalry Division, was an inspiration. His deep respect and affection for the American soldier, the GIs, the citizen-soldiers, shined like a beacon, turning me toward the men who, for half a century, have carried in their memories countless untold stories of courage, devotion, and heroism.

To Joyce Maddox, Amy Moore, and Warwick House Publishing for producing the maps, sketches, and tables used in this work—thank you.

My deep and sincere appreciation to Gen. Robert Sennewald, United States Army (Ret.), for reviewing the manuscript and providing the foreword—and to the Association of the United States Army and the Naval Institute Press for sponsoring and publishing this work. I am honored for having had their confidence and support.

For my patient, loving, and supportive wife, Veronica, who has stood by me and accepted all the "ups and downs" a large, complex writing project inevitably stirs—my deepest appreciation, enduring love, and adoration.

I

THE FIRST HALF

A War of Maneuver

THE KOREAN WAR WAS LIKE NO OTHER WAR AMERICA HAD FOUGHT
since the Declaration of Independence. First labeled a "police action" by
President Harry S. Truman, a label he would come to regret, later called a
"limited war" and, finally, "the forgotten war," to the American soldier, both
the citizen-soldier and the professional, it was war. All of it. Pure war. Pure
hell. A special kind of hell.

Early on, the bitter fighting earned from the American GI the label "the
forgotten war," which preceded the not so endearing description, "yo-yo
war." The latter term emerged from the GI's vernacular the first eighteen
months, as the contending armies swept down, up, down, and up the Korean
peninsula and ground to a halt near its waist, north of Seoul, the Republic
of Korea's capital.

A 27 August 1951 letter from Lt. David R. Hughes eloquently expressed
one young professional soldier's thoughts about life and death on the ever-
changing line between opposing forces during the first half of the war. He
was the company commander, K Company, 3d Battalion, 7th Cavalry Regiment, 1st Cavalry Division, and a graduate in the United States Military

Academy's class of 1950, the West Point class which would earn the painful distinction of being the most bloodied of all academy classes whose members fought in the "Land of the Morning Calm." By August 1951, he was a veteran, having entered the war in the first days of November, in far North Korea, as a K Company infantry platoon leader:

Again from Korea. Again from a mountain top.

Yesterday I took out a patrol. It was Sunday . . . a Sunday without services . . . a Sunday out in that troubled land that lies between two armies. There is no room for a church on our misty hill in this lonely land of many battles.

No, the day seemed only like a wet, slick day anywhere, and I wondered, as we moved down the slopes to seek out our enemies, why the feeling of Sunday had so completely deserted me. But the ridges, and the woods, and brush, soon pulled our bodies into a shallow sort of fatigue, and thinking became tiresome. We wandered far, under the fitful skies.

Then, a group of Chinese who had been waiting, opened up and shot our lead man . . . and we suddenly became involved in a short, sharp struggle of grenades and bullets. But we, at a disadvantage, had to pull back without our dead soldier.

Yet we knew what we had to do, and soon we set out again to risk much to get to him. This time we moved—not to gain knowledge, for we knew about our foe—not for ground, for we were turning back— not for glory, for we had been there a long, long time. We returned into a holocaust of bullets to recover the symbol of someone who had been so alive a short while before—and we returned in the hope that we, too, would be treated in the same way, were we ever there.

We set out, taut in every nerve, moving in a high-tension sort of way. I happened to look at the wet, bony wrist of someone beside me. He gripped his rifle with a chalky hand. Flesh and caution, against the savagery of bullets and sharp little fragments. . . .

We set out . . . an intense group of men . . . under that terrible . . . broken sound of artillery, and the snicker of machine guns in the bushes. Then, in a final, fearful second of confusion—in a second of awful silence, one gutty private crawled up, and with the last ounce of his courage, pulled our soldier back to us.

We had succeeded. We started back, rubbery legged and very tired . . . feeling a little better, a little more certain there would be a tomorrow.

We had done something important. We were bringing our soldier with us.

Then it was night, and the rain was soft again. We drew up on a nameless ridge and dug into the black earth to wait for the enemy, or for the dawn. The fog moved in among the trees. I sat for a long time looking at the end of the world out there to the north.

Nine months in a muddy, forgotten war where men still come forth in a blaze of courage. Where men still go out on patrol, limping from old patrols and old wars.

Weary, jagged war where men go up the same hill twice, three times, four times, no less scared, no less immune but much older and much more tired. A raggedy war of worn hopes of rotation, and bright faces of green youngsters in new boots. A soldier's war of worthy men—of patient men—of grim men—of dignified men.

A sergeant sat beside me. For him, twelve months in the same company, in the same platoon, meeting the same life and death each day. Rest? Five days, he said, in Japan, three days in Seoul . . . and three hundred and fifty-seven days on this ridge! Now he sat looking, as I was, at the same end of the world to the north.

Nine months, and I am a Company Commander now, with the frowning weight of many men and many battles to carry. A different, older feeling than of a platoon leader.

New men . . . I must calm them, teach them, fight them, send them home whole and proud . . . or broken and quiet. But get them home. Then wait for new replacements so the gap can be filled here, that gun can be operated over there.

There is much work to be done. I must put this man where he belongs, and I must send many men where no man belongs. I must work harder and laugh merrier . . . and answer that mother's letter to tell her of her lost son. Yes, I was there . . . I heard him speak . . . I saw him die. So, in many ways, I must write the epitaph to many families.

There is always that decision to make as to whether a man is malingering or sick . . . whether to send him out for his own sake, and for another's protection, or return him for a necessary rest. And one must never be wrong.

One must be ready and willing, always, to give his life for the least of his men.

Perhaps that is the most worthwhile part of all this . . . the tangible sacrifice that an infantryman, a soldier, can understand.

I see these things still I am slave
When banners flaunt and bugles blow
Content to fill a soldier's grave
For reasons I shall never know

Now it is raining again. The scrawny tents on the line are dark and wet, and the enemy is restlessly probing. It will not be a quiet night.[1]

When the line between the two armies stabilized near and across Korea's thirty-eighth parallel in October 1951, the term "half-war" became another commonly used term, although from another perspective, on the home front it had been a "half-war" from the beginning. Half the American population was daily interested in, affected by, or directly involved in the war in faraway Northeast Asia. For the other half of the American populace, it was life and business as usual. Guns and butter.

As for President Truman's administration, its attention was justifiably divided between Europe, with the cold war threat imposed by the Union of Soviet Socialist Republics and its allied East European client states, and Asia, with the North Koreans and their Chinese allies. The North Koreans and Chinese were the growing communist threat rearing its head in Asia. The fear of a possible surprise attack initiated by the Soviets to begin World War III was a valid security issue for the the American government. The war in Korea, backed by Soviet arms and advisers as well as Soviet pilots flying air combat missions, and Communist Chinese "volunteers" numbering in the hundreds of thousands, was strongly believed by key figures in the administration to be a possible strategic diversion preparatory to the main thrust into a Europe still recovering from the ravages of World War II. America's European Allies were not anxious to become embroiled in a World War III, or anything that might remotely lead to another worldwide conflagration.

Not Prepared to Fight

In Korea, among GIs, "yo-yo war" was an apt name. For Republic of Korea (ROK) and American soldiers, and, later, forces from seventeen other United Nations member states, the first eighteen months in Korea were marked by vicious fighting which surged up and down the peninsula. From 25 June until 15 September 1950, for United Nations forces, primarily ROK and American, it was the kind of war all soldiers despise: scrambling to piece together divisions, regiments, battalions, and companies that were not combat ready; a harried rush to the battlefield; confidence overflowing while underrating a disciplined, determined, well-trained and -equipped enemy; then stinging defeat, withdrawal, retreat, sometimes "bug out," delay, block, and in nearly every clash with the rapidly advancing North Korean Peoples Army (NKPA), the In Min Gun, heavy casualties:

According to Gen. William F. Dean, who commanded [the lead elements of the 24th Infantry Division] in the early days in Korea, they had come "fat and happy in occupation billets, complete with Japanese girlfriends, plenty of beer and servants to shine their boots." These were not the same battle-hardened troops who had swept across the Pacific and defeated the elite Japanese units in an endless series of bitter struggles in tiny island outposts. Fewer then one in six had seen combat; many had been lured into the service after the war by recruiting officers promising an ideal way to get out of small-town America and see the world. "They had enlisted," wrote one company commander, T. R. Fehrenbach, "for every reason known to man except to fight." Suddenly, after the invasion there was a desperate need for manpower. Men on their way back to America to the stockade, were reprieved and marched, still in handcuffs, to Yokohama. They would be allowed to fight in Korea as a means of clearing their records. Only as they boarded the planes and ships on their way to Korea were their handcuffs removed. When word of the North Korean invasion reached members of the 34th Infantry Regiment in Japan, the first reaction was, "Where's Korea?" The next was, "Let the gooks kill each other off." On the night of June 30, Lt. Col. Charles B. (Brad) Smith, commanding officer of the 1st Battalion, 24th Division, was called by his commanding officer and told to take his battalion to Korea. At the airport, General Dean told Smith his orders were simple: "When you get to Pusan head for Taejon. We want you to stop the North Koreans as far from Pusan as we can. Block the main road as far North as possible. Contact General Church [the division commander, who had flown from Tokyo to Taejon in the middle of the night].

"If you can't locate him, go to Taejon and beyond if you can. Sorry I can't give you any more information. That's all I've got. Good luck to you and God bless you and your men."[2]

Col. John H. ("Iron Mike") Michaelis, commander of the legendary 27th Infantry Regiment's Wolfhounds and one of the early heroes of the war, had another perspective. American troops did not know their weapons or even the basics of infantry life and survival:

> They'd spent a lot of time listening to lectures on the differences between communism and Americanism and not enough time crawling on their bellies on maneuvers with live ammunition singing over them. They'd been nursed and coddled, told to drive safely, to buy War Bonds, to give to the Red Cross, to avoid VD, to write home to mother—when someone ought to have been telling them how to clear a machine gun when it jams.
>
>> "Michaelis . . . [noticed] that the American soldiers had become prisoners of their own hardware or, in his words, 'so damn road bound that they'd lost the use of their legs. Send out a patrol on a scouting mission and they load up in a three-quarter-ton truck and start riding down the highway.'"[3]

To make matters worse, most of the commanders of American units in the early fighting in Korea were men who fought in Europe. American soldiers were not the only ones roadbound and not conditioned to fight the battles for the hills of Korea—the high ground. With some few exceptions, the same could be said of their commanders. And equally important, both soldiers and their commanders were unaccustomed to fighting guerrillas who would infiltrate their flanks and strike in their rear. Guerrilla warfare mixed with conventional warfare was the way of both the North Koreans and Chinese. The initial lack of American preparedness to fight front and rear at the same time exacted a tragic toll in the early days of the war.

Trading Space for Time

Thus began those first three months, when the South Koreans and Americans were fighting a desperate defensive war. By 28 June, Seoul had fallen. In the first five days, the ROKs, and then the Americans, promptly committed and began building up air and naval support, of necessity buying time while the overpowered ROK Army, and soon thereafter units of the

U.S. Eighth Army, gave ground toward the shrinking toehold, later dubbed the "Pusan Perimeter" by the press. After five days, in which President Truman and his Cabinet were reaching key decisions, including the decision to commit ground forces to the fight, the U.S. Army began committing inexperienced, ill-equipped, and woefully undertrained combat units as rapidly as possible. "Task Force Smith," as Brad Smith's reinforced battalion was called, was the lead element of the 24th Infantry Division, the first American division to enter the desperate fight to hold the lower half of the Korean peninsula. Then came the 25th Infantry Division. At the same time the U.S. Army was filling up and training divisions to follow the 24th and 25th Divisions into the ground war. Next came the 1st Cavalry Division, then the 7th Infantry Division, at Inchon.

While delaying and giving ground, the race was on to avoid another debacle similar to the defense of the Bataan Peninsula, the disastrous, early World War II defeat of American and Philippine units at the hands of the Japanese Empire on the main island of Luzon. To avoid a similar fate in Korea, there was an urgent need to reinforce and build solid, offensive-capable strength inside the rapidly shrinking perimeter.

When the Korean War started, the American Eighth Army, weakened by the sharp, post–World War II reduction in the U.S. Armed Forces, was composed of four badly understrength divisions stationed in Japan. The Department of the Army, working with the ROK government and the Eighth Army, rushed to fill the Eighth's four divisions with Korean Augmentees to the United States Army (KATUSAs) at the same time stripping combat experienced American noncommissioned officers from other units, such as the 1st Cavalry, to fill leadership positions in the first two divisions deploying to engage the NKPA—and backfilling the other two divisions with NCO and officer replacements sent from units elsewhere: "The 1st Cavalry Division began landing unopposed and piecemeal at Pohang on 18 July. 'Johnnie' Walker warmly welcomed the 1st Cav [and 'Hap' Gay] into the Eighth Army. That [the division] had been gutted of 750 key non-coms to beef up the 24th Division and now numbered only 11,000 men (7,500 below full wartime strength) was apparently discounted."[4]

Maj. Gen. Hobart R. "Hap" Gay, the 1st Cavalry commander, had been Gen. George S. Patton's chief of staff in Patton's Third Army in Europe in World War II and was riding in the car with Patton when the accident that proved fatal for the brilliant tactician and mercurial leader occurred. Gay unabashedly boosted Walker to Patton while Patton's chief of staff and the two had become Patton's closest lieutenants. "The old Third Army cohorts Walker and Gay were back in harness, working another battlefield."[5]

By 26 July, less than a month after the American ground forces had entered the fight, and just eight days after the 1st Cavalry had come ashore at Pohang, General Walker conceded his holding actions north and west of the Naktong River might not succeed. Though he emphatically told his staff there would be no talk of a withdrawal, he also directed them to develop a plan to pull back behind the Naktong River. For the first time there was quiet talk in his staff there might indeed be another Dunkirk in the offing. The reference was to the defeat and emergency evacuation of the British Expeditionary Forces from the European continent in early World War II, when the German Blitzkrieg stormed through Holland, Belgium, and France, cutting off and pinning the British against the English Channel in the port and on the beaches of Dunkirk.[6]

Walker was on a short tether with General MacArthur's General Headquarters (GHQ) in Japan, and MacArthur would have none of Walker's planned withdrawal to the Naktong River line. When Walker called MacArthur's chief of staff, Maj. Gen. Ned Almond, seven hundred miles away in Japan to ask permission to pull behind the Naktong and displace the Eighth's headquarters back to Pusan, Almond, after hanging up the phone, went immediately to see MacArthur to bring the pessimistic assessment from Walker. He suggested the pullbacks could have devastating effects on the entire Eighth Army and could result in another Dunkirk. He recommended MacArthur and some GHQ staff members fly to Korea and personally assess the circumstances and confer with their field commander.

MacArthur agreed and about ten o'clock the next morning, 27 July, MacArthur and a few of his staff members, including Almond, arrived in Taegu. The three senior officers conferred together privately for an hour and a half, and as usual, MacArthur did most of the talking. He laid out his plans for the near term. The 2d Infantry Division, the Marine Regimental Combat Team (RCT), and the Army's 5th RCT from Hawaii would soon arrive in Pusan to reinforce the perimeter. Yet another plan was taking shape for a landing at Inchon. "There would be no Dunkirk in Korea." Walker came out of the meeting chastened.[7]

Stand or Die

Finally, when the shrinking Pusan perimeter was squeezed small and tight, Walker, under pressure from General MacArthur, on 29 July called on his three division commanders and their staffs, one location at a time. He gave them each a pep talk, which, as matters turned out, was not well received. His talk became famous—or infamous—as Walker's "stand or die" speech. After outlining the reinforcements they would soon receive, he went on to say,

> We are fighting a battle against time. There will be no more retreating, withdrawal or readjustment of the lines or any other terms you choose. There is no line behind us to which we can retreat. Every unit must counterattack to keep the enemy in a state of confusion and off-balance. There will be no Dunkirk, there will be no Bataan. A retreat to Pusan would be one of the greatest butcheries in history. We must fight until the end. Capture by these people is worse than death itself. We will fight as a team. If some of us must die, we will die fighting together. Any man who gives ground may be personally responsible for the death of thousands of his comrades. . . . I want everybody to understand that we are going to hold this line. We are going to win.[8]

The exhortation was pointless. There was a good line behind which they could retreat: the Naktong River. And over the next several days the 1st Cavalry and 25th Division were forced to fall back another fifteen miles. But the front did not collapse and the Eighth did not fall back to water's edge. Walker, because of the shrinking perimeter, could shift forces laterally, easily, to meet and reinforce against threatened breakthroughs, frustrate enemy attacks, all the while reinforcing and building strength. At the same time, the NKPA's lines of communication and resupply were lengthening and increasingly exposed to interdiction by air and sea firepower. In arriving at the Pusan Perimeter, however, "The Americans and ROKs had paid a ghastly price. By August 1 the American ground forces had incurred a total of 6,003 casualties, the majority (3,610) in the 24th Division. In all, 1,884 Americans were dead, 2,695 were wounded, 523 were missing, and 901 were prisoners of war (POWs). This carnage was nearly three times that incurred in World War II on D day at bloody Omaha Beach (2,000) and nearly double the American casualties at Pearl Harbor (3,600) and twice those at Tarawa (3,000). To the Army's amazement, it was later confirmed that on this same date, August 1, ROK Army casualties stood at an appalling 70,000."[9]

By 2 August the Pusan Perimeter was compressed into an upright rectangle about one hundred miles tall and fifty miles wide. It was bordered by the Naktong River on most of the left (or west), the Sea of Japan on the right (east), rugged mountains on the top (north), and the Korea Strait on the bottom (south).[10]

Surprise and Breakout

Then came General MacArthur's startling 15 September strategic surprise at the ROK's west coast port of Inchon. Four aircraft carriers and fire from four cruisers (two American and two British), six destroyers, and three rocket-firing landing craft pounded enemy defenses and local transportation facilities for two days while the offshore area was swept clear of mines. The arrival of another carrier increased naval support, and the sizable force remained offshore, providing air and gunfire support, on call from the ground troops after initial landings.[11]

The United States' 1st Marine Division, a ready, well-trained division, still led by many veterans of the successful World War II Pacific island–hopping campaigns, came ashore at Inchon. The landing, in some of the most extreme tidal conditions at any port in the world, surprised the North Koreans and immediately threatened to cut supply lines and trap overextended NKPA divisions still on the offensive far to the southeast. The In Min Gun was battling furiously to collapse the Pusan Perimeter and drive the remaining UN forces off the peninsula. The Army's 7th Infantry Division, better equipped and trained than any of the Eighth Army's other three divisions, and infused with eight thousand ROK soldiers who had briefly trained with the division in Japan, arrived at Inchon on 16 September and began coming ashore on 18 September, adding to the woes of the NKPA. The 7th's commander was Maj. Gen. David G. Barr.[12]

The North Koreans, with their extended supply lines coming under increased artillery fire; U.S. bombing from strategic, tactical, and carrier based air units; devastating naval gunfire support in coastal areas; and two enemy divisions in their rear, collapsed, and hurried northward. Simultaneously, fresh American and ROK units in the Pusan Perimeter went over to the offensive and followed in pursuit of the NKPA. Most North Korean divisions dispersed into small groups, abandoned heavy weapons, and moved rapidly northward through the central mountain country that marked the spine of the peninsula to avoid the trap sprung at Inchon. Although many were captured, the remainder were preparing to regroup and fight another day: "Marine troops crossed the Han River below Seoul on 19 September and advanced rapidly on the city. Meanwhile, having secured Suwon, [31st Infantry Regiment troops], 7th Division . . . late on 26 September linked up with advance elements of the 1st Cav, which was leading the breakout from the Pusan beachhead. [The 7th Division's 32d Infantry Regiment] crossed the Han south of Seoul and entered the outskirts of the capital city. The columns advancing from the north, south and west encountered strong resistance; but Seoul fell on 26 September."[13]

Pursuit

The pursuit of the NKPA on through and past the South Korean capital of Seoul, and all across the peninsula, turned into a rout, as American and ROK forces pressed northward. In the eastern half of the peninsula, the ROK's pursuit was unabated. By 14 October they overran and had rolled twenty miles past the North Korean port of Wonsan. The overwhelmed, rapidly retreating In Min Gun was unable to organize defensive positions. The 1st Marine Division came ashore again at Wonsan on 26 October, followed a few days later by the Army's 3d Infantry Division.

When the NKPA stormed across the thirty-eighth parallel in June, the 3d Infantry had been hurriedly brought to full strength, trained, and in October deployed from Fort Benning, Georgia. The Army's 7th Infantry Division, which had come ashore with the 1st Marines at Inchon in September, joined the pursuit of the crumbling NKPA when the 7th came ashore again in an administrative landing on 29 October, much farther north, at the east coast port of Iwon. Rapidly advancing ROKs had taken Iwon days earlier: "After their annihilating defeats, in which they had lost 135,000 men as prisoners since mid-September, the North Korean forces showed little aggressiveness. By the end of the month the 24th Infantry Division [in the western half of the peninsula] had advanced to within a few miles of the temporary North Korean capital of Sininju."[14]

In late October and early November, it appeared the war would be over by Christmas. Excesses of optimism, confidence, complacency, and eager thoughts of "home by Christmas" subtly infected the UN Command and eroded both reality and caution. The rapidly advancing divisions pressed forward on narrow roads by truck and armored vehicle convoys through the steep, winding canyons, and shallow valleys between low hills, ever northward into the widening far North Korean land mass. As the advance progressed, the divisions were becoming more widely dispersed and channeled, incapable of rapid lateral moves to provide mutual support. High mountains on either side of valley roads made radio communication increasingly difficult.

Chinese Communist "Volunteers" Intervene

In America's strategic intelligence apparatus and General MacArthur's Far East, United Nations, and Eighth Army Commands, there were growing indicators of serious trouble ahead, both from the enemy and in interpreting and acting on the disturbing trends seen in enemy troop movements and reactions. However, the information gleaned from intelligence gathering did not slow the headlong rush to the Yalu River. The objective remained a rapid end to the war.

Whether due to inability to provide strategic intelligence to tactical units, rapidly moving UN units, overextended and overtaxed lines of communication, a failure to confirm or believe reports, a denial of the obvious, not wanting to bring General MacArthur bad news, wanting to tell him what he wanted to hear, or a combination of all these factors, the consequences were to be disastrous:

> There has been much discussion as to why the Chinese Communists were able to obtain such complete surprise for their offensive which began in late November.

General MacArthur [gave] the following explanation:

> Political intelligence failed to penetrate the iron curtain and provided no substantial information of intent. Field intelligence was handicapped by the severest limitations. Aerial reconnaissance beyond the border, which was our normal source of field intelligence, was forbidden. Avenues of advance from border sanctuary to battle area, only a night's march, provided maximum natural concealment. No intelligence service in the world could have surmounted such handicaps to determine to any substantial degree enemy strength, movements, and intentions. This left ground reconnaissance in force as the proper, indeed the sole, expedient.[15]

While the race to end the war was still on, the allied armies were once again ready to be brutally surprised, this time by an estimated three hundred thousand Chinese Communist Forces (CCF) "volunteers" who, under cover of darkness, were moving across the Yalu River, headed south.

On 1 November, from night's icy cold darkness and the surrounding hills, the collision began as they descended on surprised, widely dispersed UN units. The first hint of deep trouble came near Unsan, in the far northwest, where the ROKs encountered stiffening resistance and the presence of Chinese soldiers was verified: "At first it was unclear if the Chinese were present in North Korean divisions or had entered the conflict in complete Chinese divisions, but it was soon learned that the latter was the case." The Chinese launched strong attacks against the ROK's 6th and 8th Divisions, driving them back toward the Chongchon River.[16]

As the Chinese entered the war in the first days of November, the scene in the vicinity of Unsan, North Korea, was out of Dante's *Inferno* and typified the grim reality to be faced by several UN divisions pressing toward the Yalu River. In the daytime a pall of smoke drifted through company areas of the 1st Cavalry Division. The night sky glowed reddish orange from the light of forest fires raging in the mountains near Unsan. It seemed as though all of far North Korea was aflame. Talk was of the 8th Cavalry Regiment's defeat near Unsan. The 8th, one of the 1st Cavalry's regiments, had been overrun and virtually destroyed by two full Chinese divisions of twenty thousand men who had fallen on the 1st and 2d Battalions of the 8th and the ROK 15th Regiment, at Unsan.

The attack came at dusk on 1 November, simultaneously from the north, northwest, and west of Unsan. "Blowing bugles, horns, and whistles and firing signal flares, the Chinese infantrymen, supported solely by light mortars, swarmed skillfully—and bravely—over the hills," notes Clay Blair. "To the ROKs and Americans, the oncoming waves of massed manpower were astonishing, terrifying, and, to those Americans who believed the war was over, utterly demoralizing."

Most of the Chinese troops were veterans of the victorious CCF campaigns against Chiang Kai-shek's Nationalist forces. Since they had no close air support, no tanks, very little artillery, and were experienced in the tactics of guerrilla warfare, they specialized in fighting under cover of darkness: "The whistles, bugles, and horns were not only signaling devices (in place of radios) but also psychological tools, designed to frighten the enemy in the dark and cause him to shoot, thereby revealing the position of men and weapons. The fighting tactics were relatively simple: frontal assaults on the revealed positions, infiltration and ambush to cut the enemy's rear, and massed manpower attacks on the open flanks of his main elements. War correspondents were to describe the attacking waves of the CCF as a 'human sea' or 'swarm of locusts.'"

The UN forces at Unsan caved in under the massive weight of the CCF. Within about two hours the ROK 15th Regiment collapsed. Attached American tanks, artillery, and antiaircraft elements began a hurried and disorderly withdrawal through Unsan to the south. At the same time the CCF drove a wedge between the loosely tied 1st and 2d Battalions of the 8th Cavalry. Both battalions gave ground, forced back onto Unsan. By ten o'clock that night, both units were out of ammunition, more or less overrun, cut off from the rear, and desperate.

The two battalions of the 8th Cavalry Regiment were cut off and surrounded, virtually destroyed. Survivors took to the hills in small bands, abandoning their equipment. There was no semblance of organization, though the commander had received orders to withdraw the remnants of the two battalions through the 3d Battalion. Withdrawal was an order there was no chance of pulling off. By this time, at about three o'clock in the morning on 2 November, the CCF was swarming into the 3rd Battalion, blowing bugles and horns. In the wild melee and hand-to-hand fighting, the battalion commander was mortally wounded, and his executive officer took command. Many men bugged out, but others heroically banded together into tight perimeters to fight to the death in a replication of the 7th Cavalry Regiment's famous Last Stand at the Little Big Horn under George Armstrong Custer.

Fortunately, the majority of the 1st and 2d Battalions of the 8th Cavalry eventually found their way out of the hills, including the three commanders. But the 1st Battalion took heavy casualties: 265 killed or captured out of about 800 men.

By daylight on 2 November, it was clear to the division commander, Maj. Gen. "Hap" Gay, that the 8th Cavalry Regiment had suffered a disaster. No one knew what was left of it at Unsan, but whatever was left certainly must be rescued. Heroic measures were necessary. He committed all three battalions of the 5th Cavalry, plus the 1st and 2d Battalions from the 7th, in a desperate effort to break through to Unsan. Without sufficient artillery and close air support the rescue could not succeed. The casualties suffered in the 5th Calvary were ghastly: 350 total, 250 of them in one battalion.

Alarmed by the heavy casualties, the corps commander ordered General Gay to cease the rescue attempt. The 1st Cavalry and the remaining units of I Corps were to pull back south of the Chongchon River. Gay, with heavy heart, ordered his battered division to withdraw, abandoning the remainder of the 8th to their fate. Enclaves of brave men fought on for several more days, inflicting five hundred or more casualties on the CCF. When it was all over, about six hundred of the 3d Battalion's eight hundred men were dead or captured.[17]

This was to be one of several gut-wrenching defeats for the Eighth United States Army, the U.S. Marines, the ROKs, and the rest of the UN forces, as the full fury of the Chinese Communist intervention began dramatically, once more altering the course of the war. The 1st Calvary Division, I Corps, and the UN forces would have to go over to the defensive. A long trek south was beginning, but not yet fully recognized, and not before the Eighth Army opened another offensive. In the three weeks that followed, UN forces in other sectors continued to press forward while contacts with Chinese units appeared to decrease, then sharply increased. On 24 November, the offensive began: "The attacking divisions advanced against light opposition until the night of 25–26 November, at which time they were abruptly halted and thrown back by a large-scale (eighteen division) attack of the CCF, which had entered Korea from Manchuria. Similarly, the westerly advance of the

X Corps, which began on 27 November, was quickly stopped by an enemy force of nine divisions." (One division varied in strength from five thousand to ten thousand troops.)

General MacArthur described the situation: "The Eighth Army and affiliated United Nations units met powerful enemy resistance along the entire line—resistance which unmasked the fiction of 'volunteer' participation and disclosed the massive deployment of the Fourth Chinese Field Army, an important segment of the entire Chinese Communist military strength, in a formation of nine corps abreast in columns of divisions to an aggregate of 27 divisions, with elements of the Third Field Army discovered in initial deployment immediately to the rear."[18]

All the while welcome additions of combat units from other UN members continued to arrive in Korea, from the Philippines, Australia, Turkey, Thailand, and the Netherlands. Advance parties from France and Canada arrived, along with additional forces from the United Kingdom and a hospital from Sweden.

The full weight of the Chinese intervention was crashing down on the UN forces and began grinding them relentlessly backward. The surprise was complete, and the losses to UN forces quickly again became staggering. The optimistic Allied forces became a frustrated, demoralized, and overwhelmed army. They suffered defeat and disaster once more, and headed south in a fighting withdrawal, to save themselves, halt, regroup, turn around, and prepare once again to go on the offensive. Entire divisions were in peril, and had to fight their way south to avoid complete destruction.

While on the offensive the center of gravity of the UN forces' two commands, Eighth Army and X Corps, were widely separated and thinly held across the boundary separating them, primarily due to the nature of North Korea's terrain. When the Chinese intervention's full force was evident, the sparsely held center of their line gradually became a widening gap due to the heavy Chinese onslaught and the decision to pull back the X Corps toward the east coast for evacuation by sea. The X Corps, composed of the ROK's Capital and 3d Divisions, and the Americans' 1st Marine, 3d and 7th Infantry Divisions, were fighting to withdraw down the eastern half of the peninsula, while the Eighth Army battled to remain intact and withdraw down the western half of the peninsula. Along the greatly extended front of X Corps the heaviest Chinese blow was directed at the Chosin Reservoir area, where the 1st Marines had just started its attack toward the west.[19]

Tragedy at the Chosin Reservoir

The first few days of December units of the 7th Infantry Division, the Bayonet Division, suffered a disaster at the Chosin Reservoir, a body of water whose name became marks of glory for the 1st Marines, and years later, for the 7th Infantry. Along a winding, four-mile stretch of road, in hills east of the Chosin Reservoir, the last scenes of an enormous tragedy were being played out. The United States Army suffered one of the most bitter and costly defeats of the war, as survivors of Task Force Faith—1st Battalion, 32d Infantry Regiment, the "Buccaneers," and 3d Battalion, 31st Infantry Regiment, the "Bearcats," both from the 7th Division—were straggling southward, dazed, exhausted, frostbitten, hundreds wounded, toward the small North Korean town of Hudong.

The task force, named for its commander, Lt. Col. Don Faith, a Fort Benning Officer Candidate School (OCS) graduate, had been cut off and withstood assaults on its defensive perimeter for four days and nights. Faith, commander of 1st Battalion, 32d Infantry, had assumed command of the task force when Col. Mac MacLean, commander of the 31st Infantry Regiment, had been wounded and captured by CCF soldiers. Because Faith's units did not have sufficient ammunition and there were hundreds of wounded requiring better care, he believed his force could not withstand another major attack. He decided they would fight their way south to Hudong, where he expected to be reinforced. The Chinese forces were dug in on hills overlooking virtually the entire route. They set up road blocks and blew two bridges.

At one o'clock in the afternoon of 1 December, his column of thirty trucks began to move. The trucks were loaded with six hundred wounded, protected by all the infantrymen that could be mustered. To give the column added protection and firepower, a M-16 half-track with quad .50-caliber machine guns and two M-19 tank chassis carrying twin 40-mm antiaircraft artillery pieces were attached. The quad-50 vehicle was in the center of the column, one twin 40 in the lead and the other giving rear-guard support.

The move began with a horrible, shattering error when preplanned Marine close air support aircraft, in their first pass, dropped napalm short, on the head of the column. The men who suffered the blow were infantrymen leading the column. The billowing, searing flames engulfed about a dozen Americans, among them two platoon leaders. Both were badly burned, one fatally. He was George E. Foster, West Point class of 1950. Then, in the ensuing eighteen-hour, four-mile, fighting withdrawal, the entire force was virtually destroyed. Of the original 2,500 Americans who comprised the task force, about 1,000 were killed, left to die of wounds, or captured and placed in CCF or NKPA prisoner-of-war camps. Only about 385 survivors were fit for duty.

Lieutenant Colonel Faith, a paratrooper, was mortally wounded in the battle. He had been selected out of OCS to be Gen. Matthew B. Ridgway's aide and was at Ridgway's side throughout World War II campaigns in France and Germany, jumping with the 82d Airborne into Normandy. On the battlefield he was intense, fearless, relentlessly aggressive, and unforgiving of error or caution. In Korea, he was one of two battalion commanders to receive the Medal of Honor.[20]

The tragedy of Task Force Faith the first two days of December was virtually overshadowed by what was occurring all across North Korea. United Nations forces were reeling southward, engulfed by the onslaught of a sudden, massive intervention by Chinese Communist "Volunteers" who, unknown to the world, actually began pouring across the Yalu River in October. By 24 November, the CCF offensive was administering punishing, demoralizing blows to UN Forces. The tide of war was once more fully reversed.

X Corps Evacuation by Sea and Air

In the intervening weeks, there were rear-guard actions to allow UN forces to withdraw southward and remain intact. The CCF leapfrogged rapidly along the hills above the withdrawing Eighth Army columns, setting up roadblocks and ambushes, harassing, launching sharp night attacks when the retreating columns drew into perimeters to defend against assaults. The Eighth continued down the western half of the Korean peninsula, past Pyongyang, past Seoul, giving up the capital city once more, moving farther south.

Down the middle of the peninsula the CCF and its reconstituting allies, the NKPA, poured slowly through the rough mountainous terrain in a growing gap between UN forces in the two halves of the peninsula. The surge of less-road-bound Chinese divisions came mostly by foot, taking advantage of the uncontested sector between the two large, separated pieces of the UN forces.

In the eastern half, the X Corps, commanded by Maj. Gen. Edward M. "Ned" Almond (Virginia Military Institute class of 1915), who also doubled as MacArthur's chief of staff, fell back before the Chinese onslaught. The X Corps separated into two enclaves, one containing the Army's 7th Infantry Division and 1st Marine Division. The two divisions, which had come ashore in September's landing at Inchon, closed into a shrinking defensive perimeter around the North Korean port of Hungnam and resisted increasingly strong attacks by the oncoming enemy.

Farther south the second enclave was established around North Korea's port of Wonsan. Forming a defensive perimeter around Wonsan were elements of the Army's 3d Infantry Division and an ROK Marine division. They gradually pulled back, shrinking the perimeter, were finally evacuated aboard U.S. Navy ships, and moved north to Hungnam to bolster the defensive perimeter there, which was under heavy pressure from the advancing Chinese and NKPA. Slowly, the forces around Hungnam contracted their defensive positions, while a massive task force of 193 ships assembled to evacuate the withdrawing X Corps. Concentrated firepower from artillery, land and carrier based air strikes, and naval gunfire from battleships, cruisers, and destroyers accompanying the task force kept the CCF and NKPA in check, unable to bring to bear sustained fire support to mount a decisive attack and drive the withdrawing forces into the sea.

By 24 December, the evacuation was complete. In all, 206,600 persons were evacuated, including 108,600 troops, 17,500 vehicles, and 350,000 tons of other cargo. In addition, airlift brought out 3,600 troops, 200 vehicles, and 1,300 tons of cargo. Nine days earlier, President Truman, concerned for a possible outbreak of general war with the Soviet bloc, declared a national emergency.[21]

The UN forces in the eastern half of Korea had been saved from the pursuing CCF. The X Corps disembarked near the tip of the Korean peninsula, in the South Korean port of Pusan, and moved north to link up with the retreating Eighth Army in the west. The two forces reestablished a continuous defense line from coast to coast in South Korea, south of Seoul.

The evacuation of UN forces from North Korea, by sea and air, had been the greatest rescue of ground forces since the evacuation of Dunkirk by the British in World War II. But the losses had been staggering since the CCF entered the war in early November. The losses worsened one day before the closure of the Hungnam evacuation.

A New Commander: Another Turnaround Begins

On 23 December 1950, while UN forces were continuing to withdraw southward before the flood of CCF manpower, as if to punctuate the bitter defeat and precipitous reversal of the war, Lt. Gen. Walton H. "Johnnie" Walker (West Point class of 1912), the Eighth Army commander, an armor enthusiast, and George S. Patton's admirer, was killed in a jeep accident north of Seoul. In Washington, D.C., reaction was swift. His replacement was Lt. Gen. Matthew B. Ridgway (West Point, April 1917), reassigned from his position as the Army's deputy chief of staff for operations and administration. On 4 January 1951, Seoul changed hands for the third time.

Ridgway had a proven track record of winning in World War II, but he confronted a daunting task. UN forces were in retreat, dispirited and demoralized, and in his mind they had all the signs of a defeated army. Though bright, aggressive, forceful, analytical, methodical, doggedly determined, energetic, and a field leader with great "presence," he needed all the help he could get, and took with him to Korea the full backing of the Truman administration and Department of Defense, in the persons of Gen. Omar N. Bradley, the chairman of the Joint Chiefs of Staff, and Gen. J. Lawton Collins, the Army's chief of staff. Ridgway's mission was to grab hold of retreating forces, expunge the pall of defeat, revitalize their battered morale, and instill the belief they could turn the tide and win. It would not be easy, but in the space of one month after he took command, the turnaround took hold.

Ridgway was given carte blanche and intended to quietly replace, not fire, commanders who had been through the "yo-yo war" and were exhibiting signs of fatigue, discouragement or defeatist attitudes, and bring in commanders he believed would once more, successfully, reverse the UN forces' fortunes, and put them firmly back onto the offensive. He started by replacing division and corps commanders who were weary of the fight, or men who seemed to have absorbed defeatist mentalities. He extended the shake-up deep into the divisions, to include assistant division commanders, chiefs of artillery, chiefs of staffs, and regimental commanders. The Eighth

Army staff also received a house cleaning. The Eighth's new commander got nearly all the replacements he asked for, and more.

One by one, using a "six-month rotation" policy, which in one case was less than six months, he replaced four of the Eighth's six division commanders—all in the four divisions which had deployed from Japan at the war's onset. He ensured the departing commanders received decorations for their service in a period of great trial and loss on Korea's battlefields. All were professional soldiers who had served their country with distinction in World War II, and he was sensitive to the crushing personal and professional impacts outright firings would bring. In the 1st Cavalry, he sent Major General Gay home, replacing him with the division's tough-minded artillery chief, Charlie Palmer, who had fought close by Ridgway in Europe. At the insistence of the X Corps commander, Ned Almond, Ridgway replaced the 7th Division's Dave Barr, who had been commanding the division just four months. The 7th's new commander was Claude B. "Buddy" Ferenbaugh, who had been a Corps G-3 (operations officer) in North Africa in 1942, assistant division commander in the 83d Infantry Division in Normandy, and was roundly approved by Ridgway when the Army chief of staff, J. Lawton Collins, selected him for duty in Korea. While Ridgway was reshaping the command structure in the American ground forces, the advancing Chinese and North Koreans were extending their lines of communication and resupply, and, absent effective air and naval support, subjecting themselves increasingly to destructive air and naval bombardment by UN forces.

In addition to bringing new blood and increased support with him, he brought bitterly learned lessons from the first five months of the war, and fresh ideas, better strategy, improved tactics, and a surging supply of newer, more effective weapons to counter enemies who were not fighting the typical conventional war. "Get off the roads and take the high ground; get out of your headquarters and command posts, go to the critical, hottest areas on your front"—these were among his admonitions to new field commanders.

They did, and by 25 January, Ridgway was ready to go on the offensive, with punishing firepower complemented with cautious, well-coordinated offensive maneuvering. Methodically, cautiously, always ensuring mutual support and massive firepower from artillery, strategic and tactical air— both carrier and land based—Ridgway's field army hammered the hundreds of thousands of Chinese and North Korean forces slowly but relentlessly northward. The UN forces surged forward. The war had once again turned around.

Ridgway's command continued a series of hammer blows to the enemy, inflicting heavy losses in the UN's first counteroffensive against the CCF and NKPA. His forces absorbed a counterattack, gave ground, and attacked again. The UN kept up relentless pressure through 21 April and continued to pound the CCF and NKPA with withering firepower.[22]

Another Commander: Truce Talks Begin and Break Off

Ten days before the UN's first counteroffensive came to a close, Gen. Douglas MacArthur was relieved of his command by President Truman. Ridgway no sooner got the Eighth turned around and in an aggressive fighting stance than he was selected to fill the position vacated by MacArthur's relief.

In April 1951, Lt. Gen. James A. Van Fleet (West Point class of 1915) replaced Ridgway, taking command of the Eighth Army and UN field forces in Korea. His work as commander was perhaps the most difficult of the four American generals who led the UN field forces during the Korean War. "Following public change-of-command ceremonies," historian Blair notes, "Ridgway met privately with Van Fleet . . . [and] made it clear . . . he would keep a tight rein on Eighth Army. 'To the extent the situation warrants, please inform me prior to advancing in force beyond [Line] Utah.' Furthermore, 'no operations in force' would be conducted 'beyond the Wyoming Line without prior approval' from Ridgway."[23]

For twenty-two frustrating months of alternating offensive and defensive position and attrition warfare, and finally, trench warfare, the UN forces under Van Fleet's command fought determinedly to gain ground, and leverage, for the truce negotiations which began in Kaesong, North Korea, on 10 July 1951. Stalemate slowly settled into the Korean War during the six months following Van Fleet's assumption of command, as did trench warfare and on and off truce negotiations which continued for more than two years after the July start.

Fueled by Truman administration fears of a complete breakdown in truce negotiations, on one hand raising the specter of a protracted "limited war," on the other hand, escalating the conflict into a general war with the Communist world, Van Fleet would face other frustrations as the war ground on, frustrations no professional soldier, or any soldier, wanted to face—increasing constraints on offensive operations which continued the remainder of the war.

Movement toward truce talks began

in a New York radio address 23 June 1951, when Jacob A. Malik, Soviet delegate to the United Nations, presented a proposal for cease-fire discussions in Korea. An unofficial endorsement of this proposal was broadcast by the Chinese Communist Government on 25 June. Finally, after preliminary arrangements were made between the field commanders, the armistice conference met for the first time on July 10. . . . The conferences were held at Kaesong until they were suspended in August. They were resumed in mid-October at Panmunjom. From the first, progress was very slow. Each minor point had to be laboriously resolved; and the talks dragged on and on, with many suspensions of meetings, until the final armistice agreement in July 1953.[24]

Though both sides had agreed hostilities would continue while negotiations were in progress, it was obvious neither side would start an all-out offensive unless talks became deadlocked or broke off completely. But the no man's land between the armies did not remain inactive in the seven-week period talks continued.

Air strikes, continuous artillery bombardment, constant combat patrolling, and offensive ground operations of battalion, and occasionally regimental, attacks characterized the fighting. The attacks were to secure key terrain, bring in prisoners, and relieve enemy pressure on the UN lines. As one operations history stated, "Except for several offensives that grew out of intermittent breaking off of armistice negotiations, this was generally the pattern of operations that prevailed until the signing of the armistice [in July 1953]."[25]

Resuming the Offensive

When the truce talks broke off in late August 1951, General Van Fleet, in keeping with General Ridgway's policy of unrelenting military pressure on the Communists, decided to resume the offensive. The objectives were to drive the enemy farther back from the Hwachon Reservoir, which supplied water and electrical power to Seoul, and away from the Chorwon-Seoul railroad, keeping enemy artillery fire from reaching those key arteries, while seizing more defensible high ground at the head of the Chorwon valley, extending west southwest along the western edge of the valley. The railroad was being developed as a major supply route for the UN forces. The seizing of the hills along the western edge of the valley, the route of the In Min Gun's main effort in 1950, would also add strength to the defense of the traditional invasion route should truce talks completely break down and the CCF and NKPA decide to try the Chorwon Valley route again.

The offensive began first in the eastern half of the peninsula, when two divisions in X Corps, the 1st Marines and the Army's 2d Infantry Division, launched heavy attacks intended to secure high ridges to the west and north of the bitterly contested area called the "Punch Bowl."

Farther west, in I Corps, the 1st Cavalry Division was one of four divisions, plus the British Commonwealth Brigade, advancing on a forty-mile-wide front from Kaesong to Chorwon.[26] On 21 September, in the area near Chorwon, K Company, 3d Battalion, 7th Cavalry prepared to go up more hills, "get off the road," and "take high ground," as General Ridgway had directed when he took command of the Eighth Army. General Van Fleet was continuing Ridgway's aggressive, methodical approach to winning battles and administering punishment to the Chinese and North Koreans. The 7th Cavalry Regiment was to be part of an effort to advance north from Line Wyoming to seize and hold Line Jamestown.[27]

On 23 September, K Company of the 7th Cavalry, including men attached to support its operation, took and held Hill 339. On the twenty-ninth, after withstanding a heavy counterattack as Chinese attempted to retake the hill, K Company rotated around the battalion perimeter and I Company replaced them. In the intervening seven days on Hill 339, K Company took fifty-four casualties from enemy artillery and mortar fire.[28]

This was merely the beginning. Four days later, on 3 October, with no replacements for their losses, K Company jumped off in the continuing Eighth Army offensive, code-named Operation Commando. A series of objectives, including two smaller hills, led to Hill 347, which, like several other hills in the vicinity, was nicknamed "Baldy."

There was "Old Baldy" and "Chink Baldy." There was a "T-Bone Hill" and an "Alligator Jaws." But "Baldy" had a particular meaning, a name coined by GIs because of the barren, hostile hill crests gouged and completely denuded of trees or foliage from constant shelling by the two opposing armies during the numerous times the hills changed hands.[29] And there was another name given Hill 347 by the GIs who toiled up and down its battle scarred slopes: "Bloody Baldy."[30]

The Taking of Hill 347

Operation Commando began in the 7th Cavalry Regiment sector, with the 4th Battalion, the Greek Expeditionary Force, to the right of K Company, and I Company on the left. At the end of the first day's fighting, the remainder of K Company's battered 1st Platoon was destroyed, and two K Company officers were critically wounded. Company G took one hundred thirty casualties, including four officers, on Hill 418, and the Greek company on the right of K took one hundred thirty-five. No units gained their objectives, and the 2d Battalion won and lost Hill 418 five times.

On 4 October, the attacking forces again started up the outlying hills toward 347, with all the support they could muster. Again K Company was in the enemy trenches, as were the Greeks, but the tremendous mortar fire and the seemingly unlimited numbers of enemy threw out K Company and the Greeks.

The next day, they tried again. The Greeks reached and held their objectives. K Company did not. Not until all the companies of the 3d Battalion attacked just after dark. K Company took the two smaller hills with seventeen more casualties, including the artillery and 4.2-inch mortar forward observers.

On 6 October, the attackers, including K Company, reorganized, while the Chinese threw three thousand rounds into the 7th Cavalry Regiment's area of operations.

Having taken the two smaller hills nearer 347 and paused to reorganize, K Company was ready to advance on their primary objective. No more replacements came. The hill was bare for four hundred yards down from the peak, which meant assaulting troopers would be completely exposed in the final lunge at the crest. The Chinese were well covered, deeply dug in with interconnecting trenches, tunnels, dugouts, and bunkers. The trenches were four feet deep, displaced down the hill a few yards below the crest.

Direct fire from below, even from tanks, could not dislodge them. They had 60-mm, 82-mm, and 120-mm mortars on the hill and supporting artillery aimed for probable approaches to their defense network.

All elements of the 7th Cavalry's 3d Battalion were committed. The assault began at ten o'clock in the morning, with L and I Companies attacking up the other side of the peak. While L Company was fighting up the hill, I Company had to turn and counterattack toward the 3d Battalion Observation Post, where senior officers in the battalion were fighting off grenade attacks on their flank.

When the first assault by K Company began, Lt. Dave Hughes, the company commander, was seven hundred yards to the rear of the company's lead elements, where he could—with maps, radio, and weapon in hand—observe and control the remaining two platoons' progress and coordinate all the supporting fires. The 2d Platoon led the attack.

The assault initially appeared successful. They reached the enemy's trenches but were forced off by intense, concentrated fire and grenades and then pinned down, losing one officer and twenty more men. In each assault the Chinese rained grenades on their attackers, including antitank grenades. Sgt. Eugene F. Chyzy, the M Company machine-gun section leader attached to K Company for the attack, remembered seeing three and four enemy grenades in the air at any one time during the assaults.

The second time up 347 that day, 3d Platoon attempted to assist, but the attack bogged down, and the remaining men had to pull back partway. In this attempt, the officer leading the 1st Platoon was wounded. K Company fell short again, having lost another officer and more men.

In the third attempt, the same thing happened. The last officer in the company, other than Lieutenant Hughes, was wounded by a grenade, breaking the attack. Sgt. Monroe S. McKenzie, now leader of the 3d Platoon, radioed Hughes. McKenzie could see only three men left in the assault element. He asked Hughes what he should do. Hughes told him, "Hang on."

There were actually now six K Company riflemen still able to fight on Hill 347. What happened next was something of which Hughes remembered little afterward.

On 7 October, when matters seemed to have once more ground to a halt on the slopes of "Bloody Baldy," his mind was working at a furious pace; he was at once reacting and acting—on automatic—putting to use all he had learned from the men who had served with him and what he had experienced in assaulting hills in the months after the 1st Cavalry Division went on the offensive again, in January.

In observing the previous three assaults, he saw what had to be done differently to reach and hold the crest of 347 that day. He began moving forward, gathering the company's headquarters element, mortar crews, and remaining forward observers and telling them they were to be riflemen. They, with him, were to continue forward and join the surviving K Company riflemen on the northeast slope of the hill. There would be a total of thirty men, including him, the equivalent of one, understrength platoon— less than one-fourth a company's normal strength.

They loaded themselves up with ammunition and as many hand grenades as they could carry. Because he had taken the forward observers as riflemen, he could no longer coordinate distant fire support—artillery and mortars —for the company. When they joined with the men pinned down on the side of the hill, he organized them for another assault.

He led Sergeant Chyzy and his M Company machine-gun section to a position where they could support the fourth assault on Hill 347. He told Chyzy they were "to fire at any enemy up there [they] could hit, even if he or other GIs were up there and got counterattacked."

He returned to the riflemen and gave them orders for the assault. They were to use marching fire—fire repeatedly as they moved forward—to keep down the enemy's fire. They were to run through enemy return fire and grenades, no matter how intense, no matter the cost, until they crossed their trenches. Then they were to turn around and come back down on the trenches from above and behind.

He moved to the front of his men, waving them forward to begin the assault up the last one hundred fifty yards toward the crest of "Bloody Baldy," shouting encouragement. The time was about one o'clock in the afternoon. Three hours had elapsed since the attack on Hill 347 had begun.

His fatigue shirt and pockets were stuffed with all the grenades he could carry. Up they went, up a hillside being savaged by heavy mortar barrages, up through air laced repeatedly with shrapnel from exploding grenades and small-arms fire from their right flank. The men faltered, slowed, wanting to once more take cover. Hughes kept going, staying in the lead and firing his submachine gun. Men began to notice, to see their commander, this young lieutenant, showing what seemed extraordinary courage and calmness in a storm of return fire, mortar rounds, and grenades. He was in the lead, showing the way. They had to follow. They did not want to let him down. They could not leave him out front, alone.

Master Sergeant McKenzie saw two men killed by enemy antitank grenades. They were the forward observers. Hughes did not slow his ascent. McKenzie and Cpl. Robert W. Holden then saw Hughes throw his weapon down, leaving it behind. His submachine gun had quit firing, jammed or empty. He began hurling grenades—and kept going. He rushed the top, continuing to throw grenades, going straight for the bunker which had repeatedly stopped the previous attacks. To McKenzie, Hughes was "pulling his men through the fire," keeping the Chinese from standing up to fire back and allowing the remaining riflemen to spread out and overrun the trench line. They followed, trying to keep pace.

Up he went for the bunker. He knocked it out and continued to throw grenades into the lateral trenches, tunnels, and dugouts. Company K's Sgt. 1st Class Arthur J. Shuld, Jr., was following not far behind Hughes when he surged the final yards toward the top. Shuld tried to keep up, but he was hit, wounded. As he was being helped back toward the aid station, he turned to see his company commander had made it to the top. The surviving K Company men were on the trench line with him, moving about, systematically throwing grenades and firing into the enemy positions.

When they reached the crest, they saw the L Company lead men coming up the other side, nearing the hill top.

Sergeant Chyzy, with his M Company machine-gun section, also watched in admiration as Hughes led the rush toward the crest of Hill 347. He saw the men of K Company hesitate, then follow. When next he saw David Hughes, he was on top of the hill, shouting for Chyzy to bring his section up. Chyzy would later say, "By his outstanding courage and leadership, Lieutenant Hughes inspired us so much that my section and myself under any conditions would stay with him to the last man."

Sgt. Ray P. Moses, K Company, said, "During the . . . push on Hill 347 . . . I have never seen such heroism and courage as that Lieutenant Hughes had shown during the attack. . . . It was only one of many times I have seen . . . his leadership and lack of fear while he was my company commander, but this was the greatest."

Corporal Holden recalled, "His coolheadedness and lack of bother for the terrible enemy fire in the attack presented an example to the men which alone held the Company together. . . . Upon being first up the hill and I being down behind him I saw he was fighting and killing like a mad man so we could get up there. Running in and out of the bunkers he threw everything he could, including Chinese grenades, until the hill was taken." One tunnel by one tunnel the men of K Company rooted the enemy out—as either prisoners or dead men.

A reinforced battalion of enemy soldiers had defended Hill 347. They were defending a Chinese division and regimental artillery command post, facts not known to K Company when the attacks began. By dark, K Company marched 192 prisoners off the hill and counted 100 dead enemy soldiers in the open, just within the perimeter of the Chinese trenches, which were only ten yards downslope from the peak and two hundred yards long, ringing the hilltop. An unknown number of enemy casualties were attributed directly to David Hughes.

There were 250 enemy dead on the hill, many in their bunkers. The 3d Battalion, 7th Cavalry suffered seventy casualties. They had captured or killed all but eighty men in the enemy battalion, according to one of its soldiers, a clerk, captured later. With all the attachments to K Company, including Sergeant Chyzy's fourteen-man Company M machine-gun section, which joined them on top, Hughes had only thirty-seven men left under his command that day, only fifteen from Company K.

The fight for Hill 347 was over—for 7 October 1951.[31]

Going Home and the Beginning of Stalemate

K Company was soon relieved from Hill 347 and rotated to another sector in the regimental front, where the 1st Battalion had just been overrun. The company stayed relatively stationary on the hills for ten more days, while the 5th and 8th Cavalry Regiments moved up to take their objectives on Line Jamestown.

The last of the men who had been with the company at the peak of the fighting were rotated out. The last K Company GIs were gone. Only Lt. David R. Hughes remained. He was the only officer for a brief period, before a few more arrived. A short time later he was reassigned as the assistant Regimental S-3 (operations officer). That was his duty when the 1st Cavalry Division was pulled out of the line into reserve and prepared to ship out to Japan.[32]

When Operation Commando began on 3 October, the 1st Cavalry was in the center of the five division drive for Line Jamestown. Commanded by Maj. Gen. Thomas L. Harold, forty-nine and a 1925 West Point graduate, "the division ran up into the dug-in CCF Forty-Seventh Army, which was determined not to yield an inch. Ghastly fighting like that on Bloody and Heartbreak ridges took place on or near hills dominated by Old Baldy":

It took about sixteen days of hard, bloody fighting for the 1st Cavalry Division to advance six miles to Line Jamestown. During this period prac- tically the entire division was engaged. The four division artillery battal- ions fired an astonishing 380,856 rounds. I Corps incurred about four thousand casualties, about twenty-nine hundred of which were in the 1st Cavalry. The [division] historian described the carnage:

"The 1st Cavalry Division was engaged almost constantly in the most bitter fighting of the entire Korean campaign. The effort required in driving an entire Chinese Army from an excellent defensive line was so great as to almost defy description. One of the regiments reported that fully two-thirds of its rear area personnel had been sent up to front line units to fill gaps left by an unprecedented number of casualties. Survivors of companies joined with remaining fragments of other com- panies to return and assault again and again the positions that had previously all but wiped them out. This maximum, around-the-clock exertion extended to every unit and every man in the division."

After the 1st Cav reached Line Jamestown, the I Corps commander, Iron Mike O'Daniel, issued orders for the Corps to hold that line and dig in. There would be no more major offensives. As the British historian wrote, "future operations would be confined to those necessary to main- tain existing positions." One month later the battered 1st Cav was with- drawn from Korea and returned to Japan, replaced by the 45th (Oklahoma National Guard) Division, which had arrived in Japan the previous spring. Having originally embarked for an amphibious landing and mopping-up operations at Inchon, [the 1st Cavalry was rushed into the Pusan Perime- ter in July 1950. The Inchon landing and mopping up] had been expected to last no longer than six weeks. [Instead,] the 1st Cavalry Division had spent sixteen terrible months in Korea.[33]

On 11 January 1952, Hughes, for his actions on Hill 347, was nominated for the Distinguished Service Cross, the nation's second highest decoration for valor. The citation accompanying his award read in part, "First Lieutenant David Ralph Hughes . . . is cited for extraordinary heroism in action against an armed enemy on 7 October 1951, near Sokkogae, Korea."

Hughes was fortunate, and he knew it. He survived unscathed. Good, brave men witnessed his act of courage in their behalf, and they had lived to tell what they saw. There were thousands more in Korea who gave their all in no less heroic acts and did not live. Sometimes their final acts were performed alone, without the benefit of witnesses. For others, no witnesses lived to tell of their courage and deeds.

But he had lived to see numerous acts of courage by men in K Company and was determined they should be recognized. While in Japan, assigned to the 7th Regiment's headquarters, he wrote scores of recommendations for decorations. After he returned to the United States, in a bitter twist of irony, fire destroyed the headquarters building, and with it, the regiment's records of Korean operations, including all the recommendations for decorations he had written for the troopers of K Company.

In March 1952, Dave Hughes boarded a Japanese ship, the *Oturu Maru*, and sailed for home. Home. The Korean War was over for him, but it wasn't yet over for hundreds of thousands more. Thousands of ROK and U.S. soldiers, and soldiers from other UN nations, would fall in Korea after K Company of the 7th Cavalry and the 1st Cavalry Division left for Japan.[34]

There were to be more, bloody battles all along the lines separating the two opposing armies before the armistice agreement took effect on 27 July 1953. The vast majority of the thousands of small unit actions which occurred in those last twenty months became routine, with a few exceptions went unpublicized, sometimes unrewarded, then were buried in painful memories, while thousands gave their all on the ground, in the air, and at sea before the armistice was signed, though the opposing armies remained essentially static after K Company's last major battle. They fell, killed, wounded, missing, captured—some dying in captivity—during the endless daily exchanges of harassing artillery and mortar fire along a stalemated front. The war had become a twenty-four-hour grind of guard and outguard duty, reconnaissance patrols, ambush patrols, and raids; heavy barrages of artillery and mortars preceding sharp, probing attempts to determine weak points in the OPLR or MLR; attacks which were carefully planned and determined attempts to breach UN lines; Allied counterattacks to regain momentarily lost outposts or foil and then close major breakthroughs; and all the brutal trench and bunker warfare that accompanied a stalemated

Pork Chop Hill as seen from a hill just south of the Chop, November 1951.
Courtesy of John R. Krull

conventional war. From the late fall of 1951 to the spring of 1953, the war ground on while truce talks continued off and on.

And another, smaller hill, an outpost taken by the 8th Cavalry Regiment a short distance to the northeast of Hill 347, achieved a blood-soaked notoriety all its own in the spring and early summer of 1953.

Pork Chop Hill was the name.

2

TO HOLD THE HILLS

IN AUGUST 1951, TWO MONTHS BEFORE OPERATION COMMANDO began, the UN armistice negotiating team and their Communist adversaries were already negotiating the position of the truce line. The CCF and NKPA delegates were continuing to press for the thirty-eighth parallel as the final truce line. The UN was holding firm to a truce essentially "in place," offering a twenty-kilometer-wide DMZ as opposed to the prior proposal of a twenty-mile-wide DMZ. The delegations met daily from 10 to 22 August. Then, on 23 August, the Communists abruptly broke off negotiations, alleging the Far East Air Forces (FEAF) had bombed the "neutral zone" surrounding Kaesong, causing the "unlawful murder of a CCF platoon leader." Investigation of the incident turned up no convincing evidence of an FEAF attack. The UN investigators concluded that "the incident was unquestionably staged by the Communists" as an "excuse to bring an end to the negotiations."[1]

While the negotiators haggled at Kaesong, Ridgway, pursuing his policy of unrelenting military pressure on the Communists, ordered ground as well as air action. The policy suited General Van Fleet. In Van Fleet's mind, the onset of talks in July began raising deep concern about the combat readiness of the Eighth Army. There was the possibility that an armistice might be reached at any hour. Few in the Eighth wanted to take chances and be the "last man killed." There was another factor. The rotation policy was changing the face of the Army. Thousands of newcomers, green to combat, were replacing the experienced soldiers—the old hands. Signs went up proclaiming, "Drive Carefully! The Man You Hit May Be Your Replacement." An inexperienced, static army filled with caution and indifference can rapidly become a vulnerable army. As Van Fleet said later, "A sitdown army is subject to collapse at the first sign of enemy effort. . . . I couldn't allow my forces to become soft and dormant."[2]

Unfortunately, on 10 September, just as Ridgway's patience was running out and he was seeking approval from the Joint Chiefs of Staff (JCS) for a military operation to take back Kaesong, an accidental strafing of the neutral zone at Kaesong did in fact occur. The error by an aircraft from the 3d Bomber Wing compelled Ridgway to issue an apology to the Communists. The JCS, owing to this incident and the need for an apology, withheld approval of Ridgway's proposed operation to recapture Kaesong.[3]

Though truce negotiations broke off, stalled in part over the issue of the negotiating site, Kaesong, liaison officers from the two sides continued to periodically meet in Kaesong. The town with the initially agreed "neutral zone" surrounding it was located south of the thirty-eighth parallel, in South Korea, but was under control of the North Koreans. Further, it was the ancient capital of Korea. The UN had voluntarily withdrawn from Kaesong to provide the neutral zone when negotiations first began in July, a fact that continued to rankle General Ridgway. The UN wanted to move the negotiating site to Panmunjom, a truly neutral site on the line dividing the two armies, five miles east of Kaesong. Liaison officers also periodically met at Panmunjom during the two-month cessation of truce talks.

Behind the scenes high-level political and diplomatic maneuverings, including intense exchanges inside the Truman administration and the Department of Defense, followed by communications with the Soviet government in Moscow, helped resolve the issue. On 7 October 1951, the day the 7th Cavalry Regiment's K Company seized Hill 347, the Communists yielded and proposed that the senior delegates resume talks in Panmunjom. Ridgway accepted the proposal, and over the following two weeks the liaison officers negotiated the size of the neutral zone and other security details. Senior delegates resumed armistice negotiations on 25 October.[4]

During the period from 25 October to 27 November, negotiations were entering a new phase in which the central issue was the location of the truce line coupled with a hoped for rapid agreement. "On 6 November, with another deadlock looming," historian Clay Blair notes, "the Communists appeared to grant the UN another major concession. They backed off their demands that the UN yield Bloody and Heartbreak ridges, the Punchbowl, and other terrain in the Iron Triangle. They proposed to accept the existing battle line as the final truce line, provided the UN would agree to it right then and there, even before the other items on the agenda had been resolved and the armistice signed, and regardless of where the opposing forces might stand at the time of signing the armistice."[5]

Give and take with the Communists continued while General Ridgway and the negotiating team remained in an intense internal debate with the JCS and State Department regarding what Ridgway saw as a de facto cease-fire in which the Communists would be insured against the effects of UN military operations, with no incentive to resolve the remaining issues on the agenda. In Ridgway's view, if their proposal were accepted, the Communists could drag out the negotiations for years without fear of UN ground forces' pressure. During the internal debate, Ridgway held determinedly to the view Kaesong should be regained, offering in exchange to pull back UN forces on the east coast.

Nevertheless, Washington officialdom and public opinion swung behind the Communists' offer. Their offer appeared a major concession in which the CCF and NKPA were giving up the thirty-eighth parallel as the final truce line:

> On November 11 a *New York Times* editorial inquired rhetorically why the delegates were "backing and filling over a seeming trifle" when they had already agreed on the "big issues" regarding the truce line. Senior officials in both the State Department and Department of Defense agreed. On November 12 [twenty-two] representatives from State and Defense met to settle the matter once and for all. . . . The JCS cabled Ridgway their views in the early hours of November 13. He was to "press for an early settlement," stipulating to the Communists that the agreement would be valid for "approximately one month." In order to reach agreement "as promptly [as] possible," Ridgway would make "such concessions as are

not significant," meaning give up his efforts to gain Kaesong. Unlike Ridgway, the JCS did "not consider" the provisional agreement a de facto cease fire. UN ground actions could still continue "even though gains and losses would not be of significance to location of demarcation line if other items agreed to within time period." Moreover, UN air and naval action would not be affected by the agreement.[6]

Ridgway, Vice Adm. C. Turner Joy, the lead negotiator, and the whole UN negotiating team were shocked. Ridgway responded with a protest to the JCS and requested yet another reconsideration. The appeal was denied, and on 14 November the JCS expressed appreciation for Ridgway's views but ordered him to do as he was told. The following day Ridgway reluctantly instructed Admiral Joy to "press for early settlement" on the battle line. The offer included the clear understanding that if all other items on the agenda were not agreed to within one month, the provisional truce line would no longer be valid.[7]

The Communists agreed in principle on 21 November but haggled over form and language and what actually constituted the battle line until 27 November, when the delegates reached "final" agreement on the truce line. Should negotiators fail to settle the other terms of the armistice, it would expire on 27 December.[8]

Meanwhile, Ridgway had ordered Van Fleet to place the Eighth Army in a position of "active defense." He authorized Van Fleet to seize terrain most suitable for defense but limit offensive action to taking "outpost positions" not requiring more than one division. However, on 27 November, when delegates reached provisional agreement on the truce line, Van Fleet, without authorization from Ridgway, issued far more restrictive orders to Eighth Army. UN forces, he wrote, "clearly should demonstrate a willingness to reach an agreement while preparing for offensive action if negotiations are unduly prolonged to this end. . . . Counterattacks to regain key terrain lost to enemy assault will be the only offensive action taken unless otherwise directed by this headquarters. Every effort will be made to prevent unnecessary casualties."[9]

The Army historian later wrote these orders amounted to a cease-fire "if the enemy so desired." They made sense and were humane, but they were contrary to Ridgway's aim of continuing "relentless" ground pressure until the enemy reached agreement on the other agenda items. Inevitably the orders leaked to the press. One correspondent wrote that Van Fleet's order had "brought Korean fighting to a complete, if temporary, halt."[10]

There was little doubt Van Fleet's orders and the press stories concerning them could undermine the UN negotiations at Panmunjom and embarrass the Truman administration. Ridgway was furious and cabled Washington that Van Fleet had "assumed a function entirely outside" his "field of responsibility." President Truman was irate as well, and publicly denounced the stories as "fake," denying that Eighth Army had ceased offensive operations. Truman made a point of publicly saying continued pressure by UN forces was the strongest incentive for the enemy to agree to the armistice. A chastened Van Fleet ordered resumption of local patrolling and stepped up artillery barrages, but the Army historian took issue with Van Fleet's orders, writing that these measures amounted to no more than "lip service."[11]

The truce line, believed to be the most important and controversial issue to both sides in the negotiations to end the Korean War, was settled. The agreement came after five months of off-again, on-again talks and further shocking casualties on both sides. Included in the agreement was the UN's one-month time limit on the truce line agreement. As Ridgway gloomily predicted, the time limit was extended again and again, until the limit had no further meaning and was dropped as a consideration.[12]

The truce line agreed to on 27 November 1951 thus became, after minor adjustments, the "final line" in the Korean War. Few would be satisfied with the agreement. In the five months of talks the UN suffered sixty thousand casualties, twenty thousand of which were American. At Panmunjom the senior delegates turned to the next two major items on the agenda: provisions for enforcing the armistice and exchange of POWs. The delegates negotiated these two items concurrently, and eventually the two became intertwined.[13]

The New Agony: More to Negotiate

On enforcing the armistice, the key issue was rehabilitation of North Korean facilities such as roads, railroads, and jet-capable airfields. The UN objective was to prevent the secret reintroduction of Communist reinforcements into North Korea in sufficient strength to overpower UN and ROK forces and reconquer South Korea. To meet that objective, General Ridgway was at first unwavering in his hard-line position the UN negotiating team should demand severe restrictions on rotation of Communist troops and "free inspections" of virtually all of North Korea by joint UN-Communist ground and air teams. Seeing Ridgway's proposal as perhaps too rigid and possibly unattainable, Washington asked him to hold off in favor of a State Department proposal. The State proposal eventually emerged as the "greater sanction" doctrine. Should China or North Korea violate the armistice and reinvade South Korea, the UN forces in the Far East would retaliate directly at Red China by air and sea.[14]

With respect to rehabilitation of facilities in North Korea, Washington at first had an extreme hard-line position, without offering reciprocal concessions, such as moderating or suspending its massive rehabilitation of South Korea. The JCS concluded the Washington position was overly harsh on the North Korean civilian population, and probably unattainable. The JCS recommended that, except for airfields capable of accommodating jets, the rehabilitation of North Korean facilities should not be prohibited.[15]

To this point in the armistice talks President Truman virtually rubber-stamped most JCS or State positions in the talks. However, on this issue he balked, showing some frustration: "Why should we allow rehabilitation of roads, railroads and other facilities except for air fields? We have expended lives, tons of bombs and a large amount of equipment to bring these people to terms. They have been able to give us a bad time even in the crippled condition of their communications and they have been able to operate effectively even without air fields?"

When the JCS responded that "it would be impracticable to keep all of [North] Korea in a state of devastation," Truman backed down.[16]

After the policy review on the rehabilitation issue, the JCS wired Ridgway new instructions. The UN team would demand prohibitions only on the rehabilitation or construction of jet-capable airfields. However, they offered no reciprocal agreement—construction and rehabilitation of jet-capable airfields in South Korea continued—and the Communists objected strenuously. Airfield rehabilitation soon became a major obstacle in reaching agreement on prisoner exchange.[17]

On 11 December, to expedite the proceedings the UN team proposed concurrent negotiations over the next item on the agenda, exchange of POWs. Had the Americans strictly abided by the rules of the Geneva Convention pertaining to POWs, this agenda item might have been settled in a few days. The customary agreement was all-for-all POW swap. For humanitarian and, some argued, propaganda reasons, the Americans introduced several unprecedented and complicated conditions for exchange of prisoners. The conditions infuriated the Communists, threw the negotiations into turmoil, led to bizarre twists and turns that enormously damaged the United States in the eyes of the world, and ultimately prolonged the Korean War another year and a half, during which time United States forces suffered thirty-seven thousand more battlefield casualties.[18]

The causes were numerous and complex, but two factors were pivotal in influencing the Americans to depart from the usual all-for-all POW exchange. One involved Chinese prisoners held by the UN. The other involved South Korean prisoners impressed into the NKPA during its invasion of the South and who later defected to or had been captured by the UN forces.

The UN held about 20,500 Chinese. It was believed that a large number of them were former Nationalist Chinese soldiers who had defected or surrendered to the Communist forces during China's civil war. Since these Chinese soldiers had, in effect, surrendered twice, they might be viewed by the Communists as unreliable or even traitorous. The Communists might punish them or even murder them upon repatriation, was the prevailing rationale. The circumstance suggested the radical idea that if these Chinese wished, they could be repatriated to Chiang Kai-shek on Formosa, instead of Communist China. If so, the refusal of these Chinese to return to Communist controlled China could result in a substantial propaganda victory for the United States.[19]

Also among the POWs held by the UN were approximately forty thousand South Koreans who had been unwillingly impressed into the NKPA. Many of these impressed ROKs had collaborated with UN forces. They and most other South Koreans held in UN POW camps had no desire to return to Communist control. Rightly believing these South Koreans were not actually "legitimate" POWs and that many, if not most, would be severely punished or murdered if returned to the Communists in the customary POW swap, the U.S. government agreed with a request from President Syngman Rhee's government that these forty thousand South Koreans should be "reclassified" and gradually released to return to their homes in South Korea.[20]

These concepts, the first questionable at best, the second just and humane, led to a larger and even more controversial decision, which was seen by some critics as a technical violation of the Geneva Convention: that all POWs held by the UN would be polled to find out where they wanted to go upon repatriation. No POW held by the UN would be "forcibly" or "involuntarily" repatriated to the Communists.[21]

Behind the scenes in Washington, Tokyo, and Seoul, the voluntary repatriation doctrine was hotly debated. Many senior American officials, including Ridgway and Joy, strongly opposed the doctrine as unworkable or probably illegal, and as certain to be unacceptable to the Communists. Those opposed to the doctrine believed it risked prolonging the negotiations and war, and possibly a complete breakdown of the talks.[22]

The chief proponent of voluntary repatriation of POWs was President Truman, who clung to the concept tenaciously. He publicly proclaimed, "We will not buy an armistice by turning over human beings for slaughter or slavery." He elaborated in his memoir: "Just as I always insisted that we could not abandon the South Koreans who had stood by us and freedom, so I now refused to agree to any solution that provided for the return against their will of prisoners of war to Communist domination. . . . As far as I was concerned, this was not a point for bargaining."[23]

President Truman took many positions and decisions with respect to Korea and the war, but his adamant stand for voluntary repatriation would be the most controversial and morally debatable. If, as the doctrine's opponents predicted, it prolonged the negotiations and the war, American and other POWs held in Communist captivity would have to endure many more months and perhaps years of cruel incarceration and possibly death. It could further weaken the Eighth Army's will to fight in that its soldiers, if captured, could not anticipate reasonable treatment or early release. Finally, voluntary repatriation posed this most difficult question: Should American and UN soldiers fight and die or suffer wounds and injuries in order to give their former enemies, many of them traitors, freedom of choice over repatriation?[24]

When delegates opened discussions on the POW issue, the UN team at first did not reveal its position on voluntary repatriation. Instead, they merely proposed an early "fair and equitable" exchange of POWs, the sick, wounded, and injured to be returned first. The Communist delegates made their position unmistakably clear, citing Article 118 of the Geneva Convention. They demanded an all-for-all swap without delay. Still concealing its position on voluntary repatriation, the UN team shifted to another tack, an exchange of POW lists. When both sides produced the lists on 18 December, each team professed shock. The Communist list contained a total of only 11,559 names, 7,142 ROKs and 4,417 others, including 3,198 Americans. On the UN list were 132,474 names: 95,531 NKPA, 20,700 CCF, and 16,243 South Koreans impressed into the NKPA.[25]

Both sides cried foul. Because of NKPA radio boasts of having captured 65,000 ROKs in the early days of the war, and Eighth Army records carrying 88,000 ROKs and 11,500 other UN soldiers missing or captured, the UN team argued the Communists were withholding approximately 88,000 names.[26]

Charges and countercharges over the POW lists and allegedly withheld names stymied the talks' progress through the remainder of December 1951. During that time, the one-month limit on the truce line expired on 27 December, but delegates ignored the formerly important milestone and continued to ignore it in the weeks and months to come.

On 2 January 1952, the UN team introduced the doctrine of voluntary repatriation into the talks. As expected, the Communist reaction was complete shock and dismay. They labeled the doctrine "absurd" and too unreasonable to discuss. Days of acrimonious debate followed, in which Admiral Joy concluded gloomily that the Communists would never concede on the issue. He was convinced it would indefinitely delay an armistice, and furthermore, the U.S. government was on "unsound ground in insisting on the principle." In his memoir, Joy wrote that stubborn insistence on the voluntary repatriation doctrine "cost us over a year of war," during which the UN suffered fifty thousand more casualties.[27]

Yet the Communists did not walk out. There were several reasons. One reason was that in its all-out effort to sell the voluntary repatriation doctrine, the UN team consistently minimized its estimate of the number of UN POWs who would refuse to be repatriated to the Communists. At the same time the UN softened its hard-line position on airfield rehabilitation and other issues relating to armistice enforcement. When, finally, the UN team unwisely and prematurely estimated that "only 16,000" UN POWs would refuse repatriation, the Communists appeared to soften their position and even tacitly approved a "screening" or poll of POWs in UN custody. While these discussions were in progress, the American government conceived a dramatic "package deal" in which it would yield completely on the jet-capable airfield issue in return for a Communist concession on voluntary repatriation.[28]

The polling of CCF and NKPA POWs began in early April 1952. The results astounded the United Nations. At the halfway mark in the polling of 132,000 military POWs, the UN found approximately 40,000 would resist repatriation to the Communists. On the basis of these figures, the UN projected that of the total of 132,000 military POWs, plus 38,000 North Korean civilian internees, only a total of about 70,000 would elect to return to Communist control. While this could be a great propaganda boon for the UN, it also posed the danger the Communists would lose face to such a degree that they would end the talks. Behind the scenes, the UN hurried along its "package deal."[29]

When on 19 April the UN team presented its preliminary estimates on the number of UN-held POWs who would refuse repatriation, the Communists were thunderstruck. Again they felt they had been lied to and duped. Bitterly angry, they denounced the UN team for treachery. On 28 April, when the UN team presented its package deal, dropping its hard-line position on jet-capable airfields and softening on other unresolved issues pertaining to armistice enforcement, the Communists gave it scarcely a glance. They walked out, recessing the talks indefinitely.[30]

The Communists' Counter to Voluntary Repatriation

After the U.S. government introduced the doctrine of voluntary repatriation into the negotiations in January 1952, the Communists launched a vicious propaganda attack against the United States in which POWs held by them and the UN became victims or instruments. The campaign consisted of three cunning, interrelated elements: germ warfare, brainwashing, and POW riots.

On 2 February 1952, Soviet ambassador to the UN Jacob Malik accused the United States of employing bullets filled with "toxic gases" in Korea. Peking, Pyongyang, and Communist organs worldwide picked up and expanded his theme, later charging that United States airmen and artillerymen dropped and fired bacteria-infected insects and shellfish (e.g., beetles, lice, ticks, rats, fleas, and clams) into North Korea. To support their claims, the Communists created faked "exhibits" and inaugurated a massive inoculation program. Finally, by torture and threats, they forced two young Air Force POWs, and later, a senior Marine Corps pilot and thirty-five other Air Force pilots, to "confess" on film, on tape, and in press interviews that they had been part of a huge United States germ warfare conspiracy. This wholly fabricated propaganda attack, supported by Communist-manipulated "demonstrations" all over the world, was astonishingly successful. The Americans' slow-footed, righteous denials were not.[31]

In parallel with the germ warfare campaign, the Communists launched an "indoctrination" program of UN POWs, intended to turn them against the West and even refuse repatriation. The program included primarily a form of mental torture, although physical isolation was also used. The mental torture consisted of endless repetition of Communist slogans, phrases, and ideas, and the exploitation of grievances, especially among black POWs. Although few POWs were directly threatened with grave harm or death, they knew thousands of UN POWs had earlier been tortured or murdered, and partly as a result of this knowledge, this Communist campaign, which became known as "brainwashing," was also astoundingly successful. Postwar studies showed that only about 12 percent of American POWs, Gen. Bill Dean among them, "actively and consistently" resisted the program. The great majority "cooperated in indoctrination and interrogation sessions in a passive sort of way, although there was a tendency to refuse to say anything obviously traitorous." Many UN POWs did sign "peace petitions" and similar pro-Communist testimonials, which were distributed in the West. Ultimately, twenty-one Americans and one Briton refused repatriation.[32]

Beginning in early 1952, the Communists allowed trained agents to be captured as POWs. The agents were instructed to organize the hard-core Communist POWs and foment riots and other disturbances inside UN POW compounds on the island of Koje and elsewhere. The purpose was to incur punitive UN countermeasures in the compounds, which the Communists could then exploit. As planned, "riots" in UN POW compounds occurred 18 February and 13 March 1952. While attempting to quell the riots, UN guards fired into the POWs, killing 89 and wounding 166. Having cunningly staged these incidents, the Communists then denounced the UN worldwide for "barbarous massacres" and "atrocities."[33]

After the Communists broke off talks on 28 April, the POW "riots" intensified. On 12 May, during a spectacular riot on the island of Koje, Communists seized the American POW camp commander, Brig. Gen. Francis T. Dodd, who, in an attempt to negotiate with the rioters, got too close. The POWs "tried" Dodd and sentenced him to death. In an effort to save his own life, Dodd signed a document, agreeing to cease immediately the "barbarous behavior, insults, torture . . . [and] mass murdering" of POWs by guns, germs, poison gas, and atomic weapons and to halt the screening of POWs for the purpose of complying with the UN's "illegal and unreasonable" voluntary repatriation program. Sent to Koje to free Dodd by military force if necessary, the new I Corps chief of staff, Brig. Gen. Charles F. Colson, decided against using force and signed a document which he believed would gain Dodd's freedom. Colson conceded that numerous POWs had been killed and wounded by UN guards and that he would do all within his power "to eliminate further violence and bloodshed." He guaranteed "humane treatment" for UN POWs and agreed that there would be "no more forcible screening of any remaining POWs in this camp." Dodd got out, but the Communists exploited the two documents as further "proof" of UN "atrocities," humiliating the United States and the Eighth Army and raising serious questions worldwide over the validity of the voluntary repatriation doctrine.[34]

After the truce talks were broken off, and while the riots on Koje were finally being brought under control, President Truman, on 20 May 1952, in a major policy address at West Point during the final days of the United States Military Academy's Sesquicentennial celebration, firmly reiterated his views on the prisoner repatriation question:

> Up to now . . . the communists have not agreed on a fair and proper exchange of prisoners of war. The communists have continued to insist that all the prisoners we have taken must be handed over to them—regardless of whether or not they are willing to be sent back behind the Iron Curtain, and regardless of what their fate would be if they were sent back.
>
> It is perfectly clear that thousands and thousands of the prisoners we hold would violently resist being returned to the communists because they fear slavery and or death that would await them. It would be a betrayal of the ideals of freedom and justice for which we are fighting if we forced these men at bayonet point to return to their ex-masters. We won't do it. We won't buy an armistice by trafficking in human slavery.[35]

Throughout the summer of 1952, the talks at Panmunjom remained deadlocked over the voluntary repatriation issue and evolved into an institutionalized propaganda forum, where the liaison officers or senior delegates met occasionally to lodge charges and countercharges. Neither side budged or offered any new proposals.

The stalemated war also became institutionalized along the truce line. The two sides continued to hurl immense quantities of artillery shells, send out patrols, and occasionally attempt larger maneuvers to gain a hill. The Eighth Army staff from time to time conceived and urged larger operations, but these were canceled or postponed indefinitely. The unpopular draft continued in the United States. The Army sent twenty to thirty thousand young Americans every month to the bunkers and ridges in Korea, to put in about ten or eleven cautious and mostly boring months "at the front," after which they returned home for discharge, with no parades or other form of community thanks or recognition.[36]

A Change of Commander-in-Chief

The Truman administration was under attack from many quarters as the presidential election year of 1952 began. The war in Korea remained an unresolved nightmare which had cost more than one hundred thousand American casualties, and appeared mired in petty haggling at Panmunjom —while more Americans died and American POWs suffered physical and mental torture. McCarthyism, however odious, was rampant and effective. Millions of Americans did not doubt that the government, especially Dean Acheson's State Department, was infested with Communist spies, pinkos, and fellow travelers. A number of President Harry Truman's appointees, including his senior Army aide and longtime Missouri friend Brig. Gen. Harry Vaughan, had been caught with their hands in the government till, creating an aura of impropriety and scandal. The president's public opinion approval ratings sank to an abysmally low average of about 30 percent.[37]

Truman had earlier decided he would not run for reelection, and sought a successor who would keep Democratic control of the White House through the 1950s. His first choice was five-star General of the Army Dwight D. Eisenhower, commander of the North Atlantic Treaty Organization (NATO) forces. Eisenhower, who was considering a run for the presidency, effectively declined being Truman's selection, when Eisenhower let it be known he was Republican. Truman's next choice was the chief justice of the supreme court, Fred M. Vinson, who was a friend and former secretary of the treasury. When Vinson also declined, Truman turned to Illinois governor Adlai E. Stevenson. He hesitated but finally accepted, and at the Democratic convention he chose Alabama senator John Sparkman to run with him as vice presidential candidate.[38]

In 1952, the minority Republican party was sharply divided. The front-runner was right-wing, isolationist Senator Robert Taft of Ohio, who, as expected, had allied himself with retired general Douglas MacArthur. If the Taft-MacArthur ticket won, Taft promised to appoint Vice President MacArthur "deputy commander in chief of the armed forces." Liberal Republicans such as Thomas E. Dewey, Henry Cabot Lodge, and others feared another resounding defeat and persuaded Eisenhower to run against the proposed Taft-MacArthur ticket. Eisenhower was reluctant to campaign for delegates but finally relented and returned to the United States on 1 June. In a tough convention battle, he defeated Taft and chose Richard M. Nixon for his vice presidential running mate.[39]

The NATO command Eisenhower left had become a prestigious, sought-after post. There was talk of promoting Eisenhower's successor to five stars, to outrank the deputy commander, British Field Marshal Bernard Montgomery, and other NATO generals. Gen. Omar Bradley, chairman of the JCS, earlier had hoped to persuade President Truman to give the post to the Army chief of staff, Gen. J. Lawton Collins, making room for Ridgway to replace Collins. Bradley, seeing the NATO command as more prestigious, now changed his mind. On 12 May 1952, Ridgway left Tokyo to relieve Eisenhower. Gen. Mark Clark, who was contemplating retirement, agreed to replace Ridgway in Tokyo.[40]

Clark assumed the Far East Command from Ridgway in the midst of the difficult POW riots in Koje. He had been the postwar commander in Trieste and, like Ridgway, had often verbally fought with the Communists. Well suited to hold a hard-line position, he firmly believed the only way to break the deadlock at Panmunjom was continuing military pressure. Accordingly, Clark drew up plans for greatly expanding ground operations, including deployment of Chinese Nationalist troops to Korea, amphibious landings behind the enemy in North Korea, and, where practicable, tactical use of atomic bombs against CCF and NKPA military targets—and possibly even air and naval attacks on mainland China.[41]

The JCS put the ground plans on hold but authorized Clark to mount renewed, massive bombing attacks on North Korea. The Far East Air Force targets included the civilian populations of Pyongyang, seventy-eight smaller towns, eleven hydroelectric plants and related facilities along the Yalu River, and an oil refinery eight miles from the Soviet border. The attacks flattened Pyongyang, caused a two-week electrical power blackout throughout all North Korea, and ignited worldwide protests, even by the governments in London and Paris. General Clark ignored the uproar and continued the FEAF bombing attacks in a vain hope to drive the Communists back to the negotiating table.[42]

By this time the chief UN negotiator, Admiral Joy, had retired, and Army general William K. Harrison, Jr., replaced him. (Harrison was an April 1917 West Point classmate of Generals Clark, Ridgway, and Collins.) Coordinating with the State Department and Department of Defense in Washington, Clark and Harrison drew up another voluntary repatriation "package offer." The package would assure the Communists of eighty-three thousand rather than seventy thousand returnees, and other minor concessions. The UN team dramatically unveiled the new offer to the Communists on 28 September 1952, as a "final offer." When the Communists rejected the "package" on 8 October, Harrison, acting on instructions from the American government, walked out. The senior delegates did not meet again for six months.[43]

Perhaps in retaliation, in early October 1952, the CCF launched aggressive ground operations along the truce line in the Iron Triangle. Responding, Van Fleet obtained permission from Clark for a limited counterattack. The result was bitter, costly fighting for several hills in the sector, including Jane Russell, White Horse, and Pike's Peak. Neither side had sufficient ground forces or the will to overpower the other, and the furious actions gradually tapered off. UN forces' casualties were heavy—nine thousand, mostly ROKs—and the CCF lost an estimated nineteen thousand. As bitterly cold weather set in, the third miserable winter of the Korean War, both sides again dug into bunkers along the truce line and once more restricted action to patrolling and massive artillery duels. The huge expenditure of UN artillery shells seriously depleted theater and Eighth Army reserves.

Gen. James Van Fleet, increasingly frustrated and grief-stricken over the loss of his airman son in an FEAF bombing raid in April 1952,[44] complained bitterly of an "ammo shortage." His charges brought a sensational but inconclusive congressional investigation.[45]

During the October fighting, the presidential campaign in the United States built up a full head of steam. The Korean War and the corruption and communism in the Truman administration were key issues. With respect to the Korean War, Eisenhower rejected extremist views and promised to work toward a just and lasting peace. Toward the end of the campaign, on 24 October, Eisenhower electrified voters with a stroke of political genius. He promised, "I shall go to Korea." Eisenhower trounced Stevenson, 442 electoral votes to 89.[46]

President-elect Eisenhower fulfilled his promise and went to Korea, arriving on 2 December for a three-day tour, including a visit with his son, John, then serving as battalion S-3 (operations officer) in the 15th Infantry Regiment. Generals Clark and Van Fleet attempted to present Eisenhower with aggressive plans to win the war militarily, including the use of Chinese Nationalist troops and atomic bombs. But the president-elect displayed little or no interest in these proposals, leaving both Clark and Van Fleet the clear impression that Eisenhower would continue the Truman policy of seeking a negotiated solution.[47]

Renewed Hope and Tighter Reins

President Dwight D. Eisenhower came to office in early 1953 with a clear mandate to end the war in Korea honorably, but his administration possessed no magic solution. As a first step the new president and his no-nonsense secretary of state, John Foster Dulles, turned to power diplomacy, or what journalists labeled "brinkmanship." First, they rescinded Truman's earlier order which had neutralized Formosa, implying they might "unleash Chiang Kai-shek" and raising the possibility that the Chinese Nationalists might attempt an invasion of the mainland. Second, at Panmunjom, New Delhi, and elsewhere they dropped discreet hints that if the deadlock in the peace talks were not soon broken, the United States might not confine the war to Korea and might employ atomic bombs in Asia.

President-elect Dwight D. Eisenhower (*left*) fulfilling his promise to "go to Korea," December 1952. He is shown here visiting the front line with Maj. Gen. James Fry, commander of the 2d Infantry Division.
Courtesy of National Archives and Robert M. Euwer

Eisenhower later wrote in his memoirs, "the prospects for an armistice seemed to improve."[48]

Prospects for an armistice may have been considerably improved by a stroke of fate. On 5 March 1953, Joseph Stalin died. The Soviet Premier, though pragmatically allying the Soviet Union with the West against the axis powers during World War II, had once more moved the Communists toward the role of implacable, hard-line adversaries of the West after the war. Ten days after Stalin's death, Georgi M. Malenkov, his successor, in a speech appeared to offer an olive branch to the West, declaring there was no existing dispute between the United States and the Soviet Union that "cannot be decided by peaceful means, on the basis of mutual understanding."[49]

Secretary of State Dulles and other cabinet members in the Eisenhower administration dismissed the speech as yet more Kremlin trickery. Eisenhower, over Dulles's objections, directly responded in a cautiously optimistic speech, titled "The Chance for Peace," challenging Malenkov to match his word with deeds, including an "honorable armistice" in Korea. Whether at Moscow's direction or by pure coincidence, on 28 March, two weeks after Malenkov's speech, the Communists suddenly responded favorably to an earlier proposal by General Clark to exchange sick and wounded POWs. Not only that, the Communists said the exchange "should be made to lead to a smooth settlement of the entire question of prisoners of war, thereby achieving an armistice in Korea, for which people throughout the world are longing." Red China's Foreign Minister Chou En-lai and North Korea's Premier Kim Il Sung followed several days later with pronouncements that seemed to soften the Communist stand against voluntary repatriation. Both leaders expressed agreement to an earlier proposal to allow a "neutral state," such as India or Switzerland, to supervise the exchange and interview Communist POWs who refused repatriation, to ascertain their true desires.[50]

The Communist overtures were accompanied by a sudden and puzzling intensification of ground activity along the truce line. These attacks were met by a new Eighth Army commander, Lt. Gen. Maxwell D. Taylor, who dismissed the intensified CCF attacks as face-saving propaganda maneuvers. Eisenhower had sent Taylor to Korea to replace the restive and grieving Van Fleet, who retired a four star general, bitterly critical of the conduct of the past two years of the Korean War. Taylor took command on 11 February 1953. He came from the Army staff in Washington, where he was Deputy Chief of Staff for Operations and Administration, and was alive to Eisenhower's desire for an end to UN casualties and an early honorable settlement of the war.[51]

On 1 March, Maj. Gen. Paul D. Adams, the Eighth Army chief of staff, signed Letter of Instruction Number One in behalf of the Eighth's new boss, General Taylor. The letter, in essence a standing order addressed to the five corps commanders whose divisions and regiments were defending the 155-mile line, conveyed the ground forces' mission in defending the Republic of Korea. Key paragraphs stated,

3.a.   (1) Continue active defense of MLR in respective zones to include mutual contact and security along boundaries between zones.

(2) Maintain and improve fortifications in corps zones.

(3) Maintain integrity of the corps and subordinate units with minimum personnel losses consistent with execution of the mission.

(4) Maintain order in respective area of responsibility . . .

x. (1) (a) Maintain the Line KANSAS in a state of readiness for immediate occupancy. No changes will be made in this line involving either a battalion or larger size position or limiting points between corps without approval of this headquarters.

(b) Maintain Line WYOMING in the I US Corps, IX US Corps and II ROK Corps in a state of readiness for occupancy for conducting a major delaying action or to serve as a line of departure for a major counterattack.

(c) Prepare other delaying or blocking positions between Line KANSAS and the present MLR upon approval of this headquarters.

(d) Prepare to occupy Line ICELAND under armistice conditions within 72 hours and commence fortifications of it thereafter on order.

(2) Utilize all available sources to obtain essential enemy information as required by current intelligence directives.

(3) Undertake no offensive action involving a unit of company size or larger without approval of this headquarters, except counterattacks to restore or maintain the integrity of vital positions.

(4) Patrol aggressively at such frequencies as required to obtain essential information, secure occupied positions against surprise, deny intelligence to the enemy, and maintain contact between adjacent units. Raids on the enemy position will normally be limited to those essential to obtaining prisoners.

(5) Review and improve current plans for defense, employing rehearsals and CPXs [command post exercises] where applicable for training reserve units in blocking, and in diversionary attack and counterattack roles. Plans will include defense against airborne and guerrilla attacks and, for flank corps, amphibious attacks and raids. These plans will envision prompt containment and destruction of enemy forces.

(6) Develop and maintain active and passive air defense.

(7) Train units in reserve with the principal objective of developing and maintaining maximum effectiveness for offensive combat.

(8) This Letter of Instruction recapitulates the terms of your operational missions. It . . . supersedes all previous instructions on the same subject.[52]

With this letter General Taylor, the Eighth Army's new boss, gave broad, unmistakable operational guidance to his corps commanders, and clearly set the tone for conduct of the ground war in its final months. He reaffirmed the concept of "active defense," and spelled out specific conditions and limitations under which raids or counterattacks would be conducted, including the size of units committed. Casualties were to be held to a minimum. Defenses would be improved and strengthened, and planning for the anticipated armistice signing would proceed. There would be no major ground offensives by UN forces, but corps should train their units in reserve to be ready to conduct offensive operations.

The enemy's objectives and means for attaining them were quite different those final months. The stage was set for some of the most bitter and costly fighting of the Korean War.

7th Division's Long Road to Pork Chop

When the 7th Infantry Division came ashore at Inchon on 17 September 1950, it was part of the Eighth Army's X Corps. After playing a significant role in the second liberation of Seoul, the Republic of Korea capital, and linking up with units of the 1st Cavalry Division south of Suwon by 29 September, the division conducted mopping-up operations in the Seoul area until 5 October, when it began moving south to Pusan. Here the division entered training for another amphibious landing, this time in North Korea, at the east coast town of Iwon. From there the 17th Infantry Regiment spearheaded a drive through Pungsan and Kapsan, and entered the key Yalu River city of Hyesanjin on 21 November. By this time a three-battalion task force of the division's 31st and 32d Infantry Regiments had moved to the eastern shore of the Chosin Reservoir, where they were attached to the 1st Marine Division. When the CCF began their second phase, or all-out intervention in the war, elements of the 7th Division along the axis of advance Iwon to Hyesanjin withdrew to the X Corps Hungnam perimeter. By 29 November, the task force in the Chosin Reservoir area was surrounded by elements of six Chinese divisions. Two days later, with the regimental commander either killed or captured and command of the task force passed to the senior battalion commander, Lt. Col. Don Faith, the hard-hit task force began a fighting withdrawal south toward the town of Hagaru-ri and, finally, was virtually destroyed. Survivors reached the Hungnam perimeter on 11 December, where the 7th Division successfully defended a sector of the contracting perimeter until completing its outloading by 19 December, and sailed to Pusan.[53]

Offloading at Pusan, the division moved north up the eastern sector of Korea and reengaged the advancing enemy as the UN forces reestablished a line stretching across the peninsula south of Seoul. During the first three months of 1951, the 7th Division advanced in the eastern sector and reached a position just south of the thirty-eighth parallel on 31 March. Shifting left to an adjacent sector the 7th continued its attack to the north, captured the city of Yanggu, and defeated enemy attempts to break through that key position during the Communist spring offensive of 1951. On moving to an area north of Chipyong-ni, the division defended this sector successfully until 21 May.

During the subsequent UN counteroffensive, the 7th led the IX Corps drive on the central front and captured the key city of Hwachon. Continuing its drive against a stubbornly defending enemy, the division reached a point southeast of Kumhwa on 17 June, before reverting to reserve status for two months. The 7th then returned to action, moving into defensive positions north of Hwachon, from which limited objective attacks were conducted during August and September.[54]

In early October 1951, the 7th Division moved into reserve for two weeks after which it shifted farther west again, into the X Corps sector, and defended positions in the Heartbreak Ridge and Punch Bowl area until February 1952. The 7th was ordered into reserve for the third time since entering Korea and remained in this status until April, when it occupied a sector in the IX Corps at the base of the Iron Triangle, east of the Chorwon Valley. Active patrolling missions in this sector lasted until 14 October when units from two infantry battalions launched a coordinated attack against Hill 598, or Triangle Hill complex. By 16 October the hill mass was seized and successfully defended until 25 October when the 2d ROK Division relieved the 7th in the Triangle Hill area. Nine infantry battalions were committed by the division in the attack and defense of the Triangle complex.[55]

Moving into reserve in November, the 7th spent six weeks in training, then moved farther left into positions on the east flank of Eighth Army's I Corps on 29 December. Here, patrolling and raiding was again the principal tactical activity until 23 March.

Life and Ceremony in the Midst of Stalemate

The American World War II armor leader and tactical genius, Gen. George S. Patton, Jr., possessed a straightforward philosophy about winning on the battlefield. "Don't let the sons-a-bitches stand still long enough to dig a foxhole," he said. The principle of the offensive was his prescription for winning battles and wars, and in 1953, at the United States Military Academy, Patton's alma mater, the Principle of the Offensive was the fourth of nine Principles of War taught in the course titled "The History of Military Art": "Seize, retain, and exploit the initiative. Through offensive action, a commander preserves his freedom of action and imposes his will on the enemy. The selection by the commander of the right time and the right place for offensive action is a decisive factor in the success of the operation. A defensive attitude may be forced on a commander by many situations; but a defensive attitude should be deliberately adopted only as a temporary expedient while awaiting an opportunity for counteroffensive action, or for the purpose of economizing forces on a front where a decision is not sought."[56]

The defensive was not listed as one of the nine principles of war. To this day, deeply embedded in the psyche of any American professional or citizen soldier, sailor, or airman is the sure knowledge that wars are not won by remaining on the defensive. Battles can be won while on the defensive—

attackers repulsed, destroyed, even defeated for a brief period, setting the stage for shifting from defense to offense. But wars cannot be won by remaining on the defensive. Initiative cannot be ceded permanently to the enemy. The battle must be taken to the enemy, to destroy or collapse his ability or will to make war. Ground war on the offensive is the war of maneuver, taking and holding terrain, which, in Korea, essentially ended for UN forces on 27 November 1951.

At the end of March 1953, the 7th Infantry Division completed its third month of occupying and defending Line Jamestown, the line the 1st Cavalry Division had bought so dearly in September and October 1951. Through 22 March 1953, the principal tactical activity by the 7th was reconnaissance and combat patrols, the latter with the mission of capturing enemy personnel and equipment, and the interception of enemy forces by friendly outguards.[57]

Life evolves and changes during the shift from a maneuvering war to prolonged trench and bunker warfare. Starkly different from the rushed, harried daily movements in a war of maneuver, trench warfare becomes an odd mixture of boredom; many of the comforts of stateside duty in rear areas; a lack of sleep during tense periods of alert on MLR, patrol, outpost, and outguard duty during daily enemy shelling; and periods of unmitigated, heart-pounding fear during fierce artillery and mortar bombardments, clouds of grenades thrown during brutal close-in fire fights, or swarming, screaming infantry assaults that end with swirling, "kill or be killed" hand-to-hand fighting. There was a routine in life "at the front" in the stalemated Korean War, however strange it might seem.

Dutifully recorded in the monthly command reports, the daily routine plus the ebb and flow of life in the 7th Infantry Division is clearly evident. From 15 February to 15 March, 1,216 men from the 7th left Korea, bound for the United States, having completed their assignments with the division. Among them were 58 officers and 1,158 enlisted men. Replacements received numbered 1,121, including 138 officers and 983 enlisted men. Additionally, the 7th Replacement Company returned 1 officer and 188 enlisted men to duty with 7th Division units, mostly men who had previously been wounded, injured in accidents, or ill.[58]

The present for duty strength averaged 15,514 during the period, including 912 officers, 104 warrant officers, and 14,498 enlisted men. The division's total authorized strength was 18,257, and the G-1 (division personnel

officer) noted both totals, concluding the division was "below authorized strength." However, a more comprehensive picture of overall division
strength, in terms of numbers, is seen when including the augmenting and
attached combat units: 2,346 South Korean soldiers (KATUSAs) integrated
into division units; an attached Colombian Battalion with 47 officers and
1,036 enlisted men; an attached Ethiopian Battalion with 47 officers, 18
warrant officers, and 847 enlisted; and the attached U.S. 505th Military
Intelligence Service Platoon composed of 5 officers and 18 enlisted, a total
of 19,878 officers and enlisted.[59]

Numbers do not necessarily provide a complete, realistic assessment of
strength, and in March the 7th Division G-1 pointed to a "serious shortage
of officers in the rank of captain, capable of commanding companies in
the infantry and armored units." The shortage of captains ready to command companies was in part due to casualty rates among junior officers,
who were platoon leaders, executive officers, and company commanders in
line infantry and armored units. Often, company commanders were selected
in the field, from among lieutenants who were platoon leaders and executive officers fortunate enough to survive the battlefield's hazards, learn by
doing, and be seen and evaluated by senior officers as ready for battlefield
command of a company. A thoughtful company commander developed a
succession plan, a priority list of who would take command in an emergency should the commander be incapacitated or killed in action.[60]

During January and February, CCF units in front of the 7th Division
maintained defense through a tight counterpatrol screen, through continuous fortification work, and by launching occasional small unit probes
against the UN outpost line of resistance. Enemy entrenching and counterpatrol activity continued the first three weeks in March, but more frequent,
aggressive enemy patrolling was evident. As a result, in the period between
15 February and 15 March, casualties on both sides began to increase.
Among U.S. troops, 3 officers and 58 enlisted were killed in action, 10
officers and 189 enlisted were wounded, 1 officer was captured, and 7
enlisted men were missing in action. From the UN units attached to the 7th
Division, 11 Colombians and 1 Ethiopian were killed in action, with 44
Colombians and 10 Ethiopians wounded.[61]

Meanwhile, behind and on the MLR and outpost line of resistance, commanders constantly measured and assessed unit effectiveness and morale. A
wary eye was always on discipline, law and order as a primary indicator of

Gen. Mark W. Clark and other senior officers depart an observation post on the crest of a hill overlooking Chinese and UN positions near Old Baldy, March 1953. *Courtesy of Don Filgo*

morale, good order, and discipline. In March, the 7th Division's staff judge advocate, the equivalent of a district attorney, reported five cases of absent without leave (AWOL) and the apprehension and return to military control of seven AWOL offenders. There were eleven trials by general courts-martial, and the judge advocate reviewed thirty-seven records of "inferior" courts-martial, trials of less serious offenses which were prosecuted in units within the division. Forty-one soldiers in the 7th received legal assistance, and one processed a claim with the assistance of the judge advocate's office.[62]

In the rear areas, chaplains, the Red Cross and United Services Organization (USO), the Public Information Office (PIO), postal services, finance services, the 7th Division Band, Special Services, the safety section, the Civil Affairs Section, Housing, and the personnel officer's awards and decorations section provided services and a slice of stateside garrison duty to units and individual soldiers rotating in and out of the bunker and trench lines along the MLR and on the outposts.[63]

Chaplains circulated throughout the division, administering to soldiers' spiritual welfare. In March, chaplains held 491 services for 17,988 persons and made 118 hospital visits, reporting 1,026 personal contacts. They furnished services to people of all faiths throughout the division sector and adjoining areas and provided character guidance lectures to incoming enlisted replacements at the Division Training Center.[64]

Soldiers' stateside links and communications home were more frequent in the stalemated war than during the yo-yo war. Postal activities received and distributed approximately sixty-six thousand pieces of letter mail and one thousand sacks of parcel post. Stamp purchases amounted to $6,390, money orders to $581,285. The Public Information Office prepared 94 general releases, 97 photo releases, 122 hometown photo releases, and 933 hometown news releases. During March, thirty-eight correspondents, all accredited by the Far East Command, visited the division area, some writing stories about men in the division. Television correspondents shot ten thousand feet of film for use in the continental United States, and radio correspondents recorded and broadcast interviews with soldiers. The same month five issues of the weekly newspaper, the *Bayonet,* were published, with thirty-five thousand copies distributed to the division's men.[65]

Special Services brought a touch of home to the division rear area with three USO shows, presenting ten performances before an estimated audience total of 8,900. Movies were favorites for bringing home to troops, with 797 movie showings attended by audience totals of 143,480. There were 268 magazine packs and 260 book kits distributed to units of the division. Special Services also reported 1,515 persons, including 101 officers and 1,414 enlisted men, were sent to Japan for Rest and Recuperation.[66]

During the maneuver war, infiltration by enemy troops dressed in civilian clothes spawned guerrilla activity and nagging, rear area harassment of UN forces on the move. This circumstance was aggravated when UN forces were on the offensive and broke out of the Pusan Perimeter, moving rapidly northward. They bypassed pockets of NKPA troops which had to be "mopped up" to avoid ambush or rear area attacks. When the Chinese entered the war and linked up with reconstituting NKPA units to drive rapidly southward again, they were effective in mixing guerrilla and conventional warfare tactics. They often slipped past the flanks and got into the rear of withdrawing UN forces, frequently blocking or cutting withdrawal routes, causing allied forces to fight their way southward.

Now, with the front stabilized, UN units could better guard against such activity, and more effectively detect and control the movement of potential guerrillas, agents, and saboteurs throughout the division sector. The increased rear area security permitted the Civic Affairs Section to bolster relief and civic action work. In March they distributed two bundles of relief clothing totaling 184 pieces of apparel for the needy in the rear area, and using twenty-two, two-and-a-half-ton trucks, delivered twenty-nine loads of logs to the Pochon saw mill to convert to lumber for the 7th Division Memorial School. The two aid stations supervised by the Section treated a total of 1,205 civilians in the rear area. They assumed responsibility for pay and administration of the division's Korean Service Corps members, some 6,500 government-hire civilians employed by the division to perform labor which included construction of trenching and fortifications, loading, transporting, and unloading supplies and equipment and retrieval of bodies.[67]

The war was still in progress in spite of the routine, garrison duty atmosphere present in the rear areas. There were many administrative reminders of the war accompanying the daily doses of patrols, raids, artillery and mortar duels—and casualties—on both sides. The 7th's Finance Section reported March disbursements as $1,544,711, saying combat-duty pay of $433,170 went to 515 officers and 9,111 enlisted. There was leadership training for junior enlisted personnel, orientations for the steady stream of replacements coming into the 7th Division and its units, and awards and decorations. Thirty-two officers and forty-three enlisted men received decorations during the period from 15 February to 15 March. Among them were fourteen recipients of the Silver Star—the nation's third highest decoration for valor—two awarded to officers and twelve to enlisted men. There were thirty-six Bronze Star Medals awarded for valor, twelve to officers, twenty-four to enlisted. The Bronze Star Medal with the "V" device is the fourth highest decoration for valor.

The prisoner of war collecting section reported two prisoners of war captured and evacuated during the period, bringing the POW total for the 7th Infantry Division to 7,055 since it came ashore at Inchon on 17 September 1950. In March 1953, the 7th Quartermaster Company's Graves Registration Section processed the remains of three officers and sixty-four enlisted men of the 7th Division. The section also processed thirty-two enlisted men of allied units and five Korean Service Corps personnel. The 7th Quartermaster Company forwarded all remains to the 293d Quartermaster Graves Registration Company in Chong Dong-Ri.[68]

Maj. Gen. Arthur G.
Trudeau, who had just
arrived in Korea, en route
to take command of the 7th
Infantry Division.
*Courtesy of U.S. Army
Military History Institute*

On 21 and 22 March, a few kilometers behind the MLR, in the midst of this strange war and the steady flow of casualties, there were ceremonies. During the month the 7th Division Band maintained a full schedule of musical entertainment. "Combos" of three- or four-piece orchestras from the band frequently entertained units within the division. On 21 March, at the division airstrip, the band participated with the division's honor guard in the arrival and change of command ceremonies for the new commander of the 7th Infantry Division, Maj. Gen. Arthur G. Trudeau, who replaced Maj. Gen. Wayne C. Smith. The ceremonies included a division review in honor of the departing commander. On 22 March, the band again participated with the Honor Guard, at the airstrip, in the departure ceremony for General Smith.[69]

The evening of the next day, General Trudeau received a welcoming ceremony from units of the Chinese Communist Forces' 67th Division, 23d Army. While truce negotiations seemed on the verge of substantive progress for the first time in months, the Communists had decided to couple the reinvigorated talks with their heaviest assaults on the 7th Infantry Division since its arrival in the I Corps sector on 29 December 1952.

3

THE FALL OF OLD BALDY

Danger on the Left Flank

AT THE BEGINNING OF MARCH, ENEMY UNITS OPPOSING THE 7TH Infantry Division were the 141st Division of the 47th CCF Army and the 67th Division, 23d CCF Army. The 67th Division was arrayed in front of the 7th Infantry Division, and the 23d CCF Army's 69th Division was deployed in front of the 2d ROK Division, which was on line on the 7th's right (east) flank. The CCF supported its 23d Army infantry units with the 27th Regiment, 1st Artillery Division, the 29th Regiment, 2d Artillery Division, and an unidentified CCF Armored Regiment.[1]

Twelve Chinese infantry battalions, ten artillery battalions, and the equivalent of one armored battalion composed the forces operating to the 7th Division's front in March. The infantry battalions were six to seven hundred men each. Ninety CCF artillery pieces were capable of firing into the division sector, and there were approximately twenty tanks or self-propelled guns operating to the front.[2]

The 7th Infantry Division defended their front with two regiments on line and one in reserve. The 31st Infantry manned MLR and outpost positions in the left (west) sector, their left flank anchored to the ROK's 12th

61

Regiment, 1st ROK Division. The 2d, 1st, and 3d Battalions of the 31st Infantry were on line, left to right, with the Colombia Battalion in regimental reserve. The 17th Regiment was responsible for the 7th Division's right sector, with the ROK's 2d Division manning the line on their east flank. The 17th's three battalions on line, from left to right, were the 1st, 2d, and 3d, with the 1st Battalion of the 32d Infantry in regimental reserve. The 32d Regiment was the 7th Division reserve as the month began.[3]

Col. William L. Hardick commanded the 17th Infantry Regiment, and Col. William B. Kern, West Point class of 1934, commanded the 31st Infantry. Col. George L. Van Way, Kern's West Point classmate, commanded the 32d Regiment. All three were World War II combat veterans.

While UN forces in the 7th Infantry Division sector continued their routine of reconnaissance, combat, ambush, and screening patrols; raiding parties; and the manning of outpost and outguard positions the first three weeks in March, signs of impending enemy offensive operations against division and Pork Chop Hill began appearing early in the month. Obvious during the first three weeks was an increase in enemy reconnaissance patrols. Almost daily, UN outguards intercepted small groups of Chinese soldiers attempting to move close and observe allied defensive positions. The enemy patrols often quickly withdrew without exchanging fire.[4]

The night of 6–7 March, a 31st Regiment combat patrol intercepted an enemy battalion apparently en route to Pork Chop from the Hasakkol area. The Chinese supported the attack with approximately eight thousand rounds of mortar and artillery rained on the hill in a four-hour period, and another one thousand rounds on Hill 347, the dominant hill mass in the division's sector southwest of the Chop. The attempted battalion assault on Pork Chop was costly to the CCF: fifty-six counted dead. There were estimates of an additional one hundred killed, and another one hundred wounded, although there was no way to verify the 31st Regiment's estimates. At 2:30 A.M. on 9 March, two enemy platoons engaged a UN combat patrol in a one-hour fire fight, raking the patrol with fire from three sides.[5]

On 10 March, two CCF platoons in defensive positions on Hill 180 engaged a Colombia Battalion raiding party intent on capturing enemy soldiers for interrogation. In defense of Hill 180, the CCF hurled four thousand more rounds of artillery and mortar on their own position and another five thousand rounds on nearby UN MLR and outpost positions. On 16 March, two squads of enemy entrenched on Pokkae engaged a UN combat

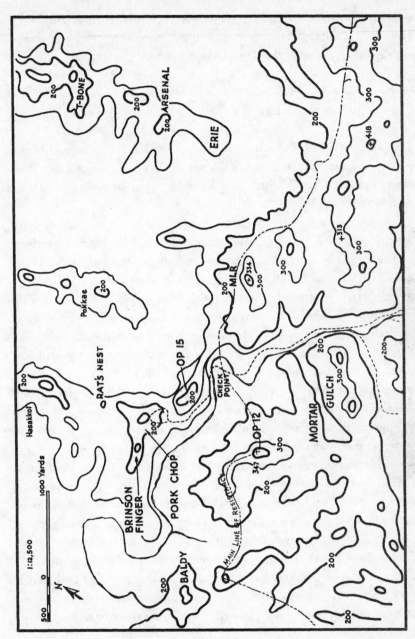

The area of battle. The dotted line shows the supply road leading to Pork Chop.

patrol for twenty minutes. Again on 18 March, from prepared positions on Hill 200, a Chinese-held outpost, an undetermined number of CCF troops engaged a UN combat patrol in a ten-minute fire fight.[6]

March 1953: In Like a Lion

The 7th Division's active defense in February included 241 reconnaissance patrols, 186 combat patrols, and six screening patrols. During the first three weeks in March the division was well on the way to matching its number of February patrols.

The size of reconnaissance patrols varied from two men to one squad of ten to twelve men. They deployed around the clock, in hours of daylight and darkness, from units manning outposts, the MLR, or in reserve immediately behind the MLR. Combat patrols, sometimes called ambush patrols, varied in strength from five men to two squads and generally consisted of an assault element and a support element. The patrols lay in ambush on known or suspected enemy routes of approach. Also dispatched with raiding missions against enemy security forces or small outposts, ambush patrols operated principally during hours of darkness. A prime objective of ambush patrols was intelligence gathering—the capture of enemy soldiers for interrogation.[7]

Support elements assisted both reconnaissance and combat patrols and varied in numbers from a squad to slightly less than a full-strength platoon. Support elements normally moved forward to positions one hundred to five hundred meters from the main force, with the mission of immediate intervention by fire and maneuver if the assault element called for assistance. Prior to departure on assigned missions, both patrols and support groups received preparatory briefings, nearly always accompanied by rehearsals or "walk-throughs" of planned operations, then debriefed on return. Battalion commanders or executive officers attended both departure and return briefings. Platoon-sized alert forces backed up patrols and support units to reinforce patrols who gained contact or to screen areas of contact.[8]

The size of outguard elements varied from two to ten men, each element armed with Browning automatic rifles (BARs), carbines, or M1 rifles, a double load of ammunition, and all the grenades they could carry. Outguard elements and patrols normally included a "wireman," a soldier with a spool of field telephone wire strapped to his back and carrying a field telephone. Wiremen provided patrol leaders the use of field telephones, a more secure means of communication between patrol or outguard leaders, and the MLR or outpost units controlling the movements of outguards and patrols. However, there were disadvantages to the use of wire communications by infantrymen, except in the case of patrols and outguards.

Should a fire fight or major enemy incursion erupt, the wire was vulnerable to frequent cuts, especially by heavy shelling or formations of assaulting enemy soldiers, at precisely the time when communications were most important. The wire also provided a clear trail the enemy could follow to locate outguard, outpost, command post (CP), observation post, or MLR positions. One former officer said, "There must have been a million miles of abandoned phone wire lying in 'no mans' land.'" In fact, in the 7th Infantry Division there was an active, continuing campaign to retrieve and reuse abandoned land lines.[9]

Patrols and outguards carried radios for backup communications. Radios were a secondary means of communication because the enemy was always listening or jamming UN operational frequencies, particularly during assaults or counterattacks by either side. When the need for rapid communications was greatest and most urgent, both the Chinese and Americans routinely jammed their adversaries' operational frequencies, effectively blocking communications, including coded messages. Prolonged use of radios on outpost or MLR positions, or during patrols also invited targeting by enemy artillery and mortar batteries because Chinese intelligence units, like the UN, used triangulation of radio intercepts to pinpoint CPs, observation posts, or other communication nodes in attempts to destroy or disrupt communication nets and adversely affect command and control of operational units.[10]

Because of inherent vulnerabilities in radio and wire communications, discipline on both was strict. Codes and call signs changed almost daily, and backup systems of visual signals and runners were necessary. The failure to use proper call signs or codes when initiating or responding to a call invariably brought a cold retort from somewhere on the net: "Station not known."[11]

In addition to routine intelligence gathering, another tipoff to the impending March CCF assault came from comparisons of February and

March numbers of enemy contacts all across the division front. The number of enemy contacts with Division reconnaissance patrols fell from four in February to two in March. The 7th Division's combat patrols made thirty-six contacts with CCF elements in February, and the number fell to roughly half in March—nineteen. In contrast, February brought seven enemy attacks, probes or interceptions by friendly outguards, and better than three times that number in March, twenty-three. While aggressively patrolling, the enemy was avoiding contact with UN patrols.

What's more, the center of the enemy's more aggressive February probing was concentrated in the left (west) sector of the division front, whereas March probes into outguard positions were all across the division front but were principally in the area of Pork Chop, Arsenal, and the Alligator Jaws. Additionally, five friendly patrols exchanged fire with enemy groups in the vicinity of Pokkae.[12]

The Battle for Old Baldy

Then, ominously, on 20 March the CCF began intensifying artillery and mortar fire across the division front, registering and concentrating primarily in the areas of Old Baldy and Pork Chop. Because of the increase in artillery fire across the entire division front, especially in the vicinity of Old Baldy and Pork Chop, Able and Baker Companies, 1st Battalion, 31st Infantry Regiment, which had been in reserve with the battalion, were moved to forward assembly areas on the night of 21 March and prepared to counterattack or to reinforce the two threatened outposts. The two companies returned to the regimental reserve area during the daylight hours of the twenty-second, while Charlie Company of the 31st remained in a nearby blocking position.[13]

The 22 March change-of-command ceremony for Generals Smith and Trudeau, and General Trudeau's assumption of command, were auspicious for more than one reason. UN intelligence, coupled with stepped-up artillery and mortar fire, and the location and intensity of enemy probes provided clear indicators of an impending assault on the 7th Division's front. Word had been passed through the chain of command and in daily intelligence briefings.

The afternoon of 22 March, Gen. Maxwell Taylor, the Eighth Army commander; Lt. Gen. Paul W. Kendall, the I Corps commander; General

Old Baldy (*left*) and Chink Baldy (*center*). Note the "cut" or "saddleback" running from Chink Baldy to Old Baldy.
Courtesy of Robert J. Schaefer

Trudeau; and Colonel Kern, commander of the 31st Infantry, discussed the tactical situation. They decided to relieve, meaning replace, B Company of the Colombia Battalion, moving the Colombians' C Company onto Old Baldy, during the early morning hours of 23 March. Orders were given to the Columbia Battalion commander, Lt. Col. Alberto Ruiz-Novoa, and the 31st Infantry's Baker Company commander, Lt. Jack M. Patteson, to effect the relief by infiltration. Small groups of Colombians from their Company C were to move from the MLR into positions on the outpost. A rifle platoon from Baker Company of the 31st would support the Colombians during the relief by occupying Company C positions vacated as the small groups moved forward from the MLR, and as the Company B Colombians moved off Old Baldy back to the temporarily manned MLR positions. Thus, as the relief progressed, the 31st's Baker Company rifle platoon was to rotate from position to position, to the right, in the right flank of the Colombia Battalion's MLR sector, and avoid leaving positions unmanned while the relief was under way.[14]

During the early evening of 22 March, Colonel Kern inspected the Old Baldy outpost. He found outguards had not been placed in position, and that men supposedly standing guard on MLR positions were not alert and in some cases were inside bunkers. After making on-the-spot corrections, he went to the Colombia Battalion command post and discussed the matter with Ruiz-Novoa. Kern, because of the findings of his inspection, spent the night of the twenty-second and the morning of the twenty-third on 7th Division Observation Post 9, and the regimental operations officer (S-3) remained in the Colombia Battalion fire-support coordination center during these hours. Enemy artillery and mortar fire decreased markedly during the night of the twenty-second and early morning of the twenty-third.[15]

At noon on 23 March, Colonel Kern was informed that the relief of the Colombians' Company B had not begun as ordered. Ruiz-Novoa revealed he had decided not to relieve Company B until 6:00 P.M. on the twenty-third. A frustrated Kern directed the relief begin as soon as possible, whereupon he was told the relief would begin at 3:00 P.M. It began late afternoon and was still in progress when the CCF launched their powerful assault on Old Baldy late that evening. Again, on the evenings of 22 and 23 March, Able and Baker Companies, 1st Battalion of the 31st, moved to forward assembly areas immediately behind the MLR, with the same missions as on the night of 21 March. Lt. Gerald R. Morse commanded Able Company, and both companies were to be ready to counterattack or reinforce on Old Baldy.[16]

The February and March probes by the Chinese in the vicinity of Old Baldy and Pork Chop had been telltale signs the outposts were major objectives in the forthcoming CCF attack. Preparations to defend against the anticipated attack had been under way prior to the night of 23 March, but the extent of the CCF's assault was surprising. The five coordinated assaults against outpost and MLR positions were the largest enemy display of force against the division in five months, and the largest display of enemy force against the division since it came on line in the Baldy–Pork Chop area for the first time, in late December 1952.

The first area hit was the MLR sector manned by Company A, Colombia Battalion, at 8:23 P.M. the evening of 23 March. Two enemy platoons from the 9th Company, 3d Battalion, 423d Regiment, 141st Division, 47th CCF Army, attacked the Colombians' positions. Then in quick succession, at 9:00 P.M., a reinforced enemy battalion from the 423d Regiment struck Old Baldy. The CCF infantrymen, coming from the west and northwest,

Air strike on Chink Baldy, 22 March 1953. This photograph was taken looking west from a position on the crest of Hill 200.
Courtesy of Robert M. Euwer

from Chink Baldy, were beginning the assault outnumbering the defenders approximately four to one. Manning Old Baldy was the Colombia Battalion's B Company, which was still in the process of being relieved by the Colombians' C Company. At approximately the same time, in the 17th Regiment sector, outpost Arsenal was hit by two enemy companies, and within five minutes after these assaults, an estimated enemy battalion stormed into friendly positions on Pork Chop. Approximately five hours after the initial attack on the Colombia Battalion's A Company, at 1:20 A.M. on the morning of 24 March, an estimated enemy company attacked the Upper Alligator Jaw, on the far right (east) division front, in the 17th Infantry Regiment sector.[17]

Meanwhile, at the Colombia Battalion's A Company, MLR position, under attack with two platoons from the CCF's 9th Company of the 423d Regiment, circumstances were beginning to improve. By 10:30 P.M., Charlie Company, 1st Battalion, 31st Infantry Regiment, commanded by Lt.

Roscoe Robinson, Jr., a black officer and 1951 West Point graduate, had been attached to the Colombia Battalion and had joined their A Company in reinforcing the MLR. The Colombian's Able Company counterattacked at 4:00 A.M. and regained their positions.[18]

The situation on Old Baldy wasn't clear initially as wire and radio communication to the outpost were soon lost, but the outpost was obviously under heavy attack. First reports from the Colombia Battalion, relayed by radio message through outpost Westview, stated the defenders held. Because of the lack of communications, the Colombia Battalion commander dispatched an officer from his battalion to Old Baldy to assess the situation. The officer returned, saying he was unable to reach the outpost because of intense enemy artillery and mortar fire on all roads and trench lines to the defense network.[19] They would soon learn the Colombians defending Old Baldy had been completely overwhelmed by the power and swiftness of the CCF assault. The battalion's casualties were staggering.

An account signed on 25 April by a just-released American POW, 2d Lt. Albert DeLaGarza gave stark testimony to the events on Old Baldy the night of 23 March. DeLaGarza, an artillery forward observer (FO) assigned to the 7th Division, in C Battery of the 57th Field Artillery Battalion, received his commission through the Reserve Officer Training Corps at St. Mary's University in San Antonio, Texas. He arrived in the division early March, with Lt. Bob Euwer, with whom he attended the ROTC camp at Fort Sill, Oklahoma. Because he was fluent in Spanish, he was attached to the Colombia Battalion as a forward observer:

At around 1900 hours 23 March 1953, I was on OP [observation post] 10 waiting for Lt. Lopes to come up and relieve me. I was to go to Westview and take over that OP. At about 1930 [7:30 P.M.], I went to the CP preparation for going to Westview. At this time the Chinks hit the left flank, I met Lt. Lopes and told him of the attack on the left flank and he left to meet the company commander. I started up the trench toward Westview. I was between Westview and Old Baldy when Chinks threw in mortar barrages. I came upon the tanks on Baldy and asked the tankers where I could observe. They pointed out a bunker and I entered it. It was an LP [Listening Post] occupied by 3 Colombians. I put my radio up and was able to contact Zebra. At this time I heard Lt. Lopes calling for Flash Baldy on the radio. The Colombians in the bunker had communications with the Company CP. None of the outguards reported the coming of the Chinks.

In about 15 minutes after I arrived at the bunker (about 8:00) the Chinks appeared and started jumping in the trenches. They didn't spot our bunker and went right on by. All this time the Chinks had a barrage falling on the finger between Baldy and Westview and the Chinks walked right through it. The 3 Colombians in the bunker with me all got hit and were killed. The Chinks kept coming in and throwing grenades. I returned fire on them with my pistol. One grenade temporarily blinded me and when I could see again 2 of the bodies had been drawn out of the bunker by the Chinks. I found a large box of grenades and threw them holding off 3 Chinks. There were 2 openings in the bunker and the Chinks found the back opening. As they started in I got behind a curtain. The Chink picked up the Carbine of one of the dead Colombians and fired toward the curtain, hitting me in the buttock. One of the Chinks moved the curtain aside and I shot him and ran out of the bunker and into another bunker. The Chinks got a man on top of the bunker who would flash a light in the bunker to spot me (all the Chinks carried flashlights). As the Chinks were closing in I threw a grenade at the door and in the confusion ran out of the bunker. I started up the trench, at this time all small arms fire had stopped. I saw Chinks all over the place. I headed toward Baldy thinking the Colombians would still be up there. As I got over the top I saw a big red Communist flag on top of Baldy (this was about 2:00 A.M.). At this time I fell down exhausted near 2 Chinks digging. One of them spoke to me and I grunted and he started digging again. I started to slip away and he and another Chink surrounded me and took me prisoner. The kept saying "follow me, follow me." They all seemed to know the words, "follow me, hello, hello Colombians, and okay." I indicated that I was tired and they let me rest but went through my pockets, taking my knife, shoulder holster and dagger. I still had a grenade in my hand with the pin pulled and they let me throw it down the hill. I was bloody from my hand wound which I had received from a grenade in the bunker. I started away with the Chinks (artillery was falling heavy now) and they made me crouch down. All the Chinks were digging in at this time. They took me to a bunker and a medic was there. The Chinks were very disorganized at this point. I feel a counterattack would have been successful at this time. The medic at the bunker tied a bandage around my hand. They let me sit down about a half hour. 7 wounded Chinks were in the bunker. The medic treated me as well as he did the Chinks. The guard then said "follow me" and I took off behind him and we proceeded down the finger between Chink Baldy and Baldy, Flash Baldy wasn't being fired now. The artillery was firing at the peak of Baldy and along the ridges. They took me to a cave with a long entrance. There were many Chinks in the cave, wounded and groaning. On the way to the cave I saw dead Chinks all over the place, too many to count. I think the cave was on the reverse slope of Chink Baldy.[20]

Company B, 31st Infantry Regiment, which had been attached to the Colombia Battalion, departed at 9:30 P.M. the evening of 23 March to reinforce the outpost. Intense enemy artillery and mortar fire slowed the movement of the company, which passed through Westview at 1:30 A.M. on the twenty-fourth, and reported Westview in friendly hands. They were ordered to continue to Old Baldy to reinforce or counterattack and reoccupy the position. By 2:00 A.M. lead elements of Baker Company reached the first bunkers on Old Baldy, began clearing them, and continued to advance. At 3:00 A.M., the enemy began bringing small-arms fire and hand grenades to bear on Baker Company's lead elements. Resistance intensified. Each time the men of Baker Company attempted to advance, they were met by intense small-arms fire and grenades. Unable to continue forward, they immediately began taking cover, reorganizing, and consolidating their positions. From 4:00 A.M. until daylight at approximately 5:30, the Chinese placed light small-arms fire and threw grenades on friendly positions, plus four rounds from a 3.5-inch rocket launcher.[21]

At daybreak enemy troops were seen moving north from nearby bunkers to higher positions on Old Baldy. They were immediately brought under fire, inflicting several casualties. At approximately 9:15 A.M. Baker Company advanced through the trench leading toward the crest of Old Baldy, and were met with an enemy machine gun firing down trench. When two casualties were sustained by Baker Company the advance stopped, and a 57-mm recoilless rifle was brought forward and fired on the machine-gun bunker from the south slope of Old Baldy. Enemy response was swift.

At 9:30 heavy enemy artillery and mortar fire began falling in the immediate area, and Baker Company's advance ground to a halt. Throughout the remainder of the morning, the Chinese continued pouring artillery and mortar fire on the counterattacking company. At approximately 11:00 A.M. enemy direct-fire weapons and heavy artillery began bunker destruction missions on emplacements held by the men of Baker Company. The devastating effect forced the forward platoon to withdraw, and with a second platoon, they established two defense perimeters to hold until reinforcements could arrive.[22]

General Trudeau had early in the fight ordered Colonel Van Way to move the 1st Battalion of the 32d Infantry Regiment forward into assembly areas, and placed it under the operational control of—attached to—the 31st Infantry should they be needed to reinforce or counterattack to reoccupy Old Baldy. Colonel Kern, the 31st's commander, directed the battalion, commanded by Lt. Col. George Juskalian, to move forward, ready to press a counterattack through Westview. With Westview as the line of departure, fast on the heels of Baker Company of the 31st, at 8:35 A.M. the morning of the twenty-fourth, came 1st Battalion of the 32d Infantry Regiment, with their Baker Company in the lead. Direct-fire support was added from Baker Company of the 73d Tank Battalion.[23]

The tanks supported from positions in the valley to the northeast, firing on the objective and the saddle between Chink Baldy and Old Baldy. The counterattack moved forward under a heavy volume of artillery and mortar fire from an enemy determined to hold the outpost they had seized from the Colombians. Attacking along the saddle between Old Baldy and Westview, the lead elements of the 1st Battalion of the 32d received small-arms, mortar, and artillery fire, resulting in heavy casualties. The assault stalled just as the lead elements started up Baldy's southwest finger.[24]

At 1:35 P.M., after reorganizing, the battalion renewed the attack and Able and Baker Companies gained the southwest slopes of Old Baldy. By 3:00 P.M. they reached and passed through the area held by the still fighting survivors of B Company, 31st Infantry. (Soon thereafter, Baker Company of the 31st was directed to withdraw to Westview.) However, between 5:25 and 6:30 P.M. the attack once again bogged down. By 10:00 P.M. that evening attacking units were in possession of only one quarter of Old Baldy and remained, holding their positions, through the night. Charlie Company, 1st Battalion of the 32d, was the battalion reserve and remained in place on Westview throughout the twenty-fourth and into the morning hours of the twenty-fifth. During the night plans were made to commit Charlie Company in a coordinated, early morning attack.[25]

On 25 March, at 4:30 A.M., the 1st of the 32d launched another attack, with Charlie Company, now commanded by Lt. Robert C. Gutner, the company's third commander in March, moving from Westview around the right front of Baldy and up the northeast finger, while A and B Companies pushed up the southwest finger. Initially, Charlie Company could move relatively unimpeded, under cover of darkness, but when daylight came, they were in plain view of CCF forces to the north, manning the Chinese MLR. First light of day brought Charlie Company fierce enemy small-arms, automatic weapons, mortar, and artillery fire, and by 9:30 A.M. the attack stalled. At 1:15 P.M. the battalion commander reported his unit's fighting strength down to four officers and fifty-four enlisted men. The 1st Battalion of the 32d had been decimated.[26]

When the 31st Infantry Regiment's commander, Colonel Kern, received the battalion commander's status report he discussed the situation with General Trudeau, and with Trudeau's and General Kendall's approvals, ordered the 1st of the 32d to reorganize, evacuate the dead and wounded, and withdraw to a designated assembly area. The withdrawal was complete at 6:30 the morning of 26 March. While the withdrawal was in progress plans were already in motion for another battalion-sized counterattack.[27]

At noon on 25 March the I Corps commander, Lieutenant General Kendall, issued a verbal order to the 7th's assistant division commander, Brig. Gen. Derrill M. Daniel, for a counterattack to reoccupy Old Baldy outpost. He told Daniel the division was to prepare a plan for his approval, that the attack would take place on his order, on 27 or 28 March, after rehearsals. At 2:15 P.M. on 25 March, General Trudeau, after further discussions with Colonel Kern, designated the 2d Battalion, 31st Infantry the counterattacking force, and the battalion pressed ahead with a plan, approved by both Trudeau and Kendall, and two rehearsals on terrain similar to Old Baldy's.[28]

When it was apparent the CCF had seized and were holding the crest of Baldy, the 7th Division began calling for tactical air support to help drive the enemy off the hill. Shortly after dawn on 25 March, as the 1st of the 32d launched its 4:30 A.M. counterattack, Fifth Air Force fighter-bombers began steadily pounding the bunkers and trenches held by the CCF. All day long the battering continued. At twenty-minute intervals, flights of four, many loaded with two 1,000-pound bombs on each aircraft, released their weapons loads on the outpost. The battering continued through the night of 25–26 March with night flying B-26s, partly in anticipation of a battalion counterattack. Though plans and rehearsals for the counterattack continued, other factors intervened to end the fight.[29]

In a conference that began at 11:00 o'clock the morning of 30 March, the Eighth Army commander, Gen. Maxwell Taylor, discussed with General Trudeau the importance of Old Baldy to UN defensive positions along the line confronting the CCF. Apparently still much attuned to President Eisenhower's and the JCS's deep concerns over casualties, Taylor concluded that both tactically and psychologically, continued attacks to retake the outpost were not merited. He directed the planned counterattack not go forward, but the plan and techniques developed be preserved to execute on order within ninety-six hours. The planned counterattack which did not materialize in March would be resurrected again, in July, under quite different circumstances.[30]

While foreclosing additional casualties, a merciful act by the Eighth Army commander, Taylor's 30 March decision was a harbinger for Pork Chop Hill in more ways than one. For the Colombia Battalion, and the men of the 31st and 32d Infantry Regiments, and the 7th Division, the decision was to prove both a blessing and a curse. The blessing was no more bleeding to retake Old Baldy. The curse was fourfold: permanent loss of Old Baldy, an enemy who retained the initiative and willingness to launch powerful offensive operations, terrible casualties in the days remaining until the armistice was signed, and another outpost increasingly threatened.

Hit by a raid on the MLR, completely overrun and driven from Old Baldy by the powerful Chinese onslaught, the Colombians' one battalion was shattered by grievous losses: 50 killed in action, 112 wounded, and 91 missing in action. The Americans' 31st and 32d Infantry Regiments, including ROK soldiers and Korean Service Corps laborers, suffered more than twice the casualties absorbed by the Colombians during the thirty-day period beginning 15 March. All but a few were on Old Baldy and Pork Chop Hill. Six times more Americans than Colombians defended 7th Division positions. Nevertheless, by any measure, the Colombians' losses were disproportionate and egregious, simply because on Old Baldy they bore the brunt of a concentrated, overwhelming enemy assault.

Afterward, there were persistent rumors the Colombians were not sufficiently alert the night of 23 March, that many had been bayoneted in their sleeping bags. Clearly, the Chinese had been planning the assault for days, if not weeks. What's more, the springboard for their overwhelming assault was Chink Baldy, and on the reverse slopes of Chink Baldy was a network of caves, tunnels, and trenches sufficient to hide the large force the CCF amassed to launch their attack. The saddleback ridge line linking the two hills offered the CCF a rapid approach to Old Baldy's defenders, a golden opportunity for surprise that the Chinese exploited. Their overwhelming numbers, use of surprise, and catching the Colombians in the midst of a relief and replacement of the outpost garrison proved too much for Baldy's defenders, and the beginning of far more serious trouble for outpost Pork Chop.

Objective: Pork Chop

Minutes after the Chinese assaults on the Colombians' outpost positions on the MLR and Old Baldy on 23 March, the 2d and 5th Companies of the 201st Regiment, 67th Division, 23d CCF Army attacked Pork Chop Hill. Five tanks supported the six-hour attack. The enemy units came from Hasakkol and Pokkae, and the supporting tanks were thought to be in the rear of Hasakkol.[31]

Manning the trench and bunker network on Pork Chop was an under-strength Love Company, 3d Battalion, 31st Infantry Regiment. Due to the stepped up enemy mortar and artillery fire beginning 20 March, particularly in the vicinity of Old Baldy and Pork Chop, Love Company, commanded by Lt. Forest Crittenden, was on full alert when the assault came. The 9:05 P.M. assault had also been presaged by a 9:00 P.M. enemy contact with a twelve-man UN support group tied into a thirty-four-man security platoon from I Company of the 31st. The security platoon and support group were occupying positions to the left front of the outpost when the support group reported they were receiving small-arms fire from an unidentified enemy to its northwest.[32]

Consistent with the prebriefed plan the patrol immediately withdrew into the security platoon's perimeter, while 4.2-inch mortar fire was directed toward the encroaching enemy. At 9:02 P.M., Love Company defenders on Pork Chop began taking heavy artillery and machine-gun fire. At the same time, outguards around Pork Chop were calling in numerous reports of movement and lights in their vicinity. Again, consistent with the prepared plan for defense, the security platoon was ordered into the MLR, to the rear of Pork Chop. Before the order could be carried out, an estimated seventy-five Chinese assaulted the patrol from the west, south, and north, cutting them off from the MLR. Defenders from the Item Company platoon repulsed the attack. Heavy mortar and artillery fire preceded two more enemy assaults, but both were driven back. Finally, in one more dogged push, the Chinese overwhelmed the remaining I Company force.[33]

Meanwhile, Pork Chop's Love Company defenders came under heavy attack by the enemy. At 9:26 P.M. the battalion CP received a report the Chinese were in L Company trenches. After a savage struggle, including hand-to-hand fighting, L Company's survivors, isolated in areas where they could not be resupplied with ammunition and were overwhelmed by weight of numbers, withdrew from the hill. Company officers who were not casualties set up a rallying point at the northern base of Hill 200. A radio message went to 3d Battalion requesting ammunition, reinforcements, and orders. The battalion responded rapidly, dispatching ammunition, calling variable time fused artillery—air bursts—on Pork Chop, and issuing orders to prepare for a counterattack. Commanded by Lt. John Hemphill, the remainder of I Company, still manning the MLR, was ordered to move up and secure Hill 200, reported to be under attack. The L Company survivors at the base of Hill 200 were to stand fast and await the arrival of Company A, 1st Battalion, part of the 31st Infantry Regiment's reserve. By 10:30 P.M. the surviving I Company platoon took control of Hill 200, unopposed, while a plan to counterattack Pork Chop with A Company and the reassembling L Company was in the making. The planned jump-off time was forty-five minutes past midnight. I Company platoon members on Hill 200 joined L Company in preparing for the counterattack.[34]

At 11:20 P.M. Colonel Kern altered the plan, directing that Able Company probe Pork Chop and if the enemy was occupying in strength to wait in a perimeter defense for Company D and further orders. If light resistance were encountered, Able Company would secure the hill. But circumstances again intervened to alter the counterattack plan. At thirty minutes past midnight, with Able Company en route to join with L Company, the Chinese launched an artillery barrage, using variable timed fuses to obtain air bursts. Able Company had to take cover to avoid heavy casualties, and remained pinned down for two hours while the barrage continued.[35]

When the artillery fire lifted, the battalion commander, Lt. Col. George M. Maliszewski, organized Companies A and L and ordered them to move out under UN artillery preparation to assault Pork Chop. The two companies attacked line abreast with Able Company on the right, and reoccupied the hill by 4:30 A.M., against only light resistance from diehard Chinese defenders who survived the artillery pounding.

Early the morning of 24 March, Pork Chop was back in the hands of the 31st Infantry Regiment, the outpost's trench and bunker network heavily damaged by the battering taken from artillery rained on the hill from both sides. Reorganization of its defense began immediately. The regimental commander dispatched a pioneer and ammunition platoon, and engineers, to help clear debris and rebuild bunkers.

The Americans took three prisoners during the 7th Infantry Division's first battle for Pork Chop. By 8 April, the American and ROK soldiers manning outpost Pork Chop, plus Korean Service Corps laborers assisting in rebuilding the Hill's defenses, recovered the remains of thirty-seven Chinese dead. Estimates were the enemy suffered an additional seventy-five killed in action and one hundred wounded. The identity of the two Chinese companies which assaulted Pork Chop the night of 23 March came from papers taken from the bodies of Chinese soldiers.[36]

Unknown to the Love Company survivors, when they first pulled back and were preparing to counterattack the night of 23–24 March, two men left behind on the outpost were continuing the fight in their own way. Their tenacity and courage were to add a new dimension to the way artillery supported the 7th Division's infantry when the enemy was swarming a network of defenses.

When the CCF began their assault on Pork Chop, 57th Field Artillery Battalion forward observer Lt. Allen Craig Felger of New Orleans, Louisiana, and 57th communications sergeant William A. Cox of Mill Valley, California, were manning a bunker, an observation post, with eight other men on the forward slope and just below Pork Chop's western and higher of two peaks on the hill. Before the Chinese hit Pork Chop, Felger could hear them coming, firing burp guns, as he peered through one of the bunker's two apertures. The night was dark, almost black. He could not see them. Then at 9:02 the CCF artillery and mortars began their thunderous barrage on Pork Chop. Shortly thereafter, disaster struck the OP.

An artillery round came directly through the aperture and in a blinding flash exploded inside the bunker. After the dust, initial shock, and confusion subsided a bit, a shaken Lieutenant Felger saw three bodies in the debris. They were all dead. One of the survivors yelled, "Let's get out of here!" The Chinese were now close. Felger and Cox decided to stay and the other five men hurriedly escaped the bunker. In the dark and confusion, everything seemed lost. Neither of the two men could find weapons to defend themselves. The Chinese overran the hill's crest and the bunker, and on three occasions came to the door and sprayed the inside with burp guns. Miraculously, they missed Cox and Felger every time, once when Felger was in a corner trying to find a pistol.

In spite of the CCF artillery round's destructive effects inside the bunker, including the loss of their "hot loop," a sound-activated wire-connected phone line to a cluster of 57th Forward Observers, Felger and Cox were able to maintain backup communications via two still-operating radio transmitters to request artillery fire missions. Lt. Bob Euwer, manning his Hill 200 OP on the east flank of Pork Chop, was the forward observer nearest Felger and Cox. Euwer was on the hot loop with them and knew primary communications with the two men had been knocked out. After the two men cleared their minds and assessed their situation, they could hear voices of Chinese outside and near their bunker, in between the explosions of incoming artillery and mortar rounds.

Felger remembered praying the Chinese would not throw any grenades into the bunker. But the prayers did not stop him from calling in VT rounds above his position whenever he heard nearby enemy voices. Their own voices masked by the sounds of mortar, artillery, small-arms, and automatic weapons fire, Felger and Cox could hear enemy soldiers talking in nearby trenches and began repeatedly calling VT on their position, taking a toll on those moving about nearby, out from under protective cover.

As time went on more enemy high explosive artillery rounds slammed into and near the bunker, and it began to give way. Thousands of rounds were gouging Pork Chop, at one point Felger counting seven hundred per minute. Both men wondered if they were going to be buried alive. One round closed the bunker door partway, and other rounds sealed the two apertures. From about 10:00 P.M. on they were sealed in the bunker. They could not leave if they wanted. From their increasingly precarious, but oddly more protected bunker, they continued to call for deadly VT on position, and there they remained in the company of three dead American soldiers until early the next morning, just before daylight, when the two men heard Americans outside.

Felger's and Cox's tenacity, ingenuity, courage, and bravery saved their lives and inflicted an unknown but undoubtedly heavy loss of life on the enemy, while unquestionably avoiding more American casualties among the men given the counterattack mission later that long night. For his actions Felger received the Distinguished Service Cross. And from the two men's crisis-born thinking came an artillery-infantry cooperative measure in the 7th Infantry that would repeatedly save UN soldiers' lives while inflicting heavy casualties among the enemy about to overrun friendly positions. In April, the 7th Division would test the new measure under fire once more, on

Pork Chop Hill. Although Eighth Army turned down the 7th Division's recommendation that the procedure for VT on position be standard throughout the five corps, neither did the Eighth prohibit its use, in spite of some expected friendly casualties.

As for Cox and Felger, two rattled soldiers, they were grateful for surviving a harrowing night. When telling the story to a war correspondent, Lieutenant Felger decided he and Cox had stayed in a "damn good bunker."[37]

In April, Lieutenant Euwer, a forward observer in C Battery, 57th Field Artillery Battalion, would have the same Pork Chop OP caved in on top of him and his FO team by a direct hit from an enemy artillery round. Three days later, after an emergency repair team rebuilt the bunker, he would again be connected by hot loop to the OP as the Chinese overran the position and Lt. Harvey "Andy" Anderson, another C Battery FO, once more called VT on position.

Assaults on Outposts Arsenal and Upper Alligator Jaw

On 23 March, the 17th Infantry Regiment occupied the east or right regimental sector of the 7th Infantry Division front. The 31st Regiment held the west or left sector of the division's front, and the 32d Regiment was the division reserve. From west to east, the 1st, 2d, and 3d Battalions of the 17th Regiment were on line, with the 3d Battalion, 32d Infantry attached, in reserve. The reserve battalion's companies occupied blocking positions on likely routes of breakthrough should the enemy penetrate the MLR.[38]

Outpost Arsenal, eighteen hundred yards from the MLR, came under attack at 9:00 P.M., simultaneous with the assault on Old Baldy. Normally a company defended this position. This night two platoons of Baker Company, 1st Battalion of the 17th, defended the position, while the third platoon occupied Brie outpost, five hundred yards south of Arsenal. Organized for all-round defense, outpost Arsenal included protection by numerous bands of double-apron and concertina wire. Overhead cover sheltered fighting and living quarters with sufficient strength to withstand UN VT-fused artillery, without injury to occupants.[39]

At 9:00 P.M. on 23 March, members of Able Company observed two red flares above Arsenal, and alerted Baker Company, occupying the position. Ten minutes later, enemy artillery and mortar rounds began falling on Arsenal. At 9:22, under flare-lit skies, an estimated company of enemy infantry was seen moving south toward the outpost from a finger of Chinese-held Hill 200. At the same time a second enemy company was observed approaching near Brie. Baker Company defenders called for and received "Flash Fire Arsenal!" and close-in defensive fires.[40]

"Flash Arsenal" closed around the hill:

Differing little from the curtain barrage of World War I days, the "flash fire" of Korean operations was an on-call, tightly sown artillery (plus 4.2 inch mortar) barrage, usually horseshoe shaped and so dropped that it would close around the front and sides of an outpost ridge. The main idea of flash fire was to freeze enemy infantry movement, blocking out the enemy force on the low ground while locking in such skirmishers as had gained the heights.

In effect, one battery fired on each concentration, 120 rounds per minute, two shells breaking into the ground every second. High explosive and proximity fuse shells [variable time or "VT" fuses] were both used in the blast, the balance varying according to terrain conditions. While a flash fire lasted, infantrymen stayed in their fighting positions.

In the usual procedure, a flash fire was delivered with maximum firepower for three minutes, the howitzers then cutting back from twelve to six rounds per tube per minute while maintaining the fire for six minutes.[41]

Most of one enemy company was inside the "horseshoe of fire" when the curtain of "flash fire" descended around the hill, but they had to advance through the close-in defensive fires. The Chinese continued advancing through the heavy artillery and mortar, and infiltrated the wire surrounding the outpost, during a sharp, violent exchange of small-arms and automatic weapons fire. At 9:37, elements of the attacking forces began entering Baker Company's trenches. The outpost commander called for VT fused artillery directly on the outpost. The close-range small-arms and automatic weapons fight became a hand-to-hand battle with the enemy assault finally stopped.[42]

Wire communication to the outpost ceased soon after the assault on Arsenal began, although radio communication continued. The Chinese were jamming radio frequencies, making communication difficult but not impossible.[43]

Firing became sporadic in the next thirteen minutes as the enemy began withdrawing through Tapsong-Dong, dragging an estimated ten dead and fifteen wounded. Friendly forces raked the withdrawing enemy with artillery, mortar, small-arms, and automatic weapons fire.[44]

At 9:40 P.M., during the beginning of the fire fight for Arsenal, one platoon of K Company, 32d Infantry, was dispatched to reinforce the platoon outpost position on Erie, and arrived at 10:20. A platoon-sized Charlie Company combat patrol, scheduled for the night of 23 March, had not departed MLR positions when the Chinese launched their attack. The attack resulted in a change to the platoon's mission, and the unit moved instead to reinforce Arsenal outpost at 1:30 A.M. on 24 March. While moving through the trenches toward Arsenal the platoon received heavy incoming enemy fire and sustained two killed and five wounded, impeding their progress and delaying their arrival on Arsenal until 2:15 A.M.[45]

After the enemy withdrew from Arsenal, friendly fire on the Chinese-held Hill 200 and other enemy avenues of approach to the outpost decreased in intensity to harassment and interdiction firing. Chinese casualties were eleven counted killed, nine estimated killed, fifteen counted wounded, and twenty-five estimated wounded.[46]

THE OUTPOST on Upper Alligator Jaw was seven hundred yards in front of the MLR, still under construction, and being fortified for manning by slightly less than one platoon when the Chinese launched their 23 March assault. On outpost duty that evening were twenty-two men from Company I, 3d Battalion, 17th Regiment, holding only one completed, covered bunker and a network of shallow trenches. Supporting artillery and mortar units completed registration of defensive fires prior to 23 March, and contingency plans to reinforce or counterattack had been prepared and rehearsed.[47]

At approximately 1:20 A.M., now fully alert Upper Alligator Jaw defenders heard noise near the northwest portion of the platoon position, triggering illumination flares. The flickering light from the flares revealed an enemy group of undetermined strength. A brief fire fight ensued, which killed the Chinese leading the force. The I Company platoon leader began preparing his men for an imminent attack. Shortly thereafter the enemy assaulted the outpost from all sides using burp guns and hand grenades. The engagement sharpened rapidly into a close-range small-arms, automatic weapons, and hand grenade fire fight.[48]

The onrushing enemy killed the American platoon leader and two sergeants a few minutes after the action began. Surviving platoon members rallied under the leadership of a corporal and succeeded in beating off the attacking Chinese. The enemy withdrew from the position, making much noise as they pulled back.[49]

While the platoon was heavily occupied driving the enemy from the outpost's positions, a second enemy force approached from the south, and after a heavy assault, occupied a portion of the outpost. Defenders engaged the enemy with small arms, hand grenades, and hand-to-hand fighting and called in defensive fires and reinforcements by radio. Prepared fires from I Company's 60-mm mortars struck the enemy, and two I Company reinforcing squads departed the Company's positions at 1:30 A.M. to reinforce the outpost. A heavy volume of enemy mortar and artillery fire falling on the company positions and approaches to the outpost prevented the reinforcing squads from arriving at the scene of the action until 2:15 A.M. When they arrived the enemy was driven from the position, and withdrew rapidly, attempting to carry their dead and wounded. Defenders directed artillery and mortar fire on the Chinese, inflicting heavy losses.[50]

Screening patrols dispatched as the enemy withdrew returned with two prisoners, one uninjured and the other wounded. The count of enemy dead and wounded was twenty-three and three, respectively, with an estimated eight wounded.[51]

Relative Quiet Returns

On 28 March, two weeks after Malenkov's speech, and before General Taylor's 30 March decision overruling another battalion counterattack to retake Old Baldy, the Communists suddenly responded favorably to an earlier proposal by Gen. Mark Clark to exchange sick and wounded POWs. When the Communists responded, they went further, saying the exchange "should be made to lead to a smooth settlement of the entire question of prisoners of war, thereby achieving an armistice in Korea, for which people throughout the world are longing." The U.S. government and the UN Command reacted to the Communist proposal, and General Taylor's refusal to permit the counterattack on Old Baldy was undoubtedly part of the UN reaction. At the same time, Taylor dismissed the intensified Communist attacks preceding their overture as face-saving propaganda maneuvers.[52]

Several days later Communist China's Foreign Minister Chou En-lai and North Korea's Premier Kim Il Sung followed this statement with pronouncements which seemed to soften the Communist stand against voluntary repatriation. The two leaders also expressed agreement to an earlier proposal to allow a "neutral state" such as India or Switzerland to supervise the exchange and interview Communist POWs who refused repatriation to ascertain their true desires.[53]

The statements from Peking and Pyongyang indicated a possible long-sought break in the deadlocked peace talks. Nevertheless, the United States viewed the remarks cautiously and, in some instances, negatively. Secretary of State John Foster Dulles and Secretary of Defense Charles E. Wilson, two of the most powerful men in the Eisenhower Cabinet, argued to reject the overtures. In the National Security Council on 8 April, both used tough language, urging a "much more satisfactory settlement in Korea." Included in their views was a postarmistice political arrangement that would virtually unite Korea and leave it divided not at Line Kansas but much farther north, "along the waist," Pyongyang-Wonsan. President Eisenhower overrode Dulles and Wilson, and approved the exchange of sick and wounded POWs as a "test of good faith on the part of the Soviets." He believed the proposed response by his two cabinet members could lead to an abrogation of the armistice, and more fighting, which the American people would not tolerate.[54]

In the first twelve days of April, while the two negotiating teams ironed out the details of Little Switch, which would begin on 20 April and extend through 3 May, relative quiet settled along the 7th Division front. On 1 April, Secretary of the Army Robert T. Stevens arrived in the division rear area, where the division's band and honor guard welcomed him with a ceremony. A similar ceremony occurred the next day when Lt. Gen. Paul W. Kendall, the I Corps commander, departed the division area. The same day, the 17th Infantry Regiment was ordered off the line into division reserve to rest, refit, and conduct training. On 9 and 12 April, the 17th Regiment's 3d and 1st Battalions, respectively, held battalion reviews.[55]

Reconnaissance and combat patrols continued with the same missions and frequency as in March. Front-line battalions normally sent one reconnaissance patrol forward daily to ensure adequate coverage of their sectors, and nightly, each front-line regiment sent out combat patrols. Work to rebuild and improve the division's OPLR and MLR trenches and overhead cover, bunkers, and firing positions continued.[56]

The first days of April were not void of enemy contacts. The majority of the early month's contacts with the Chinese were in the vicinity of the Alligator Jaws complex and had been preceded the last week in March with increased fortifications improvement by the enemy, vehicular sightings and troop activity to the north of the complex. Almost immediately thereafter, a series of probes and patrol clashes occurred on and near Alligator Jaws.[57]

On 4 April at 2:05 A.M. outguards engaged an estimated fifty enemy. After a brief fire fight the outguard wisely disengaged and directed supporting fires, dispersing the enemy with one Chinese soldier counted killed in action. Ten minutes later the same night a combat patrol engaged approximately five enemy. After a ten-minute fire fight, directed supporting fires forced the enemy to withdraw, with three estimated wounded in action. On 5 April there were two reports of contact on the OPLR in the area of the Alligator Jaws. At 11:01 P.M. a combat patrol engaged an estimated Chinese platoon. After a fifty-two-minute fire fight the Chinese withdrew under cover of approximately one hundred rounds of supporting fire from their mortars. During the fire fight the defenders prevented an attempted enemy envelopment of the patrol. The frustrated attempt to close on the patrol resulted from supporting fire from the patrol's support element plus fire from positions on the MLR.

Enemy casualties were five counted killed in action, six counted wounded, and seven estimated wounded. At 11:10 P.M., while the combat patrol was still engaged in their fire fight, two enemy squads probed another nearby area on the Alligator complex, using small arms and automatic weapons supported by machine-gun fire and an estimated two hundred rounds of mortar and artillery fire. The enemy withdrew after a ten-minute fire fight. Two more brief contacts with small groups of enemy occurred: at 11:40 P.M. on the sixth and 12:05 A.M. on the seventh. In both cases the Chinese received fire which caused them to disperse.[58]

Again, on 10 April outpost defenders sighted and fired on an unknown number of enemy soldiers, apparently causing them to withdraw. The final probe of the Alligator Jaws OPLR was 11:00 P.M. the night of 16 April, when an estimated enemy platoon assaulted an unoccupied outpost. American artillery and mortar fire was called in on the position, and the enemy withdrew after a thirty-minute fire fight.[59]

Farther southwest, directly south of now Chinese-held Old Baldy and in front of the American MLR, was outpost Dale, normally manned with one platoon. On the MLR, the 1st Battalion, 31st Infantry Regiment was occupying the center battalion sector with three companies on line and Company I, 3d Battalion of the 31st in regimental reserve, on call in a nearby forward assembly area. Baker Company of the 31st was in the center company sector of the 1st Battalion, with one of its platoons forward on outpost Dale. In the three days preceding 16 April, Dale was the subject of unusual amount of attention, perhaps an indicator the Chinese intended to penetrate the MLR southeast of Old Baldy.[60]

The increasing hints of an impending major assault on Dale came at 4:55 the morning of 13 April when a Chinese patrol of unknown strength probed the outpost. At 10:30 P.M. the night of the thirteenth, an estimated enemy platoon attacked, followed less than four hours later by another estimated platoon-sized attack. Defenders repulsed each attack with the help of supporting artillery and mortar fire, but the supporting fires destroyed or heavily damaged many of Dale's fighting positions and trenches. Then came 16 April, four days before Operation Little Switch began. The CCF launched a series of powerful assaults on the 7th Division front.[61]

In parallel with repeated enemy probes of Alligator Jaws and Dale outposts the first half of April, defenders of outpost Pork Chop experienced similar enemy attacks. Through interrogation of captured enemy soldiers, intelligence analysts concluded the Communists' purposes were to discover the strength and location of friendly defenses, gain combat experience for inexperienced troops, and ultimately seize and hold key terrain. Intelligence officers' conclusions understated the more obvious conclusion. The fact was, the loss of Old Baldy in late March, and the decision not to make a determined effort to eject the enemy from that key hill, had spelled increasingly serious trouble for Pork Chop.[62]

Old Baldy was west-southwest of Pork Chop, at the left end of an arc of four powerful enemy strong points now ringing the outpost on three sides. Proceeding from west to east around the arc, the other enemy strong points were Hasakkol, directly north of the Chop, Pokkae to the northeast, and T-Bone, farther to the east-northeast. All four were at least 100 meters higher in elevation than Pork Chop's sharply peaked 234-meter summit. From the tops of all four the Chinese could look down on a hill ill-formed for all-around defense and too loosely tied in to the supporting American positions. And from behind the ring of four strong points the Chinese could pound Pork Chop with mortars. Longer ranging artillery multiplied the fury of the shelling and the unpleasant consequences for defenders. As a result of the hill's position and Chinese frustration at being unable to permanently eject its defenders, day after day more enemy artillery and mortar rounds fell on its few acres than on the rest of the entire 7th Division.

Behind Old Baldy, to the northwest, lay the less obvious but more solid reason for Old Baldy's threat to Pork Chop—Chink Baldy:

Old Baldy, scabrous after months of battle, a mountain looking like a refuse dump, more cheated by nature than abused by man, was unsuited for mounting of an attack. While its superior heights outflanked Pork Chop and made the manning of Westview [a UN outpost almost within a stone's throw of Old Baldy] seem like wanton defiance, it was much too naked to afford a concealed approach. The companion peak, Chink Baldy, was more suitable. Tree growth, rock outcroppings and conveniently spread fingers which descended unevenly to the low ground gave it tactical privacy. So it was to this platform, [Chink Baldy], that troops looked, wondering if an attack would come.[63]

There was one more factor not obvious to troops on the UN line manned by the 7th Infantry Division:

The superior heights held by the enemy concealed from ground observation a still more formidable characteristic in the Red Chinese defensive front. They had organized their high ground in true depth by sweating their soldiery and making the most of their press gang labor. Compared to this monumental work, Eighth Army's "deep front" was a hollow shell.

An airborne observer looking beyond Old Baldy or any other main bastion in the enemy line would have reported roughly, as follows: To a depth of more than 20,000 yards, the Reds had entrenched and bunkered the ridges. Their defensive works had ten times the depth of any belt of entrenchments in World War I. The lines of the main trench systems were traced by our air photo interpreters; it was hard and repetitious exercise because the enemy was diabolically clever at camouflage.

Finally, on the acetate the picture looked like a giant spider web with successive main lines joined by communication trenches along transverse ridges. Shells and bombs could be rained on this system day long with little chance of finding a soft target. A miss by a few inches, and the projectile was wasted. Further there was no way of knowing, at a particular moment, which part, if any, of the works under observation was manned.

Every tactical group on the enemy side had multiple firing positions within the general position; underground tunnels connected one position with the others.[64]

The huge, spider-web complex of trenches, bunkers, and deep underground caves was both the product of Chinese guerrilla warfare against the Japanese, then the Chinese Nationalists, and an effective defensive counter to the firepower advantage resident in the UNC's artillery and aircraft. And in April, to give powerful teeth to any onslaught by massed Chinese infantry, artillery units capable of firing into the 7th Division sector numbered ten battalions, deeply revetted and camouflaged. Estimated at 75 percent strength, nine guns per battalion, their firepower included four battalions of 122-mm, two battalions of 105-mm, and four battalions of 75-and 76-mm guns—approximately ninety guns total. Additionally, there were an estimated twenty tanks and self-propelled vehicles mounting 76- and 85-mm guns, all revetted or hidden in caves, carefully camouflaged, and usually moved only at night.[65]

Old Baldy's seizure by the Chinese in March also dictated adjustments and expansion in Pork Chop's defense network. The left flank, the western sector, needed to be strengthened, with greater depth and more firing positions to counter infantry assaults that could be launched from the areas behind Baldy. Approaches from the vicinity of the two much higher Chinese strong points, Old Baldy and Chink Baldy, led to the left rear of the American outpost. To make matters worse, the long shank of the Chop was Brinson Finger, a three-quarter-mile extension of the ridge that ran from the hill's peak west, sloping gradually downward toward Baldy.

Though designed for all-round defense, as were nearly all American outposts, an infantry company could not adequately defend the entire hill, because defenders would be overextended, and subject themselves to easy penetration of the perimeter. The reason a determined enemy could easily penetrate Pork Chop's perimeter on the left flank was almost self-evident. On Brinson Finger, the trenched and bunkered perimeter of Pork Chop crossed over the ridge line as it circled from the north, or front slope of the hill, peaked at the ridge line's crest, then dropped down the south slope of the Finger, as it circled back toward the east to close the perimeter's loop. Heavy, simultaneous, parallel assaults by enemy formations coming from the vicinity of Old Baldy, attacking from west to east along the front (north) and rear (south) slopes of Brinson Finger, could quickly overwhelm either a single or reinforced infantry platoon manning that sector.

Though Pork Chop's April defenders could readily see the peril to their left rear when Baldy fell the last days in March, and began immediately to adjust and strengthen defenses, time was working against them. The Chinese were wasting no efforts in taking advantage of Old Baldy's position of superior observation heights relative to Pork Chop, the large hill's most important commanding strength. The Chinese now had unobstructed lines of sight into the Pork Chop defenders' flank and rear, and could routinely observe work in progress to strengthen the Chop's defenses.

Also under direct observation was an approximately one-thousand-yard stretch of Pork Chop's lifeline. The hill's jugular vein was the access road which ran from the MLR checkpoint behind Hill 200, around the northwest toe of 200, across the valley between Hill 200 and Pork Chop, and climbed to the outpost's evacuation landing, from where it continued down, back to rejoin itself in the valley between the two hills. In that one-thousand-yard interval, when the two armies were locked in brutal fire fights, men and vehicles transiting the road would frequently run a deadly gauntlet of enemy artillery and mortar fire.

No sooner had the March battle for Pork Chop ended than the CCF began readying itself for another assault. On the Chop rebuilding and strengthening began, a race against time. The second major assault came soon enough, and was worse.

4

UPPING THE ANTE

THE FIRST PROBE OF PORK CHOP IN APRIL CAME ON THE THIRD, AT
9:05 P.M., when, predictably, an undetermined number of enemy
approached from the north and west, from the area of Chink Baldy. As the
Chinese moved toward the outpost, a mix of three hundred enemy artillery
and mortar rounds began falling on the defenses. UNC artillery and mortars responded with directed fire, dispersing the enemy. Again, at 1:30 A.M.
the morning of 10 April, eight enemy soldiers were engaged by a combat
patrol. After a brief but intense small-arms fire fight, the combat patrol
withdrew at 1:35 A.M. and directed mortar and artillery fire on the Chinese. One enemy soldier was counted killed in action. The two probes
were outward indicators confirming intelligence gathered through other
sources:[1]

> For almost a week the word had been out. No mere rumor, it was spread
> to the squads on the authority of the [7th] Division G-2 that the Commu-
> nist enemy would make a "main effort" at Hour 2300 [11:00 P.M.] on 16
> April. The word had leaked from the other side and that was good reason

to believe it. The reason lay in a contradiction within the fighting system of this peculiar Chinese enemy. Though his tactics—his movement of forces on the battlefield—reflected the extreme rigidity of an autocratic state, his manner of handling vital information was democratic to the point of recklessness.

When a battle plan was decided by the high command, its essentials were passed down the line until finally even rifle squads were permitted to chew them over. The theory was the troops got a "good feeling" from knowing the secret. It made them think that the plan was the best possible one. At least that was the American explanation of the Chinese reasoning.

So when any agent or other line-crosser brought word that a Communist attack was imminent, it didn't lessen his credibility that he specified the hour and place.[2]

In April, enemy psychological warfare was consistent with their March efforts. On average, every other night, loudspeaker broadcasts wafted through the night air, most unintelligible because of wind conditions or other normally interfering noises, including the sporadic firing and explosions of artillery and mortar rounds, lofted into the lines of the two armies. On 15 April, in the vicinity of Chinese-held T-Bone, a woman's voice announced, "If the UN goes home, the CCF would go home to China and leave Korea." Her broadcast preceded a man's voice encouraging the UN forces to "come over and get good chow," followed by the threat, "If you don't, we will come over and kill you."[3]

The next day, two leaflets were seen floating in the air in the vicinity of T-Bone:

DEATH IN VAIN ON T-BONE HILL

To you, to your family, your life is the most precious thing in the world.

But what is your life worth to the brass hats?

On January 25, on T-Bone Hill, northwest of Chorwon, men were sent to die to provide a show for visiting newspapermen and generals.

The visitors were given nicely prepared mimeographed programs, bound in colored covers, so they could follow what the brass hats called "Operation Smack."

While they watched, men of Easy and George Companies, 31st Regiment, Seventh U.S. Infantry Division were ordered against Chinese positions, got within 15 yards of it, and were mowed down!

This was too raw even for some congressmen in Washington. Rep. Clare Hoffman demanded an inquiry. Rep. William Brady asked Defense Secretary Wilson if the Army "was putting on a show with actual killing for visiting firemen, using human guinea pigs."

In Boston, Mass., draft board member Chester Wicks, himself a veteran, submitted his resignation, saying, "I just don't want to have any part in sending boys to Korea to die in any exhibition."

But General Lawton Collins, Army Chief of Staff, said he approved the operation and "there would be many more like it."

AMERICAN SOLDIERS! NO ARMY IN THE WORLD HAS EVER ALLOWED ITS GENERALS TO TREAT THE MEN LIKE THIS. YOUR GENERALS ARE BECOMING LESS CONCERNED ABOUT YOUR LIVES. THIS WAR IS NOT IN THE INTEREST OF THE PEOPLE. NOBODY BUT THE AMERICAN BIG-SHOTS WANT IT TO GO ON.

IT'S NO DISGRACE, BUT AN HONOR, TO QUIT THIS UNJUST WAR!

At the top of the leaflet was a very clear lithographic print of an American soldier who appeared to be badly wounded. The leaflet referred to a highly publicized January operation conducted by units of the 7th Division against the Chinese. Briefed in advance to American war correspondents and distinguished visitors, "Operation Smack" proved costly and embarrassing, and when reported in the press indeed stirred heated controversy in the United States.[4]

On 16 April, the loudspeaker broadcasts continued:

From the superior height of the enemy-held ridge named Hasakkol, the light breeze of early evening brought to Pork Chop Hill the sound of music. For some minutes it continued, rising, then fading out according to the caprice of the wind. Men were singing in chorus. It was a mournful chanting, faint, tremulous and uncanny. And though the voices were high-pitched, there was a muted quality to the music, as if it came out of a deep well. Now it became lost in distance again and the men [of Easy Company of the 31st], who had paused to listen resumed their supper of steak, French fries and chocolate ice cream.

A private said, "It sounds like they're gathering in the tunnels."

Another answered, "O.K., as long as they stay there."

Asked a lieutenant, "But what does it mean?"

"They're prayer singing," said the interpreter. "I can't hear the words, but I know the music. They're getting ready to die."

Said the lieutenant, "Maybe we ought to be singing, too."[5]

Another Time Around

The growing number of enemy seen in front of the 31st Regiment sector, plus other intelligence information, including the expected exact time of attack, increased tension and heightened the state of alert in all the 31st's battalions. At 7:15 P.M. the evening of 16 April, about the time the eerie sounds of mournful singing floated from the Chinese-held line to the men on Pork Chop, the regimental commander, Col. William B. Kern, notified the battalion commanders to expect an enemy attack that night. General Trudeau called Colonel Kern at 9:00 P.M., telling Kern to expect an attack "in two hours." The 31st was ready and waiting. The 2d Battalion of the 31st had been on 100 percent alert since 1:00 A.M. the morning of 16 April.[6]

Maj. Robert S. Swayze's 2d Battalion of the 31st manned the MLR sector and outpost Pork Chop to the front of Hill 200. The battalion's Easy Company, commanded by 1st Lt. Thomas U. Harrold, West Point class of 1951, was on outpost duty. Behind the 2d Battalion's MLR positions, in blocking positions prepared to execute counterattack plans, were the 3d Battalion's King and Love Companies, commanded by 1st Lt. Joseph G. Clemons, Jr., and 1st Lt. Forrest G. Crittenden, respectively. The 3d's I Company, commanded by 1st Lt. John A. Hemphill, was in a blocking position behind the 1st Battalion, ready to counterattack in that sector. The 1st Battalion sector included outpost Dale. The 3d Battalion commander was Lt. Col. John M. Davis.[7]

Shortly after the beginning of evening nautical twilight, all outguards in the 2d Battalion sector departed on schedule, and reported in position by 8:00 P.M. As they moved from the MLR into forward positions they undoubtedly heard the same eerie sounds of singing coming from the lines of the 201st Regiment, 67th Division, 23d CCF Army. Three companies of the 201st's reinforced 2d Battalion were preparing to assault Pork Chop. The first to throw itself bravely against the outpost's defenses was 5th Company, plus reconnaissance elements of the 67th Division. Next came 4th Company as reinforcement early on 17 April. Finally, the 201st Regiment's 6th Company flung itself into the maelstrom before the 2d Battalion withdrew on 18 April.[8]

The first reports of enemy action in the UN's 31st Regiment sector came at 10:05 P.M. when a regimental observation post reported a fire fight of undetermined intensity in the Colombia Battalion sector. Shortly thereafter, a flare ignited above the Colombian position and the fire fight ceased. Relative quiet once more descended in the 31st's sector, and tense waiting continued.[9]

As was the routine, and as ordered, Easy Company, manning Pork Chop, dispatched a patrol of six men, plus five from Fox Company, to the front of the outpost. Though Harrold had been told of the expected enemy assault, he apparently saw no reason to argue for cancellation of the scheduled patrol, planned several days in advance. While intelligence seemed convincing, many commanders considered such information to be rumors, nothing more. It was prudent to err on the side of caution and put patrols out front to ensure there were no surprises.

At 10:45 P.M. the patrol saw enemy movement in front of its position and requested the commitment of its support element. The support element responded, but shortly thereafter all communications with the patrol and support element were lost. An intense artillery and mortar barrage began falling in the 2d Battalion sector. Simultaneously, outguards north and west of Pork Chop sighted an undetermined number of enemy to their front and, using sound powered phone, the "hot loop," attempted to report their observation to the company commander. Once again, communication lines had been severed, and the report did not reach Lieutenant Harrold. Unknown to Harrold, Easy Company was rapidly entering a crisis.

With its strength already less than normal—at ninety-six men including medics, artillery observers, and engineers—and with outguards and a patrol totaling twenty-six men deployed forward, the company was ill prepared for a determined, well-planned enemy assault. Outguards were in pairs, deployed in a semicircle 125 to 300 yards from the main position. Worse, Lieutenant Harrold, having passed the word to his chief subordinates and comfortable all his men knew to expect an attack that night, was to learn that few had ever received word of the impending attack. The outguards and patrol had no inkling of the impending assault. To them, the evening, though always tense on such assignments, was routine tense, and expected to remain routine.[10]

At 10:58 P.M., Harrold reported enemy mortar and artillery beginning to fall on his position. Ten minutes later the 2d Battalion commander, Major Swayze, ordered Easy and George Company outguards to return to their company positions. Few heard the order, as most were either cut off from communications, overwhelmed, pinned down by enemy artillery and mortar fire, wounded or killed, or had taken matters into their own hands and run for cover in their companies' primary defensive positions.[11]

Lacking information about the situation to the front of Pork Chop, cut off from communication with Battalion, and hearing small-arms and automatic weapons fire increasing on Pork Chop's left shoulder, Lieutenant Harrold was now convinced matters were rapidly deteriorating. He stepped to the entrance of his CP and fired a red parachute flare over Pork Chop, signaling, "We are under full attack." Men in George Company spotted the flare and called it to battalion. Within seconds Harrold fired a second red star cluster, meaning, "Give us Flash Pork Chop." Pork Chop was indeed under full attack and he was requesting a mixture of friendly variable timed fused (VT) and high-explosive artillery fire to close in and directly on the outpost. The star cluster partially malfunctioned, some of the shell's contents ricocheting off the entrance's facing into the interior of the bunker, setting fires. The CP's occupants temporarily abandoned the bunker to fight and extinguish the flames, then reentered.[12]

The emergency signal from Harrold required an immediate visual response from Battalion. Major Swayze ordered the reply, and at 11:06 P.M., six illuminating flares burst high over Pork Chop, signaling that antipersonnel artillery rounds, VT, fused to explode seventeen yards above ground, would fall on the position in approximately two minutes. To every UN soldier who saw the signal or heard the shouted warnings of "VT incoming!" there was only one meaning: take cover. Exploding VT rounds sprayed deadly cone-shaped patterns of shrapnel downward onto surfaces below. To soldiers in trenches or bunkers with well-constructed overhead cover, the sound of VT shrapnel hitting the surface above them was like soft rain. But the rain was murderous to friendly or enemy soldiers caught in the open without protective cover. At 11:09, VT artillery began falling on the outpost.[13]

At this time, the rate of enemy mortar and artillery fire increased along the entire 31st Regiment front, with heavy barrages falling on outposts Pork Chop, Dale, and Westview. At 11:16 P.M., an estimated two enemy companies attacked outpost Dale in the 1st Battalion sector. Baker Company was responsible for defending Dale.[14]

On Pork Chop, at 11:25, a silence returned to the hill. Lieutenant Harrold had still not seen any enemy soldiers in the vicinity of the company

CP, but he had heard the approaching sounds of small-arms and automatic weapons fire decrease to virtual silence on the left flank of the hill. The absence of firing and the silence in communications were ominous, and he correctly concluded 1st Platoon no longer existed as a fighting unit. The outpost's west shoulder was defenseless. At 11:30, he reported to battalion an undetermined number of enemy in the trenches and again requested VT be placed on position. At the same time, Lieutenant Anderson, an artillery forward observer in the CP with Harrold, requested continuous VT fire and illumination and that flash fires be brought in closer.[15]

The silence also told Harrold the Chinese were reorganizing at the scene of 1st Platoon's destruction, preparing to push on and take possession of the entire outpost. As he viewed circumstances, there was no longer an American garrison defending Pork Chop, and he radioed his conclusions to battalion. Major Swayze's battalion CP relayed the information to regiment, and Colonel Kern took the report at face value. Shortly before 2:00 A.M. on 17 April, Kern sent word he was dispatching one platoon of Fox Company and another from Love Company to attack up the rear slope of Pork Chop to reinforce Easy Company. At two minutes before midnight Fox Company's platoon was already on its way. Some time later Love Company's platoon departed for Pork Chop. Harrold received word of Kern's order, and assumed the two platoons would come up the rear slope in attack formation. The attack never materialized.[16]

The Fox platoon got lost in the night and did not arrive to complete its mission. The Love platoon moved out rapidly on its mission but had not been told the hill was swarming with Chinese. In spite of the artillery, mortar, small-arms, and automatic weapons fire on Pork Chop in the preceding hour, the platoon leader evidently took literally the statement they were to "reinforce" and marched his platoon up the rear slope in a closed column—and square into the teeth of a Chinese machine gun emplaced on top of the chow bunker. A short burst from the enemy gunner inflicted a few minor casualties and total surprise on the column, which promptly recoiled and ran back to the valley. After the Love platoon slipped away, Chinese mortar and artillery barrage fire swept the valley. This was the beginning of a long, bloody forty-eight hours on Pork Chop Hill.[17]

Incoming artillery ceased in the vicinity of outpost Dale by 12:36 A.M. the morning of 17 April, although friendly VT was still being fired. Just one minute earlier an I Company platoon arrived on Baker Company's MLR position, planning to reinforce outpost Dale, which was five hundred yards in front of the MLR. At 12:45 A.M., the situation on Dale was still in doubt, and it was uncertain whether the reinforcing platoon could successfully reach the outpost.[18]

Colonel Kern then received information the Communists were reinforcing their troops on Dale. At 1:30 A.M. he ordered Item Company, minus the one platoon already moving toward Dale, to immediately counterattack. At 1:50 Baker Company, commanded by Lt. Jack M. Patteson, reported the reinforcing platoon previously dispatched had been forced to withdraw.[19]

At 3:15 A.M., all available VT fires were placed on Dale, and under his personal leadership Lt. Col. George M. Maliszewski, commander of the 1st Battalion, launched the assault. Two platoons from I Company, commanded by Lt. John A. Hemphill, plus one platoon from B Company were to secure the outpost. The counterattacking forces, which had split to come at the enemy from two directions, contacted their adversaries at 3:59. For the next thirty minutes a bitter small-arms, hand grenade, and hand-to-hand fight ensued. In those thirty minutes, the Americans either killed, captured, or drove the enemy force from Dale. The outpost reported "secure" at 4:50 A.M., but Maliszewski received serious wounds and had to be evacuated. A Chinese grenade exploded under him, blowing off his right foot. Hemphill, who continued battling until the outpost was retaken, received several shrapnel wounds, including a serious head wound. He refused to be evacuated until the fight ended.[20]

While the counterattack on Dale was coming to a successful conclusion, the situation on Pork Chop was more tenuous. Though Lieutenant Harrold and Easy Company's dwindling number of survivors held the CP and nearby bunkers, the Chinese controlled most of the Chop.[21]

At 3:30 A.M., Colonel Kern ordered Lt. Col. John N. Davis's 3d Battalion to counterattack Pork Chop with Companies K and L, with the mission of restoring complete control of the outpost. Kern's regiment was now fully committed all across its sector, and at 4:05 he informed General Trudeau that one company was counterattacking Dale, two companies were counterattacking Pork Chop, and all reserves had been committed. Trudeau acknowledged the situation, and began drawing on the division's reserve, the 17th Infantry Regiment. He released the 2d Battalion of the 17th to

Colonel Kern's operational control. Kern ordered the battalion, commanded by Lt. Col. James R. Tully, to move to a forward assembly area adjacent to the CP of the 2d Battalion, 31st Infantry.[22]

In the meantime, Companies K and L, which had spent a quiet night in a reserve position behind Hill 347, moved toward their line of departure for the first full-scale counterattack on Pork Chop. Lieutenant Clemons's K Company was 135 strong and had had a late meal and caught a few hours' sleep. When the call came at 3:30, trucks were already on their way to move the two companies to positions behind Hill 200. K Company was ready when the convoy arrived.[23]

Each rifleman carried three or more grenades. In each platoon were six BARs with twelve magazines per weapon. Ammo bearers were to carry five boxes of ammo for each light machine gun. Lieutenant Harrold, the Easy Company commander, wounded by grenades but still holding on in the CP on Pork Chop, recommended each platoon carry a flame thrower and heavy rocket launcher. The two counterattacking commanders took his advice.[24]

By 4:30 A.M., K and L Companies reached their assault positions, and immediately launched the counterattack. King Company moved up the south slope of the hill with two platoons line abreast and one in reserve at the base of Hill 200 on its south side. Lieutenant Clemons's company would have to make the assault without the support of his weapons platoon, which had been detached to assist in holding outpost Westview, also under attack. As a substitute for the weapons platoon supporting Westview's defense, a platoon from the 73d Tank Battalion was to give direct support to King Company.

The two Love Company platoons moved toward the hill in columns from the east, one moving along the military crest of the ridge line and saddle back which gradually curved from Hill 200 to join the east shoulder of Pork Chop. The second column moved generally parallel to the first, farther down the slope, parallel to the road, which also curved left as it climbed toward the trenches and bunkers. Approximately halfway to the two companies' objective, the Chinese controlling the hill's heights began pouring heavy machine-gun, small-arms, and grenade fire into the ranks of both, temporarily halting the advance. Enemy fire had taken a heavy toll, particularly among officers and noncommissioned officers. After hesitating briefly, both companies reorganized, resumed their advance, and began clearing the hilltop, moving from bunker to bunker.[25]

As the retaking of trenches and bunkers continued, the men from King Company were completely surprised when they came upon a few beleaguered Easy Company holdouts in their CP at 6:00 A.M. None were aware five wounded Easy Company survivors, including their company commander, were holed up in the CP.

Clemons, on seeing the ranks of King Company's two platoons depleted by half, requested his reserve platoon to come forward. In the meantime, a decimated Love Company at last closed on the positions taken by King Company, but not before the two converging forces fired on one another, wounding two more from the already devastated Love Company platoons. When finally the remnants of Love Company joined with Clemons's men, there were only ten remaining to assist Clemons's men in retaking the remainder of the hill from the Chinese. They were commanded by one of the surviving Love Company officers, Lt. Arthur A. Marshall. Sixty-two had started with Love Company's commander, Lt. Forrest J. Crittenden, who fell, wounded in the assault. Lt. Homer F. Bechtel took command and was quickly struck down by a grenade.

With all this, the job was not yet done. The Chinese still controlled half the Chop, including the crest, and the two forces were closely intermingled, mostly hugging rocks and pits dug by artillery rather than risking the trenches and bunkers more frequently struck and caved in by artillery.[26]

At 6:30 A.M., as the sun was edging toward the horizon, Pvt. George Atkins brought news to Clemons. Looking westward from a high knob on Pork Chop he saw "many Chinese" moving toward the outpost from the general direction of Old Baldy and Chink Baldy, and from Hasakkol, to the north. Clemons called on the radio. Would the artillery plaster the area where the movement was headed and drop a curtain in the valley between Pork Chop and Hasakkol? The requested fires at first did not come, so Clemons turned to three medium tanks in a 73d Tank Battalion platoon attached to King for support. They were still idling around the base of Hill 200, approximately five hundred yards rearward. He called them forward to the low ground west of Pork Chop, where, with direct fire, they diverted the enemy approaching from the west, northwest. However, the tanks were not in position to break up the enemy heading south from Hasakkol, toward the Chop.[27]

At 6:24 a requested air strike struck Hasakkol. Coordination of the tactical air mission required the artillery to hold its fire in the vicinity of the strike. Beginning at 8:45 A.M., and every thirty minutes throughout the day, all across the regimental front, air strikes continued. To the casual observer and the uninformed, tactical close air support and interdiction missions appeared glamorous and exciting to observe, even fun, but aircrews flying the air strikes knew differently. It was a hazardous business.

Chinese troops and antiaircraft gun crews were well trained and disciplined. Sensitive targets such as outpost and MLR troop positions, vehicles such as trucks and tanks, automatic weapons, artillery pieces, and ammunition storage areas were well defended. The resulting heavy volume of concentrated defensive fire directed toward individual aircraft making low passes to bomb, rocket, or strafe enemy positions often took their toll. Attacking aircraft, which usually flew parallel with the MLR to avoid dropping weapons on friendly troops, were targets deserving the wrath of concentrated enemy fire because of the powerful, damaging weapons loads they delivered.

In the meantime, at 6:35 A.M. George Company from the 2d Battalion of the 17th Regiment received orders attaching it to the 3d Battalion, 31st Regiment. George was to reinforce King and Love Companies, still fighting to expand their grip on Pork Chop, but virtually stalled by heavy casualties and the steady pounding of artillery and mortars.

Commanded by Lt. Walter B. Russell, Jr., George Company ran into deadly enemy artillery and mortar fire, while moving to reinforce. Reinforce was the operative word in Walt Russell's mind, as information about King Company's dire straits had not come clear to Colonel Davis, Clemons's battalion commander, who gave the orders to Russell. Operating under the belief George Company would not be facing heavy enemy resistance, Russell deployed his company in a column of platoons and moved parallel to the access road which led toward the King Company CP, near the "evacuation landing." Harsh surprise greeted George Company, as enemy soldiers who had taken trenches and bunkers on the heights added their small-arms and automatic weapons fire to the continuing enemy artillery and mortar fire along George's approach to the hill's crest. In spite of taking an estimated thirty-five casualties from the shelling, and small-arms and automatic weapons from enemy soldiers still clinging doggedly to their hard won positions on the hill, George Company moved up the south slope, shifted their attack toward the east, and closed on the outpost by 7:30.

The greater part of two squads from George's 1st Platoon connected with Clemons at 8:14. Until then Clemons had not known any part of the Buffalo Regiment was in the area. He was surprised when he heard a pleasant voice ask, "Will you please tell me the situation here?" Clemons raised his eyes to see his brother-in-law and 1951 West Point classmate, Walt Russell, with whom Clemons had had lunch a week earlier. Clemons said, "Now what in hell are you doing here?" He told Clemons his mission was to reinforce King Company. The George Company mission was the first indicator to Clemons that his commanders did not understand the precariousness of the situation on Pork Chop.

George Company immediately began assisting in mopping up and reorganizing the defenses. As George arrived on the hill's crest, they observed fifty to one hundred Chinese fleeing down the north slope. At 8:30 Clemons reported the hill secure. His men had bagged five prisoners, in addition to killing and wounding an unknown number of enemy. Nevertheless, King's position was not nearly as strong as thought by the battalion, regiment, or division commanders. And for King Company, matters would get much worse as the already bloody day wore on.

King of the 31st

For King, the fight had been under way for four hours and they had moved hardly more than one mile. Though the morning was cool and fair, a typical day in Korea's loveliest season, canteens were empty, most having been used to satisfy the thirst of wounded. Grime fouled many weapons, requiring frequent cleaning to avoid their jamming. Men were busy using toothbrushes, the infantryman's weapon-cleaning tool easiest to carry and use, in spite of sporadic enemy small-arms and automatic weapons fire. At 10:00 A.M., with his radios knocked out, only thirty-five tired King men available, ten survivors from Love, and twelve exhausted Easy soldiers rescued in the push down the trench line, Clemons gave command of the outpost and defense of the hill's right (east) shoulder to Lieutenant Russell. George from the 17th, King, and Love Companies and a few men from Easy of the 31st set about clearing trenches and strengthening the battered defense network.[28]

But there was more trouble ahead. While Clemons and Russell reorganized to defend the portion of Pork Chop that King, Love, George, and Easy survivors had managed to hold or retake—the right shoulder of the hill and the area surrounding the command post—other decisions were about to be made, and other decisions postponed, that would leave King Company in desperate straits. Crucial information about the seriousness of King's predicament had apparently never been clearly presented to Clemons's senior commanders, Davis, Kern, and Trudeau.

Clemons and Russell moved into Harrold's old CP. Russell informed Lieutenant Colonel Davis, his operation battalion commander, he was assuming command of the hill's defenses. "Negative, negative," came the reply. Then, using Russell's radio, Clemons told battalion, "I must have water, plasma, more medical assistance, flame throwers, litters, ammunition, and several radios." At 11:00 A.M. Korean Service Corps bearers reached the chow bunker bringing a load of C-rations and water. Due to the intensity of barrage fire on the hill, distribution of these supplies to men in the forward foxholes was no longer possible.

At noon, the battalion S-2 (intelligence officer), Lt. James Blake, entered the CP with a written message for Clemons from Lieutenant Colonel Davis, the battalion commander. Any Easy and Fox Company survivors were to be sent to the rear immediately, and George Company was to withdraw promptly at 3:00 P.M. Clemons responded, "Take this message back. Tell them I believe the crisis here is not appreciated either by Battalion or Regiment. I have very few men left. All are exhausted. Russell has only fifty-five men left. When they go out, it is not reasonable to expect that we can hold the hill." Battalion acknowledged the message one hour later but did not amend the order.

By noon, the flame throwers, ammunition, and litters Clemons requested arrived at the foot of Pork Chop, carried by eight Korean Service Corps cargadores. The barrage-swept crest caused a change of heart, and for safety's sake, in the early afternoon, when the defenders could have used the cargo at the embattled summit, the bearers stayed in place on low ground. Their mission failed. The eight Koreans remained, hugging cover 175 yards shy of their intended destination.

During a brief lull in the fighting, Lt. Walt Russell faced one of war's brutal choices, and an incident he would remember the rest of his life. He and Joe Clemons had decided to make their way through the trenches to the chow bunker where M-39 armored personnel carriers (APCs), used in resupplying the defenders, had off-loaded water, an increasingly precious commodity. En route to the bunker, Russell encountered a private from one of George Company's platoons. The soldier was sitting down alone in a roofless area midway in the communication trench, leaning against its wall. Russell stopped and, knowing the soldier's platoon needed him, asked the private, "Where's your platoon?" "I don't know," came the reply. Concerned the soldier had no support in sight, could give no support to any of the hill's dwindling number of defenders, and was exposed to persistent incoming artillery and mortar rounds, the company commander ordered, "Go find your platoon." Without hesitation, the soldier firmly replied, "No."

Russell didn't hesitate. He drew his .45 pistol and, moving to place the muzzle against the soldier's head, ordered again, "Go find your platoon. That's an order. See this pistol. You know what it can do." There was a brief, frightening pause for both the soldier and his commander. Then the soldier got to his feet, turned, and walked up the trench line toward the area held by Pork Chop's defenders. A shaken Russell wondered, and to this day still wonders, what he would have done if the soldier again refused to obey his order.

But there was an answer to the long-remembered question and some comfort for both men. When George Company came off the hill later that day, the private had survived to leave the hill with them. Russell saw him again in the company's assembly area to the rear of the MLR, but the two did not speak. The incident undoubtedly became a difficult memory for both.

The final irony for Clemons and King Company came when Lt. James Barrows, a division public information officer, entered the CP with two staff photographers at 2:45 P.M. The three had dared the enemy artillery and mortar fire that stopped the Koreans at the base of the hill, coming to take pictures of what Barrows believed was a successful American action. Clemons, now genuinely frustrated, said, "Forget the pictures. I want you to carry a message to Battalion." He wrote, "We must have help or we can't hold the hill." Barrows left immediately, and battalion acknowledged the message in less than an hour. Still no amended orders.

Separately, and unknown to Clemons, shortly before 3:00, Walt Russell sent his own message, in the clear, to Lieutenant Colonel Davis, the battalion commander. Russell used the George Company radioman's code. Clemons's radios were out, the other major reason Clemons attempted relinquishing command of the hill's defense to his brother-in-law. Russell, on the 3d Battalion of the 31st's net, to Davis, his operational boss, "Blue 6, George 6, over."

"George 6, Blue 6, over."

Using the radioman's code to hopefully avoid understanding and reaction by the enemy, he then told Davis that George Company had fifty able-bodied men left to fight and King Company had only twenty. He urged Davis to pull King off the hill instead of George.

Russell's request was simple and logical given the circumstances on Pork Chop's battered crest. If one of the two companies must leave the hill, common sense and reason said King should be ordered off the outpost. Should the 201st CCF Regiment launch another assault against the Chop's defenders, King did not have enough men to hold; they would be overrun. Russell's radioman, and other George men with him in his CP, heard his broadcast, and were not pleased at the prospect of an affirmative reply from battalion. But they needn't have worried.

"George 6, Blue 6, negative, negative. George execute how able immediately." "How able," was American GI vernacular and radioman's code for "haul ass." Davis did not hesitate to refuse the request. The fight for Pork Chop was still Colonel Kern's, the 31st regimental commander's fight, and command lines had to be clean and uncomplicated. Responsibility for defense of Pork Chop still rested with Davis's battalion.[29]

Whether an oversight by Clemons due to fatigue, the result of professional training which emphasized brevity in communications, or an unwarranted optimism on the part of his commanders and their staffs, his messages to the rear apparently did not state clearly enough the critical point: the severity of King Company's losses. What is more, though Walt Russell's message to Clemons's battalion commander might have clarified the serious predicament existing on Pork Chop, Clemons never heard Russell's message. Both Battalion and Regiment in the 31st knew Clemons well, accepted his distress calls as valid, and believed the Pork Chop force was "dead beat"—exhausted. When Colonel Kern called Division to urge that King, if not relieved, be reinforced, he emphasized the physical exhaustion of the force, and not its losses. Division, still more remote from the fire fight, was even more upbeat and optimistic and did not sense the urgency in Clemons's twice retransmitted messages. Unknown to Clemons, there was another, more complex issue at stake. Though the fight was local, the issue was national.[30]

Division's more complex question was, Is Pork Chop ultimately worth the price in blood? If the hill were abandoned, the Communists would strike next at Hill 347, the dominant hill on the UN MLR and, indeed, among all the hills in the vicinity of Pork Chop. If the fight proceeded, Pork Chop might become another battalion-a-day battle like Triangle Hill. So division asked a decision of I Corps. Corps asked Eighth Army, and Eighth Army asked Far East Command. "Do you really want to hold Pork Chop?" Less than a month earlier, General Taylor, expressing the same dilemma a different way, decided to call off further counterattacks and cede Old Baldy to the Chinese. Now the same question, and while senior officers wrestled the decision a shrinking picket squad continued holding desperately to the Chop.

After division heard Kern's request in behalf of King and Love Companies, the answer was, "There will be no help for the time being." It was not a hard-nosed refusal. Rather, Trudeau wanted to be certain the fight was in earnest before committing another company. But in the meantime, there was only one sure way to know the circumstance of Pork Chop's defenders. General Trudeau and his assistant division commander, Brig. Gen. Derrill M. Daniel, flew in a chopper to Davis's battalion CP to learn how King was faring. They landed at 3:00 P.M., exactly the time Lt. Walt Russell pulled George Company of the 17th out of the Chop's works and led them down the hill. In seven hours he had lost half his command.[31]

As Lieutenant Russell led his George Company column off the hill, six Korean bearers, taking advantage of the lull, climbed to the chow bunkers carrying the flame throwers. Some of King's men tried to bring the flame throwers forward. They did not have the strength to lift them.[32]

Clemons's King Company was down to twenty-five men, including Lieutenant Marshall and his Love Company survivors. The day's fighting cost King eighteen killed and seventy-one wounded. The remainder could not be stretched across the crown of the hill, not without risking certain death. Clemons gathered the men and led them as a tight group to the highest point on the left side of Pork Chop. Earlier they had been a rifle company. Now they were three squads, isolated, clinging to a defensive island.

Within the perimeter, eight or nine of the worst-spent men sought cover next to sandbagged walls in three partially collapsed bunkers. The others moved into nearby shell craters not deep enough for good cover. Lacking the strength to wield the small entrenching tools they carried, they used spoons, knives and bayonets, trying to widen and deepen their roofless shelters. Though the early morning had been a typically cool beginning to a comfortable April day in Korea, they had sweated profusely in the steep climb and constant scramble for cover, fighting for their lives every step of the way. No water had arrived to refill empty canteens, and most had minor wounds. Ammunition was low and resupply was virtually impossible. Using toothbrushes, they listlessly cleaned and recleaned weapons to ensure they would have a last desperate line of defense. After deploying the small band of defenders, Clemons returned to the CP with one radioman and a runner, effectively isolating himself from the remainder of the hill's defenders. Another defender later joined the trio. Clemons needed to protect the company's remaining radios left with him by George Company, and be in the best position to make contact when reinforcements came.

Now began four hours of pounding by enemy artillery and mortars, as they zeroed in on the high point held by the small band of men from King and Love. They no longer talked to one another, and they did not move except when an exploding shell shook them from their exhaustion-induced lethargy. Added to the fury of the shelling, from in front of them came a random, intermittent rain of bullets. Occasionally a grenade sailed in, but none of the defenders saw a single human target, merely one explanation as to why so few fired their weapons. Fortunately, the enemy did not know the other reasons. Ammunition was scarce, and most no longer had the strength to raise a weapon to their shoulders and fire. "We lay there and took it," said Cpl. William H. Bridges. As S. L. A. Marshall wrote so many years ago, "There is no more moving entry in the record of King, that young Americans too exhausted to fight may still obey such group discipline as their enfeebled resources permit."

In spite of King's and Love's precarious circumstances, there was a saving grace in the enemy artillery and mortar fire the late afternoon and early evening of 17 April. Not only were the two companies' remnants hemmed in, the Chinese holding the remainder of the hill were kept out, partially by the artillery—and perhaps were also convinced unspent, carefully conserved fury awaited them within the small perimeter. They decided to let their artillery and mortars do the job, undoubtedly intending to wait until dark to mount a final assault.[33]

As for Clemons and the three men in the CP, even if they tried to return to rejoin the small band of defenders inside the nearby perimeter, they probably would never have made it. Chinese snipers and grenadiers came through the unguarded slopes around the CP, from both sides of the trench, keeping the four pinned in the bunker. Having no choice, Clemons and his three men picked up their rifles and fought to keep from being overrun. Because of their fight for survival, an hour was lost before Clemons could return to his communications.[34]

The Message Gets Through

At approximately 4:40 P.M., there was a brief pause in the fighting, and Clemons called his battalion commander, Lieutenant Colonel Davis, on the radio. "We have here about twenty men who are still unhit. They are completely spent. There is no fight left in this company. If we can't be relieved, we should be withdrawn." General Trudeau was in Davis's CP when the message came through. The message had the effect of a fire alarm, galvanizing Trudeau into action. Until then information was fragmentary, the picture blurred. Trudeau knew the enemy had punished King, but he did not know the desperate straits of Pork Chop's defenders. Now that the day was almost gone, he was aware the hill could not be held unless additional troops moved toward it quickly as the night. The questions were, Where would he get them, and how many were needed?

Pork Chop's defenses were near total ruin, and could provide cover to no more than a few men. Enemy artillery would not let up as long as the Chinese held most of the hill. Trudeau flew back to the 7th Division CP to consult with the other generals and with Colonel Kern, already en route to the CP by chopper. It was there the decision was reached at higher levels. Trudeau spoke with Maj. Gen. Bruce C. Clarke, I Corps' new commander, asking and being reassured if Trudeau spent more men to regain Pork Chop, he would not later be directed to withdraw. Once he received assurance, he attached the 2d Battalion of the 17th Infantry Regiment to the 31st. Since George Company of the 17th had already lost half its command in the day's fighting, Kern now had two rifle companies available to win the fight. The 1st Battalion of the 17th was also directed to move to the Pork Chop area, but not put under Kern's operational control. Trudeau wanted

A wounded American soldier is helped to a waiting APC for evacuation from Pork Chop during a lull in the fighting the afternoon of 17 April 1953.
Courtesy of National Archives and Robert M. Euwer

to keep a string on 1st Battalion until circumstances proved the fight could not be won without committing more units from the 17th.[35]

Kern immediately called Captain King of Fox Company of the 17th, and directed him to move his company onto Pork Chop and relieve Clemons's force as soon as he could make ready. The time was 6:00 P.M. Responsibility for defense of the outpost now passed from the 3d Battalion of the 31st to Lieutenant Colonel Tully's 2d Battalion of the 17th, which remained attached to the 31st Regiment. Relief of King, Love, and Easy Company survivors began at 8:05 and ground to a halt at 10:30 P.M. Held up for a period by heavy enemy artillery and mortar fire, a last minute, beleaguered defense of a surrounded CP, and a requested "Flash Pork Chop" to ward off another enemy counterattack, at midnight the last members of King, Love, and Easy infiltrated from their positions on the hill.

By the time the last of the three companies' survivors left Pork Chop that night, King and Love Companies had for twenty hours been riding briefly, walking, running, sweating, and toiling uphill with heavy loads of ammunition, rations, and other necessities at night; dodging artillery, mortars, machine guns, small arms, and grenades—and fighting desperately on into the daylight hours to retake and hold the outpost. Already exhausted, they then had to reorganize themselves and prepare for counterattacks they were certain would come. In the next four merciless hours, only three men, among all the King and Love survivors in the small perimeter at the crest of the hill, actually fired their weapons. When relief came, fourteen had survived relatively unscathed, but sick and shaken. Of the fourteen, seven were Americans, the remainder ROKs.[36]

Fox of the 17th

The relief by the 17th's Fox Company did not come without cost—and another crisis. Captain King lost some hours getting his company on the road. He wanted to ensure the men were well equipped and ready. In the end, the delay probably cost Fox excessive casualties.

Enemy artillery and mortar fire, though slowed somewhat in the afternoon, kept pounding away, taking their toll. The relief in fact was a counterattack, because the Chinese were coming again—in force. The enemy's preparation was already under way when Fox Company began to move. The company left its line of departure at the base of Hill 200 under cover of darkness, at 8:40 P.M., two platoons line abreast, angling up the south slope of the outpost's northeast finger. Intensity of enemy artillery and mortar fire increased, raking the valley between Hill 200 and up the south slopes of Pork Chop. Though Fox lost nineteen casualties before they could even engage the enemy, their advance persisted, and they contacted the hill's defenders at 9:15 P.M. An hour later the expected enemy counterattack began.[37]

On the radio, a call for "Flash Pork Chop" temporarily scattered the enemy formations and stalled their counterattack. Had not an alert 2d Lt. Earle L. Denton, a surviving, heroically fighting Love Company platoon leader, called in the flash fire when radios were being repeatedly jammed by the Chinese, the developing counterattack would have caught the relief of the outpost's exhausted defenders midstream. In the flickering light of artillery-fired illumination rounds, Denton had seen a body of Chinese crossing the valley from Hasakkol toward Pork Chop. Calmed by the Americans' flash fires, incoming from enemy artillery and mortars also ceased at 10:42, permitting the relief of King Company to proceed.

No sooner did Fox Company's defenders begin settling into position than the fury increased again. At 12:55 A.M. the morning of 18 April a company-size enemy force attacked, and four minutes later succeeded in reaching the outer edges of Fox Company's trenches. The call went out again for VT, directly on position. The inverted, cone-shaped, killing air bursts drove the attackers to cover, but they would come again, this time at 1:30 A.M., when an estimated 150 more surged up the west slope of Pork Chop. The sound of enemy small-arms and automatic weapons fire began increasing, and fifteen minutes later word came through artillery channels from a forward observer in the Fox Company CP. The CP area was surrounded and many defenders were wounded. Fox Company, which had lifted the siege of a nearly overrun King Company CP, now faced a second wave of assaulting enemy, and were once more engaged in a bitter, close-quarter, hand-to-hand battle for trenches and bunkers.

Colonel Kern, the 31st Regiment commander, now convinced the situation on the outpost was again approaching a crisis, asked for commitment of additional units from the division's reserve. General Trudeau approved his request, saying, "If we've got to counterattack again, lay it on before first light." Kern committed Easy Company of the 17th, commanded by Lt. Gorman C. Smith, also West Point class of 1951, to counterattack Pork Chop. At the same time, Trudeau released 1st Battalion of the 17th if needed to hold the hill. Easy and Able Companies of the 17th would finally secure Pork Chop Hill thirty-six brutal, costly hours after the initial assault by the CCF's 5th Company of the 201st Regiment.[38]

Easy of the 17th

Lieutenant Smith's company, along with the entire 17th Regiment, had been in Division reserve on 16 April, when the Chinese launched the assaults on Arsenal, Dale, and Pork Chop. Easy was at Camp Indianhead, and Smith had been putting the Company through intensive training while refilling from the stream of replacements constantly flowing into UN divisions. Early on the evening of the sixteenth, on order, Easy moved from Indianhead into a forward assembly area behind the 31st Regiment's MLR positions to provide a counterattack force if needed for the expected battle.[39]

In the period after the fight for Pork Chop began, Lieutenant Smith observed and followed the action with great interest, and began formulating a plan, should his company be committed. Old Baldy offered enemy observers an elevated, unobstructed view into the rear of Pork Chop, and the valley between Hill 200 and the Chop. He learned four infantry companies, one at a time, were badly mauled crossing through the valley between 200 and the Chop, and up the outpost's south slopes. The killers were a gauntlet of fire along the access road plus long-registered areas of enemy mortar and artillery fire tearing into the valley and up the south slopes of the hill. Further, the enemy had seized most of the high ground on the hill. During daylight or under illumination at night, Chinese soldiers on the crest of the Chop could see UN units approaching from behind Hill 347, look down on Hill 200's MLR positions, into the valley between the two hills, and thus were able to see approaching UN formations as they repeatedly counterattacked to retake the outpost. They could thus bring more misery to counterattacking units by adding small-arms, grenade, and automatic weapons fire to the shower of enemy steel from artillery and mortars.

The plan evolving in Smith's mind was risky, even daring, and his battalion commander, Lieutenant Colonel Tully, would need convincing. Smith would take his company east along the south base of Hill 200, parallel to the stream, and angle up toward the saddle between 200 and the MLR to the east. Easy would then turn left, to the north, northeast and proceed through the saddle, its concertina wire, move around Pork Chop's base to the front of the northeast face of the outpost, then sweep up the northeast finger toward the crest. In the final lunge up the hill, their backs faced the enemy on Pokkae. The route, if followed at night, would give them a good chance of evading observation from Baldy, and the heretofore inevitable rain of artillery and mortar rounds.

The lieutenant was so certain of the idea, he called his men together twenty-four hours prior to receiving the assignment, and briefed them in detail on the plan, explaining why he believed it would work and what each element in Easy Company would do. When the time came, Easy was ready to move, with no additional instructions needed. He sold Tully on his idea, saying, "If I have to reinforce that ridge, I want permission to move through the front door." Five minutes after the order came, Easy Company was under way.[40]

At 1:22 A.M. they crossed their line of departure. "While Easy Company worked its way along the base of Hill 200, Smith's forward observer, Lieutenant Clark, laid a covering barrage in the valley east of Pork Chop, about 200 yards beyond the assault column." The protective move risked calling attention to Easy's presence on the flank and rear of the Chinese at the top of the hill, but they did not see what was coming. The barrage continued as Easy charged up Pork Chop's east finger, apparently still not alerting the Chinese to the danger. At 2:50 A.M. Easy Company was fully deployed across the shattered crest of Pork Chop, with the 31st Regiment's Colonel Kern receiving a report the outpost was secure.[41]

Siege at the Company Command Post

In the final minutes of Easy Company's surge onto and across Pork Chop's crest, 2d Lt. Earle L. Denton, a platoon leader in Love Company of the 31st and one of those extraordinary young officers who shined like a beacon when confronted with chaos and danger, was participating in an apparent last stand in the CP now held by Fox Company. About midnight, he and his small group of Love Company survivors had been similarly hemmed in in the CP with King Company commander Lt. Joe Clemons and Fox Company's Captain King, and had been saved at the last minute by some forceful, heroic actions by Love Company survivors who decided to stay with their young, now-acting company commander.

When the first siege of the CP was lifted, Clemons and Denton and the rest of the CP holdouts were ready to depart the hill, the last of King and Love Companies to start down the hill following their relief by Fox Company. Also in the CP were five wounded soldiers, on bunks, awaiting evacuation. Clemons and his men started rearward, and Denton and his men were about to follow, when Captain King said to Denton, "I don't know this position at all. Could you stay awhile and help me?" Denton agreed, and his six-man "palace guard" elected to remain with him. Among the six was a hard-boiled pint-sized soldier from Brooklyn, Pfc. John L. Baron. Baron was described as "a case; the boy talked a blue streak of profane obscenity and thus far in the fight had done little else." S. L. A. Marshall, in his classic story of the April battle, *Pork Chop Hill*, described what happened next:

Clemons had been gone one and one-half hours when the fight flared, [about the time Easy Company crossed their line of departure headed toward the northeast finger of the hill]. There were sounds of movement from the roof as of men tearing at the sandbags. Through the top of the CP door sailed three grenades, as if a leaning man had made the toss from above. Two blew off harmlessly. The third grenade exploded metal into one of the American wounded.

Then a Chinese came through the door triggering a submachine gun. Denton was shot through the leg and hand. Other bullets hit Captain King and one of his men, Sergeant Robertson. Shooting from the floor, Baron cut down the gunner with one burst from his carbine, yelling, "Take that, you ——— son-of-a-bitch!"

Again the Chinese on the roof grenaded through the doorway, and in the same instant, a second burp gunner aimed his weapon through the embrasure. The grenade exploded under the bunk of a wounded man who had already lost a leg. Chambliss, Newton and Ford [three of Love Company's men], blasted toward the embrasure and killed the Communist gunner before he could fire. Once more, Baron jumped into the open trench and, spinning, fired at the roof. The grenadier fell and his feet dangled above the CP door in the morning.

He would have been dead in three more seconds anyway. As Baron rebounded into the bunker, three 122-mm artillery rounds landed in salvo, two crushing in one corner of the roof, the other exploding into the bunker's sandbag base and caving in one side of it. One round cut a yard-wide hole in the ceiling and showered fragments over the bunks holding the American wounded.

Hit again, they screamed and sobbed hysterically.

Denton cried, "Shut up! I don't want any cry babies in here. Nobody but good men in my company!"

That silenced them immediately.

Baron shouted, "Jesus Christ, this is worse than Custer's last stand."

Asked Denton, "Were you there, too?"

"No," yelled the kid, "but I've read about it."

Denton's radio was still working. He had already been in touch with two Quad-50s [four .50-caliber machine guns mounted on a tracked, self-propelled vehicle] which had parked halfway down the finger waiting for the moment when they might assist the infantry fight. It flashed over his mind that if the eight .50 machine guns could put a grazing fire over the roof, the Chinese could be kept from grenading through the hole blown by the artillery. Denton called the Quads, "Can you give it to me now—all the fire that you've got—put it right over the CP roof?"

Came the answer, "Which roof Lieutenant? From where we sit all of the bunkers look alike." And it was too true, as Denton reflected.

He dropped the instrument, grabbed a grenade and wired a flare to it, then looked for a willing hand. Again it was Baron who volunteered to go into the trench and pitch the improvised light on the roof to mark the target for the Quads. He went, grenade in one hand, carbine in the other. As he made the upward toss, a Chinese burp gunner, ten yards away, opened fire. The burst cut three buttons from Baron's jacket without breaking the skin.

Yelling, "You ———— son-of-a-bitch!" he whirled with his carbine and emptied a magazine into the man.

With the light came the deluge. The Chinese correctly read it as a signal for help in some form. Earlier, their attack upon the bunker was a random effort, the unorganized forays of a few determined individuals. Now, as if on order, they pressed on it in large numbers, coming from all sides, grenadiers throwing and machine gunners firing as they ran screaming toward the central target.

The men inside the bunker knew now that they were beaten. The noise was overpowering. No one moved toward the trench. Denton did not try to form them for the last round.

Baron had walked over to the man with the missing leg. He had seemed to be lapsing into deep sleep. "I watched him," said Baron, "hoping he would make it; it kept my mind off things." Suddenly the man stirred and propped on his elbow, crying, "Save the ammo! For Christ's sakes save the ammo! Don't waste another bullet!"

Sergeant Falk spoke, "Nothing can help us now but prayer. That's what I've always heard about spots like this."

Denton said, "Well, Falk, if you can pray, go ahead."

Falk started, "Our Father—who is in heaven—forgive—forgive us our debtors—Oh, hell, Lieutenant, I don't know it, I just don't know it."

During the moments of this fervent supplication, reverent in spirit if not in language, they were all silent. (Later, they quoted Falk's prayer verbatim as if it were etched in the memory.) Then as Falk said the last words, outside there was silence also, broken only by the crackling of rifle fire at some distance. Gone was the oppressive rattle of the burp guns and the fury of the oncoming grenadiers. The storm ended as suddenly as it had risen.

Easy Company of the 17th Regiment had arrived on Pork Chop . . .

To Denton and his assistants, the fact of deliverance was at first unbelievable. Once again the irrepressible Private Baron jumped into the trench to see what was happening. His first impressions are given in his own words, "There's a ROK soldier going by me, firing a BAR, going to town. Jeez, can that guy use a weapon! Leave him alone and he'll go clean to China. Hey, and there's a hot shot of a little kid, just a small punk, hasn't even got a man's voice yet, screams like a girl, but he's all over the place, doesn't seem to know how to turn that carbine off. Jeez, what a guy, the little bastard's a one-man army."[42]

According to the 17th Regiment Command Report for April 1953, Easy lost not one single man on the way to the crest of Pork Chop. But Lt. James Forton, platoon leader, 2d Platoon, Easy Company, remembered differently, and shed more light on the company's ascent to Pork Chop's crest the early morning hours of 18 April. An Officer Candidate School graduate, after being drafted from his hometown of Tonawanda, New York, in September 1951, he arrived in Korea and joined his platoon seven days before the Chinese struck Pork Chop. One of six—all the Easy Company officers—

wounded in those early morning hours, he wrote home just after returning to his company from the hospital:

Easy Company moved up behind Hill 347, with orders to be prepared to either reinforce or counterattack in the event of an attack on Pork Chop. Ten, eleven, twelve o'clock and everything was quiet. We had blankets sent up, preparing to spend a restless, but warm night. I had been with the company about a week, and all this seemed like games at Benning. About 12:30 a flare lit up the area, then another, and then everything broke loose. The games were over. Word came back in less than a half-hour that Pork Chop had been overrun and we were to counterattack immediately. Hasty company and platoon orders were given and we moved out in a dispersed column by twos.

As we moved past the battalion aid station, we formed a single line and followed the creek out to the cut in Hill 200. The company moved over the cut, through the wire to the valley, and then to the base of Pork Chop. There we fixed bayonets and began the long climb, with the second platoon following the first and third up the hill. No opposition met us until the three-quarter mark, when we began taking fire and started taking casualties. We pushed on, reaching the crest of Pork Chop, where we stopped to reorganize. We had suffered about fifty percent losses at that point. Little potato masher grenades seemed to be coming from everywhere, with burp gun fire all around us. It was now close to three A.M. and all hoped for daylight to come.[43]

The route of Easy's advance boxed in the Chinese, coming at them from their flank and rear. Completely surprised, several groups of Chinese soldiers who saw an escape route fled down the northern fingers toward the valley and enemy-held Pokkae. Easy's rapidly advancing skirmish line trapped others in front of the debris defended by Fox men. The Chinese soldiers caught in the closing vise died fighting.

Unfortunately, another problem reared its ugly head. Sgt. James N. Butcher, Fox Company of the 17th, born in a coal mining town in West Virginia, and later moved to Charleston, West Virginia, vividly recalled,

In the early hours of the morning the shellfire slackened enough to organize a thin trench line facing uphill toward the Chinese held crest. Flares continued to light the sky as though it were daylight. As we awaited dawn, one of our lookouts yelled that he saw a Chinese skirmish line moving slowly up the hill to our rear about 300 yards away. They did not have steel helmets [part of Easy Company's attempt to confuse Chinese who might sight them from Hasakkol or Pokkae] so we concluded that they were Chinese. With enemy holding high ground and firing machine guns into our positions we were afraid we would be caught between two bodies of enemy troops. We now had to make a last ditch stand against the forces coming up the hill. We assumed that this would be our last stand —a suicide stand—and we wanted to make the best of it. We knew, at that moment how Custer must have felt at the Battle of the Little Big Horn. We waited and watched as the shadowy figures moved toward us. Then one of the men on my left thought that the approaching line of shadows was getting too close and he tossed a hand grenade at the closest figures. It burst a few yards in front of them and they speeded up their charge at us . . . now firing and yelling as they made their assault. We began to take aim at the advancing figures.

The first voice I heard coming from the advancing troops was in English. "Wait! Hold your fire!" Someone yelled, "They're Americans!" The yelling got closer, then one of the advancing troopers, an officer from Easy Company, nearly out of breath, recognized our helmets and called for his troops to hold fire and move into the trenches.

We were ecstatic over the turn of events. The officer in charge, angry at first that we opened fire on his skirmish line, was surprised to find anyone alive on the hill because he had been informed that the Chinese held the hill and that no Americans were left.

In spite of the news Fox Company was still fighting on Pork Chop, Gorman Smith knew it was not over, the hill not yet secure, though a momentary lull settled over the Chop. Some of the more determined, tough, disciplined, battle-hardened Chinese soldiers lay low, biding their time, hiding in the battered bunkers and trenches, waiting for the next assault wave. As S. L. A. Marshall wrote, "This was the typical, well-seasoned reaction. In two years of trench warfare, the Red Chinese soldier had become like Brother Fox. Any part of earth was his cover and he had learned to bide his time."

Easy and Fox Companies did not have long to wait. At 3:20 A.M., reinforcements from the 201st CCF Regiment counterattacked once more, this time up the north finger of the Chop. When their reinforcements hit Easy and Fox defenses, enemy snipers which had burrowed into the hill emerged from their holes and reentered the fight. Defenders were now suffering more casualties on Pork Chop.

Another Enemy Surge

Meanwhile, beginning shortly after midnight and throughout the remaining hours of darkness, at Captain King's Fox Company request, flare dropping aircraft and artillery and mortar illuminating rounds bathed the north side of the hill in flickering light. Fortunately, the flares did not give away Easy's climb up the right shoulder and northeast slopes of Pork Chop, while permitting the hill's defenders to see approaching enemy formations, and giving the men of Fox and Easy Companies the ability to bring defensive artillery and mortar fire to bear. Illuminating the north side of the outpost, and keeping the south side in relative darkness and shadow, also minimized casualties of already hard hit units which had been relieved and were departing the battered outpost.

Approximately 4:00 A.M. searchlights mounted on the beds of two-and-a-half-ton trucks, parked on roads along the 7th's MLR in the vicinity of Hill 347, and sweeping the "no man's land" between Pork Chop and the Chinese outpost line, picked up the movement of approximately seven hundred Chinese troops—another battalion—coming from the area near Chink Baldy, headed toward Brinson Finger. The division was conducting tests with searchlights, mounted on truck beds, and later tanks, tied into the artillery net. The forward observer accompanying the searchlight battery called for a fire mission, with the enemy battalion's location and direction of movement, and heavy artillery and mortar fire boxed in the battalion, shredding it with heavy casualties.

Nevertheless, the situation worsened again, when at 4:29 A.M. the remnants of the shattered but determined enemy battalion, approximately one company, climbed Brinson Finger on the outpost's left flank, engaged the defenders with hand grenades, and gained the heights. At 5:05 A.M., Gorman Smith, the Easy Company commander, requested that units on the MLR take Brinson Finger under fire with all available weapons.[44]

When Colonel Kern received the first message that Easy Company was once more under assault, he reacted swiftly. He called General Trudeau and said he thought it time to commit the additional battalion of the 17th Regiment. The division commander replied, "No, we're chewing up one battalion a day. We can't keep it up. Send just one company. Then withdraw the extra company the moment we get the position under control." When the 4:29 A.M. message was relayed to Colonel Kern he ordered Able Company of the 17th to reinforce Pork Chop, and at 4:35 the company departed their forward assembly area.

At 4:18, Lieutenant Colonel Tully, 2d of the 17th, who had learned of Easy and Fox Companies' plight, ordered Walt Russell to prepare the remainder of George Company to reenter the fight and reinforce the outpost. With the 1st Battalion's Able Company now on the way to Pork Chop, Walt Russell's half-strength company remained in reserve, then later moved to refit, refill with replacements, retrain, and fight another day.[45]

At 6:20 the morning of 18 April, Company A, 1st Battalion, 17th Infantry joined with Easy and Fox Companies of the 2d Battalion on Pork Chop. Wounded in Able Company's assault was an infantryman, Cpl. Dale Cain of Phoenix, Arizona. Dale falsified his age and enlisted in the Army in March 1950. He was sixteen. At the conclusion of basic training in Fort Ord, California, and two weeks leave, he reported to Camp Stoneman, California, where he soon received orders for Japan and the replacement center at Camp Drake. Follow-on orders sent him to join Charlie Company, 17th Regimental Combat Team, 7th Infantry Division. After intensive training with the 7th at Camp Fuji, Japan, he came ashore at Inchon on the west coast of the Republic of Korea in September. He remained with the division as it provided security on the south side of the recaptured capital city of Seoul, and linked up with the 1st Cavalry Division, which drove north from the Pusan Perimeter.

He made the long trek with the 7th Division and its 17th Regiment as the units reboarded ships, came ashore at Iwon, North Korea, on the peninsula's east coast, and drove north toward the Yalu River. At a base camp in far North Korea, the long arm of federal and military law caught up with the still underage soldier and returned him home for discharge. The Army discharged him at Camp Stoneman on 31 December 1950, but his journey through the Korean War was not yet over.

In 1952, at age eighteen, he was no longer underage and did not need his parents' permission to enlist—and he reenlisted, with the understanding he could rejoin his unit in Korea.[46] He wanted to help the Korean people fight for their freedom. Back to Camp Stoneman, thence to Camp Drake again, and finally to Able Company of the 17th and Pork Chop Hill on 18 April 1953, came Dale Cain. His brief April fire fight on Pork Chop Hill was not his last—only a beginning. The next and most severe test came less than three months later, and began three weeks before the armistice ended the fighting in Korea.

Half an hour after Able Company linked up with Easy Company the morning of 18 April, incoming artillery began decreasing. At 7:06 the hill's defenders reported enemy artillery once more increasing, while A, E, and F Companies continued mopping up operations. Shortly before daylight, quick action by an artillery forward observer shattered a final enemy attempt to reinforce Pork Chop. He spotted an estimated company of approximately one hundred men in the open, moving from Pokkae south into the valley toward the outpost. Within two minutes after the initial observation eight battalions of artillery fired three to five rounds per gun on the lucrative target. Only one enemy soldier was seen to have moved from the area after the fires were lifted.

At 8:30 A.M. Colonel Kern ordered Maj. Earl Acuff, commander, 1st of the 17th, to assume responsibility for the defense of Pork Chop, and to infiltrate Easy and Fox Companies back to the MLR. Lt. Gorman Smith, whose company boldly turned the tide early that morning, assembled the remainder of both companies and requested maximum smoke be laid on Pokkae and Hasakkol at 10:00 A.M., to cover the withdrawal. The smoke rounds fell as requested, and after reaching friendly lines at 10:30, Easy and Fox Companies departed for Camp Steward. On Pork Chop, enemy artillery tapered off as the day wore on. With transportation provided by medics and M-39 Armored Personnel Carriers, the evacuation of wounded and dead continued. The open-top M-39 APCs, tracked vehicles, were a godsend and lifeline to Pork Chop. They had been used throughout the battle to evacuate the wounded and dead, and resupply the hill's defenders. Only one had been struck by mortar or artillery fire during the battle, wounding the two-man crew.

Six infantry companies, the equivalent of two infantry battalions, less the men manning the battalions' heavy weapons companies, had been committed across the valley in front of Hill 200 to hold outpost Pork Chop, after the Chinese assault the night of 16 April shattered and almost destroyed Easy Company, 2d of the 31st. Easy Company of the 17th, which had turned the tide the early morning hours of 18 April suffered thirty-two casualties, including all five of its officers wounded. Three of Easy's soldiers were killed in action.[47]

The Chinese lost untold hundreds killed in action, and probably more than a thousand wounded while bravely crossing the valleys and fighting their way up the slopes of Pork Chop in the face of murderous, defensive artillery and mortar fires. Those who made it to the crest fought determinedly to hold the heights for nearly forty-eight hours. Bodies of 116 CCF dead were found and searched for documents by counterintelligence, and many more bodies were retrieved by their fellow soldiers and carried from the field. Fifteen of their number were taken prisoner.[48]

S. L. A. Marshall wrote poignantly of other casualties: "Shortly after Pork Chop Hill, I attended a memorial service for the battle dead of one battalion. It did honor to 73 men. But they had been given no other honor by their country for the victory which they had helped win; it drew no headlines, nor did the voices on the national radio give adequate testimony. There is a great deal of iron in war. There is also irony."[49]

Marshall wrote that April's Pork Chop was an artillery duel, saying the battle was "a minor affair as to infantry numbers." The battle's weight, as measured in metal and supporting rounds fired, validated the guns' victory when compared to the "relatively few riflemen who struggled to hold the outposts, doing it with their flesh when their weapons would no longer work." In the forty-eight-hour period spanning the battle for Pork Chop, Brig. Gen. Andrew P. O'Meara, the 7th Division's artillery commander, kept nine battalions of artillery, including one from the adjacent ROK 2d Infantry Division, operating in support of 7th Division units. During the first twenty-four hours the guns fired 37,655 rounds in defense of Arsenal, Dale, and Pork Chop. The heavies fired 9,823 rounds and light howitzers—the 105s—fired 27,832. The second day, after Arsenal and Dale were saved, and Pork Chop raged on, the supporting fires built up to 77,349. It is noteworthy that neither of these totals include the deluge of killing artillery rained on and around Pork Chop by the enemy. Nor do they include the thousands of mortar rounds that fell on the hill and surrounding slopes from both sides of "no man's land."

The twentieth-century history of thunderous artillery duels yields interesting comparisons with the April 1953 Korean War battle. Never on Verdun's World War I battlefield were guns worked at any rate as on Pork

Pfc. Melvin Lucas (*left*), Company K, 31st Infantry Regiment, brings in an enemy prisoner at bayonet point he captured on Pork Chop, 17 April 1953. *Courtesy of National Archives*

Chinese prisoners taken under guard from Pork Chop by soldiers from Company I, 17th Infantry Regiment, 17 April 1953. *Courtesy of National Archives and Robert M. Euwer*

A medic from the 7th Infantry Division dresses the wounds of an enemy prisoner captured during the battle for Pork Chop. *Courtesy of National Archives*

After having his wounds treated, an enemy prisoner captured during the battle for Pork Chop receives a cigarette from a 7th Infantry Division medic. *Courtesy of National Archives*

Chop Hill. The World War II battle for Kwajalein Island in the Pacific, America's most intense shoot during that war, was of lesser measure than Pork Chop Hill. In terms of rounds per hour, weight of metal against yards of earth, and the total output of the guns, the April battle for Pork Chop deserves a place in history. At the time it set an all-time mark for artillery effort.[50] But come July, a new record would be set.

When the April fight was over, the hill was as battle-scarred and picked clean as Old Baldy. The outpost's cratered slopes would not bloom again soon, not until after the late July armistice. Rusty shards, empty tins, and bones were too well planted there, said S. L. A. Marshall.

The Chinese did not breach Pork Chop's defenses again until the first week of July, when, for five agonizing days in one last desperate thrust by the CCF, thousands of men from both sides would spill their blood and fight to the death on this small, brutally tortured hill.

5

REBUILDING

ON 20 APRIL, TWO DAYS AFTER EASY AND ABLE COMPANIES OF THE 17TH secured Pork Chop, Operation Little Switch began in Panmunjom, approximately twenty-five miles southwest of the outpost. The exchange of sick and wounded POWs continued to 3 May. It was an extraordinary operation governed by elaborate security measures, and the two sides accomplished the exchange without notable incident. The UN returned a total of 6,670 POWs: 5,194 NKPA, 1,030 CCF, and 446 civilian internees. In exchange, the UN received a total of 684 POWs: 471 ROKs, 149 Americans, 32 Britons, 15 Turks, and 17 other UN personnel.[1]

Among those received by the UN before 25 April was 2d Lt. Albert DeLaGarza, the artillery forward observer attached to the Colombia Battalion, wounded and taken prisoner on Old Baldy in the early morning hours of 24 March. He was more fortunate than most UN POWs, many of whom were captured early in the war and remained in captivity for the duration. Except for his relatively brief period in captivity, DeLaGarza's POW odyssey was not unusual:

About a half hour later they took me from the cave and walked me about 4 miles west past hill 190, 180 and 177, along the river. After that I lost my sense of direction. They then took me into a cave dug into the side of a hill on the north bank of the river. All along the route I walked I saw a constant caravan of medics with stretchers headed toward Chink Baldy. I thought of escape knowing I could go to the left but the constant stream of medics made it impossible. All the time I was walking along the river our artillery was firing at the bottom of the slope and at the bottom of the river. Also many flares were coming in and lighting up the area. I expected to get hit by the artillery but got through all right. I think the cave was toward hill 222 running away from the river. I was in the cave 3 days and 3 nights. 7 or 8 air strikes hit on the hill during this time but didn't hurt the cave at all. The cave was back in the mountain with a tunnel about 100 yards long. All along the tunnel walls were wounded Chinks lined up in a solid line of stretchers. I was put with 3 Colombians and we had to sleep in a small corner on some sacks of coal. We were fed twice a day, rice and bread. We got water whenever we asked for it. They would bring us a can for urination. None of us had to defecate during the 3 days. After 3 days they put me and another Colombia on a stretcher and walked approximately one half mile. Then they put me on a large affair (similar to the body of a car). Cables were tied to it and they pulled it to the other bank of the river. Then we had to walk again approximately 3 or 4 miles. We left the cave about 0500 hours. After we crossed the river we walked until about 0700. They kept hurrying us because they were afraid planes would spot them. As we crossed the hills we heard an artillery battery nearby, it sounded like 122s. (right of tit from OP 10). About 2 of every 5 Chinks we passed were armed with a carbine. Everywhere we walked we saw caves. At about 0900 we stopped at a bunker. There was a man with a PRC 10 [radio] powered by a BA 70 monitoring our [radio] channels. I could not understand what was said on the radio but it was working perfectly. The man at the radio asked if anyone could speak English. I indicated I could and he asked my name and they searched me again. They took my lighter, watch, mirror, etc., but later gave back all but the lighter and pocket knife. I was there all day, that night and until noon the next day. I was interrogated all that time. I had removed all identification but had a letter in my pocket so they immediately knew my name and organization. They asked about 7th Division Artillery. They knew the artillery battalions and regiments they supported. I think the bunker was the battalion CP. While I was being interrogated a very trim looking officer with clean mustache and high collar came into the bunker and everyone jumped to attention. He wore no insignia but it is my thought that he was the battalion commander. He stayed throughout my interrogation with the interpreter translating for him. He had the interrogator bring me a large map and insisted that I point out to him the location of our artillery positions. I told him I did not know the location of the artillery positions, and this made them violently angry. I told them I did not have to know the location of our artillery positions to be able to adjust artillery fire. At first they didn't believe this but finally seemed satisfied with this. They told me of the prisoner of war lenient policy which was a guarantee of safe conduct and good care if I would agree to cooperate and give them the information they desired. When I refused information pertaining to the location of the firing batteries, they said I probably could not be guaranteed safe conduct. However, later they told me that I would not be harmed and would be sent back farther to the rear. 8 of us (7 Colombians and myself) left this bunker and proceeded to the rear under guard. We traveled roughly a week, walking during the day and sleeping in bunkers at night. We saw several knocked out trucks which had straw mats over them. We finally came to a very large river which we crossed at night on a large barge, which held several trucks. The barge was pulled by cables from one bank to the other. There was a large tunnel on the side of the bank into which the barge was pushed into during the day. Our guard finally got us a ride on a truck, and we were taken to a small village. There we were interrogated by a woman and three men. They offered us cigarettes and treated us very nicely. They wanted to know all about the counter fire machine [counter battery radar], and what it looked like, how it operated, and the tie in between it and artillery. They also wanted to know about the organization of a field artillery battalion, and how we were able to mass our artillery fire. They also want to know how good their artillery was and what results they had. I was interrogated along with the 7 Colombians and was their interpreter while they were being interrogated. They wanted to know all about the first Army unit organized in Colombia, when the Colombia Battalion got to Korea and how many casualties it suffered. They were very much interested in the raid on hill 180 by the Colombians. They wanted to know the reason for the raid and the casualties we suffered. At the village I saw an infantry company move out equipped with mortars, 57s, 60s, and light machine guns. They had pack mules for transportation. They told me I was the second forward observer that had been captured. They said the other man was from the 49th FA Bn and he was captured during the attack on hill 598 last October. I cannot remember his name though they told me his name. His radio sergeant whom they also captured was Sgt. [name not readable]. He was captured at the same time.[2]

The Mission: Hold at All Cost

While Little Switch was in progress, the 7th Infantry Division command report for March was being compiled and prepared to send on to the I Corps historian, resident in the corps' operations staff, the G-3. Signed the same day Albert DeLaGarza signed his POW debriefing following his release by the Chinese at Panmunjom, the report contained General Trudeau's thoughts after a tumultuous one-month period in command of the division. The two major assaults on the division front by the Chinese in late March and mid-April caused him to look closely for ways to strengthen the 7th's "active defense" all across its sector. "In as much as this report is submitted at a time when I have completed one month in command of this Division," Trudeau noted, "during which period two heavy actions have been experienced, I consider it desirable to record my principal conclusions on the current situation."[3]

Beginning with a discussion of *Defensive Dispositions*, he wrote,

The selection of positions is generally good, especially with respect to observation, terrain obstacles, and natural routes of communications. However, the sector is very wide in terms of manpower and firepower. It is evident that with fronts so extended that front-line battalions must commit all their rifle companies on the MLR and outposts, depth to infantry positions behind the MLR is provided by limited counterattack forces. Such forces consist of minimum regimental reserves; a division reserve comprising elements relieved periodically for rest and rehabilitation; and the division tank battalion.

The principal means of gaining depth (space and time) with respect to the main defensive position is by pushing forward relatively strong outposts whose mission is to hold at all cost. Although these outposts are all less than one mile from the MLR, the task of reinforcing them while under attack is normally difficult and requires elements from the MLR, thereby temporarily weakening the main battle position. However, such outposts in effect constitute islands of defense. They provide mutual support for each other, serve as patrol bases, and limit the infiltration of hostile forces against the MLR or into areas immediately adjacent thereto. Balancing all factors involved, I consider the deployment of the available forces in my sector to be good.[4]

In the final paragraph he appeared to be crystallizing his thoughts and expressing his views on the March abandonment of Old Baldy, when, as a newly assigned division commander, he was unable to persuade Gen. Maxwell Taylor of the need for another counterattack to retake that outpost. He went on to emphasize the risks of abandoning any more major outposts:

Abandonment of the major outposts would increase the risk of loss of some important centers of resistance on the MLR to a point that would be hazardous. The loss of certain such centers of resistance would threaten the integrity of the entire position and might seriously tax my capabilities to restore it. Furthermore, with respect to abandonment of major outposts, a consideration is its probable psychological effect upon the enemy's estimate of the situation. I believe he would interpret such a withdrawal as a confession of weakness and an invitation to assault essential MLR positions.[5]

The Chief Engineer and the 13th Engineer Battalion

Maj. Gen. Arthur Gilbert Trudeau was an engineer, the number fifteen graduate in West Point's 405-man class of 1924. In a career of mostly engineer construction and military training assignments, including command of the 1st Cavalry Division in Japan in 1952–53—after the division was pulled out of Korea—he came to the Republic in March well prepared to take command of an infantry division. His engineering skills were especially suited to command a division needing well-constructed, fortified defenses on a long-stabilized, deeply entrenched line. Now, after one month, he saw clearly in his own mind that Pork Chop's shattered defenses must be rebuilt, strengthened, and markedly improved to reduce casualties and avoid losing the outpost to the Chinese. Prior to writing his *Organization of the Ground* in the March command report, he had already verbally outlined to his staff and commanders the improvements he considered necessary on a shattered Pork Chop, all other division outposts, and the MLR. Work was already under way when he wrote,

The organization of the ground in this sector is inadequate for determined and protracted defense against heavy infantry-artillery attack. (There is no serious threat of armored attack in this sector.) The present organization of the ground leaves much to be desired and extended efforts are being made to improve the defenses. New work is now being prosecuted vigorously.

The principal weaknesses are as follows:

(1) Limited strength prevents occupation of positions near the forward base of hills to obtain the best fields of fire, especially flanking and grazing fire.

(2) Many bunkers for automatic weapons are not well designed; few are sited or employed to provide fire to flanks. Generally they are used only to fire to the front.

Rarely are they dug down so that the normal slope of the terrain can be restored upon completion. As a result, most bunkers have distinct profile and consequently offer choice targets for enemy destruction.

(3) Trenches vary from shallow to too deep. Many have long, straight sections that increase hazards from enfilade fire in close-in fighting. Very few have overhead cover except at points where fighting or sleeping bunkers join. Many of proper depth (6'-6") contain no firing steps. In most cases, no effort has been made to cover sandbags with natural earth to improve concealment. Few trenches exist on the reverse slopes; thus there is a lack of secondary firing positions to the flanks and rear.

(4) Fighting bunkers, in addition to many structural weaknesses, are frequently located so that they give a false sense of security for close-in fighting and become death-traps.

The same may be said for numerous sleeping bunkers which are integrated with the fighting trenches.

(5) Protective wire needs improvement. The most common weaknesses are:

(a) Failure to repair existing wire

(b) Insufficient number of bands of wire

(c) Outside band within grenade range of trenches

(d) Dependence on concertina rather than single and double-apron fence.

(6) Communication wire invariably poor, due to failure to bury it in trenches and approaches. This causes general failure of wire communications during attacks and is highly wasteful.

(7) The concealment effort has been inadequate, and far below that of the enemy in quality. Many installations are openly exposed to the front; others are poorly camouflaged. In this connection there has been little or no attempt to prepare dummy positions.

(8) Minefields are not well recorded. Apparently successive units have placed mines without insuring that locations were precisely plotted and made known to relieving troops. Enemy fire has further upset such locations. In consequence, mines are now considered more hazardous to us than to the enemy, and there is a reluctance to lay additional ones.

The essence of improving the techniques in this field revolves around the following points, with due consideration for available units, manpower and firepower:

(1) Careful selection and development of positions, based on thorough study of observation, field of fire, concealment, obstacles and communications. Development of positions for actual all-around defense.

(2) Broken trenches traces to minimize artillery and small arms enfilading fire. Frequent covered sections of trench and shelters to permit cover from enemy artillery and VT fires on our own positions. Adequate depth to trenches, installation of firing steps, and restoration of natural earth and slopes insofar as practicable.

(3) Sightings of automatic weapons to the flanks for maximum effect to provide final protective fire and maximum coverage of intervening terrain.

(4) Construction of properly designed bunkers to minimize any changes to contours or profile of natural terrain.

(5) Separation of sleeping (living) bunkers to reduce absence of men from firing positions during periods of close combat.

(6) Location of protective wire beyond grenade throwing distance and with due regard to best final protective line of automatic weapons. Wire must consist of multiple bands of single or double-apron fence interspersed with flares and when practicable personnel mines.

(7) Carefully selected emplacements for searchlights, anti-aircraft and anti-tank (tank) weapons. Dummy emplacements are also desirable.

(8) Well-defiladed communications trenches and routes of approach.

(9) Buried sand-bagged wire lines.

(10) Good distribution and storage of all types of ammunition and essential supplies.

(11) Reasonable sanitary arrangements.

(12) Improvement of concealment, camouflage, and dispersion.

(13) Further effort to record existing mine fields.

(14) Continuing and systematically planned improvement of all positions.

Trudeau continued, "A training memorandum outlining these techniques will be published. Furthermore, a selected piece of terrain will be organized as a model for the instruction of all newly assigned officers and senior non-commissioned officers. In addition a relief model of that area will be constructed."

The 7th's commander touched on other key factors in the division's readiness to fight, including the Air Section and its night operations capabilities, logistics, the division's officers and enlisted men, offensive capabilities, and decorations:

The availability of improved aerial cameras and reproduction equipment greatly enhances the contribution that can be made within the division to provide our own photographic intelligence data promptly.

Night operations of division air sections can be greatly expanded. The proven ability of the L-20 aircraft to carry 40 M-6 illumination flares (L-19 can carry 14) gives the division an improved method of providing illumination of the battlefield. This is essential to supplement searchlights and reach defiladed areas in rugged terrain. It is more effective and less expensive than the use of illuminating artillery shells. In this sector, division aircraft capabilities compared to Air Force flare-carrying aircraft (C-46) are as follows:

ITEM	L-20	C-46
Effectiveness	Excellent	Good
Time to reach target	15 minutes	75 minutes
Length of illumination	2 hours	7 hours
Cost per hour of operation	$22.00	$100.00
Size of crew	3	7

Night reconnaissance by division light aircraft is highly effective. Enemy vehicular traffic halts in the presence of our low flying reconnaissance planes. Accurate observations far exceed what would be expected due to intimate knowledge of the sector acquired by our pilots. Hazards from anti-aircraft are approximately one-tenth of those in daylight.

Evacuation by army helicopters (L-13) at night is highly effective. With two litter-bearing Division helicopters, nine seriously wounded casualties have been successfully evacuated during four nights of heavy fighting.

Turning to logistics, Trudeau observed, "The availability and distribution of supplies and equipment is excellent. Motor vehicles are old; many have been rebuilt in Japan. Emphasis on maintenance has kept the vehicles operative in the present situation. However, the maintenance effort clearly shows that the present vehicles could not long support mobile operations." He then recorded his observations of the officers and enlisted men in the 7th Division:

Officers

As a whole, my officers are competent, loyal, courageous and well oriented.

Second lieutenants are well selected and generally well trained. As noted above, I believe they require better preparation for current operations in Korea, particularly with respect to defensive organization of the ground.

Enlisted Men

Group identification is always lacking to some degree, due to rapid turnover. Under good officer and NCO leadership, some units leave nothing to be desired; however, unfortunately, not all reach this standard. By and large, the United States soldier is a splendid fighting man.

The average squad presently consists of five or six Americans (at least one negro), one Puerto Rican and three KATUSAS. . . . Language difficulties are not so great as might be expected. A very large number of KATUSAS have served with the Division for more than two years (some 700 since before the Inchon landing).

He then took up the question of offensive capabilities, capabilities that had not been put to the test for nineteen months:

The only offensive action is periodic reconnaissance and combat patrolling (using up to platoon-sized units), occasional company (minus) size raids and counterattacks of company and battalion strength as required to restore overrun positions. Consequently, the capabilities of the Division remain untested with respect to mobile, offensive action in a fluid situation. Nevertheless, the fact that the combat arms have been subject to considerable combat, coupled with a keen sense of mission, insures that the Division will give a good account of itself in any situation. Training in offensive action will be stressed when units are not on line.

Writing about decorations, Trudeau reveals himself a commander who sees the division, its KATUSAs, and all its attached Colombian and Ethiopian troops as one unified command, noting that he is unable to decorate the KATUSAs and UN troops as they deserve to be:

A family of United Nations decorations is urgently needed. The system for and limitations in providing U.S. decorations for personnel of UN contingents leaves much to be desired. The Division Commander cannot issue an "On the Spot" award for heroism to a KATUSA soldier even though all other members of his squad, patrol, etc. are decorated and despite the fact that often he has the longest period of service of any in the group. Similar restrictions prevent any prompt recognition of heroic action by personnel of foreign units. Relaxation of restrictions on the award of the Silver Star and Bronze Star Medal (Valorous) would provide an expeditious but temporary solution. United Nations decorations are the proper answer in my opinion. Psychologically, there are additional advantages that seem apparent.[6]

Trudeau's penetrating April critique of the 7th Division's—and Pork Chop's—defenses made clear much work was ahead. Aside from Old Baldy, which had fallen into Chinese hands in March, Pork Chop, for a variety of reasons, was the next most significant outpost in the division sector and had taken the worst and longest pounding in April's battles. The 7th Division Engineer, Lt. Col. Earl L. Icke, doubled as the commander, 13th Engineer Battalion (Combat), and to the engineers fell the tasks of designing, assembling the needed materials, leading, participating in, and supervising the reconstruction of Pork Chop's defenses. Work began in April, immediately following the bitter fight to hold the hill.

A tough, crusty, no-nonsense engineer, Icke had high standards, was intensely demanding, and was determined to rebuild the hill's defenses so they would not collapse again. He was known among the Eighth Army's engineers as "the meanest damn battalion commander in Korea." In reality, General Trudeau, commissioned in the Corps of Engineers, was the division's chief engineer. His first troop duty assignment following his commissioning was the 13th Engineers. In a sense, Trudeau was now back home with his old unit. Nevertheless, his division chief engineer, Lieutenant Colonel Icke, also knew why the defenses on Pork Chop so readily crumbled under the weight of Chinese artillery and mortar rounds.

The bunkers had been constructed over an extended period of time preceding the April battle, supervising and working under fire, side by side with KATUSAs and Korean Service Corps (KSC) laborers. Battalions assigned responsibility for defense of the Chop normally rotated their three rifle companies onto the outpost at five to seven day intervals, but the infantrymen on outpost duty could not participate in rebuilding the positions.

While on outpost or MLR duty, the infantry slept primarily in the daytime, although fitfully because of harassing enemy mortar and occasional artillery fire as well as the disrupting effects of construction in progress. The infantry stood "radio guard" and scaled back observation duty during daylight hours, because they had to remain alert at night, when the enemy was routinely active. With rebuilding work possible only during harried daylight hours, in open trenches on the north slopes, visible to nearby Chinese forward observers on higher hills, the 13th had gradually built the bunkers and trenches while almost daily dodging incoming artillery and mortar rounds. Facing incoming rounds and almost daily casualties among the infantrymen and anyone else on the outpost, the engineers, their KATUSAs, and KSC laborers had done the best they could in shoring up the Chop's defenses prior to the CCF's April assault.

In addition to all the weaknesses identified by General Trudeau, the results of harassed construction were doorways, embrasures, and firing apertures were not square or level, floors were not level, and walls, including sandbag walls and vertical members, were not plumb. Each of these factors contributed to weakened overhead cover. When the artillery and mortar barrages fell in April, the defensive network became an easy victim of collapse and cave-in, and the death traps Trudeau described in his critique following the March and April battles. And that said nothing at all about the placement and orientation of firing positions and bunkers intended to anchor the hill's defenses.

The 13th Engineer Battalion, a combat unit with Able, Baker, Charlie, and Dog Companies, which, like the infantry companies, were infused with KATUSAs, organized and trained to support all 7th Division units, but primarily infantry units on the MLR and OPLR. Each engineer company was assigned to support an infantry regiment. Thus Able Company normally supported the 17th Infantry, Baker the 31st, and Charlie the 32d. Dog company was "general support," which meant they provided engineering support to other combat and combat support units organic or attached to the 7th Infantry Division, such as artillery battalions, the 73 Tank Battalion, medical companies, and other units. They also provided general support to the 13th Engineer Battalion's other three companies.

Within each of Able, Baker, and Charlie engineer companies, a platoon supported one of the three infantry battalions in the regiment. When a company within the supported infantry battalion was ordered to counterattack, one squad from an engineer platoon was dispatched to participate in the mission and placed under the command of the infantry company commander. For example, for counterattacks, the 1st Squad, 1st Platoon of the engineers' Able Company was attached to the 17th Regiment's Able Company, 2d Squad to Baker Company, and 3d Squad to Charlie Company. After the company's mission was complete, the attached squad of engineers was released back to their engineer company, and hitched a ride to their respective bivouac areas.

Able Company of the 13th Engineers had an excellent reputation. If Lieutenant Colonel Icke identified an officer or enlisted man who needed some discipline, solid training, and an education in the finer points of being a good combat engineer and in knowing what it meant to support line infantry and other units—some straightening away, in other words— he invariably sent the man to Able Company and its commander, Capt. James A. Brettell. Brettell was an equally tough, no-nonsense company commander who had a most unusual background and had met his crusty engineer battalion commander in a most unusual way.

Brettell graduated from high school at the age of sixteen during World War II, immediately signed up for the draft, and was drafted, but his falsified age was discovered. Undeterred and intent on doing his part in the war, with his mother's approving signature, and still sixteen, he took another avenue that was entirely legal for a sixteen year old during World War II: he joined the Merchant Marines. He took his "boot camp" under the Coast Guard's tough regimen and shipped as a crewman on tankers—not the safest profession in Wolfpack-infested shipping lanes across the North Atlantic to England. From the tanker he watched a more cautious, now-beaten German U-Boat strategy at work late in the European war. Instead of wholesale assaults from all sides, the Germans attacked and sank the trailing ships in the convoys, which fortunately was never the lot of his tanker. Then he found himself on a tanker off Okinawa in the Pacific near the end of the war, during the hellish Kamikaze attacks on the American invasion fleet. His ship received no Kamikaze hits, but was struck by a Japanese bomb which earned him a piece of shrapnel, and his tanker heavy battle damage and a war-ending trip home accompanied by the Navy's aircraft carrier *Franklin,* which was also sporting severe battle damage from the battle for Okinawa.

Immediately after World War II, Brettell enlisted in the Army at age eighteen, and it was off to Fort Benning for Officer Candidate School and Fort Belvoir to Engineer Officer Basic. From there it was Europe for four years, where in Austria he married the daughter of an officer. Back in the States in 1951, he was assigned to the Shore Battalion of the 369th Engineer Amphibious Regiment at Fort Worden, Washington, and from there with the Shore Battalion to the Nevada nuclear test site. There he built combat positions and displays, and led troops in mock assaults toward ground zero following each detonation in eight nuclear weapons tests.

Next came aviation training at San Marcos, Texas, where his physical stature was gaged "too big" for the Army's airplanes. From San Marcos he went to Fourth Army Headquarters at Fort Sam Houston, Texas, where he received orders for the Far East and Eighth Army. When he left for Korea, his wife stayed in San Antonio taking care of their two-and-a-half-year-old daughter and a newborn son.

How did he get to the 7th Division and 13th Engineers? When he arrived at Eighth Army in Seoul, Korea, he began pressing for an assignment to a line division. While in his boss's office reiterating his wishes for duty in a division, the phone rang. On the other end of the line was "the meanest battalion commander in Korea" telling Jim Brettell's boss, "I need an engineer captain right now!" The response? "I have one sitting right in front of me." Said Lieutenant Colonel Icke, "I'll come and get him," and he did.

Captain Brettell would learn much, quickly, under the tutelage and driving intensity of his new battalion commander, and it was all good.

In Able Company, "Bulldozer Able," the other three 13th Engineer companies, and the battalion staff, were some extraordinary men, including Capt. Joseph K. Bratton, who became the 13th's S-4, the battalion supply officer. When Bratton traveled by train from Inchon to the 7th Division, he was the senior officer among fourteen officers destined for the division, one to be a company commander in the 13th. The new engineer company commander was severely wounded within a week after he arrived, and at the end of the war, Bratton was one of two among the fourteen who had not been killed or wounded.[7]

But it would take more than the engineers to rebuild the defenses of a shattered Pork Chop Hill beginning 18 April 1953.[8]

Korean Service Corps laborers, Korean civilians employed in support of UN divisions on line in Korea, and other rear area units were crucial in rebuilding and improving Pork Chop and other defensive positions along the line, as well as sustaining combat operations. Commanded by ROK Army officers, six thousand laborers in the 101st KSC Regiment, and the 3d Battalion, 102d KSC Regiment, a total of twenty-four companies, supported the 7th Infantry Division. Nearly all were Korean men either too old or too young to serve in the ROK Army, which meant there were young boys among the laborers.[9] Throughout most of April, the division allocated six KSC companies in support of each of the two regimental sectors; nine companies to the 13th Engineers; two companies to the technical services, 7th Division Headquarters and division rear; and one KSC company to headquarters, 7th Division Artillery.[10]

The Lifeline

Among several missions assigned the 13th Combat Engineers was maintenance of Pork Chop's lifeline—its access road. The access road came forward from the division rear area, passed behind Hill 347, through the checkpoint behind Hill 200, then turned northwest to run parallel with Hill 200 and crossed a small stream bed. It then wound around the base of Hill 200, climbed up a relatively steep grade to the outpost's evacuation landing, and returned more steeply downhill, rejoining the access road and forming a loop intended to avoid conflicting return traffic and the necessity of a widened road. The evacuation landing was just outside the entrance to what later became known as the "engineers' tunnel," the main covered trench which went past the company CP and supply bunkers located underneath the hill's crest, and connected with Pork Chop's entire trench and bunker system.

Maintenance of the access road was important in all weather conditions. Most months the spring-fed creek passing behind Hill 200 and in front of Hill 347 was a dry stream bed, but the 13th needed to anticipate Korea's monsoon season and work especially hard before and during to keep the access road, and the entire division road net, passable. Vehicles using the access road off-loaded mostly at the evacuation landing. Their cargoes were the necessities of life and battle for Pork Chop's defenders, including rations, water, medical supplies, ammunition, weapons, explosives, construction materials for strengthening the trenches and bunkers, communications wire equipment, and other items. On the return trip they transported wounded and dead from the hill to collection points behind the MLR for pickup and shuttle to aid stations, hospitals, or the quartermaster unit where remains were processed to graves registration. Although the engineers' tasks appeared "routine," they were anything but routine.

The access road was also the route taken by APCs loaded with engineers, their KATUSAs, and KSC laborers on and off the hill during rebuilding of the Chop. At staggered and varied times daily the construction crews, which included a few augmenting troops from division reserve units, departed from behind the MLR early in the morning, remained on the hill to work ten to sixteen hours, and returned to their cantonment areas late in the evening. Remembering their experiences with some embarrassment, two former engineers recalled that when riding the M-39s, the open-topped APCs, Americans, KATUSAs, and KSC laborers rode side by side inside the vehicle. When later the boxlike closed-top APC, the T-18, came into service, the engineers and KATUSAs rode inside the vehicles and the KSC laborers rode outside, on top, obviously much more exposed to enemy fire than the men inside.

On at least one occasion KSCs riding on top of T-18s became a sore point. Lt. Richard White, platoon leader, 3d Platoon of the engineers' Able Company, took a work crew of engineers and KSC laborers to Pork Chop early one morning, accompanied by a brand-new ROK Army lieutenant assigned supervisory and leadership responsibilities for the KSCs. As usual, the KSCs rode on top of the APC. Late in the day, when a T-18 came to pick up the work crew, the ROK lieutenant, on seeing the Americans and KATUSAs again load inside the APC while the KSCs climbed on top, proclaimed to the KSCs in Hangul, the Korean language, "If the Americans and KATUSAs ride inside, KSCs should ride inside."

White was confronting an immediate problem. If he relented in the face of the young officer's demand, there was not room for everyone to make the return trip. Another APC would need to be dispatched or the vehicle would have to make a second round trip. The covered T-18s were new, undergoing operational tests, scarce in number, and beset with maintenance growing pains in this tough, combat environment. Moreover, if he relented, a precedent would be established doubling the demand on the small APC fleet of vehicles. White decided to take a different approach to the problem.

He called upon two of the biggest, strongest American engineers he could find, explained the situation, and asked them to pick up the ROK lieutenant by each arm, bodily if need be, and deposit him inside the APC. Then White crawled on top of the T-18 to sit down with the KSCs. Dick White had entered a whole new culture.

As the vehicle's crew was loading up the inside with American and KATUSA engineers, getting ready to move, the KSCs clamored up on top, sat in a circle, and all interlocked arms and legs and held hands with one another, including Dick White, preparing for the return ride. And ride they did. No one man would fall off the vehicle unless all the KSCs, including White, fell off.

When they returned to the checkpoint behind Hill 200 and unloaded, the 13th Engineers, ROK Army lieutenant, and KSCs went their separate ways to their bivouac areas. The ROK Army lieutenant was never seen again. He had been embarrassed in front of the KSCs, had "lost face," while the KSCs continued to ride on top of the T-18s plying back and forth to rebuild Pork Chop's defenses.

Rides from the checkpoint behind Hill 200 to Pork Chop and back were wild, because approximately one thousand yards of the road were under direct observation by Chinese forward observers on Old Baldy. CCF artillery batteries had long since plotted and registered the entire route, and if the Chinese decided to "fire for effect" at vehicles or troops plying the road, they could make life both hectic and frighteningly miserable. The GIs had a name for the section of road rounding the foot of Hill 200: "Clobber Corner." At Clobber Corner, vehicles were closest and most exposed to the deadly combination of observers on Old Baldy and well-hidden batteries of CCF artillery revetted in caves behind the Chinese MLR.

What is more, the Chinese Army's still common use of guerrilla warfare meant UN forces had to be on their guard against "line crossers" from the north and unconventional warfare units infiltrating and causing havoc in rear areas. Line crossers could lay hidden in wait, plot the locations of bunkers, command and communications nodes, artillery positions, road nets, and assembly areas, and call or signal artillery or mortar rounds into rear areas. Lone vehicles with their drivers, even individual soldiers walking along roads or trails, could suddenly find themselves under heavy assault, depending on the whim of a line crossing artillery or mortar observer, observers on Old Baldy or in MLR observation posts, or simply a randomly fired salvo of harassment and interdiction rounds. Snipers and ambushes were also the missions of line crossers and small groups of infiltrators from the rear.

How did the engineers maintain Pork Chop's access road? The 13th's Dog Company would truck rocks to the checkpoint behind Hill 200, and KSC laborers off-loaded the rocks onto APCs. Then the APC crews drove the diesel-engined, tracked vehicles along the road and, at the desired point, opened the doors at the rear of the vehicle allowing the engineers and KSC laborers to shovel and push rock out of the vehicle onto the road section needing maintenance or repair. Later, when the monsoon rains started, the APCs began washing out and deepening potholes as they made their trips back and forth to the evacuation landing. To solve that problem, the engineers would load the APCs with sand bags filled with rocks, and drop the bags into the potholes and ruts.

Servicing the monsoon-washed potholes under fire was not fun, and stopping a vehicle on the access road en route to Pork Chop was never a good idea. But sometimes, especially prior to the monsoon season, preventive maintenance of roads was absolutely essential and stops were necessary—to build culverts across roads, for example, or to dig and reinforce drainage ditches alongside them, all to ensure the lifeline remained passable during the rains.

One night, Lieutenant White accompanied an armored, cab-covered bulldozer to grade and improve the access road to Pork Chop. He was the

A T-18 APC coming up the Pork Chop access road toward the landing and turn-around area during the rebuilding of the Chop's defenses, June 1953. Note in the background the trenches on the ridge and the "saddleback" on Hill 200.
Courtesy of James R. Goudy

bulldozer operator's guide for the trip. Each carried a "handy talkie" radio, the hand-held radio. The night was particularly dark, the best time to do the maintenance work. No lights allowed. Lights would draw mortar, artillery, or sniper fire. The operator could barely see the big dozer's blade in front of him, never mind an acceptable distance beyond the blade. Dick White's job was to walk backward up the access road, just in front of the huge blade, and give simple commands to the operator as to direction of movement and other necessary adjustments to improve a heavily traveled road, used by heavy vehicles.

Mortar rounds fell periodically. The Chinese could hear the diesel engine but could not see the target and could not get the range: "Right. Left. Raise the blade. Lower the blade. Stop. Back blade." Under the circumstances, a stumble while walking backward, uphill, at night, in front of and close to a moving bulldozer with limited visibility was not a good idea, even with radio contact between guide and operator. Then when they reached the landing, Dick White had to "walk" the big dozer back down the return road.[11]

A light moment while working the 7th Division's road net. *Left to right:* two Korean Service Corps laborers and Corporals McCandless and Torrence (*in the culvert*) of the 13th Engineers.
Courtesy of James R. Goudy

Improvements for night operations were also needed, and M.Sgt. Jim Goudy, platoon sergeant, 2d Platoon, Able Company of the 13th Engineers, was given the task of improving the road to permit safer blacked-out dashes up to the evacuation landing and back on the access road, by APCs, jeeps, and other vehicles occasionally used for transport to the Chop. Goudy took two squads of soldiers with him. At night, if the weather was calm and guns were silent, sound carried a long distance. Soldiers on both sides of the line were excellent listeners, especially the "old hands," and the sounds of generator and vehicle engines, gasoline or diesel driven, were easy to hear. So were the sounds of sledgehammers.

When Jim Goudy and his men drove metal stakes with low level light reflectors on them into the ground at night, at 20 to 30 foot intervals, to enable vehicle drivers to follow the road at night, they took extra precautions to avoid the unwanted surprise of artillery, mortar, or sniper fire. They carefully wrapped each stake with burlap sufficient to mute the collision of sledgehammer heads and metal stakes, as they drove each one into the ground. There was a sense of urgency accompanying every stake driven.

There were no nearby trenches or bunkers in which to take cover should the enemy hear the sound of their presence and choose to fire at Jim Goudy and his two squads of 13th Engineers.[12]

The 13th maintained not only the Pork Chop access road but also the entire division road net and put three shifts on duty to keep roads open. The road net, nearly all dirt but potentially a muddy quagmire during the monsoon season, had to be maintained around the clock, in all kinds of weather, ready to sustain the weight of tanks and other heavily loaded vehicles. Passable division roads were essential to adequately defend the 7th's sector, because the division's companies and battalions had to remain cocked and ready to go—fluid—be able to move laterally from one regimental or battalion sector to another, rear to front and front to rear. When major battles were in progress, as occurred on Pork Chop in March and April, roads were heavily trafficked as units moved on the division transportation net frequently, shifting from bivouac, training, and reserve areas to assembly areas, lines of departure, counterattack or blocking positions immediately behind the MLR, onto outpost duty, or to man MLR positions in a different sector of the line. Rock was the material of choice to help keep roads passable.[13]

Motor pools frequently dispatched convoys of trucks to load infantry companies and move them from bivouacs several miles in the rear to forward assembly areas or checkpoints in other battalion or regimental sectors. Add to that traffic the flow of vehicles carrying wounded and dead off the outposts or MLR to clearing and collecting stations, aid stations, and hospitals, and the picture emerges of considerable transportation activity, day and night.

Weather was ever a factor in combat operations in Korea, and no less important along the stalemated front in the spring and early summer of 1953. Korean weather is a contrast of extremes. Summer heat reaches over 100 degrees Fahrenheit, with high relative humidity. Winter cold plunges at times to 40 degrees below zero. Precipitation patterns are typical of rice-producing regions in which long dry periods are followed by intense periods of rain and monsoon winds. Winter snowfall is not excessive, but the winds blowing out of the north create miserable periods of blowing snow and bitter cold. Weather perennially impacted the tempo of operations all along the line. Large-scale tactical operations are difficult at best, and nearly impossible during the monsoons, and the same was true during winter, as the Eighth Army learned early in the war. Summer heat and humidity particularly tested infantrymen to their limits of endurance, especially when moving in mountainous terrain with combat gear.

It is also noteworthy that the extremes of winter and summer monsoons also offered the best masks for tactical surprise, which the Chinese exploited frequently to offset to some degree the advantages in artillery and air power possessed by UN forces. Spring and fall obviously provided the best weather for ground operations.[14]

Rebuilding and the Never-Ending Stream of Replacements

Added to the rebuilding of trench and bunker networks so necessary to the successful defense of the Chop, any other outpost, and MLR positions was the constant turnover of personnel and the orientation training and retraining which inevitably accompanied the influx into Korea of twenty thousand to thirty thousand American soldiers each month. Of the approximately three hundred thousand Americans in Korea during the stalemated war, only fifty thousand, one of every six, manned the 155-mile defense line. The flow of replacements to combat and combat support units was particularly high, a hundred percent average turnover rate in infantry companies every four months.[15] Several factors combined to drive the high turnover rate.

The point system devised to equitably encourage soldiers to serve on the line also determined when they might be rotated off the line and returned home, as did the extraordinarily high casualty rates among infantry units. Thirty-six points was the magic number that theoretically earned soldiers a ticket home—or at least out of higher point zones, usually after nine months to a year, depending on how rapidly they accrued the necessary total. A soldier in battalion headquarters forward to the MLR or OPLR, received four points per month, the highest number of points per month he could receive. From battalions rear through regiments to division was the three-point zone, from division to corps was two points, and from corps to Eighth Army and farther to the rear, one point. Thus the time to accrue thirty-six points took longer if the soldier remained in the rear area.[16]

However equitable the system appeared, it also carried adverse effects into units on the line. The protracted peace talks and the point system kept

American soldiers ever aware of caution and risk avoidance. "I don't want to be the last man killed in the war," was a frequently verbalized thought. As men came closer to achieving thirty-six points, care, caution, and avoidance of increased risk—primarily duty on the MLR or outposts—were the watchwords, and a few would find constructive ways to avoid four-point areas on or near the line. In the extreme there were a number of self-inflicted gunshot wounds intended to affect evacuation from the four-point zone, or perhaps, if serious enough, a return trip stateside. Not a common occurrence, such drastic action to avoid service on the line or in the four-point zone, if found out, could earn the soldier a court-martial.[17]

In turn, commanders and senior noncommissioned officers were attentive to casualty rates, wounded returned to duty, total points accumulated by their men, and how many times they had been in the midst of heavy engagements or in deadly fire fights while on patrol. The results were experienced platoon leaders and company commanders occasionally held back or prematurely rotated from outpost or MLR duties toward the end of their assignments and replaced with inexperienced men. The effect was to deprive units of badly needed, combat-wise leaders just when they were needed the most—when the units might become embroiled in a fight.

Compounding the problem were the high casualty rates in infantry companies and their attached engineer squads during heavy engagements. The March and April battles on Pork Chop—indeed, any major battle throughout the war—offered stark testimony to the extraordinarily high percentage of casualties suffered during heavy, extended contact with the enemy.

King Company of the 31st Regiment in the April battle was one of many examples. Capt. Joe Clemons's company began their movement from the assembly area toward Pork Chop the early morning hours of 17 April with 135 men. By midnight 18 April, fourteen of their number remained, and seven were KATUSAs, the rest killed, wounded, or missing—and the missing either captured or dead.

Needed: Company-Grade Officers

To make matters worse, officers and noncommissioned officers repeatedly suffered disproportionately higher casualty rates, stripping away company leadership at crucial moments, and causing a perpetual shortage of experienced company grade officers—with accompanying accelerated turnover rates. Casualty rates analyzed at war's end clearly illustrated the price of leadership for the American officer and noncommissioned officer in the Korean War, and the rates were driven by battles similar to those experienced on Pork Chop in March and April.

A typical example of casualties taken by a line infantry company in Korea is Easy Company of the 17th Infantry Regiment, from 28 April 1952 to war's end. Broken down to show losses by rank, type of casualty, and enlistment status, data showed 67 percent of Easy's losses were suffered by privates, 28 percent by noncommissioned officers, and 5 percent by officers. However, when the analysis is based on the number of men in each rank grouping, the results reflect the heavy price paid by the company's leaders. As a group, privates suffered 34 percent of the casualties, noncommissioned officers 49 percent, and officers 86 percent. From another perspective, the analysis shows that for every 10 men in each rank grouping, 3.6 privates, 4.9 noncommissioned officers, and 8.6 officers became casualties. The data also show that draftees' and regulars' casualties were in the same ratio as they appeared on the company rosters. High casualty rates among company grade officers were typical, as Easy Company's experiences in April amply demonstrated—and would be again in July.[18]

The reasons for the high loss rates among officers and noncommissioned officers in line infantry companies were straightforward. Company commanders, platoon leaders, senior noncommissioned officers, platoon sergeants, and squad leaders were often out front leading counterattacks, making them early casualties of high volume enemy fire. Additionally, they were often targets identified by enemy soldiers with the specific intent of decimating the company's leadership and grinding an attack to a halt or breaking the will of leaderless defenders.

Leadership training and thoughtful commanders and platoon leaders who had succession plans in place should they be killed or incapacitated, and informed their men who would succeed them in an emergency, prepared their units well for such a contingency in battle. The designated successor would, when his commander or leader fell, normally pick up the leadership mantle without pause. The preparation did not always mean the line of succession would actually work in battle, that someone would always step forward to take command when unit leaders were cut down. But such preparation did increase the likelihood action would continue toward accomplishing the planned mission, in spite of hard hit leadership ranks. There were numerous instances when corporals or privates in line companies emerged fiery, inspiring leaders in the heat of wild hand-to-hand melees and high casualties among officers and noncommissioned officers.

Combined but Not Fully Integrated

There was one other irritant operating just beneath the surface in American combat units in the Korean War—integration. The infantry company's authorized strength was 195. In the 7th Division there were on average two KATUSA soldiers integrated in each of the four twelve-man squads of an infantry platoon. In each company, there were three rifle platoons and one weapons platoon, plus a headquarters element. On average there was one Hispanic and one black soldier in each squad. There were five officers authorized for each company, four platoon leaders, normally second lieutenants, a first lieutenant company executive officer, and the commander, a captain.

Attached to the 7th Division was a Colombian Battalion and an Ethiopian Battalion. The integration of KATUSAs and Hispanic and black Americans into the division and its line units, plus the attached Colombian and Ethiopian battalions, created language, ethnic, and cultural barriers that needed to be overcome daily. For the Koreans, and attached Colombian and Ethiopian units, interpreters and the exchange of liaison officers, and KATUSAs who were given English language training, helped solve many problems. The pressure cooker of common danger plus the motivator of common mission seemed to erase most of the remaining irritants and potential barriers to combat efficiency.

However, despite some modest progress, integration of America's black soldiers, and to some degree, Puerto Ricans, was slow. In *Battle at the 38th Parallel: Surviving the Peace Talks at Panmunjom,* author Joseph E. Gonsalves, former member of Easy Company, 17th Regiment, during the Korean War, explained:

When the conflict began in 1950, the U.S. military, as well as the rest of the country, had yet to come to grips with integration. In the Army, blacks tended to be assigned to combat support units such as port units, transportation truck companies, and quartermaster companies. There were also combat units, such as the 24th Infantry Regiment of the 25th Division, which were organized much in the same manner as black volunteer regiments in the Civil War, with black enlisted men commanded by white officers.

Integration of the Armed Services had been set in motion by Executive Order 9981, signed on 20 July 1948 by President Harry S. Truman. However, by 1950 only the Air Force had complied. The key that opened the Army to compliance was a cable to Washington in May 1951 by General Ridgway, containing a recommendation that the 24th Infantry Regiment be deactivated and all other black units in the Eighth Army be desegregated, because they had proven to be "ineffective in combat." The driving force behind Ridgway's recommendation was that in May 1951, thousands of qualified black replacements existed in Japan, while units in Korea were starving for manpower. Thus, pragmatism and the need for a more efficient organization finally won over a century of prejudice. By the end of 1951, all direct combat units in Korea had been integrated. However, even at the end of the war in 1953, ten percent of the blacks in Eighth Army were still serving in segregated combat service support units.

During the final year of the war, twelve percent of Easy Company's strength consisted of black personnel. They served in all enlisted ranks except master sergeant and all assignments except first sergeant. Of the thirty-three company officers identified, Lieutenant Cary, who served as executive officer from April 1952 until October 1952, was the only black. Prejudice existed in the company, as it certainly did in the Army; however, any impact it had on our combat efficiency was not apparent. The prejudice was transparent to most of us, but where it existed, it was dealt with between those involved, not breaking out into the open.

A blatant example of prejudice existed on company rosters submitted to regiment every month. These rosters listed all personnel, including officers, assigned to the company by name, rank, serial number, and duty status. The rosters also included a breakout list of "Class II Personnel."

In one hundred years the Army had come to at least acknowledge the existence of blacks in its combat units, but felt compelled to group them under the heading of "Class II Personnel." It did not feel compelled to list any of the other ten racial groups in separate listings. The number of blacks on its roster was typical for the company throughout the period [28 April 1952 to 1 August 1953]. The range of assignments, rank, and ratio of duty status between combat and combat support assignments was a typical mix for the company, except for the absence of senior NCO personnel. Three of the PFCs on the list were promoted to corporal during their tour and one of the corporals eventually made SFC [sergeant first class]. It should be noted that all three of the combat support personnel initially served time as riflemen. Blacks in the company were certainly exposed to the same hazards and took the same risks as nonblacks. Nine of the seventy-one black personnel who served were killed.

Gonsalves goes on to say that two of Easy Company's black soldiers, Cpl. Raymond A. Watson and Pfc. Moses Jones, Jr., won Silver Stars for valor, Watson for actions during the April battle for Pork Chop and Jones in the July battle, when a Puerto Rican, Pvt. Marcellino Rosa-Cordero, also won a Silver Star:

> Although technically not a segregated unit, the all–Puerto Rican 65th Infantry Regiment was considered by many in the Eighth Army to be in the same category as an all-black unit, and consequently, suffered under the same prejudices. It was, however, not covered by Ridgway's desegregation recommendation and continued as an all–Puerto Rican unit until January 1953 when the bulk of its personnel were transferred to other Eighth Army units and integrated. The 65th was then reconstituted as a fully integrated unit. As a result of Ridgway's decision, Easy Company was on the receiving end of experienced personnel of the 65th. The forty-three Puerto Rican personnel in the company during the final year of the conflict served well, suffering twelve casualties including four who died. Two were awarded the Bronze Star and one the Silver Star for heroism. Private Marcellino Rosa-Cordero's courage in the face of the enemy, as noted in his citation for the Silver Star, reflected the true capability of Puerto Rican personnel.[19]

Near the end of May, Lt. Robert M. Euwer, reassigned from forward observer in the 57th Field Artillery Battalion to replace a 15th Self-Propelled Anti-Aircraft Artillery platoon leader, received a lifelong memory of the positive effects of integration and the disquieting pain of segregation and discrimination. The platoon was dug in, reveted, on the line near outpost Westview. Its leader, First Lieutenant Wright, was completing his assignment in Korea and was scheduled in a few days to return home to South Carolina, at which time Euwer would assume Wright's duties. Wright took

Euwer to all the platoon's gun positions on the line, showed him the position of the infantry unit the platoon supported, and pointed out the target areas in front. They went to the infantry battalion command post to meet with liaison officers from artillery, mortar, and tank units. Bob, in addition to being a platoon leader, would be the liaison representing the self-propelled AAA.

During their first meeting Wright told Euwer he was black, a surprising revelation because, in Bob Euwer's words, "He was lightly colored and could have passed for white." During the time Wright spent with Euwer before he left for South Carolina, he expressed his anxiety about returning home because of the hatred and discrimination that existed there. It upset Wright to talk about it. He would sip from a bottle of Vodka that he pulled from his locker.

Later, when Wright returned home, he exchanged several letters with his replacement. Conditions at home were as bad as he feared they would be, and he yearned to be back in the 15th AAA "where I could be treated as an equal." He told Bob the fact that he "could pass himself off as white" only compounded his anguish. It was the first time Bob Euwer realized how bad racial discrimination was in America, and drove home the point that service in combat was a great leveler which would sweep away barriers threatening mutual trust among soldiers, and survival in war.[20]

Capt. Juan Raigoza, 48th Field Artillery Battalion liaison officer to the Ethiopian 2d Battalion, would also confront the ugly effects of discrimination when, on invitation of an allied officer he befriended, he accompanied a member of the Kagnew Battalion on rest and recuperation (R&R) in Tokyo. Juan was more fortunate than Bob Euwer. He would be able to strike a different kind of blow for freedom.

Task for a Bulldozer

In spite of all the detractors and obstacles the 13th Engineers faced, rebuilding of the Chop proceeded. Each day for two and a half months beginning immediately after the April battle, twenty to twenty-five men, mostly Americans and KATUSAs from Able Company, plus small numbers of troops from division reserve units and twenty-five to thirty KSC laborers, made the trip back and forth to the hill. Working only during daylight hours because night construction operations were not possible, each member of the 13th's work crews spent approximately twenty-five days a month on the hill, pushing hard to complete the rebuilding.[21]

Initially, infantry company commanders rotating on and off Pork Chop for outpost duty were assigned responsibility for the overall improvement project, with the engineers providing the technical support, the bulk of the labor force, materials, equipment, and know-how. But this arrangement proved unsatisfactory. To remedy the problem of a frequently rotated project manager, an infantry field grade officer, the 1st of the 17th's executive officer, Maj. Billy E. Fritts, was given responsibility to oversee the Pork Chop project and ensure its operational utility and effectiveness.[22]

In cooperation with the infantry and consistent with the command critique and guidance given by General Trudeau and Colonel Icke, the 13th, working with the 17th Regiment, developed a new bunker and trench plan for Pork Chop's defenses. As work progressed in May and June, Capt. Jim Brettell, with Major Fritts, walked Pork Chop's defense network, where Fritts selected and designated locations for fighting bunkers including positions for automatic weapons, command post and supply bunkers, observation and listening posts, and sleeping bunkers, all to be interconnected with reinforced, covered trenches. In some cases bunker locations selected were part of the pre-April defenses, and were expanded in size and strengthened with heavy structural members.[23]

Clearing of debris from the old trench network, and digging, began immediately after the April battle ended. Meanwhile the 13th Engineers' S-4, Capt. Joe Bratton, the battalion supply officer, scoured South Korea to obtain materials while the engineers developed simple, standard-design plans for each type of bunker and fighting position. The plans included standard sizes for bunker and trench excavation and standard, precut structural and reinforcement members for walls and overhead cover, with the necessary materials and tools for easily assembled "kits." In the vicinity of the battalion CP the 13th set up a sawmill-like, bunker kit production area for cutting, assembling, and packaging the kits, using steel straps to keep the kits bundled. The kits were then hauled by the engineers' Dog Company to the checkpoint behind Hill 200, thence via APC to the Chop, ready to be assembled on site.[24]

The Covered Trenches

A key factor in the entire project was expanding and strengthening overhead cover throughout the defense system. The rebuilding plan included widening and deepening trenches, and increasing and greatly strengthening overhead cover in selected areas of the trench network, as well as in bunkers. The overhead cover for trenches was intended to provide defenders better cover from artillery and mortar fire, as well as quick access to cover should "on position" VT from friendly artillery be necessary.

As spring inched toward summer and the inevitable oppressive humidity and heat bore in, the work became harder. Americans and KATUSAs necessarily wore body armor—flak vests as they had been called by aircrews during World War II—to protect against the daily harassing artillery and mortar rounds falling on the Chop. While body armor was important,

Two soldiers from 2d Platoon, Able Company, 13th Engineers, constructing trench cover and bunkers on Pork Chop, late June 1953.
Courtesy of James R. Goudy

and lessened casualties from incoming, the vests added weight and more heat to the daily grind. The work was heavy, tough, dehydrating, and fatiguing. Water, always a precious commodity on the hill, became more so.

The work began with clearing debris and digging out caved-in trenches, then the collapsed bunkers which were to be enlarged, strengthened, and reused. Digging was not only hard, but it brought sometimes frightening surprises, and all too often sad reminders. The sad reminders were the bodies of GIs and enemy soldiers found, still buried beneath the dirt and debris of the hill's battered defenses. The GIs remains were placed in body bags and taken to the evacuation landing for removal by graves registration. Enemy soldiers' remains were piled up for later disposal, usually in mass graves.[25] The men of Pork Chop Hill were working and fighting on hallowed ground.

Heart rates and cold sweat would definitely increase when an unexploded artillery or mortar round was struck during digging. Another skill for which selected engineers were trained was explosive ordnance disposal. Whenever possible, they normally solved the problem of a dud by blowing the round in place. They first pasted a blob of plastic explosives to the dud, then inserted a fuse and blasting cap—and lit the fuse. Hopefully, that would do the job, but sometimes the old World War II caps and fuses failed to fire.

Lt. Richard White's platoon sergeant, M.Sgt. Houston Long, planted explosives on an unexploded 155-mm artillery round uncovered halfway up the main trench from the evacuation landing. It failed to explode. The fuses were cut to burn in one minute. When it failed the engineer waited five minutes, then went back and snatched the cap and fuse, made up another, and tried again. Long replaced the fuse and it failed again. He replaced that fuse, a third failure. By this time Long had broken out in a cold sweat. White: "Long, let me go up this time." He replied, "Hell no. I started it and damn it I'll finish it." He had one more failure and finally blew it on the fifth try.[26]

One of the first trenches cleared was the main trench which opened onto the evacuation landing at the hill's rear, and went forward, gradually sloping upward, to the northwest from the landing, underneath the crest of the hill. Structurally reinforced, the covered trenches, which gave the appearance of tunnels, branched out and progressed into areas where the crews expanded the digging to excavate from inside the hill and build heavily reinforced fighting bunkers. However careful the crews were it was impossible to hide work in progress from the enemy. From their elevated vantage points on the surrounding hills, CCF observers could see nearly every shovel of dirt tossed and every structural member being installed in Pork Chop's defense network.

The last step in building fighting bunkers was to carefully construct fan-shaped firing apertures in each, with the narrow end of the fan at the inside wall of the bunker. The fan-shaped apertures provided gunners traverse and elevation for fields of fire planned for each bunker. Construction crews' plans included mounted and anchored wire mesh in each aperture to keep the enemy from throwing grenades through the aperture into the bunker. Nevertheless, apertures did not afford defenders sufficient, wide-angle views of the terrain in front of their bunkers. Enemy soldiers could approach the apertures from angles and areas outside the fields of view, with explosive charges, grenades, or automatic weapons, which often proved fatal to the men inside.

The bunkers were thus built as much as possible from the inside out, to avoid disturbing the hill's natural contours, hold enemy observation to a minimum, and reduce the probability of being well-plotted, inviting targets for enemy artillery. The entire network formed a closed, generally elliptical perimeter, somewhat broader on the west shoulder of the hill, across and underneath the ridge of Brinson Finger. The layout improved strength on the left flank, oriented to defend against enemy avenues of approach from Old Baldy, Chink Baldy, and Pokkae, while improving defensive capabilities facing into other avenues of approach from the north and northeast. The closed perimeter also provided all-around defense with alternate firing positions in the hill's rear.

From the outset of rebuilding, trenches and bunkers also received serious attention from the 13th Engineers. In the succeeding two and a half months, construction crews widened and deepened usable existing trenches and, where possible, widened them sufficiently to allow stretcher bearers to pass and defenders to walk erect throughout the network. They dug additional trenches where the plan called for them.

Rather than sharply zig-zag trenches to reduce enemy enfilading fire, the engineers achieved the same effect by digging new trenching with curved bends. Trench roof construction included heavy vertically and horizontally laid structural members, with two layers of sandbags on top of water draining, fire resistant material, plus approximately two feet of earth on top of

Corporal Girgenti and a KATUSA, members of Able Company, 13th Engineers,
pause briefly while rebuilding trenches and bunkers on Pork Chop, June 1953.
Behind and above them is a net over the work area to limit enemy observation. Note
both are wearing body armor, and the Korean is wearing the 7th Division shoulder
patch.
Courtesy of James R. Goudy

the sandbags. Strongly roofed trenches were intended to reduce casualties
from daily shelling, avoid collapse due to heavy barrages, and limit the ability of enemy soldiers to penetrate the trench network.[27] The main trench,
which went past the entrances to the outpost CP and supply bunkers, and
opened onto the evacuation landing, had twenty-two layers of sandbags
for overhead covering at the entrance.[28]

While enemy observers on the higher hills could not be denied a view of
all the work in progress on the outpost and the remainder of UN defenses
in the 7th Division's sector, there was much the Chinese could not see. The
extent and quality of the work was not visible. The 7th Division was building a system of bunkers that would be increasingly difficult to defeat as
progress toward 100 percent complete drew nearer.

But among the Chinese soldiers of the 23d Army and its 67th Division
were many seasoned veterans, and they found creative ways to carefully
reconnoiter, learn, and map Pork Chop's defenses—its strong points and
vulnerabilities. There were indeed vulnerabilities in Pork Chop's defenses,

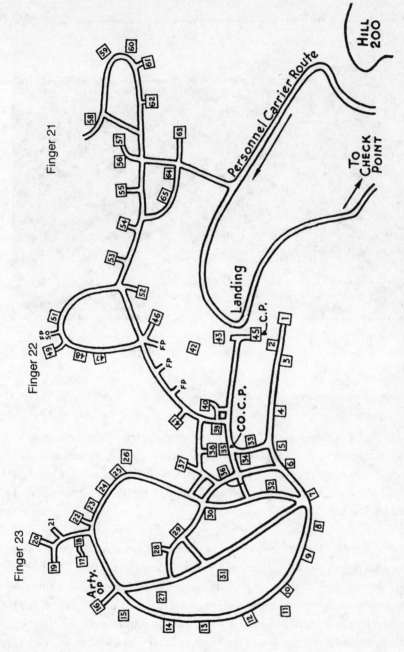

The Pork Chop bunker and trench system as rebuilt following the battle of 16–18 April 1953.

The south face of Pork Chop, as seen from an MLR position on Hill 200. Note the not-yet-covered main trench leading toward the outpost's crest (*left*), the trench leading off the access road (*right of center*) toward the trenches on the ridge, and one large bunker and a smaller one adjacent to the access road (*left of center*). *Courtesy of Jack Roberts and John W. Phillips*

not the least of which was a network not yet complete when the most violent assault came in July. And ironically, the strengths built into the outpost's defenses by the Americans and their South Korean allies in the end would work against the units given the mission of counterattacking and retaking the hill.

WHILE LITTLE SWITCH was ongoing the final ten days of April, and strengthening of the OPLR and MLR was in progress on Pork Chop Hill and the remainder of the 7th Division's sector, senior delegates at Panmunjom resumed talks after a six-month hiatus. They turned their attention to the final major agenda item and obstacle to a cease-fire, the exchange of the main body of POWs, plus other, far less significant unresolved issues. Unfortunately, they soon mired in endless debate over which "neutral" nation or nations would supervise the exchange of the main body of POWs, and other petty issues. The American government's hopes for an armistice seemed to once again be slipping away when the discussions degenerated into bitter name calling and the delegates recessed to explore alternatives.[29]

The CCF and NKPA had already begun planning and preparing for a powerful series of attacks to push forward to the thirty-eighth parallel. The bloodiest two months of the entire war would soon begin.

Replacements in Love

In New Milford, New Jersey, and Indianapolis, Indiana, the last ten days in April, two lieutenants graduated from West Point with the class of 1952 were preparing to leave their wives, having received orders which would eventually take them to Able and Baker Companies respectively—1st Battalion, 17th Regiment. Lt. Richard T. Shea, Jr., hometown Portsmouth, Virginia, and Lt. Richard G. Inman from Vincennes, Indiana, were classmates at West Point, and in the spring of 1952, they were on the Army track team together.

Dick Inman, the oldest son of the Vincennes High School football coach, lettered on the Army football team in the fall of 1951 and loved his family, hometown, and state; while attending the infantry course at Fort Benning, he requested his next assignment be Camp Atterbury, in the Hoosier state just outside Indianapolis. Above all sports he loved football, though he was on a championship high hurdle relay team at the Penn Relays in Philadelphia the spring of 1952. Dick also loved to write. He particularly loved to write poetry, and he wrote poetry exceptionally well.

While at Camp Atterbury, he visited home and family as much as possible, and on a blind date he met and fell in love with an elementary school teacher, Barbara Kipp, from Fort Madison, Iowa. In addition to her elementary school teaching, she was teaching reading and writing night courses to young soldiers at the Army post.

A whirlwind romance ensued, and they began to consider marriage. After Dick received orders for Korea, indecision about marriage troubled him, but they both decided to follow their hearts and married on 28 February 1953. Seven weeks later Dick left by commercial airplane for Seattle, Washington. There he boarded a troop ship for Japan and Korea, the route taken by the great majority of soldiers destined for Korea.

Dick Shea, who at age seventeen enlisted in the Army prior to the end of World War II, took technical training and education at Virginia Tech for a year and served in the occupation forces in Germany. He eventually earned promotion to sergeant in the communications field, and began running in GI Olympics competition. He obtained a regular Army appointment to West Point, and went to the United States Military Academy prep school at Stewart Field in Newburgh, New York, for one year. In the spring of 1948 he met Joyce Elaine Riemann at a Red Cross dance at Stewart Field. They too fell deeply in love. He entered West Point in the summer of 1948, and two years later they decided to marry immediately after he graduated from West Point.

While at West Point he became a star record-setting track and cross-country athlete, and his track and field teammates, who included Dick Inman, elected him team captain. For a period of time he was considered a possible Olympic athlete, but he and Joyce together decided he would concentrate on their lives and his chosen career in the Army. They were married right after graduation, and he, too, went to Fort Benning's infantry course, then to airborne (jump) training before receiving orders for Korea.

When Dick Shea boarded a commercial airliner at LaGuardia Airport in New York City in late April, Joyce was expecting a baby. Their parting that day was not easy. They felt the same emotional tugs Dick Inman and Barbara felt in Indianapolis, the same feelings soldiers and their wives and families have always felt when confronted with war and its uncertainties.[30]

6

CALM BEFORE THE STORM

BOTH THE 67TH DIVISION OF THE 23D CCF ARMY AND THE 7TH INFANTRY Division needed to refill with replacements, refit, retrain, and rebuild after the furious Chinese assault on Pork Chop in April. In May, the Chinese pulled their battered 201st Regiment off the line, into reserve, replacing it with the fresh and apparently better disciplined 200th Regiment. The exact location of the 201st's new reserve position had not been determined by the end of May. The 201st had been on the line for five months and had suffered heavy casualties, especially during the March and April battles.

In the Hasakkol-Pokkae area the 2d Battalion of the 200th Regiment relieved the 2d of the 201st. The 1st Battalion, 200th Regiment relieved the 3d Battalion of the 201st on T-Bone. The 200th held their 3d Battalion in reserve. In the area to the front of the 7th Division's left, elements of the CCF 1st Army replaced the 421st Regiment, 141st Division, 47th CCF Army. As the month progressed, the CCF gradually replaced on-line units of the 47th Army with units from the 1st Army.

The 7th's line infantry and intelligence units noted evidence of the 200th CCF Regiment's discipline in their operational security. Screening patrols found bodies of Chinese soldiers devoid of any documents or unit identification, and the 200th's camouflage and track discipline were better than any time during the previous five months the 7th Division had been in contact with the CCF. The absence of documents on the bodies also suggested Chinese soldiers were either being searched before they departed their defenses on patrol or raids, or were voluntarily leaving any personal identification or documents behind. Also noted were the increasing number of times the enemy was able to approach UN positions at night, undetected, with up to company size units. While success at being undetected might have been indicative of insufficient alertness on the part of the 7th Division, it also indicated improved discipline and tactical training by the 200th Regiment.[1]

In parallel with a shift in enemy patrols and raids toward the 7th Division's eastern—right—sector during the month of May, the Chinese increased psychological warfare activity, particularly loudspeaker broadcasts using ongoing peace talks as a theme. To augment their efforts, for the first time since the 7th came on line in the Chorwon Valley in December 1952, the Chinese fired propaganda leaflet shells all across the division front.[2]

The UN's and 7th Division's dominating control of the air above the battlefield permitted both aerial observation of CCF activities by the 7th's Observation Section and the ability to supplement other sources of intelligence. During May the section flew 132 combat missions, totaling 169 hours. The Signal Company flew 32 missions. Nineteen supplemented the Air Force's 18 photo missions to detect enemy activity and installations, and another 13 to detect camouflage, analyze fortifications, and estimate construction on the friendly MLR. The Observation Section countered the CCF psychological warfare by dropping approximately 362,000 propaganda leaflets in May.

Airborne excursions above the line of contact between the two armies were invariably met with a hail of ground fire. Pilots estimated approximately twenty thousand rounds of mixed antiaircraft, automatic weapons, and small-arms fire were thrown at the observation aircraft and helicopters during May's flight operations.[3]

General Trudeau's April assessment of the need for improvement in what he termed "organization of the ground" brought early May reorganization and realignment of defense responsibilities on the 7th Division's front. On 2 May the division front became a three-regiment front, instead of two with one regiment in reserve. With three regiments on line, each regiment kept two infantry battalions on line, with one in regimental reserve. The shifting and moving of forces began prior to the realignment of responsibilities which took effect on 3 May. The realignment of sector responsibilities permitted commanders to assign troop labor from their reserve units and increase emphasis in constructing and strengthening defenses within their sectors.[4]

Prior to the reorganization, the 17th Regiment Buffaloes with two battalions from the 31st Infantry, occupied the left regimental sector of the 7th Division front. On 3 May the 17th Regiment assumed responsibility for the center regimental sector, with a two-battalion front. The 1st Battalion of the 17th took the right battalion sector, and on 15 May the 3d of the 17th moved into the left battalion sector. On 19 May the Colombian Battalion, now attached to the 17th, replaced 1st Battalion units on their MLR positions, while 1st Battalion retained responsibility for defense of outposts in the Arsenal-Erie complex. The 31st Regiment Bearcats defended the division's left sector and the 32d Infantry Regiment the right, with the Ethiopian Battalion attached to the 32d.[5]

Unit rotations onto and off outpost positions normally occurred every seven days, and continued throughout the division's sector realignments. Periodic relief and rotation onto and off MLR positions continued, by battalion within regiments rather than a regiment at a time.

While the reorganization progressed, the daily routine of combat and reconnaissance patrols continued. Each regiment normally sent one combat patrol a night to intercept, ambush, and capture groups of enemy attempting to move toward friendly positions. In daylight hours two reconnaissance patrols from each regiment moved forward of MLR or OPLR positions to observe enemy activities, and gather additional intelligence information on strength and dispositions.[6]

Another Try for the Chop

Action began early in May for the 17th Infantry. An estimated enemy company attacked a squad-sized outpost Snook at 11 P.M. on 4 May. Outguards detected the enemy incursion early, warned Snook's defenders, and they were able to fight off the larger enemy force inflicting heavy casualties. The fire fight continued until 12:45 A.M. on 5 May when the enemy withdrew. Though the small outpost held in the sharp one-hour fire fight, and the enemy withdrew, ending the action, its defenders suffered heavy casualties, reporting three killed and eighteen estimated wounded.

On 8 May at 2:40 A.M., five days after the 7th Infantry Division's reorganization began, the Chinese struck Pork Chop again, this time less forcefully than in March or April. Easy Company, 2d of the 17th was on outpost duty, the fourth company to take its normal rotation onto the Chop after the April fight. Easy Company, led by its commander, Lt. Gorman Smith, had broken the back of the 201st CCF Regiment's April assault with its bold move around the east flank of the outpost and up the northeast slopes to surprise the Chinese. Easy was a proud unit with an excellent reputation, and was not prone to overstating or understating the facts presented them.

For reasons to this day unclear—perhaps due to the reorganization in progress, breakdowns or misunderstandings in communication, or failure to make entries in the battalion or division operations journals—the May assault on Pork Chop appears to have been underreported. One estimate of the attacking force was more than "battalion-size," an estimate found in platoon leader Lt. Bob Hope's personal account. The second estimate was an enemy company, found in the 17th Regiment's command report for May. Strangely, the 7th Division command report for May 1953 made no mention of an assault on Pork Chop by an enemy unit of any size, while the 17th Regiment report states friendly forces suffered one killed and fourteen wounded in the company-sized attack. An article written for the *Army Combat Forces Journal* in 1955 by Col. William R. Kintner, former commander of the 3d Battalion of the 17th, described the May assault by the Chinese as a "reconnaissance in force" in which the Chinese hit all the outguard positions in front of Pork Chop.

Lieutenant Hope, who arrived in Easy Company after the April battle, described the attack:

> During the attempt my platoon was dug in on the extreme right of the hill, when word came back from our outguards that the Chinese were massing in attack position on Old Baldy. It was my first time on Pork Chop and my first experience with a major Chinese attack. I was scared to death. We immediately recalled our outguards, requested illumination,

and called for flash fire all around the perimeter. The artillery not only preregistered their fire, but were on standby to fire immediately when a flash fire request was called into the fire control center. We did not have to wait long. It was heavy and fell directly on the massed Chinese troops. In the artificial light, you could see the gaps being blown in the Chinese ranks as the fire rained down. The attack never got going. As a result of problems learned during previous attacks, the flash fire impact areas had been zeroed in much closer to our positions than previously. As a result, most of the casualties that we suffered were most likely due to friendly fire. It was estimated that the Chinese lost 1,400 men, all due to the flash fire. They never got close enough to our positions.[7]

The close-in final protective artillery fire—flash fire—provided the men of Easy Company in the early morning hours of 8 May indicated important lessons from the April battle had been well learned. In April outguards from Easy Company, 31st Infantry, were rudely surprised by the abrupt, swift movement and attack by two companies from the CCF 201st Regiment. Before the outguards could warn the company commander the enemy was upon them and communications were severed. This time, alert outguards from Easy of the 17th observed and reported enemy movement and attack preparations early. The alert early reporting bought time to bring the company to the ready, inform battalion, call in the outguards, illuminate the area to Pork Chop's front, bring final protective fires in close, and decimate the assaulting force.

In July, the enemy would be much wiser, and use a different set of weapons to breach the Chop's much improved, stronger defenses.

Discovery of the Rat's Nest

Following the repulsed enemy assault in the early morning hours of 8 May, Easy Company dispatched a patrol under cover of smoke to screen the area for information that might be found on the bodies of Chinese soldiers, for possible wounded who could be taken prisoner, and to check for the presence of other enemy units in the area. The patrol unexpectedly came upon an assault position, a complex of interconnected caves and tunnels large enough to hide an entire company. The find was not comforting.

The complex was approximately five hundred yards directly north of Pork Chop's crest on both sides of the steeply sloped Finger 23, which ran north, gradually descending from the Chop's crest. The openings to the complex of caves were on both slopes of the finger, facing west, east, and some north. Thus the entrances could not be easily detected from the ground or air because of their orientations with respect to the MLR, Pork Chop's defense network, and the normal flight tracks of observation and reconnaissance aircraft. Soon dubbed the "Rat's Nest" by intelligence, operations, and men on the line, the area was an obvious, additional jump-off point for future assaults on Pork Chop. The discovery triggered planning and actions intended to make the position unusable by the Chinese. The location and geographical orientation of the complex's entrances made the Rat's Nest the subject of growing attention and frustration over the next several weeks as air strikes and artillery failed to destroy or damage the complex.[8]

WHEN THE negotiations at Panmunjom resumed in plenary session in late April, the U.S. government's hopes for an armistice revived. The representatives of the two sides immediately focused on the exchange of the main body of POWs and other far less important issues. But within days the discussions mired in endless arguing and finally bitter name calling about the lesser issues as well as which "neutral" nation (or nations) would supervise the exchange of prisoners. When the discussions degenerated into name calling, the delegates recessed to explore alternatives and the U.S. government's hopes for an armistice seemed to be slipping away once more.

Gen. Mark Clark, still convinced military pressure was necessary to force the Communists into an armistice, proposed another massive Far Eastern Air Force bombing campaign against the North Korean civilian population. Gen. O. P. Weyland, Clark's air chief, pointed out there were no cities or towns left anywhere in North Korea and instead proposed FEAF wipe out the North Korean rice crop, predicted to be 283,000 tons, and starve the Communists into submission. The campaign began on 13 May and continued two weeks. The target was a complex of earthen irrigation dams in the vicinity of Toksan and Chasan, about twenty miles north of Pyongyang.

Large formations of F-84 fighter-bombers attacked the dams day after day, with some success. While the damage to the rice crop or the degree of starvation inflicted upon the North Koreans could not be precisely assessed, bomb damage assessment photos showed sufficient flooding of the paddies and roads for Weyland to conclude the campaign's success was "perhaps the most spectacular of the war." However, closer examination of aerial reconnaissance photos and other intelligence revealed the enemy reacted rapidly by repairing their road and rail nets within seven days, to keep ample supplies moving to their armies.

As the assault on the earthen dams wound down on 25 May, the Chinese launched a powerful offensive all along the line, primarily against the ROKs, while attacks in the 7th Division sector were somewhat more restrained. Whether the enemy was restrained or active in taking the initiative, the 7th's vigorous, never ending patrol schedule had its detractors and critics.[9]

While the daily, twenty-four-hour routine of scheduled combat and reconnaissance patrols appeared to cost little and the count seemed rather boring and mundane, typical daily and monthly totals of patrols were considerable. With each of six battalions on line sending 3 patrols a day, thirty days a month, the division dispatched 540 patrols a month. At the end of the month, the total number of casualties accumulated as a result of 540 "active defense" patrols was always painful. And the casualties suffered in an active schedule of patrols did not count the killed and wounded which came from daily interdiction and harassing artillery fire by the Chinese. All too frequently random, unexpected artillery single shots or battery salvos would strike an outpost or MLR position catching unsuspecting GIs at the wrong place at the wrong time, with tragic consequences. When probing attacks on outposts occurred, the Chinese sometimes overran outguards, as was the case in their April assault on Pork Chop.

In May, the 7th Division counted forty contacts with the enemy, twenty-three patrol contacts, the remainder either intercepts of the enemy by outguards or enemy-initiated probes of outpost positions. The contacts were spread across the division's front, but with the exceptions of Pork Chop and Arsenal, most were in front of outposts Yoke and Snook.

On 14 May a Charlie Company ambush patrol from the 17th Regiment lay out front of the northwest finger of outpost Arsenal. Composed of a ten-man assault element and a twelve-man support element, the patrol engaged in two brief, sharp fire fights with two groups of enemy. The first engagement lasted twenty minutes. The second began shortly thereafter and ended at 2:35 A.M., when the Chinese withdrew. Charlie suffered one KIA and eleven WIA, and a screening patrol counted five KIA, with another ten estimated WIA.

On 15 May, a reinforced squad from Able of the 17th manned outpost Snook located about a thousand yards forward of the MLR. During the hours of darkness two outguard groups of three men each moved into position out front of Snook. Later that evening an estimated enemy company attacked the outpost, sending one force to block the main reinforcement route from the MLR to Snook, and the other as an assault element. Moments prior to the assault, to the north and west of the outpost approximately one hundred yards, the two outguard groups engaged the approaching enemy with small arms and automatic weapons. The enemy's divided forces then attacked Snook from two directions at 11:04 P.M. using automatic weapons and grenades, and during the assault overran and killed one of the outguards. Snook's Able Company defenders used small arms and grenades to fend off attempts to seize the outpost.

At 11:20, the enemy began extremely heavy shelling on outposts Arsenal and Erie and MLR positions in the 1st Battalion sector. Artillery and mortar fire began falling on Snook at 11:24, and at nine minutes past midnight on 16 May, the commander on Snook requested reinforcements. In response to the request, twenty-five men departed the MLR at twenty-one minutes after midnight to reinforce the outpost, but by fourteen minutes after midnight all small-arms fire ceased on Snook. The enemy was withdrawing. At that time, casualty evacuation began, as did screening of the battle area. By 12:45 A.M. all firing ceased and outguards returned to reoccupy their original positions.[10]

Ethiopia's Unknown Battalion

The Ethiopian Army's feisty pre–World War II performance against Fascist Benito Mussolini's supposedly far superior, invading Italian Army established a high standard and an excellent reputation for the African nation's soldiers. Thus, their performance and reputation were well known and accepted as fact among the West's professional soldiers long before the Korean War. The Ethiopians were eventually overwhelmed by Il Duce's armed forces in 1936, but not before the Italians were severely bloodied and embarrassed. Trained by the British Army, they acquitted themselves well. And when Emperor Haile Selassie sent his Imperial Guard to fight in Korea, his soldiers did not disappoint.

S. L. A. Marshall's classic work, *Pork Chop Hill, The American Fighting Man in Action, Korea, Spring 1953,* is the story of the April battle for the outpost. However, in a chapter titled "The Incredible Patrol," Marshall tells of the 19–20 May CCF assault on outpost Yoke. At the time, Yoke and another smaller outpost, Uncle, and the MLR to the rear of Yoke were defended by the Ethiopian 3d Battalion of the Imperial Guard, Emperor Haile Selassie's defenders of the realm. Marshall's account, resulting from interviews with patrol members before and after the engagement on Yoke, introduced the "Incredible Patrol," in part, with these words:

Sometimes the bravest meet death with their deeds known only to heaven.

If another reason is needed for now unfolding the tale, there is this, that of all troops which fought in Korea, the Ethiopians stood highest in the quality of their officer-man relationships, the evenness of their performance under fire and the mastery of techniques by which they achieved near perfect unity of action in adapting themselves to new weapons during training and in using them to kill efficiently in battle.

They could not read maps but they never missed a trail.

Out of dark Africa came these men, thin, keen eyed, agile of mind, and 95 percent illiterate. They could take over U.S. Signal Corps equipment and in combat make it work twice as well as the best-trained U.S. troops. When they engaged [the enemy], higher headquarters invariably knew exactly what they were doing. The information they fed back by wire and radio was far greater in volume and much more accurate than anything coming from American actions.

Their capacities excelled also in one diversionary aspect of the soldierly arts. There are no better whisky drinkers under the sun. They take it neat, a full tumbler at a time, without pause or a chaser, and seem abashed that Americans can't follow suit. This unexampled skill might properly become a proper object for research by a top-level military mission.

Their one lack was good press. The Turks, the ROKs, the Commonwealth Division and others in the medley got due notice. But the Ethiopians stood guard along their assigned ridges in silence unbroken by the questions of itinerant correspondents. They were eager to welcome strangers and tell how they did it. But no one ever asked.

If to our side, at the end as in the beginning, they were the Unknown Battalion, to the Communists they were still a greater mystery. When the final shot was fired, one significant mark stood to their eternal credit. Of all the national groups fighting in Korea, the Ethiopians alone could boast that they had never lost a prisoner or left a dead comrade on the battlefield. Every wounded man, every shattered body, had been returned to the friendly fold.

That uniquely clean sheet was not an accident of numbers only. Knowing how to gamble with death, they treated it lightly as a flower. On night patrol as he crossed the valley and prowled toward the enemy works, the Ethiopian soldier knew that his chance of death was compounded. It was standing procedure in the battalion that if a patrol became surrounded beyond possibility of extraction, the supporting artillery would be ordered to destroy the patrol to the last man. That terrible alternative was never realized. Many times enveloped, the Ethiopian patrols always succeeded in breaking the fire ring and returning to home base. If there would be dead or wounded to be carried, the officer or NCO leader was the first to volunteer. When fog threatened to diffuse a patrol, the Ethiopians moved hand in hand, like children. Even so, though they deny it, these Africans are cat-eyed men with an especial affinity for moving and fighting in the dark. In most of the races of man, superstition unfolds with the night, tricking the imagination and stifling courage. It is not so with the Ethiopians. The dark holds no extra terror. It is their element.

Of this in part came the marked superiority in night operations which transfixed the Chinese. It hexed them as if they were fighting the superhuman. The Ethiopian left no tracks, seemingly shed no blood and spoke always in an unknown tongue. Lack of bodily proof that he was mortal made him seem phantom like and forbiddingly unreal.

That may explain why, toward the close, everything done by the Ethiopians seemed so unbelievably easy, even under full sunlight. We watched them from Observation Point 29 through glasses on a fair afternoon in mid-May, 1953, in as mad an exploit as was ever dared by man. Under full observation from enemy country, eight Ethiopians walked 800 yards across no-man's land and up the slope of T-Bone Hill right into the enemy trenches. When next we looked, the eight had become ten. The patrol was dragging back two Chinese prisoners, having snatched them from the embrace of the Communist battalion. It was only then that the American artillery came awake and threw smoke behind them. They got back to our lines unscratched. So far as I know, this feat is unmatched in war. How account for it? Either the hex was working or the Communists thought the patrol was coming to surrender.

This brazen piece of effrontery took place only three days after the fight of the Incredible Patrol. These were actions by men who had never previously been under fire.[11]

In Korea, from the beginning, the Ethiopians proved themselves tough, disciplined fighters, who gave no quarter in a scrap. The emperor personally conveyed this admonition to his soldiers when they departed for the Republic of Korea: "I want every man to return, dead or alive." The meaning? "Fight to the end. Leave no one behind. Return home every man who falls." No one knows for certain if they lived up to their emperor's orders to perfection, but there was no doubt these men, his most loyal soldiers, tried mightily. And as Marshall wrote, the numbers said the score was perfect. When the Ethiopian Battalion engaged units of the CCF's 67th Division, the Chinese knew they had been in a fight.

Capt. Juan Raigoza, an American officer of Mexican descent, knew the Ethiopians' Kagnew (pronounced Kan' yu) battalion well. He was the 48th Field Artillery Battalion liaison officer to the 2d Battalion, which rotated out of the 7th Division in late April 1953. Juan was more than ten years in the U.S. Army when he first became acquainted with the Ethiopians.

Drafted in 1941, in his third year of college, he was in the Aleutian Islands in June 1942 when the Japanese sent a diversionary naval task force toward the Aleutians, and their main fleet steamed to its near destruction at the battle of Midway. Juan was in antiaircraft defense. His skill was working with a relative new piece of equipment called radar, when the Japanese bombed the Aleutians' Dutch Harbor. From the harbor's shore he watched in stunned disbelief as a Japanese fighter shot down a Navy PBY seaplane just as it was lifting off the water. His instinctive reaction was to grab an unmanned .50-caliber machine gun, fire at the enemy airplane, and try to bring him down. His instincts also told him to lead his quarry—aim ahead of him—and hope the fighter would fly through the stream of bullets. He did not bring the enemy down but thought he saw some hits.

Later, his performance of duty and education earned him entry into Officer Candidate School, where infantry was his branch of choice. Between World War II and Korea, he was one of the thousands of reserve officers mustered out of the Army as the force dramatically shrank. At the time the Army was in dire need of skilled junior officers and leaders, asking its reserve officers to reenlist on active duty as master sergeants, that they might be recalled as officers when the Army expanded again. He reenlisted, and six months later came the opportunity to regain his officer's commission. This time he entered commissioned service at the Presidio in San Francisco and asked to attend the artillery school. He then volunteered for Korea, and when he arrived he was asked, "Where do you want to be assigned?" He wanted his World War II unit—the 7th Infantry Division.

Brigadier General O'Meara, the 7th's artillery commander, insisted on meeting all officers coming into his battalions. Juan met him at breakfast in a tent at 7th Division Headquarters in mid-1952. Juan asked for bacon, eggs, and Tabasco sauce. O'Meara eyed him for a moment and said, "I know where I'm going to send you." Replied Juan Raigoza, "Where, Sir?" With a twinkle in his eye, O'Meara said, "I want you to be the artillery liaison officer to the Kagnew Battalion, the Ethiopians. They love Tabasco sauce and hot food, too," he chuckled. "Yes, Sir," said Juan, and he lived and fought beside the Ethiopians' 2d Battalion until they rotated home in late April 1953. What did he learn about the Ethiopian soldiers and their officers?

As the American artillery liaison officer from the 48th Field Artillery Battalion he worked daily with the Kagnew battalion commander, the battalion operations officer, the S-3, and the S-2, the intelligence officer. Though he was the liaison officer, he doubled as the battalion fire control coordination officer. He coordinated and forwarded requests for artillery and mortar fire which came to him from the battalion's companies, specifically from the artillery forward observers—one American FO assigned to each company. At battalion and in each company, Juan and the FOs worked side by side with an Ethiopian counterpart. The setup was excellent, and worked well.

Juan never forgot the first day he, as a captain, met Lt. Col. Assfaw Andargue, to get acquainted with these men from a faraway north African land. Colonel Andargue spoke excellent English. After Juan reported and was invited to sit down, the colonel gazed at him a moment, and said, "You're not American."

"Sir, I'm an American—we're from all over the world: Scandinavia, Europe, Africa, South America, Canada, Asia, Central America."

"But you don't look like an American. What nationality are you? When did you come to the States?"

"My ancestors came from Mexico at the turn of the century. I was born in Los Angeles, California."

"Ah—Mexico. Mexico is our friend. When the Italians invaded Ethiopia in 1936, Mexico was one of very few nations in the old League of Nations to stand up for Ethiopia and loudly protest the Italian invasion as aggression. They demanded the League take prompt action to stop the aggression. The Mexicans will always be our friends. You will always be our friend."

From that moment on Capt. Juan Raigoza was included in the lives of Ethiopia's officers and men of the 2d Kagnew Battalion. Juan knew them as fierce fighters, and as moral, full of integrity, and proud. The great majority of their officers were trained at Scandinavian or European military academies such as L'École Polytechnique in France and Sandhurst in Great Britain. And yes, they all loved Tabasco sauce and kept an ample supply on hand. Later, when Captain Raigoza's mother sent him some jalapeño chili peppers, they tasted the peppers as well and asked him to "have the lady send more."

How fierce and aggressive were the Ethiopians? Sgt. Gebrasadik Gebreheyot, a member of the 2d Battalion and holder of his country's coveted Haile Selassie Medal, was a master at night patrol. When the 7th Division came back on line in the Chorwon area during the Christmas season of 1952, the Communist Chinese as usual greeted new arrivals with propaganda broadcasts and even large signs containing slogans they changed periodically. The propaganda signs, like the loudspeaker broadcasts, were blunders, indicating the Chinese did not have the linguists available to communicate with the Ethiopians, and brought laughter to both Ethiopians and Americans. The signs and broadcasts urged UN troops to alternately surrender into the "kind hands" of communism or bring about tears of homesickness, but they were in English, not understood by the great majority of Ethiopian soldiers. Sergeant Gebreheyot took matters into his own hands. One night he fixed his bayonet to his rifle and slid out into the darkness. Twenty minutes later he sighted a Chinese soldier painting a new slogan on the board. Using his bayonet, which he liked and knew how to use, he quietly killed the Chinese soldier and brought back the sign board.[12]

As a unit the Ethiopians had been together a long time. Their NCOs were experienced, stable, knowledgeable leaders who could quickly pick up the leadership mantle in a fight, if need be. And, of course, they were the emperor's crack troops, his most loyal, devoted soldiers. And they were black, which placed Juan Raigoza in more than one circumstance he will never forget.

The battalion S-2, a captain, invited Juan to accompany him on a rest and recuperation (R&R) leave to Japan. In Japan, they went out to dinner one evening, intending to meet other American soldiers at a restaurant.

When they met the group and were getting ready to sit down, one of the Americans announced he "didn't sit down at a table with niggers." Juan was never certain if his Ethiopian friend knew the meaning of the word—his English was not that good—but he flew into a rage. He told the Texan bluntly, "Let me tell you, you stupid son-of-a-bitch, this man is one of our allied soldiers. He's a hell of a proud fighter, and a damn good one, as they all are—while you sit on your ass here in Japan and make those remarks. That's an insult, and can cause a diplomatic incident. You either sit down with us or get out. I'll take this all the way to the Eighth Army if I have to." Juan made his point forcefully, and his ties with the Ethiopians were bound more tightly.

On another occasion, a *Stars and Stripes* writer in Seoul published a piece in the paper which stung the Ethiopians. He wrote, completely erroneously, complaining about Ethiopian mechanics who habitually "took hammers to vehicle engines that malfunctioned, and simply beat on them." The "fact" had absolutely no basis in fact, and implied mechanical ignorance among the Ethiopians. The Ethiopians, nonplused, did not know what to do about the ridiculous piece of writing and came to Juan. He took care of it with a blistering phone call to the reporter in which he asked him a few pointed questions to learn what he knew about vehicles.

"Why do you put antifreeze in a car?"

The reporter answered, "So you can start it in winter."

Juan ripped into him with a thorough explanation about expansion of freezing water, cracked engine blocks, and a few other pertinent facts, and then proceeded to chomp on him until he got an apology.

Juan also learned the Ethiopians were Coptic Christians, the original early, before-Christ Christians, who spoke the Coptic tongue in their religious ceremony. They were devout, had a chaplain in their battalion, and consistently invited him to their religious ceremonies—and Juan was not a religious man, not by most standards. He "believed in the Ten Commandments and the Articles of War," as he put it.

What of the Ethiopians as aggressive fighters? American artillery had a well-deserved reputation among the Chinese. Deadly accurate, able to rapidly concentrate huge volumes of fire in or around specific points or areas, the Americans, like the Chinese, occasionally launched brief harassment and interdiction (H&I) concentrations on known or suspected enemy activity, including assembly and bivouac areas. As the Ethiopian Battalion's fire control coordinator, Captain Raigoza was reluctant to permit supporting American artillery battalions to conduct H&I missions in the Battalion's sector. Ethiopian soldiers had their own form of harassment and interdiction, and could appear from out of nowhere on the Chinese side of the line. Juan's fear was random American H&I fire could hit Ethiopian friendlies quietly but aggressively at work in an area known to be controlled by the enemy.

As S. L. A. Marshall wrote, the Ethiopians did not read or carry maps, but they never missed a trail. To help the Kagnew Battalion solve the problem of calling in artillery support, Juan and his counterpart devised a simple scheme of colors and numbers to mentally overlay the battalion's sector. Using the Ethiopian flag's colors, green, yellow, and red, and the directional words "left" or "right," they established a grid and coordinated it with supporting artillery units. The artillery targeting scheme lived beyond Juan Raigoza's assignment with the 2d Battalion, and was to prove, along with their love of Tabasco sauce and jalapeño chili peppers, a life saver and wholesome addition to victory on the battlefields fronting the Ethiopian battalions. These were the men of the Kagnew Battalion as Juan Raigoza knew them.[13]

When the 3d Battalion arrived in the division area to relieve the 2d Battalion, there was the usual soldierly grumbling in the 2d about their being "late going home," while the 3d came into the division with the usual competitive, soldierly brashness and bravado: "The 3d is a better outfit than the 2d." Grumbling and boasting aside, the Ethiopian battalions, the unknown battalions, more than earned a deservedly sparkling reputation within the Americans' 7th Infantry Division.

Additional testimony to the way the Ethiopians viewed their mission came from Second Lieutenant Samuels, an American forward observer assigned to their 3d Battalion from the 48th Field Artillery Battalion. When Samuels reported to the company commander at his CP, the two soldiers standing guard smartly at attention, outside their commander's bunker, immediately impressed the lieutenant. When he entered the bunker, it at first appeared quite dark, but after his eyes adjusted to the dim light he saw the commander sitting at a candle-lit table. The commander enthusiastically welcomed him, and gave him a detailed orientation on the mission, the disposition of his platoons, and the enemy confronting the company, complete with thorough explanations using maps. When he was through,

Left to right: Brig. Gen. Derrill M. Daniel, assistant division commander, 7th Infantry Division; Lt. Col. Wolde Yohannes Shitta, commander of the Ethiopian Battalion; an unidentified Ethiopian officer; and Major General Trudeau. *Courtesy of U.S. Army Military History Institute*

he paused and added matter of factly, "If the Chinese come, you stay with me. I'll be the last in this company to die."[14]

The 3d Ethiopian Expeditionary Force, Korea (EEFK) Battalion arrived in the 7th Division area on 21 April to replace the 2d Battalion, which headed home after completing its year in Korea. Attached to the Americans' 32d Infantry Regiment, which was in division reserve at the time, the 3d entered training 24 April after being issued arms and equipment left by the departing 2d Battalion. Training continued through 9 May with emphasis on weapons training, especially the 81-mm mortar, and the 57- and 75-mm recoilless rifles. The Ethiopians also received training in the principles of patrolling, small unit actions, and raids, with special attention to communications training on the AN/PRC-10 radio.[15]

When the 3d Battalion completed training on 9 May, the division's reorganization into a three-regiment front was in progress, and the 32d Infantry had been assigned to defend the division's right flank sector. Not long afterward the 32d Infantry moved into its new position on the MLR, and the 3d Ethiopian Battalion received its baptism of fire. The evening of 19–20 May came the assault on outpost Yoke, and there, about seven hundred yards north of Yoke the Chinese first met a fifteen-man ambush patrol, the "Incredible Patrol," from Kagnew Battalion's 1st Company. Next the oncoming Chinese ran afoul of one officer and fifty-six enlisted men in the 1st Platoon, 3d Company, a reinforced platoon manning Yoke.[16]

Capt. Behanu Tariau commanded 1st Company, which, with the remainder of the Ethiopian battalion, manned a section of the MLR, including Hill 327, the next highest point to the east of Hill 347 and 334 on the 7th Division front. Hill 327 overlooked Uncle and Yoke, approximately eight hundred yards to its front, both entrenched all around their summits, with wire entanglements covering their slopes.

At 11:00 P.M. on 19 May, the leader of the patrol, twenty-two-year-old 2d Lt. Zeneke Asfaw, with his second in command, Cpl. Arage Affere, leading the column, started their march. They descended at a running walk from Hill 327 to the valley below. Their mission was to proceed to a position about eight hundred yards to the right front of Yoke, and there attempt to ambush a Chinese patrol and take prisoners—the routine mission of an ambush patrol. In thirty-five minutes they reached the bottom in front of Hill 327, a trail distance of a mile and a half, and continued toward the disputed "no-man's-land" north of Yoke and between the two armies. By 11:40, Asfaw and his patrol had seen no enemy. He decided to halt.

The patrol had come upon a concrete-walled irrigation ditch. Asfaw surveyed their location, and recognized they had found a tailor-made position to provide cover. He was standing at a 90-degree bend in the concrete wall, with the elbow of the bend pointing directly at T-Bone, a well-known hill mass occupied by the Chinese. Within a few yards of the bend in the ditch three trails crossed. He decided to deploy his patrol behind the protective cover of the concrete wall, distributing his men evenly, with one Browning automatic rifle on each flank.

Just in time. No sooner had he deployed his men and accustomed his eyes to the dark and terrain in front of their position when he observed a lone Chinese standing in the clear about 300 yards in front of the patrol's position. While he held his gaze on the lone figure to their front, the number of men congregating around the scout grew to a platoon. They simply stood in place, as if awaiting a signal. The platoon-sized group was a tempting target for their automatic weapons; however, at three hundred yards their fire would only scatter the enemy, probably with little effect. Still, the target was vulnerable to American artillery, and Asfaw knew he had the communications to call in massed fire.

Shortly after midnight, at 12:15 A.M., as the Chinese assault force was beginning to assemble to the front of Lieutenant Asfaw's patrol, enemy mortar and artillery rounds began falling on the Ethiopian MLR, and on outposts Yoke and Uncle. Approximately five hundred rounds fell on the MLR positions and another fifty to sixty fell on Yoke in the hour preceding the assault which surged onto Yoke. Still Lieutenant Asfaw's patrol held its ground, remaining undetected by the oncoming Chinese.[17]

Asfaw switched on his radio to call battalion. The radio did not connect, and he spat in disgust at the technical failure. In hindsight, the failure to get through to battalion on the radio proved a blessing in disguise. The Chinese assault force, assuming they had not been discovered, continued massing their troops. Asfaw, observing the assembling force grow to two platoons, repeatedly told himself he was here to capture prisoners. The enemy still did not move. Quick math told Asfaw his fifteen men would be confronting close to one hundred men. Fair enough. He crawled along the ditch quietly cautioning his men to maintain silence and hold their fire until he gave the word.

When the Chinese moved toward the well-concealed patrol, the move was not in columns but in a V-shape like a flight of wild geese, the point heading directly for the apex of the ditch. Throughout the build-up and movement of the enemy to the patrol's front, Asfaw concentrated his gaze on the approximately two-platoon force. Now he shifted his gaze toward the files at the far ends of the V coming toward them, and caught sight of two more groups of enemy he had not seen. To his left about five hundred yards was another Chinese company, marching single file. They had passed his flanks, moving directly toward Yoke. Instinctively he looked to the right and saw another company had outflanked him, and was marching toward 1st Company's position on the MLR. Then came the realization of the entire picture unfolding before him. He was witnessing the beginning of an assault by an entire Chinese battalion.

The enemy force advancing toward the patrol was within two hundred yards of their position as the column to Asfaw's left was almost on the foot of Yoke. His radio was still out, but for the first time he noticed a ten foot high mound to his immediate rear. Thinking the mound might be blocking the line of sight radio signal, he began moving to his left, whispering to his men to stand ready, and testing his radio every few feet. The sounds of enemy artillery and mortar rounds masked his whispered commands to his soldiers and continuing attempts to call battalion on the radio. The enemy was almost upon the patrol.

Eight enemy soldiers were within ten yards of their position when Asfaw shouted "Tekuse!" (fire). The entire patrol fired simultaneously cutting down all eight Chinese at the point of the V. At the same time, the two BARs on the flanks of the patrol poured enfilading fire into both wings of the V, fifteen yards farther to the patrol's front. The totally surprised Chinese lost another dozen men before they could react, throw themselves down, and hug the ground. The Ethiopian patrol continued firing and throwing grenades.

At that moment Lieutenant Asfaw's radio made the long-sought connection and he received a friendly reply. Here is the transmission recorded in the battalion combat journal as a 1:25 A.M. message, "The enemy came. I stopped them. Now they surround me. I want artillery on White Right."

The Ethiopians were using Juan Raigoza's targeting scheme, changed to the colors red, white, and blue, to control supporting artillery fire. They blocked out in colors areas on the map where they likely would need fire support, and simply called for fire on "Blue Left" or "Red Right." In Asfaw's own hour of emergency, he was ignoring the enemy to his front, hoping to shatter the columns moving against Yoke and Uncle.

The enemy fell back about thirty yards and split into two smaller groups. One remained in place and attempted to keep the patrol pinned down while the other tried to flank the patrol on its left. Asfaw did not amend his artillery fire request, and instead simply shifted some of his men to the left, certain grazing fire would slow the enemy's movement. As he later said, "By then I had steadied and was enjoying it."

Within three minutes, the American barrage fell right where Asfaw called it. The big 155s lighted the valley with illuminating shells. Their glare provided the young Ethiopian lieutenant a ringside seat as killing rounds tore into the column, killing some Chinese, scattering others. Against Yoke's skyline he also saw figures in silhouette moving against the outpost, and guessed the enemy had penetrated the works, which he reported on the radio.

The close-in sounds of small-arms and automatic weapons fire during his patrol's fight kept Lieutenant Asfaw from noticing the Chinese massed heavy artillery fire on the MLR, Yoke, and Uncle. The sharp and concentrated barrage cut all communication wires and forced men back into their bunkers.

Second Lt. Bezabib Ayela and many of the fifty-six men in Ayela's reinforced 1st Platoon of 3d Company, on Yoke, could hear rifle fire and grenades faintly but did not know the ambush patrol was in a fight with the enemy. Artillery erased the distant sounds of firing promptly at 12:15 A.M. when incoming rounds began to fall on the MLR, Yoke, and Uncle. Ayela's field phone went dead and both his radios were hit. Ayela moved from post to post yelling, "Berta!" (stand by), bringing his platoon to 100 percent alert. But the noise and no sight of the enemy kept him from warning of an imminent attack.

At 1:53 A.M. the CCF fired three red flares above the rear slope of Yoke, signaling the advance. Ayela ran along the trench toward the flares, knowing the enemy fired them by hand. At the rear parapet he could hear voices chattering from downslope. From the Kagnew Battalion's ridge to the south a searchlight's beam cut through the dark, bathing Yoke's rear with light. Ayela raised himself to the embankment and saw at least a squad of Chinese working their way up the slope, through the rocks, not more than thirty yards away. Cpl. Ayelow Shivishe was with Ayela and survived to tell the lieutenant's story.

A short distance from Ayela were thirteen riflemen and one machine gunner, covering the back slope, but in the wrong position to see the approach of the squad of enemy soldiers. Before he could fire or cry out, the sounds of shooting and a piercing scream right behind him drew him back the way he came. Two squads of Chinese had come up the side of Yoke, killed a BAR man, and jumped into the main trench. He ran for the Chinese at full speed, rifle in hand, and was blown up by a hand-thrown bomb—a Chinese "potato masher" grenade with TNT wrapped and shaped around it for use against bunkers. The brave young Ethiopian lieutenant never knew what hit him.

The weapon weighed three to three and one half pounds and was roughly the size of a human head. Two pounds of TNT gave the device the explosive force of five to six American grenades. To assemble the weapon, the Chinese tied the TNT to the grenade with torn pieces of cloth, exposing the wooden handle for carrying and throwing. Additionally, the inventive Chinese attached a strip of rag to the entire bundle as a handle so that it could be carried by an alternative means. Apparently intended for use against bunkers, much like the American satchel charge, it was too heavy and awkward to be thrown as far as a grenade. Nevertheless, it was a potent antipersonnel weapon if exploded inside a bunker or near unprotected soldiers. Both the Ethiopians and their allies were seeing the weapon in the 7th Division sector for the first time.[18]

After the firing started on Yoke, two groups of enemy about three to four hundred yards in front of the 1st and 2d Companies fired on the Ethiopian MLR positions with a machine gun and small arms. A small number of enemy also opened fire on outpost Uncle from one hundred yards north of the outpost.

When the explosion killed Ayela, Corporal Shivishe went flat in the trench and emptied his M-1 rifle into the enemy group. He saw three men drop. Shivishe knew Yoke's defenders were now leaderless, but no one else did. He ran the other way around the trench to tell Sgt. Maj. Awilachen Moulte he was in command. As he made the turn, the Chinese on the rear slope came over the parapet and into the trench—but not unopposed. Pvt. Kassa Misgina, the machine gunner, heard the noise and rushed to the breach. He cut down the first three men. Then matters got worse.

His gun jammed, and an enemy grenade exploded, driving shrapnel through both legs. The deep wounds did not stop him. Misgina handed the gun back to a rifleman, yelling to him to undo the jam. He then grabbed a box of grenades, stepped to where Ayela had been those few seconds, and resumed the fight to block the Chinese route into the perimeter. Misgina believed, correctly, if he kept them ducking for cover, they could not rush. Thus, he stood on the parapet and hurled grenades, one after another.

In the valley, Lieutenant Asfaw, leader of the still-unscathed patrol, knew nothing of the ordeal on Yoke, nor did his commanders on the ridge of Hill 327 to the south. Unlike every other man observing the battlefield that night, Asfaw alone could see all parts of the big picture. From his place in the irrigation ditch he saw all the enemy formations go forward, past the patrol's position. He knew the observers on the high ground did not have a complete picture of the battle because of the lower ridges that blocked their view. They could only catch glimpses of the unfolding assault. He had seen the American artillery shatter the enemy's assault force on the front slope of Yoke, but that fact was hidden from the commanders observing from the MLR.

Asfaw now concluded his task was to destroy the Chinese battalion using artillery, and he was the only observer in a position to call in fires with no "overkilling"—friendly fire casualties. He also realized that halfway success calling in artillery on the patrol's flank would ultimately doom the fifteen men. Retreating survivors would converge within the draw which was his escape route to the rear. The survivors would reinforce the company which was moving around his left flank, and from that direction the concrete-walled ditch provided the patrol no protection.

He watched the artillery pound the Chinese on the lower slope of Yoke for fifteen minutes, while the enemy column moving toward the 1st Company's ridge took no incoming from the Americans. The reason Asfaw left the column untouched was the force's progress was slower because of the steep, higher hill. During the same interval the Chinese platoons to his front continued their crawl around the patrol's left flank and were now even with his position.

He looked to his right rear once more, and saw the enemy column moving toward the MLR was fifty yards short of Hill 327's main slope. Now was the time to call in the artillery. He radioed his color and direction coded instructions, which were being relayed from outpost Uncle to battalion, and from there to the fire control coordination center. Artillery came in right on target, shredding the ranks of the CCF assault force headed for 1st Company. The devastating response from the 48th Field Artillery Battalion began dissolving the enemy column, and its survivors recoiled, falling back toward Asfaw's patrol.

As the survivors fell back toward the patrol's position, the enemy company to Asfaw's left continued their crawl toward the patrol's left rear. To counter their slow progress, he moved a few more riflemen to the left to continue the grazing fire, keeping the enemy pinned to the ground, their progress slow and costly. In this circumstance, though the patrol's withdrawal route was still open, Asfaw made another crucial decision. He would fight it out here, in the irrigation ditch.

Here was a young Ethiopian lieutenant having his first experience under fire, and he had accepted a role and responsibility few men would relish. Perhaps even more extraordinary, he was displaying a sense of timing rarely found in a division commander.

On Yoke, when Corporal Shivishe ran to tell Sergeant Major Moulte he was now in command, Moulte's first act was to run to Lieutenant Ayela's body to see if he might still be alive. The same bomb that killed the lieutenant had felled two enlisted men. Moulte yelled for a stretcher bearer, then gathered six men and passed each an armful of grenades. He sent a scout five yards in front of the group and they moved silently, in a low crouch, from the rear toward the front of Yoke, on the heels of the Chinese who had killed Ayela—and entered the trench network. Approximately thirty to forty-five yards from their starting point the scout gave an arm signal, hand out, pointing the direction for the grenade shower. Came the throw from all seven, and explosions dead center among the enemy group. Complete surprise. Some Chinese were killed and others scrambled for safety, climbing up the trench wall.

In the dim night light Moulte clearly saw six Chinese silhouetted against the sky. Carrying a BAR, the sergeant major could have cut down all six, but did not fire a shot. Later he said, "I don't know why; I just didn't think of it."

Moulte ordered the six men to carry on and hunt down the invaders, and then doubled back to check the situation on Yoke's rear slope. The jam in the wounded Private Misgina's machine gun had been cleared. Misgina, with his machine gun and one BAR man supporting him, were keeping the Chinese at bay. Downslope in front of Misgina's gun, Moulte counted ten dead Chinese. Beyond them he counted approximately thirty Chinese, all obviously living, who revealed themselves while momentarily grenading uphill toward the trenches. But the distance to the trenches was too great, and the bombs fell short, exploding among their own dead.

Adding to the mounting resistance to Chinese attempts to come in Yoke's back door was another factor. While the fighting was in progress all across Yoke's rear sector, which faced the MLR and Uncle, a machine gun on Uncle maintained fire into the assaulting enemy's rear. While the Chinese may have taken some comfort in their approach to Yoke's rear, the machine gun on Uncle was reminding them they were in perhaps the worst kind of crossfire.

Intermittent radio communications, ever a problem in the midst of a hot fight, had been repeatedly frustrating to Lieutenant Asfaw his first night at war. They were also plaguing Sergeant Major Moulte on Yoke, and the platoon manning Uncle. But somehow the temperamental signals managed to function at crucial moments and thinking men made important, correct decisions to effectively work around their patrol's and outpost defenders' inability to tell their commanders they were in trouble and needed support.

Because of interrupted radio communications, battalion did not know Asfaw's patrol was in trouble and had been in a fight for thirty minutes. Asfaw's first message to get through was picked up by 1st Company's platoon on Uncle. Because 1st Company's radio also was intermittent, the relay from outpost Uncle bypassed 1st Company, and Capt. Addis Aleu, the battalion S-2 (intelligence), heard only a brief warning originating from Asfaw: "Main movement against Yoke . . . fire White Right." Captain Aleu could only speculate about developments, because at that moment the radio on Uncle cut out. But 1st Company's commander, Capt. Behanu Tariau, in his hilltop Observation Post 29, could see the skirmish on Yoke's rear slope. During the period 1st Company CP could no longer raise battalion, Tariau overheard the message relayed by Uncle, saying the patrol was engaged.

Then for fifteen minutes, the critical period when Moulte and his men were fighting off the Chinese attacking from the rear, Captain Tariau's radio cut out. The company commander's anxieties mounted, as did his feelings of helplessness. With the aid of the searchlight bathing Yoke's rear slope he could see the Chinese massing on Yoke's rear slope, but without communication he could not act. He was in touch with no one. Then quite suddenly his radio cut through again.

Captain Tariau told his artillery forward observer, Second Lieutenant William W. DeWitt, to hit Yoke directly with VT (proximity fuse) fire and illuminating shells. DeWitt passed the order upward to Lt. Col. Joseph W. Kimmitt: "Fire Flash Yoke Three!"

At 2:10 A.M., five minutes after Tariau's call for artillery fire on the position, exploding VT rounds had the effect of driving Yoke's remaining, exposed defenders to their bunkers while slashing into the ranks of Chinese caught in the open. For thirty minutes, killing VT rained on Yoke. Tariau then requested a curtain barrage on each side of Yoke, to box in the enemy survivors. The company commander considered for a moment the idea of expanding the barrage across the outpost's forward slope, then thought better of it. Asfaw's patrol might be falling back toward Yoke's defenses. Captain Tariau need not have worried. Asfaw remained steady in the irrigation ditch with his patrol, still enjoying his first fight.

By now the Chinese who had been slowly, carefully completing the half-circle across the patrol's rear were spread out in a skirmish line one hundred yards distant, between the patrol and Yoke. As expected the first stragglers retreating from the fires on Yoke, Uncle, and the slope in front of 1st Company, were beginning to join the still-prone skirmish line. This was Asfaw's moment. He had nailed his flag to the mast. The patrol's ammunition gone except for rounds in the chambers of three M-1 rifles, it was win or lose. If he could not successfully call artillery on the swelling ranks to their rear his fifteen-man patrol would be overwhelmed.

Asfaw gave the message to Uncle: "Fire Blue Right!" Uncle relayed the message to Captain Triau, and he transmitted it to the artillery. If the patrol leader's guess was right the concentration would crush the Chinese to his rear and fall short of his position. Two suspenseful minutes passed before the answer came. The barrage fell dead on target and raked the enemy line from end to end. Asfaw kept the fire coming for ten minutes. When it lifted, nearly all quiet. No more fire came from the patrol's front or immediate rear.

Fragments of the two main enemy columns continued to drift back toward the patrol's position, and the fight periodically flared for the next two hours. Asfaw knew the survival of his men depended on the radio and the accuracy of his calls for artillery. There were times when the stragglers retreating from the two outposts regrouped and came within fifty yards of the ditch, but Blue Right never failed him. More than once he called for barrage fire on all four sides of the patrol, closing the enemy's escape routes to T-Bone Hill while protecting his men from a now better armed enemy.

By four o'clock in the morning the battlefield was finally quiet. Asfaw could see no sign of a live enemy. The patrol arose and stretched, relieved the close call was the right call and satisfied they had done a good night's work. Asfaw radioed another message: "Enemy destroyed. My men are still unhurt. We have spent our last bullet." Now unarmed, the patrol expected a recall. The answer was unexpected.

Captain Aleu's message to Asfaw: "Since you have won and are unhurt and the enemy is finished, you are given the further mission of screening the battlefield, examining bodies for documents and seeking capture of any enemy wounded." The new mission, begun at 4:30 that morning, brought another four or five miles of marching and occupied the patrol for two more hours. Daylight had come and birds were singing when the lieutenant's patrol reentered the MLR.

On the ground within 150 yards of the patrol's irrigation ditch Lieutenant Asfaw counted seventy-three Chinese dead. On the slopes of Yoke and in its trenches were thirty-seven more enemy bodies. Men on Yoke saw the Chinese carry about ten more killed or wounded off the slopes of the outpost. In the rice paddies forward of Uncle were more bodies, still not counted. The usually accepted battle ratio of four wounded for every one mortally hit meant Asfaw and his men effectively eliminated an entire Chinese battalion. To top off the patrol's seven hours of excitement, they captured one prisoner during their sweep of the area.

S. L. A. Marshall, who fifty years ago personally interviewed key participants, and listened to the patrol's debriefing, wrote the original account of the 19–20 May 1953 battle for Yoke. He said of them, "As a feat of arms by a small body of men, it was matchless. No other entry in the book of war more clearly attests that miracles are made when a leader whose coolness of head is balanced by his reckless daring becomes attended by a few steady men. Victory came not because of the artillery but because Asfaw believed in it, willed it, then planned it."[19]

It was a marvelous first fight for the Ethiopian 3d Battalion, and a young lieutenant and his incredible patrol who did everything right. They soundly thrashed a fresh, disciplined enemy who had come at them from several directions at once, and made the Chinese battalion pay dearly for their assault.

Ironically, the 32d Infantry's combat operations history, while acknowledging credit due to Lieutenant Asfaw's patrol and the Ethiopian defense of Yoke, downgraded the results of the Ethiopian 3d Battalion's first battle in Korea. The 32d dispatched an Intelligence and Reconnaissance platoon into the area the afternoon of 20 May. The platoon captured a wounded

Chinese prisoner, who was interrogated along with the other prisoner captured by Lieutenant Asfaw's patrol. There was a considerable disparity between the patrol's body count of 110 obtained by S. L. A. Marshall during his debriefing and review of the entire action, and the forty-four contained in the 7th Division's history. The 7th's "Battle Records Board," whose president was Lt. Col. Earl C. Acuff, formerly the battalion commander of the 17th Regiment's 1st Battalion, provides a possible clue to the disparity. "Reports of the number of enemy sighted appear to be exaggerated. They are much larger than the figures which were obtained from the two prisoners, whose interrogation was considered fairly reliable."

The Battle Records Board debriefed, reviewed and critiqued engagements the 7th's assigned and attached units fought, and made conclusions and recommendations—today called lessons learned—based on the critiques. The 20 May battle for Yoke resulted in at least one conclusion that, in the face of American commanders' drive to continue an active defense and avoid casualties, never became a recommendation. The Battle Records Board observed that "the enemy used grenades much more than Burp guns in the fight on the outpost. The Chinese probably thought the troops on Yoke would hide in the bunkers and they would be able to take it by grenading the bunkers. When the Ethiopians got out of the bunkers and fought from the trench, they obviously upset the Chinese plans for taking the outpost."

The board concluded, "The enemy can be more easily defeated in their attacks if more of our troops would fight from the trenches."[20]

On 19 May, while the division reorganization to a three-regiment front was continuing, and as the 3d Kagnew Battalion was about to receive its baptism of fire, the Colombian Battalion moved on line as the right flank battalion in the 17th Regiment sector. The Colombians had been in reserve, and were now attached to the 17th, and relieved the 1st Battalion of the 17th, though the 1st Battalion retained control of outposts Arsenal and Erie.[21] As reconstruction and strengthening of Pork Chop Hill's defenses continued, the ability of defenders to fight from its trenches decreased. Subjected to almost daily shelling by mortars and artillery, overhead cover was a premium commodity devoutly wished and aggressively pursued. As overhead cover for trenches increased, so did the likelihood of battles fought bunker to bunker, inside the covered trenches, and the evolution of the "death traps" General Trudeau sought from the beginning to avoid. No defense is impregnable. The acid test for Pork Chop's improved but not yet complete covered trenches and greatly strengthened bunkers would come in July.

The Virginian Takes Command

The day the Kagnew Battalion fought off the Chinese assault on outpost Yoke, a new battalion commander arrived in 1st Battalion, 17th Infantry. Lt. Col. Beverly M. "Rocky" Read, a class of 1941 Virginia Military Institute distinguished graduate, had followed in his father's footsteps at VMI. Not only was his father a track and field athlete, and graduate in the class of 1916, he was later the track coach at the Institute, and when Bev Read was a cadet, he too was an athlete on VMI's track and cross country teams his freshman and sophomore years. An aggressive World War II combatant in the Pacific, he served on the 24th Infantry Division staff in the Philippines campaign. Among other duties, he flew on numerous special observation and reconnaissance missions in light aircraft, deep into Japanese held territory—with no escort.

In the spring of 1945, he nearly lost his life on a daring one-man reconnaissance mission to identify and map enemy defenses on Japanese-held Samal Island. His close calls on the hazardous mission included a two-hour night swim through shark-infested waters and near death from a guerrilla outpost he approached in the dark. The plan was for Major Read to approach the island in a small skiff, but the craft sank, forcing him to swim, pushing his pack before him. His guide, a German Jewish refugee who had lived on the island, came with him. The distance was not great, but tides and cross currents kept the two from shore, and it was not until two hours later they pulled themselves on the beach nearly exhausted. The next morning Filipinos offered to show him the sharks that made this particular stretch of coastline their playground.

Bev Read completed his mission, traveling twenty-five miles in Japanese held territory, and returned with a thorough assessment of Samal Island's defenses. Undoubtedly his excellent physical conditioning, and his legs, contributed to his success.

A reserve officer, he left the Army after the war, and beginning in 1946 taught English two years at Washington and Lee University in his home town of Lexington, Virginia. Offered a regular commission in the Army he returned to active duty in 1948. In May 1953, when he took command of the 1st of the 17th, he met another Virginian, also a track and cross country athlete. First Lt. Richard T. Shea, Jr., a former enlisted man who graduated in West Point's class of 1952, was captain of Army's 1952 track team. Come July, the two men would have far more in common than a home state and a love for the sports of track and cross country.[22]

As THE FEAF bombing campaign against the earthen dams wound down on 25 May, the Communists launched powerful offensives nearly all across the UN line. The attacks came mostly to the east and west of I Corps. To the west the assault forced the Americans' 25th Infantry Division into a withdrawal from hilltop outposts east of Panmunjom. To the east of the 7th Infantry sector, the main CCF force struck ROK-held positions in the central front near Kumsong. "The offensive caused complete chaos and for a time posed grave dangers. Under the weight of the CCF attack, several ROK divisions broke and bugged out, leaving great gaps in the line. [Gen.] Maxwell Taylor, [the United Nations and Eighth Army commander,] plugged the gaps with reserve ROK divisions and finally stopped the retreat. Typically, and fortunately, the CCF offensive soon ran out of steam and the situation stabilized."[23]

While the enemy offensive picked up a head of steam on the central front, a movie company came into the 7th Division area 26 May. Paramount Studios of Hollywood began work on a full-length, three-dimensional feature film titled *Cease Fire,* produced by well-known movie mogul Hal Wallis. There were frequent special services programs and United Services Organization (USO) shows cycling through division areas all across the front after the line stalemated and stabilized in November 1951. But this was different. The members of the 7th were told the production company would remain in the area thirty to sixty days, and the film would star men of the division.

A significant number were eventually involved in the making of *Cease Fire.* One was Lt. David L. Bills, West Point class of 1951, and an engineer officer in Lieutenant Colonel Icke's 13th Engineer Battalion (Combat). Bills, an acknowledged explosives and booby-trap expert and battalion supply officer in the 13th, accepted the assigned project with enthusiasm and interest. Here was something new and totally different. He would be providing engineering support to the film company and helping produce movie special effects, including simulated combat scenes. Two and a half months hence, while making a trip from a film shooting location in Seoul back to the 13th Engineers to pick up additional materials to use in the production, Bills would receive a very different mission, a mission no one in the 7th Division hoped for or expected.[24]

On 27 May, Lt. Richard G. "Dick" Inman, of Vincennes, Indiana, and Baker Company, 1st Battalion of the 17th Infantry Regiment, turned his thoughts once more to home and family:

A lot has happened since I last wrote you. . . . I'll tell you all I can get down before I retire. I have to rise at 3:00 o'clock . . . [tomorrow] morning to work my platoon on outpost digging detail out front, so I'll have to make this short. . . .

Tomorrow night I'll "tag along" on a patrol to gain some experience. Should be a fair chance to learn something. I've been taking my platoon out each day to dig on the two major Battalion-sector outposts, "Arsenal" (farther) and "Erie" (nearer). That has become almost routine in the last few days. Nothing happens very often, although a few mortar rounds came in on us a couple of days ago. Old Joe Chink is funny—he may see a company of men, marching or riding somewhere and just sit and watch them. On the other hand, one man may be walking on the road and the gooks'll throw a whole barrage in on him! Like I say, it's a phony, crazy, out-of-date war and I'm glad the world doesn't know what it's like. When the Chinese hit, they hit hard, but they don't hit very often. . . .

I wish I could be home to see everyone and play with Bonnie. Sweet little gal,—

Barbara loves her as much as I do. And I miss talking and living the good, solid Hoosier life of my former days! I guess I'll be able to pick that up quick enough when I return, tho! I wish so badly I were home with my wife and folks, among the dear old souls of our Vincennes! . . .

I leave my love and thanks to you for writing as often as you have. I'll write, myself, whenever I can, but time is extremely precious here, and I have loads to do! But—I'll do my best!

'Til then—don't work too hard, and I'll be thinking of you!

Love to all,

Dick[25]

During Baker of the 17th's rotations onto and off outposts Erie and Arsenal in May, Pfc. Buster Duncan from Aurora, Illinois, a medic attached to Baker Company, listened at night to Chinese loudspeaker broadcasts, and the inviting, silky voice of "T-Bone Till," as the GIs called her. Her repertoire included a welcoming announcement for "the men of Baker Company of the 17th Infantry Regiment"; nostalgic, popular American music intended to stir homesickness; and the names and hometowns of selected members of the company. She then abruptly changed the tone to the less melodious and nostalgic, and after naming several soldiers on the outpost, would ask individually, "I wonder who your wife is sleeping with tonight?" Occasionally, the broadcasts ended with a more deadly change in tone—the abrupt, onrushing sound of incoming enemy mortar or artillery rounds which shook and tore at the outposts.

The broadcasts, though sometimes entertaining to seasoned "old hands," created tension and uncertainty among replacements new to MLR and outpost duty. Already apprehensive, inexperienced troops wondered how the Chinese knew their unit names, individual names, and hometowns. Then, as the artillery and mortar rounds began coming in, the men cursed as they scrambled for cover to avoid the spray of wounding and killing shrapnel which accompanied the exploding enemy rounds. Unease, fear, nostalgia, memories of home, family, wives, girlfriends, attempts to stir mistrust and anger, then an abrupt change to mortal danger. This was psychological warfare on the line, Chinese style.[26]

The UN used psychological warfare as well, intended to erode the enemy's morale, exacerbate and exploit known differences between the Chinese, North Koreans, and the Soviet Union. In May the UN reported 18 loudspeaker teams broadcasting in Korea, with 1,198 separate broadcasts totaling 312 hours to the CCF and 308 hours to the NKPA. Typical themes included "USSR Tricks China," "Mao Serves Any Russian Master," "The North Korean Government Is a Tool of Russia," and "Why Fight Russia's War?"[27]

United Nations intelligence operatives, spies, and saboteurs were reporting information which affected the selection of such themes. While UN intelligence rated the morale and quality of CCF soldiers good, the NKPA soldiers' fighting qualities and morale were considered poor. North Korean civilians were complaining Chinese soldiers treated them badly, actions that stirred the ancient resentment of perceived Chinese "arrogance." There were similar strains expressed by the NKPA, creating tensions between the two battlefield allies.[28]

Intelligence reports also indicated that within the CCF other kinds of stresses could be exploited. The CCF was said to be increasingly using political officers to lead in the attack, while beforehand holding "spiritual mobilization" meetings with their soldiers. During attacks platoon leaders commanded squads and sections.[29] It seemed reasonable to conclude the "political officers" had established themselves as firmly accepting the Communist doctrine, and the heavy casualties being sustained by the CCF were adversely affecting morale, calling into question soldiers' loyalties.

IN MID-APRIL, as both Dick Inman and his West Point classmate, Lt. Richard T. "Dick" Shea, Jr., were preparing to leave for Korea, a fierce fight erupted on Arsenal, then defended by E Company, 2d Battalion of the 32d Infantry. The battle cost eight dead and seventeen wounded. But there had been no major Chinese assault on Arsenal or Erie during the approximate one-week rotations of 17th units into and off the two outposts' positions—not while Dick Inman and Dick Shea were there.

As Lt. Dick Inman wrote home again on 27 May, and the month was coming to a close, the 7th Division's regiments, battalions, companies, headquarters, and staffs were already compiling data and other information accumulated for their monthly command reports, which would be summarized in the division's May command report. The division historians, a small section within the division G-3, the operations staff, compiled and drafted the report, usually completed the third week of the succeeding month. The reports, like most writing in military and corporate organizations, were invariably cold, perfunctory, factual in content and tone, and generally void of emotion, except for an occasional flair of boasting and unit chest beating by an enthusiastic, loyal historian. Such documents are less easy to compile and write when a maneuver war is in progress, when rear area living is far less like garrison living stateside or in a well-established overseas location where the host nation is at peace. Nevertheless, the reports contain information recording the enormity of effort put forth in war by an infantry division, its supporting units, the Army, and the Department of Defense.

In May, 84 officers and 1,697 enlisted men rotated to the Zone of Interior—the continental United States. Replacements coming in to the division numbered 4,517, including 132 officers and 4,385 enlisted. As replacements continued to pour into the division, the never ending cycle of orientation and training also continued, as did rest and recuperation leaves, and numerous other activities and functions intended to keep the division in fighting trim, while being ready to move if necessary.

A comparative analysis of arriving and departing enlisted men, by grade and time in grade, revealed "local conditions require the rapid promotion of men of limited experience and, more important, indicate the rapid advance to responsible positions made necessary by the present replacement system. Many . . . advanced to responsible positions in Korea are not necessarily qualified in all phases of Army life. Their knowledge of this fact, coupled with the lack of assurance that they will have more than one year of duty in the United States before returning to Korea, acts as a deterrent on their enlistment."

Of greater interest to the Americans' national command authority and the men fighting the war were the casualty reports, which heavily influenced the flow of replacements, and eventually hit the news outlets back home. In the 7th Division, General Trudeau was making himself felt. He insisted that not only should American casualties be reported each month, but also KATUSAs, Colombians, and Ethiopians. Casualties sustained by the 7th Division sharply decreased in May, compared with the months of March and April, a welcome but somewhat deceptive fact.

Battle casualties for U.S. troops included 2 officers and 39 enlisted men killed in action, and 7 officers and 152 enlisted men wounded. The Ethiopians lost 9 men killed in action and 47 wounded, most the result of the 20 May battle for Yoke. The Kagnew Battalion's brief but stirring defense of the outpost eleven days after joining the "Buccaneers" brought death or wounds to more then 5 percent of their number. Koreans augmenting the 7th Division in May suffered seven killed and twenty-nine wounded, all enlisted men. When viewed from the perspective of the United Nations, though South Korea was not a UN member nation, the totals from the four nations were far more imposing: 57 killed, 235 wounded—and that ignored the casualties to KSC laborers who endured considerable risk in their work.

Officers, men, and women serving in the 7th Medical Battalion had seen something else in March and April's fluctuating, sometimes overwhelming stream of wounded coming from the line through collection points, aid stations, and the Medical Clearing Company into the Mobile Army Surgical and Evacuation Hospitals, and on into the general hospitals in Japan or the United States. "A standing deficiency in application of tourniquets has existed throughout the Division, and was not ameliorated by approaching the problem in technical channels. Tourniquets, when applied on the battle-field, have been almost always ineffective and very often not attempted at all when indicated. Therefore a training directive was issued to insure that all troops forward of the regimental command post received additional instruction on applying tourniquets."[30]

Necessary almost daily on the line, the ability to successfully apply tourniquets was not a skill needed only by "docs," the medics, the "angels of mercy" who daily risked their lives beside the men in the infantry and other combat arms. It was for all UN soldiers, and particularly for those forward of regimental command posts.

Equally surprising were the May nonbattle casualties among the Americans, one officer and 469 enlisted men. Most were eventually returned to duty; however, in April the division lost thirty-three men to gunshot wounds, most through accident, but some suspected as intentionally self-inflicted. In May the command began reducing the number of casualties caused by careless handling of firearms. For the more extreme, suspected intentional gunshot wounds, commanders imposed punishment upon officers and enlisted men who, upon investigation, were found to have been guilty of carelessness or of exercising "poor command supervision." Recognizing that fatigue contributed heavily to accidental injuries, the division approximately doubled its rest and rehabilitation area to accommodate 150 men each third day, for a forty-eight-hour rest period. The increase came while five-day R&Rs to Japan continued in May, numbering 1,403. The number was near the monthly division R&R average. These two approaches to reducing nonbattle gunshot wounds and other casualties appeared to bring almost immediate downward trends in the losses. There were several other measures taken to help: increased overall emphasis on safety, such as improving and better maintaining the division road net; improved weapons and ordnance handling and training, and further reduction of fatigue through other means, notably the reorganization of the division front.[31]

Sometimes commanded solutions intended to cure a problem have unintended consequences. Such was the case with the threat of court martial action against a commander when a soldier in his command self-inflicted a gunshot wound. While the intent of the stern action was to cause commanders to be more attentive to the morale and mental states of men in their command, and thus prevent self-inflicted gunshot wounds, in at least one case the result was quite different. Lt. Robert M. Euwer, the newly assigned platoon leader in the 15th AAA Battalion, in late May walked head-on into a battery commander who ordered him to take exactly the wrong action as Euwer's first duty in his platoon.

A soldier had deliberately shot himself in the hand in an effort to get a quick, no-return trip stateside. The battery commander, a captain, ordered Lieutenant Euwer to write a report of the injury as battlefield related. Bob Euwer, against his will, obeyed his new commander and in the years ahead wondered what story the GI in question told his family or children about how he won the Purple Heart in Korea.[32]

The reorganization of the division front from two regiments to three brought operational improvements, plus morale and welfare benefits to the troops—also cutting into fatigue. Among the gains was each regiment's ability to maintain unit integrity, a much sought after quality, particularly when training or fighting together. General Trudeau took advantage by directing commanders to more rapidly rotate units occupying outpost and MLR positions. The more frequent rotation reduced the number of days, nights, and hours on alert, and exposure to harassing enemy mortar and artillery fire.

The division road net was not only critical in terms of the ability to shift or relieve units manning the MLR and outposts during "routine," quiet, nonbattle periods along the line, but in rapidly reinforcing or committing reserves during a battle. In a battle, companies and battalions almost always moved by convoy at night, blacked out (no lights), because that's when the Chinese launched their assaults or the UN prepared to reinforce or counterattack. Poorly maintained roads hampered responsive moves of forces, especially at night when blacked-out movement was slowed further by narrow, winding roads—movement also affected by the enemy's predilection for night guerrilla operations.

For example, in May the division transportation officer dispatched 818 trucks. Of these, forty supplemented rail coaches moving troops to Seoul for R&R. He cleared 316 outsized vehicles to move on division roads, while military police and transportation officers and men regulated eighteen convoys which also moved on the road net—nearly all operational unit moves responding to training needs and the battlefield situation.[33]

Armored Personnel Carriers

When the engineers, infantrymen, and KSC laborers began rebuilding and improving Pork Chop's defenses and improving the road which was the outpost's lifeline, the use of armored tracked vehicles, M-39s, to haul men, materials, and equipment to Pork Chop became routine. Two-and-one-half-ton trucks, or any vehicle with air-inflated tires, were far too open and vulnerable to haul men all the way forward to the OPLR. It was either walk from assembly areas or blocking positions forward, and haul materials and equipment using cargadores, or use armored tracked vehicles which offered far greater protection against small arms, mortars, artillery, and automatic weapons.

During the CCF's 16 April assault on Pork Chop, a few M-39 resupply missions, including evacuation of wounded on return trips, had proved the vehicle's value in sustaining the hill's defense while reducing casualties. General Trudeau recognized that the outpost's key but precarious position necessitated increased M-39 use. The vehicle's speed, load carrying capability, better armor protection, and ability to navigate difficult roads and terrain made it an obvious choice to support the increasingly threatened outpost. While the vehicle offered numerous advantages, its most salient feature was the reduction of troop exposure to enemy fire as they moved from the MLR onto the hill.

To better perform the mission General Trudeau directed the 7th's staff to organize a Provisional Armored Personnel Carrier Platoon within the Regimental Tank Company assigned the 17th Infantry Regiment. When the platoon first activated in April, the 17th Infantry provided an officer platoon leader, two noncommissioned officers for section leaders, twelve enlisted drivers, and two enlisted mechanics. Five M-39s came from various units within the division.

An M-39 normally carried a squad of soldiers and their combat loads, but twenty men frequently rode from the checkpoint behind Hill 200 on the dash around "clobber corner" to Pork Chop's evacuation landing.

Normally, ten to eleven M-39s could bring an entire infantry company forward, including its fourth platoon, the weapons platoon. With the weapons platoon detached to another location supporting the company, the infantry company's move onto the Chop required seven to eight M-39 loads.

The vehicle's design afforded drivers, positioned in the front, considerable all-around protection. If they chose, drivers could sit down, close the overhead hatch, and completely "button up" in the driver's compartment—and have enough protected visibility to still safely navigate the roads. The vehicle offered passengers some measure of protection but considerably less than its drivers.

Passengers and their cargo entered and departed the vehicle through rear doors. They sat on the floor of the vehicle to remain out of enemy sight and avoid aimed, random, or barrage fire and gain the best possible protection from the vehicle's armor, which was not heavy. Though M-39 drivers and passengers were always mindful of the potential for a direct hit in the passenger compartment by a mortar or artillery round, or overhead exposure to deadly shrapnel from VT rounds, it was a marked improvement over trucks, and became commanders' and medics' vehicle of choice to evacuate wounded and dead from Pork Chop to collection points and aid stations just behind the MLR.

At the end of the month, medical officers took note of another new APC which began entering the 7th Division's inventory with the receipt of the first six on 17 May: a boxlike, well-armored, completely covered tracked vehicle. General Trudeau had been arguing strenuously the vehicle was sorely needed in the 7th Division. He prevailed, and the T-18E1 began field testing immediately, while being modified to accommodate four litter cases, two stacked on each side of the vehicle's interior. The medical officers wrote, "The new personnel carrier, T-18 was first employed this month to transport personnel to and from forward positions. Initial reports indicate that they are a great improvement over the M-39 for transport of casualties."

At the same time, a less optimistic report on the T-18's performance came from the 17th Infantry Regiment:

The cost of maintenance far overshadows the usefulness of the T-18 Armored Carrier, due to the following reasons:

(a) The front volute bumber springs are not strong enough. Three (3) springs have broken on three (3) different vehicles in one (1) weeks operation.

(b) The front shock absorber bracket mounting bolts are not large enough. Twelve (12) of these bolts have sheared off in one (1) weeks operation.

(c) One road wheel suspension arm has broken in three (3) days operational period.[34]

The T-18, like its open-top M-39 predecessor, included doors that could be opened by the driver, but the armored cover on the newer vehicle gave passengers and cargo much more effective all-around protection from hostile fire, while concealing the vehicle's contents from the enemy.

Before General Trudeau left Japan and command of the 1st Cavalry Division in March to take command of the 7th Division, he knew the T-18 was coming into the Army's inventory and wanted to organize a motorized infantry battalion equipped with the new APC. He decided he would seek reassignment of the late Gen. George S. Patton, Jr.'s, son, Lt. Col. George S. Patton III, as the battalion commander in the 1st Cavalry Division. Trudeau had not been successful before departing for Korea, but knew the T-18 was coming off the production line, and remained convinced of the vehicle's value to the infantry. He was even more firmly convinced during the April battle for Pork Chop, when he and the I Corps commander attempted to get a firsthand, close-up look at the situation on Pork Chop the afternoon of 17 April. That was the afternoon the survivors of Easy Company plus a few from Fox of the 31st; Lt. Joe Clemons and King Company, 31st Infantry; and George Company, 17th Infantry, were fighting desperately to hold onto the outpost, calling for reinforcements and resupply.

As the George Company commander, Lt. Walt Russell, later recalled, "Throughout the [April] battle for Pork Chop we never saw one field grade officer on the outpost."[35] Though neither Trudeau nor Walt Russell's battalion or regimental commanders set foot on the hill during the furious forty-eight-hour fight, Walt Russell did not know his division commander had at least tried to get a close-up look at the defenders' situation that afternoon. What occurred the afternoon of 17 April became the rationale for Trudeau to eventually win his fight to get T-18s in the 7th Infantry Division.

Using the observation helicopters allocated to division and corps commanders and their staffs, Generals Trudeau and Clarke agreed to an airborne rendezvous above the checkpoint behind Hill 200—which was on the MLR—to evaluate the situation on Pork Chop. Trudeau knew well that enemy observers on Baldy could call for mortar and artillery barrages along Pork Chop's lifeline, almost at will, because of their unobstructed view of the road, Hill 200, and into the Chop's rear.

Clarke was late arriving. If there was one thing the Chinese had, especially considering the UN's domination in the air war, it was an intensely active antiaircraft defense along the line of contact. Trudeau's helicopter came under heavy enemy fire—with flak bursts clearly visible and near. The division commander and his helicopter pilot decided to land at the checkpoint behind Hill 200. When Clarke arrived, he and Trudeau walked to the front side of Hill 200's defenses where they had a clear view of Pork Chop. They saw firsthand the road leading to the evacuation landing, and the potential for devastating artillery and mortar fire on anything that moved across the valley between 200 and the Chop.

Years later General Trudeau recounted what occurred after his 17 April trip to meet General Clarke on Hill 200:

I went to G-4 [supply] of Army to try and get some of the new personnel carriers, which I knew were in . . . , and my answer was that they couldn't be released because they were being saved for an armored infantry battalion. Well, this was a situation like I told you about before, when I needed the flares to quickly get light over my positions, and they said, "You can't have them, they're Air Force property." I said, "Goddamnit," and I got them anyhow, thanks to Dick Moyer, who was the G-4. I had the same proposition here. I had to go to General Taylor, and he released [the T-18s], I don't know how many . . . , maybe it was eight. It made all the difference in the world in getting supplies up there, and also getting men, and furthermore had the advantage that the enemy didn't know what the hell we were doing. They didn't know whether we were moving in men or supplies, whether they were reinforcements or supplies. And of course it was saving a lot of men evacuating casualties. It was the first time [the T-18s] were used in combat.[36]

Though the T-18 would go through some maintenance, repair, and replacement growing pains in May and June, its operational availability increased as time progressed. The second week of July, under the pressure of circumstance, the Provisional Armored Personnel Carrier Platoon grew rapidly to fifty-eight men, twenty-one M-39s, and six T-18s. The vehicles would be life savers for many men defending Pork Chop Hill.[37]

The Brash Young Corporal from Boise

During the month of May, in long days of toil and sweat on Pork Chop, Able Company of the 13th Engineers continued hard at work rebuilding and strengthening the outpost's defenses. Supporting the 17th Infantry Regiment, Able Company's platoons and squads took their turns, along with infantry companies rotating on and off the outpost, men dispatched from the regiment's reserve units, KATUSAs, and KSC laborers.

In 3d Squad, 2d Platoon of the 13th's Able Company, nineteen-year-old Cpl. Dan D. Schoonover of Boise, Idaho, took many of his days on the hill. Dan's company commander, Capt. James A. Brettell, at the request of another company commander in the 13th, had earlier accepted Dan's transfer into Able Company. The requesting commander regarded Dan as somewhat of a troublemaker, perhaps a bit of a malcontent, who, to the commander's mind was not doing well and was causing mischief. Brettell, the battalion's older, more experienced company commander, was looked upon as the officer who could take unpolished, rough-edged, energetic young soldiers and trim the rough edges, make them solid soldiers, and perhaps even turn them into leaders.

In Brettell's company was Dan's older brother, Pat. Pat's service in Korea, which began prior to his younger brother's arrival in the 13th, inspired and motivated Dan's enlistment. Dan wanted to "go to Korea to be with his brother," and on enlistment undoubtedly requested assignment to the same unit. Once arrived in the ROK, Dan's urge to serve beside his brother could have been his unspoken, hidden reason for unhappiness in another 13th Engineer company, and the real reason for his move to Able Company. Whatever the reason for Dan Schoonover's move to Able Company, his tough, realistic, no-nonsense commander drew the line with "no" when Dan requested that he and Pat be put in the same platoon. Each platoon supported one of the three infantry battalions in the regiment. When a battalion engaged in combat operations, each squad in the engineer platoon was committed to one of the infantry companies, when the company was committed to a counterattack. Jim Brettell was adamant. He did not want to risk having the two brothers attached to the same battalion, never mind the same infantry company, should the battalion or company be committed to a fight.

In the scheme of things, 1st Platoon of Able Company normally supported the 1st Battalion, Buffalo Red, of the 17th, and 2d Platoon of the 13th supported 2d Battalion, Buffalo White, while 3d Platoon supported 3d Battalion, Buffalo Blue. Dan Schoonover's squad was normally trained, ready, and on call to support George Company, Buffalo White. In May, Dan Schoonover got the break he wanted. Blond, handsome, athletic-looking, smart, ambitious, and full of energy and scrap, Dan was ready when opportunity came knocking at his door. The lively, brash, hard-working young man from Boise, Idaho, excitedly wrote home to his mother on 30 May 1953, Memorial Day in the United States:[38]

> The people on top of the ladder around here must like my efforts, as I am a squad leader now. I was an assistant a week ago, but the squad leader went on R & R (rest and rehabilitation), so I took over while he was gone. We were working on Pork Chop then, and I worked the squad pretty hard so we could get off the hill sooner. Ended up getting more work done (even if we were putting in 16 hours a day) than anybody else.
>
> The company commander thought so much of it, he made me squad leader after the old one came back. Now the old one is taking my orders. Pardon my boasting about my progress, but it makes me feel so good I had to tell you.[39]

Brash young corporals who possessed the spark of determination, fight, and leadership were among hundreds who provided a different kind of spark and shining light in the month of July 1953, when all would be put to the test.

7

SIGNS OF TROUBLE

THOUGH MAY 1953 HAD BEEN RELATIVELY CALM IN THE 7TH DIVISION'S sector, and the rebuilding and strengthening of Pork Chop's defenses continued at a rapid pace, the rest of the 155-mile UN line had seen a substantial increase in enemy-initiated offensive operations. In terms of frequency and size, the increase was 50 percent compared to March totals, and it exceeded the first three months' combined total by 25 percent.

Beginning 11 May, the CCF and NKPA launched a series of limited objective attacks with forces ranging in size from company to regiment. For the most part their offensive operations struck at outpost and MLR positions held by the ROK II Corps and the U.S. I Corps, west of the 7th Division's sector, with smaller scale assaults in the U.S. X Corps sector. While combat was more extensive than at any time since October 1952, Eighth Army intelligence concluded, "There were no indications . . . the enemy intended to exercise his accepted capability of launching a general offensive. It appeared rather that the Communist objective was to seize key terrain features and to strengthen the positions of enemy negotiators at Panmunjom by assuming an attitude of offense."[1]

At the end of May, outpost Horseshoe and one outpost on the northern slope of Finger Ridge in the ROK 8th Division sector; Wire Ridge in the ROK 5th Division area; and outposts Elko, Vegas, and Carson in the 25th Division sector, defended by the Turkish Brigade, had fallen into enemy hands. The Turks had repeatedly fought off Chinese assaults on the outposts for three days in counterattacks and fierce hand-to-hand fighting, inflicting heavy casualties on the Chinese. As had been the case with Old Baldy in March and outposts taken in April, persistent, repeated, heavy assaults by the CCF finally resulted in decisions to cease counterattacks and order defenders to abandon the outposts.[2]

With restarting, then stalling, then restarting of negotiations after Little Switch, political tensions increased, both between UN allies and the enemy, and between the South Korean government and its allies. As May came to an end and June began, it was clear truce negotiators were approaching agreement on the last major issue on their agenda, the exchange of POWs. The real possibility of an armistice seemed at hand, and was the subject of several conferences involving General Taylor, General Clark (the commander-in-chief, United Nations Command), the American ambassador to Korea, President Syngman Rhee, and members of the UN staff at Panmunjom. It was an effort to constantly review plans, to ensure all parties were geared to act according to the terms of the agreement should it come to pass, while maintaining a posture of strength and readiness to continue fighting should the talks fail or the CCF and NKPA violate the agreement and resume their offensive. All the uncertainty and work toward settlement, as well as the issues that would follow, also needed discussion with key members of FECOM in Japan, and the Eighth Army staff in Seoul.

At the same time, the enemy initiated more aggressive offensive operations, while the South Korean government increased public statements expressing opposition to an agreement that did not reunify Korea. Several mass demonstrations on Seoul's city streets emphasized the viewpoint expressed by President Rhee. The statements' and demonstrations' effects were disturbing to the ROK's allies, including the Eighth Army and UNC, and General Taylor queried the city government, where Eighth Army was headquartered. Seoul's Mayor Kim responded with a letter saying in essence that "the demonstrations against the truce in Korea had been spontaneous, but . . . future demonstrations would be orderly and controlled inasmuch as they would be conducted only after having coordination . . . [with] . . . the Chief of Police of Seoul and the Provost Marshall, Seoul City Command."[3]

The Next to Last Signature

June was to be another relatively quiet month for the 7th Infantry Division and the men rotating on and off Pork Chop. Aside from the normal combat and reconnaissance patrol activity at the beginning of the month, and frequent contact with the enemy during patrols, the Chinese offensively probed division outposts only three times, though the frequency of CCF reconnaissance patrols increased considerably, particularly in front of Pork Chop. Aside from two brief fire fights in front of Pork Chop on 3 and 6 June, aggressive enemy offensive activity appeared muted near the outpost.[4]

The first of two most notable assaults on the division front came on 4 June, when the Chinese again sent an estimated enemy company against men from 4th Company, Kagnew Battalion, who manned outposts Yoke and Uncle.[5]

The battle began at 9:12 P.M. when Ethiopian outguards detected and exchanged small-arms and automatic weapons fire with an unknown number of Chinese located north and west of Yoke. The Ethiopians' senior officer on Yoke ordered the outguards back into the perimeter when the enemy force was 150 yards west of Yoke, and asked for artillery and mortar illumination to locate and assess the size of the enemy force. Then shortly before 9:30 he called for "Fire Flash Yoke." The steel curtain of artillery fire closed around the outpost beginning half past the hour.

The enemy set up machine guns on the north finger and west side of Yoke, near the valley floor, to support their attack. At 9:42, two groups of Chinese attempted to assault the outpost's defenses from the east and west, using small arms, automatic weapons, and grenades. Ethiopians manning Uncle and MLR positions to the south directed mortar, automatic weapons and tank fire on the north and west flanks of Yoke, and artillery "flash fires" continued thirteen minutes from the time the first rounds hit. The enemy's attempt to work through the artillery curtain ringing Yoke, and other supporting fires from flank and rear, did not succeed. The firing then became sporadic as the CCF troops attempted to evacuate wounded and dead from the north and west slopes of the outpost.

At 3:35 A.M. the following morning, the Chinese made one more attempt to overrun Yoke, when two machine guns, each approximately 150 yards to the front and rear, opened fire on the outpost. Under cover of the machine-gun fire a small group moved up the west flank of the position but finally

Pork Chop as seen looking northeast from Hill 347, June 1953. Note the primary (*nearer*) and secondary (*right of primary*) crests of Pork Chop (*right of center*); Chinese-held Hasakkol, the high peak slightly left of center; Brinson Finger, the long "shank" of the Pork Chop, which runs from the primary crest almost due west toward Old Baldy; and the Chinese-held Pokkae (*far right center*).
Courtesy of Robert J. Schaefer

broke contact ten minutes later when met with small-arms and automatic weapons fire. At 3:50 A.M. the enemy withdrew, and quiet returned to Yoke and Uncle.[6]

Amid war's clamor senior delegates at Panmunjom continued talking and making progress. By 4 June they agreed on the mechanics of the main POW exchange, and most of the details of the armistice had been worked out.[7]

On 4 June, Lt. Dick Inman, 2d Platoon, Baker of the 17th, wrote home again:

I'm extremely sorry that I have not been able to write as often as I would like to; I hope there will not be too many occasions in the future which will see similar lapses in my letters to you. Right now . . . I'm on outpost duty on "Erie," the outpost hill out in front of the M.L.R. in the 17th Infantry sector. Erie lies right behind the outpost, "Arsenal," which together with Erie, forms a twin combination that the Chinese have been unable to break since 1951. . . . Presently, Arsenal-Erie is the only place the Chinese have failed to attack along the entire 155-mile front in their recent effort to obtain "bargaining points" for the current "peace-talk-truce-armistice-prisoner-exchange" squabbles. I guess they have despaired of gaining anything in our sector, since they've tried so often and failed. They've given it all up as a lost cause, I believe—the capture of the outposts, I mean. I hope they continue that train of thought, since I'm largely in charge of the defense of Erie now. However, Arsenal, the farther of the two hills from the MLR, is in greater danger than Erie is. . . .

Right now we're concerned with digging our positions better—hard! [We're] making trenches, bays for vehicles, tunnels, bunkers, and fighting positions all over the place! Also, we are beginning to erect dummy positions and fake firing bunkers, etc. It's all part of a plan to confuse the gooks, who are in the habit of learning the outlay of our positions down to the last trench and bunker before they attack. . . .

I don't want to scare you . . . but I've been under mortar fire twice now. Yesterday, the last time, I was sitting on a couple of ammo cans, and a piece of shrapnel about the size of the end of my middle finger missed my old wooden head about two inches and slapped against the ground below me. I was going to send the piece to Barbara, but reconsidered, thinking it would make her worry all the more! So don't tell her! I'll tell her when I get home. . . .

Must close now and inspect my positions. Tell Bonnie to be a good girl and write a letter to me when she can. I miss her and all of you so much. Got the pictures from Barbara that Admiral took—Love, Dick.[8]

Four days later, on 8 June, both sides signed a repatriation agreement, clearing away the issue which had deadlocked the negotiations for eighteen months.[9] Confidence was growing in the Eighth Army and the UN Command. Only a few minor technical issues stood between more fighting and the silence of Korea's guns. Other factors intervened, however, including evidence the CCF and NKPA were not through yet. Seen in early June were indicators of significant movements by enemy forces, a thinning of forces holding positions on each coast, and clear evidence the UN's adversaries were building up strength on the central front, opposite the sectors held by the ROK's II Corps and the U.S. IX Corps, which included the ROK's 2d,

9th, and Capital Divisions. The enemy's intentions were not entirely decipherable, but they clearly could be interpreted as signs of more trouble ahead—more fighting. But troubles of a different sort were to intervene a few days later.

Rhee and the Surprise Prisoner Release

In the beginning of June, 7th Division realigned regimental boundaries within the division's sector, as adjustments continued in the reorganization into a three-regiment front. The 17th Infantry Regiment's boundary shifted farther left. The day prior to the signing of the POW repatriation agreement, 2d Battalion assumed responsibility for defense of Hill 347, in the regiment's left sector. The 1st Battalion of the 17th, previously responsible for defending outposts Pork Chop, Erie, and Arsenal, was relieved of responsibility for Erie and Arsenal, effective 10 June, and moved into MLR positions on Hill 200, while retaining responsibility for the defense of Pork Chop. To the 1st Battalion's right was the Colombian Battalion, and the 17th's 3d Battalion occupied Erie and Arsenal, where Dick Inman's 2d Platoon, B Company had been on outpost duty and improving defenses.[10]

Two days later, while news of the POW agreement spread, Lt. Dick Shea in Able Company told of the good news and the regiment boundary's shift to the left in a letter to his wife Joyce:

9 JUNE 53

Darling Joyce,

Our battalion has shifted, and we are in a new area now, and I have a new task, much similar to some of the other work I was doing before, but with more responsibility. Also I have my own log underground bunker, having with me our medics and part of our supply detail. I am fortifications and labor officer, and have two sergeants who oversee about 60 Korean Service Corps laborers. Now we are engaged in digging in deeper, putting sturdy log and earth covers on our trenches, and building new fighting and sleeping bunkers. It is a lot of work, but it is really a good project, for the completed works afford excellent cover from enemy artillery. The KSCs do most of the digging, and our engineer platoon which is attached to the company places in timbers and log walls already notched to fit. So the hole is dug to specifications, the KSCs lug the lumber up to the position, the engineers put the pieces together, then the unit is covered up and the ground leveled. That way the position is difficult to detect, as well as being formidable enough to stand even the heaviest bombardment. It is interesting to move hundreds of yards along our positions completely underground, through tunnels from one underground room to another. The sides are shored like a mine, in fact so much so that one boy who had worked in coal mines in Pennsylvania has been very helpful to the engineer platoon. Jim Deitz, you will remember I saw him the other day, is here with the engineer platoon. We see Dick Inman ever so often. He is strong in his belief that the Reds mean business on peace this time, but I cannot entertain any such hopes as yet. They appear to be playing the old game and only when it happens will I believe it, and then I shall be greatly pleased of course. We have heard, but not read, that the PW [prisoner of war] pact was signed, and that today they recessed after we were all expectantly awaiting further agreement, possible signing of the armistice.[11]

In the meantime, the patrol and probe battle went on on the 7th Division front.

At 9:30 P.M. on 10 June outguards in front of outpost Dale, to the west, southwest of Pork Chop, reported an undetermined number of enemy moving toward their position. Shortly thereafter they estimated the number to be twenty-five and opened fire with small arms and automatic weapons from their positions. A reinforced platoon from Charlie of the 31st was manning Dale when approximately two enemy platoons began their probe. Almost simultaneous with the beginning of the fire fight, Chinese approximately 100 yards north of Dale fired three green flares. The platoon leader on Dale called his outguards back into the outpost positions. At 9:55, enemy mortar and artillery rounds began falling on Dale at the rate of two to three rounds per minute, and three minutes later, the outguards reentered the defensive positions.

The Charlie Company platoon leader then immediately directed prearranged mortar and artillery fire. An intense small-arms, automatic weapons, and hand grenade fire fight began at 10:00 P.M. as the oncoming CCF platoons attempted to assault the outpost from the left (west) flank. American artillery "flash fires" blanketed Dale's north slopes for three minutes then shifted farther north to seal off enemy reinforcements and the route of withdrawal. The Chinese supported their attack with long-range recoilless rifle and automatic weapons fire from Old Baldy and Chink Baldy, but to no avail. At 10:10, the Chinese force withdrew without pressing their attack into the outpost's defenses. By 11:00 P.M. Dale's outguards were back on position, with communications reestablished.[12]

On 14 June, while relative calm kept its hold on the 7th Division front, and the ROK government was still expressing its opposition to the emerging terms of the armistice agreement, Gen. Maxwell Taylor continued to voice his belief the armistice could be signed at any moment. In a statement broadcasted on the Armed Forces Korean Network radio he informed soldiers of the Eighth Army, "The possibility of an armistice has increased to the point that we must consider what a signing would mean to the Eighth Army. A good soldier never allows himself to be surprised by the course of events, so it is up to all of us to study this matter of an armistice and prepare to discharge our duties if an armistice is actually signed.[13]

Lieutenant Shea's sketching abilities were to be particularly useful to the 1st of the 17th's, and Able Company's, defense of Pork Chop Hill in July. The same day the Armed Forces Network broadcasted General Taylor's statement, he wrote Joyce:

> My job as I told you, was concerned with improvement and engineering
> of fortifications. The sketch that I have included is the original one I
> made by covering every foot of the hill, going into every position in
> the course of two days. Thereafter I made six tracings, mounted them,
> covered them with acetate, and made them sector property of the hill,
> meaning they remain on position when units change. Lt. Roberts, [the
> company commander], desires that when we take over our next hill, a
> sort of semi-reserve position when we have completed this mission, I
> have prepared sketches of those fortifications. I welcome the opportunities as it keeps me busy, and I like it much, giving my fingers plenty of
> training.

A day earlier, when A Company returned from outpost duty, Dick was assigned as platoon leader of fourth platoon, the company's heavy weapons platoon. He explained in his 14 June letter to Joyce that the platoon consisted of three 57-mm recoilless rifle crews and a section of three 60-mm mortars, and the platoon supported the operations of the company by fire. His platoon numbered approximately forty men. He added, "We are in reserve at this time, resting contentedly by day behind the MLR, moving up at night as a counterattack force in case the line needs reinforcing. It is good experience and well for me that I take over the fourth platoon at this time rather than when we are occupying an outpost."

Dick Shea was settling comfortably into A Company:

I am well pleased with this company, and with the officers and men. It is difficult to say whether a company is best or not because you do not know the others as well as your own. But I do know we have the much desired spirit necessary and the feeling of warm cooperation needed for a line unit. I would not trade for anything, though I suppose one finds much merit in any group of men this far forward. Lt. Stewart and Lt. Barr are first and third platoon leaders, Lt. Wilcox second, Lt. Greenwell Executive Officer and [Lt.] Roberts CO. Sergeant Young is administrative first sergeant and Sgt Hovey field first sergeant. I will write you a little more about each one in my letters to come.[14]

Though mass demonstrations expressing Korean antipathy for the proposed armistice remained common during May and June, attitudes of the demonstrators and the text of the banners hundreds of them carried appeared more conciliatory as weeks went by. Then, four days after General Taylor's 14 June public statement, a crisis erupted, a crisis not precipitated by the CCF and NKPA, but by President Syngman Rhee.

Without warning, sometime between midnight and dawn on 18 June, approximately 25,000 of 33,600 NKPA, anti-Communist POWs escaped and shed their uniforms, having been aided by their ROK Army guards. Awaiting their release, ROK National Police assisted the fleeing prisoners in finding refuge, including food, shelter, and clothing. President Syngman Rhee promptly announced the mass escape had been planned and carried out on his order, and responsibility for the outcome was solely his.

Rhee did more than release the prisoners. He declared virtual martial law in South Korea, forbade all ROK Army personnel and civilians to continue working for the UN Command, and alerted senior ROK Army commanders to prepare to fight on, armistice or no armistice.[15] While the effects were immediate and disconcerting for South Korea's allies, powerful, ancient Korean history lessons were at work in Rhee's and his people's minds.

When World War II ended with the partition of Korea at the 38th parallel, the entire peninsula had been freed of forty years of a brutal Japanese occupation which began during the Russo-Japanese War. For hundreds of years prior to the Japanese occupation, Korea's history was filled with warring, powerful neighbors—out of Russia, China, and Japan—running rampant up and down the peninsula, and all, in turn, battling and, when they won, harshly repressing the Korean people and their strong drives for national identity and independence. What is more, their powerful neighbors all seemed to express attitudes and feelings of arrogant superiority in dealings with the Koreans.

Once Communist-trained Kim Il Sung launched his invasion in 1950, intent on crushing any semblance of a democratic South and gaining control of the entire peninsula, Rhee and his supporters were passionately inflamed by Kim's brutal onslaught, and became ferociously determined the Communists would be driven out of Korea. Rhee would not go quietly at the notion he and his people must now compromise with the new Communist emperor to the north, who had under his control roughly half the number of Korean people as lived in the fledgling democracy to the south.

Moreover, in Rhee's eyes, there were other old, gnawing issues. While there were early and increasing signs Kim Il Sung was building his armed forces to strike southward, and tensions were rising on both sides of the thirty-eighth parallel, the United States pulled its last ground forces—the 7th Infantry Division—off the peninsula. At the same time the American government attempted to keep internal Korean animosities in check by restraining the South Korean armed forces' buildup to counter the growing threat in the north. The military imbalance between the adversaries continued to grow until the Communist dictator decided it was time to strike. Kim was convinced the United States would not intervene, and the South Koreans were so weak he could gain a quick victory. These were all bitter pills for President Rhee, an avowed Korean nationalist with an American education and strongly democratic leanings.

But Rhee's well-founded frustration and anger would not be allowed to carry the day in the new world of growing, nuclear-laced, East-West, democratic-Communist superpower confrontation, especially in an era when the Western nations were in no mood to spark what they believed would be World War III.

When the twenty-five thousand anti-Communist POWs rushed out of their compounds and melted into the South Korean population and countryside, the UN, American government, South Korea's allies, and the Eighth Army were presented a harsh dilemma. Numerous conferences followed, involving Generals Taylor and Clark, other UN officials, and U.S. Ambassador Briggs, all aimed at evaluating the situation and determining the best course of action. The conferences continued through the end of June.[16]

While hurried efforts were under way to find the best means to resolve the contentious issues the incident unleashed, the American ambassador and Generals Clark and Taylor tried in vain to convince President Rhee to reverse course and support the armistice agreement. Rhee was adamant. In the United States, momentum gathered in the American government for actions to bring Rhee around. Assistant Secretary of State Walter Robertson, President Eisenhower's representative to confer with Rhee, would arrive in Seoul on 25 June.

In the meantime, faced with increasing CCF and NKPA attacks along the central front; twenty-five thousand supposedly anti-Communist former POWs loose in the UN's rear areas; and Eighth Army unity menaced, General Taylor moved to blunt the Communists' attacks, bolster rear area security, and ensure ROK Army units would remain engaged with the enemy. Before the month of June ended, he redeployed three UN divisions to reinforce or counterattack to meet the Communists' attacks. As for the released prisoners, rounding up twenty-five thousand North Koreans rapidly scattering throughout South Korea would be impossible. Taylor could not commit the forces to a mission certain to be futile.

Restrained Operations and an Apology

There were other troubling issues surfaced by President Syngman Rhee's actions. The American government and its UN allies feared another extension of the war. The Communists, already engaged in strengthening the central front and assuming a stronger, more aggressive offensive posture, might break off the negotiations entirely, greatly prolonging a war growing increasingly unpopular and controversial, especially in the United States. Some painful steps were in the offing, and Taylor, undoubtedly acting under instructions, promptly took other measures when the POWs were released on 18 June.

He directed his five corps commanders to cease all combat patrols effective that day, until further notice. They were to continue reconnaissance patrols but there would be no UN-initiated contacts with the enemy. The I Corps commander, General Clarke, received Taylor's instructions and immediately passed them to his division commanders and they, in turn, passed them to regimental commanders and on to the battalions. Lt. Col. Rocky Read, commander of 1st Battalion, 17th Infantry, also received Taylor's 18 June guidance, although he probably was not aware of the source of the directive.[17]

In the 1st Battalion, which occupied Hill 200 on the MLR and rotated companies on and off Pork Chop every five to seven days, the order to cease all combat patrols delayed an operation which had been in the planning stage since late May, a raid on the Rat's Nest. Units of the CCF 200th Regiment, 67th Division, could now, with the benefit of restrained allied operations, continue digging deeper, fortifying, laying in supplies and ammunition, and bringing troops into the complex of caves, fortifications, and trenches a short distance directly north of Pork Chop. UN reconnaissance patrols could move forward of Pork Chop day and night, observe, and report their observations. Air attacks and artillery fire could continue as needed, the 1st Battalion's infantry companies could continue planning and rehearsal of the raid, but there would be no raid—not in June.

In China, North Korea, the Soviet Union, and its client states, for more than thirty-six hours, nothing was said of the prisoner release in the state controlled presses, while the American government and its UN allies scrambled to confront the dilemma Rhee's actions posed.

In a bid to ensure the truce did not fall apart, Gen. Mark Clark and the chief UN negotiator, Lt. Gen. William Harrison of the Army, delivered a written apology to the Communists, specifically blaming Rhee for the "escape" of the twenty-five thousand NKPA. The Communists grudgingly accepted the apology in a meeting with Harrison on 20 June: "They suggested that Clark track down the 'escapees' and reimprison them for a proper exchange, but knowing full well that this task would be impossible, they did not press the issue. Instead, they rightly posed the larger questions:

What was to be done about Syngman Rhee? Could the UN Command bring him under control? Would an armistice include the ROK government? If not, would the ROK government abide by its terms, or would it continue the war alone?"[18]

The delegation sent to Seoul by President Eisenhower, and led by Assistant Secretary of State Robertson, conceived a three-step strategy for negotiations with President Rhee. Their objective was to secure Rhee's cooperation on the armistice. In applying the first step, they intended to reason with the ROK president, promising a long-term mutual defense treaty, full support for a twenty-division ROK Army, and untold billions in military and economic aid. If the first step failed, the delegation would try a gigantic bluff. Rescind the previous offers and threaten to withdraw all American forces from the peninsula, leaving the South Koreans to their fate. If the bluff failed, they were prepared to stage a coup d'état, code name Operation Everready, and replace Rhee with a more amenable South Korean leader.[19]

More Letters Home

On 22 June, while the prisoner release crisis swirled in the South Korean, American, and allied governments, Dick Shea again wrote Joyce: "I have a few moments, then I must clean my weapon, and perhaps tomorrow, rather tonight I mean, I will have some more time to write. At present I'm in my sandbag command post (similar to one of those in the watercolor) at the base of a cliff." He carefully explained that his platoon was still in "semi-reserve," and their 60-mm mortars were indirect fire support for A Company. The mortars were positioned on a ridge to the rear of Hill 200, which was part of the MLR, and with their high, arching rounds could reach the "main battalion hill," Pork Chop, a thousand yards to their front. A forward observer was on Hill 200, with the company. "He phones back, or radios, where mortar rounds are landing, and adjusts fire from there to get us on the enemy."

With respect to the 57-mm recoilless rifles, he explained they were usually attached to rifle platoons and were direct-fire weapons. That is, the high velocity of fired rounds resulted in a nearly flat trajectory, making the 57-mm essentially a "line of sight" weapon.

Like Dick Inman, Dick Shea took note of the combined forces of the UN while he continued to map the company positions and learn the intricacies of the company's defensive positions:

Yesterday morning I set out at nine o'clock to the right end of our line, the ridge of which 200 is the left end. I went to the Colombian unit on our right, Company "B," Colombian Battalion, and mapped the positions of the platoon which joins first platoon of our company. I understand why so many people take Spanish in school. I expected great difficulty talking with them, but the military terms are so similar that it was quite easy. Platoon: palatoona; Squad: escuadra; grenadier: granadero; Sleeping bunker: dormitoro (dormitory); Company Commander (captain): Commander (el Capitan). And when I wished to record weapons and fields of fire, if the weapon was not actually there for me to see, I only had to ask for "machine gun" or BAR, as they understand since they are Americano weapons they use, and to determine the caliber only had to write down 30 or 50 and have them point to the correct one.

In the course of the day I went from their sector down the ridge through 2000 yards of trenches and fighting positions to Hill 200, mapping every position. . . . By dark I turned [the five foot long map] in to the company commander.

His thoughts then flowed from the more artistic side of him, dreams of longing for home and family, then his wakening to the sounds of gun fire, which seemed at first a part of his dream:

It is so pretty here. One regrets the caution that must be maintained, but does not forget it. Neither I nor anyone I know of forgets why they are here, even in moments of appreciation of the beauty of this country. The thought always runs: Such a beautiful land, why must this devastation go on; the hills are so bright in the sun, but this is no place to go walking. . . .

Last night I dreamed about [my brothers] Bill and Bob and me, and Pop was holding a big party in the large field in front of James Farm house, a squash field—and we were running all around setting up things, the three of us, so we could give a shooting demonstration he had commanded to back up a boast he had made. I woke up, and there really was shooting going on all right. . . .

Now I say good afternoon. . . . I love you immeasurably, and I am miserably lonely, xoxo Dick[20]

On Thursday, 25 June, Baker Company's Dick Inman wrote:

Dearest Family,

I have a little time to write this morning, so I thought I'd drop you all a bit of "un-newsy" news.

Today marks the beginning of the fourth year of the war in Korea. I am just as tired of the war as I would be had I spent all three years over here. However, things over here are rapidly "coming to a head," so to speak. You can just about feel it in the air—at least I imagine that I can! Either there'll be a truce, a withdrawal of U.N. troops, a U.N. offensive (very unlikely, I think), a Chinese offensive, or a movement of U.N. troops or U.S. troops into reserve support! "Somethin's gonna come o' that!," anyway.

We'll just have to wait and see—but probably not too long. Again I'll have to say, "By the time you receive this, you'll know more than I now know!" Things are happening so quickly, y'know.

. . . I got official notice that my Purple Heart has been awarded to me. I was top of a list of about 60 men on the orders for award! Holy cow! I am all right, if you think I may be hiding something. After looking in the mirror, tho', I believe I'll be carrying a scar above and to the left of my left eyebrow. Not too big, probably, but noticeable. I consider myself blessed that that mortar fragment hit where it did, instead of an inch lower. I'm lucky that I still have two good eyes! Ah, well—"the breaks of war . . ."

The company is busy rehearsing and re-rehearsing an imminent raid on a trouble spot near Pork Chop—don't know whether or not we'll be permitted to go thru with it or not—it takes an approval of the—yes, that's right—*Department of the Army* to put the plan into action! It'll be quite an affair—we'll have such support that we feel almost flattered—all the Army has will be turned toward our area—if our company is chosen for the attack, we will have been given a real honor, more or less a nod over the other companies in the battalion—and, as a result, our morale is pretty high!! I feel personally good because my platoon has been appointed as the platoon to do the real job—demolitions, and destruction of the positions, plus screening for the entire raiding party. I hope everything turns out all right.

Yesterday and the day before I had time to work on a little personal affair. About half a month ago I received a letter from a Major Paul O. Siebeneichen, who is in charge of the guided missiles research and development work at Redstone Arsenal. He told me to transfer from Infantry to Ordnance Corps, and then request an assignment to Redstone. Now, I've never had a definite affinity for the branch of Ordnance, but if that's the branch which handles the Army's missile program, I guess I'll accept it!

So, yesterday and the day before I set the wheels in motion for a branch transfer to Ordnance. This morning the papers . . . went to regiment. . . . [They] have to go to division, Eighth Army, and then to theatre, and finally to Washington. So, maybe (in a year or so!!) I'll be in guided missiles finally! I sure hope so. I think that field offers so much future. I'd kinda like to get into it. Perhaps a branch transfer would remove me from this Korean mess. On the other hand, maybe the war will prevent my getting the transfer. If it does come, the Lord knows when it will.

Things here don't change. Rumors are running rife all through the G.I. Armies. Intelligence reports conflict: reported heavy Chinese movement *south* in some parts—and reports of them pouring *concrete* bunkers in others; one indicative of offense, the other of defense—who knows?

I know *one* thing! I'd sure like to be home! I would swim in Rainbow Beach with everyone, play with Bonnie, talk with my folks, make love to my wife, and, generally, live again! Maybe this Korean business will end before too long. Let's all hope so. Sometimes the future is so uncertain! But I've so far refused to be bitter, although I have pretty good attacks of fierce nostalgia now and then! But that's all included in our privilege to live and love. I miss you all very much.

Write soon.

Love, Dick

P.S. Sorry I dropped the first two pages in the mud.[21]

Dick Inman's second experience with a Chinese mortar barrage earned him his first Purple Heart. When he wrote of the mortar attacks on 4 June, he had not told Barbara or his family of the wound or the near miss to his left eye. His "P.S." referring to the mud on the first two pages of the letter verified that Korea's monsoon was in progress.

On 26 June, the day after Dick Inman wrote of his purple heart and plans for the future, the Communists were continuing to build their strength along the central front, predominantly in areas facing ROK divisions. The CCF buildup on the central front, to the right of the 7th Division, posed a serious threat to the entire UN line. As a result, General Taylor and the Eighth Army staff concentrated heavily on preparing to defend against a major assault. Still wrestling the POW release crisis in Seoul, and uncertain of the enemy's intentions across the rest of the 155-mile line, the Eighth Army staff was slow in taking the wraps off combat patrols in the east and west flank corps, the corps which anchored the line on each coast. Not until 29 June, in the face of the growing enemy threat, did the 7th Infantry Division receive authorization to resume combat patrols.

In the 1st Battalion of the 17th Infantry Regiment, plans and rehearsals to raid the Rat's Nest had continued. Prior to the 7th Division's reorganization, 3d Battalion of the 17th had been rehearsing for the mission, but they now had responsibility for defense of another sector. With the division front organized into a three-regiment front, and each regiment's sector with three battalions on line, the question of which company in the 1st Battalion would receive the mission depended largely on the weekly rotation onto and off the Chop, and when the raid would be given the go-ahead.[22]

The monsoon season now brought frequent rain. Dick Shea wrote Joyce on Monday, 29 June, describing the monsoon's effects:

> We had been behind hill 200 all night, the artillery thundered and flashed, and flares lit up the sky and valley, but the incoming was elsewhere and we slept sound, though chilly, under a sky that held no rain for us this night at least. But the creeks and streams are swollen and swift. The monsoon season is upon us, and everywhere the roads and trails turn to mud, then knee deep soup. Yesterday our vehicles began using snow chains to combat the mud. Going to the bivouac area where our company is quartered, Scotty, the driver, drove his jeep along the stream bed, which was smoother, better road than the oozing earth on the bank above. Last night as we were to move at seven, I went ahead with a small detail of men, two jeeps and a trailer, to build a foot bridge across the now raging torrent of the bubbling little stream I have described to you, behind 200. As the men pulled back yesterday at dawn, they had to wade knee deep in water, and we did not want them to get wet clothing and boots and have to sleep out in them all night.

Though rumors and optimism about a truce still permeated the UN lines, the buildup on the CCF's central front increased the likelihood of continued strong offensive activity by the Chinese. The rain storms that swept the peninsula almost daily rendered American air power less effective, and the enemy would surely take advantage. Dick's 29 June letter to Joyce told of Able Company's mission as the monsoon season continued: "This reserve company has the mission of blocking the valley road leading to our outpost position, the hill [Pork Chop] beyond 200, so each night we must move up in case we are needed. But it has been quite some time since the Chinese bothered our sector. Therefore we only keep our communications, radio and telephone, 'hot' (someone listening on the loop from all CP's) all the time and the bulk of the men sleep. They pull the telephone shifts like guard."

He had begun his letter,

Dearest Joy,

I love you sweet girl—I'm tired and sleepy but I could love you so snuggled in your arms. . . . Yesterday I went to mass and communion at Regimental headquarters, and I served mass. And afterwards Father Ruesnock invited me to eat with him at the mess there, and we had an enjoyable meal. He is about 32 and very interesting to talk to, and the time went by quickly. I left the company at 10:30 but did not return before 2:00. . . .

. . . Just this morning I learned that Harold Scharmer is in this company, the first platoon. I saw him lay down a letter addressed to a family in New Milford, and I asked if he lived there. The mail clerk told him I lived there, but I said no but you did. He said he lived there 11 years but now they were in Paramus. I asked if he knew Don and Joyce Riemann and he said that he did, that he played soccer with Don. He's a very fine boy, this morning with his rifle slung across his shoulder, his helmet slightly askance, looking healthy enough, not too tall, slight of build, about 5'8", with a two days growth of blond beard. I will see him more often and will keep an eye on him because it helps when someone here watches out for you. I know I have people taking care of me, and they don't say so, but things indicate that.

Then he turned to the welfare of the forty soldiers in his platoon:

One comes back from the front . . . tired, and so we have a few hours each morning of rest. The reason I was up and met Hal Scharmer was because I was trying to obtain cots for the men in the company here I had found sleeping on the ground. They accept most anything, and had I not decided to look into our 12 tents before turning in myself they would have had to pile brush on the muddy floor, about 12 men together. They have such a hard time getting anything they want, if it is not there they do not expect it. I have told them to complain to me about anything they need. . . .

Then he wrote of his duty toward his men, and his responsibilities as an officer:

The duty of the officer has always been toward the men first, but the trend is toward self-comfort. There are things that seem impossible which are only made so by rank stupidity and laziness—but I have found that a good psychological kick in the right place gets things moving. There is no reason why this war should not be conducted on a 24 hour basis. I am here and my only interest in the thing is that I must do it, and as I must, I will, until as quickly as I can I can come home. What I am doing will make the time go swiftly for I am always busy—not doing what I am told to do, for then I would lay back and ride with many others, but what I know should and must be done, which my fair one, does not include close contact with one individual known affectionately by those in the ranks as Joe Chink. To wait to do only what you are told to, to me appears to be a miserable existence.

Then came Dick Shea's unit spirit, humor, and love of art:

. . . Yesterday afternoon I spent making three signs to add to those already along our roads. All other units have something:

A BRIDGE TO BUILD, A ROAD TO DOZE
CALL ENGINEERS, YOU BUFFALOES

IT ONLY TAKES A LITTLE MORE TO GO FIRST CLASS.
GO BY BUFFALO.

FROM THIS LOFTY VANTAGE POINT YOU ARE PRIVILEGED
TO VIEW THE BEAUTIFUL PASTURES NOW
ROAMED BY THE WHITE BUFFALOES.

But even our battalion hasn't been mentioned yet. So I made these up with ammunition box tops painted olive drab, with red and gold lettering and gold crossed rifles which I carved out of slats.

Last night on the way to the bridge we put them up right at the cross roads near battalion forward headquarters. They look sharp.

. . . Now I will sign off because I must catch a few hours of sleep. . . . Good morning sweet, I love you—I answer letters tomorrow. Now I sleep, now I love you, tomorrow I be with you again, soon such a tomorrow, I pray.

All my love, forever and ever,

Dick

In the three-way correspondence of family, Barbara Inman, still the new bride, wrote her husband's parents frequently. On 30 June she wrote of her fears for Dick Inman's safety:

Dear Folks,

. . . The last time I wrote I told you I hear from Dick about every other day. Then, suddenly his letters stopped coming—and I *finally* heard from him yesterday. 2 letters. (I imagine you did too.) So, my heart left its crowded place in my throat and stomach flipped back into place. He has been on outpost duty for three weeks—a while back he seemed so pleased that his platoon was commended by two command- ing officers and given the critical position on Pork Chop—but he was so thankful in his last letter to be off of that "hot spot."

Seven of his men were pretty seriously wounded . . . he hadn't had a bath since the first of June, ate C-rations for two weeks, and was bone tired. (Said he'd lost weight.) Then, in his second letter, his spirits were high—he was rested, had a chicken dinner, showered, shaved, and even had a new pair of fatigues—then he had to finish his letter abruptly because he had been ordered to take his platoon out to clear some Chi- nese near the hill. Half the time I don't know what to think—whether he's fighting, or pulled back or what. The latest news broadcasts con- cerning the fighting on the Central Western Front have pretty much set me on my ear—he drew a diagram once of his position and the ROK 1st Division that has been doing so much heavy fighting were to the left of Dick's Regiment. I can't help worrying and hating this whole mess—but I just know in my heart that Dick will be all right. He has been gifted with so much—such a good mind and such capabilities, that he has a much bigger mission in life. Still—I'm so disgusted with "truce" meetings. Maybe (and it *is* possible) I don't understand many things behind the headlines, but I think the U.S. should pull their troops out of Korea. Well, I won't go into my views on the subject, but the strongest emotion I've felt all day is *Anger.* (Oh, I "emote" all the time anymore.) . . .

. . . To keep me from getting melancholy and bored, Dick also gave me quite a task concerning his book. . . .

. . . I still write to Dick every day, but I'm sure running low on news—one of these days I'll be listing what I've had to eat for each meal.

Bonnie, Mary Jo tells me that you've become quite an expert swimmer and diver. You put me to shame.

I hope you have some success with your garden.

Write when you have time.

All my love,

Barbara[23]

At the end of June, Eighth Army intelligence estimated total enemy forces in Korea numbered 1,090,900 with approximately 353,000 at the front, an on-line increase of 42,300 over May. Included in the more than one million total were an estimated 10,000 Soviets and their satellite personnel. On line were eight CCF armies with elements of seventeen divisions in contact and ten in reserve, an increase of five divisions since 31 May. At the eastern end of the line were two NKPA corps, with five divisions at the front and one in reserve, a total of 262,000 troops. The Eighth Army estimated the enemy suffered 16,600 casualties in June pursuing their increasingly aggressive "limited objective offensives."[24]

Aside from the more aggressive limited objective attacks in June, Eighth Army and 7th Division intelligence took note of other activities that spelled trouble for UN forces and the 7th in July. Eighth Army informed General Taylor that counterbattery fire by CCF artillery doubled to approximately five thousand rounds. The 200 percent increase inflicted twelve killed in action and forty-four wounded in UN artillery units, plus three guns damaged, two slightly; forty-eight trucks damaged; and four bunkers destroyed. The 7th reported 105 rounds of 152-mm enemy artillery struck the division's sector—fired from units facing the ROK's II Corps, to the right of the division. This was the big gun's first appearance in the enemy's artillery arsenal, and its range and striking power were impressive.[25]

Major Units under Eighth Army Control, 30 June 1953

U.S. I Corps	U.S. IX Corps	ROK II Corps	U.S. X Corps	ROK I Corps	ROKA	KMAG	Army Reserve
1st KMC RCT	ROK 2d Div	ROK 6th Div	ROK 7th Div	ROK 21st Div	Northern Security Command	Advisory Groups with ROKA units	ROK 11th Div (less Div Arty)
U.S. 25th Div, Kimpo Provincial Regt, Turkish Brigade	U.S. 2d Div, French Bn, Netherlands Bn, Thailand Bn	ROK 8th Div	ROK 20th Div	ROK 15th Div	ROK 22d Div		5th RCT (less Arty Bn and Engr Co)
Commonwealth 1st Div	U.S. 3d Div, Belgian Bn, Greek Bn	ROK 3d Div	U.S. 45th Div, Phil 14th BCT		ROK 25th Div		187th Airborne RCT (less Arty Bn)
ROK 1st Div	ROK 9th Div	ROK 5th Div	U.S. 40th Div				
U.S. 7th Dv, Colombian Bn, Ethiopian Bn	ROK Capitol Div		ROK 12th Div				
1st Marine Div							

Abbreviations

Arty	Artillery	KMAG	Korea Military Advisory Group
BCT	Battalion Combat Team	Phil	Philippines
Bn	Battalion	Prov	Provisional
Div	Division	RCT	Regimental Combat Team
Engr	Engineering	ROKA	ROK Army

(1)	17th Infantry Regiment
(2)	31st Infantry Regiment
(3)	32d Infantry Regiment
(4)	73d Tank Battalion
(5)	48th Field Artillery Battalion
(6)	49th Field Artillery Battalion
(7)	57th Field Artillery Battalion
(8)	31st Field Artillery Battalion
(9)	15th AAA (AW) Battalion
(10)	13th Engineer (C) Battalion
(11)	7th Medical Battalion
(12)	7th Reconnaissance Company (Attached 25th Division)
(13)	7th Military Police Company
(14)	7th Signal Company
(15)	7th Quartermaster Company
(16)	7th Division Band
(17)	7th Replacement Company
(18)	707th Ordnance Battalion
(19)	Headquarters and Headquarters Company

Attached Units

(1)	Kagnew Battalion, Ethiopian Expeditionary Forces in Korea
(2)	Colombian Battalion
(3)	187th ROKA Field Artillery Battalion
(4)	7th Counter Intelligence Corps Detachment
(5)	505th Military Intelligence Corps Detachment
(6)	2d Platoon, 567th Ambulance Company
(7)	3d Platoon, 61st Engineer Searchlight Company
(8)	1st Platoon, 388th Chemical Smoke Generating Company

In the 7th Infantry Division, the end of month casualty figures came in from the regiments, battalions, and companies. June's totals remained substantially the same as for May. Among the Americans, 1 officer and 38 enlisted men were killed in action, with 7 officers and 154 enlisted men wounded. The Ethiopians lost 2 killed and 16 wounded, and the Colombians 3 killed and 16 wounded. KATUSAs, South Korean soldiers fighting as members of American units, suffered 4 killed and 31 wounded. The totals for the four allied countries represented in the 7th Infantry: 48 killed in action, 224 wounded.[26]

Uncertainty remained. Though many serving in Korea believed the armistice could come any moment, no one could say with the slightest bit of confidence when it would come. Communist pressure on the central front remained intense, the POW release crisis unresolved, while the 7th Division's July combat and reconnaissance patrols were to continue as scheduled—plus one planned raid on the Rat's Nest.

The "quiet," if it could be called quiet, gave scant hint of the hell about to visit Pork Chop Hill.

8

THE BEGINNING

ON 2 JULY, BARBARA AGAIN WROTE TO DICK INMAN'S MOTHER
and father:

> Just me again. I wanted to send these pictures. Doesn't it make you
> angry and helpless to look at those barren, dismal hills and know that
> is what we're (Dick) is fighting for?
>
> I haven't heard from Dick since I last wrote you. I certainly hope that
> by this time they have put him on R&R (rest and rehabilitation). He's
> never mentioned to me that he was due for it, however Dick Finch . . .
> told me that the soldiers are kept on the front for six months—then sent
> back for 5 days.
>
> By the way, if you get a magnifying glass and look at the pictures,
> you can see black dots in the sky—which are either shells exploding or
> airplanes.
>
> Hot weather is still prevailing here. (That's my news item from
> Iowa.)
>
> Lots of Love,
> Barbara[1]

The same day, Thursday, 2 July, Dick Inman wrote home once more:

Dear Family,

Sorry I haven't written lately, but of course there's always plenty to keep a fella busy around here. I always enjoy getting your letters. Thank you for continuing your writing even tho' I'm not able to answer as often as I'd like!

Things haven't changed much here. We're still up on the line, and tonight I go on combat patrol to the east side of Pork Chop. The 17th Infantry must be indispensable to the front-line duties of the Army! I don't think we'll ever be pulled into the rear! I suppose my grandchildren, and your great-grandchildren, will still be slugging out this slow, "unreal" war—sometimes things look rather bleak as far as the future is concerned, but sometimes things look fairly (relatively) bright. Of course, whenever I think of coming home, I get a glimmer in these bleary eyes again! My future is in the hands of God and the ebb and flow of universal fortune! I don't think a man could be in combat long without realizing or learning to believe in a sort of predestination. And I suppose it's true that there's no such thing as an atheist in a foxhole. War has a settling influence on some people, I think. I think a lot of things over here, but mostly I just think about you folks and Barbara and home in general.

Sometimes the homesickness in my heart wells up so that I feel I'll burst with it. But I've resigned myself to this type of existence for some time to come. I'll either be so happy to get home that I cry all over myself, or I'll be so numb I'll just sit and stare at the old familiar surroundings in Vincennes and Indianapolis. When the time comes, I'll certainly be glad to get back in the good old U.S.A.!

I've been overseas for some 2½ months now, but it seems like 2½ years! I can just remember what it feels like to walk down a city street and look at the carefree people, the signs, and the busy buildings and streets—traffic! I say I can remember—but I have almost forgotten what it feels like! By the time I return to home and loved ones I shall have forgotten! But "that's the breaks of war," so they say over here.

You know what I'd like, if you could send it to me somehow—airmail, if possible—a copy of the good old Vincennes Sun-Commercial! I'd read it through with misty eyes and trembling fingers, from front to rear! That would be a good parcel—a piece of home, more or less! Could you arrange it, please?!

Tomorrow afternoon I'm going to have my picture taken! It will be taken by a Public Information Office man for an article in Sports Magazine. I guess they want pictures of men who were "prominent" (ahem!) in Army (West Point) athletics and who are now in Korea. . . . I guess I'll give them a real heart-breaking picture and story!

Barbara has the names of possible publishers to whom she'll send letters and copies of the "book" we have fitted together. I figured she hasn't anything to do and you folks have so much to do that it wouldn't be fair to have you handle all of our business. Now, she may need a lot of help so if you have a good idea of any publisher or "pusher" for the book, write her a letter and advise her further. It's sorta hard to conduct business from 9,000 miles away!

Anything you think up may come in handy so be sure to tell her of any outlet you think of. You have a couple copies of the thesis yourself, so do with them—send them—what and where you will!

Well, I must go to briefing now. Rounds are coming in fairly often right now! See you all soon—Love to all—

Dick—[2]

In the steady flow of correspondence from Dick Inman were copies of poems he hurriedly scribbled during free moments. Among them was "My Toys," which told of a boy's toy soldiers and armies and the reality of war as he now saw it:

> When I was quite a little boy,
> I used to get a thrill
> At playing with my soldier toys
> Back in the old sand-hill.
> I would wage imaginary battles
> While my toy soldiers would run
> Thru the make-believe roar and rattle
> Of a make-believe machine gun.
>
> And all the day long I used to sit
> With my warriors 'round the room,
> And use my Red Cross First-Aid Kit
> To bandage up their wounds,
> Or play at being grenadier,
> Or armored tank, or plane.

When I was small I had no fear.
In play there was no pain.

But, now that several years have passed,
I have a new outlook.
No longer is this game of war
Come from a picture-book.
For I learned soon after my childhood days,
And it's not been long since I was small,
That war was different from my play.
War wasn't that way at all!

Now the smooth sand-hill is jungle swamp,
And the toy soldier is me.
But where is that pillow-chested pomp
And the royal artillery?

What has become of my clean little toys,
And the beautiful sky blue,
The newly pressed clothes, the juvenile joys,
And the light hearted life I knew?

The roar of the play machine-gun
Is so loud that it hurts my ears
And the fun I had with the First-Aid kit
Has now changed into fears
The fear of grown men living still
With a leg half-missing, or a hand that's gone,
Being carried from the smooth sand-hill
To a first aid station at the break of dawn.

And the shiny soldiers that cluttered the porch
Now splash in the sticky mire
With the tanks and the trucks . . . And the hot sun's scorch,
And the bombs, and the smoke, and the fire . . .
And when the little toy soldier runs,
It's not in children's play,
But it's for cover from enemy guns,
'cause wars are played that way!

So the sickness that tugs within my chest
Is not the fever of tropic parts,

But the black disdain of war, and the next,
That's forever in my heart.
For now I know what it's all about
Why good men have to fall—
It's because most people haven't found out
War isn't that way at all.[3]

In early June, plans had been set in motion to destroy the Rat's Nest. Throughout the second half of the month, increased enemy activity was reported all along the 7th Division front, and was most evident in the area of Hasakkol. Specifically, the enemy was engaged in an intensive fortification program, providing positions from which an attack could be launched against the division. Observers noted revetments from which Chinese artillery pieces were capable of firing into the division rear areas, and sharply increased enemy armor activity was noted in the area in front of the 7th, with armored vehicles firing into friendly positions.[4]

In June, the 1st Battalion of the 17th began rehearsing to raid the Rat's Nest, but, as previously indicated, Eighth Army prohibited aggressive ground action from 18 to 29 June, due to the prisoner release crisis and ongoing truce negotiations. Dick Inman alluded to the raid in his 25 June letter home, saying B Company was rehearsing for an important mission, and his platoon had a central role in the operation. However, hope remained the Rat's Nest could be destroyed without committing ground troops in an assault. Any raid aimed at Chinese outposts or MLR positions implied possible heavy casualties, because operations would have to be conducted against well-prepared, deeply dug, fortified positions in close range of the enemy's MLR positions on Hasakkol and Pokkae.

The Americans fired numerous artillery and mortar barrages at the Rat's Nest, and called in air strikes. The artillery barrages included the heaviest, most destructive weapons in the field, 155-mm and 8-inch guns, but it was virtually impossible to loft rounds directly into the cave entrances. Both types of weapons had generally south to north trajectories, thus the west, east, and north facing openings to the complex gave the Chinese good protection against incoming artillery and mortar rounds. Three air strikes failed to hit the complex.

Among the air strikes was a night drop on 3 July, a full load of thirty-three 500-pound, high-explosive bombs from a B-29 piloted by 1st Lt. Paul R.

Trudeau (not related to the 7th Division commander) and carrying a crew of nine more, including the copilot, 1st Lt. William J. "Pat" Ryan, West Point class of 1951. Diverted from their primary target because of weather conditions and the priority assigned the Rat's Nest, they flew radar guided to the target and released the bomb load at an altitude of three thousand feet on a single pass over the area northeast of Old Baldy. The bomb run paralleled the MLR to ensure a better chance of hitting the assigned target without stringing the bomb load into UN positions.

An aircraft flying above and parallel to an MLR guarantees sharp enemy reaction, clouds or no clouds, especially the CCF and NKPA. The diverted B-29 mission proved no exception. The big bomber came under heavy fire from CCF defenders and due to battle damage, Lieutenant Trudeau made a decision to recover at Itazuke Air Base, Japan, where depot level repair facilities could quickly get the big aircraft back in commission. When they landed there were 168 holes in the aircraft.[5]

On Saturday, 4 July, American Independence Day was at hand. The Communist pressure near Kumsong was increasing, as were preparations in front of the 7th Division—and plans were well under way for a heavy CCF attack on the central front. The Eighth Army, I Corps, and the 7th Infantry Division had some far less ambitious plans of their own.

Charlie Company's Raid on the Rat's Nest

The May discovery of the Rat's Nest by the 17th's Easy Company screening patrol was a clear indicator the enemy was moving relentlessly toward Pork Chop with the intent of close-in, short-notice assaults. Under cover of darkness the CCF's 200th Regiment was slipping men, equipment, ammunition and other essentials into the cave and tunnel network, where, during the day, the Chinese burrowed deeper, tunneled ever closer to the Chop, and added to their assembly area, essentially undetected and untouchable. This was the tipoff the Chinese planned to attack Pork Chop in force, but no one knew when. The fortifications could hide a substantial number of soldiers, and a prisoner confirmed the CCF kept a company in reserve in caves within the complex.

Time was running out. If the Rat's Nest was not destroyed, the threat to Pork Chop increased. The raid on the complex became a necessity, and

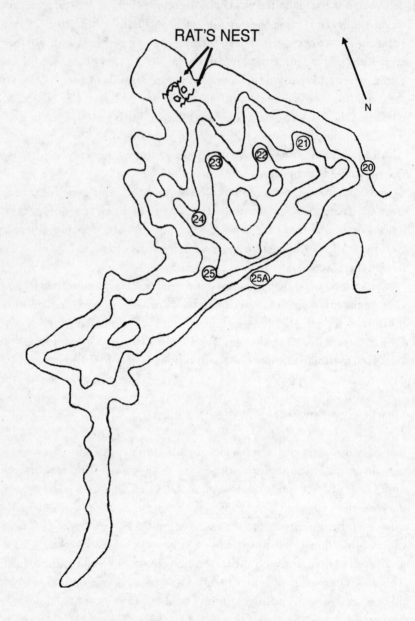

RAT'S NEST

N

20
21
22
23
24
25
25A

Charlie Company, 1st Battalion, 17th Regiment's raid on the Rat's Nest,
4 July 1953. Numbers 20–25A represent outguard or listening posts and
identify key ridges or "fingers" on Pork Chop.

Charlie Company, the 1st Battalion's reserve company, drew the mission. Able Company was on outpost duty on Pork Chop and Baker Company manned the MLR on Hill 200.

During the period from the Rat's Nest's discovery until the mission began, Charlie Company rehearsed seven times, three times at night and four during daylight hours. Most of the rehearsals came in the period between 29 June and early the morning of 4 July, the day intentionally selected for the operation. Right from the beginning, the 1st Battalion commander, Lt. Col. Rocky Read, heavily involved himself in planning and preparation for the raid.

The 1st Battalion was Rocky Read's battalion, and he was a highly respected commander who led by example. As a thirty-four-year-old commander who led by example, he was physically fit, tough, possessed high standards, and demanded his officers and men meet those standards. He asked nothing of his men he would not ask of himself. If any of his companies received an operations order, he would be there ensuring his men were well trained, had a carefully worked out plan, were prepared with everything they needed to perform the mission—plus all the support necessary to make the operation go as planned and be successful. If there was a "hot spot," a fire fight involving one of his infantry companies, Read would go immediately to take a firsthand look at the situation. He was the consummate professional soldier, and as the raid on the Rat's Nest would soon demonstrate, was also a sensitive, compassionate commander.

The raid plan required Charlie Company to go by truck to the assembly area which normally doubled as the reserve company blocking position behind Hill 200. There they received final instructions, a double load of ammunition, and all the grenades they could carry. After dark the company moved three rifle platoons in column, in two single file columns, one on each side of the access road, from the assembly area onto Pork Chop. Able Company, on outpost duty, occupied the Chop's defensive positions, and the early morning raiders would pass through Able en route to their objective.

The maneuver plan called for one rifle platoon, in the assault, to sweep the enemy positions and a rifle platoon, minus the platoon's weapons squad and one rifle squad, to follow in close support. The sweep would be from west to east from Finger 24, across the valley between 24 and Finger 23, and up the western slope of 23, through the enemy positions. The detached weapons squad, with two .30-caliber machine guns, and the rifle squad would move north on Finger 23, which connected Pork Chop and Hasakkol. The weapons squad would set up and fire on the route coming from Hasakkol to prevent the enemy from reinforcing. The rifle squad would go forward and make contact with the enemy, then pull back, to draw the Chinese away from their positions. When the enemy reacted from their main positions, the leader of the assault group would give the order to begin the sweep of the main enemy positions using automatic weapons and hand grenades.

Following immediately behind the initial screening and assault force, the support platoon minus, with its first squad in a skirmish line, would sweep for friendly casualties. The second squad, equipped with five-pound TNT satchel charges to place in enemy fortifications, would assist in evacuating casualties after throwing their charges. One weapons squad was to provide fire support and flank security on the west flank. Each group would lay communication "hot loop" wire from the departure positions on Pork Chop to their initial assault position. A third platoon, commanded by Lt. Anthony M. Sutera, would remain in reserve on Pork Chop, providing fire support, prepared to reinforce or extricate the raiders if trouble developed, and send screening patrols when the raiders returned. Radio silence was to be maintained by each group until contact with the enemy.

Lt. John J. Drury commanded the assault platoon, which departed Pork Chop's positions at 2:15 A.M. 4 July. The 1st Squad led off, followed by the 2d, 3d, and 4th Squads. The 4th Squad, the weapons squad, dropped off the column and set up some distance down Finger 24, to cover the other three squads by firing on Hasakkol, and protecting the west (left) flank of the raiders. The squads of Lieutenant Banfield's support platoon, commanded by Sergeant Dennis and Sergeant Woods, moved out fifty yards behind Lieutenant Drury's platoon and formed a skirmish line.

As Drury's assault platoon and supporting squads moved down Finger 24, Master Sergeant Cazzort's diversionary force moved out onto Finger 23 and down toward Hasakkol, past an outguard position, with one weapons squad and one rifle squad. Approximately 200 yards past the outguard position (OG 22) the weapons squad, led by Corporal Brownell, set up their two machine guns. From there Sergeant Cazzort and Corporal Weathers led the nine-man rifle squad to the point of Finger 23. Shortly thereafter, a planned six to eight minutes of friendly mortar preparation fire struck the

Rat's Nest, followed by the ten-man diversionary force's move forward to make contact with the enemy. As Sergeant Cazzort and his men started forward, a heavy concentration of enemy mortar rounds began falling among them, and he ordered the force to move back to shell and bomb craters twenty-five yards to their left rear. Corporal Weathers yelled he had been hit. Cazzort jumped from the shell crater, went to Weathers's aid, and helped him withdraw to the bottom of Finger 23, on the east side.

WHEN ENEMY mortar rounds began falling among the raiders, answering preplanned countermortar fire, assisted by MSQ-10 radars behind the MLR, came soon thereafter. The counterbattery fire came from the 49th Field Artillery Battalion and other UN artillery and mortar batteries supporting Charlie Company. The volume of artillery, mortar, and other supporting fires from both sides picked up rapidly. Before the raid ended near sunup, 57- and 75-mm recoilless rifles, M-46 Patton tanks with direct firing 90-mm guns, M-16 track vehicles with quad .50-caliber machine guns, all on or in front of the UN MLR, had joined the battle in support of Charlie Company. On the left flank of the raiders' platoons, on Finger 24, Sgt. William Webb's weapons squad, with its two machine guns, joined with Corporal Brownell's weapons squad on Finger 23, the raiders' right flank, with frequent supporting bursts into Chinese positions which had shown themselves with muzzle flashes. Before the fight ended Webb's two guns would fire approximately two thousand rounds and Brownell's, fifteen hundred.

The supporting UN fires did not go unanswered. The enemy quickly determined the origin of the force bearing down on their positions, and recognized that UN reinforcements and operational commands would most likely be coming from Pork Chop. The CCF's mortar and artillery rounds began falling on Pork Chop and likely avenues of reinforcements for the raiders, and before night turned to day, approximately thirty-four hundred rounds would fall on and near the outpost. Charlie Company's two machine-gun squads also did not go unanswered. The enemy could see their muzzle flashes as well, and lobbed mortar rounds into their areas— fortunately with little success. Both squads kept steady pressure on the enemy throughout the operation, in spite of the CCF mortar fire, tenacity that did much to increase the operation's success and avoid more Charlie Company casualties.

Once in a position out of the mortar fire, Sergeant Cazzort set up a horseshoe-shaped perimeter, facing toward Hasakkol and the Rat's Nest. When enemy mortar fire ceased, the squad began receiving small-arms fire from the front of Hasakkol and Pokkae. Corporal Brownell's weapons squad, having planned to rejoin Cazzort's diversionary squad, started to move toward their position, but saw six soldiers coming toward them fifty yards away. Brownell believed Cazzort's squad might have been confused and were coming to join them instead. Brownell yelled at the six men, who promptly hit the ground and opened fire. They were Chinese.

Private First Class Lewis heard the enemy shots go past him and saw Brownell fall, wounded in the foot. Corporal Brownell ordered the machine guns to set up again and fire on the enemy. Brownell then returned fire and saw several run back toward enemy positions east of Finger 23. Some in Sergeant Cazzort's squad saw the Chinese retreating from Brownell's machine guns, and opened fire. They believed they saw three wounded. Brownell next called the Charlie Company commander, Lt. James J. Balduzzi on Pork Chop and told him he had been hit.

A few minutes after the supporting mortar fires lifted, and while the diversionary force was engaged, Lieutenant Drury's platoon started the assault element's sweep from Finger 24 toward 23. Sergeant Johnson's squad was on the left, extended into the valley between Hasakkol and Pork Chop. Corporal Wilson led the center squad, and Corporal Crouse commanded the right flank squad, nearer to Pork Chop's defenses. They moved down the east slope of Finger 24 and up Finger 23's west slope. In the valley they discovered an irrigation ditch six to eight feet deep with ten to twelve tunnels running upward, toward Pork Chop. Two of the assault platoon's men, who were in the irrigation ditch, fired into the tunnels and threw grenades. As the assault advanced up the western slope of Finger 23, all members of the platoon began to fire into every cave and position they saw.

As the three squads in the assault platoon pushed farther up the western slope of Finger 23, Corporal Wilson's center squad heard the sound of burp guns firing, but the sound seemed distant, as though coming from the east side of Finger 23. When the assault platoon reached the crest of the finger they encountered a wounded Chinese soldier. Three Americans opened fire, killing him. The assault platoon continued with marching fire until they reached the eastern side of the ridge, where they ceased fire, and continued toward Finger 22. When they crossed 22's crest, they flushed three more Chinese soldiers who fired at the raiders, then ran for the valley between Hasakkol and Pokkae. Drury's men returned fire, drawing a yell from Master Sergeant Cazzort. The return fire had passed above Cazzort's two diversionary squads.

Drury's platoon, less Sergeant Johnson's left flank squad, continued their withdrawal around the base of Pork Chop, moving into the valley between Fingers 22 and 21, while Sergeant Cazzort moved his two diversionary squads up 22, and picked up the wounded Corporal Brownell, who had not been evacuated. Johnson's left flank assault squad, led by Drury's platoon sergeant, Sergeant Craft, had begun to lag behind the platoon's line of advance because concentrations of enemy mortar were continuing to fall between them and Corporal Wilson's center squad. When Drury, with Wilson's and Crouse's squads, reached Finger 22, Johnson's squad had fallen 150 yards behind the line of advance, and Drury had noticed most of the enemy mortar rounds apparently aimed for the assault platoon were falling to their right, farther up Pork Chop's slopes, and heavy concentrations were falling on the outpost. Both Drury and Craft decided the best routes of withdrawal into Pork Chop's defenses were up the east and southeast slopes of the outpost. Drury brought Wilson's and Crouse's squads up the hill's east shoulder, and Craft and Johnson brought Johnson's squad farther to the southeast, up over the cut between Pork Chop and Hill 200.

Five minutes after Lieutenant Drury's assault platoon began their advance from Finger 24 toward the Rat's Nest, Lieutenant Banfield's support platoon, with its satchel charges, moved toward the objective. Sergeant Dennis's squad was on the left, toward Hasakkol, with Sergeant Woods's squad on the right, toward Pork Chop. As they moved out, enemy mortar rounds began falling with greater accuracy on Banfield's two squads. Nevertheless Banfield's men pushed on.

As they proceeded up the western slope of Finger 23, an enemy soldier suddenly raised up in his fighting position, preparing to fire. Pvt. Nathaniel Waite caught sight of him first, and fired before he could react. Waite saw him fall to the floor of his protective hole, and kept moving. Private First Class Bettencourt and another soldier discovered a large pile of spoil—evidence of digging—and a deep cave running under a large rock. Bettencourt heaved a TNT charge into the cave. Farther left, toward Hasakkol, Sergeant Dennis threw a charge into a tunnel dug into the east side of Finger

23. To Dennis, the explosion sounded "far away," convincing him the tunnel was deep.

The support platoon's two squads began moving more slowly, becoming separated by the mortar barrage. Wood's right flank squad began encountering grenades and small arms as they neared shell craters on the east slope. Enemy mortar and artillery concentrations increased to heavy as they approached the crest of Finger 23, but they continued through, firing at the enemy positions as they moved over the top. Grenade fragments and small-arms fire wounded Sergeant Woods and a medic. Mortar shrapnel wounded another man, as the enemy barrage continued intense, finally driving Woods's squad back over the crest, dragging their wounded, to take cover in the craters. Circumstances forced Woods to alter his squad's planned route of withdrawal, and he elected to return, bringing the wounded up a more direct route, Finger 24.

Sergeant Dennis's left flank squad was receiving small-arms fire from the south slopes of Hasakkol and numerous mortar rounds were landing near the right flank of his squad. They pressed their advance, continuing to fire into enemy positions, and throw charges and grenades into tunnels and caves. Over the top of Finger 23, down into the valley between 23 and 22, and over the crest of 22, they went. Having lost wire communications immediately after the raiders opened fire, and unable to contact the company CP on their radios, Dennis was finally able to radio Sergeant Cozzart's diversionary force, which was ahead of them. Shortly after crossing Finger 22, Dennis's squad picked up wounded Private First Class Hernandez from Sergeant Cozzart's force. Dennis and Cozzart, who had three wounded with him, agreed the best route to bring the wounded back onto Pork Chop was through Outguards 20 and 21. Enemy mortar fire on Finger 22 was too intense.

When Sergeants Dennis and Cozzart reached the outpost, and counted their men, two were missing: Private First Class Sullivan and a KATUSA, Lee Kil Yung. A screening patrol was immediately organized in Charlie Company's 3d Platoon, led by Lt. Anthony M. Sutera. In the 3d Platoon, the Charlie Company reserve platoon for the raid, several men had already been wounded by the enemy's artillery and mortar barrage which had been falling on the hill for more than three hours. Wilson, Lopez, Olivares, and Matthews had all been hit. When Matthews left to be evacuated he handed Cpl. Henry Baker his BAR. Henry, from Portland, Oregon, and squad leader in the platoon's 3d Squad, went with the screening patrol.

The patrol included a radioman, the platoon sergeant, S.Sgt. Harold H. Hackett of Mattoon, Illinois, the 3d Squad's leader, Baker, and three other men. Both missing men, when last seen, were believed to be in the area between Fingers 23 and 24. Private Sullivan, when last seen, was on the east side of Finger 23, firing his BAR toward the low point on 23—"the cut"— between Hasakkol and Pork Chop. Thus the screening patrol planned to move down the valley between the two fingers.

Harold Hackett had volunteered for the Army immediately after completing high school, at the age of eighteen, entering 12 June 1951. He attended basic at Fort Leonard Wood, Missouri, and went to antiaircraft artillery training at Fort Bliss, Texas, for six weeks before being assigned to Fort Meade, Maryland, as a radar operator. While at Fort Meade, he met his future wife, Phyllis, who lived in Cressona, Pennsylvania.

While at Meade, once a week at Reveille formation, he heard an announcement of overseas assignments available. One week he decided to volunteer. He did, and was told, "You're going to be an infantryman." From there he went to Indiantown Gap, Pennsylvania, for infantry training, then received orders to report to Fort Lewis, Washington, on 10 November 1952, destination Alaska. He and Phyllis decided to marry and said their vows on 1 November. After a brief honeymoon he left for Fort Lewis, and she remained at home in Cressona.

As is often the case in wartime, orders change, and Harold, after three to four weeks at Fort Lewis, departed by ship to the 1st Cavalry Division in Japan. When he arrived in Japan, the 7th Division was still in Korea, refilling and retraining after its battles at the Iron Triangle and service at the POW camps on the island of Koje Do. The 7th needed replacements badly, and the Army changed his orders again.

He went by ship to Pusan, then by train to the 7th Division, where he arrived in Charlie Company late January. From winter's cold, through Charlie's several tough engagements, into sweltering, monsoon muggy July, and now Harold Hackett found himself "on point" with a screening patrol, looking for two of Charlie's own, both missing after the raid on the Rat's Nest.

The patrol moved out at early daylight, down the valley between Fingers 23 and 24, Harold in the lead—"on point"—carrying his M-1 rifle, armed and ready, the radioman close behind, and Lieutenant Sutera at the rear of the patrol. Henry Baker, carrying his newly acquired BAR, was toward the rear of the column, near the platoon leader. They carefully worked their way down the valley, and after some distance, Harold saw a body to his right front, sitting erect. At first he concluded it was Lee Kil Yung, the missing KATUSA. He carefully approached close enough to see it was the booby-trapped, bloated body of a Chinese soldier. Suddenly the sound of heavy machine gun fire began echoing loudly off the valley walls, and everyone in the patrol hit the dirt. At first, Harold believed the fire was coming from Pork Chop—supporting fire. Then the sound of more firing told him it was not. He aimed his rifle toward the area he believed the enemy was firing from, a bunker on the slope of Finger 23, and squeezed off only one round before the enemy gunner found his mark.

A burst of fire struck the ground close by Harold Hackett, just to his right, and one round came in above his rifle stock, tearing through his right cheek, just beneath the cheek bone. Instinctively, he jumped up and ran ten to fifteen yards to the rear to escape the fire, and the patrol began pulling back toward Pork Chop's defenses. Henry Baker opened up with covering fire, at first backing up the hill. He then saw Hackett climbing the hill, obviously wounded in the face. Baker moved back downhill, took Harold's rifle to lighten his load as the platoon sergeant climbed back toward Pork Chop under his own power, and entered the trenches, bleeding.

A medic gave him first aid and took him to Pork Chop's evacuation landing, where a T-18 APC was backed up to the entrance of the engineers' tunnel, loading. He walked through the doors for the ride down the access road. Enemy artillery and mortar rounds continued to fall on the Chop, its south slopes and in the valley between the outpost and Hill 200. The APC's driver instructed everyone on board, "Tie yourselves in good! We're getting the hell out of here!"

Next came the wild, hurried ride down the hill, around "clobber corner" to the collection point behind Hill 200. From the collection point behind Hill 200, Harold Hackett went by litter jeep to the battalion's aid station and finally to a Mobile Army Surgical Hospital (MASH) for a two-week stay.

Behind him, on Pork Chop early the morning of 4 July, the company commander, Lieutenant Balduzzi, organized another screening patrol, intent on taking a route through the cut between Pork Chop and Hill 200, moving northwest around the east shoulder, across Fingers 21, 22, and 23 in front of the Chop, and hopefully finding Charlie Company's two missing men. The plan included smoke in front of Hasakkol and Pokkae. Artillery laid in the smoke rounds, but the smoke was ineffective. The Chinese sighted the screening patrol, and drove them back with well-placed mortar fire.

When Lt. Col. Rocky Read received word of Charlie Company's casualties, he pleaded with General Trudeau to let him send another patrol to retrieve the two missing soldiers. Trudeau, a tough, yet sympathetic commander, denied Read's request. The frustrated battalion commander lifted his eyeglasses from the bridge of his nose and brushed tears from his cheeks as he listened to Trudeau's denial of the request. Read suffered as nearly all combat commanders do, wondering if he had made the right decisions and adequately prepared his soldiers for the mission, though he well understood a rescue attempt would likely mean more casualties and a questionable probability of success.

The Rat's Nest was damaged but still intact. Among the raiders Charlie company suffered thirteen wounded in action, with two missing, one of the two believed killed in action. Returning raiders counted three enemy soldiers killed and four wounded. Estimates were four more killed and another three wounded. The raiders claimed seven tunnels partially destroyed.[6]

The counts and estimates did not include CCF killed or wounded by the heavy volume of supporting UN fires in the four hours of sporadic fighting and heavy, almost continuous shelling by both sides. Though damage inflicted by Charlie Company's demolition charges proved insufficient to delay an attack by the Chinese, the men of Charlie Company, 1st Battalion of the 17th Regiment, had had the satisfaction of taking the offensive against the enemy for the first time in many months, if only for a limited objective.

A tired but proud Charlie Company came off Pork Chop on 5 July and rotated into MLR positions on Hill 200. Among them were the company's complement of medics, assigned from the 17th Medical Company. One was Cpl. Oral Grimmet, a West Virginian, who was "in charge"—the medics' leader. Another was James McKenzie, who tended the wounds of Wilson, Lopez, Olivares, and Mathews before they were evacuated that morning. None could know, however, serious trouble loomed for Able of the 17th, the men now manning Pork Chop. Nor did they have any inkling of the steady pounding they would take before they returned to the Chop four days hence. Sgt. Henry Baker would return to the Chop with Charlie Company, a platoon sergeant replacing S.Sgt. Harold Hackett. Next time on the hill, Henry Baker would carry the BAR Mathews handed him. The enemy had made plans, too, beginning several weeks earlier. A bitter struggle was in the making.

Baker Company Ambush Patrol

Before Charlie Company returned from its 4 July raid on the Rat's Nest, Baker Company had already received another mission, an ambush patrol out front of Pork Chop the night of 6 July. Lt. Dick Inman, who had been on combat patrol around the east side of Pork Chop on 2 July, received the assignment from Baker company commander, Lt. William J. Allison. Inman would lead the patrol of twenty men plus one other officer through the outpost's east sector and down the north slope. Accompanying him would be twenty-one men, nearly all from his 2d Platoon.

Typically, the patrol would be divided into assault and support elements of ten men each, not including the patrol leader. Lt. Lloyd W. Brubaker, the new 1st Platoon leader who had arrived in Baker Company a week earlier, was to lead the patrol's support element. Staying behind to act as leader of 1st Platoon in Brubaker's absence would be S.Sgt. Anton Cicak, the platoon sergeant. Among the remaining twenty men on the patrol were Pfc. Irwin Greenberg and Cpl. Harm J. Tipton, both of Baker Company's 2d Platoon, and Pfc. Clarence H. Mouser, a forward observer from the heavy mortar platoon, in Dog Company, the 1st Battalion's heavy weapons company. Greenberg would be in the assault element, Tipton and Mouser in the support element with Lieutenant Brubaker.

On 5 July, while Baker Company was in its reserve assembly area, Dick Inman briefed and rehearsed the patrol. Baker Company had taken its normal rotations onto Pork Chop, and except for brand-new replacements, its men had participated in the outpost's rebuilding and were familiar with the map and layout of the hill's defense network. Ambush patrols normally were men with experience on the line, and had been on day and night reconnaissance patrols. The capture of at least one prisoner was consistently an objective of an ambush patrol. An ambush patrol, nearly always a night mission, was not for green replacements unacquainted with patrol procedures or the enemy's behavior on the battlefield.

For communications and operational control, the 1st Battalion attached the patrol to Able Company's 2d Platoon, led by Lt. D. Willcox, whose platoon anchored the right, or eastern, sector of Pork Chop defenses. Inman's assault element was to move downhill out of the 2d Platoon area, angling down Finger 21 into a position in front of Able Company approximately ten yards below the outguard position, beyond a footpath, or Choggie Trail, as the GIs referred to it. The support element was to remain to the rear of the assault element, in position to provide covering fire if the assault element got into a fire fight, or needed to withdraw under attack. The support element would also double as a screening patrol if circumstances required.

Dick Inman and his patrol were to be tied into Able Company's communication net by wire—a hot loop—plus radio as a backup, and procedures between him and David Willcox included prearranged, brief calls, each signaling specific information or actions required of Dick and his patrol should fighting erupt. Otherwise, radio silence was the norm.

The patrol's rehearsal included various scenarios, or problems, involving enemy contact, and how the patrol would react to the contacts. Reentry and alternate rendezvous locations within Able Company's positions were identified, in the event they were called back into the perimeter while under attack.[7]

The evening Inman rehearsed his patrol, Chinese psychological warfare officers blared one of their frequent loudspeaker broadcasts at Able Company. From the hillsides to the north, Pork Chop's defenders first heard soft music, which faded in and out with shifts in the summer evening breezes. Then voice broadcasts began, and defenders heard demands they surrender. If they did not, the loudspeakers proclaimed, "You will all die." No prisoners were to be taken. "We will take Pork Chop even if we have to wade through blood."

The threat was not new. It was merely another broadcast in what had become standard nightly news over the nearly two years of trench warfare. The Chinese read off the names on the company roster over their loudspeakers the night Able Company rotated onto outpost duty. Nevertheless, the words and reading of the roster did not comfort green replacements just arrived on the outpost, nor was it popular with the more battle hardened veterans. Cpl. Dale Cain, a veteran who had traipsed up and down the Korean peninsula in two enlistments, had heard most all the loud-speaker broadcasts before but remained impressed by the lieutenant who had introduced himself as Dick, Dick Shea.

Cain, a radioman and switchboard operator in "Batt-Comm," in the 1st Battalion CP, where he had been recovering from wounds, including a broken foot, received on Pork Chop when Able Company was ordered on the hill in April, was now back on outpost duty. His wounds during the short, furious fire fight the morning of 18 April were insufficient to war-rant evacuation from the peninsula but sufficient to finally warrant his being kept off the line and sent to Batt-Comm until they healed. Prior to Charlie Company's raid on the Rat's Nest, Dale was told his battalion commander, Lieutenant Colonel Read, had received a request from the Able Company's executive officer, Lieutenant Shea. Shea wanted his return to the company, which was on outpost duty on the hill.

He was to report to Lieutenant Shea, be a radio operator for the com-pany, assist Shea in setting up another CP, and reinforcing and strengthen-ing Pork Chop's defenses. For the first time, when Dale Cain came back on the Chop, he met and began working closely with Dick Shea. Shea was supervising work to strengthen and improve fortifications, ensuring ade-quate ammunition, grenades, communications, rations, water, medical sup-plies, and weapons that were clean and ready. The company commander had been warned of aggressive offensive operations by the Chinese and, with his executive officer and platoon leaders, was preparing to defend against a strong attack.

Shea took Cain to a bunker near the company CP, from where they could see across the valleys north of Pork Chop. He explained to Dale what he wanted him to do, and for the next three days they worked together, preparing to better defend the outpost. By the end of the first day, Dale Cain and Dick Shea had carried boxes of C-rations, ammunition, grenades, and containers of water into the bunker, and Cain had set up a communi-cations net.

The net included a PRC-10 radio with an outside radio antenna, a phone hookup, and sound-powered, hot-loop phones patched to four Listening Posts. The installations complete, he ran communications checks with Able Company's primary radio operator, forward [artillery] observer, and battalion locations. Cain was frequently at Shea's side as he made the rounds to bunkers and firing positions between 6:00 and 9:00 P.M. each evening 2, 3, 4, and 5 July. In those four days, Dick Shea made an indelible impression on a young Corporal Cain, who had first served in Korea in the early, frantic days of the war, as an underage sixteen year old who had successfully lied about his age, to enlist in the Army and "go to Korea." Cain particularly noted Shea's response when the Chinese loudspeakers were blaring their messages. When Shea saw or heard the younger GIs' expressions of fear, he would reassuringly put his arm on their shoulders, giving them words of encouragement: "Don't let it get to you. Everything's going to be OK. We're in good shape."

When Shea made his rounds with Cain close by, they checked all the company's positions, including Pvt. Robert E. Miller's fighting position. Bob Miller, a rifleman in 1st Platoon, had become acquainted with Lieutenant Shea as well, in an easygoing, humorous way. He admired the company's new executive officer. He knew Shea was a "true leader." Shea was greatly interested in the men's morale, a "Do as I am doing" officer. He pushed the men hard to be ready at all times and talked to Miller about the subject, as he did others, checking to see Miller had an adequate supply of ammunition and grenades and telling him to keep his rifle clean. At five o'clock each day, soldiers fired a clip or a short burst of ammunition from rifles and automatic weapons to ensure weapons were clean and in good working order. Dick Shea, he said, "wouldn't ask anything of soldiers he wouldn't do himself." He would fight beside the GIs, put his life on the line with them.

Miller noticed Shea was always neat and clean in appearance, despite the long days on outpost duty, on the MLR, or in a bivouac area when Able Company was in reserve—and his combat boots were always shined when the company was out of the dirt, dust, muck, and grime of outpost duty. Even on outpost duty, and on the MLR, Shea's appearance always set an example. Shea liked to challenge his men to maintain their appearance and cleanliness, from head to toe. One day, while the company was in reserve, Miller decided he would take up the Virginian's challenge and polish his combat boots to a high shine—then compare them with Shea's. He did, which delighted Shea and drew complimentary remarks about Miller's appearance and boot shine. For his trouble, Miller took much good-natured ribbing from the men in his squad. Miller was describing what other men in A Company knew of Dick Shea, and the night of 6 July, Bob Miller would need everything he learned.[8]

LATE THE afternoon of 6 July, Baker Company boarded two and a half ton trucks and moved from their reserve area to the checkpoint, up against the bluff near the end of a finger which descended from Hill 347 toward the floor of the valley behind Hill 200. Trenches followed the finger's ridge line down from the crest of Hill 347, part of the MLR trench and bunker system. At the checkpoint was a medical bunker—the collection point for wounded coming off the MLR or Pork Chop—a communications bunker, and an armor bunker near which a platoon of M-46 Patton tanks routinely parked, with one M-46 reveted next to the bunker.

The tanks were part of the blocking force intended to keep an enemy assault from penetrating the MLR and advancing up the road which crossed behind Hill 347 deeper into the division rear. All vehicles traveling the road to or from Pork Chop, or tanks or other armored vehicles on fire missions beyond "Clobber Corner," passed through the checkpoint. The checkpoint also served as one of two control points for scheduling APCs on and off Pork Chop, the other located on the outpost in the bunker adjacent to the evacuation landing.

Sunset on Saturday, 6 July, was 7:58 P.M. Near dusk, Baker Company formed two files, platoons in column, and walked from the checkpoint toward the defiladed blocking position at the base of Hill 200's south slope. They followed the tank trail, which branched right, off the access road, crossed the valley floor and spring which ran between the checkpoint and Hill 200, toward "Clobber Corner." The small spring Dick Shea had referred to in his letter to Joyce was no longer a spring. It had been raining heavily for five days, and it was raining when Baker Company waded across the swollen, rapidly flowing stream. The crossing necessitated the men's care to avoid being swept off their feet or slipping down and fouling their weapons in the deepening, muddy water. With the company were medics, including Pfc. William J. "Buster" Duncan and Pfc. William Helliean, a black soldier.

Lieutenant Inman's patrol split off from Baker Company and made for Pork Chop. As part of the planning for the battalion reserve mission, the company commander instructed his platoon leaders, should there be an assault by the CCF, and their company was committed to reinforce the hill's defenses, they would rendezvous with the members of the ambush patrol, in the positions the platoons normally occupied when they were on outpost duty. Except for a few new replacements, the officers and men were all familiar with the outpost and its defense network. The 1st Platoon, led by acting platoon leader Sergeant Cicak, would join Lieutenant Brubaker in the hill's right flank positions, at the platoon CP. Inman and 2d Platoon members usually occupied the left sector of the hill.

At 8:30 the evening of 6 July, Dick Inman's ambush patrol left A Company's 2d Platoon defenses and angled downhill to take up their positions in the north slope, spread west to east, straddling Finger 21.[9] A heavy rain was soaking the ground and trench networks already wet and muddy in the full-blown monsoon season. The storm meant more trouble for weapons daily cleaned of grime splashed into their moving parts. In the confusion and dashes through mud in a night fight, a dropped weapon, stumble, or fall into the muck could quickly render a weapon useless, jammed by wet, soupy grit. This night the heavy rain portended far more trouble than jammed weapons.

Able Company: Surprise in a Monsoon Rainstorm

As in April, intelligence had picked up information of an impending CCF assault in the 7th Division's sector, expected 6 July, probably near 11:00 P.M. As before, however, an assault precisely where, by how many, and on what objectives, was not known. The 7th Division chain of command had been alerted, and presumably the lessons of the March and April battles had been well learned. If so, all patrols out front of the MLR this night had also been told to be especially alert, although at least one rifle company commander had, in the past, chosen to withhold such information until his company's patrols were in place out front of the MLR or outpost positions.

In May evidence surfaced that all was not well in the hazardous missions of outguards and patrolling. The evidence regarding patrols appeared in monthly command reports, primarily the result of April's bitter fighting and S. L. A. Marshall's critiques of outguards, patrols, and unit actions being made available to General Trudeau and battalion and regimental commanders. Marshall bluntly criticized the practice of putting ambush patrols out front when intelligence appeared persuasive a major assault was expected on a specific date. He also identified a number of instances in April when, prior to posting, outguards had not been passed the word of a likely enemy assault. He further noted outguards often did not know how to react if the enemy suddenly appeared in force, obviously intent on attacking the outpost or MLR positions the outguards were responsible to warn of the enemy's approach.

In Able Company on outpost Pork Chop the night of 6 July 1953, whatever the status might have been in other companies manning other positions on the 7th Division's line, the supporting Baker Company ambush patrol, Able Company's outguards, its company chain of command, and the men on guard duty inside the perimeter had the information needed, were alert and ready. Word had definitely been passed, and on order of the company commander, at 5:00 P.M. all Able company weapons were again fired to ensure they were clean, operable, and loaded.[10]

Nevertheless, this night the Chinese found a way to surprise Able Company and the 7th Division, in spite of efforts to forewarn, the line regiments' training, heightened alert, and intense preparations to defend.

Under cover of the rain storm, a reinforced CCF battalion of more than seven hundred men began moving toward the left and right flanks, center, and rear of Pork Chop. The darkness and heavy rain had several effects, all bad. It masked sound, limited the ability of individual soldiers and forward observers to see much beyond three feet, hampered communications, and made UN tactical air support virtually impossible. The enemy had planned and timed their assault almost perfectly.

At 10:25, Pvt. Robert E. Miller, a rifleman in 1st Platoon, was asleep in Bunker 32 not far from Able Company's CP, Bunker 35. He was preparing for a turn on guard duty later that night. Corporal Cain and Lieutenant Shea, the executive officer, were in their bunker near the company CP, where Cain, Shea, and a medic slept and worked and Cain operated the additional company radio. The men were not asleep. Shea was acting company commander because Lieutenant Roberts, the commander, was off the hill. Cain's radio was on and fully operational, and, as always, he was attentive to traffic on the company and battalion nets. Able Company's outguards were in place in OG positions 20 through 25A, tied into the company's and platoons' hot loops.[11]

At the battalion checkpoint behind Hill 200, Pfc. Emmett "Johnny" Gladwell, a medic in the 17th Medical Company, was also in his bunk sleeping, while one or two other medics were sitting at a table writing letters by candlelight. The rain made sleep easier. Johnny, like all medics, was usually called "Doc" by the GIs, a term spoken in tones of admiration and respect. He was in a large, well-reinforced medical bunker. The checkpoint served as a collection point, the first stop for casualties coming off the outpost or MLR. From there the wounded were taken, usually by litter jeep or truck, to the battalion aid station, a mile and a half farther to the rear.[12]

Across the road from the medics' bunker was a tankers' bunker, where armored personnel slept—some of the men of the provisional platoon who maintained and operated the APCs which plied on and off Pork Chop's evacuation landing, and tank crews for the two platoons of tanks emplaced or parked temporarily at the checkpoint. A communications bunker was also at the checkpoint, an important part of the 1st Battalion's communications net linking the outposts and MLR.[13]

Frequently on duty in the communications bunker was Pfc. Robert L. Wilson of Tupelo, Mississippi. The jeep driver for 1st Lt. John Dashiell, the company commander of Easy Company, 17th Regiment, Wilson had been wounded in both legs on 6 February. He was hit by shrapnel from a mortar round while on a raid from outpost Uncle against Chinese-held bunkers on T-Bone. After a stint in the hospital and operations to remove some of the eighteen pieces of shrapnel, he was returned to duty. The company commander selected him to be his driver after Robert went on two more patrols with legs out of shape and not responding well when time to run during a fire fight. In addition to doing communications duty at the checkpoint, he ran wire when lines went down or were cut. This night he was driving to the communications bunker in his jeep, preparing to take his turn assisting the battalion and his company.[14]

At the battalion aid station two miles farther to the rear, Pfc. Lee Johnson, a West Virginian and close friend of Johnny Gladwell, also a West Virginian, was in the large aid station bunker sitting at a table writing a letter home by candlelight. Since shortly after ten o'clock, Lee had had an urge to go to the nearby latrine, dug a safe, sanitary thirty yards distance from the aid station, just across a small stream. Because of the rain, he resisted the urge, in spite of growing discomfort.[15]

A few miles to the southeast of 1st Battalion's aid station was the 32d Regiment headquarters and CP. Sgt. 1st Class Paul Anderson, a regular Army noncommissioned officer and the communications chief in regimental headquarters, was responsible for seventy-seven enlisted men on duty, in shifts, in the comm center. The center encrypted and sent the 32d headquarters' outgoing messages, and received incoming messages destined for the regimental commander and his staff. Paul had been a platoon sergeant in King Company of the 32d for forty-five days beginning in January. He knew the sound and power of artillery and mortar rounds, whereas most men under his supervision had never been on the line. Tomorrow, 7 July, Paul Anderson would complete his tour in Korea and begin the journey stateside, but a month earlier CCF artillery had convinced him he had better dig a small bunker into the hillside, for himself, at the base of the south slope of a hill about seventy-five yards from his communications center. He had been unsuccessful in convincing the soldiers under his supervision to do the same.[16]

Meanwhile, in the aid station bunker at 1st of the 17th's aid station, at 10:25, Pfc. Lee Johnson was about ready to relent to nature's insistence, when he heard a sharp, nearby explosion which shook the bunker. He recognized the sound immediately as an incoming artillery round.

Then in quick succession two more explosions, nearer. This was more than occasional harassing fire. Someone ran to the door of the bunker and yelled, "Hope no one in here has to go to the crapper. The place has just been blown all to hell!" Stunned, Johnson was slow to react at first. Then he remembered he had restrained himself for the better part of half an hour. His rain-imposed restraint probably saved his life. The incoming also meant the beginning of long sleepless days and nights for Lee Johnson and every other medic in the 7th Infantry Division, particularly in the 17th and 32d Regiments.[17]

Twenty-two-year-old Pvt. Henry Bakker from Rock Valley, Iowa, a mechanic in the 17th Medical Company motor pool, heard the exploding artillery rounds nearby. He was in his sleeping tent one hundred to two hundred feet from the motor pool. With other men in the tent, he scrambled to take cover in their foxholes at the base of the south slope of the hill a short distance to the north of their bivouac area. He had seen bodies of soldiers on stretchers with ponchos over them outside 17th Company's aid station and holding point during past battles. He would see many more in the days ahead.[18]

At the same time, rounds began slamming into the 32d Regiment's headquarters area, and Paul Anderson made for cover in the bunker he had dug into the hillside. By digging his bunker in the hillside, he had intended to ensure he completed his Korean tour of duty, still healthy. Not surprisingly, when the incoming began to hit and rattle the headquarters area, he was soon visited with formerly skeptical soldiers from the comm center, busily digging into the same hillside.[19]

At the checkpoint behind Hill 200, Lee Johnson's friend, Johnny Gladwell, felt the effects of incoming at almost the same instant Johnson had, except the enemy artillery was far more accurate. The first round to hit the checkpoint was a direct hit on the medics' bunker. The force of the explosion threw Gladwell from his bunk onto the floor, blew out the candle, knocked over the soldiers sitting at the tables, and momentarily filled the air with dust and gritty sand. Miraculously, no one was hurt. Their hard, spare-time work strengthening the bunker's overhead cover with extra bracing and layers of crushed rock and sandbags had done well for the men inside.[20]

Easy Company's Robert Wilson was just driving up to the checkpoint in a jeep when incoming began to fall. He quickly stopped his jeep, jumped out, and scrambled for cover underneath a nearby APC. When the shelling finally stopped, he discovered the APC was loaded with grenades.[21]

AT 10:25 P.M. the CCF had begun thunderous mortar and artillery barrages all across the 7th Division front, and into the division's rear areas. On the division's right, the Chinese launched similar barrages on the ROK 2d Division's MLR and outposts. On Pork Chop, in the bunker near the company CP, Pvt. Bob Miller awoke with a start, jolted to sleepy confusion by the sound of artillery slamming into the hills and valleys to the south of the outpost. All hell's broken loose, he thought. He left the bunker and entered the tunnel headed toward his fighting position wondering what was going on. Someone yelled at him to get his rifle. He turned around and ran back through the covered trench toward the squad's sleeping bunker to get his M-1 rifle, which was on a rack inside and above the bunker door. He turned left to enter the covered cross trench which passed the door of his sleeping bunker, and as he neared his bunker he was greeted by the sight of six or seven dead American soldiers lying nearby in the trench.[22]

Almost immediately Dale Cain's radio came alive with traffic. He was swamped with calls. From the outguards—the LPs—he heard reports of enemy coming in large numbers. He heard a patrol [the Baker Company ambush patrol] call in from somewhere in the valley below. "We're coming in." There were calls indicating the enemy was coming in on the outpost's left flank. Trouble was brewing—quickly. Dick Shea grabbed his helmet and hurriedly left the bunker, heading toward the threatened area. It was the last time Dale Cain saw Dick Shea.[23]

In the left sector of the outpost, in the 1st Platoon's 4th Squad, the weapons squad, Pvt. Harvey D. Jordan manned a water-cooled .30-caliber machine gun. Harvey and his ammo bearer, a KATUSA who doubled as the other half of his gun crew, immediately tensed at the sound of the heavy CCF barrage falling on the MLR and into the rear areas. They anxiously peered through the bunker aperture into the darkness and rain. To Harvey's right in another bunker was Pvt. David H. Johnson, with another machine gun. Johnson was on the hot loop talking with Jordan and the outguards on the slopes below their bunkers. Both Jordan and Johnson heard outguards' alarmed calls on the hot loop: "They're coming! They're coming! We're coming in!" Johnson saw them, too, and exclaimed, "Here they come!" Then the hot loop went dead.[24]

In the bunker to Harvey's left was Pvt. George Sakasegawa, from Salinas, California. Manning a BAR with his squad leader, Sakasegawa was of Japanese ancestry, and as a boy during World War II he had been interned with his parents in a camp in Poston, Arizona. He had two older brothers who fought in the famed 442d Regiment in Italy during that "good" war. Now, as a result of being drafted while in the University of California at Santa Barbara, here he was confronting onrushing waves of Chinese infantrymen on Pork Chop Hill.[25]

Within a few minutes flares fired by artillery and mortars began shedding their flickering light on the north slopes of the outpost and the valley between Hasakkol, Pokkae, and the Chop. In Private Miller's fighting bunker was his squad leader, Cpl. Charlie Brooks, who manned a BAR. As soon as the enemy artillery started, Brooks left the bunker to check the readiness of squad members at each of their firing positions, then returned.

He got his Browning automatic rifle ready and peered through the firing aperture, rain and flare lit sky, down into the valley below. In the valley, not far down the north slopes of Pork Chop he saw what appeared to be hundreds of Chinese infantrymen surging uphill. Brooks and the men in his squad, which included seven American and two ROK soldiers, watched and waited.[26]

The watching and waiting seemed both interminable and terribly brief. Luck is unpredictable at any time, and especially in war. At longer ranges, shells and bullets are random in their effects. They are not aimed at specific individuals. They are barrages or concentrations zeroed in on coordinates marking geographic locations on maps and the earth's surface, where the enemy is regularly observed or likely passing through; covering or supporting fire with rifles or automatic weapons aimed at areas or points where the enemy is known or believed to be; fields of automatic weapons fire preplanned for machine guns on offense or defense for the same reasons artillery or mortar barrages occur. Nevertheless, from long ranges heavy, concentrated artillery and mortar barrages, and covering machine gun fire, can decimate infantry units caught in the open, ricochet and rip through openings in bunkers, ruthlessly smash through overhead cover, cave in trenches and bunkers, and wreak havoc on defenders.

Day or night, at long range, overwhelming numbers of onrushing enemy infantry are both awe inspiring and fearsome sights. As their distance closes, and if their ranks are not shredded by artillery, mortars, grenades, and automatic weapons, defenders confront the harsh reality of close quarter, hand-to-hand fighting with the possibility of being overwhelmed by sheer weight of numbers. This is one of many times fear can destroy defenders' rationality and increase the killing on the battlefield.

At the end of a final surge in an infantry assault which carries overwhelming numbers into trenches and bunkers, when showers of hand grenades have failed to stop the advance, matters are far different, and far worse. Pistols, rifles, and submachine guns, fired in a close, seething, vicious fight, are aimed point blank at specific threatening targets, the closest enemy soldiers. With ammunition gone or weapons malfunctioning, bayonets, knives, rifle butts, empty weapons of any kind, fists, even helmets swung like clubs become brutish necessities for killing and survival.

The temptation to flee, run away, "bug out," take cover, hide, "go to ground"—not participate—hovers over soldiers, ready to pounce on and smother the will to stand their ground and fight. But retreat into a whirlpool of single-minded, all-consuming self-preservation is a disaster for individual soldiers, and potentially far more disastrous for fellow soldiers around them. Mutual support, one for another, must be the watchword.

Such fear-driven actions are intolerable for officers responsible for leading soldiers who are owed the best possible leadership an officer can give. Officers and noncommissioned officers are expected, and must deliver, a calming influence and correct, rational decisions under the most irrational circumstances. They are expected to radiate a lack of fear, exhibit unbending self-control and consistent steadiness, when inside they may be swimming in fear, terrified.

If in the attack or counterattack, the enemy rushes defenses with overwhelming numbers and firepower, defenders' luck is far more likely to run out. Luck did run out for many in Able Company late the night of 6 July 1953, for the CCF had sent overwhelming numbers against them, a ratio approximating four or five to one, at least equal the weight of the assault on Old Baldy's Colombians in March.

At 10:38, A Company reported to Battalion, "Receiving small-arms fire." The hill was about to be engulfed with swarms of enemy infantry. Another A Company soldier in Brooks's squad, Pvt. Angelo Palermo, said the attack looked like a "moving carpet of yelling, howling men—whistles and bugles blowing, their officers screaming like women driving their men up the hill." And as usual, among the lead elements of Chinese infantry, were young boys twelve to sixteen years of age, carrying no rifles or submachine guns, but loaded down with grenades and trained to pick up weapons others dropped, American or Chinese, and use them.[27]

As soon as the artillery began Lt. David Willcox called his outguards and Dick Inman's ambush patrol back into A Company's 2d Platoon sector and started rounds to check his platoon positions. When he reached the area of Bunker 51, where the patrol was to reenter the platoon position, some of Inman's assault element had already made their way into the perimeter, rejoining the support element. Inman was outside the position waiting for the last man to come into the trench. Private First Class Mouser, the forward observer from Dog Company, the 1st Battalion's heavy weapons company, and attached to the support element, saw Inman reenter the trench.[28]

BEFORE THE rising tide of CCF attackers reached the barbed wire at the outer perimeter on the center and left shoulder of the hill, men manning bunkers in those sectors received a second surprise. The Chinese had planned well and were ready to strike hard and fast. The rebuilding and strengthening of Pork Chop's bunkers and covered trenches was approximately 80 percent complete.[29] There were necessarily sections of trenches with no overhead cover, intended to have firing steps to permit defenders to fight from the trenches, but there were few firing steps completed.

Coming up the north slopes of the Chop, they were in five groups. One group of approximately two platoons surged toward the boundary between the 1st and 2d Platoons of Able Company, straight toward that part of the network nearest the covered trenches leading from the north slope's trenches and bunkers to the company CP, which was underneath and slightly east of the hill's highest point. Apparently intending to breach the perimeter, and enter the trenches between the two high points on the hill, they would cut the defenses in half and be in a position to rapidly overrun the covered trenches to the company CP. Another two platoons rushed directly toward the right center of Lieutenant Willcox's 2d Platoon sector, along and just east of Finger 22, intending to penetrate near the platoon CP, which was directly underneath the second highest point on the outpost. They were on a direct route to seize the secondary crest and pin defenders in place. The largest group, an estimated company, made straight for the hill's crest, intending to overwhelm defenders occupying bunkers on and either side of Finger 23, the long ridge line running across the valley toward Hasakkol. In the meantime, two more platoons, in separate groups, moved over the top of Brinson Finger, turned north onto the south slope and into the valley between the outpost and Hill 200. One intended to penetrate the left rear, while the other was aiming for the evacuation landing.[30]

In the two and a half months after the April battle, while Pork Chop's reconstruction progressed, Chinese reconnaissance patrols and observers on the higher hills near the outpost undoubtedly observed and mapped every single bunker and trench on the front slope of the hill, especially the positions of Pork Chop's automatic and direct-fire weapons. Invariably, the CCF used the intelligence well in their planning. The enemy came with carefully prepared assault teams. Each team had a definite objective and used bazookas, satchel charges, and flame throwers. Some used yellow

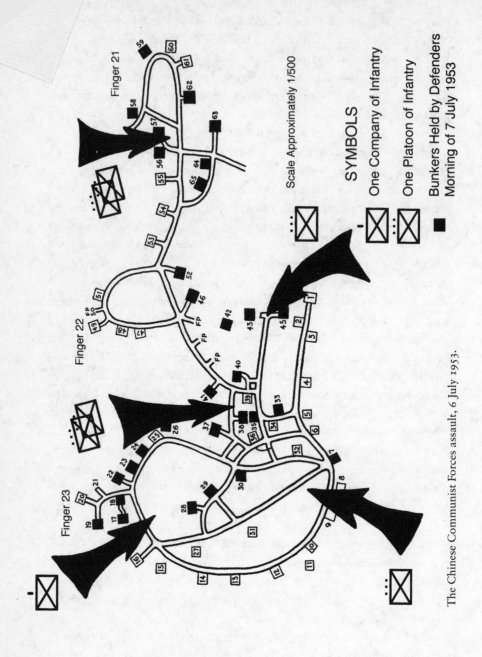

SYMBOLS

⊠··· One Company of Infantry

⊠ One Platoon of Infantry

■ Bunkers Held by Defenders
Morning of 7 July 1953

Scale Approximately 1/500

The Chinese Communist Forces assault, 6 July 1953.

View from a trench on the south side of the crest of Hill 200, looking west toward the peaks of Old Baldy (*left*) and Chink Baldy (*right*), illustrating the enemy observer's ability to observe the rear of both Hill 200 and Pork Chop.
Courtesy of Jack Roberts and John W. Phillips

sulfur sticks to produce acrid fumes, forcing men out of their bunkers.[31] Just before the enemy formations reached the defense's wire and broke over the trenches and bunkers, powerful, direct-fire weapons began bunker busting attacks on automatic weapons positions across the north face of Pork Chop. In 4th Squad, 1st Platoon, the effect was immediate and devastating.

Within an instant after the hot loop went dead, cutting communications with outguards and Pvt. Dave Johnson and his machine gun crew farther to Harvey Jordan's right, a direct-fire round, perhaps from a recoilless rifle

or T-34 tank's 85-mm gun, slammed into the adjacent bunker to his immediate right. The well-aimed round killed the two BAR men inside and
critically wounded the squad leader, who began screaming in pain. The
explosion knocked a large hole in the wall between the two bunkers, partially caving in both.

The squad leader continued to scream in pain. When the air cleared
somewhat and Jordan began recovering, he saw he was unharmed. He
attempted to fire his machine gun at the onrushing enemy. It spit one round
and quit. The explosion had damaged the weapon. He and his KATUSA
ammo bearer started throwing grenades. The next thing Harvey Jordan
remembered, an enemy grenade landed in the bunker aperture and exploded
in a blinding flash, knocking him backward to the floor while spraying
shrapnel into his right arm, and a piece that struck his right eye. His body
armor saved his life, but his KATUSA ammo bearer was dead.

When his vision cleared momentarily, he could not see from his right
eye. He looked up through the collapsed wall and ceiling of the adjacent
bunker. Standing on the lip of the trench line, silhouetted against the flare
lit sky, peering down into the wrecked bunker, Jordan could see Chinese
soldiers with burp guns pointed down into the bunker. He could hear his
squad leader screaming, "Kill me! Kill me! End it!" Suddenly Lieutenant
Barr, Jordan's platoon leader, appeared at the entrance to Harvey's bunker.
The squad leader's cries persisted.

"Do you have any grenades?" Barr asked. "No, all we have left are illumination grenades." "Give me one," Barr replied. Jordan handed him the
grenade; Barr pulled the pin and flung it through the opening into the collapsed bunker. It came to rest next to the squad leader, then fired, radiat-
ing a brilliant light which blinded Jordan and the Chinese soldiers standing
on the lip of the trench.

When the grenade's flare burned itself out, Barr was gone, and the Chinese reappeared at the lip of the trench, raking the bunker walls and floors
with their burp guns, killing Harvey Jordan's squad leader. Then, mercifully for Jordan, all went dark.[32]

In the bunker to Harvey's left, the mass of Chinese infantrymen soon
overwhelmed both George Sakasegawa and his squad leader. They held
their fire until the enemy was almost upon them. Sakasegawa remembered
emptying what seemed an entire clip of ammunition into one man, and he
did not fall. The enemy hurled grenades at their firing aperture, one of

them finally finding its mark. A blinding explosion. Sakasegawa received shrapnel wounds in his buttocks and both legs, but fortunately he could still get up and walk.[33]

THE CHINESE had moved forward onto Pork Chop under cover of the rain storm, one of several coordinated diversionary jabs which simultaneously struck at outposts Snook and Arsenal. At Arrowhead, an outpost six miles to the northeast in the ROK 2d Division sector, another major assault was under way. On Pork Chop, it was a saturation attack in such force that it quickly divided and isolated defenders, who could not support or reinforce one another. Communications within the positions were soon gone.[34]

When Dick Inman's ambush patrol returned to the A Company perimeter on the right shoulder of the hill, apparently with no one wounded or missing, incoming mortar and artillery had become intense.[35] In Charlie Brooks's squad on the left shoulder, suddenly, without warning, the entire area outside, above, and around their trenches and bunkers seemed alive with enemy soldiers. Everyone in 1st Platoon was in a fight for his life.[36]

In the center between the two high points on the hill, the Chinese swarmed into the trenches connecting the 1st and 2d Platoon positions, pushed on over the crest toward the rear slope, and battled their way toward the company CP. M.Sgt. Howard C. Hovey, Able Company's field first sergeant, was on duty in the CP when the assault came. Within minutes he and other Able Company soldiers were in a fierce fire fight to keep the enemy from seizing the CP.

On the right flank of the hill, contact was soon lost with the 2d Platoon's leader, Lt. David Willcox. After making his rounds to check platoon positions and see that Dick Inman's patrol was pulling back as enemy artillery continued, Willcox returned to his platoon CP. When he entered he immediately received a call from Pfc. Richard Baker, 4th Squad, who with Pfc. George H. Cunningham manned a machine gun in Bunker 53. "The Chinese are all over us!" he shouted above the noise. Baker had no more time.

Cunningham, the gunner, cut down a Chinese soldier, twenty feet in front of the firing aperture, hitting him in both legs. A hand grenade exploded in front of the bunker, knocking out the gun. The crew immediately reported the situation and Willcox, on hearing the report, promptly left the CP, heading toward the machine gun positions in Bunkers 54, 53, and 41.

Cpl. William R. Garman left the CP, following behind Willcox about ten feet, and witnessed some of what followed. Garman saw his platoon leader meet the machine gunner, Corporal McAuvic, from Bunker 54 and the two continued toward 53 and the damaged gun. McAuvic was carrying an M-1 rifle. As they were about to enter the bunker, enemy soldiers attacked both with grenades and burp guns but did not bring them down. They continued toward Bunker 41, but enemy soldiers pouring into the defenses "like a waterfall" in front and behind separated the two men, isolating Willcox between the two bunkers. The two men engaged in furious fighting to eject the Chinese from trenches near the left boundary of the platoon's sector, as well as the observation post at bunker number 54, which the enemy had taken.

In the melee David Willcox found himself in two violent, close quarter fights. He emptied his .45- and .38-caliber pistols at close range, killing five or six enemy soldiers in each encounter, before he was attacked by a Chinese soldier who came at him after David emptied both pistols and did not have time to reload.

David Willcox routinely carried three knives: his bayonet, a hunting knife he brought from the States, and a knife made from the steel of a Samurai sword in Japan. In the ensuing hand-to-hand struggle, Willcox killed the soldier with a knife. To his horror he realized he had killed a boy thirteen to fifteen years of age, a fact that haunted him for years.

He fought his way back to Bunker 53, and at a fork in the trench encountered Corporal McAuvic—with McAuvic's M-1 pointed at Willcox's face. Willcox had lost his helmet and his hair, typically, was crew cut. When the M-1 was shoved in his face, he croaked, "Mac?" certain he was about to be killed. "Lieutenant?" Voice recognition saved Willcox, and the two joined Cunningham, Baker, Pfc. Jesse Foster Jr., and four others who eventually took cover with them then were pinned in the bunker, isolated and without communications. When he came into the bunker, he told the men inside, "I was jumped. My carbine was knocked into the mud. When I picked it up, it only fired one more round. I've got to get a weapon I can depend on." Willcox, who entered the bunker with an open back wound, was given first aid by Richard Baker, who years later could "still feel the lieutenant's uncovered back bone with [his—Baker's] fingers."

A shaken Willcox asked McAuvic why he did not kill him when they encountered each other in the trench. Replied the corporal, "I knew it was you. The Chinese aren't that tall."

Once treated, Willcox posted himself at the entrance to the bunker, and kept the enemy at bay throwing grenades handed him by the men inside. While they fought with their weapons from inside the bunker, he continued throwing grenades until an enemy grenade landed nearby and exploded, wounding him again, this time in the leg. The men helped him back inside, and sandbagged the entrance to keep enemy grenades out. They remained in the position for approximately sixty-four hours, fighting off repeated enemy assaults. From outside the bunker the wounded Chinese soldier's moans could be heard gradually weakening throughout that first, long night.[37]

Lt. Dick Inman and his Baker Company patrol did not know the enemy also entered the trenches in the eastern sector of the outpost's defenses, between the patrol and the 2d Platoon's supply bunker. The Chinese had already overwhelmed several bunkers and trench segments in both sectors. Vicious, bloody hand-to-hand and close-quarter fighting was in progress as small groups of soldiers confronted one another in the alternating dark and flare-lit night.

Dick gathered his men and reminded them they would rendezvous with Baker Company, which would be the first company committed to reinforce Pork Chop if the battalion commander responded to the radio request. In the meantime the reassembled patrol must attempt to reach the 2d Platoon supply bunker, near the CP, where ammunition and grenades were stored.

As they moved toward the 2d Platoon CP, they could hear whistles, horns, and shouting Chinese infantrymen outside the trench and above them. In areas with no overhead cover enemy soldiers were just outside the lip of the trench throwing grenades into their path. To drive the Chinese back, they threw grenades from the dwindling supply they carried, and fired their rifles and automatic weapons at fleeting individuals and groups of enemy soldiers moving in the flickering, eerie glow outside the trenches. When they approached bunker 54 they met a rain of grenades thrown from inside the position, which had been seized by the enemy. Dick's men responded with grenades thrown toward the bunker entrance, trying to kill or dislodge its occupants.

A soldier emerged carrying a flashlight, yelling, "Prisoner! Prisoner!" There was momentary uncertainty as to whether he was Chinese or American, until he was recognized as an enemy soldier. One of the Americans shouted "Kill him," but Dick said no, they would take him prisoner. The Chinese soldier came forward with his hands up, and one of Dick's men started to search him. Suddenly, Cpl. Harm Tipton, a member of Lieutenant Brubaker's support element, caught sight of a grenade thrown from the darkness. He yelled, "Look out!" and every man scrambled and dived for cover as the Chinese soldier bolted and ran round a turn in the trench.

The grenade's explosion stunned but apparently did not wound anyone seriously. Recovery was quick, and they fired down trench, but were uncertain whether they hit the fleeing enemy. They pulled back a short distance from bunker 54, and Private First Class Mouser noted Dick Inman was limping. He had either turned his ankle or been wounded in the leg, perhaps by the grenade.

Inman decided again to fight their way through to the 2d Platoon supply bunker, but they were again driven back by Chinese grenades. Most of the patrol's weapons had quit firing. Ammunition was low, some weapons had jammed, and his men had no more grenades.

He and Brubaker decided to gather the men who had functioning weapons and send the others down the back side of the hill to the evacuation landing. They divided the remaining patrol members into two groups. The plan was to run parallel to the trench, making for the supply bunker and A Company's 2d Platoon, with Inman's group on the lower side, and Brubaker's group on the upper side of the trench. Brubaker and a soldier with a BAR would provide covering fire as his group ran past bunker 54. Inman's carbine and Pfc. Irwin Greenberg's rifle were all that remained operable for the men moving along the lower side. Inman would provide covering fire with his carbine. He radioed the patrol's situation, and probably their plan, to Lieutenant Willcox. He told Willcox he had a broken leg.

They moved out, undoubtedly in a low, running crouch, with Inman first out of the trench, stopping to provide covering fire so his men could rush past him toward the supply point.

Corporal Tipton and the three or four men who had no operable weapons stayed behind, waiting to make a run for the evacuation landing. They watched as both groups left the relative safety of the trench and disappeared into the blinding muzzle flashes, grenade, mortar, and artillery explosions, the buzz of bullets, and the shouts and screams of Chinese infantrymen seemingly everywhere on the hill. Brubaker and the man carrying the automatic rifle returned shortly, telling Tipton they could not get through because there were too many Chinese. Both had been wounded and headed for the evacuation landing.

Tipton decided to find Dick Inman's group to warn him and went around the lower side of the trench, moving east toward the 2d Platoon area, only to discover the group pinned down by burp-gun fire and grenades. He came up behind Irwin Greenberg, and Greenberg told Tipton that Inman had been hit and was lying on the ground about fifteen yards away. Greenberg told Tipton he would provide covering fire with his rifle if Tipton and a soldier from Able Company, Sgt. Alfredo Pera, would make a run to pull Dick to safety.

Irwin Greenberg squeezed off only one round before his rifle jammed, as Corporal Tipton and Sergeant Pera dashed to retrieve Dick. He was lying on his back. Harm Tipton got his hands underneath Dick's shoulders and Sergeant Pera lifted his feet. Tipton noted Dick was unconscious, and saw what he knew to be a massive, fatal wound on the left side of his head.

They started downhill with him, toward the concertina wire, which they would follow east to the trench leading to the evacuation landing. Chinese soldiers caught sight of them and began hurling grenades. Tipton and Pera had gone only five to six feet, desperately trying to carry him to safety, when a grenade exploded in their midst, wounding both men. Dazed and bleeding they could no longer carry Dick Inman and staggered downhill to the east, toward the 2d Platoon supply point where medics later treated them and they were evacuated to a field hospital.

The grenades kept coming, more of them. Irwin Greenberg and the men with him made their way past the second row of concertina wire, toward the west, to shelters near the evacuation landing and the tunnel leading to the Company CP. Their rifles had quit firing. They could neither attack nor defend save for their sheathed bayonets, their trench knives. Their circumstance was the same for tens, perhaps hundreds of Chinese and American soldiers isolated from their units, alone or in small groups. Men were moving about inside and outside the trenches of Pork Chop, many with inoperative weapons or out of ammunition, encountering one another in the confusing swirl of fighting, often hand to hand, trying, if they were wounded, to leave the field or help other wounded to safety, fighting to take and retake bunkers, firing positions, and trench lines—and survive.[38]

The hillsides, trenches, and bunkers were rapidly becoming littered with dead and wounded. Small clumps of defenders were isolated in bunkers and trench segments, fighting often against overwhelming numbers, running out of ammunition, unable to resupply themselves or join with others for mutual support. Communication between isolated pockets was impossible unless someone had a radio. The field telephones were dead, the wires cut by shelling or, if buried, sometimes shorted at the splices due to continued heavy rain.

From somewhere on the outpost a call came over the division communication net, "Flash Pork Chop! Flash Pork Chop!" Greenberg heard an American soldier yelling, "Take cover! VT's going to come in!"[39]

Within moments American artillery responded—massively. At 10:41, sixteen minutes after the first Chinese artillery rounds began crashing into the 7th Division sector, the division artillery reported to the division's CP, "Flash Pork Chop in progress." Not only did close-in defensive fires come pouring in, a request for VT on position brought added killing power to the artillery's response.[40]

"Flash Pork Chop" closed around the hill, sealing off attackers caught inside the steel horseshoe-shaped curtain around the outpost, while temporarily shielding defenders against follow-on assault waves. The VT exploding in the air above the outpost tore into the Chinese infantry caught in the open and hemmed in by the "flash fires." Those able to take cover inside bunkers, covered trenches, or in semiprotected shell craters could survive the killing air bursts unscathed. But "flash fires" and VT would not break the back of a determined enemy. There was only a pause. The battle was just beginning, though "flash fires" repeatedly dropped a steel curtain around the outpost as the night progressed, and defenders intermittently requested VT on position.

To compound what was rapidly becoming a serious situation, at 10:56 an Able Company call on the radio net reported enemy automatic weapons fire hitting the evacuation landing, which was adjacent to the main trench and engineers' tunnel leading into the Company CP and nearby supply point. The enemy was in the rear of the defense network, on the south side of the hill. Pork Chop was temporarily cut off, the access road interdicted.[41]

At 11:02 another call reported enemy coming into the trenches in the left sector, and that the enemy partly occupied the left sector. This was the area toward which Dick Shea had rushed when the first calls came over the radio Dale Cain was monitoring. Shea, the acting Able Company commander, called for immediate reinforcements. The Chinese were around and above the Company CP, on the crest of the hill.[42]

In the meantime, at division, regimental, and battalion CPs, radio and phone traffic filled the communications net, as hurried spot reports from Pork Chop came in with calls for reinforcements—and were passed up the line. Enemy artillery and mortar barrages falling on the MLR and into key targets in the rear areas punctuated the obvious. Though brief and hurried the information coming from Able Company made clear the situation was deteriorating rapidly. Important decisions were necessary, fast.

The Chinese had launched a major assault on the 7th Division's front, and it was becoming clear Pork Chop was the objective of their main effort. The power of their onslaught had carried into the outpost's perimeter, taken the hill's crest, and temporarily cut off its defenders. Before the night was over the defenders would count nine waves of attacking Chinese infantry.

Lieutenant Willcox's 2d Platoon had lost all communications with the company CP, and his platoon was now isolated on the right shoulder of the hill.[43] Inside the covered trenches and bunkers, Able Company was engaged in vicious, close-quarter, hand-to-hand fighting. Groups of defenders were cut off, one from the other, fighting almost entirely from their bunkers using rapidly dwindling supplies of ammunition and grenades which had been laid into the bunkers for just such an eventuality. Sometimes two or three men were fighting three times their number.

In the battle for the company CP, M.Sgt. Howard Hovey inspired the men around him. The highly respected "old man" of the company, a World War II veteran and an infantryman who had fought in General Patton's Third Army in France and Germany and helped liberate a Nazi death camp, was due to leave Korea soon. He planned to return home to his wife and three children, including ten-year-old twins Dean and Melanie—and retire.[44] This night he showed he was no "old man," and he was not ready to retire.

When word reached the CP the Chinese were coming into the trenches on the west shoulder of the outpost, he ran to a nearby trench to direct a hail of fire on the enemy, several times temporarily repulsing CCF attempts to overrun Able Company positions near the CP. When the enemy briefly relaxed their pressure, but held positions near the CP while they reinforced, he recognized the danger to the entire post. He returned to the CP, armed himself with a carbine and grenades, and moved from the cover of the trench where he could see advancing enemy soldiers approximately fifty yards away.

He charged them, pouring crippling fire and throwing grenades. His aggressive assault inflicted numerous casualties and checked their advance. Though wounded by automatic weapons he continued firing until wounded again, critically, by a napalm grenade. Believing the lives of others were still in danger, he grabbed another carbine and more grenades, and left the bunker area once more. He maintained his stand and kept firing his weapon and throwing grenades until mortally wounded by a grenade's direct hit. He fell in a bitterly contested area, where, like many others on Pork Chop, he could never be reached. His determined aggressiveness, courage, and valor in defending the CP held the enemy back, permitting its safe evacuation and setup at an alternate location adjacent to the evacuation landing.[45]

Able Company's losses in dead, wounded, and missing were heavy, but it was impossible to count them or the survivors of the first wave of CCF assaults. Most of Able's automatic and direct-fire weapons had been knocked out or taken, and the company's survivors were fighting desperately to keep from being completely overrun. The Baker Company ambush patrol had been decimated in the trenches, one of its officers dead, the other wounded and out of action, at least four enlisted wounded, and the rest out of ammunition or carrying fouled, inoperable weapons.

1st of the 17th's Reserve: Baker Company

Throughout the month preceding the attack the 17th, on order from division, held a company in reserve, and at night moved it into a blocking position immediately behind Hill 200. In the carefully selected, defiladed position the reserve company could react quickly to block enemy attempts to penetrate the MLR by advancing along the Pork Chop access road toward the checkpoint. From the blocking position the reserve company could also react rapidly to reinforce Pork Chop if needed. At the same time soldiers in the blocking position could take cover in bunkers at the base of Hill 200, well shielded from enemy artillery, but not entirely free of mortar

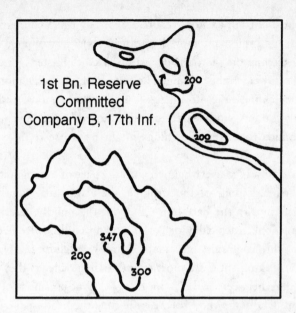

1st Bn. Reserve
Committed
Company B, 17th Inf.

Company B, 17th Infantry, departed the blocking position behind Hill 200 on foot at 11:08 P.M. on 6 July 1953, planning to reinforce Company A. The company arrived on Pork Chop at 12:37 A.M. on 7 July and immediately counterattacked.

rounds, which could be lofted high and dropped into the assembly area. Until the artillery and mortar barrage started at 10:25, the area where companies had taken up the blocking position had been virtually free of mortar attacks. Not so this night.

Baker Company suffered their first casualty on 6 July shortly after the barrage began, one man wounded by mortar shrapnel. Medic Buster Duncan watched the evacuation of his friend Private Coons, who received his fifth Korean War wound before the company left the blocking position that night. It was a wound that could well have saved his life. Baker soon entered the fight on Pork Chop.[46]

The thunderous artillery and mortar barrage immediately heightened Baker Company's alert status. They were ready when the call came from 1st Battalion at 11:02, to reinforce Able Company. They began moving out of their assembly area six minutes later. The 1st Platoon, led by acting platoon leader Sgt. Anton "Tony" Cicak, was lead in the column of platoons.

In two files, one on each shoulder of the access road, Baker Company moved around the foot of Hill 200, past Clobber Corner, drawing ever nearer the battle for Pork Chop. Lieutenant Allison, the company commander, with his radioman, moved up and down the column, passing instructions, keeping the platoons closed up. Medics Buster Duncan and William Helliean were in the column. The sounds of exploding mortar and artillery, the crackling, staccato rattle of automatic weapons, and small-arms fire grew louder—and nearer—as they moved farther up the access road. The sounds told everyone things might be worse than expected. They were.

Able Company was so overwhelmed with the pace of events on the outpost in the first half hour of the struggle, there was little time to pass specific information to the battalion CP about the rapidly deteriorating situation. Thus, Baker departed for Pork Chop absent knowledge of Able Company's plight. Their mission remained simply, "Reinforce Able."

They began taking sporadic mortar and artillery fire as they angled across the valley between Pork Chop and Hill 200, but most of it was falling on Pork Chop and the MLR. By the time the head of the column neared the evacuation landing the entire company had been forced to slow down and move to the right shoulder of the road, the uphill side, to be nearer cover. As they moved closer to the rear slope of the outpost they came under small-arms and occasional automatic weapons fire. Finally, at 12:37 A.M., 7 July, Baker Company called the battalion CP, reporting their arrival on the hill. While Allison could talk with Able Company on the radio, they had not yet made contact with the company.[47]

Contact with Able Company on the radio and a quick survey of the situation resulted in Allison's abandoning the planned rendezvous with Baker's ambush patrol. From a position near the entrance to the main covered trench, looking uphill, the company commander and men in the 1st Platoon could see Chinese soldiers silhouetted against the flare lit sky at the crest of the hill. The enemy already controlled the crest and were jumping into the trenches on the reverse slope, attempting to take the trench and bunker system, and fight their way downhill toward the evacuation landing. Undoubtedly in part due to a request from Able Company, he ordered an immediate attack, not yet aware of the enemy's approach from the west, toward the evacuation landing's rear—or their seizure of the hill's east crest. The enemy was about to gain control of Pork Chop's lifeline.

Not until 2:24 that morning did a call come from Able Company saying Baker had closed with them. In the interim, Allison found a wounded

Lieutenant Brubaker among the growing number of wounded in the large bunker immediately adjacent to the "engineers' tunnel." Brubaker undoubtedly told him of the shattered ambush patrol and defenders' dire straits at the hill's summit.[48] Allison, still in contact with Able Company via radio, later made another decision, changing Baker's mission.

Circumstances dictated their defense of the outpost's rear, to include the evacuation landing, the main supply bunker—full of weapons and ammunition—which was adjacent to the access road, the entrance to the main trench (engineers' tunnel), the two bunkers adjacent to the entrance, which included the bunker sheltering the wounded, and the hill's lifeline, the access road which climbed the hill's southeast slope to the evacuation landing.[49]

In the meantime, during periods when the rain tapered off or briefly stopped, forward observers on Hill 347 and a few men in Able Company could see groups of enemy approaching Pork Chop, intent on reinforcing their newly won positions. In addition to "flash fires," and VT on position, friendly artillery and mortars took the reinforcing groups under fire, while directing counterbattery fire on enemy artillery and mortar positions. From the MLR positions near Pork Chop also came close support fire.[50]

This was the beginning of a long, agonizing forty hours for the men of Baker Company.

9

HOLDING TIGHT

WHILE THE 1ST BATTALION'S BAKER COMPANY WAS EN ROUTE TO Pork Chop, reports from Able Company to the battalion CP continued intermittently and were relayed to the 17th Regiment, then to division. General Trudeau received enough information within the first hour to know Pork Chop's defenders were in danger of being overrun. In division reserve was 2d Battalion of the 32d Infantry Regiment. At 11:40 P.M. the 2d's commander, Lt. Col. Royal R. Taylor, received alerting orders from division. Be ready to either reestablish the position or counterattack.[1]

At 12:55 A.M. Able Company reported an unknown number of enemy on the crest of the hill, that Able occupied the center portion of the hill north and west of the APC landing, and Baker Company was engaged in a fire fight on the right finger of Pork Chop. Five minutes later they reported hand-to-hand fighting in the trenches.[2]

The Baker Company fire fight reported to battalion began when Lieutenant Allison ordered an immediate attack and the company started to move uphill toward the crest. Baker's column of platoons along the access road were in an excellent position to simply turn right, lay down a high volume of grazing fire up the slope, and begin moving uphill in the attack. When the company's 1st Platoon, led by Sgt. Tony Cicak, reached the small bunker next to the entrance of the main trench, the column stopped and took cover on the uphill side of the road. Allison, moving down the column, told Cicak, "They've taken the commo trench between the two sectors of the defenses. Instead of going in the tunnel to reinforce, we're going up the hill and take them out of the trenches."

A machine gun was set up to the right of the bunker nearest the entrance to the main trench. Tony Cicak was to deploy the 1st Platoon to the right and on top of the main trench, that the machine gun could give crossing, grazing fire from outside and behind their right flank. The other two platoons would follow behind 1st Platoon. With the advantage of good covering machine-gun fire upslope, and on command, they moved forward, initially making good progress fifty to seventy-five feet toward the hill's crest. The flares were lighting up the north slopes of the outpost, but the rear slopes were in dark and shadow. The Chinese were coming over the crest, silhouetted against the flares' light, heading for the straight section of trench on the reverse slope, but could not see into the darkness. The grazing fire was taking its toll. The fight continued for approximately twenty minutes.

In spite of the heavy casualties inflicted on the Chinese, the CCF kept coming. 1st Platoon's standard ammunition load was getting low, and soon would be gone unless replenished. Baker Company could no longer press the attack. Lieutenant Allison ordered the platoons to fall back and hold the main supply bunker.

To defend the rear of Pork Chop, he gave instructions to the company to redeploy back along the access road, and hold the entrance to the main trench, two other nearby bunkers next to the road, and the trench leading from the access road to Able Company's 2d Platoon CP, which was underneath the crest in the right sector. One of the two bunkers was a large, heavily reinforced bunker originally intended to be a mess hall for hot meals brought to the outpost. Now, the bunker was a haven for wounded who had walked or been carried off the hill or out of the main trench. Baker Company had become, for the moment, the outpost's rear area defenders against enemy coming over the crest of the hill, and the two CCF formations which had circled over the crest of Brinson Finger, attempting to encircle the outpost and take its defenders from the rear.

Baker Company men began assisting the wounded, taking them to shelter in the large bunker adjacent to the main trench entrance, then clearing weapons and resupplying themselves with ammunition as they deployed along the road.

While helping the wounded to the bunker, Tony Cicak encountered a soldier inside, who had a gash in his cheek. The bunker had front and back entrances and some light came through the doorways. The platoon sergeant could not see any other evidence of a wound. "Where are you hit?" asked Tony. "In the cheek," came the reply. "Any place else?" Tony asked. "No." "What the hell are you doing here? Get back to your platoon," Tony snapped.

Baker Company's move uphill seemed to have stalled the enemy's downhill advance from the trench line toward the evacuation landing—at least for a while. Cicak and Allison moved into a position near the entrance to the main trench. Standing, seemingly safe from observation, they could look uphill toward the crest. Tony saw two enemy soldiers coming downhill from the trench, toward the perimeter wire and the evacuation landing. Allison was standing next to Cicak's right shoulder. Cicak fired. Allison, stepping around behind to Tony's left, with his right hand on Tony's right shoulder, peering uphill, the company commander asked, "Did you get him?" Replied the platoon sergeant, "I think I did. Looks like he's hanging on the wire."

At that instant, Tony Cicak felt a slight jerking motion on his right shoulder, and heard a sound behind him. He turned his head to look. The company commander had disappeared from view. Tony's first thought was, he slipped in the mud and fell. He glanced down, expecting to see the company commander get back on his feet. Allison was dead, struck in the head by a sniper's bullet.

Another soldier stepped in to grab Allison. Two more bullets zipped through the position, and the sound told Tony they were fired from the right shoulder of the hill, near the crest. "Get back!" he exclaimed. He scanned the darkness below the crest. Two more muzzle flashes. He noted them, called to a BAR man and told him to put a magazine into the notch where the muzzle flashes were seen. After the BAR man responded with his automatic weapon, no more sniper fire came from the area.

Not long afterward, Tony Cicak, still positioned near the entrance to the main trench, witnessed an incident forever etched in his memory.

Suddenly, from the darkness on the right rear shoulder of Pork Chop, came a bright light, which for about four or five seconds bathed a large section of the southeast slope in an eerie, false daylight. Someone had inadvertently triggered a trip flare not far below the hill's secondary crest. There, clearly illuminated, four soldiers wearing American battle dress were coming downhill toward the access road. Two were carrying their rifles slung on their shoulders, one on each side of a third man, obviously wounded, whom they were half carrying, half dragging downhill, his head down. Behind them was the fourth, rifle poised to provide covering fire. In those few instants, before they could react, from a bunker above and behind, a machine gun opened fire. Cicak watched helplessly as all four men went down. The hill went dark again. He convinced himself he was uncertain of their fate. Maybe they had not been hit. Maybe they had hit the dirt before the machine-gun's bullets found them. Maybe they all came home. He will never know, but he has always wondered.[3]

As the night wore on, Baker Company established contact with Able and they both fought to clear the main trench and retake bunkers. Bugles were heard intermittently, heralding successive attacks, and at 2:35 in the morning of the seventh, Able Company reported enemy in the trenches at the CP, the trench blocked, and enemy soldiers placing small-arms fire down trench. At 2:51 another request for reinforcements came, and yet another at 3:47, for reinforcements to man bunkers that had been cleared of the enemy by counterattacks. Baker Company later swept over the hill, retook at least nine bunkers in the left sector and cleared part of the central sector near Able Company's CP. Some time later, Company A reported the enemy had overrun Pork Chop, withdrawn slightly, and then attacked again, but the right sector—David Willcox's 2d Platoon—was holding.[4]

Before the night ended, Tony Cicak and other Baker Company men became aware the Chinese had seized at least three bunkers on the rear slope of the right sector, placed machine guns in them, and were in commanding positions to rake the evacuation landing and the access road stretching from the landing to the trench entering the right sector. One gun had first shown itself when its crew opened fire on the four soldiers caught in the light of the trip flare. Tony had definitely pinpointed the weapon's position. It had to be knocked out. He moved back down the access road past the entrance to the 2d Platoon trenches, and stopped a T-18 with a .50-caliber machine gun mounted forward on the vehicle's top, coming uphill. He climbed on top, and talking through the open hatch to the crew, pointed out the one enemy gun's location as best he could. He explained the gun had to be knocked out, and asked the T-18 crew to place their heavy machine gun's fire on the Chinese position.

The vehicle commander responded, "You know where it is. You fire." Tony Cicak obliged him. The gun spit out three or four rounds and ruptured a cartridge, a potentially hazardous condition if the gunner attempts to clear the cartridge and keep firing. While Tony was pondering what to do next, a 57-mm recoilless rifle round, a dud, fired by the Chinese blasted out of the darkness and, fortunately, bounced off the side of the T-18. The driver yelled, "We better get the hell outta here!" They gave Tony a quick ride to the evacuation landing, unloaded their cargo, reloaded, and left for the return trip. The problem of the enemy machine-gun positions would not be solved until shortly before noon, 7 July.[5]

Preparing to Commit the Division Reserve

When the artillery and mortar barrages began at 10:25 the night of 6 July, 2d Lt. MacPherson Conner, Dick Inman's and Dick Shea's West Point classmate, was with an ambush patrol in front of the MLR, in the 32d Infantry's sector to the right of Pork Chop. Mac Conner had been in Korea three weeks, and was platoon leader of the 1st Platoon, Easy Company, 2d Battalion of the 32d. He was an observer on the patrol from another company, a step toward completing his battlefield orientation. His battalion was in 7th Division reserve.[6]

A few days earlier Conner had reconnoitered Pork Chop, to become familiar with the terrain in front of the MLR and the outpost's defense network. En route he encountered Inman, also his West Point classmate. Baker Company was having a hot meal. Since Conner's company had been eating K-rations for several days he joined them for the hot meal and talked briefly with Inman.

Now, the night of 6 July, when enemy artillery opened fire, the patrol Mac Conner was with was also promptly called back into the MLR, but the CCF did not attack their position. Unknown to Conner, at 12:45 A.M., before he was released to return to Easy Company, General Trudeau had ordered Conner's battalion commander to move one rifle company to the blocking position behind Hill 200, ready, on order, to be attached to the 1st Battalion of the 17th.[7]

When Mac returned to his company on the MLR, he decided to go into a bunker and get some rest. He fell asleep, unaware his company would be moving soon. It's well he did. The nights and days soon became long and miserable. He eventually caught up with his company on Pork Chop early the morning of 7 July.

Lieutenant Colonel Taylor assigned the mission to Easy Company, and the move by truck to the assembly area behind 200 began. At 2:25 A.M. the company commander reported Easy closed in the assembly area, ready to reinforce or counterattack the outpost. As soon as the report came in from Easy Company, Col. Benjamin Harris, the 17th Regiment commander, requested General Trudeau to release the company to the operational command of the 17th. Trudeau granted the request, and Harris immediately passed Easy's operational command to Lt. Col. Bev Read, 1st of the 17th commander.[8]

Easy Company was getting ready to move its first platoon to Pork Chop. Accompanied by Rocky Read, who was going forward to assume personal command of the outpost's defense, the company's lead elements departed the blocking position by APC at 3:48 A.M. Bev Read and the lead platoon of Easy Company reported arriving on the hill at 4:08, and Read began to take stock of the situation. In the meantime, Easy's company commander passed word back to find Mac Conner. The company was on Pork Chop.[9]

The defenders needed help. Able and Baker Companies had taken back some of the bunkers, but there were not enough men available to keep advancing. To hold bunkers taken required more infantrymen. Dead and wounded were sheltered in all the trenches and bunkers making traffic through them difficult.

Near daylight Read called Colonel Harris. He had been everywhere on the hill he could possibly go. He intended to hold the remainder of Easy Company at the blocking position, owing to the large number of men already on the hill. He would occupy all the friendly positions with able-bodied men now on Pork Chop, evacuate the dead and wounded, and then bring the remainder of Easy Company onto the outpost. Able and Baker of the 17th, and one platoon of the 32d's Easy Company, with the aid of APCs, carried out Read's plan during daylight hours on 7 July, and the last of Easy Company arrived on the outpost 5:30 P.M. that afternoon.[10]

This jeep took a direct hit from an enemy mortar round, 7 July 1953.
Courtesy of National Archives

Emerging Patterns in Artillery, Mortars, and Tactical Air

In the first hours of the battle, in spite of the chaos and fury, certain patterns emerged, most not new, yet all would mark the days ahead. In the hours between the opening barrage at 10:25 P.M. 6 July and 5:30 the afternoon of 7 July, the enemy fired a total of approximately twenty thousand rounds of mixed artillery and mortar rounds onto Pork Chop, Hill 200, and Hill 347.[11] Hill 347, on the MLR with its summit the home of several observation and listening posts, also received special attention because its crest overlooked all the hills held by the Chinese in the vicinity of the Chop.

The UN artillery battalions and mortar sections, more efficient and in many respects more deadly, answered with devastating fire of their own, along with direct-fire weapons such as M-46 tanks' 90-mm guns, 57- and 75-mm recoilless rifles—some mounted on jeeps to avoid becoming fixed targets—twin 40-mm rapid-fire antiaircraft guns, and quad .50-caliber machine guns mounted on half-track vehicles. Close-in defensive flash fires on the front slopes and flanks of Pork Chop, VT on defenders' positions, concentrations placed on enemy assembly areas—Hasakkol, Pokkae, and the Rat's Nest, for example—and avenues of approach used by reinforcing CCF units or small groups coming from those assembly areas, routes in the valley and along the north and south slopes of Brinson Finger from Chink Baldy and the rear of Old Baldy, plus counterbattery fire were the answers to the CCF. All added to the enemy's deadly fire and near endless thunder which crashed on, and around, and shook Pork Chop.

The almost constant fire from both sides surged at times to mind-numbing crescendos for men at both receiving ends of the barrages, as assaults, counterattacks, and reinforcements swept back and forth across the hill and its approaches.

The enemy, with the advantages of higher elevations than Pork Chop, ringing it on three sides, and the ability to observe the valley between the outpost and Hill 200, as well as most of the rear area immediately behind Hill 200, could lay in heavy artillery and mortar concentrations almost at will. The entire outpost, including its front and rear slopes, access road,

49th Field Artillery Battalion 105 howitzers behind the 17th Regiment's MLR, fired to support the 17th during the July battle for Pork Chop.
Courtesy of Robert J. Schaefer

the valley between Hill 200 and Pork Chop, front and rear slopes of Hill 200 and the valley behind it, could be repeatedly hammered with ease.

Once the battle began, the problem for Pork Chop's defenders was compounded when the Chinese gained and held the outpost's crest. They held the high ground doggedly, which gave them additional, closer observers of approaches to the outpost from the MLR. In the daytime, and to a lesser degree at night, they could observe troop movements and resupply activities on the access road, the valley between the outpost and Hill 200, and the front slopes of 200.

As in the April battle, the CCF's infantry seemed to have no aversion to assaults through their own artillery fire, and the Chinese artillery and mortar crews did not hesitate to lay heavy concentrations of high explosive fire, with impact fusing, in the midst of their own soldiers, especially if their secured positions on the hill were in danger of being retaken. As S. L. A. Marshall observed, the battle-hardened Chinese veterans would merely seek cover, wait out artillery and mortar barrages on position, then come out of their holes and fight—almost entirely at night.

Enemy assaults came at night with near overwhelming force, ratios of three or four to one, sometimes more, but were prepared with a well-thought-out plan and carefully targeted assault team objectives. They would attack, fall back, regroup, and attack again and again, and they were brave, resourceful, and prepared to make the most of weapons and ammunition captured in their assaults. They could quickly turn American weapons on their former users.

Despite the UN advantage of more, more efficient, and deadlier artillery and tactical air power, the Chinese were able to offset those advantages considerably by revetting their artillery, tanks, mortars, and self-propelled guns deep in caves. They could move their weapons forward to cave entrances, rapid fire quick volleys and concentrations, and pull back into the cave. Only precisely placed counterbattery rounds or tactically delivered aerial munitions, directly into the mouth of a cave, had a reasonable chance of silencing an artillery piece.

When weather permitted the UN to use Allied, Air Force, and Navy fighter-bombers, pilots encountered a formidable front-line CCF air defense system, and troops and vehicles well camouflaged, dispersed, and seldom moving in the daytime. Lucrative, hard targets were more difficult to find, with artillery pieces and tanks deeply revetted and camouflaged, or rolled well back from firing positions in camouflaged mouths of caves.

The Chinese routinely operated at night, seldom in daylight hours, specifically to offset the UN's artillery and night tactical airpower assets, which were fewer in number and far less effective than in daylight hours.

To counter the CCF's reliance upon night operations, the UN fired and dropped airborne, parachute-suspended illumination rounds throughout hours of darkness and heavy contact. They supplemented the flares with mobile truck and a few tank mounted searchlight batteries constantly on the move along the MLR, switching on and off to avoid becoming easy targets for artillery, mortars, or infiltrating snipers. The intense effort to turn night into day over the attacking enemy was kept to the north of Pork Chop. Keeping the outpost's south slopes and MLR in darkness or shadow complicated the ability of the CCF to interdict reinforcements and resupply.

Primarily because of five preceding days of monsoon rains, in the first hours of the battle Communist artillery and mortars began taking a toll on the return section of the access road, which looped through the evacuation landing and descended to rejoin the main road in the valley. Soon the section was impassable, and for the engineers, too hazardous to repair because of enemy fire. The return section, the latter third of the loop, from the landing back to rejoin the access road in the valley, had been built to allow increased traffic flow and improved resupply. Its use was intended to avoid two-way traffic except on the easier maintained valley floor, a wider road, or at least passing areas, coming uphill to the landing, with inevitably slowed and reduced traffic uphill—and turnarounds at the landing. Because of the return road's and adjacent embankment's steep grades, rain-driven erosion washing onto the road, the enemy's frequent shelling, and infiltrating snipers, the engineers abandoned attempts to keep the section open soon after the Chinese launched their attack.

The CCF assault on the rear of the outpost that first night, nearly severing the outpost's lifeline, made the M-39 and T-18 APCs indispensable in Pork Chop's defense. In the coming days, APC traffic to the evacuation landing and back would increase rapidly, severely taxing the new, still not fully field-tested T-18 and its crews—and the access road. The two vehicles became necessities in more ways than one, carrying reinforcements, command and reconnaissance parties, counterattacking companies, ammunition, grenades and other explosive charges, weapons, rations, medical supplies, water, communications gear, and men and materials needed to keep the access road open in the face of heavy monsoon rains and frequent enemy shelling.

In a few instances, the T-18s serving Pork Chop's defenders became weapons platforms. The vehicle included gun mounts, and among the round trips from the checkpoint behind Hill 200 to the evacuation landing were APCs with .50-caliber heavy machine guns occupying the mounts.

For Pork Chop's defenders and attackers, the sum of these huge masses of firepower, and the brutal, close-quarter, hand-to-hand fighting on and beneath the hill's surface, brought an indescribable hell. Neither side could remove the dead and wounded caught in the small, alternately owned, fiercely defended no-man's lands between trench sections and bunkers. As a result, both sides could merely watch as the wounded, dead, and dying accumulated in trenches and bunkers ringing the hill, areas endlessly contested. In the first hours the smell of death and shattered latrines began permeating the air, aided by the rivulets of rain and mud. Walks through trenches at night often brought the sickening sounds of decaying, punctured, or shattered bodies, and detached limbs squeezed under foot. Even in daylight hours, often the dead's bodies could not be seen because they were covered by thin layers of dirt and debris from caved-in trenches, roofs, and walls of shattered bunkers. Men living in the nightmare, wrenched with emotion and numbed by fatigue, did the best they could to ignore the scene around them— and grabbed moments of restless sleep to get ready for the next assault.

From the bunkers and trenches controlled by the Americans and their KATUSAs in the left and center sectors of the hill, during the fighting and the brief lulls that followed, wounded, some under their own power, others assisted by one or two medics or infantrymen, made their way down the slopes to the bunker at the evacuation landing. Those who could moved through the defense network to the main trench, or bunkers connected to the main trench, where they waited for evacuation.

On the east shoulder of the hill, where Able Company's 2d Platoon was isolated with a few of Baker Company's men, wounded began accumulating in bunkers cut off from one another, plus bunker 64, the platoon CP. In that sector, evacuation from inside or outside the trench network was hazardous at best. During the first night of fighting, enemy snipers, who had taken or slipped into trenches, bunkers, and other concealed areas on the south slope, could cut down anyone that moved in the open, or whose head got above the trench leading to the access road east of the evacuation landing.

Behind the MLR, by late afternoon of 7 July men and women in the 7th Division's medical companies had already been on their feet nearly eighteen hours as the wounded began streaming through the collection points and aid stations to the rear, toward the two mobile army surgical hospitals, one a Norwegian MASH. This was only the beginning. Would it ever end?

A Bright Shining Light

In every war there are men who shine like bright lights when the situation is desperate, even hopeless. They are rocks, unshakable, calm, deliberate, able to make rational decisions amid terrifying, irrational, chaotic, life-threatening conditions. They seem to radiate their energies, their souls, and reach outside themselves to help or lead others, showing absolutely no concern for their own safety, and every consideration for their men and the mission they are given. They are golden, marvelous under pressure, and strengthen everyone around them. Their voices, the fire in their eyes, their presence, though they might be wounded—even mortally wounded—lift others to fearless, determined action, urged on by an unspoken, unbounded confidence in the rightness of their actions. Such men can draw magnificent responses from those around them. There were many such men in the last battle for Pork Chop Hill.

When the enemy assault began, and the waves of Chinese infantry moved against the heights of Pork Chop, Able Company's acting commander, Lt. Dick Shea, in addition to organizing and leading counterattacks, circulated among soldiers' positions, checking, steadying, directing, and redistributing ammunition. He knew Pork Chop well, having been heavily involved in the reconstruction, mapping and sketching the entire layout, and strengthening Able Company's defenses in the three days prior to the CCF assault. In the dark he was able to move quickly and confidently from one position to another. "Don't worry," he said. "Help will be here in the morning. We've just got to hang on till then. We can make it."

As he moved about, he learned which bunkers were in friendly or enemy hands, where ammunition, medical aid, and other supplies and support were needed—information later valuable to Lieutenant Colonel Read and the hill's defenders. During his movements he carried ammunition to positions he could reach, where defenders reported running low in ammo.

Shortly after dawn on 7 July, a group of Chinese soldiers rushed down a trench line, attempting to expand their hold on the outpost. They overran several of the soldiers Dick Shea rallied, before they encountered him. He used his .45-caliber pistol to cut down four or five of the enemy before he ran out of ammunition. He then ran forward with his trench knife slashing and kicking, killing two more of the enemy. His raw display of courage caused the remaining, nearby Chinese soldiers to retreat.

He took advantage of their momentary confusion and led a group of soldiers in another counterattack down the trench line, chasing the enemy from a number of positions they had overrun. As a result of the attack Pork Chop's defenders in that area regained better observation of enemy-held slopes and movements, as well as better fields of fire.

Able Company, then Baker Company, and combined members of both companies launched successive counterattacks toward the center and left, to retake bunkers, firing positions, and heights overrun in the initial onslaught and the surges of repeated Chinese assaults. In that first night Dick Shea organized two or three such attacks, leading men from both companies.[12]

1st of the 17th's Rocky Read

First Battalion commander Lt. Col. Rocky Read, with the 32d Regiment's Easy Company commander and one of his platoons, arrived on Pork Chop about 5:30 the morning of 7 July. Shortly after arriving and surveying the situation, Read decided to set up the battalion CP in bunker 45. When he considered the situation inside the engineers' tunnel, the enemy on the forward slopes and crest of the hill and in the covered trenches near the Able Company CP, as well as the company CP's smaller size, vulnerability to loss of communications, and nearness to enemy-controlled positions, the new location clearly remained the best choice. Easy of the 32d's company commander collocated his CP in Bunker 45 as well.

Bunker 45, large, divided into two rooms, one approximately twenty feet by twenty feet, the other sixteen by sixteen, was strongly reinforced, and opened onto the evacuation landing and the trench running from the evacuation landing to the outpost's main trench entrance. The bunker also had a rear entrance, through which occupants could exit to observe the hill's south slope and the valley between Pork Chop and Hill 200. The bunker's position on the hill's reverse slope also offered the best location for communications with supporting and supported units and their commanders. Antennas were more rapidly and easily set up and were less vulnerable.

Wounded soldiers were already being sheltered in the larger of the two rooms in the bunker, when the battalion CP was set up in the adjoining room. It had become, along with the main trench, a makeshift collection point for loading wounded onto APCs for the return trip to the collection point behind Hill 200.[13]

WHEN LT. MacPherson Conner was awakened from his sleep, he caught a jeep to the checkpoint and an APC to Pork Chop. His company commander was already on the hill in Bunker 45. Colonel Read had given the go-ahead to begin bringing the rest of Easy Company forward as the wounded and dead were being evacuated, and Conner's commander wanted the remaining platoons to move out. Easy Company was to take up counterattack positions inside the tunnel and trenches of Pork Chop. Within the hour, Mac had been transported by armored personnel carrier to the evacuation landing and went into Bunker 45 to be briefed on the company mission.

It was daylight by the time he and his platoon arrived on Pork Chop. His commander told him his platoon's mission was to hold the engineers' tunnel. During the furious fighting the night before, the Chinese had several times tried to fight their way into the tunnel. Commanders knew the tunnel, Pork Chop's main trench, was essential to successful defense of the hill. As circumstances evolved, the entrance to the main trench would be one of the prime locations for safely collecting and holding wounded until they could be evacuated by armored personnel carriers.

After receiving his mission Mac made his way into the tunnel, into what was already a crowded, confusing collection of American soldiers fighting to hold or retake bunkers and firing positions in the defense perimeter. The tunnel was almost full, two men abreast. Mac worked his way forward through the tunnel, reconnoitering the position his platoon would defend, and refamiliarizing himself with that part of the defense layout the defenders still owned.

There were lateral entrances along the tunnel, through which defenders could enter the web of trenches linking Pork Chop's bunkers, firing positions, and CPs. There were openings leading vertically from the ceiling of the tunnel to the surface of the hill above. Through the vertical shafts Mac and his men could hear the voices of Chinese soldiers, talking. At times the Americans could hear calls in English for defenders to surrender. All too frequently the enemy threw grenades down the shafts or through the lateral trench entrances into the tunnel.

During the lull in fighting the morning of 7 July, Mac, his platoon, and Able and Baker Company men who remained in the tunnel set about improving their position. They stacked sandbags three to four feet high across entrances from the tunnel into connecting trenches dominated by the enemy. The sandbags would decrease the enemy's success in throwing grenades through the entrances, and force the Chinese to crawl over the stack, one at a time, enabling defenders to concentrate their fire and pick off attackers. In addition the Americans dug defensive positions into the sides of the tunnel. The recessed positions allowed defenders to take cover while opening up a center lane in the tunnel should the enemy succeed in bringing automatic weapons to bear, down trench, as they had the night before. To avoid grenades thrown from above, down the shafts into the tunnel, soldiers were told to stay back from shaft openings.

Along toward noon, the Chinese began throwing grenades at the far, northwest end of the tunnel, apparently intending to fight their way in. Mac Conner immediately responded, rushed forward up the tunnel's slope toward the sound of explosions, and in the darkness, slipped and fell on an ammunition can, cutting his right index finger to the bone. He held the finger, bent, to stem the flow of blood, until the action quieted. When he finally released pressure on the cut he bled profusely. He searched out a medic, and found one in the darkened tunnel, near the Able Company CP.

While the medic was taping up the cut, a distinctive, familiar voice heard behind him caught Mac's attention. He had not heard that voice in a long while.

"Is that Dick Shea?" he asked.

"Yeah, who is that?" came the reply.

"Mac Conner."

"Oh—Mac Conner!"

Shea told Conner the Chinese had earlier fought their way into the tunnel. They placed small-arms fire down trench, and a burp gun killed M.Sgt. Howard C. Hovey, the Able Company first sergeant, during the fight to drive them back from the CP. He told Conner, "A platoon [the 2d Platoon, in the right sector] is cut off, and I can't get through to them." He also told Mac, "Dick Inman called in and said he had a broken leg."

Shea could not know what happened to Inman in the few minutes following the initial Chinese assault and the radio call telling of a broken leg. The ferocious, seesaw fighting and disrupted communications on Pork Chop made it difficult to know what the situation was from moment to moment. There was no way to stop and count soldiers present for duty. Wounded soldiers, walking or assisted, out of ammunition or carrying inoperable weapons, and unarmed soldiers who had lost or abandoned their weapons, were individually making their way to bunkers and the tunnel near the evacuation landing, in hopes of receiving medical aid, evacuating, or rearming themselves to fight.

Now Easy Company of the 32d gathered in the tunnel to counterattack in hopes of occupying and holding positions that had been retaken after Baker Company swept over the hill in the dark early morning hours.

Mac Conner's platoon counterattacked to drive the Chinese from the tunnel near the CP, while Dick Shea made another attempt to fight his way to rejoin the isolated Able Company platoon on the right flank. He was beginning the second in a series of close range and hand-to-hand encounters with the enemy.[14]

The situation remained chaotic, however. The Chinese firmly held the western sector and the defenders held tightly to the eastern sector and part of the center sector, including the engineers' tunnel toward the rear of the hill. But neither side could advance and hold their gains. Friend and enemy were interspersed in the trenches and bunkers dividing the two tightly held sectors. Though some bunkers had been retaken by defenders, there were not enough men available to keep advancing, as infantrymen had to hold bunkers they had retaken.

Hand-to-hand fighting for the trenches and bunkers of the outpost was intermittent throughout the day. Friendly and enemy forces continued to reinforce. The remainder of E Company, 32d Infantry, came onto Pork Chop via APCs, and offloaded into the tunnel near the CP. By 5:30 P.M. the entire company had joined in the defense of Pork Chop. The Chinese reinforced with groups of five to ten men at a time, slowly building up their casualty-thinned ranks, and their strength.[15]

Sporadic but well-placed enemy small-arms, mortar, and artillery fire fell on Pork Chop during the day. The weather continued wet and rainy, with a low overcast which denied defenders badly needed close air support. The APCs continued to evacuate and resupply the outpost. Without them it would have been impossible to reinforce, since Chinese artillery and mortars systematically interdicted the road to the evacuation landing.

Agonizing Decisions

With the morning light on 7 July came a lull in the fighting. In Charlie Brooks's bunker in 1st Platoon the bitter all-night swirl of fighting had taken its toll. No one was dead but grenades hurled through the bunker aperture wounded nearly everyone inside. One tore off Bob Miller's right leg, just below the knee, and shattered his left leg. Another squad member, Paul Sanchez, put a tourniquet on Miller's right leg and bandaged the other, saving Miller's life, but they remained hemmed in the bunker.

Chinese held nearby bunkers and were blocking the tunnel leading past the company CP toward the evacuation landing. Worse, they were getting low in ammunition, with no end in sight, nor any sign of more ammunition, reinforcement, or relief. A second grenade thrown through the aperture exploded between Brooks's legs without doing the serious damage done to Miller.

During the first night and on into the day more men came into the bunker, until seven men were there, including Brooks, Miller, Paul Sanchez, one of the squad's ROK soldiers, and a lieutenant. The officer had no helmet on, and was carrying a .45-caliber pistol. His conversation was at times confused and incoherent. The men soon realized he was dazed, in shock, and out of his head, probably suffering from "battle fatigue."

By late afternoon, Brooks had a half clip of ammunition remaining in his BAR and everyone else was nearly out of ammunition. "What are we going to do?" was the question being asked earlier in the day. At first Brooks said, "We'll hold on. Reinforcements and ammo will come." Neither came. Now the questions and discussion became more intense. In the middle of it all, the lieutenant put his pistol to the head of the ROK soldier and demanded his helmet. The ROK soldier was angry and frightened. Brooks, to defuse the situation, persuaded the young Korean to give the lieutenant his helmet, telling him, "I'll give you mine."

Finally, late in the afternoon, after discussion of their predicament, they agreed they would have to leave the bunker, somehow, and get to the aid station at the evacuation landing. The only way out, Brooks convinced them, was through the aperture, out onto the loose shale slope on the front side of the hill, and quickly around the hill to the rear. Miller would have to stay. They would get help to him. Though his rifle was not operating, there was a half case of grenades they could leave next to him. Thus Charlie Brooks and five other men from the bunker left through the firing aperture and made their way to the makeshift aid station next to the evacuation landing and told the medics about Bob Miller, the nature of his wounds, and where he was located.

About dusk on 7 July, Charlie Brooks and the other five soldiers left Pork Chop Hill on armored personnel carriers. There would be many years of buried remorse and wondering before Charlie Brooks learned that Bob Miller survived his ordeal.[16]

THE LULL in fighting early the morning of 7 July came after the Chinese launched a furious early morning assault to overrun bunkers still held by Able and Baker Companies on the north slope in the western sector of Pork Chop. Harvey Jordan, who had lost consciousness soon after he was wounded in the initial enemy onslaught the night of the sixth, waked the morning of the seventh to find two Chinese soldiers standing over him, both brandishing burp guns. He was their prisoner, and later in the morning he was led down the north slope of Pork Chop toward enemy positions on Hasakkol.

George Sakasegawa and his squad leader, who left their bunker the night of the sixth to continue the fight from a commo trench, had survived a harrowing night, cut off—isolated in the trench, unable to rejoin other men or resupply themselves with ammunition. The rain of enemy artillery and mortars repeatedly forced the two men to "hit the dirt" deep in the trench to avoid more wounds or instant death. When the killing bursts tapered off they fought, using their dwindling supply of ammunition.

The next morning they saw the Chinese assault on the bunkers in their western sector, moving relentlessly toward them. The enemy moved along the hill's forward (north) slopes, from bunker to bunker, systematically throwing satchel charges in each one, and then cutting loose with flame throwers into entrances to ensure there were no survivors. With ammunition virtually gone and no way to fight out of their predicament, the two had little choice but to surrender. Anything else would have been suicide by explosives or fire. They, too, became prisoners.[17]

Commanders Forward

The flow of situation reports from Colonel Read's CP to the 17th Regiment CP gave impetus to additional preparatory and contingency decisions by Col. Benjamin T. Harris, the regimental commander. During daylight hours and the relative lull in enemy activity, Harris ordered reconstitution of reserves and the move of additional companies into position to further reinforce or counterattack Pork Chop. He directed relief of Easy Company, 17th Regiment, from Hill 327, by Company B of the Colombian Battalion. Additionally, he ordered the forming of provisional companies to be ready to occupy MLR and adjacent reserve areas, relieving rifle companies for defense of Pork Chop.[18]

The provisional companies' manpower came primarily from company and battalion administrative sections, the 17th's Intelligence and Reconnaissance Platoon, Pioneer and Ammunition Platoon, and other support organizations in the 17th's rear area. These were men who, for a variety of reasons, normally did not rotate onto the MLR with rifle companies to engage the enemy. The forming of provisional companies sent rumors, questions, and apprehension rippling through rear area units and headquarters. Were the Chinese about to overrun Pork Chop and penetrate the MLR?[19]

Harris's decisions came during a day when General Trudeau, feeling he could not gain adequate knowledge of the situation from secondhand reports, decided he would go to the Chop for an on-site look. Another company counterattack by another division reserve company was under consideration. Lieutenant Colonel Taylor alerted Fox of the 32d to be ready, but the line of departure, timing, objective, and direction of approach to Pork Chop was not yet decided.

There was much on Trudeau's mind. He knew the situation was tight, the defenders had taken heavy losses, and he needed to decide what to do.

He needed to decide when to replace the two units which had been there the longest. Able of the 17th had been on the hill for five days before the bitter night-long fight, and Baker Company had been on their feet all night, joined the fight before midnight, and had already lost their company commander and at least one other platoon leader.

Trudeau had walked the bunkers and trenches in the two preceding months, when Pork Chop was being rebuilt. He knew its strengths and weaknesses, knew it was stronger than in April, but also knew such fortifications could not indefinitely withstand the pounding being administered by the CCF artillery. He had been told the enemy had temporarily cut the access road, continued to shell it, occupied bunkers overlooking the entrances to the CP and main trench, and though driven back from the evacuation landing, had infiltrated snipers at night to make life hazardous for anyone in the open on the south slopes. Members of Trudeau's staff advised him, "You don't belong out there." But the division commander decided otherwise.

Shortly before noon, knowing insignia of rank made an inviting target, General Trudeau traded his star-studded steel helmet for the one worn by his jeep driver, Sgt. 1st Class Albert F. Clampert, of Leavenworth, Kansas. He then took the other rank insignia off his uniform, rubbed mud over the sergeant's stripes on Clampert's helmet, put it on, and entered the aft doors of a T-18 bound for the Chop. Sergeant Clampert delighted in the humorous experiences that came with wear of the general's helmet, with its two stars, but circumstances would be quite different for Trudeau and the officers accompanying him.

With Trudeau was Colonel Harris, the 17th's commander, Maj. Joseph E. Noble Jr., 2d Battalion commander, and the 2d's operations and intelligence officers—Lt. Ken Swift and Harry Ess—Noble had been ordered to prepare his unit for a counterattack on 8 July, when 2d Battalion would relieve the 17th's Able and Baker Companies on position, and the 2d would assume responsibility for defense of the outpost. The three officers were going to reconnoiter Pork Chop, and make plans for the counterattack.

About noon the APC came to a stop on the evacuation landing. By the time Trudeau's APC arrived, Colonel Read, through early morning experiences on the hill, and probably the advice of its defenders, had already instructed men in the bunker and near its entrance to provide covering fire

The checkpoint south of Hill 200. Shortly before noon on 7 July 1953, General Trudeau, Colonel Harris, and Major Noble boarded an APC here bound for Pork Chop. Note the APC parked in the stream, the access road crossing the stream, and a tank configured as a flamethrower (*left foreground*).
Courtesy of National Archives

anytime someone had to leave or enter the position on foot. Read undoubtedly ensured General Trudeau would receive similar cover when he left the APC to enter the command post bunker.

From there, Trudeau, Harris, and the reconnaissance party spread out through the bunkers and trenches controlled by Able and Baker Companies, and Easy of the 32d, to take the on-site look each needed. Read likely accompanied Trudeau. Noble, Swift, and Harry Ess went separate directions through the trenches to make their own assessments.[20] For Trudeau it was a sobering experience, one he would remember the rest of his life. He noted the men lining the walls of the trenches and congregated in the bunkers were fatigued and downcast. He saw them as dispirited, their morale low. He knew his policy of forty-eight hours in a fight must stand. He must arrange Able and Baker's relief no later than 8 July. And he encountered one other circumstance that left an indelible impression on him.

As he walked through one of the covered trenches near the main trench, a sergeant came toward him, bent forward, straining, carrying an American soldier slung over his shoulder, the soldier's upper body draped down the back of the man carrying him. When the sergeant passed Trudeau, the division commander noticed the soldier being carried was obviously gone and was bleeding heavily from the mouth. A soldier standing nearby began to cry, sobbing. Trudeau sensed trouble. Believing the soldier's behavior would ripple through men already exhausted and demoralized, the thought of "doing a George Patton" flashed through his mind. He recalled, "I damn near took a crack at him." Trudeau's thought was an instant recollection of the famous Patton slapping incident in North Africa during World War II, when Gen. George S. Patton, Jr., visiting wounded in a field hospital, slapped a frightened soldier who had no visible signs of a wound—after the doctors accompanying Patton told him the soldier had "battle fatigue."

Trudeau's better judgment prevailed. He took the soldier aside and quietly talked to him, trying to calm him. Then the division commander continued his on-site look at the situation on Pork Chop, never knowing if he had steadied the soldier and avoided more serious effects. He would never know how much crying had already occurred on the outpost that first night, and would continue in the days ahead.

General Trudeau's firsthand look at the situation on Pork Chop did make clear friendly and hostile groups were mixed together in the bunkers and adjoining sections of the trench network, and positions frequently changed hands. Though outside, on the surface of the hill, a daytime lull appeared in progress, inside the trench and bunker network, hand-to-hand fighting continued intermittently throughout the day. Sporadic but well-placed enemy small-arms, artillery, and mortar fire continued throughout the day. He also learned the high rates of fire and grenade use by defenders were depleting ammunition and grenade supplies, and more communications were needed. During the day the Chinese were continuing to reinforce in small groups of five to ten, gradually building up their strength on the outpost preparatory to more assaults that night. When he returned from the hill that day, he immediately called a staff meeting and told his staff in no uncertain terms what the men defending the hill needed. At the top of the list were ammunitions and communications equipment.

Nevertheless, Trudeau was convinced the hill could be held. And the commanders and reconnaissance party accompanying him decided their next moves in the desperate struggle to hold Pork Chop Hill. The stage was set for a night counterattack. In view of enemy observation and artillery concentrations, a daylight counterattack appeared impractical. The Chinese occupied the bunkers on the highest ground on Pork Chop. Should the counterattack mission be to seize and hold these bunkers or to sweep the Chinese off the hill?[21]

The 17th's commanders opted for a night sweep. With a few hours to prepare for the mission, Fox Company, 32d Infantry, planned to exploit a possible surprise and support the counterattack with defenders on the hill.[22]

Angels of Mercy

Between noon and one o'clock on 7 July, Pfc. Jim McKenzie, a medic from the 17th Medical Company, came on Pork Chop via an APC, riding with men from Easy Company of the 32d Regiment, who were reinforcing the 17th's Able and Baker Companies. With him was Pfc. Jackie McWhirter, also a medic. Both had been ordered forward in support of Able Company. This was Jackie's first time on either the MLR or an outpost. Until now, the closest he had been was in moving wounded from the collection point behind Hill 200 to the battalion aid station, farther to the rear.

When they off-loaded from the carrier McKenzie went into bunker 45 Lieutenant Colonel Read's command bunker, and a collection point for evacuating wounded from the hill. As soon as McWhirter stepped out of the APC, he saw a wounded soldier nearby, sitting on the ground, with part of a heel blown off. He immediately went to his aid, patched him up as best he could, and put him on an APC to the checkpoint behind Hill 200.

In Korea, nearly all medics carried weapons, usually the lighter semiautomatic M-2 rifle—the .30-caliber carbine—and a pistol. Jackie McWhirter was an exception, but only partly by choice. He did not carry a weapon while serving as a medic in the rear areas, and when the order came to go forward, there were none available in his medical company.

The UN forces learned early in the war that, contrary to practices during World War II, medics should not wear white arm bands with the traditional red cross symbol, or the same white circular field with a red cross painted on the center front of the medics' steel helmets. The North Koreans and Chinese disregarded the Geneva Convention and used such insignia as aim points, making medics targets. Consequently, medics were not distinguishable from GIs, except by the canvas, olive drab bags they carried, which the GIs quickly learned to recognize.

As soon as he arrived in Bunker 45, Jim McKenzie began doing what he had been sent to do. From the entrance to the bunker a trench led into the engineers' tunnel approximately thirty feet to the west. Propped against the wall of the tunnel entrance was the first of several wounded soldiers waiting to be evacuated. They needed to be moved out of the tunnel into the bunker to clear the tunnel entrance, permit better care, and get them closer to the access road to load onto personnel carriers. McKenzie began bringing them into the bunker. Like all tasks on Pork Chop, the job was not easy and was hazardous at best.

In the thirty feet of distance to the tunnel entrance, the trench wall height shallowed, making it impossible to stand up and move a wounded man through the area without exposing both the medic and the wounded to enemy snipers or skirmishers. To move the first wounded soldier into the bunker, McKenzie strapped his carbine over his back and crawled on his hands and knees through the shallow area of the trench. He then laid the wounded GI on the ground, on his back, with his head pointed toward the bunker. McKenzie straddled him on hands and knees, with the soldier holding onto him with his arms around McKenzie's neck, and then, with much effort, slowly, painstakingly crawled toward the bunker entrance, dragging the wounded soldier underneath him. When he finally reached Bunker 45 and got the man situated, he realized he had worked hard to get the man to safety. He also discovered he had lost his carbine. When he went to the bunker entrance and looked up the trench, the weapon was gone. It was needed elsewhere. This was the beginning of better than two days of nonstop toil to save as many lives as possible.[23]

Throughout the day on 7 July, Baker Company of the 17th continued defending Pork Chop's rear, threatened by three bunkers the enemy seized the night of the sixth. Sgt. Tony Cicak, and others within the remaining half of 1st Platoon pinpointed the three positions in the east sector of the hill, below the crest on the rear slope. The bunkers were above and astride the trench leading from the access road to Able Company's 2d Platoon CP, looked down on the access road and evacuation landing, and now housed enemy machine guns. The guns had to be knocked out.

The Patton tanks in the two platoons of tanks parked in a blocking position at the checkpoint behind Hill 200 could not be used. Their 90-mm guns were too powerful and could kill nearby Pork Chop defenders. First, a U.S. Marine Corps amphibian track vehicle, with a 75-mm mountain howitzer, parked at the base of Hill 200 would try direct fire from across the valley behind Pork Chop. The first round ruptured, and after several attempts to repair the weapon, the vehicle turned around and left.

In the supply bunker next to the access road were 3.5-inch rocket launchers, a powerful antitank weapon. Tony and one of his platoon members each shouldered a rocket launcher, and began firing at the bunker apertures, taking the nearest one first. They succeeded in putting rounds into the two nearest targets, knocking out the guns, but failed to hit the third bunker, 115 yards distant. About six more rounds failed to hit home. Just after Tony fired another round and missed again, his platoon member let fly with another. It went straight into the aperture and triggered a large secondary explosion—either ammunition or grenades stored in the bunker with the machine gun.

As darkness approached on 7 July, defenders increased watchfulness, knowing night would bring more enemy assaults. The evening before, some of Baker Company's men had fought their way into trenches and bunkers on the south slope. Medic Buster Duncan fought beside them, firing his M-2 carbine, throwing grenades, and stopping to aid the wounded when needed. A twenty year old from Tennessee's Appalachian Mountains when he was drafted, he saw all the fear, rage, chaos, horror, killed, and wounded he cared to see for a lifetime.

He witnessed the killing of a wounded Chinese soldier who had lost an arm below the elbow, pulled himself over the edge into the trench, and with motion and sounds begged for water. A BAR man shot the enemy soldier in the face. In the night, walking through the trenches, Duncan found himself walking on the dead and pieces of the dead.

As first light came to Pork Chop's defenses, from the trench he could see the head of a Chinese soldier in the barbed wire directly in front of him about twenty feet. Looking to the west, bodies and parts of bodies seemed everywhere in the trench, and many more dead lay close by, on both sides of the trench. Duncan spent most of his day walking through the trenches, treating the wounded, but in the afternoon, when fighting seemed to have died down, he entered a bunker. Standing guard outside was an American soldier. When he pushed the heavy canvas flap aside, he startled the men crowded inside. Reflexively, they pointed their weapons at him, and at the same instant someone yelled to keep them from firing. Some in the bunker were wounded, and he treated them.

Near evening twilight on 7 July, Duncan heard a soldier calling for a medic. When he walked toward the voice, an American soldier appeared and motioned him to his position. Approximately a squad of men he did not know wanted him to accompany them to the front side of the hill, at Finger 22, while they set napalm charges in anticipation of the night's fighting.[24]

While Tony Cicak and his platoon were taking out enemy-held machine-gun positions in the rear of Pork Chop the afternoon of the 7th, on the south side of Hill 200 a fight of another kind was about to begin.

A Bridge Too Near

When the 13th Engineers received word of the CCF assault on Pork Chop, they were already heavily engaged in maintaining the 7th Division road net, which was being severely taxed by the monsoon rains. Nevertheless, Capt. Jim Brettell ordered the 13th's Able Company to "fall out"—assemble—dressed for battle, with steel helmets, body armor, and their infantry-supporting counterattack combat load: weapons, ammunition, bangalore torpedoes, mines, radios, water, and rations. Only Brettell's officers knew it was a drill. It was an exercise Brettell called frequently, but it was well he called one again for the entire company. Some soldiers were not ready.

Lt. Richard White learned a couple of his men in the 3d Platoon did not have their basic weapons, the M-1 rifle, or ammunition. Another could not find his weapon and showed up sporting a BAR, authorized only for infantrymen. The drill gave platoon leaders the opportunity to ensure every man was properly equipped to support infantry companies in the counter-attack.

While Fox of the 32d and Pork Chop's defenders prepared for the 7 July night counterattack, the outpost's lifeline, its access road, was facing another threat—not from the enemy, but from rising water fed by six days of monsoon rain. At twilight on 6 July, when Baker of the 17th walked from their trucks parked at the checkpoint, along the tank trail, to the blocking position behind Hill 200, they waded the rising stream between

A jeep assigned to the Ethiopians' 3d Battalion attempts to ford a stream swollen by monsoon rain, 7 July 1953.
Courtesy of Ed Puplava

the checkpoint and the blocking position. The small, narrow, inches-deep spring was now a fast-growing, swirling, and potentially dangerous river. By the time Easy of the 32d began moving by APC from the checkpoint to Pork Chop early the next morning, it was evident the stream might soon wash out the existing road-based bridge. Two large sixty-inch culverts allowed water to pass under the road, but the rapidly rising water would soon overwhelm the culverts. When General Trudeau's APC crossed the existing bridge shortly before noon, matters were worse. A Bailey Bridge needed to be built over the top of the road in case it were washed out, or Pork Chop's jugular vein might be cut by mother nature.

The impetus for the hurry-up mission to build the bridge belonged to Army engineers, and Trudeau, the 7th's boss, undoubtedly turned to Lieutenant Colonel Icke to get the job done. Early the morning of 7 July, Capt. Jim Brettell, the 13th Engineers' Able Company commander, had already been given the task of taking an on-site look at the location. Brettell and the platoon sergeant of 2d Platoon, Jim Goudy, drove down the access road, past the checkpoint, and over the crossing. They parked on the north side of the stream to hopefully remain out of the enemy's sight as long as possible. In combat, nothing is easy, and life is always hazardous. Time was of the essence and this mission was particularly hazardous.

No matter where in the valley behind Hill 200 a bridge might be built, the enemy could observe its construction from Old Baldy. There were no bunkers nearby to take cover from easily adjusted artillery or mortar fire. The bunkers at the blocking position were too far away. Time did not allow the construction of bunkers, revetments, or deep foxholes, and the bunkers at the blocking position must be kept open to shelter reserve or counter-attacking units called forward to defend the Chop or MLR.

Worse, the 13th Engineers were combat engineers, not bridge-builders. While they might be able to obtain the prefabricated Bailey Bridge module to do the job, most had had no training in bridge building since attending branch engineer schools. The best solution to getting the bridge in place quickly was to call in a Corps of Engineers bridge building company. The 13th requested I Corps to dispatch the company to do the job.

At the same time Capt. Joseph K. Bratton, the 13th Engineers' aggressive supply officer, began a communications search to locate a bridge module which could be rapidly moved to the selected construction site. He learned I Corps had the material, got the OK to move it and the necessary trans-portation and construction vehicles, and asked the 13th's Dog Company to begin loading and hauling forward.

While Bratton and Dog Company were searching out transportation and materials, and the request for the bridge building company was going to Eighth Army, Brettell and Goudy, the platoon sergeant in Able's 2d Pla-toon, surveyed the existing bridge and its approaches. As the two men sur-veyed the site, an incident occurred they both were to remember the rest of their lives.

Among the platoon sergeant's many skills was mine clearing, and as he and his company commander walked through an area thirty yards off the southeast approach to the culverts, Jim Goudy stepped on something metal-lic with his left foot, and heard—"click." He instantly froze, keeping his body's weight on the left foot. He and Jim Brettell knew he had stepped on a mine, and Jim Goudy knew what kind. It was a malfunctioning antiper-sonnel mine, a "Bouncing Betty," normally triggered by a trip wire. The trip wire had been previously severed, and Goudy had stepped directly on the mine. If he lifted his foot to run or dive to ground, he would not be able to escape the explosion and shrapnel spray.

Goudy looked at his company commander and said, "What do I do now?" Said Brettell, "I don't know—let me think." Brettell looked around. They were out front of MLR positions on the finger running down toward the checkpoint from Hill 347, and in full view of CCF observers on Old Baldy. Whatever they did had to be done quickly.

Brettell realized the area was strewn with boulders. He told Goudy, "The only thing I can do is build a revetment against your leg with some of these boulders, then you jump over it and get to ground as quickly as you can." Goudy, still frozen in place, said, "OK," and Brettell went feverishly to work. To Brettell the revetment building seemed to take two hours, but only minutes passed before he built a knee-high wall against Goudy's left leg. Brettell said, "That's all I can do, Goudy. I'm going over there behind that big boulder and you jump over the wall and hit the ground as quickly as you can."

Goudy did, and when he jumped, the mine was propelled into the air. Normally, the Bouncing Betty springs straight up eight to ten feet, then explodes, but this one did not. Instead, it went up at an angle, and away from Brettell and Goudy, the fan shaped explosion and shrapnel spray pattern tilted so one side of the fan was horizontal and the other side pointed straight down. Both men escaped without a scratch, completed their survey, and drove back to the company area to call battalion with the results. Brettell asked when the I Corps' bridge builders would arrive.

The I Corps solution was no solution. Their bridge builders were already heavily involved elsewhere in a higher priority mission. The Corps' higher priority mission meant the 7th Division and 13th Engineers would have to do it on their own, and they did, although the lack of recent training and skills meant the work would take longer.

Icke tapped Brettell and "Bulldozer Able," Able Company of the 13th, to do the job. The bridge building task fell to 2d Lt. Jim Dietz's 2d Platoon. Second Lt. Richard White's 3d Platoon was to provide security while work was in progress. White, an OCS graduate from Pensacola, Florida, had entered the University of Florida's school of engineering, but left the university to enlist as an infantryman after his older brother, 1st Lt. William L. White, in the 7th Division's 49th Field Artillery Battalion, was killed in action in the battle for Hoengsong, on 12 February 1951. Dietz was a 1952

West Point graduate, a classmate of Dick Shea, Dick Inman, and Mac Conner. In no more than a few minutes after word came Able Company would build the bridge, Jim Goudy came up with a manual explaining how to build one, and training began.

It was nearly dark when the bridge arrived at the crossing. But that was only the beginning. The bridge trucks were big "Brockway" trucks with double construction booms on the beds. They were so big the engineers had great difficulty turning them around in the confined area of the bridge site. Worse, the Chinese knew the implications of the rising waters for Pork Chop's defenders and the CCF's ability to quickly secure the hill. They saw what the 13th was about to do, and let the engineers know they objected.

Mortar rounds later began falling on a regular basis. Able Company was beginning work that would last all night long and into the next morning, while darkness closed around them, the monsoon rains continued, and the enemy kept the construction site under fire. Had a bridge building company been available, the ninety-foot span would have been completed in four to five hours. The bridge building began the night of 7 July, a night long remembered by the 13th Engineers and many others.[25]

Night Counterattack

Before the 17th Infantry Regiment's commander, Colonel Harris, went forward to Pork Chop with General Trudeau at midday on 7 July, he continued plans to aggressively defend the outpost. He ordered Maj. John Noble, the 2d Battalion commander, to prepare his unit for a counterattack. Because the 2d manned positions on and behind Hill 347, Harris subsequently ordered an intricate series of unit moves and reliefs to free the 2d's rifle companies for counterattack. Additionally, he had previously ordered the forming of provisional companies to hold in reserve positions or man the MLR.

In late afternoon, the Colombians' B Company relieved the 2d Battalion's Easy Company, which manned the west sector on Hill 347. Another unit from the division reserve, the 32d Regiment's George Company, relieved the 2d of the 17th's Fox Company in the east sector of 347. One of the provisional companies relieved the 2d of the 17th's George Company, in reserve behind 347. The stage was set for a follow-on battalion counterattack approximately 3:00 P.M. the afternoon of 8 July. In the interim, beginning late afternoon on 7 July, the fury on Pork Chop began once more escalating.[26]

At approximately 7:30 P.M. a T-18 APC stopped on the outpost's evacuation landing to unload. For nearly two hours, Baker Company's Tony Cicak manned a .50-caliber machine gun mounted atop the vehicle. On board and close by were eight boxes of ammunition he could use. The driver sat inside, hatch open, so Tony could be the driver's observer and give him directions if need be. While unloading proceeded, the armored vehicle–gun combination provided heavier firepower countering CCF attempts to come in the outpost's back door. Cicak could swivel the weapon 360 degrees and attack any area where muzzle flashes indicated the enemy was firing on defenders.[27]

About dusk, from an observation post on Hill 200 came the report a company-sized CCF unit was moving toward the right rear of the outpost, up the slopes of the cut between the Chop and 200. The 17th's Charlie Company was still manning MLR positions on 200. Sgt. Henry Baker, who had been a squad leader in Charlie's 3d Platoon, the reserve platoon during the raid on the Rat's Nest, and was now the platoon sergeant, had just posted six outguards on the front slope of Hill 200, and returned to his position on the MLR. The outguards were from Sergeant Crawley's platoon, and Crawley was manning a machine gun overlooking a trail leading from 200 to Pork Chop.

Among the outguards was draftee Cpl. Raldo Horman from Louden, Iowa. Raldo, a member of 3d Squad, 2d Platoon of Charlie, was a rifleman. Issued a BAR when he first arrived in Charlie Company, his weapon of choice was now the M-1, the result of previously running out of BAR ammunition at the wrong time in a fire fight.

When Raldo and two other squad members arrived at their three-man outguard position, they discovered the "hot loop" phone line had been cut. One of the men went back to get a wire spool and ran another set of lines to reestablish communications. When he returned to their position, reconnected the phone, and checked it for operation, the line was again dead. They immediately thought the line had been cut again—that the enemy was in the area.

Suddenly, all hell broke loose. The sounds of blowing whistles, shouts, screams, small arms, burp guns, outgoing (friendly) artillery and mortars exploding on the eastern slopes of the cut between 200 and Pork Chop echoed in the valley between the two hills. Enemy artillery and mortars also began falling on Pork Chop, its south slopes in the vicinity of the evacuation landing, in the valley between the two hills, on 200, and intermittently behind 200, in the area where the 13th Engineers were building a bridge across the swollen stream. Apparently the enemy objectives were to seize the access road and evacuation landing, block any reinforcements destined for the hill, and cut the defenders' lifeline. A forward observer on Hill 200 called in artillery and mortar fire on the enemy formation, with some success, but the Chinese pressed forward. The suddenness of the CCF assault convinced Henry Baker the enemy had been lying in wait when he posted the outguards. Raldo Horman, at one of the Listening Posts, now had no doubt the enemy had been lying in wait. (Soldiers often referred to outguard positions as listening posts, or LPs.) With communications lines severed, he did not have to wait to be called back to the MLR. He and the other two men with him began crawling on their bellies, back to the Charlie Company positions.

On Hill 200's crest, Henry Baker went to Sergeant Crawley and said, "I'm going to get the LP." Crawley replied, "You can't. I'm going. They're my men." Baker responded, "Then I'm going with you," and they both started moving carefully down the trail toward the LPs. In the darkness he saw figures coming up the trail toward them. In the half mile in front of their position, the noise coming from Pork Chop's right rear indicated the Chinese were everywhere. Might the figures be enemy soldiers trying to slip into Charlie Company's positions?

Baker and Crawley tensed, stopped, peered intently into the dark, and prepared to challenge the intruders. Henry Baker remembered his training. If you challenge unidentified intruders with, "Halt! Who goes there?" and the answer comes back, "GI," assume it's the enemy. Came the reply, "GIs." A tense silence.

Baker pulled the spring-loaded bolt on his BAR full back and released it, sending rounds into the chamber and barrel. He then slipped his finger onto the trigger, ready to fire. In the next instant he heard a low voice. "Baker?" It was Pvt. Thomas Irvine who spoke and saved the lives of Charlie Company's six outguards. They were within a hair's breadth of being cut down by a hail of automatic weapons fire from Baker's BAR. Had he pulled the trigger, he would have been haunted the rest of his life by an accidental assault on soldiers who, in battle, meant everything to him. Throughout the years since that July night, Baker has wondered why he did not act on his first impulse and open fire—at a time when impossible-to-understand randomness, treachery, hair-trigger decisions, and chaotic danger intervened often as the difference between life and death.[28]

In Pork Chop's rear, the Chinese approaching through the cut between Hill 200 and the outpost triggered a furious fire fight from friendly trenches and on the evacuation landing, undoubtedly the result of enemy holding the crest attempting to sandwich the outpost's rear area defenders. Enemy artillery and mortars continued the pounding. The Chinese were again trying to fight their way downhill toward the landing. Lieutenant Colonel Read reported the fire fight to the 17th Regiment at 9:15. While the fight was in progress, the Chinese were attempting to reinforce their men holding the hilltop. A call went from defenders to the artillery requesting VT on position.

On the evacuation landing outside the CP, Sgt. Tony Cicak was busily engaged with the heavy machine gun. He and the APC driver did not get the word VT was on the way, and a round exploded in the air—close. Tony felt a nearby "ping" and instantly heard the driver screaming, "They blew my leg off! They blew my leg off!" Cicak looked down the open hatch. A large shell fragment had gashed the driver's leg like a saber. He gave the man first aid, called for a medic, and told him the driver would have to be evacuated. Later, another driver took control of the APC for the return trip.[29]

Plans had been in motion since early in the day for the Chop's defenders to join in a night counterattack by another company which would approach from the southwest and west, along Brinson Finger. The reported 9:15 fire fight on the evacuation landing came fifty-three minutes after the counter-attacking company from the 7th Division's reserve battalion left its line of departure. Easy of the 32d was already on Pork Chop. Fox Company would be next.[30]

Fox Company, 2d Battalion of the 32d Infantry Regiment was to proceed down the north slope of Hill 347, continue to the north, cross the valley and its swollen stream, climb up Brinson Finger's south slope in column—then turn right and sweep west to east on Brinson Finger. The concept was a hurriedly planned, surprise night counterattack against the Chinese holding the left flank and crest of Pork Chop. With only a few hours to plan and prepare, Fox Company faced significant obstacles.

The plan selected was not simple, and the night operation complicated the company commander's and platoon leaders' control of both the unit's move to the attack position and the assault. A night-time, single-file march through barbed wire in totally unfamiliar terrain, across a swampy valley and a stream swollen by heavy rains was difficult at best. The long night trek in steep terrain precluded carrying more than the normal ammunition and weapons load for a counterattack. Though participation of the Chop's defenders had been planned and coordinated, and the belief was a night counterattack with their participation would surprise the Chinese, as time progressed, the changing situation on the outpost complicated Fox Company's already complicated mission even more.

As laid out in the plan, Fox Company passed through the MLR positions on Hill 347, departing at 8:23 P.M., and descended the north slope. In single file, a necessity to maintain sufficiently closed-up spacing and control during the move to the assault position, F Company's men still struggled to stay together.

On 6 July, Pvt. Emory Ballengee, a Fox Company BAR man from Rupert, West Virginia, had relaxed with the company in division reserve, in its second day off the line. He was still a junior man in his rifle squad, and it was the habit of some squad leaders to assign the most junior men in their squads to carry the BARs. Emory arrived in Korea on 14 May, after being drafted the previous November at the age of twenty. He had never been in a fire fight. Though he had been on the line, gone on patrol, heard and seen artillery and mortar rounds fall nearby, he had never seen or heard barrages like the thunder he heard the night of the sixth. Still, though he later learned enemy shells had fallen in the division rear, none hit the Fox Company reserve bivouac that night. Circumstances changed abruptly on 7 July, when in the early afternoon, the siren sounded in the reserve area, signaling "assemble combat ready."

The company formed up, helmets, weapons, body armor, ammunition loads, rations, water, plus armed medics with first aid bags, and climbed aboard two and a half ton trucks which moved them to an assembly area on Hill 347, near the line of departure. They climbed down from the trucks and shortly afterward Emory Ballengee's long night of 7–8 July began.[31]

Pork Chop as seen from an aperture in OP 12 on Hill 347. When Fox company of the 32d Infantry Regiment departed 347 the night of 7 July, they crossed the stream shown in the lower left corner, climbed up Brinson Finger, and turned right to counterattack uphill toward the crest of the outpost.
Courtesy of Ed Puplava

The company climbed over the crest and started downhill as dark came and rain fell intermittently. As Fox Company's long single file began its trek, in the valley below and to their right front, behind Hill 200 and in view of CCF observers on Old Baldy, the 13th Engineers were beginning their night of bridge building under fire. Less than an hour later the men of Fox could see flare lit skies and hear the sounds of artillery, mortars, small arms, and automatic weapons echoing through the valley between Pork Chop and Hill 200, as renewed fighting raged near the evacuation landing.

Right behind Emory Ballengee in the column came his assistant gunner and ammunition carrier, who, in addition to BAR ammunition, carried his own M-1 rifle and ammo. Emory, like everyone else in the column, was scared. He carried one belt of ammunition in addition to the magazine loaded in his weapon. Down its tortuous way Fox Company went, sloshing through the dark, across a swampy valley and the waist deep stream.

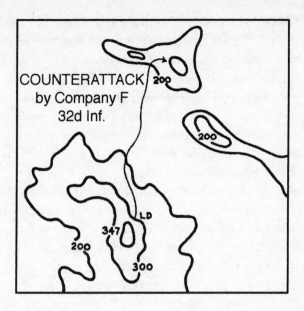

The counterattack by Company F, 32d Infantry. The company departed Hill 347 on foot at 8:23 P.M. on 7 July 1953 and began the assault at 1:35 A.M. on 8 July.

Emory heard sergeants passing the word, "Keep it closed up. Keep the pace. Keep the man ahead of you in sight. When you wade the stream, keep your rifles over your heads."

The stream was swift, footing not easy. Emory could no longer see his ammo bearer, and saw very few men after crossing the stream. Then came the climb up Brinson Finger, where men found the steep, rain-soaked hill required the use of rifle butts shoved hard down onto the wet ground to assist in the pull. Emory and his ammo bearer were separated. He never saw him again.[32]

By the time Fox was laboring up Brinson Finger, still undiscovered by the enemy, fighting at the evacuation landing had tapered off. Baker of the 17th's Sgt. Tony Cicak was standing guard on the left side of the entrance to the main trench, next to the evacuation landing. Opposite him on the right side was Private Connally, in Cicak's platoon. Though fighting had died down somewhat, the Chinese had grown wiser. They were keeping their heads down in their own positions, but quietly attempting to infiltrate downhill, get on top of bunkers and the openings to covered trenches, and hurl grenades inside.

With no warning, a grenade hit the front side of Connally's helmet and exploded in a blinding flash, knocking both men down. Tony took shrapnel in the face and neck. When he recovered his senses, he thought for sure he was terribly mutilated, and Connally must be dead. Connally was down, not moving—at least not for a brief period. Then Connally stirred and got to his feet. "I'm OK," he said, and he was OK—miraculously unhurt. Tony? He walked in the bunker where the wounded were collecting, and a medic put a bandage on his neck, which he later removed when the bleeding stopped. The bandage was too tight.[33]

Fox Company covered the one or two miles to the objective in almost five hours, reaching the enemy bunkers undetected. En route, no artillery or mortar rounds fell in the company's vicinity—at least not yet, and only occasionally did Emory Ballengee notice flares lighting the sky. At 1:35 A.M. 8 July, came the report Fox Company was in the western trenches, almost unopposed. They had surprised the enemy. When Fox Company reported their success, they received a mission change. They were to stop the sweep and seize the crest of Pork Chop.

When Fox began their assault uphill toward the outpost's crest, Chinese holding the high ground fought back with intense small-arms and automatic weapons fire. Enemy artillery and mortars began finding the range, while the fire fight drained the company's limited supplies of ammunition and grenades. During the night the Chinese committed another battalion to reinforce CCF units battling to hold Pork Chop and seize the evacuation landing. In the sharp fight for the crest, Fox gained some trenches, but eventually began running short of ammunition and grenades, and was unable to eject the enemy from their tightly held positions. The company then attempted to fight its way east, around the south side of the hill, to establish contact with defenders holding the rear areas, but the effort failed. As twilight neared, enemy artillery and mortars, which had not been pinpointed for American counterbattery fire during the night, began saturating the company's positions, causing heavy casualties.[34]

Throughout Fox Company's fight another angel of mercy was fighting to save lives and the wounded. Pfc. Hugh D. Porterfield was everywhere, disregarding the heavy enemy fire all around him, seeking out the wounded, and giving them aid. When the order came for Fox Company to pull back and fight their way toward the evacuation landing, he passed the word, helped direct the pullback, and assisted the wounded. Then, moving through heavy enemy mortar and artillery fire, he made the rounds of positions believed vacated, to ensure no wounded were left behind.[35]

Pvt. Robert L. Pothoof, a radio operator, was a critical link in the entire Fox Company counterattack. Despite continuing artillery and mortar fire, his radioed reports, requests, and responses to questions kept units on Pork Chop in close coordination with Fox Company's whereabouts and movements as the fight progressed. In between the necessary communications he several times joined the fighting to keep their position from being overrun.[36]

At one point in the relentless shelling, Lieutenant Colonel Read, in the CP at the outpost's evacuation landing, counted five rounds a second falling in the area atop Pork Chop, on the slopes, and around the landing. The earth was pulsating with the roar of explosions, the bunker shook and shuddered, and dust permeated the air inside. Medic Jim McKenzie, inside the CP with the wounded, put his head down and prayed, thinking it would never end.[37]

During the same period, Jackie McWhirter was in the bunker where Jim McKenzie was, tending to wounded. He put his head down and prayed, too—a different prayer. He prayed he would be wounded and evacuated from the hill. He had been through an incomprehensible day.

He earlier heard the cries of a man seeking aid, down the hill from the CP bunker. He could see a waving hand above a pile of fallen timber, the man evidently trapped beneath it. McWhirter couldn't tell if he were a friend or enemy and hesitated. Finally, he could stand the pleading no longer, and took two GIs with a stretcher with him, out the front door and down the hill, hoping to pull the soldier to safety. The soldier was an American, and with intensified enemy small-arms fire making the trip hazardous down and back, Jackie and the two GIs pulled and carried him to the safety of the CP.

Matters were to get much worse the next day, when he worked his way up the hill to the trench on the south side of the east shoulder of the hill. He witnessed a scene that never left him. Wounded and dead, Chinese and American, littered the trench. They seemed everywhere, and he spent the remainder of that day aiding and moving the wounded and carrying the dead to stack them near the entrance to the main trench.[38]

AT 4:25 A.M. on 8 July, Fox Company reported the enemy had it surrounded. They were ordered to withdraw. Remnants of Fox and their wounded started down the south slope, withdrawing across the valley toward the MLR and Hill 347, or moving toward the evacuation landing's CP and medical bunker.[39] Emory Ballengee was one of the wounded who struggled back across the valley.

During the fire fight, he, like many others, encountered showers of Chinese grenades. At one point, while on the ground, he believed he saw three enemy soldiers silhouetted against the sky. He raised up and fired the BAR. Three grenades immediately fell nearby, exploded, and shrapnel hit his lower left leg and foot. He could not get on his feet or walk. It was still dark, but he knew twilight was near. The most he could do was sit up, and in the sitting position, use his arms and right leg to lift and drag his lower body and left leg backward down the hill. If he could not drag himself downhill and across the valley, he would surely die. So began Emory Ballengee's desperate struggle to survive.

Slowly, painfully he lifted and pulled himself down the south slope of Pork Chop Hill, in the sitting position, backward. He prayed to God, "If you get me off this hill, I'll serve you." Daylight came. He saw smoke grenades being thrown above and to his right, near the evacuation landing —cover for APCs being loaded with wounded. He could see remnants of Fox Company walking off the hill to the south toward Hill 347, some helping wounded. All moved slowly across the valley and the stream, toward safety.

He struggled past a lieutenant who was on the ground, his foot missing. There were no medics in sight. Standing near the swollen stream was a soldier with both his eyes hanging from their sockets, against his cheeks. Two soldiers came to Emory's aid and helped him across the stream, where they flagged down an APC returning from Pork Chop and loaded him on top. The APC took him to the collection point behind Hill 200. He was taken on another vehicle to the battalion aid station, and from there the doctors sent him through the medical system, for evacuation by air to a hospital in Osaka, Japan. The war was over for Emory Ballengee, and he buried the memories of his only fire fight—and Pork Chop Hill.[40]

The counterattack by Fox Company of the 32d Infantry Regiment in the early morning hours of 8 July failed to achieve its objectives. Time had been too short to plan for a mission requiring careful preparation under the best of circumstances, but the growing pressure on the outpost offered no reasonable alternative to the night counterattack. The changed mission, with the objective of driving the Chinese from the hill's crest, complicated their mission even more. In spite of the outcome and Fox Company's heavy losses, the timing of their assault spoiled an enemy attack aimed at the evacuation landing and its connecting road.

The rest of the outpost's defenders were now running low on ammunition of all types. Had the landing fallen into Chinese hands, the entire outpost would have been isolated, starved of resupply, and lost. The disruption and delay of CCF reinforcements, and assaults on the rear, allowed the hill's defenders to reorganize and continue the fight. Remaining elements of Fox Company were able to withdraw down the south side of the outpost, where the wounded were evacuated by armored personnel carrier. The remainder of the company withdrew through the valley between Hill 347 and Pork Chop.[41]

Behind Hill 200, while the bitter night fighting raged for Pork Chop's crest, access road, and landing, Able Company of the 13th Engineers, with their KATUSAs and KSC laborers, were fighting their own battle to keep the outpost's lifeline open. The bridge across the rising stream had to be completed, soon. The delivery of the bridge module and equipment at dark was the start. Darkness, while valuable in reducing the accuracy of enemy artillery and mortar attacks, did not stop the Chinese from trying. Rounds fell steadily all night.

Richard White's 3d Platoon set up security, posting its men primarily as outguards to the south and west, astride likely avenues of enemy approach from Old Baldy and Chink Baldy. Combat engineer troops with M-1s and one machine gun were the security. Mostly they were to keep their eyes and ears open. After setting up the security screen, White decided to offer bridge building assistance to Jim Dietz and his platoon. He had had some experience in building Bailey Bridges.

Each bridge panel was five feet by ten feet and weighed 560 pounds. The bridging material and equipment were on the north side of the stream underneath a nose on Hill 200, on a hill cut, to hide the activity as much as possible from the Chinese on Old Baldy. The plan was to assemble the bridge, a section at a time, on rollers, then push the assembled sections across the top of the road and culverts. Once the Bailey Bridge was in place and anchored to its approaches on both sides of the stream, if the culverts and road gave way to rising water, the Bailey would remain in place, able to sustain the 7th Division's heavy vehicles. Brettell and Goudy believed sixty feet of bridge would do the job.

After constructing the first three sections, the engineers learned they could no longer push the joined sections toward the south side of the stream. With rain-slicked footing there were not enough men available. They hauled in a D-7 bulldozer to the site, and as sections were assembled the bridge builders pushed toward the other side.

Shortly after midnight, Richard White decided to take a short break and had just taken a seat on the bridge rail. The first mortar round came in and landed in the stream, upstream. The second landed in the stream, downstream. The next two rounds landed in the road, one at each end of the bridge. Everyone ran for cover. He made the mistake of running to the exposed end of the bridge to take cover, away from the protection of a ditch which ran parallel to the stream, and the hill cut, which were on the north side of the stream. Once he recognized his mistake, he did not want to cross the bridge in the open, so decided he would work his way across in the stream, on the upstream side.

All went well until he reached the culverts. They were running overfull. He made it past the first culvert, still on his feet, but half way across the second lost his footing. The next instant he was clinging to the culvert's edge in a raging torrent, thinking, here I am going to drown in a stinking culvert, and will be washed into North Korea. Fear works wonders in an emergency. He managed to pull himself across the second culvert and out on the bank.

He saw several men had taken cover underneath the Bailey Bridge, and it occurred to him the bridge was the enemy's target—not the safest place to take cover. He crawled toward them and grabbed the foot of the first man he reached. He shook his foot and yelled, "Let's move up!" A funny thought struck him as soon as he spoke—a poor choice of words. The soldier's answer confirmed White's thought. "I'm under this damn thing as far as I can get!" Considerable persuasion was necessary to convince the engineers under the bridge to take cover elsewhere, but he finally succeeded.

Shortly thereafter, Richard White heard men on the security detail yelling for help. A member of the machine-gun crew had been hit. The quickest way to the wounded man was over the bridge. He ran across the bridge and made his way to the machine-gun position. Because of the dark, he could not see but learned one of his KATUSAs, an ammo bearer and assistant gunner, was hit in the legs. The South Korean soldier moaned but did not speak. Helped up, White began taking him back across the bridge. From out of the darkness, Sgt. Jim Goudy ran to them and assisted in getting the Korean to safety and evacuation to the battalion aid station a couple of miles to the rear.

Mortar rounds continued to fall periodically throughout the remainder of the night. In the midst of the long night of work and "take cover," there was both humor and pathos among the men of Bulldozer Able. The engineers noted an eight to ten foot embankment was near the north approach to the bridge, the best place to take cover from mortar barrages. When rounds started coming in, Goudy and others made for the embankment, leaped over the side, and backed up into the sitting position against the bank. On one occasion, Goudy leaped over the side; his helmet came off in midflight, then hit him in the head when he hit bottom before the helmet did.

When the mortar rounds came in another time, he jumped over the edge, landed to back up against the bank, and in the dark discovered a four-foot-long piece of heavy, six-inch-by-sixteen-inch timber. He tried to stand the big piece of wood on end in front of him for added protection. He felt someone else's hands tugging on the timber, but could not see his competitor. "Who in hell is pulling on this?" he demanded. A voice replied, "This is Captain Brettell." The tug of war ended.

A sadder case was that of a young jeep driver who had been in Korea a considerable period of time. When the shelling began he found a niche for cover, and lay there frightened and trembling the whole night. Richard White failed to coax him out, nor would orders budge him. He had "gone to ground," consumed with fear, terrified, shattered, unable or unwilling to perform under fire. The next morning his company commander, Jim Brettell, took the soldier in his jeep to the battalion aid station, and he entered a hospital. The war was over for him. He was a hazard to himself and others.

Work halted frequently when it was necessary to take cover from incoming. Casualties came one after another, but by 6:00 A.M. on 8 July a sixty-foot span bridged the stream. That was not the end of pushing a Bailey Bridge across the swollen stream. Rising waters again threatened the bridge, this time the abutments. Able Company's engineers returned the next morning and added thirty more feet to the span. Because they stored unused materials at the site, additional construction held up traffic only two hours.

The bridge on Pork Chop's access road was the bridge too near the enemy. The courageous work by the engineers was costly: thirty-eight wounded in thirty-six hours, a few seriously. But none were killed in action, and inexplicably not once did the enemy hit the bridge with a mortar round.[42] The APCs kept grinding relentlessly across the bridge and up the access road, carrying the wherewithal for battle to the outpost's defenders, returning with weary men relieved from the fighting, the wounded, and all the dead the hill's defenders could reach. Pork Chop was preparing for another day, and plans were well under way in the 17th Regiment to launch a battalion counterattack the afternoon of 8 July.

10

BATTALION COUNTERATTACK

THE CCF'S NOW-OBVIOUS, SINGULAR OBJECTIVE OF SEIZING PORK CHOP from the 7th Division, and possibly penetrating the MLR at the north end of the Chorwon Valley, clearly indicated the hill was a key terrain feature standing in the way of a breakthrough. The Chorwon was the primary invasion route used by the NKPA in 1950. The collapse of defenses on Pork Chop could permit the Chinese to flank MLR positions on Hill 200, get into the rear of 200, and move south on the road from the outpost into the rear of Hill 347. Along the MLR, going from the east to the west coast, Pork Chop and Hill 347 anchored the line at a significant bend, from a slightly angled east-west orientation, more sharply to the southwest. Should the CCF break into the Chorwon Valley with sufficient force, they would threaten the rear of UN divisions manning positions in the hills northeast and north of Seoul.

To the east of the 7th Division sector, outpost Arrowhead, in front of the ROK 2d Division's MLR, was also under intense attack. Arrowhead offered an alternate route into the Chorwon Valley. Penetrations in both areas would open a wide gap in the UN line. The assaults on Pork Chop and Arrowhead could either be major attacks intended to penetrate the UN MLR and, in the eastern two-thirds of the peninsula, force a rollback of the entire line toward the thirty-eighth parallel, or major diversionary attacks intended to draw in Eighth Army reserves prior to the CCF's launching heavier attacks against the ROKs to the east—with the same objective: roll back the line to the thirty-eighth parallel or farther.

On 7 July planning began for a battalion counterattack on Pork Chop the afternoon of 8 July. At midnight of the seventh, Maj. John Noble, the commander of 2d of the 17th, received alerting orders. Easy and George Company commanders, in turn, were told by Noble their units would carry out the counterattack mission. Plans included facilities for both wire and radio communications. The two attacking companies were to lay wire as they moved to assault positions, and each was completely equipped with radio and alternate operators designated for all communication equipment. Expecting a night-time CCF counterattack following the two-company assault, the 2d Battalion's Fox Company would be prepared to reinforce George and Easy Companies.

Artillery battalions and supporting mortar sections drew up preparatory plans for fire on all known enemy artillery and mortar positions within range of Pork Chop. Easy Company's 60-mm mortar section prepared to support from a position at the base of Hill 200's south slope, near and slightly east of the approach to the Bailey Bridge. Engineer demolitions teams from the 13th Engineers attached to counterattacking companies would destroy hasty fortifications prepared by the enemy to hold the outpost.

The original plan was two companies line abreast, moving across the valley from Hill 200 to Pork Chop, but the plan was altered:[1]

At a conference at the 17th Infantry CP at 8:00 A.M., 8 July, General Maxwell Taylor, Eighth Army commander; Lieutenant General Clarke, I Corps commander; Major General Trudeau, 7th Division commander; Colonel Harris, 17th Regiment commander; and Major John Noble, commander, 2nd Battalion, 17th Infantry, whose battalion was to make the next counterattack, completely reviewed the situation.

The decision was made to launch a two-company daylight attack in the middle of the afternoon. The attack was to be preceded by twenty minutes of preparatory [artillery and mortar] fire . . . , with surrounding

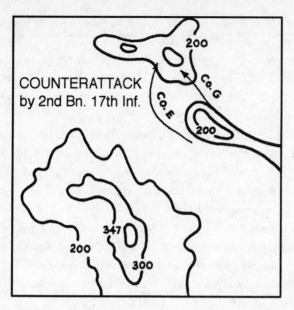

COUNTERATTACK
by 2nd Bn. 17th Inf.

200

Co. G

Co. E

200

347

200

300

The counterattack by 2d Battalion, 17th Infantry. The battalion departed Hill 200 on foot and began the assault at 3:40 P.M. on 8 July 1953.

enemy observation posts to be smoked and enemy mortar and artillery positions neutralized. Troops were to be moved by truck to the checkpoint [behind Hill 200]. Company G, 2d Battalion of the 17th was to attack to the east side of Pork Chop and secure high ground, jumping from a line of departure on the forward slopes of Hill 200. Company E of the 2nd Battalion was to follow the stream bed [at the base of] the reverse slope of Hill 200, attack up the western side of Pork Chop, and tie in with G Company on the high ground. Special instructions were issued to the troops to stay out of the trenches until they were on their objective.[2]

General Taylor, whose policy was "undertake no offensive action involving units of company size or larger . . . except counterattacks to restore or maintain integrity of vital positions," undoubtedly came to examine the 7th Division's plan as well as review the situation. At 10:00 A.M. he authorized the planned battalion counterattack.[3]

Early the morning of 8 July, shortly after artillery fire slackened, Chinese soldiers launched a localized attack down a trench line on a finger of Pork Chop, which was across a deep gully from an opening in the engineers' tunnel. Mac Conner and two of his riflemen, hidden inside the tunnel on the enemy's flank, apparently unobserved, could plainly see the attack in progress. Conner and his two riflemen kept a steady fire on the right flank of the assaulting Chinese, wiping out the right half of the attacking element. It was the last offensive action by the Chinese in the vicinity of the tunnel for the duration of his stay on Pork Chop.

A short time later, Conner again encountered Dick Shea, his West Point classmate, in the tunnel leading to the Able Company CP. Shea's cheek showed a small gash and his neck evidenced a cut or bullet crease, superficial wounds incurred in the hand-to-hand and close-quarter fighting the night before. Conner sported the bandaged finger from his fall onto the ammunition can during his platoon's counterattack to drive the enemy from the tunnel near the Able Company CP the morning of the 7th. Shea told Conner that Able and Baker Companies were being relieved of responsibility for defense of outpost Pork Chop, and again expressed frustration at being unable to reach the isolated 2d Platoon.[4]

Consistent with General Trudeau's policy of sending in fresh units to relieve others engaged in fighting for thirty-six to forty-eight hours, Lieutenant Colonel Read had been alerted to evacuate the wounded and dead, and move Able and Baker Companies off the hill, to give Easy and George Companies more freedom of movement in the counterattack. Easy Company of the 32d would briefly assume responsibility for defense of the Chop while the evacuation was in progress—and until the 2d Battalion, commanded by Major Noble, assumed the mission.[5]

Able Company's 2d Platoon had held firm on the east flank, and Lieutenant Colonel Read had told Dick Shea to establish contact with the platoon and come off the hill with them. In the brief second encounter with Mac Conner, Dick Shea was explaining he had to reach the platoon but had been unable to get through. He was going to try another foray, but did not know how he was going to reach them.

"Are you OK?" Conner asked.

"Yeah," Shea replied.

Conner knew Shea would not leave Pork Chop without the men he was assigned to bring off the hill. He put his hand on Shea's shoulder. "Don't get yourself killed."

Shea replied earnestly, "Don't worry. I won't, Mac."[6]

Able Company's Heroic Private

While the Army, Corps, and Division commanders were making plans for the afternoon assault by Easy and George Companies, more heroics were in progress on Pork Chop. Pvt. Robert E. Miller was being readied for evacuation with the wounded of Able and Baker Companies, and Dick Shea and Jim McKenzie were preparing to assist David Willcox's 2d Platoon. Though the two companies were to be relieved when Major Noble's 2d Battalion took over responsibility for the defense of the hill, Able Company's 2d Platoon had to continue to hold the east shoulder of the hill until relieved by G Company in the midafternoon counterattack.

Pvt. Bob Miller's abrupt awakening in the first minutes of the 6 July assault by the Chinese turned into a nightmare. Told to grab his rifle, throughout the night he engaged in a series of close-quarter fights with enemy soldiers swarming into the 1st Platoon positions near the company CP. Everywhere he turned, almost without pause, it seemed there were Chinese infantrymen. He repeatedly hurled hand grenades, emptied his rifle, and reloaded, firing at fleeting figures and small groups of enemy soldiers. His rifle eventually quit firing, and he hurled grenades and had grenades thrown at him—until one came through the aperture, exploded at his feet, tore off his right leg below his knee, and shattered his left.

Finally, on the afternoon of the seventh, Charlie Brooks asked Miller if he could hold on while the rest of the men went outside the trench and bunker network to get assistance for him. For Brooks it was an agonizing decision. They had attempted several times to fight their way through the trenches and tunnel to get aid for him. Miller understood his circumstance, and theirs. His rifle was jammed, but he agreed to remain by himself if they would leave him a case of hand grenades. They did, and moved him out of the bunker into the trench, away from the entrance, propped against the wall where he could see both directions. Next to him was the case of grenades.

For what seemed like hours he waited. Every time he heard Chinese voices approaching, he threw a hand grenade toward the sound. Each time the grenade exploded, the voices stopped. Later, another squad member, Angelo Palermo, who returned to the 1st Platoon after fighting in another sector of the hill, came down the trench, identifying himself to Miller.

Palermo was dumbfounded to learn Miller was left behind, alone. Miller explained why and showed him the supply of grenades, telling Palermo how he was defending himself and noting he had used up only a fourth of his supply—that he was all right. Palermo said he believed the tunnel was clear of enemy now and he would go get a medic. He rechecked Miller's bandages, saying, "They'll be OK 'til help arrives," and left.

Again it seemed hours passed. Day had turned to night after Brooks left. Then Palermo had gone for help. Now it must be near morning. Bob Miller continued to hurl grenades at approaching sounds of Chinese soldiers. Suddenly he heard the roar of a flame thrower, behind him, around the corner, coming from the direction of the company CP. He yelled, "What the hell are you doing? Cut that damn thing off." He breathed a sigh of relief when he heard an American voice say, "He's one of us."

Soon he was carried on a litter down the tunnel past the CP. As his litter bearers approached the tunnel entrance he could see reinforcing soldiers lining the walls. He saw the expressions on their faces as he passed them. He knew some, on seeing him, were receiving their first dose of war's reality.

He had had no food or water since the afternoon of 6 July, and asked if anyone had a drink of water. A soldier said, "Here's my canteen. Take it. You need it more than I do." After taking a drink, Bob Miller offered the canteen back to him. "You keep it," he said.

At approximately 10:00 A.M. 8 July, Bob Miller was evacuated from Pork Chop Hill on an APC. He did not know the soldier who gave him a drink of water and his canteen; he did not ask his name. But over the years he has yearned to know, while inside he has said his thanks to the soldier many times.[7]

Preparations to Relieve Able's 2d Platoon

The morning Bob Miller was evacuated, Dick Shea and Jim McKenzie both were to make their way to the 2d Platoon area on the right flank of Pork Chop. Lieutenant Colonel Read earlier had told Dick to contact the platoon and prepare them to leave the hill before George and Easy Company counterattacked that afternoon. Men from George Company, attacking up the east shoulder of the hill, would relieve Able Company's 2d Platoon. Dick was to come off the hill with David Willcox's platoon.

The Chinese had continued to hold bunkers and trenches between the company CP and 2d Platoon's perimeter, isolating David Willcox and his men from the rest of the company. The most severely threatened area of Pork Chop remained in the left and central sectors, the west shoulder of the hill, manned by 1st Platoon. The 1st Platoon and men from Easy of the 32d were keeping the Chinese from overrunning the bunker formerly housing the company CP, which was almost directly beneath the crest of the hill. Thus reinforcements coming onto the hill were consistently off-loaded from APCs near the entrance to the engineers' tunnel, to shore up the more severely threatened areas, and retake areas held by the enemy.

There were other reasons 2d Platoon had not been reinforced sufficiently to be relieved with the rest of A Company. Because the center and left of Pork Chop were under constant pressure from the Chinese, Read could not pull men from the most threatened areas to fight their way through and reinforce 2d Platoon, which was holding its own. Additionally, repeated enemy shelling and assaults on the rear of Pork Chop made reinforcement, replacement, resupply, and evacuation of wounded and dead only slightly less hazardous than fighting in the open or from the trenches and bunkers on the front slope of the hill. Persistently troublesome interdicting enemy fire along a one thousand yard section of access road leading to the south entrance to the platoon's defense network hampered efforts to reinforce. Further, the trench leading to the 2d Platoon CP did not offer as much cover from enemy fire as the covered main trench leading to the company CP.

To gather the force necessary to move out of the trenches and bunkers near the company CP and attempt reinforcing the right sector was next to impossible. There were seldom enough men to hold positions retaken with counterattacks. Going outside the defense network onto the northern slopes in localized counterattacks, as when Dick Inman's patrol attempted fighting its way to 2d Platoon positions that first night, would be costly to already beleaguered, exhausted troops. Worse, given the confusing intermixing of American and Chinese held positions, there was an added hazard of "friendly fire" casualties unless Americans and KATUSAs chose to identify themselves during counterattacks.

Day or night, it was virtually impossible to use daily passwords, because communications and contact did not extend to isolated defenders. The certainty of who was to the right, left, in front or behind defenders vanished the night of the initial Chinese assault, and was seldom restored anywhere on the hill. Voice identification was not reliable. Visual identification risked instant death. Defenders were tense, ready to shoot first and ask questions later. When the situation did improve, it could immediately deteriorate in the next Chinese assault, or the next American counterattack.

The morning of the 7th, Rocky Read personally intervened to stop Dick Shea from exposing himself to enemy fire during an attempt to eject Chinese from a trench section near the company CP. Now, the morning of 8 July, from Bunker 45, Read personally covered Shea with rifle fire to keep enemy heads down and permit Shea to get to the area where the surviving men in Able Company's 2d Platoon were fighting to hold the hill's right flank. The battalion commander saw Shea safely enter the platoon's perimeter when Shea dashed the seventy-five yards back down the access road and turned left into the trench leading toward the platoon CP in Bunker 64.[8]

Some time later, Jim McKenzie was covered by machine-gun fire as he traversed the same route to 2d platoon, to provide medical aid and prepare wounded to be evacuated. He reached Bunker 64, where he stayed, tending wounded. Late in the day he would be swamped by casualties, as the George and Easy Company counterattack swept onto Pork Chop and was decimated by enemy artillery and mortar fire.[9]

The First Wound

The morning of 8 July, after Mac Conner's second brief encounter with Dick Shea, he went outside the tunnel with one of his men. Their purpose was to throw grenades uphill toward enemy soldiers who had been repeatedly hurling grenades at the men in Mac's platoon. The foray resulted in the wounding of the man accompanying Conner. He unsuccessfully attempted to pick up and throw a live Chinese grenade back at the enemy, and it exploded in his hand. Nevertheless, Conner decided a more forceful excursion outside the tunnel could get the Chinese off the hill directly above them.

He laid out the plan for his men, and they were successful in driving the enemy off the area immediately above the tunnel. However, the cost was heavy, and it stuck with Mac the rest of his life. One of the platoon's sergeants was killed by enemy automatic weapons fire from much farther up the hill.

While Conner and his men were outside the tunnel, and were successful in driving the Chinese off nearby ground, they witnessed a veritable rain of grenades from farther up the hill, most falling among the enemy's own soldiers below. Conner's move outside the tunnel made clear to him that numerous Chinese were holed up all over the top of the hill, and a major attack would be needed to dislodge them. He decided to keep to his orders. He did not want to lose any more of his men. He would take no more offensive actions, not until he was ordered to launch an assault the next morning. While his platoon took no more offensive actions on 8 July, before the day was over, Mac Conner was wounded for the first time.

In midafternoon, he finally paused to eat some C-rations. He was sitting near an opening at the lower end of the tunnel, spooning fruit from a can, when a mortar round exploded adjacent to the opening, knocking him backward onto the ground. A piece of shrapnel punctured his right arm and lodged in the bone near his elbow. The wound was not incapacitating, and he remained on Pork Chop.[10]

George Company Enters the Fight

Pfc. John W. Phillips was a radioman on a forward observer team in the 81-mm mortar platoon of H Company, the 2d Battalion's heavy weapons company, when orders came for How Company to detach an FO team to support George Company's counterattack. After the war, as years passed, he chronicled his reminiscences of those five days of battle on Pork Chop. His recollections are paraphrased in the following paragraphs.

When the Chinese assault on Pork Chop began in the heavy rain the night of 6 July, Phillips and other FOs had been in the headquarters squad of the mortar platoon in a combination fire direction center (FDC) and sleeping bunker dug into the hill at the mortar position behind Hill 347. Promptly called into action, there was little the mortars could do in the heavy rain storm that first night. Although they did some firing in defense of Pork Chop, the artillery did most of the work that night. Such weather is difficult and dangerous for mortar crews, and infantry units that might receive the mortars' supporting fire. Rain wets externally mounted powder increments on the rounds causing misfires and short rounds.

In the rainstorm that night John's buddy, Bryant W. Robison, and others from the 81-mm mortar platoon spent an active night in the pouring rain manning the OP on Hill 347. They helped medics and others care for the wounded and evacuate the dead and wounded from incessant shelling of the hill and attacks against outpost positions. It was often difficult or impossible to carry litters through the trenches, so litter bearers had to get out of the trenches onto the surface, which exposed them to enemy fire.

On 7 July, 81-mm mortars from 1st Battalion's heavy weapons company, Dog Company, moved from 17th Regiment's reserve position, and John Phillips saw their mortars set up behind Hill 347 across a draw from How Company's position. That morning, on the side of the hill near Dog Company's position, John also saw litters covered with blankets and ponchos laid out in neat rows. Graves Registration Service troops were moving among them.

In the heavy weapons companies, as well as the battalion staffs and other supporting units, rumors were flying about the intensity of the Chinese attack of the previous night. Matters seemed to be getting desperate, almost frantic. Under the direction of the OP on Hill 347, John's mortar platoon fired almost continuously, mostly on the approaches to and front slopes of Pork Chop as well as Hasakkol. Rumors were the whole central front was being attacked, particularly the ROK Army units on the 7th Division's right, and that the ROKs were being overwhelmed and pushed back. Also heard, correctly, the Chinese possessed much of Pork Chop.

Sources of the rumors, and some facts, were from the small FDC switchboard in John Phillips's platoon. The FDC was connected by wire to the OP on Hill 347, company headquarters, the How Company machine-gun platoon which was protecting the left flank of Hill 347, and 2d Battalion headquarters. In the mortar platoon's headquarters squad, the platoon sergeant and others constantly talked on the hot loop with men in the platoon's OP. The men in the OP continued their daily routine of taking turns returning to the mortar position for food and supplies. Both over the phone and in person they brought reports of what they were seeing; attacks by the Chinese, fighting in the trenches, and constant bombardment by both sides. They had been manning the OP so long that they knew every land feature in front of them.

Although several M-46 Patton tanks with their standard armament of 90-mm guns were routinely in hull defilade on the crest of Hill 347, the 17th Regiment moved other tanks by road to the rear of 347, and they dispersed down the draw in a blocking position, in case the Chinese breached the MLR. Traffic on the road, which cut across the abandoned rice paddies to the rear of the How Company mortar position, picked up considerably. Trucks, jeeps with and without trailers, ambulances, and litter jeeps shuttled back and forth. John Phillips and other newcomers to the 7th Division knew something big was happening, something most had never seen before. From behind Hill 347, it appeared the attack was centered on Pork Chop Hill. The outpost was being severely tested, but the Chinese had not struck Hill 347 or 200 with troops. Mortars and artillery were enough. Pfc. John Phillips's turn to "go up on Pork Chop" came after noon on 8 July.

John's platoon leader told him and Cpl. Robert A. Keith they were being sent to battalion headquarters to be attached to a rifle company as an FO team. They had less than a half hour to prepare, and gathered their gear quickly. Phillips had his own steel pot (helmet), flak jacket, and M-1 rifle, but needed much more. In the platoon was Sergeant Lehrke, an experienced FO due to rotate home any day. Whenever possible, short-timers were not sent into a pitched battle, so Lehrke traded his coveted automatic M-2 carbine for Phillips's semiautomatic M-1 rifle. Lehrke helped him strap some "banana clips"—oversized carbine magazines—end to end with commo tape and loaded them to the top. Banana clips carried thirty rounds each, rather than the fifteen rounds in the standard box magazine. Three banana combinations gave John 180 rounds without reloading magazines, plus another sixty in four box magazines.

The platoon's communications chief installed a new battery in a PRC-10 radio and helped strap it on a backboard along with a new spare battery in its plastic bag, plus a thermite grenade to destroy the radio in case of imminent capture or overrun. The FO carried field glasses, a lensatic compass, and a map. Both men knew the concentration numbers for fire missions, some firing data, and were familiar with terrain features. Corporal Keith had been on the Chop before, but John Phillips had not.

Master Sergeant Jackson, the platoon sergeant, checked the two men for other necessities: dog tags, first-aid bandage, bayonet, extra ammo, toothbrush, scratch paper, pencil, cleaning patches, and no personal effects such as wallets, pictures, or jewelry. John Phillips's former Marine brother had taught him about carrying mortar range cards and toilet paper in his helmet liner, and about carrying an extra canteen of water. Now loaded with gear, John routinely carried a can opener on his dog-tag chain and a spoon in his pocket. The FO, Corporal Keith, carried two personal weapons, both an M-1 rifle and a .45-caliber pistol. He wore a full M-1 cartridge belt and carried several magazines for the pistol.

The road and gap over the hill to the rear of Hill 347 was periodically receiving incoming harassing rounds, but considerable traffic was coming to the front and returning to the rear. This day traffic was heavier and included trucks carrying troops and ammunition, tanks, and a few APCs, along with ambulances and litter jeeps. The two men crawled in a jeep and the platoon leader's driver took them through the gap over the next hill to the rear, to the large battalion bunker housing the CP. More blanket- and poncho-covered litters were along the hillside near the CP, and graves registration people were working among them. Ten to fifteen trucks were also spaced along the side of the road, filled, they assumed, with various supplies, ammunition, and rations. When the two reported in, Battalion S-3 (operations) assigned them to join George Company, already on the road down the draw toward the checkpoint behind Hill 200. They reboarded the jeep and sped back down the hill which passed behind 347 and down the draw toward George Company.

John Phillips and Robert Keith left the mortar platoon in bright midday sunshine with scattered clouds. As the afternoon wore on the sky became heavily overcast, the precursor to typical monsoon rain squalls. To himself, John reasoned the smoke and dust rising from the continuous shelling in the vicinity of Pork Chop made the overcast heavier and darker than normal. As they neared the usually fordable stream which ran beside the narrow road, a few of the 13th Engineers were still working on the Bailey Bridge.

When Keith and Phillips caught up with George Company, it was deployed in a long single file at the base of the south slope of Hill 200, awaiting orders. The soldiers waited, spread out and in cover in the blocking position, because mortar rounds were occasionally falling in the area. When the FO team reported to the company commander, 1st Lt. Robert Brobst, a division artillery FO team, which included 2d Lt. Edward B. McAllister from the 49th Field Artillery Battalion, was already with Brobst. As in Easy Company, both the artillery and mortar FO teams would remain close to the commander, his radioman, and headquarters element throughout the time George Company was on the hill.

While the men waited, a jeep-towed trailer pulled up and unloaded more cases of all sorts of ammunition for George Company. With the now louder sounds of artillery and mortars coming from the front, no one needed encouragement to increase his personal ammunition supply. Everyone picked up even more ammunition bandoleers, hand grenades, machinegun cartridge boxes, and other ammunition.

While George Company waited behind Hill 200, the mortar FO team tried a radio check with their platoon behind Hill 347, and were quickly offered a helpful relay. The voice spoke perfect English but his eager, polite tone and helpfulness gave him away as Chinese listening on the FO frequency. The FO team went off the air. The PRC-10s ("handy-talkies" carried on the back) and "walkie-talkies" were short range radios, did not carry far in Korea's hills and mountainous terrain, and the Chinese frequently intruded on tactical frequencies, or jammed them with chatter and noisemakers. Planned alternate frequencies daily passed to all radio operators were the counters to Chinese intrusions and jamming.[11]

Among the men of George Company the afternoon Phillips and Keith arrived to join them were Cpl. Robert Northcutt, squad leader and machine gunner in the weapons squad of a rifle platoon, and Cpl. Dan D. Schoonover, a squad leader in Able Company of the 13th Engineers. Schoonover, the brash young corporal from Boise, Idaho, had brought his squad of combat engineers, each carrying a satchel charge in addition to a rifleman's weapon and ammunition load.

Earlier in the day, when George Company was in its assembly area, Bob Northcutt received word of an attack order from his new, replacement platoon leader when the lieutenant called a meeting of the platoon sergeant and four squad leaders. The platoon leader told them they were going to attack Pork Chop that afternoon. Bob Northcutt had fought on the Chop in April. He knew this one would be no easier.

Before departing their assembly area, the men prepared for what lay ahead. At the company supply point, they were told to draw ammunition and high explosive grenades—all each man could carry. Northcutt told every man in his squad to carry as many belts of machine-gun ammunition as they could. The company then moved by open-topped two and one half ton trucks from their assembly area to the checkpoint behind Hill 200. En route to the checkpoint, the convoy passed close to an 8-inch field artillery gun battery, which fired a salvo just as Bob Northcutt's truck passed. The explosive roar of outbound artillery startled everyone and affected North-cutt's hearing for hours. From behind the bluff hiding the checkpoint from observers on Old Baldy and Chink Baldy, they moved on foot to the block-ing position behind Hill 200.[12]

As Easy and George began moving to their lines of departure, APCs were arriving on Pork Chop with more ammunition and supplies, and on the return trips evacuating Able and Baker Company men, plus the wounded and dead. By 2:30 in the afternoon, Able and Baker had been evacuated, except David Willcox's 2d Platoon of Able Company, while Easy of the 32d moved to fill and hold the positions being vacated by the evacuation. The removal of wounded and dead continued until late in the afternoon and early evening of 8 July.[13]

While George Company moved into position to assault the east finger of Pork Chop from Hill 200, Easy Company, commanded by Lt. John Dashiell, was assembling to proceed parallel to the stream, around the northwest foot of Hill 200, cross the valley, and climb Brinson Finger. One of his platoon leaders was Lt. Bob Hope, who had been on Pork Chop in May—Hope's first fire fight on the outpost. When the Chinese launched the May assault, estimated to be from one company to one battalion in strength, Hope had seen the enemy unit shattered by well-directed artillery fire. This time would be far different.

Dashiell's jeep driver, Pvt. Robert Wilson, previously wounded, fully recovered, but not yet reassigned to 1st Platoon, would be staying behind, on duty at the communications bunker at the checkpoint. Dashiell wanted Wilson to remain at the checkpoint where he could check on Easy Com-pany men coming off the hill. Robert Wilson was an "old hand" in Easy Company and knew all but a few of the newer replacements. Part of the counterattack plan included setting up an Easy Company mortar position at the base of Hill 200, out of sight of the Chinese on Old Baldy, and a short distance from the north approach to the Bailey Bridge.[14]

Undoubtedly concerned about the use of a skirmish line or some other tactical formation in the face of heavy artillery and mortar concentrations expected when their assault began, George Company planned a single file movement from Hill 200 to Pork Chop's east shoulder. Deployment of the company into a tactical formation in broad daylight on the front slopes of

Hill 200 would permit enemy observers on Old Baldy and Pork Chop's crest to better concentrate and adjust CCF fires, and inflict more casualties. By moving rapidly, single file, downhill from 200, and along the west slope of the cut between 200 and the outpost, and up the back slope of the Chop just below the crest, casualties would be lessened. Once consolidated on the hill, they would attack west, up the trench line, but staying out of the trenches and bunkers.

The order to stay out of the trenches and bunkers was to ensure that counterattacking companies kept moving outside, on the hill's surface and rooting out the enemy clinging to the crest of Pork Chop. Once the enemy was swept off the crest and cleared from bunkers and trenches, then the two companies would have complete control of the outpost. The plan, to move rapidly, was reinforced with instructions not to stop and assist wounded while on the move between Hill 200 and the objective. Medics would follow behind and retrieve the wounded.[15]

At 3:00 P.M. George Company left the blocking position, single file, and started the climb up a shallow, hip-deep trench, toward the crest of Hill 200. As the climb continued the trench gradually deepened to six to seven feet at the crest. A rifle platoon, squads in column, was the lead element, followed by Corporal Northcutt's machine-gun squad. Well back in the column was Lieutenant Brobst, his command element, and the forward observers.[16]

The point of departure for George Company was a solidly roofed firing bunker on the front slope of Hill 200. Since 200 was lower than the crest of Pork Chop, the point of departure was hidden from enemy observers on Old Baldy, Hasakkol, and the Rats' Nest. However, the Chinese holding Pokkae and the crest of the outpost could clearly see the entire front slope of Hill 200 and would be able to see the lead elements of George as soon as they started their move toward the Chop.

At the firing bunker, a young George Company sergeant was acting like a starter at a race. Pvt. John Phillips recalls:

As each soldier, squad, or small group filed up the trench to the bunker and the line of departure, he checked that we did a lock-and-load on personal weapons. (With all the yelling, noise, artillery bursts, and small arms snapping around, troops can get so nervous that they forget to load their weapons.) The sergeant could glance out the bunker aperture at the troops who had gone before, so he could regulate the pace. The sergeant reminded each soldier to keep his head down, to maintain the standard, combat zone, five-yard separation, and to keep moving to the top of Pork Chop. Maybe five or six wounded were inside the bunker and on litters in the adjacent trench awaiting evacuation, and a medic was working among them.

Suddenly it was World War I all over again. At the sergeant's signal, each person put his right foot on the firing step, swung his left leg up and over, and clamored out of the trench outside the bunker, over the top, and started down the slope toward Pork Chop. No one had any idea what was over the top or down the slope or what had happened to those who preceded him. For all we knew a Chinese machine gun was cutting down everyone on the path. All we knew was that when your turn came, you went. Shells were falling sporadically in the area where we were. This caused you to hunker down and try to pull your head into your body like a turtle. But mostly the shells were crunching on Pork Chop to which we were headed. Also some sounds of small arms fire including machine guns crackled, but I have no idea who was firing at whom.

When I went over the top, I immediately discovered that there was a path and the path was fairly steep. Down the slope I went, running very fast. Part way down gravity took over, I lost my footing, fell down, and rolled or slid maybe ten yards, got up, ran on to the bottom, and trotted across the wide, flat area. We went through some barbed wire. It was a very long, lonely run to the base of Pork Chop. Then I started up the Pork Chop finger following the general path and those before me. By this time the Chinese observers to the north on Pokkae, Old Baldy, the crest of Pork Chop and other positions had noticed the reinforcements; so, about one-fourth of the way up mortar shells were falling all along the finger on both sides. The Chinese had been shooting at those hills as long as we had, and they had them perfectly registered.

The slope of the Pork Chop finger was fairly steep. With the loads we were carrying, the humid July afternoon heat, the mortar and artillery fire incoming, and the roar of friendly artillery fire outgoing, we actually began to spread out much more than the minimum five yards. This was not a glorious infantry charge. Since we had not been ordered into an assault formation, we were hoping that GIs held the slope of the hill and the top of the hill, and that we were indeed reinforcements. But no one was certain.

After we started up the slope, we were no longer running, but walking in a crouch. A few troops were crawling and some were slowly jogging. We were loaded and struggling, sweating profusely, gasping for breath, and very worried about what was happening all around, and what lay ahead. From the slope, you could see the constant blanket of air bursts of VT above the forward slope, just below the crest. Several people around me went down either from wounds, fear, or exhaustion. But our orders were to keep moving, and common sense said those were good orders.

As we climbed the finger, I remember passing a black medic on my right who was helping a hobbling wounded guy back down the slope. I hope they made it back to Hill 200, but I doubt it. Somehow I remembered Sergeant Knox from basic training. "Don't stop! Keep moving through it! Your chances are better." I clearly remember having a round go off in front of me, maybe ten or twelve yards at the most, filling the air with dirt, debris, and shrapnel. I kept moving and stepped in the churned shell hole, still soft, hot, and smoking. Then another shell went off behind me where I had been seconds before. I did not get a scratch from either shell, but, if I had stopped for the first one, the second one would have landed on my head. For the time being, Sergeant Knox's advice was holding true. I stepped in a number of hot, smoking shell holes on the way up the slope.

On the top of the hill, no skirmish line had been formed and no sweeping of the hill was taking place. . . . Artillery and small arms fire were too intense to stay erect on the surface. Perhaps the earlier arrivals had tried to stay on the surface and move west along the crest. . . . I do not know. At the top I momentarily crouched down beside a bunker to catch my breath, assess what was going on, and try to spot the group I was supposed to be with sweeping the crest of the hill. I did not see any troops on the ridge line in front of me or along the rear slope near the ridge line I remember. I looked back down the steep finger up which we had climbed, and troops were still straggling up. Since at that moment no one could move on the surface, everyone was entering the trench line as he reached it and he could find a place. Everything was chaotic. Platoons and even squads had disintegrated as units. What was left of the full rifle company quickly clogged the trenches. All forward movement stopped. Everyone knew we should keep five yards apart, but there was no place to go. We could not move forward, and there was no going back. I have no idea how long it had taken from Hill 200 to the top of the finger of Pork Chop, but it was hot as hell, and everyone was exhausted, gasping for breath.

Into the Trenches

John Phillips's recollections continue:

Everyone was bunched up as the lead elements cautiously moved forward against they knew not what. A few direct hits on that section of the hill at that moment would have killed and wounded dozens. The squads and platoons seemed to have lost unit integrity, but the little headquarters group I was with reassembled and never totally disintegrated. For what seemed like a long while, the company headquarters group did nothing except stand packed in the trench as officers and senior noncoms tried to assess the actual situation, get organized, and decide what to do next. . . .

After a while some rifle squads were reorganized, and we advanced westward with the CO's team through the trench lined with men. Pork Chop defenses had changed greatly since Keith had last been there. In that part of the hill, extremely deep commo (communication) trenches had been dug and roofed with timbers and sandbags against the constant shelling. In some places the trench was dim because of the overheads, but in many places the overheads had received direct hits and were caved in, open to the sky. Between April defense and July defense, the trenches had been dug so deep (they seemed eight or ten feet deep) that there was no way to get out of them. I knew for sure that we were all dead then because a lone Chinese crawling on the surface of the hill could have grenaded the trench and killed us all. Only intense VT artillery fire on the surface probably kept that from happening. That particular section of the trench was blown in.

In one long section the bottom of the trench was so littered with bodies that in many places they were several deep. We had no time to move them and no place to which to move them. You had to step on them to move forward. I do not know whether the dead were already there when George Company arrived or whether they were from the lead elements of George Company. Chinese could have been among them. They were the first battlefield dead I had been close to. I tried not to look at them, but you could not walk on them without looking at them. We all resembled each other in age and dress. If the Chinese had just created that mess, they lifted or shifted their fires or retreated too soon. A little more of whatever had caused that chaos would have wiped out the remainder of the entire company.

We advanced westward in the trench along the crest to a place where the trench was completely blown in and barricaded with timbers. You could not tell whether it was a deliberate barricade or whether the over-head had just fallen that way in an explosion. Nobody seemed to know where the enemy was or where other friendly troops were in the maze of trenches and bunkers with which most of us were not familiar. If George Company had been briefed before they left Hill 200 on what to expect on Pork Chop, I did not hear it. Although Chinese were thought to be on the other side of the barricade, no one fired down the trench either way. An officer sent for a combat engineer with a satchel charge, and we backed down the trench around the bend for him to blow the barricade.[17]

Bob Northcutt remembers well what the soldiers of George Company were told: "If men go down, wounded, don't stop to help them. Keep going. Medics will come along behind and pick them up."[18]

Also attached to G Company was a demolition squad from Able Company, 13th Engineer Battalion. The squad leader was the young corporal from Boise, Idaho, nineteen year old Dan Schoonover. The squad's mission was to use satchel charges to dislodge the enemy from hastily erected fortifications, bunkers, and other covered defenses the Chinese had seized.

When Easy and George Companies moved off the line of departure, both encountered murderous artillery and mortar fire. Bob Northcutt remembered George Company lost many men to wounds from artillery and mortar fire before they left the line of departure on Hill 200. Counter-battery fire from the Americans could not possibly locate and silence all the Chinese mortar and artillery pieces which had been registering on the outpost and 200 for weeks. The weather continued overcast, locking out American air support which might otherwise favorably tip the firepower balance.

Nevertheless, both Easy and George aggressively pressed their attacks through the withering fire. In addition to the holocaust of artillery and mortar rounds, Chinese soldiers holding high ground on the east side of the main crest of the hill, and in Able Company's 2d Platoon sector, raked George Company with intense automatic weapons and rifle fire and a rain of grenades. The company's officers and noncommissioned officers were struck down, one by one, wounded or killed. Easy Company experienced a similar circumstance approaching from the west.

With their leadership shredded, both assaults lost momentum and bogged down. As John Phillips recalled, in spite of instructions to remain out of the trenches and bunkers until on their objectives, the devastating enemy fire left the men of G Company little choice. The awful toll drove them into trenches and bunkers for survival, with many pinned down in the vicinity of Bunkers 60 and 61. When the attack began to falter, it became once more a series of isolated struggles between small groups of surviving Chinese and American soldiers. Squad leaders had become separated from their squads, platoon leaders and platoon sergeants from their platoons, the company commander from his platoon leaders. The ability to control the company as a unit immediately became difficult, if not impossible.[19]

Under the withering Chinese fire, Cpl. Bob Northcutt and his machine gunners scrambled up the steep slope toward the left center area of David Willcox's 2d Platoon defensive positions, taking cover as best they could in badly battered, caved-in trenches. He too saw the dead and wounded in the trenches. When his platoon leader and platoon sergeant fell, wounded, he rallied survivors to continue the advance. They moved a short distance past the small headquarters element of Lieutenant Brobst, his radioman, the first sergeant, and the FO teams, and encountered two enemy-held bunkers from which the Chinese were taking a toll with machine guns.

Northcutt ordered a base of fire be placed on each bunker and crawled forward from the right, underneath the enemy crossfire. Although painfully wounded by fragments of an enemy mortar round, he continued to assault the right bunker and succeeded in killing the enemy gun crew with hand grenades. After shifting supporting fire to the second bunker he crawled to its side entrance and killed its occupants with his last two grenades and pistol fire. Later, the survivors of his platoon and squad—few in number and out in the open—were forced to withdraw into a defensive perimeter by withering enemy artillery and mortar fire. The perimeter he set up was under cover as much as possible, and was separate from the perimeter containing Lieutenant Brobst and his company headquarters element. Neither had communication with the other.

Once into the perimeter Bob Northcutt called for Private First Class Schneider to come forward with machine-gun ammunition boxes. They needed to prepare for the expected Chinese night counterattack. Bob returned his gaze in the direction of the enemy and heard a loud explosion behind him. He turned to see Schneider's head gone, his body slumped against the side of the trench. Bob Northcutt had no choice. He began moving about collecting ammunition and weapons abandoned by the wounded and fallen with the dead. They were in for a long night.[20]

For his squad and all soldiers manning machine guns and other heavy weapons, such as mortars or recoilless rifles, life in battle was always difficult and could be terribly brief, especially if they could not fire their weapons from inside well-constructed and reinforced bunkers, or move quickly to another position if they were not well hidden by other forms of cover. When a fight was in progress, once enemy forward observers identified machine-gun or heavy weapons positions they immediately called in artillery and mortar fire. The pounding was relentless until incoming rounds found their mark—if the crew did not quickly move after firing a few rounds. Bob Northcutt lost two of his men that terrible day: Private Schneider, decapitated by the incoming round, and Private First Class Denton, who completely lost control of his emotions that night and stormed forward out of protective cover, up and over the hill's crest, toward the enemy, while Bob screamed at him in vain to come back. He never saw him again.[21]

The hail of enemy fire, heavy fighting, and the confusing intermixing of enemy and friendly-held positions soon convinced Cpl. Dan Schoonover his squad from Able Company, 13th Engineers, could not conduct their assigned demolition mission. Instead, in the midst of the desperate fighting, he voluntarily employed his men as a squad of riflemen. He forged ahead, leading them up the hill in the assault.

When an artillery round exploded on the roof of an enemy bunker, he ran forward and leaped into the position, killing one Chinese soldier and taking another prisoner. A short time later, when George Company soldiers were pinned down by fire from another bunker, he dashed through the hail of fire, hurled grenades in the nearest aperture, then ran to the doorway and emptied his pistol, killing the remainder of the enemy. His actions enabled troops to resume their push forward to Pork Chop's east crest.[22]

It was late in the day of 8 July, about 6:00 P.M., when the counterattack stalled. George Company lost nearly half its men, killed or wounded. The remainder, bereft of officer and NCO leadership, remained isolated, hugging the safety of battered and collapsed trenches, and a few in bunkers.

Success of the counterattack was crucial to successful disengagement and withdrawal of Able Company's 2d Platoon. Every man in the 2d Platoon was exhausted after forty-four hours with no sleep and sporadic, heavy fighting. Nearly 80 percent of those able to fight were wounded. If G Company could not keep the Chinese at bay and occupy positions vacated by 2d Platoon, relief of defenders on the right flank could stall completely. If the Chinese massively reinforced in that area, which they had shown they were willing to do, 2d Platoon could be completely overwhelmed, causing collapse of Pork Chop's defenses.

No one knows for certain what Lieutenant Dick Shea saw or was thinking when the George Company counterattack bogged down. He undoubtedly recognized the stalled attack meant the 2d Platoon relief could not proceed as long as G Company remained pinned down and had lost most of its leadership as well as its forward momentum. He probably recognized the situation had reached a critical stage in which the entire operation's success was questionable. He was that well trained, that well versed, and undoubtedly concluded the 2d Platoon relief could not possibly occur unless the men in G Company somehow aggressively resumed the offensive. Dick Shea made a crucial decision.

He ordered another soldier to take responsibility for leading the 2d Platoon's survivors off Pork Chop. He then moved to assist and organize approximately twenty George Company soldiers, and led a series of localized counterattacks, keeping pressure on the Chinese and off the men of Able Company's 2d Platoon. They confronted an enemy machine-gun position. He maneuvered, while under fire, to within a few yards of the position, threw two hand grenades, then moved in after the grenades, firing his carbine as he closed on the enemy. He killed the three-man crew, silencing the machine gun.

It was still daylight. He sensed a lull in the fighting, a hesitation by the enemy, and determined to launch another counterattack to eject the Chinese from the trenches and bunkers they had taken.

Attacks down the trench line were not effective, the trenches too narrow and crowded to bring the fire power of more than one or two men at a time. The most effective way to break the enemy hold was to move out of the trenches where more firepower could be brought to bear from above, into the trenches and bunkers.

He moved from man to man. "OK. We're ready." Then, "Let's go!"

He led a running assault on Chinese positions in Pork Chop's right flank sector, intent upon overrunning them. He was hit and went down.

He got up and continued moving forward, yelling to his men, "Get going!" For the fifth time in less than two days he refused to leave to obtain medical aid.

The Chinese held their positions, shifted forces and reinforced to meet the counterattack. Dick Shea, among a dwindling group of attacking GIs, was last seen in the eastern sector of Pork Chop, engaged in furious hand-to-hand fighting. They were apparently overwhelmed by sheer weight of numbers, as the enemy continued to reinforce and launched their own battalion size counterattack. There was no further communication from him, no way to get to where he had last been seen, and when 2d Platoon finally pulled off Pork Chop on 9 July, he was not among them. No surviving American soldier witnessed Dick Shea's death.[23]

Fox Company, 2d of the 17th

While fighting was in progress 8 July, the enemy continued to reinforce and resupply their troops holding the crest, and north and west slopes of Pork Chop—clear indicators of a follow-on counterattack after Easy and George Companies launched their assaults. Plans proceeded for Fox of the 17th to reinforce Easy and George, and the remaining Pork Chop defenders from Easy Company of the 32d Regiment.

Pvt. Paul Serchia from Niagara Falls, New York, and Pvt. Arthur R. "Buzz" Lowe from Oakfield, New York, met in basic training at Fort Devens, Massachusetts. They became friends, and both were at Camp Drake in Japan en route to Korea when they received their assignments to the 7th Division. When they arrived in the 7th, they were sent to the 17th Regiment and finally to Fox Company. Serchia went to the 3d Platoon, Lowe to the 2d Platoon. Both were riflemen, carrying M-1s, but early on Serchia had carried a BAR on patrols, a "privilege" sometimes earned by the most junior men in the infantry squads, because the BAR was the heaviest weapon in an infantry squad. Later he and Lowe carried carbines with spectra scopes on patrols, a night-vision device which permitted the user to pick out silhouettes of enemy intruders moving at night.

While at Camp Drake, Serchia met two more New Yorkers, both from Buffalo, right next door to his hometown of Niagara Falls. Vito Smeraldo and Frederick "Fritz" Shelgren were both attorneys serving as GIs in the infantry, in Easy Company. The morning Easy Company and Fritz Shelgren pulled off Hill 347, headed to Pork Chop, the men of Easy passed close to Fox Company. Paul described Fritz as a "little guy who always wore his helmet low in front, over his eyes." As Fritz's company went past Fox that morning, he yelled at Paul, "We're going over to Pork Chop. We'll get together later for a beer." That's the last time Paul Serchia saw him. Not until much later did he learn Fritz was killed in action.

About 1:00 P.M. on 8 July, Fox left on foot from Hill 347, en route to the assembly area at the blocking position behind Hill 200. During preparations to move out, Paul Serchia received a surprise. His first sergeant told him he was to carry a flame thrower on this mission. Serchia had received no training on the use of one of the 7th Division's more than three hundred flame throwers. He had received a demonstration but no training. A buddy lightened his load for him by trading weapons with Serchia, giving him his M-2 carbine in exchange for Serchia's M-1. To augment the carbine, he was given a .45-caliber pistol.

Pfc. Eugene Urban of Los Angeles, California, also received a surprise after he departed Hill 347 en route to Pork Chop. He was a gunner on a 60-mm mortar in Fox Company's 4th Platoon, the company's weapons platoon. His platoon provided supporting fire to Charlie Company for approximately three hours during the raid on the Rats' Nest on 4 July—his birthday. But today most of the men in his platoon were to leave their mortars behind, at the checkpoint. They were to once again become riflemen in the battle for Pork Chop.[24]

It was not raining that afternoon, as radio operator John Phillips had observed, but it was hot, becoming progressively overcast and humid, and the hike to the blocking position was long. Still, it was the first time in several days Paul Serchia's fatigues were dry. Unfortunately, Chinese observers could see Fox's movement, and CCF artillery and mortars began shelling them during the long, almost four-hour march to the blocking position. They took cover several times to reduce casualties, slowing their progress and adding to their frustration. They waded the waist-deep stream instead of crossing the bridge, and Paul, carrying the flame thrower on his back, struggled to keep his footing. He fell on several occasions, got swept off his feet, and had to ask for help to cross. No help came until his best friend, Frank Guthrie from Canton, Georgia, came back, pulled him on his feet, and helped him to the bank.

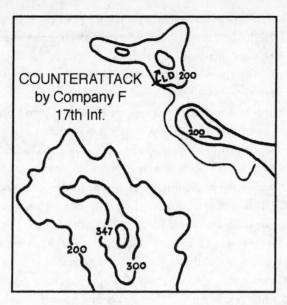

The counterattack by Company F, 17th Infantry. The company departed Hill 347 on foot at noon and boarded APCs behind Hill 200 for the move to Pork Chop. The assault began at 5:30 P.M. on 8 July 1953.

The move on foot from Hill 347 to the blocking position behind Hill 200 proved costly. Before Fox Company reached the assembly area, where they loaded on T-18 APCs, they took forty casualties. Because they had eaten no lunch, and the company commander needed to give them final instructions for the assault, there was a twenty-minute rest break at the blocking position, during which they were fed C-rations. As Serchia recalled, their new commander, Captain Flaherty, told them they were going to off-load at the APC landing on Pork Chop, deploy in a skirmish line, assault uphill, seize two machine-gun bunkers held by the enemy, and reinforce Easy and George Companies. To the uninitiated, the mission did not sound difficult.

The move to Pork Chop by T-18s began at 5:30 P.M., approximately thirty minutes before the Easy and George Company counterattack bogged down. Paul Serchia and his friend Frank Guthrie were in the first vehicle, with the company commander. When Fox Company closed on Pork Chop and readied themselves for the assault, it was approximately 6:00 P.M. Second Lt. Steven H. Wood from Locust, New Jersey, leader of Serchia's platoon, assisted the company commander in organizing Fox Company into a skirmish line, with 3d Platoon on the right, 2d in the center, and 1st on the left.

Then came the next surprise. Captain Flaherty passed the word up and down the line. "Fix bayonets!" Serchia, with his carbine and flame thrower, could not "fix bayonets." Art Lowe could, and did.

As Serchia remembers, after bayonets were fixed, the company commander said, "Let's climb the hill!" Nobody moved. After several of the same commands, still no one moved. Finally, Serchia said to Guthrie, "Screw it Frank. Let's start it off." At the same time, their platoon leader, Lieutenant Wood, farther to the right in the skirmish line, was urging 3d Platoon forward. The line began to move. Lowe, in the 2d Platoon, had just exited his APC when he saw Wood leading the 3d Platoon assault.

Lowe's 2d Platoon was to the left of the main trench. As with Baker Company the night of 6–7 July, an assault up the south slope of the Chop allowed the effective use of grazing fire. Lowe's platoon used marching fire, rifles held at the hip, pointed uphill, firing as they advanced. Serchia began having trouble with the flame thrower almost immediately. It was heavy and awkward. The hill was steep. He and others nearby had to crawl, sometimes on their stomachs. Eventually, he took the flame thrower off his back to drag it uphill, but later lost his grip, and it tumbled back downhill. From now on the fight would be with his carbine, pistol, and grenades. The first time he attempted to fire his carbine, the weapon malfunctioned.

Still, Fox Company pushed on uphill. Paul Serchia took a piece of shrapnel in his left arm from a mortar round, but he bandaged it to stop the bleeding and fought his way into a bunker. In the trenches the fighting was periodically hand to hand. He remembered at one point standing above a trench, his friend Frank Guthrie shouting to him to look at the bullet crease in his helmet. Paul saw one small hole in Frank's helmet. Underneath the steel pot the ricocheting round had creased his friend's helmet liner.

The Chinese answer to the Fox Company assault came quickly, and the intensity of the fire fight picked up. On the right flank, one by one, Sgt. 1st Class Britton T. Thompson, Pfc. Goldman Strunk, Sgt. George Zegaig, Cpl. Kenneth Johnson, and Pvt. Art Lowe, all in Fox Company, became witnesses to acts of extraordinary courage, bravery, and heroism by Lieutenant Wood.

As Wood led the 3d Platoon uphill toward the trench on the south side of Pork Chop's east shoulder, his men were pinned down and halted by enemy machine-gun fire from a bunker to his left. Disregarding grenades and intense small-arms fire, Wood circled to his left, moving toward the enemy-held fortification, and threw three grenades into the bunker. The grenades knocked out the machine gun and killed at least four enemy soldiers, permitting his platoon to resume the advance toward Pork Chop's crest.

When they reached the crest, the enemy greeted them with a hail of grenades and small-arms fire from the trench below the crest on the north slope of the hill. An exploding grenade blew off part of Wood's ear and wounded him in the face. He refused medical aid, and continued leading and encouraging his platoon and other Fox Company men in the advance.

As darkness approached they began receiving enemy grenades thrown from nearby trenches. Wood stood up, exposing himself to enemy fire, and threw three more grenades into the trench. He saw additional enemy soldiers coming through the trench toward them, and opened fire with his carbine—which quit firing. He then picked up an M-1 rifle and killed five more Chinese soldiers, suffering additional wounds in his hands. Again, he refused medical aid, this time from Cpl. Kenneth Johnson, a medic who offered to bandage his hand. In refusing the aid, Wood said to him, "Save it for the boys that may need it." While clearing the trench he found five American soldiers hemmed in a bunker and freed them.

Someone in Fox Company called a cease-fire. They were running out of ammunition. Quiet came for a bit—but firing resumed. Soldiers began replenishing ammunition from the supply point on the APC landing. With the approach of darkness, Art Lowe saw flare light from above the north slope of Pork Chop, silhouetting what seemed an inexhaustible supply of Chinese soldiers coming over the crest of the hill, raining grenades on Fox Company soldiers. The enemy soldiers were big men. Mongolians he thought.

The barrage of grenades caught Paul Serchia while he was on the ground taking cover from the explosives thrown in his direction. One hit his helmet and dropped to the ground next to him. Instantaneously he thought of picking it up and throwing it back. The next instant he remembered from basic training. "Lay there, turn your head away, and wait for it to go off," which he did. It seemed minutes passed before the explosion jolted him. When the grenade exploded, he felt shrapnel in the side of his head, left arm, and buttocks. Shortly, a medic came to his aid, cut off the legs of his fatigues and bandaged him. About 7:30 soldiers assisted him back down-hill to the large bunker housing the CP and wounded awaiting evacuation.

In the confusion and chaos of night fighting, a group of Fox Company men, including Art Lowe, got separated from the rest of the company and took cover in a bunker apparently not controlled by the Chinese. When they went inside, they found a dead American soldier.

Lieutenant Wood, though still bleeding from wounds, guided Fox Company soldiers in establishing a defense perimeter, and continued helping other wounded down the hill to the evacuation landing. Finally, about 11:00 P.M., he agreed to some first aid. Art Lowe, Lt. Steven Wood, and surviving men from Fox Company remained on the hill through the night of 8–9 July, until they received word Fox was to be pulled off Pork Chop.

About 6:00 A.M. Paul Serchia was taken off the outpost in an APC with a load of wounded, then by helicopter from the battalion aid station to the Norwegian MASH, where surgeons removed the shrapnel. From there he was taken by train to an airfield for evacuation by plane to a hospital in Japan. He arrived at the hospital approximately 11:00 P.M., 11 July, his 21st birthday.[25]

DURING THE late afternoon hours, while Easy and George Companies were battling for control of Pork Chop and Fox Company was moving into position to reinforce, APCs continued their frequent round trips to resupply the outpost in anticipation of another night counterattack by the Chinese. On return trips the vehicles evacuated casualties. While the resupply and evacuation of wounded and dead continued, defenders holding the outpost reorganized, also anticipating the night counterattack. During the same period forward observers saw large groups of enemy reinforcing Pork Chop from the vicinity of Hasakkol and the Rats' Nest, and immediately requested artillery fire. The enemy advanced through the well-placed fire with characteristic disregard for casualties.[26]

The failure of the 2d Battalion counterattack the afternoon of 8 July had been a near miss, and plans were already in progress for another counterattack in case it did not succeed. At the early morning command conference that day a tentative decision had been made to laterally move the 17th Regiment's 3d Battalion from the right flank sector of the regiment's line, and prepare them for another counterattack on Pork Chop should the Easy and George Company assault fail. The 3d Battalion's sector included the equally vulnerable Erie-Arsenal outpost on the tip of T-Bone. There was excessive risk in replacing the 3d's Love Company on the often-hit Arsenal while a battle was in progress on the adjoining outpost. Instead the 2d Provisional Company of the 17th Regiment, a company formed from headquarters and service troops, plus other combat able troops from the 17th, replaced I Company on the MLR.

While Colonel Harris was taking aggressive action the morning of 8 July to prepare the 17th Regiment for follow-on counterattacks, General Trudeau ordered the 32d Regiment commander, Col. George L. Van Way, to relieve the 3d Battalion from its positions on the MLR, and replace it with the Ethiopian Battalion. In the event the attacks by the 2d and 3d Battalions of the 17th Regiment failed to dislodge the enemy, the 3d of the 32d would be required to either counterattack or relieve friendly elements. The Ethiopians relieved the center and right companies in the 32d sector by 5:00 P.M. on 8 July, while George and Easy of the 17th were battling to gain ground on Pork Chop. The Ethiopians then relieved the left MLR company and units on outposts Yoke and Uncle at 3:12 A.M. 9 July. The 3d of the 32d was designated the Division Reserve Battalion when it closed in its assembly area at 5:10 the morning of 9 July.

The last of the 17th Regiment's Item Company came off the line at 5:30 the afternoon of 8 July, half an hour before the E and G Company counterattack came to a halt, torn apart by heavy mortar and artillery fire, and the determined resistance of Chinese holding the crest of the hill.

At 6:05 P.M., the 3d of the 17th's King Company was ordered to move to an assembly area near the Pork Chop checkpoint, and fifteen minutes later Maj. Charles H. Costigan, commander of the 3d, reported to Colonel Harris and received a briefing on the situation. At 10:30 that night Costigan received orders to prepare a counterattack with two companies, arriving on position at first light. The plan was to send both companies across the cut to the right of Hill 200's crest, then west along the base of the hill to form skirmish lines opposite Pork Chop. The intent was to avoid observation from Old Baldy, intense enemy artillery and mortar concentrations known to be in the valley south of Pork Chop, and assault rapidly across the valley from 200, south to north over the crest. While King and Item Companies were on the move, and before Major Costigan received orders to launch another battalion counterattack, the Chinese struck hard at the Chop again.[27]

Defensive Perimeters and a Long Night

Before dark on 8 July, George Company's headquarters element set up a defensive perimeter, as did Cpl. Bob Northcutt, his surviving squad and platoon members, and other separated pockets of Pork Chop defenders. Pvt. John Phillips, the radio operator on the How Company 81-mm mortar FO team, described what occurred:

> The George Company commander and the headquarters team retired back along [the] trench a few more yards [from the barricaded section] and set up a CP in a couple of bunkers that were still intact and in the connecting trench on the crest of the finger. It seemed to be George's assignment to hold that section of Pork Chop because the company CP and headquarters unit stayed anchored in that area most of the rest of the time George Company was on the hill, that is, for the next 48–50 hours. When it began to get dark, an officer or the first sergeant set up a defensive perimeter for the headquarters unit. Someone from George and I were assigned night defensive positions in a small fighting bunker, maybe five feet wide by five or six feet. Corporal Keith, the FO, sat in the trench outside the entrance under an overhead, the safest spot he could find and where Lieutenant Brobst could find him. He had been wounded in an earlier action and did not want an oak leaf cluster on his Purple Heart.
>
> The bunker looked down one side of the finger and back toward Hill 200. The bunker turned out to be an excellent position for our FO radio because the flexible radio antenna sticking out the aperture gave optimum, almost line of sight, transmission to our platoon OP on Hill 347. However, even though the bunker faced the way it did, it was not completely protected because the Chinese could and would envelop any outpost and attack from any side, and the rear was usually the most vulnerable side. They could come across the paddies from Pokkae to the north or Hasakkol to the northwest and assault the flank, the finger, or the rear, cutting off escape, reinforcement, or resupply.
>
> Several times between reaching the hill, and about midnight, I tried to raise the OP on the radio, with no success. Either the American-speaking Chinese were on the channel pretending to be GIs offering oh-so-friendly assistance for a relay, or Chinese chatter and noise jammed the frequency.
>
> As a radio operator, I had been instructed never to use a unit's or person's real name over the air or even over a field telephone. The Chinese monitored most radio transmissions and had even been known to tap

into wire communications with English-speaking soldiers. I suppose all radio and telephone operators had been similarly instructed. But the American English of the Chinese was so convincing, it was difficult to believe they were not GIs. They may have been persons who had lived or studied in the United States.

Every unit in Korea had a radio and telephone call sign that changed every week or so. The How Company 81-mm mortar platoon call sign for that week was Horsehair Nan Six. The call sign for our OP on Hill 347 was Horsehair Nan Six Eight, and my call sign was Horsehair Nan Six Niner. I said it so many times during those three days on Pork Chop that the call sign burned indelibly into my memory. . . .

The accounts in the records say that only half of George Company made it to the top of Pork Chop unscathed [on 8 July]. . . .

Lieutenant Brobst had lost half his company through absolutely no fault of his own. We all just followed our orders. Anyway, we stayed on the hill until late afternoon on 10 July. I was never far from Lieutenant Brobst. Often the George Company radios were not working or the frequencies were jammed by the Chinese. Many times [he] would give an order or report, and I would relay it over the radio because the mortar platoon had a radio relay on the crest of Hill 347 behind us. As far as I am concerned, he gave good orders at the right time. Several times when the Chinese were about to overwhelm us, he ordered fire support requests which I relayed to the rear and which came in time to save or protect us.[28]

Approximately half an hour before Easy and George launched their battalion counterattack, Sgt. Cordell Hadley, platoon sergeant of 4th Platoon, Easy Company's weapons platoon, completed the setup of Easy's 60-mm mortar section behind Hill 200. The four mortars and twelve men comprising the section were to provide fire support, primarily to Easy Company, in the assault, and to other targets called to them from their FO, located on Hill 347. The weapons platoon's recoilless rifle and machine-gun squads would leave their heavy weapons behind and go as riflemen with the rifle platoons.

The mortar section set up in open, already prepared, sandbagged revetments twenty-five yards north of the stream, to the northeast of the Bailey Bridge, and approximately fifty yards from the south slope of Hill 200—hidden from enemy observers on Old Baldy. The position was three hundred yards to the northwest of the checkpoint, across the valley and its stream, between Hills 347 and 200.

The 4th Platoon, along with the rest of the company, had been told that morning they were "going back to Pork Chop." Cordell Hadley, a veteran of twenty-six patrols, had arrived in Easy Company the last week in October 1952, during the final days of the fierce fighting in the Iron Triangle. On patrols he began as a wireman, carrying spools of wire on his back, to unwind, and permit patrol leaders' reliance on the more secure telephone, rather than radio communication. He was with the company on their 18 April counterattack on the Chop, when they broke the back of the CCF's attempt to seize the hill, and he was twice wounded. He was on the Chop again, in May, when artillery broke up another attack on the hill. Older than many draftees, and married two years when he was drafted at the age of twenty-five in February 1952, he became a platoon sergeant for Easy Company's 2d Platoon—and now the platoon sergeant for the weapons platoon.

The mortar section's fire plan called for approximately twenty minutes of preparatory barrage fire on a time table, with fire adjusted afterward by the FO positioned on Hill 347. Ammunition included high explosive and white phosphorus rounds. They opened fire and continued steady supporting fires for approximately two hours.

At the checkpoint, Pvt. Robert Wilson, Lieutenant Dashiell's jeep driver, and Pvt. Otto Glander began shuttling boxes of 60-mm mortar rounds by jeep from the supply point to feed the high volume of fire lofted over Hill 200 to the front slopes of Pork Chop. Rather than follow the access road across the Bailey Bridge, they followed the tank trail across the stream at the east end of the valley, then along the base of Hill 200, to reduce risk of observation and avoid giving away the position of the Easy Company mortar section. Enemy mortar rounds came in far too regularly, but Wilson and Glander timed their impacts to make the hurried trips with their cargo of mortar rounds, and reduce the risk of being hit. After ten or eleven round trips, and reloading the vehicle for another run, Wilson turned to get into the jeep. The Easy Company first sergeant, M.Sgt. Freddie Webb, stopped him. "Don't go back," he said. "They've been hit."

The hit was devastating. A few minutes earlier, Cordell Hadley had been taking fire mission orders from the FO, on the PRC-10 radio, adjusting fire when needed. The FO had been telling him their fire was consistently on target, hitting the Chinese accurately. Suddenly, Cordell saw ten to twelve incoming rounds impact approximately fifty yards away, right at the base of Hill 200. He knew instantly their mortar position would be bracketed—close—with the next salvo, and yelled, "Take cover!" Matters quickly got far worse. The next enemy salvo was a direct hit, and set off a secondary explosion among the mortar rounds stacked nearby. Virtually the entire section was killed or wounded. Only one man, Pvt. Donald Haikawa, was relatively unhurt and able to walk. Cordell Hadley had a deep wound in his right thigh and a fractured leg.

As soon as he recovered from the blast, Hadley looked around at the shattered mortar position and told Haikawa to run to the checkpoint and have an APC come pick up the wounded. Haikawa ran, and in a few minutes returned, riding in an M-39, open-topped APC to pick up the wounded. When they carried Cordell Hadley into the APC, he did not know how many of his men were dead and how many were wounded.

From the checkpoint, a T-18 took them to the battalion aid station. From there, for him, the trip was by bus and train to a hospital in Pusan on 10 July. The next day it was into surgery, followed by air evacuation to a hospital in Japan, where he remained until September. The war was over for Cordell Hadley the afternoon of 8 July 1953. He came home. Several men in his mortar crews did not.

Pvt. Robert Wilson would see many from Easy Company come off Pork Chop early in the forty-eight hours the company battled to retake the hill. Among the first he saw was his wounded company commander, Lt. John Dashiell, along with his company executive officer. A less seriously wounded platoon leader, Lt. Bob Hope, took command of Easy's able-bodied men remaining on the Chop and fought them well.

Another wounded Easy Company officer who came off Pork Chop early the evening of 8 July was 2d Lt. Samuel E. Daniel, platoon leader, 3d Platoon. Beginning minutes after the company's assault on the west shoulder of Pork Chop, shortly before Cordell Hadley's mortar section was struck by a salvo of enemy mortar rounds behind Hill 200, Cpl. George B. Chandler, 2d Lt. George W. Sutton, and Pvt. Billy G. Smith witnessed Daniel's extraordinary acts of heroism.

Faced with the same relentless barrage of mortar and artillery fire as that faced by George Company on the hill's east shoulder, Easy Company's riflemen began taking casualties as soon as they deployed into skirmish lines for the assault. Daniel was hit with shrapnel about the face and neck before his platoon was fully deployed for the move uphill toward Pork Chop's crest.

At 3:30, immediately after the advance began, his platoon was pinned down by machine-gun fire from an enemy held bunker. He did not hesitate. Unassisted, he rushed the bunker with his carbine and grenades, killed the gun's crew, and silenced the weapon.

His platoon remained pinned down, this time by a second enemy machine gun farther in front of their position. Samuel, though wounded, again moved forward and silenced the gun, killing its crew. In spite of his wounds he twice led his platoon over the outpost's crest, only to run short of ammunition, necessitating withdrawals to replenish ammo, assist wounded, and reorganize. During the second withdrawal to a trench providing reasonable safety, he became aware that one of his men had received serious wounds and was unable to pull back.

The time was now 4:05 P.M., little more than a half hour after Easy Company's assault began. Daniel immediately went forward to within ten yards of enemy positions to bring the wounded soldier with him. Daniel was hit again, this time in the leg, while he was assisting the wounded soldier. In great pain, Daniel held on to the soldier and kept coming toward safety until his leg gave way. When he fell, he kept the man in his grasp and dragged him the remaining distance to the trench. Still in great pain, and unable to move about, he refused evacuation and directed the platoon's organization in a defensive position.

Repeatedly asked to consider evacuation, he refused, insisting he wanted every soldier more seriously wounded than him to be evacuated first. Not until all the men in his platoon who were more seriously wounded than him were evacuated did he finally agree to leave Pork Chop Hill. He left with the everlasting respect of all who had seen him repeatedly risk his life for his men.[29]

Once more flares lit the forward slopes of Pork Chop as night closed around the hill. The expected enemy counterattack began at 9:48 P.M. All weapons available to support Pork Chop's defenders opened fire against every known and suspected enemy assembly area and reinforcing route. The Chinese pressed their attack on the west shoulder of the hill, hitting an already battered Easy Company and forcing Fox Company to withdraw approximately one hundred yards. The enemy again bore down with more reinforcements in spite of heavy, accurate artillery fire. The Chinese continued their assaults, battalions in column.[30]

Behind the 7th Division's MLR, from their sector of the line, King and Item Companies, 3d Battalion of the 17th Infantry had earlier in the day begun moving left toward the checkpoint and blocking position behind Hill 200. To move the 3d Battalion to the left, and ensure the MLR remained fully manned, the 17th's commander, Colonel Harris, ordered the activation of the 3d Provisional Battalion to relieve the 3d Battalion, previously responsible for the right battalion sector in the 17th Regiment's area. At 6:20 P.M. the 2d Battalion commander, Major Costigan, reported to Colonel Harris to receive a briefing on the situation. At 7:00 P.M., two and three quarter hours before the expected CCF counterattack materialized, King Company completed their move into the assembly area near the checkpoint.

At 10:30, while the CCF counterattack was in progress on Pork Chop, the 17th's commander ordered Major Costigan to prepare for a two-company counterattack against the outpost, to begin at dawn. At 11:00 P.M. Costigan received a warning order, and at 11:45, the 3d Provisional Battalion staff reported they were in place to assume responsibility for defense of the 17th Regiment's right battalion sector of the MLR.

Following these unit moves and the warning order from Colonel Harris, the 3d Battalion began planning and coordinating the details of their attack plan, including routes of approach, communications, objective areas, and fire support; however, time was not on the side of complete planning. Item Company had not arrived in the preattack assembly area before it was time for the two companies to depart the attack position, if the planned counterattack was to take advantage of pre-dawn darkness. Major Costigan knew Item Company was en route and, undoubtedly with Harris's approval, decided to press ahead to avoid having the two companies taken under artillery and mortar fire while deploying for the assault. Thus King Company departed the attack position on schedule, anticipating Item Company would soon arrive and follow on behind them. By 3:00 A.M. the morning of 9 July, King Company was at the checkpoint moving forward to attack positions located at the rear of Hill 200. The stage was set for another battalion counterattack against the Chinese holding doggedly to the north slopes and crest of Pork Chop Hill.[31]

11

THREE COMPANIES
AND A PLATOON

FROM THE LENGTHENING BATTLE WHICH HAD RAGED FROM 6 JULY through the night of 8–9 July, several patterns emerged. The Chinese displayed an unwavering determination to reinforce and resupply its soldiers holding the crest and north slopes of the outpost. Repeatedly they sent small groups of men to reinforce during daylight and launched heavy counterattacks at night, usually a battalion or more.

Relentless CCF artillery and mortar attacks on high ground taken back or under counterattack by defenders invariably drove the Americans and their KATUSA allies to cover on the surface of the hill, out of fighting trenches and positions into covered trenches and bunkers, where they waited out the barrages to avoid heavier casualties. In those areas still held by the Chinese, enemy soldiers were furiously digging in deeper, expanding their one- or two-man fighting positions when they were not fighting—that they could save themselves from the killing air bursts of American VT rounds they knew would come during Chinese counterattacks or heavy reinforcement.

The intermixing of friendly and enemy held bunkers and trenches, and the inability of American commanders to know who held which positions at any given time complicated defenders' problems and severely hampered their ability to take advantage of their edge in firepower and accuracy. American artillery repeatedly fired flash fires when the Chinese launched assaults, but there were limits to how close in they could come without hitting their own positions with destructive high explosive rounds.

American VT rounds wreaked lesser but painful havoc among the outpost's defenders, as it was impossible to alert all of them when commanders, platoon leaders, or forward observers requested artillery on position. Communications were badly hampered at best, completely cut off at worst, and to send runners across the surface of the hill to pinpoint friendly positions was often tantamount to sending men to their deaths. Both defenders and enemy were keyed to shoot first and ask questions later.

Further, American and supporting ROK artillery could not fire high explosive rounds with contact or delayed fuses at the Chinese burrowing into the crest of the hill. Infantrymen and artillerymen feared hitting friendly troops in the open or American and ROK soldiers holed up in bunkers and covered trenches.

The Chinese had firm control of the north slopes and crest of the hill, and at night, the flares lighting the front slopes inhibited defenders from venturing onto those slopes to counterattack the enemy. Instead, they tended to stay under cover, and attempt to fight from bunkers and covered trenches. While staying under cover was necessary to avoid casualties, their fields of vision, and consequently their ability to defend from inside bunkers, were limited. Further, their difficulties were complicated by an enemy willing to crawl forward at night and throw grenades into covered trenches and bunkers, while also infiltrating snipers into the rear.

The Chinese's dogged retention of the crest was a continuing thorn in the side of defenders trying to wrest control from them, particularly during daylight hours. The enemy now had extra sets of eyes to observe areas to the rear of Pork Chop, and report troop movements obviously intended to reinforce defenders, or counterattack. Intense mortar and artillery fire consistently tore into companies moving on foot across the valley between Hill 200 and Pork Chop. If defenders came on the outpost in APCs and disembarked to reinforce or counterattack, enemy mortar rounds soon fell on the south slopes, where CCF artillery was less effective because of shallower shell trajectory.

On the rear slopes of Pork Chop, the enemy faced a stalemate of their own. Though the CCF kept up an almost steady rain of artillery and mortars on the outpost and MLR positions behind it, their attempts to force their way over the crest and downhill to the APC landing and access road were consistently met with intense, grazing small-arms and automatic weapons fire from defenders looking uphill. Alternatively, if the situation demanded, devastating fire from friendly units manning the MLR could pound the enemy on the south side of the hill, while the outpost's defenders took cover in bunkers and trenches.

As the fight progressed the 7th Division continued to increase the role of APCs in resupplying the hill's defenders, bringing fresh troops for counterattacks, reinforcement, or relieving defenders, and evacuating the wounded and dead. The Chinese thus far had been totally unsuccessful in cutting the access road, slowing or stopping the flow of APCs on and off the outpost.

On the other hand, the Chinese faced the task of resupplying their troops entirely with manpower—carrying everything by hand or on their backs. What's more, the awful toll of enemy wounded and dead continued to accumulate on the outpost throughout the days and nights of fighting. The CCF, apparently fully intending to fight to the bitter end, were braving deadly allied artillery and mortar barrages to reinforce or counterattack, and were unable to evacuate the mounting toll of casualties piling up around their troops. The heavy losses they were taking just to reach and hold their objective, left insufficient manpower to keep pace in carrying off their growing numbers of dead and wounded.

The Americans and KATUSAs faced the bitter reality that they could not possibly reach all their wounded and dead. Many were buried or partially buried in caved-in trenches and bunkers, their locations unknown or interspersed with Chinese-held positions. Further, the Chinese were notorious for booby-trapping the dead, even their own. As a result of these factors and the continued fighting, the trenches on the north slope were a horror of dead and wounded from both sides, as were, to a lesser degree, the trenches on the south slopes.

In preparing to send patrols against the CCF on the stalemated front, detailed planning, including rehearsals, had been routine. Prior to the major assault on Pork Chop, training in the 7th Division's rear areas included the tactics, techniques, and procedures of patrolling. The canceled battalion counterattack on Old Baldy in March had been rehearsed by the 31st Infantry's 2d Battalion on terrain similar to the large outpost's hill mass. The 1st Battalion of the 17th's raid on the Rat's Nest had been rehearsed several times before the early morning assault of 4 July. Now, as in April, when the Chinese were daily reinforcing and nightly committing counterattacking battalions, reinforcing and counterattacking companies from the Americans' 17th and 32d Regiments had not the time to rehearse or adequately plan before being committed to the outpost. All training ceased soon after the initial Chinese assault of 6 July.[1] Companies and battalions hurriedly moved to attack positions, and seldom had time to thoughtfully plan and prepare for their missions.

In the 7th's rear areas, the need to rapidly react to counter the CCF's waves of attackers set in motion one unit move after another. The division and regimental commanders confronted a chain of chessboard actions, relieving units in reserve or on the MLR, to permit their move into the stream of companies and battalions thrust into the fight to drive the enemy off Pork Chop while attempting to ensure the MLR and other outposts remained fully manned and capable of withstanding additional CCF assaults. The commanders' successive tactical decisions and the necessity to support and relieve the units committed to the fight, plus high casualties and inability to adequately orient and train replacements, in turn brought the entire rear area alive, and necessitated sending fresh, less trained replacements into units on the MLR.

The division road net, already affected by the monsoon rains, now carried the burden of numerous truck convoys, many at night and blacked out, moving troops from bivouac, assembly, and reserve areas to the checkpoint behind Hill 200. From there they either rode APCs onto the outpost or walked, deployed in tactical formations, and fought their way onto the hill. In addition to troop movements the heavily trafficked road net bore the additional loads of trucks and other heavy vehicles carrying ammunition, supplies, and water to the checkpoint behind Hill 200, where APCs picked up the loads and moved them forward to Pork Chop.

Then came the surges of wounded and dead coming off the hill on the APCs' return trips, as commanders diverted the needed transportation to evacuate the accumulating casualties from the outpost. Pork Chop was a company-sized outpost, and both sides were now committing battalion-sized formations in repeated assaults. As the fight continued, it became essential to periodically evacuate the wounded and dead, which relieved congestion and overcrowding in the temporary aid stations, bunkers, and trenches where the wounded were being held. The need to evacuate the wounded and dead was not only a matter of caring and compassion, but an important operational essential. Their movement off the hill reduced the burden of caring for them by the men who were trying to fight the battle. Following, and sometimes accompanying, the wounded and dead, came men whose units had been relieved after forty-eight hours or more of fighting—units returning to the rear with far fewer men than when they arrived on the outpost.

At the medical collection points, holding areas, aid stations, and hospitals, the nearly constant flow of wounded included Americans, KATUSAs, KSCs, and a few enemy soldiers. They moved progressively to the rear by APCs from Pork Chop to the checkpoint, then by litter-equipped APCs, ambulances, trucks, litter-bearing jeeps pulling trailers, and helicopters, to aid stations, field hospitals, and evacuation hospitals. And on the other side of the MLR a few captured American soldiers were seeing evidence of the terrible toll of casualties the Chinese were absorbing as a result of their relentless assault on the outpost.

Counterattack

At 3:00 in the morning of 9 July, King Company, 17th Infantry, left its attack position on the south side of Hill 200 and crossed the line of departure—the cut or saddle in 200, above the blocking position, east of the hill's crest. From there the company descended to the bottom of Hill 200, and moved west along the base. Item Company, which arrived in the attack area before the last of King departed, followed fifteen minutes behind King, to ensure both companies stayed in their respective zones of attack. King's sector of attack was the east shoulder of the Chop, the sector the men of George Company were fighting to wrest from the Chinese. Item Company's zone was farther west, the area Fox and Easy Company were battling to retake.

Traveled in darkness, the route from the line of departure for King and Item reduced the probability of detection unless enemy observers on Pokkae should discover them. Moving along the east base of Hill 200 both companies could temporarily mask themselves from detection by observers on Old Baldy and the crest of Pork Chop. Surprise was the hoped-for outcome,

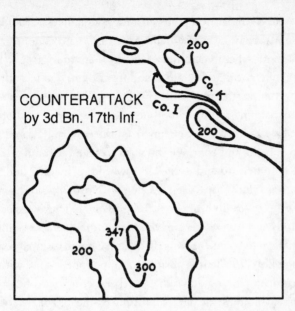

The counterattack by 3d Battalion, 17th Infantry. The battalion moved by trucks to the checkpoint. Beginning at 3:00 A.M. on 9 July 1953, it deployed on foot through the cut on Hill 200, then along the north base of Hill 200 to skirmish lines.

as well as avoiding the devastating effects of intense enemy artillery and mortar fires known to be well registered in the valley south of Pork Chop.

While some of the King and Item veterans knew and were familiar with Pork Chop and its defenses, many were not. That factor, along with the hurried, late move of Item Company to the assembly area did not help and resulted in one platoon and one squad being separated from the remainder of Item. The separated platoon and squad instead joined with King Company in its assault on the outpost's east shoulder. At 4:15 A.M. the assault began.

As soon as the enemy detected the attack, intense artillery and mortar fire began falling on both companies. Caught in the open in a near perfect skirmish line, both companies immediately began taking heavy casualties. In spite of the heavy concentrations of fire tearing at them, King and Item fought their way uphill and succeeded in entering the main east-west trench lines, and then converged toward one another. By 5:45 King Company established physical contact with elements of George Company, on the outpost, and cleared all enemy from the east shoulder of the hill up to and including

Bunker 48. Item Company, a platoon and a squad less than intended strength, fought their way up the main west-east trench line, skirting the crest of the outpost, where a determined enemy fought furiously to hold on.

Once King, plus the platoon and squad from Item, tied in with George Company, they launched an assault which passed through the small, isolated perimeter held the entire night by George Company's Cpl. Bob Northcutt. The attack was to clear the enemy from the eastern half and forward slopes of the outpost and continue the push to take the main crest of the hill. Isolated well forward and to the left toward the dividing line between the two sectors of Pork Chop's defenses, neither Northcutt nor his men had slept or had water to drink throughout the long night. They were nearly out of ammunition, and he was certain that one more enemy assault would likely overrun them. Now, as the King, Item, and George Companies' assault passed through Bob Northcutt's position, a sniper opened fire with deadly effect, momentarily pinning down the attackers. Northcutt, heartened by the reinforcements joining the fight, and stung by the loss of two of his soldiers during the counterattack late the evening before, reacted to the sniper's sudden appearance.

Snipers characteristically hide themselves well, attack selectively and swiftly, then pull back into hiding to avoid having their location pinpointed. The most common way to draw a sniper out of cover is to present a target—an elusive target that will cause the sniper to fire again, miss, and give away his position. Bob Northcutt, a quiet, unassuming, modest man, made a deliberate decision. He would be the bait to find the sniper. He thoughtfully, carefully, and quickly presented himself as a target, causing the sniper to give away his position. Then Northcutt charged him, killing him with rapid-fired rounds from his pistol.

Northcutt's self-sacrificing act of courage and valor broke loose the stalled assault on the Chinese-held crest of Pork Chop, but in the ensuing attack he was hard hit in his right arm by shrapnel from an exploding enemy shell—his second wound. A medic administered morphine and temporary first aid, and though Northcutt could walk, the medic told him he must be evacuated. He protested. He wanted to stay and fight. But the medic insisted. His wound was not to be taken lightly. Against his wishes, he relented and worked his way downhill to the CP, the large holding area for the evacuation of wounded.

A T-18 APC later evacuated him and other wounded to the battalion aid station. There he received another dressing to stop the bleeding and an ambulance took him to an evacuation hospital farther to the rear. Later he traveled to the hospital in Pusan, and was flown from Pusan by C-124 transport to a hospital in Japan. By the time Bob Northcutt left the hospital three to four weeks later, the truce agreement was signed, ending the fighting. He returned to his unit for a few days, then left for the continental United States, having officially earned more than the thirty-six points necessary for rotation home.

In 1954, at Fort Knox, Kentucky, Sgt. Robert Northcutt stood in the reviewing party at a battalion parade honoring his service on Pork Chop Hill. At the parade, a general order was read in the name of the president of the United States and the commander-in-chief, Far Eastern Command, awarding him the nation's second highest decoration, the Distinguished Service Cross, for "extraordinary heroism . . . in keeping with the finest traditions of the military service."[2]

THE RENEWED, bitter fighting at daybreak on 9 July very nearly brought success to King and Item Companies. Their assault surged toward the crest of the hill, joined by George, Easy, and Fox Company survivors, as well as men from Easy Company of the 32d Regiment. But once again, heavy artillery and mortar fire, joined by a storm of small-arms and automatic weapons fire from the well-dug-in Chinese on the crest of the hill, bogged down the assault. By 9:00 A.M. Item Company had only one officer left and King Company had none. Both companies had lost their commanders, and fighting once more trailed off into scattered, small group and individual battles for safe cover and survival. In Easy of the 32d, which had laterally shifted to defend the outpost prior to the 2d Battalion counterattack the evening of 8 July, plans had been prepared to join the King and Item Company assault.

Inside the tunnel early the morning of 9 July, Mac Conner's platoon had received orders from their company commander to launch an assault of their own, in coordination with the I and K Company counterattack. Another Easy Company officer was assigned to Mac's platoon to participate in the assault. The platoon had lost both its noncommissioned officers, one killed the preceding day when Conner and his men had cleared the

Chinese from the hill immediately above them, the other pulled from the platoon to be the company first sergeant.

When Conner led his platoon out of the tunnel onto the hillside they moved into the maelstrom of artillery, mortar, automatic weapons, and small-arms fire already tearing at the ranks of Item and King Companies. The officer assigned to the platoon was promptly hit, wounded in the leg, and went down. Mac led on, moving a short distance up the hillside, shouting encouragement, urging his men forward. All the men were wearing body armor. He felt something hit him in the left side, and remembered looking to his left, puzzled, wondering what it was. At that instant an explosion on the ground directly below his groin lifted him off the ground and spun him around completely. He landed on his back, feet up slope, and slid backward down the hill into the arms of his men.

He was grievously wounded, the pain agonizing. His men pulled him back inside the tunnel, and medics began working on him. He felt paralyzed from the waist down. His testicles swelled to the size of softballs. Because of heavy bleeding, and apparent extensive injuries, the "docs" were fearful of severe internal injuries. They could not give him morphine. To make matters worse, the fierce fighting would keep him and the accumulating wounded in the main trench for several hours before APCs could begin their evacuation. The pain mercifully overwhelmed Mac Conner. He remembered nothing more until he awakened in a Norwegian Mobile Army Surgical Hospital a day or more later. He then learned he had been first hit in the left side by fire from a submachine gun. A bullet had entered his left thigh and lodged against his hip bone.[3]

By 6:53 the morning of 9 July, the 3d Battalion attack's forward progress essentially ended, shattered by a relentless enemy barrage of artillery and mortars, estimated at 7:00 A.M. to be three hundred rounds per minute falling on the American units and their KATUSAs. At 9:00 A.M. control of the surviving elements of I and K Companies passed to Major Noble, commander of the 2d Battalion, which retained responsibility for defense of the outpost. Major Noble now had under his command elements of Companies E, F, G, I, and K of the 17th, and E Company of the 32d, plus Able Company's 2d Platoon, still holding the right flank with survivors of the 8 July George Company counterattack.

An air strike on Hasakkol. The monsoon rains let up on 9 July, and UN commanders believed air strikes on Chinese reinforcing and resupply routes would cause the
enemy to relent in their attempts to seize Pork Chop.
Courtesy of Ed Puplava

At daybreak came the summer sun and sweltering heat. The odor of
decaying bodies and blown-up latrines, which had permeated the air since
the first day of the battle, was more overpowering with each passing day.
Water was a precious commodity. Despite the frustration of four failed,
major counterattacks and heavy casualties, American commanders believed
air attacks on reinforcing and resupply routes, and enemy exhaustion from
three days of continuous fighting, might cause the Chinese to give up first.
In hopes of finally tipping the balance they prepared another attack, this
one by Charlie Company, 1st Battalion of the 17th, the same company that
conducted the 4 July raid on the Rat's Nest.

In the morning prior to Charlie's relief from the MLR and subsequent
late afternoon assault, the machine-gun platoon of How Company, 2d
of the 17th's heavy weapons company, walked onto Pork Chop. The men
of the machine-gun platoon and their leader, Lt. Raymond N. Clark,
began the long trek to the Chop a day earlier, and he later wrote detailed
recollections of the platoon's odyssey.[4]

Double Time to Pork Chop

Raymond Clark enlisted in the Army toward the end of World War II, and served in the infantry, Signal Corps, and as a communications specialist in a B-17 bomber group in the 9th Air Force, based in Germany. He completed OCS nine months before his May 1953 assignment to the 7th Infantry Division as the platoon leader of the machine-gun platoon in How Company, 2d Battalion of the 17th Regiment. After he arrived in H Company he learned he was replacing a platoon leader who had been wounded in the April battle for Pork Chop.

In the period after his arrival in the 2d Battalion, H Company refilled with replacements following the April battle, went through intensive training, and, in his judgment, became a well-prepared, disciplined company with improved morale. His platoon built to an overstrength unit of fifty-five men. During that period, 2d Battalion's sector defense responsibilities included Hill 347, Hill 200, and Pork Chop, and he and others in his platoon had helped rebuild the defenses on Pork Chop, as well as improve the defenses at other positions on the MLR, including Hills 200, 347, and 327.

When July rolled around, Clark's machine-gun platoon was on the far left flank of the 17th Regiment sector and from their position could not see Pork Chop Hill. The outpost was hidden from view by Hill 347. He and thirty-five men in the platoon occupied a blocking position in a narrow valley on the left flank of Hill 347, between the hill and outpost Westview, manned by the 31st Infantry Regiment. One squad from the platoon was on Hill 347, on the MLR, in support of 2d Battalion rifle companies. In the valley, Clark and his men were armed with a .50-caliber machine gun, four .30-caliber light machine guns, four .30-caliber heavy machine guns, two 3.5-inch rocket launchers ("Bazookas"), M-1s, carbines, and enough ammunition and grenades for a major battle.

When first assigned to the blocking position, Clark concluded both the position and mission were unusual for a machine-gun platoon; nevertheless he decided he and his men would make the best of it, and steadily improve their defenses. They set about doing so, and developed a formidable strong point in the MLR, right at the boundary between the 17th and 31st Regiments.

The complex included a huge 250-gallon high-pressure flame thrower taken from a tank and delivered to the platoon by men from the 707th

Ordnance Battalion. The flame thrower included about one hundred feet of firing hose. To house the weapon in protective cover and ensure rapid response in a fight, the platoon built a bunker next door to their CP, also housed in a bunker. They were anxious to test fire the flame thrower but quickly learned three discouraging lessons.

The weapon was just as dangerous to the gunners as it was to the enemy, since the high pressure knocked the gunners off their feet. Firing into a minefield could result in unanticipated fireworks, both in the mine fields and from battalion headquarters. Last but not least, the men from the 707th Ordnance Battalion did not like to come to the front lines to refill and pressurize the tank.

Until the 6 July assault on Pork Chop, How Company's machine-gun platoon saw little excitement or action on the line, except when gun crews participated in patrols, or, on one occasion, when a Chinese defector, a major in an operations (G-3) staff, walked in to their position and surrendered. But the night of the sixth marked an abrupt change from the routine. Though they could not see Pork Chop from their position, they could hear artillery and mortars, and see flares lofted to the north of the outpost. They could also see and hear heavy support fires delivered from Hill 347.

They were on alert all night and throughout 7 July, expecting a diversionary push by the Chinese into their valley or against Westview to their immediate left. News of the action in progress was scarce since their only reasonably secure communication line was one phone to the company CP. Their detached squad on Hill 347 was ordered down to join them, and during the night of the seventh, Clark received a call telling him the platoon would be relieved early in the morning, that they should report to the H Company CP behind Hill 347. The next morning the relieving machine-gun platoon appeared on schedule, but a snag immediately developed.

To Clark's chagrin, the first lieutenant insisted the platoon evacuate all its troops and equipment before the lieutenant would accept the position. Normally, during relief and replacement of a unit, tripods and ammo remained in place because they had been zeroed in, ready to fight. The men quickly exchanged guns one at a time, and then the troops being relieved quickly departed, because both units are vulnerable. Clark argued the point, but the lieutenant persisted, remaining fixed on keeping his "new equipment and clean ammo." The ammunition was still sealed in cans inside bolted wooden boxes. Ray Clark gave up arguing, and except for the flame thrower, had the platoon's gear loaded in their two jeeps and trailers, and headed out via Road 46 to their company CP, behind Hill 347.

When they arrived at the company CP he learned of "a big enemy push against Pork Chop, with elements of the 17th and 32d Regiments already chewed up, and the 2d Battalion of the 17th now being committed." Single rifle companies were being fed in one at a time because there was not room on the Chop for additional units to maneuver. He was told to prepare the platoon to move to Pork Chop. The company CP would remain in place behind Hill 347. The mortar platoon, which had been in action from the beginning, was to stay in place, across the road in a draw, and the recoilless rifle platoon was to continue in action from Hill 347.

To prepare for their move onto Pork Chop, the platoon left its .50-caliber and .30-caliber heavy machine guns, light machine gun tripods, and other extra gear and items in supply. They bolted bipods and shoulder stocks on the light machine guns, cleaned and checked their ammo, filled canteens, and passed out grenades. According to his job in the platoon, each man carried an M-1 rifle, carbine, or assault machine gun plus a .45-caliber pistol, ammo belts, helmet, flak jacket, hand grenades, canteen, first aid packet, poncho, rifle grenade launcher, rifle grenades, and bayonet. In addition, several men wore pack boards loaded with machine-gun ammo cans.

They were told to bring rocket launchers with ammo to blast bunkers occupied by the enemy. They carried two launchers and eight rounds of ammo strapped to pack boards. Because the Army did not issue suspender-type harnesses much of the gear hung around their waists. In addition to his regular gear, Clark carried a set of field glasses and a compass. At supply he traded his carbine for a .45-caliber "grease gun"—a submachine gun—thinking it would be more useful in the trenches. He also carried a .25-caliber Beretta automatic pistol in the pocket of his flak jacket as a "getaway" gun.

The platoon had no communication equipment, either for use among themselves or for contact with their company or other units. The platoon medic was told to carry a second field medical kit and extra morphine.

After completing preparations, the platoon went to assist How Company's mortar platoon, which was firing from the ravine across the road from the CP. The machine gunners carried ammunition to the mortar crews. The mortar crews had already burned out two tubes since the battle began. They were firing rapidly while swabbing the tubes with mops dipped into buckets of oil, attempting to keep the tubes cool. The mortar base plates, which normally sit on the surface of the ground, had been driven about one foot into the dirt from the repetitive firing recoils.

While the machine gunners were assisting the mortar platoon, they saw Fox Company of the 17th march from the rear, up over Hill 347, in the direction of the fighting. Bringing up the rear of the long column were a large number of stretcher bearers, an ominous sight Clark would never forget. While Fox Company moved past the mortar platoon, he was asked to select five men for a "dangerous job." The men were taken away on a truck, leaving the machine-gun platoon with approximately fifty men.

At dusk, open-topped two and a half ton trucks arrived to load the How Company machine-gun platoon, and they started north on road 46D and then west on road 45 heading for the APC loading site at the check-point near Hill 200. The distance was only three miles, but the ride took several hours. The blacked-out trucks crept slowly through the fog and darkness, stopping frequently for unknown reasons.

Clark rode in the last truck, and during one stop, a blacked-out American jeep roared up behind and crashed into its rear. The small convoy remained long enough to evacuate the jeep's two injured soldiers, and push the damaged vehicle off the road. They arrived at the APC loading site about midnight 8 July, and checked on the status of the APCs. Two were operational, one an M-39, the other a T-18, but no more trips would leave that night because of intense fire on the access road to Pork Chop, and the fear of ambush by Chinese patrols in the valley.

The bunkers at the checkpoint, always a beehive of activity, were full and were especially active twenty-four hours a day because of heavy fighting on Pork Chop. As a result, the machine gunners of H Company were not invited to stay inside with the APC crews, medics, and other support personnel. Instead, they were told they could remain behind the nearby dirt levee, into which the bunker was dug. The platoon crowded behind the levee, next to the bunker, attempting to get some rest in the rain that had started falling. The long night's trip and restless hours in the rain were the prelude to the platoon's first casualties.

As dawn broke a concentration of artillery or mortar fire suddenly fell on the bunker and among the unsheltered platoon. Five of Ray Clark's men were wounded, including two squad leaders, and the platoon's KATUSA sergeant, who was also the platoon's Hangul (Korean language) translator.

As the sergeant was being loaded into an ambulance, he promised Clark he would be back. Ray Clark never saw him again. He reasoned the ROK Army took the KATUSA from the hospital, as they were always looking for trained soldiers for duty in their units. The Korean sergeant's loss was sharpened by the fact Clark considered his KATUSAs normally the best gunners in the unit. In training he used them as instructors. They had been with the platoon considerably longer than other soldiers, were technically more proficient and better than American soldiers at cleaning, assembling, and operating weapons. His platoon was now down to forty-five men.

About 8:00 A.M. on the ninth, an hour before Maj. Joseph E. Noble, Jr., the 2d Battalion commander, assumed command for the defense of Pork Chop, an officer in the APC bunker told the Company H platoon leader that a message from the battalion commander ordered the platoon to proceed on foot to the outpost. Upon arrival he was to report to Major Noble at his CP. On receipt of the message Clark started immediately, leading his platoon single file, east across the valley toward Hill 200, toward the cut above the blocking position.

They crossed the valley without incident, waded the swollen stream, climbed the south slope trench on Hill 200, to the cut, turned left into the single MLR trench, and moved west, all the way to the last bunker, which faced Pork Chop from the west end of Hill 200. The distance covered from the APC loading site was over half a mile but was difficult for Clark's troops because of the heavy and bulky equipment they carried through the narrow trench.

At the bunker he halted his platoon, and looked over a long, bare downhill slope that ended at a small stream. Across the stream was the access road APCs plied back and forth to the outpost. The distance from where he stood on Hill 200 to the road on Pork Chop was another half mile. The enemy on Old Baldy, Chink Baldy, and Pokkae had observation and direct fire on the slope the platoon must now descend.

While Clark was gazing at the area to find the best route, Capt. Gorman Smith, the assistant regimental S-3 (operations), came out of the bunker and asked him what they were doing. Smith, as a lieutenant, had commanded Easy Company during the April battle for Pork Chop, and the platoon leader was surprised to find him on Hill 200. Clark thought S-3s were usually with their commanders. Unknown to Clark, he and his platoon were passing through trenches manned by Charlie Company of the 17th, and in the next two hours Charlie would be pulling off Hill 200, replaced on 200 by a refilled, reconstituted Able of the 17th. Charlie Company was about to revisit Pork Chop Hill.

After a short discussion with Smith, Clark decided his machine-gun platoon should start moving, as they were partially exposed to the Chinese in their present location. It was now nearly noon on 9 July with a brilliant sun beating on the platoon, temperature nearing one hundred degrees and the humidity high. He passed word to the platoon sergeant at the rear of the column. "We're going to double time to Pork Chop."

Leading the platoon over the top of the trench, he started downhill on the run. After going approximately one hundred yards, he ran into a previously unseen, sturdy, barb-wire fence, which temporarily halted progress. A nearby body dressed in American fatigues lay doubled across the wire, and it became the bridge for the How Company platoon to quickly cross and move on.

The Chinese were apparently taken by surprise by the platoon's movement, because Clark reached the bottom of the slope, crossed the stream, and was nearing the APC road when the first incoming rounds hit. Although not wounded he was knocked to the ground a few seconds. His platoon members helped him up and they continued, walking uneventfully up the access road toward the APC landing, under partial cover of the road's embankment. He and his men were winded and sweating profusely from the long run, but apparently no one had been hit—although he could not be certain. One of his squad leaders was missing.

He dispersed the platoon, under cover, and proceeded up the road to the APC loading area, accompanied by Staff Sergeant Johnson, one of the two section leaders in the platoon. Johnson, a regular Army soldier from Philadelphia, and an extremely cool and efficient NCO under fire, had been decorated for past valor.

Inside the CP bunker Major Noble was sitting in the right corner by a Coleman lantern, dressed in battle fatigues, undershirt, and combat boots. A short, squat middle-aged man with a large "Buffalo" mustache, he was engrossed in reports and maps while conversing on the phones or radios, or with men nearby. With his Buffalo mustache he was displaying his 17th Regiment esprit. Each year, the Buffaloes, as the 17th called themselves, held a contest to see who could grow the biggest Buffalo mustache. Although he looked tired and was sweating heavily in the heat and smoke of the bunker,

Noble portrayed his usual calm, detached, cheerful self while outside fighting raged periodically, and the bunker was jammed with equipment, water cans, ammo and ration boxes, as well as artillery and mortar forward observers, communications men, medics, wounded, and dying.

Clark reported to Noble, as Noble's message to him at the checkpoint early that morning had ordered. Noble said he was glad to see Clark and his platoon, but no, he had not ordered them to come on foot. He expressed surprise he and his men had made it to the outpost without heavy casualties. Then he gave Clark his first set of orders on Pork Chop Hill. "Set up the machine guns to fire on the upper slopes to keep the enemy down and to silence the automatic weapons sweeping our lines." Noble knew another company, this time Charlie Company of the 17th, would be arriving on the outpost later in the afternoon.

Clark and Sergeant Johnson left the CP. The trench in the area of the CP was not suitable because it was too deep, with observation uphill insufficient. Back down the return APC road they found the trench joining Bunkers 1 through 5 still under friendly control. Two enemy automatic weapons were firing from the summit into the area. Clark instructed one of his sections—two machine guns and their crews—to take the enemy weapons under fire. They either hit the two enemy gun crews or they moved, because the Chinese ceased firing from those two positions and were not a problem again. Clark found no other good firing positions, and dispersed the remainder of his platoon under cover.

Clark reported back to Noble for further instructions. Noble told him his immediate problem was loss of control on the hill. As the senior officer present he commanded all troops on Pork Chop regardless of their parent organization. Most of the officers and NCOs from the 17th and 32d units were casualties. With the loss of officers and NCOs, chains of command and unit cohesiveness were gone. He was commanding many individuals instead of units, and most individuals and small groups were fighting independent of one another, without mutual support.

Many bunkers, as well as covered and open trenches, had collapsed during the fighting. However, of pressing concern to Noble were the many wounded not receiving care. Some had been in collapsed bunkers and open trenches since the start of the battle. Some of our troops walked over the wounded, sat on them, and ignored them. There were no doctors or aid stations on the hill, and very few medics, although the primary CP—the one occupied by Noble, his staff, and forward observers—and the platoon CP on the right shoulder of the hill were both being used as collection points for wounded. Major Noble ordered Clark to use excess machine-gun platoon members to set up collecting points and aid stations to collect, treat, and evacuate the wounded. He would arrange APC support to get them off the hill.

Accompanied by Sergeant Johnson, the platoon leader ran to the "chow and sleeping bunker" through the incoming fire. A sturdy one-room bunker, approximately ten feet by thirty-five feet, it was built on top of the ground on the inside of the APC road. Approximately eighty yards to the east of the CP, with its back dug into the side of the hill, the bunker had in the past offered a central point where the hill's defenders were served hot food and ate under cover. During the day it was used for rest for men on night duty.

The platoon leader ordered all able-bodied men out, and he and Johnson set up their first collecting point, with the machine-gun platoon's medic in charge. Clark then sent some of his soldiers through the nearby trenches to spread the word and help carry in the wounded and dead. Both Americans and KATUSAs began to arrive and soon filled the bunker. They piled the dead against the outside wall. A small number of Chinese were also brought in and treated.

T-18s started arriving and Clark and his men loaded them for evacuation. They put the dead on the troop compartment floor, then the walking wounded made their way in and sat back out of the way. Finally, they placed wounded on stretchers on top of the dead. In two to three minutes they could load one APC and send it on the return trip to the checkpoint behind Hill 200. The entire time the evacuation was in progress enemy artillery and mortars continued to fall, causing additional casualties.

Among the Wounded

Fox Company's Pfc. Eugene Urban was among the wounded that afternoon. About 2:00 P.M., he received a serious head wound from grenade shrapnel. After a night of fighting in which he picked up a BAR to use against two enemy held bunkers, he and two other men were on the east shoulder of the hill, working to the west. They were closing in on an enemy-held bunker on the south slope, just below the ridge line—throwing grenades. Suddenly, the Chinese struck back. The man in front of Eugene was hit hard by an exploding grenade, knocked down, and tumbled downhill into the barbed wire. Before Eugene could react, two more grenades came at him. He turned to run, intending to "hit the dirt," but another explosion quickly followed. He was knocked down, and felt his helmet had been hit by something, but felt no pain. He got to his feet, checked his helmet, and realized it had indeed been hit by something, in the right front, in the area of his forehead. There was a small hole, but it appeared his helmet liner was only scratched.

He decided to seek medical attention at the evacuation landing. A medic examined him and asked, "Did you get hit by a rock? Do you feel OK?" He replied, "Yeah, I'm OK." There was a small hole in his helmet, the helmet liner, and a minor wound to his forehead, but no bleeding.

The medic checked and bandaged his head and sent him back to his company. He climbed back up the hill to Fox Company. About three hours later, while he was standing guard at the north entrance to a trench, he began feeling badly. A fellow soldier asked him if he was all right. "You don't look so good." Eugene did not feel good, but he did not know why. Finally, another medic examined his wound and told him he should be evacuated from the hill immediately. When he rode an APC back to the checkpoint, he went by ambulance to a MASH, where he learned a piece of shrapnel penetrated the right frontal lobe of his forehead, to a depth of two and a half inches.

The next day he was in an Army hospital in Seoul for surgery, an early, long trip home, and to this day many visits to veterans' hospitals.[5]

A 60-MM mortar round slammed into the road near Lieutenant Clark, and he received a minor but painful wound in the throat. Later in the afternoon, at the same location, he was hit again by 60-mm mortar shrapnel, which lodged in his right cheek. Sergeant Johnson took a hit in his right hand from the same shell. Several men from the How Company machine-gun platoon received wounds and were evacuated that afternoon. Others not as seriously wounded refused evacuation.

Sad, difficult memories inevitably grow from these experiences. Clark recalled two men carrying a soldier on a stretcher toward the aid station. While passing an upright timber they carelessly slammed his arm against it. He immediately told them to be careful and placed the soldier's arm on his chest. One of the two carrying him said, "It's OK, lieutenant, he's dead." For some reason, Clark felt foolish for not realizing the soldier was dead.

In the trench below the APC landing, where Clark's men had set up two machine guns, he set up another collecting point and aid station. The trench had become a haven for Item and King Company wounded hit during the early morning when their skirmish lines were caught in the open with a devastating enemy mortar and artillery barrage. He could not find a bunker intact, but found a large hole in the middle of the trench where a bunker had stood or one was being built. The hole had no overhead cover but the walls were sturdy and it was about eight feet deep. At the moment it was full of troops crowded in for protection.

He directed them out so he could set up an aid station. No one moved. He pulled out a white phosphorus grenade, removed the pin and announced he would count to three and then drop the grenade into the hole. Within seconds the hole emptied, except for the seriously wounded. He put one of his squad leaders in charge, then started collecting the wounded in nearby trenches. He told his NCOs scouring the trenches for wounded to get the riflemen on their feet fighting again. As he went through trenches, he sought out NCOs and put them in charge of nearby troops. By midafternoon, Lt. Raymond Clark and his platoon had successfully evacuated all the wounded and dead they could safely locate—approximately 150 American and South Korean soldiers. The evacuation began before Charlie Company of the 17th came on Pork Chop that afternoon, and continued throughout the company's move onto the hill by APCs.[6]

Charlie Company Counterattacks

Charlie Company had been defending Hill 200 since the battle began. They needed to be replaced on their position before they could attack enemy units on Pork Chop. Several reliefs and movements of various units freed them to enter the fight. While the evacuation of wounded was in progress on the outpost, a reconstituted Able Company, filled almost entirely with replacements, completed relief of Charlie from their sector of the MLR, Hill 200, at 2:10 P.M.

The break in the weather, while beneficial to tactical aircraft striking enemy supply lines, gun positions, and troop assembly areas north of Pork

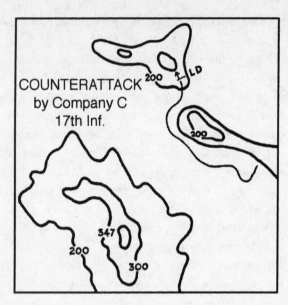

The counterattack by Company C, 17th Infantry. The company was relieved from MLR positions on Hill 200 and boarded APCs for the move to Pork Chop. The assault began at 3:23 P.M. on 9 July.

Chop, also benefited Chinese observers on Old Baldy, Chink Baldy, and Pokkae. Observers on Old Baldy could see Able Company's move across the valley from the checkpoint toward Hill 200, and undoubtedly concluded another counterattack was in the making.

While the relief of Charlie Company was in progress, the Chinese stepped up their artillery fire on the MLR and Pork Chop. On the outpost, Raymond Clark remembered the shelling as "a never ending inferno of explosions from Chinese and U.S. weapons." CCF artillery and mortar barrages falling on Hill 200 during the change caused numerous casualties. Exhaustion and three days living under constant barrage and oppressive heat, reduced Charlie Company's combat effectiveness. Nevertheless, the Company began the move from Hill 200 by APCs at 3:23 P.M., and closed on Pork Chop at 4:59 under an intense barrage of enemy artillery and mortars. As Charlie deployed for the assault uphill, the company immediately was engaged in a fierce small-arms fire fight.

Cpl. Dan Peters, the mortar section squad leader in the company's weapons platoon, was in one of the ten loads of troops shuttled forward

View of Hill 200 and Chinese-held Pokkae (in the center of the valley beyond 200) from an aperture in OP 12 on Hill 347. Note the MLR trenches and bunkers along the ridge of 200, just above the lower edge of the aperture.
Courtesy of Ed Puplava

for the assault. His platoon's 57-mm recoilless rifles and mortars were not used in support of the company. Instead, Peters and men in the platoon moved ammunition and supplies forward to sustain the counterattack. Consequently, his platoon suffered fewer casualties compared to the three rifle platoons.

The company was to attack up the slope on the eastern shoulder of the hill, retracing approximately the same route King Company took early that morning, except Charlie Company had the advantage of moving to the assault via APCs rather than on foot. The APCs considerably reduced their exposure to enemy fire during the trip from the assembly area behind Hill 200.

In spite of heavy enemy fire, which took the life of Lt. James J. Balduzzi, Jr., the company commander, their counterattack was the most successful to date. The commander was leading the first element when he was killed near the crest of the hill, and the counterattack temporarily faltered. Lt. Frederick K. Kamaka from Honolulu, Hawaii, the executive officer, was leading the second element of the assault. When the first element was pinned down near the crest Kamaka came forward to lead in a fierce, aggressive assault that surged to the top of the hill.

Joined by Sgt. 1st Class Richard G. Beacher of Eufala, Alabama, and Sgt. Donald D. Swope of Woodbine, New Jersey, Kamaka and his men ran from one enemy bunker to the next, throwing grenades and firing into the doorways and firing ports, killing or taking prisoners any enemy soldiers that dared show themselves. After securing the crest on the right shoulder of the hill, Kamaka set up machine guns on the company's flanks, in order to hold the position.

When Dan Peters came on the hill in an APC, bringing ammunition, he left the vehicle and entered a seven foot deep trench. Enemy fire was heavy—artillery and mortars. Though the trench was seven feet deep, it was not covered where he was, and Peters's instinctive reaction was to keep as low to the ground as he could, and crawl on his belly to bring the ammunition where it was needed. He quickly learned he could not carry ammunition and a rifle while crawling on his stomach. He leaned his rifle against a wall of the trench and continued the ammunition delivery. When he came back to retrieve his rifle and another load of ammunition, the rifle was gone. More startling, as he crawled back and forth in the trench, he noticed wounded men were walking past him, standing fully upright. He wondered, "What in the hell are those crazy bastards doing?" As day wore on toward night, however, Dan Peters, like the walking wounded, became increasingly desensitized to the dangers surrounding him, and was soon walking upright in the hell that was Pork Chop.[7]

Cpl. Oral Grimmet, the most senior medic attached to Charlie Company listed his hometown as Judson, West Virginia. Carrying his carbine, medic's bag, and a supply of grenades, he came on Pork Chop behind the assault wave. At first there were few wounded, and he fought beside Charlie's infantrymen as they battled toward the crest of the outpost. When he finally reached the trenches on the south slope, near the crest, the sight that greeted him became his work through the night on into the afternoon of 10 July. As others had seen before he arrived, the trenches were littered with the dead and wounded, Chinese, Americans, and a few KATUSAs.

The bunkers were crowded with wounded, dying, and men staying off the surface of the hill to avoid the killing mortar and artillery rounds—or who had lost their weapons, run out of ammunition, or simply wanted to avoid the fight. He eventually entered Bunker 64, the platoon CP for 2d

Platoon, Able of the 17th, now a collection point for wounded on the east shoulder of the hill. There he went to work, doing what he was sent to do—treat the wounded. Before the night passed, he threw many grenades, sometimes uncertain whether they were targeted on fellow-soldiers or the enemy. The enemy moved in close in the dark, and it was never easy to discriminate between friend and foe without putting one's life at great risk.[8]

Squad leader and BAR man Cpl. Henry Baker, who inherited Harold Hackett's BAR after Harold was wounded in the Rat's Nest raid, remembered the Chinese on Pork Chop's east shoulder were surprised by Charlie Company's sudden, swift onslaught. Many were caught in the open in the trenches, and Henry killed a large number with his adopted, and now favorite weapon. His mind's eye and his camera captured a small bit of the horror of Pork Chop's trenches, the kind of horror he did not see when his platoon was in reserve on the outpost during the raid on the Rat's Nest. He was among many Americans who came home remembering the dead from both sides intermingled, waist deep, in the heavily contested, stalemated sections of Pork Chop's trenches.[9]

Before dark Charlie Company made substantial gains and cleared the Chinese from most of the right finger of Pork Chop—but failed to clear the enemy from the entire hill. In spite of the fierce fire fight for the crest of the hill's right shoulder, they succeeded in gaining a portion of the high ground in the vicinity of Bunkers 48, 49, and 50, only to be forced to withdraw to trench positions cleared during the assault.[10] Perhaps their greatest achievement was the relief of David Willcox's 2d Platoon of Able Company, permitting their evacuation from the hill.

A LATE arrival to join King Company on Pork Chop the afternoon of 9 July was Pvt. Jim Leal, a medic. King Company was taken off outposts Erie and Arsenal. Jim asked King Company's senior medic permission to go back to the regimental medical company for a short R&R, which was normally two days. The morning of the ninth, he learned King Company was on Pork Chop. Carrying his carbine and medic's bag, he hitched a ride on an ambulance from the 17th Medical Company to the checkpoint. When he arrived at the checkpoint to board an APC for the outpost, he noticed many news and television cameras were present. He also encountered the first of several sobering sights burned into his memory in the next twenty-four hours—medics washing the blood off stretchers in the nearby swollen,

A dead Chinese soldier, and the feet of a dead American soldier next to him, in a Pork Chop trench, July 1953. The Chinese soldier had just killed the American using the entrenching tool seen beyond the GI's foot when a burst from an American BAR cut him down.
Courtesy of Henry G. Baker

Dead Chinese soldier in a Pork Chop trench.
Courtesy of Henry G. Baker

muddy stream. When he climbed aboard a T-18 and rode to Pork Chop, there were no photographers riding forward to the outpost. Then he saw the APC was loaded with all types of ammunition and asked himself, "What in the hell am I doing here? If we get hit, I'll never be found!"

When he walked out the rear doors of the APC onto the landing, he saw the bodies of numerous dead soldiers stacked next to the supply building, outside the entrance to Pork Chop's main trench. Lieutenant Clark, medics already on the hill, and Clark's H Company platoon members had begun the grim task of collecting the third large group of dead and wounded to be evacuated in the three days since the Chinese launched their attack.

As Jim Leal entered the engineer's tunnel, he also noted the ammunition stacked outside the supply building not far from the bodies. Inside the tunnel he learned from the Chop's veterans, "Don't go through open trenches. There are snipers. Your company, King Company, is on the top of the hill on the east shoulder."

Leal grabbed some supplies, went back out the tunnel entrance, and was surprised to see "grease guns"—.45-caliber submachine guns—lying on the ground near the supply building, with Cosmoline still on them. A heavy barrage of enemy artillery and mortars began, and he returned quickly to the tunnel to take cover until the firing slowed. He then made his way carefully to the area King Company was holding, and was first greeted by a sergeant who knew him. "Where the hell have you been?" he asked. Leal explained, then moved on toward a bunker where wounded were being treated.

En route, the greetings were decidedly more friendly. "Doc, how ya' doin'?" The night of 9–10 July was a night Jim Leal would long remember.[11]

Miracle in Bunker 53

When relief came, Jim McKenzie was still tending wounded in Bunker 64. The devastating casualties taken in George, King, and Item Companies' earlier counterattacks flooded the already overflowing bunker with wounded and dying. Among the wounded was another medic who knew Jim. In the dark he called Jim's name, but when the man shined a small light on his own face, McKenzie had difficulty recognizing him because his face was covered with blood.

As relief and evacuation drew near, Jim McKenzie helped move the wounded and dead from the 2d Platoon CP to the evacuation landing. McKenzie did not know it, but the term "Doc," given the medics by the GIs, was more than a mark of respect. Medics were special people, truly angels of mercy, and the soldiers knew it. The medics saw all the horror, all the ugliness, but sheltered a deep well of compassion within them, inside the steel shell which gave them the strength to keep at their difficult task under the most extreme conditions.

Like Jim Leal in King Company, among Jim McKenzie's most vivid memories of 9 July was the image of American dead, stacked like cord wood at the edge of the evacuation landing, waiting to be moved on APCs. Lying on top was a Latin American soldier, perhaps Puerto Rican, his face young, so young. His fatigues were clean, freshly laundered, and his combat boots showed little wear and mud. The young soldier's life on Pork Chop Hill had been dreadfully brief.

In Bunker 53, David Willcox and seven other men had held firm for nearly sixty-four hours, before Charlie Company freed them from the bunker late the afternoon of 9 July. Four were wounded, and David was in a seriously weakened state when he heard shouts of "We're Americans, Charlie Company!" He had to be helped from the bunker by the other men. He had received thirteen puncture wounds from grenade shrapnel, with one leg being particularly hard hit. Now, late afternoon on the 9th, he was carried on a litter and placed on the ground just outside the trench leading to the 2d Platoon from the access road. He remembers lying on the litter gazing up at what seemed a beautiful sky he had not seen for days. Yet he knew he was not entirely safe. He reached for a nearby sandbag and pulled it to cover his groin. A heaven-sent American soldier appeared out of nowhere, and poured some clear, warm water into his dirty helmet. The water tasted marvelous, "like champagne" to David Willcox, in spite of its color. Forty-three years later, at a reunion, David Willcox was to learn the American soldier who appeared from nowhere to give him water was Jim McKenzie. Jim had helped carry him on a stretcher to await evacuation by APC.[12]

From those nearly three days of hell in a small place, David Willcox carried an unforgettable, glowing memory, among many memories he wished to forget. Near the end of the long ordeal in Bunker 53, there was growing doubt the eight men would get out alive. Water and food were gone. Their ammunition and a case of nearly 150 grenades were running low, and they were all exhausted. Richard Baker remembered David Willcox, at one point in their ordeal, handing his .38-caliber pistol to one of the men not wounded, saying, "If I don't get out, see that Dick Shea gets this."

They had early in the fight sealed the bunker door with sandbags to keep the enemy from finding them or throwing hand grenades through the door. Over the bunker's firing port they firmly anchored a wire mesh similar to chicken wire, to keep "potato mashers," Chinese grenades, from being hurled through the firing port. There was a small new testament Gideon Bible in the bunker, in David's possession. He said, "I'm not a very religious person, but I think it's time to pray." He suggested they take turns reading passages out loud, and begin by joining together in saying the Lord's Prayer. After they recited the Lord's Prayer, he began with the first reading, then passed the Bible to the next man.

During a pause in the action, while they were taking turns reading the Bible, suddenly they heard a slight noise at the entrance to the firing port, and looked up to see an American grenade, firing pin pulled, lodged in the wire mesh. Instantaneous, absolute silence followed, and the certainty they were all dead. American grenades were far more efficient killers than Chinese potato mashers.

Then, after what seemed an eternity, just as abruptly as the grenade appeared before their eyes, the wire mesh loosened its grip, and the grenade fell from view. The explosion which followed, always startling, was harmless. The men in Bunker 53 knew a miracle had occurred.

Among the eight men evacuated from Bunker 53 late the afternoon and early evening of 9 July were Lt. David Willcox, Corporal McAuvic, Pvt. Richard Baker, Pfc. Jesse Foster Jr., and Pfc. George H. Cunningham, all from the 2d Platoon, Able Company of the 17th Infantry Regiment.[13]

Fire Extinguisher Forward!

When How Company's machine-gun platoon leader, Lieutenant Clark, reported the results of the evacuation of wounded to Major Noble, the 2d Battalion's commander gave him a new task. Troops on the hill needed to be resupplied. Clark was to learn what was needed, send word back with the APC drivers, then receive, distribute, and store the cargoes of supplies brought on return trips. The supplies needed were at the checkpoint behind Hill 200.

Clark was already ahead of the task. During his travels searching for, assisting, and moving wounded to the newly established holding points, the troops told him their needs: water, food, bandages, morphine, grenades, ammo, and a few needed rifles. He wrote out a precise list with priority and amount, and sent it to the rear with an APC driver. Instead of sending what he asked for and could handle, the APCs brought loads of explosives and ammunition. At first his men stored these supplies in a bunker constructed around a large metal container located about ten feet into the main covered trench, on the right side.

After this bunker was crammed full of supplies, he and his men stored boxes of ammo, grenades, shaped charges, and 60-mm mortar rounds in a smaller bunker built against the outer wall of the larger bunker, facing the APC loading area. Eventually they ran out of room and had to stack supplies on the ground, in the open alongside the small bunker.

The supplies sitting in the open were set on fire by an incoming mortar round. There was no fire fighting equipment on the outpost, and Clark feared an explosion would destroy the CP and nearby trenches. Sergeant Johnson, Clark, and the platoon medic began picking up burning boxes, carrying them across the APC landing, and throwing them over the edge of the landing, down a sharp, almost sheer one hundred foot cliff.

The fire was continuing and threatened a major explosion if not extinguished. During the thirty minutes they worked to dispose of the burning ammo boxes, the three men were knocked off their feet several times by explosions. Other times they had to take cover, anticipating explosions because they could not pick up boxes on fire. While they rushed to dispose of the burning ammo boxes outside the bunker, a call went from the CP for the 13th Engineers to dispatch a fire extinguisher via an APC. The Charlie Company fire fight was still in progress on the crest of the hill, and mortar rounds were still falling periodically in the area of the access road and landing.

Lt. Jim Dietz, leader of the 2d Platoon in the 13th Engineers' Able Company, rode out to Pork Chop on an APC, bringing the large fire extinguisher and its fifteen-foot hose. The APC rolled to a stop on the landing, turned around, backed toward the burning supplies, and stopped. The doors opened, Jim Dietz walked out with the hose, and quickly began pouring suppressant on the fire. Mortar rounds were continuing to fall and two landed at some distance, one on each side of the APC. Dietz saw the rounds hit, was certain the enemy mortar crews had bracketed their position, and was equally certain the next salvo would be on target.

The mortar rounds stopped. Dietz was not convinced. He had spent the night of 7–8 July dodging mortar rounds along with his men while they built a Bailey Bridge behind Hill 200, under the enemy's observation. The moment the supply bunker fire was out, he threw down the hose and made for cover. The expected direct hit never came, and after a respectful pause, the hose was taken into the APC, and Jim Dietz rode back, unscathed, across the Bailey Bridge, to the checkpoint behind Hill 200.[14]

Lieutenant Clark decided to stop the resupply. On the evacuation landing Pork Chop's defenders were being inundated with supplies they could not use or store. At 5:15, on the crest of Pork Chop's east sector, Charlie Company stopped an enemy counterattack.[15]

Another Long Night

In spite of Charlie Company's successful counterattack, the situation on Pork Chop Hill the night of July 9–10 was little different than the night before, and in some respects was worse. There were men on the outpost from six companies of the 17th Regiment, plus Easy Company of the 32d. Major Noble had almost no staff to assist him in controlling the outpost's defense, and communications with the various units on the hill were virtually nonexistent. American and Chinese-held bunkers and trenches remained intermixed, some having merely changed hands in the preceding twenty-four hours. The Chinese still held the tail of the Chop—Brinson Finger—most of the hill's north and rear slopes, and the crest.

Many forward observers sent to Pork Chop during the preceding days' counterattacks were no longer paired with their company commanders, but with their high-powered radios, were able to pass information to senior commanders. The disconnected pockets of infantrymen were less fortunate. With their battered communications net, they were less able to transmit a clear understanding of the situation. "Piecing together a comprehensible picture received from so many, and often so conflicting reports, was almost impossible." Because there were men from so many different companies on the hill, and their company commanders, platoon leaders, and NCOs had taken such heavy casualties, Major Noble was commanding a large number of individuals, not cohesive units.

Noble's review of the situation as the day wore on, and his communication of the facts to senior commanders, made clear the number of wounded, coupled with the disorganization of remaining effectives on the hill, made it difficult to either maintain control or launch additional counterattacks. The result was the evacuation of the dead and wounded which began 9 July, and a plan to relieve the remainder of the three battalions of the 17th Regiment on Pork Chop on 10 July. APCs were to be used for the evacuation and relief, and by evening twilight on the 9th, nearly all of the wounded and dead had been evacuated.

As the plan evolved, the 3d Battalion of the 32d Infantry would replace the departing able-bodied defenders, fight their way onto the hill if necessary, and prepare the Chop for another battalion counterattack on 11 July. Additionally, the 1st Battalion of the 32d would attack, with a supporting, diversionary battalion attack on Old Baldy—if Eighth Army approved.

At 8:00 P.M. on 9 July, General Trudeau called General Clarke, the I Corps commander, and asked him to commit a reserve regiment, permitting the 7th Division to proceed with its plans to relieve the hill's defenders and reestablish firm control of the outpost. Clarke agreed, and plans were set in motion to relieve the entire 32d Regiment in the east sector of the 7th Division front. During daylight hours on 10 July the 25th Infantry Division's 14th Regiment, less its tank company, would displace forward and relieve the 32d Infantry. Attached to the 14th would be the 69th Field Artillery Battalion, and Company B, 65th Engineer Combat Battalion.

Circumstances intervened to knock out part of the plans. As Item Company of the 32d arrived behind Hill 200 at midnight on 9–10 July the Chinese launched a series of attacks on Pork Chop which continued until dawn. Simultaneously the enemy shelled the MLR and roads leading to the battalion CP. Commanders thus suspended relief of 17th Regiment units until the situation became clearer. The 17th continued to hold the outpost.[16]

In Lt. Ray Clark's mind the scene on the outpost after dark the night of 9 July was bizarre. From hills along the MLR, two huge spotlights, called "moonbeams" by the GIs, lit up Pork Chop in a brilliant, unnatural white light. In addition, constant explosions, hissing, and burning of mortar and artillery-fired flares forward, over, and behind the hill added more light to the strange scene. The entire area for several square miles was brilliantly illuminated the entire night. Much of the American artillery used included VT to stop the enemy and drive them into cover, as the Chinese launched a series of attacks prior to midnight. After midnight fighting slackened for a while, before resuming with greater intensity.

During the brief lull, a radio call from an American observation post on Hill 347 to the CP on Pork Chop asked who was marking targets on the outpost's summit, and for what reason. Marking targets was a term describing soldiers' use of a kit of white panels spread on the ground in patterns to signal pilots where to strafe or bomb. The call puzzled the men in the CP. This was not an activity anyone expected GIs would be engaged in on the crest of Pork Chop Hill—day or night, and especially at night.

Lieutenant Clark took his field glasses outside and scanned the hill's summit. Two Chinese soldiers were putting on white shorts and undershirts. They apparently found a GI pack and were taking advantage of their booty regardless of their surroundings. Forward observers in the CP quickly relayed information to the artillery and shells soon fell on the spot the two Chinese were last seen.

During the night, Major Noble, accompanied by one of Ray Clark's squad leaders acting as a guide and guard, made the rounds of trenches held by defenders. When the two men returned, they brought two Chinese prisoners they had captured, their wrists bound behind their backs with communication wire. Noble instructed Clark to take the prisoners to the rear and turn them over to the S-2 (intelligence officer).

The next APC arrived, unspooling and stringing communications wire out the back of the vehicle, the primary means of reconnecting phones during the battle. Ray Clark told the sergeant in charge of the wire stringing operation to take the prisoners to the rear and hand them over to the S-2. The sergeant became excited and argumentative, saying he thought they ought to be shot "on the spot." Clark changed his tone to an order, telling the sergeant to guard and evacuate them when he departed. He heard the APC leave with the prisoners as he went about his other work.

After fighting died down somewhat about midnight, Ray Clark looked for a safe place to eat and take a nap. After climbing over the supplies in the large supply bunker, uncovering a GI who had the same idea, he cleared a spot in the rear of the bunker where he could sit and nap. It was not only relatively safe but he could see and guard the entrance as well as the roof of the CP bunker, in case they had unwelcome visitors during the night. Among the supplies where he sat was a loaded .45-caliber pistol in a holster, which he strapped on his belt "just in case." Nothing unusual happened the remainder of the night, not in the supply bunker, and Clark was able to get some rest. However, to the rear, in the 7th Division, 32d and 17th Regiment CPs, other factors were weighing in the fight for Pork Chop Hill.

At 2:15 A.M. on 10 July, fighting again became intense, with a noticeable increase in artillery reported. At 3:00 A.M. the enemy again counterattacked the outpost in force, resulting in an urgent call from Major Noble for additional reinforcements. The request prompted a decision to commit Company I, 3d Battalion of the 32d in a reinforcing role, with orders to fight its way onto the position. As did Charlie Company, Item of the 32d prepared to move to Pork Chop Hill by APC.[17]

Decision in Seoul

On 9 July, while fighting continued on Pork Chop, Arrowhead, and other sectors of the front, South Korea's President Syngman Rhee agreed to cease attempts to obstruct the armistice. For three tumultuous weeks, the nearly two years of on-again, off-again armistice negotiations had hung in the balance. Rhee's opposition and orchestration of "public opposition" to the truce provisions, his 18 June orders to release twenty-five thousand NKPA POWs, directions to his field commanders to continue the fight in spite of the looming truce agreement, and unyielding insistence that Korea be unified under his government had failed to sway his allies. In a complete reversal, he declared his government would "endeavor to cooperate fully and earnestly" in what he believed would be a continuing effort by the United States and the United Nations to unify Korea by political action.[18]

President Rhee's altered stance came after President Eisenhower's task force promised the long-term mutual defense treaty, full support for a twenty-division ROK Army, and billions in military and economic aid. A collective sigh of relief swept through allied governments. Theoretically, only "minor technical issues" remained to be negotiated, namely, the final line of demarcation.

Unfortunately, for some months the CCF had been building their strength on the central front, preparing for a final paroxysm of bloodletting. Eighth Army's intelligence assessment of the enemy's intent in the final weeks of the war, contained in its July 1953 *Command Report,* concluded,

> Although an armistice appeared imminent during the first days of July, the enemy apparently was determined to seize key terrain features and create the impression that the closing days and hours of hostilities would be recorded with the Communist forces in an offensive which could be claimed to have forced the UN to sign a truce. In order to attain the objectives which appear at best to have been somewhat nebulous, the Communists seemed willing to make lavish expenditures of men and material. At the same time, the Chinese demonstrated their forces in Korea are better organized, better trained, better led, and better supplied than at any time since their entry into the Korean conflict.[19]

In the 7th Infantry Division CP the night of 9 July, when General Trudeau requested I Corps' General Clarke to send a regiment to relieve the 32d from the division's right sector, another plan was being discussed, a plan intended to break the CCF's hold on Pork Chop. Trudeau wanted to commit the 2d Battalion of the 32d Infantry in a battalion counterattack on Old Baldy, on 11 July. Trudeau's idea came from the 31st Regiment's March counterattack plan, previously rehearsed by the 31st and now pulled "off the shelf" to blunt the CCF assault on the Chop.

Trudeau reasoned a surprise attack to retake Old Baldy would divide both the CCF's attention and their artillery, and take the pressure off Pork Chop. The Chinese were massing all their artillery on the outpost. As a retired Lt. Gen. Arthur Trudeau explained years later, "[The Chinese] are not as flexible as we are, and I figured that before they could change and remass their artillery on Baldy, that we would be on the damn hill."[20] At the same time seizure of Old Baldy would deprive the Chinese of observation posts on the large hill and hamper their ability to see into Pork Chop's and the MLR's rear, behind Hill 200, an advantage costly to the 7th Division and gained by the CCF when General Taylor called off the 31st Infantry's planned counterattack at the end of March. Trudeau firmly believed the CCF was attempting a penetration of the MLR in the center of the division's sector.[21]

On the surface, chances appeared good that Taylor would approve the plan to retake Old Baldy with another battalion counterattack. He had already approved two battalion counterattacks on Pork Chop, committing two of a battalion's three rifle companies each time, and another was to begin tomorrow morning. Plans did not work out as Trudeau hoped. The renewed CCF counterattacks on the Chop, the enemy's apparent total disregard of their continuing heavy casualties, and perhaps the turn of events in Seoul caused Eighth Army to revert to the policy contained in General Taylor's 1 March Letter of Instruction.

Trudeau's plan was approved, but he was told he could only commit one reinforced rifle company in the assault. The 7th Division commander knew from March and April experiences with outpost battles, one company would not be sufficient. If a single rifle company were successful in such an assault, it would inevitably need to be reinforced to hold the outpost. Chink Baldy was next door to Old Baldy, and the Chinese could quickly counterattack in force. He would be sending a single infantry company against a hill far too large to attack and hold, and he did not want to send a unit he knew full well he would have to withdraw after a bitter fight. Trudeau decided against pursuing the idea.

He remarked with some bitterness years later, "I don't want to say where this went for the final decision. It went several echelons above me, I know, and I don't know which one finally said no. They didn't quite say no. They authorized me to attack, as I recall it, with not more than a reinforced company. Whereupon I said, 'I can't do it,' because this is just sending men out that couldn't possibly take their objective, and I'm just not going to do it. So I didn't. This was an indication of the limitation of authority that is now placed on a commander when you can't fight a battalion."[22]

More heroics, acts of valor and sacrifice, and far more difficult decisions were in the offing in the last battle for Pork Chop Hill.

12

FINAL DECISIONS
AND SURPRISES

ITEM COMPANY OF 3D BATTALION, 32D INFANTRY, ASSEMBLED JUST before dawn on 10 July and began moving via APCs, with instructions to relieve defenders in the eastern sector of Pork Chop. King Company would follow, also transported in APCs, to take over responsibility for the western sector. Though intense fighting had been in progress during the hours after midnight, when Item Company arrived at 5:45 A.M., the threat of a stiff fight did not materialize and the relief continued. The 3d Battalion's Love Company remained in an assembly area to the rear, in battalion reserve.[1]

Among the men arriving on Pork Chop with Item Company of the 32d Regiment that morning was Pfc. Louis Salovich, from Portland, Oregon. A rifleman, Louis carried an M-2 carbine. When he walked off the APC, his platoon moved up Pork Chop's south slope to positions near the crest on the east shoulder of the hill. They were not yet aware they would be relieving surviving able-bodied soldiers from the 17th Regiment's George, Fox, King, and Item Companies who were holding the east shoulder of the hill and had repeatedly attempted to push westward and secure Pork Chop's crest. Though a stiff fight did not materialize when Item of the 32d arrived, the night the 10th would be quite different, and dramatically change Louis's life.[2]

Throughout the early morning, APCs under constant fire moved men to Pork Chop, with King Company closing on the hill at 9:45 A.M. The APCs returned to the checkpoint loaded with weary 17th Regiment soldiers, plus their wounded and dead.[3]

While the 32d Regiment's King Company moved onto the Chop early that morning, Lt. Raymond Clark, the leader of H of the 17th's machine-gun platoon, came upon several of his troops at the entrance to the main trench yelling at a man out in the open about fifty yards from them. The man was above the chow bunker, on the south slope of the hill, near the barbed wire. Extremely dirty and disheveled, he wore only a ragged fatigue jacket and trousers, with no helmet or shoes. He was moving aimlessly about, firing a rifle into dead bodies, perhaps even wounded men, and into bunkers in his vicinity. The area was still contested and Clark and his men had not recovered all the casualties.

The man laughed and danced about as he fired his rifle. It was obvious he had suffered a complete mental collapse. Clark yelled at him to come in. He responded by waving at the lieutenant, with more laughing, dancing, and gunfire. Ray Clark asked one of the KATUSAs to call to him in Korean. The same response. He next tried Chinese, which one of the KATUSAs spoke. Again, the same response.

Clark told Sergeant Johnson to stop the man's shooting rampage. Johnson borrowed a BAR from a nearby rifleman, set the bipod on the parapet, and fired a burst at him. The man fell, lay a moment, then got up and went into his routine again. Johnson fired again. The man fell and stayed down. Later, Clark looked toward the area and saw the man had crawled to a fence directly behind the chow bunker, where his body hung on the wire.

As the temperature rose later in the morning, Clark detected a vile odor coming from the APC landing, where a mass of flesh lay in the road, covered by flies. The discovery vividly illustrated the hatred and rage generated in a few men among the thousands caught up in the deadly, stalemated, close-quarter struggle for Pork Chop Hill. The platoon leader asked a couple of nearby GIs what it was. They replied, "Those are the two Chinese prisoners from last night."

According to the two, the communications sergeant forced the two prisoners to lay in the road and ran over them with the APC. There was little left of their bodies after being run over by armored vehicles for several hours. Clark obtained shovels from the supply bunkers and told the two GIs to shovel the remains over the side of the nearly vertical slope. They started to do as they had been ordered but began retching and were unable to continue. Clark then asked two KATUSAs, and they quickly disposed of the remains.

Before King of the 32d began arriving on the 10th, Major Noble, the 2d of the 17th's commander, told Clark that he, Noble, had been ordered to relieve and evacuate all troops on the hill, that they were being replaced by fresh troops. Noble directed Clark to take charge of loading and dispatching them, beginning with the wounded, then in order, the units which had been on the hill the longest. They were to depart from the APC landing using the APCs which brought in the fresh units.[4]

Among the wounded Lieutenant Clark's platoon assisted in evacuating on 10 July was King of the 17th's Pvt. 1st Class Richard A. Baughman, a radio operator involved in the battalion counterattack the morning of 9 July. Richard, whose hometown was Blue Mound, Illinois, was in the National Guard's 44th Division, 130th Regiment Service Company, when the division was called to active duty and later ordered to Fort Lewis, Washington. In December 1952, he received orders to Korea.

After the April battle on the Chop, Richard learned much about Pork Chop Hill. He traveled the access road, and using communication wire hooked to Chinese soldiers' bodies helped remove their sometimes waist-deep dead from its trenches. He assisted in searching their pockets for intelligence gathering purposes, and smelled the odor of burned flesh—the result of flame throwers used during the battle.

He participated in the rebuilding of the outpost after the April battle. He also learned there were two large, permanently emplaced flame throwers on Pork Chop, one on each north slope flank of the hill's defenses. They were the same type as the one installed and fortified by the 707th Ordnance Battalion near the west shoulder of Hill 347, where Lt. Ray Clark's machine-gun platoon was when the battle began on the sixth.

The night of 9 July, after King of the 17th counterattacked the outpost early in the morning with 188 men, the company's ranks were shredded in the heavy fighting. The Chinese, as had been their habit, launched another heavy assault, complete with artillery, mortars, burp guns, and grenades. Richard had come on the hill as the radio operator for his platoon leader.

He brought with him his carbine and a PRC-10 radio carried on a back board. Before the night was over, his radio antenna—a sixteen-foot antenna off a Russian T-34 tank—was shot off, and his hand-held mic was hit and knocked out, making his radio useless. Accustomed to firing a rifle mounted with a sniper's scope, he threw down his carbine, frustrated he could not hit the enemy with it.

During the close, bitter fighting he found a .30-caliber light machine gun and fired it with great effect. He then returned the borrowed gun, and began looking for an M-1 rifle—until an incoming artillery round found its mark beneath him, sending him cartwheeling downhill. The artillery round did more damage than shell fragments in his chin and the center of his left cheek. His platoon leader ordered him off the hill.[5]

The 32d Regiment Relieves the 17th

Word of the relief spread rapidly, and Lieutenant Clark found himself surrounded by troops trying to crowd into each APC as it unloaded the arriving soldiers from King of the 32d. Clark had to get tough.

He decided he would have to use his grease gun as a "ticket puncher." Each time he called a unit designation many of the troops, and especially the KATUSAs, crowded forward. Clark then required the senior man from each company to personally vouch for each person before he was allowed on an APC. Some companies needed only one APC to evacuate.[6] King of the 17th was typical—they had only twelve remaining of the 188 who fought their way onto Pork Chop thirty-six hours earlier, including medic Jim Leal who arrived on the outpost the afternoon of the ninth.[7]

Jim Leal's twenty-four hours on Pork Chop were filled with sights and sounds he's never forgotten. After carefully working his way from the main trench entrance to the area held by King Company, and being greeted by the sergeant who was irritated by Jim's late arrival on the outpost, he started through the trenches treating and moving the wounded to safety in locations they were being collected. While moving through a trench on the south slope in broad daylight, he was startled and horrified by an awful misstep. He heard a squishing sound and looked down to see he had stepped on the stomach of a dead American soldier—a young, blond lieutenant partially covered with dirt rained on his body by exploding shells. There were two more bodies in the same area. The sound became a sickening, repulsive sound and his most vivid memory of a day he wished he could forget.

In the hours ahead he picked up his carbine to help fight off enemy attacks which surged onto and across the outpost beginning before midnight and again at 2:10 A.M. the morning of the 10th. An officer ordered Jim and a black medic to move over the crest to trenches and bunkers to join men on the north slope in defending against the wave of Chinese attackers. Flares illuminated the north slope of the hill and the valley below. The enemy kept coming. Both men started firing but soon ran out of ammunition. Jim had a "bad feeling" and realized "we have to get the hell outta here." They had no choice but to fall back and take cover; they did not have the means to defend themselves. Shortly thereafter American artillery—VT rounds—began exploding over the hill and broke the enemy assault.

Now, on the tenth, King Company's first sergeant was told by radio to evacuate Pork Chop. Leal reported there were more men along the trench line and went looking for them. He helped move wounded downhill to the collection point. One APC, an open-topped M-39, was his ticket back to the checkpoint, and all twelve piled onto the vehicle. On the return trip, Leal believed he was in the last APC bringing King Company off the hill. He was not aware there were no other King Company survivors except the men on this vehicle. He was among the last of King Company—all others had been killed or wounded.

On the ride back to the checkpoint, he saw an APC on its side, apparently hit or turned over by enemy fire. The vehicles crew was outside on the ground. Leal hollered for the M-39 driver to "Stop! We need to pick up the injured." Some of the K Company men riding with him protested loudly. "No! Keep goin'. Let's get the hell outta here." "Stop!" shouted Jim Leal, and the driver stopped. Leal and another medic exited the vehicle, and brought the two men to the waiting M-39 for the return to safety—and treatment of their injuries.[8]

Finally, it was time for Lt. Ray Clark and his H Company machine-gun platoon to leave Pork Chop. When they did, his platoon numbered fifteen to eighteen men, a far cry from the fifty he brought with him from Hill 347—nevertheless, a larger number than several entire companies could count leaving the outpost that afternoon.

A T-18 carried most of the platoon, and the rest, including Clark, rode an open-topped M-39. He rode in the assistant driver's seat, with his head out, above the open hatch. They roared down the hill at full speed, bouncing and being thrown about, past the overturned M-39, and around clobber corner, all the while collecting a thick layer of dust. They closed up behind a slower moving T-18. The M-39 driver, determined to shorten their exposure to enemy fire, stormed past the heavier vehicle and forded the stream rather than use the Bailey Bridge.

At the checkpoint they boarded a truck and rode to the battalion bivouac area, where Clark took an immediate count of his platoon. Still fifteen to eighteen. He then drove to the division medical company to look for wounded from his platoon. Most had already been sent to a MASH, and he never saw them again.

At the medical company Clark found his missing squad leader, who had disappeared during their run downhill from Hill 200 and up the road to Pork Chop at noon on 9 July. The squad leader was sitting in the sun, reading comic books. He said he had a case of "nerves" in the trench on Hill 200, and took off. He had lived up to his platoon nickname of "Bug-out."[9]

When the remaining men from George Company came off the hill that afternoon, tragedy struck its members hard. As their commander, 1st Lt. Robert G. Brobst, Jr., and his jeep driver, Cpl. Thomas M. Bixler, were about to leave the checkpoint, a salvo of enemy mortar rounds slammed into the area, scoring a direct hit on the jeep. Both men were mortally wounded.[10]

BY 5:50 in the evening, the relief on Pork Chop was complete, with Major Noble, the 2d Battalion of the 17th commander, and the men from the 17th Regiment evacuated. Item and King Companies of the 32d were believed to be the only American units on the outpost.[11]

When I Company of the 32d Infantry relieved the remaining 17th Infantry units on the eastern flank of Pork Chop, Cpl. Dan Schoonover, 13th Engineers, voluntarily stayed, manning a machine gun for several hours. A comrade implored him to leave the hill with George Company's few survivors, but he refused, saying, "Some of these other men are married and have families. I'll stay." He subsequently joined Item Company's assault on enemy emplacements. When last seen he was operating a BAR with devastating effect until he was mortally wounded by artillery fire.[12]

At 4:00 P.M. the afternoon of 10 July, Lt. Col. Royal R. Taylor temporarily took command of the 32d Regiment's 3d Battalion, and Pork Chop Hill's defenders. Taylor, a World War II combat veteran and member of the 82d Airborne Division in Europe, proved himself an inspired combat leader during a harrowing twenty-four hours on Pork Chop Hill, when the Chinese struck again and again. Throughout the ordeal by fire endured by the 3d Battalion of the 32d Regiment, Royal R. Taylor was one of many bright, shining lights seen on Pork Chop in the five-day battle. Right from the beginning, when he boarded the APC for the ride to Pork Chop late the afternoon of 10 July, he set an inspirational tone for the men of the 3d Battalion.

Prior to his assumption of command, and while he was being briefed into the existing situation, Taylor sent his executive officer, Maj. Reginald G. Watkins, ahead of him to the outpost to temporarily take command of the hill's defense, when the 17th Regiment was relieved and defense of the hill passed to the 32d Regiment. Watkins arrived on Pork Chop at 4:00 P.M., reconnoitered friendly positions, and began conferring with company commanders preparatory to finalizing plans for a counterattack later that evening. Taylor arrived on the Chop by APC shortly thereafter, and the two men conferred, agreeing the counterattack should commence at 6:00 P.M. On Taylor's ride to the outpost, enemy artillery and mortar fire was intense and continuous.

Throughout the period Taylor was discussing the counterattack with his executive officer in the outpost CP, enemy artillery rounds were falling on the hill at a rate of three rounds per second. After the two officers discussed the counterattack plan, Taylor climbed into another APC and returned to the division CP to brief General Trudeau and Colonels Van Way and Lonning on the situation and the planned counterattack. As events unfolded throughout the long night of 10–11 July, plans for the counterattack changed.[13]

At 8:50 the night of 10 July an enemy company attacked the King Company sector on the west shoulder of the hill. Commanders called in all available supporting fires, and after a forty-one-minute fire fight, the Chinese withdrew. In response to the again increased tempo of enemy attacks, Lieutenant Colonel Taylor ordered Love Company into the assembly area behind Hill 200, to be ready to reinforce or counterattack if the enemy succeeded in further penetrating defenders' positions. The company closed in the blocking position behind 200 at 9:42 P.M.[14] At 10:30, after ensuring

Love Company was in the blocking position behind Hill 200, prepared to counterattack or reinforce, Taylor returned to the Pork Chop CP under withering artillery, mortar, and sniper fire to take command of the outpost's defense. His plans and preparations were none too soon.[15]

Death in a Shallow Trench

When Louis Salovich, a draftee, rode an APC onto Pork Chop Hill with Item Company of the 32d Regiment early the morning of 9 July, he did not have any idea how his life would be changed. He arrived in the company on 1 June while they were in a blocking position in the area behind the Ethiopian Battalion. After his arrival, Item remained there for five days, then 3d Battalion replaced the Ethiopians on the MLR. From the MLR he could see the 17th's Charlie Company raid the Rat's Nest from Pork Chop the morning of July Fourth. Then, on 7 July, after having seen from a distance the fury unleashed on Pork Chop the night of the sixth, the men of Item Company received word they were being relieved from their positions on the MLR. Pork Chop was the eventual destination.

The officers and men of Item Company undoubtedly expected the worst when the APCs delivered them to the Chop's landing. The lack of stiff resistance when they arrived was surprising. But the test, as had been the case every night beginning 6 July, came beneath the alternately dark and flare-illuminated skies.

Louis's squad members stayed in bunker 63 and 64 for approximately an hour and a half, until Item Company was organized in positions to support King Company, coming on the hill soon after Item Company arrived in the east sector. King would move up the south slope and in the engineers' tunnel, in the hill's western sector, and push toward the outpost's highest point, relieving the 17th's soldiers in that sector. Item's company commander wanted his men in position to provide supporting fire.

He directed them to spread out along the trench toward bunker 51 and relieve 17th Regiment soldiers. Louis and others entered bunker 54, while other Item soldiers relieved men holed up in bunker 53. The door to 53 was sandbagged, and when its 6 or 7 occupants came out and walked past Louis and the men in 54, the obviously pleased men shook his hand and told him they were happy to be out. One handed him a clip of ammunition for his carbine. Another said, "Take no prisoners. Those sons-a-bitches won't."

He remained in bunker 54 until toward dusk, when he and a group of seven or eight moved farther west toward bunker 51. There was a barricade of railroad ties between 52 and 51, and because of the darkening sky, they could not see past the barricade. He was told to stand watch. Suddenly the Chinese started throwing "potato mashers" from the darkness. Louis and the men with him opened fire, but could not see their adversaries. He remembered someone saying "Salovich! Where's he at?" Immediately thereafter incoming artillery and mortars began hitting perilously close. Bunker 52 took a direct hit about 9:00 P.M. A second round lifted him off the ground.

When the dust and debris cleared momentarily he could see three or four men were down, hit by shrapnel. He was too—grievously. In his right hand and right ankle. He could not crawl. His right foot was turned completely backward and almost torn off. His rifle stock was splintered, and he took half of it to make a tourniquet to stop the bleeding. Someone managed to call the company commander on a radio or phone, for medics. He was soon picked up on a stretcher and moved into bunker 54. His company commander came into the bunker and told the medic to give Louis two shots of morphine. It would be awhile before he could be evacuated.

Sometime later he was carried past bunkers 63 and 64 on a stretcher, into the shallow, three foot deep trench near the access road, to be moved to the APC landing. Two medics appeared out of the darkness to carry him to the collection point, where he would be held until loaded on an APC. One of the medics said, "I want to go get that 45 [caliber pistol]," and went back toward an APC. The other said, "I'll stay here with him."

Mortar rounds suddenly started falling nearby. The medic was standing up in the trench next to Louis. Louis told him to "Get down!" The next instant a round landed close by, slamming the medic up against the trench wall. He careened off the wall and pitched forward across Louis Salovich's body. The medic was dead. Louis Salovich lost consciousness.

He dimly remembered being evacuated on an APC, a short ride to the battalion aid station, then a trip on a litter-bearing jeep to a MASH. When they were taking him out of the trench, someone asked him if he remembered seeing an ROK soldier in his bunker. "No," replied Louis. He later learned the ROK soldier was in fact a wounded Chinese soldier, quietly lying unnoticed, in hiding.[16]

11 July

At 2:14 A.M. on 11 July, an unknown number of Chinese attacked and succeeded in penetrating positions occupied by Item Company, on the east shoulder of Pork Chop. A short fire fight ensued, after which the enemy fell back out of the trench line, and Item restored its positions. Shortly thereafter, American intelligence informed senior commanders of an impending battalion counterattack by the Chinese, before daylight. To counter the expected enemy assault, Lieutenant Colonel Taylor alerted Love of the 32d to be ready to counterattack.

At 3:30 A.M., a heavy assault by an estimated battalion of Chinese infantry hit the left flank of I Company, and succeeded in overrunning the left and center platoons. At 4:18, Love Company departed its assembly area by APC and attacked on the left flank of Item Company.[17]

When King Company's 1st Lt. Thomas M. Armour received word of the enemy's penetration of Item Company positions, he also learned from his battalion commander of Love Company's counterattack, with instructions that King should attack from west to east and help drive the enemy from the right shoulder of the hill. Armour personally led King's assault from the west. After King, Love, and Item Companies succeeded in retaking some of Item Company's positions, Armour supervised and assisted in evacuating wounded, resupplying his men, and then organized the King Company perimeter to hold its position. Next, he took up a forward position where, with a radio, he could direct supporting fire from the MLR.[18]

Another King Company soldier distinguished himself on 11 July. During one of his company's counterattacks on the well-entrenched Chinese, Pfc. Rother Temple from North Carolina, and his comrades, were pinned down by intense mortar and machine-gun fire. Temple moved into an exposed position and unloaded a hail of fire from his weapon into the enemy-held position. As his squad withdrew, he remained in the open and continued to fire. Only after his entire squad reached safety did he move

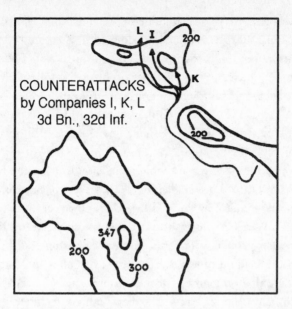

The counterattacks by I, K, and L Companies, 32d Infantry. The companies moved by trucks to the checkpoint and by APCs to Pork Chop. I Company arrived at 5:45 A.M., and K Company arrived at 9:30 A.M. on 10 July 1953. L Company departed the checkpoint at 4:18 A.M. on 11 July.

toward cover. On his return toward cover, he received wounds mandating his evacuation.[19]

In Item Company, Pfc. James W. Lee, an Alabama soldier, served as a constant inspiration to his fellow soldiers, by repeatedly exposing himself to heavy enemy small-arms fire and grenades, in attempts to deny the Chinese key positions. He moved about the surface of the hill and fought heroically from trenches and other vantage points, personally accounting for numerous enemy casualties. His devastating fire and complete disregard for his own safety lifted the spirits of his fellow soldiers.[20] There were many others whose actions in the final twenty-four hours of fighting on Pork Chop proved them extraordinary soldiers.

Throughout the long night and into the late afternoon of 11 July, the battalion commander, Royal R. Taylor, performed acts of bravery, courage, compassion, valor, and selflessness which were more than extraordinary in the eyes of those who witnessed his example.

By the time of his second trip back to Pork Chop by APC the night of 10 July, the Chinese had already launched the first of their night attacks, and were hitting the access road and evacuation landing with snipers and small-arms fire, as well as continued shelling by artillery and mortars. The APC stopped about ten yards from the CP entrance, and Taylor was the first to exit the vehicle, urging the other occupants to follow. He made for the CP entrance, but his radio operator, Corporal Durulla, injured his knee jumping from the APC and could not walk. As soon as the enemy saw the injured soldier, the intensity of small-arms fire aimed near the APC increased.

There were other soldiers available to assist Durulla, but when Taylor turned and saw Durulla down, he immediately came back to assist him to safety in the combination CP and aid station. Once everyone was inside, Taylor next led several soldiers to positions where they took the snipers under fire. After the men were in position to begin suppressing sniper fire, he directed the loading of wounded into APCs, while under continuing small-arms fire all around him. The medics and other soldiers assisting the wounded to board the APC saw their battalion commander aggressively giving first priority to the wounded. The result was similar performance from men who had been bystanders under cover.

Once he completed these tasks, Major Watkins briefed him on the situation. Taylor then ordered Watkins off the hill with instructions to supervise resupply and evacuation. After learning the defenders' circumstances, he passed orders to the company commanders and began organizing the CP. First Lt. Obel H. Wells described the CP as "littered with serviceable and unserviceable equipment and waste." Taylor noted a group of men with no assigned job and assigned each work to do in cleaning up the CP.

The men were reluctant to step outside the CP to dump the debris. Taylor did not order them out. He simply took an armload of trash, stepped out into the open in spite of the enemy fire, and threw it out of the CP. The men promptly followed suit and in short order cleaned out the bunker. The gestures of participation and clean-up, seemingly insignificant, lifted the men's morale.

While Taylor and the men with him were establishing security for the CP, the enemy struck the ammunition storage and CP bunkers with an incoming salvo of white phosphorous rounds, setting off an explosion in the storage area, and fire in both the storage area and CP. Taylor ordered the CP evacuated, with relocation of the wounded into the nearby covered main trench, which was secured by King Company. The CP occupants' move through the open into the trench promptly drew increased enemy small-arms fire, which struck an already wounded soldier near the battalion commander. Taylor helped the wounded soldier to safety. Once inside the new CP, he looked back to see another wounded soldier lying in the open near the just vacated CP. He ran back outside and dragged him inside the new CP.

Once inside, Taylor began reorganizing the new CP. He provided covering fire for Lieutenant Wells when he had to return to the burning CP to retrieve a radio to set up communications. Taylor's covering fire successfully pinned down the sniper. Wells was almost overcome and blinded by smoke as he tried to make his way back to the new CP with the radio. Taylor came out of the CP, met him, and led him to safety.

A few minutes later they discovered they had insufficient radio batteries. Several men volunteered to return to the burning CP for more batteries. Taylor first cautiously surveyed the burning ammunition storage area and saw 3.5-inch rocket launcher rounds on fire. He knew an ammunition explosion was imminent, and refused to let his men attempt the grab for batteries. Instead, the battalion commander chose to make the dash. When Taylor was five yards out of the new CP, the ammunition exploded, caving in the old CP bunker and burying the equipment inside it. Miraculously Taylor was uninjured.

All during the night and the following morning the Communists kept up a steady pounding of the outpost with artillery and mortars. The covered trench took several direct hits, wounding more men. When the enemy assaults began in earnest shortly after 2:00 A.M., Taylor positioned himself near the south entrance to the main trench, where he would be among the first the enemy encountered if they succeeded in overrunning the rear slopes of the hill. At one point he handed out grenades to all the defenders in the tunnel, including the wounded, telling them if the enemy penetrated and they all fought they would drive them back.[21]

When Love Company arrived on the hill to launch their counterattack, Taylor left the confines of the covered trench and moved among the men of the battalion, encouraging them and coordinating local counterattacks. At one point, while he was in another bunker, it took a direct hit from an artillery round, and caved in, trapping him inside.

His men communicated his plight to Regiment and began working to dig him out. In Hill 200's outpost 12, the 3d Battalion S-3, Capt. Robert W.

Lewis, received an order from the regiment's new commander, Colonel Lonning, to go forward in an APC, dig Taylor out, and obtain information on the tactical situation. When Lewis arrived he assisted in digging and pulling Taylor from the caved-in bunker, essentially unharmed. Taylor filled Lewis in on the tactical situation. While they were talking a medic standing two feet from Taylor was hit and killed by a sniper. When Lewis reentered the APC to return to Hill 200, the vehicle's driver told Lewis he had been ordered to contact Taylor and request that he return to the MLR. The battalion commander declined and refused medical treatment, stating he would remain with his men. He stayed on the Chop until late afternoon, 11 July.[22]

Though King, Item, and Love Companies were successful in restoring some of the positions overrun by the Chinese, and at daylight the 3d Battalion of the 32d retained control of a substantial part of the Chop's defenses, there were signs of trouble ahead—again. The night of intense fighting resulted in heavy casualties in all three companies, raising again the need to evacuate wounded and dead, resupply, and prepare for another night of enemy assaults.

By Saturday, 11 July, the battle had been raging for five days, virtually nonstop. To regain full control of an outpost defended by one company, rifle companies from five American infantry battalions in two regiments, all with KATUSAs in them, were committed to the fight. Intelligence gathered during the action now confirmed at least one entire Chinese division had been committed against the hill's defenders, sometimes two battalions in one assault wave. The enemy seemed willing to accept any cost to hold their gains.

When the daily command conference convened at the 7th Division CP on the morning of 11 July, Gen. Maxwell Taylor, the Eighth Army commander, Gen. Bruce Clarke, I Corps commander, and Gen. Arthur Trudeau, the 7th's commander, discussed the relative benefits of continued counterattacking and occupation of the outpost. At the end of the discussion, summarized in the 7th Division Command Report for July 1953, Taylor reluctantly announced his decision to withdraw from Pork Chop:

It was obvious from the size of the enemy forces already committed that the Chinese were determined to take and occupy the position. Furthermore, it was quite possible that the enemy intended or had intended to

SF Jazz Trail Ride?

Tom! E Bay Men's Grp

Ed - Maybe it was really that
you were angry with Trish!

John __ Same __

Ed → ᚨᚨ → M. Connolly

→ It hurt me →

Q: last week

Satisfied, Curious and worried

attempt a MBP [Main Battle Position] penetration. The continued reinforcement and counterattacking on the part of friendly forces was considered fruitless in view of the expected toll of casualties and the complete
loss of tactical value of Pork Chop. . . . Since the enemy had committed
elements of two regiments [the 199th and 200th of the 67th Division],
and probably elements of a third regiment in his attempt to take the position, coupled with an estimated 4,000 enemy casualties, the decision was
made to evacuate Pork Chop in a deliberate daylight withdrawal.[23]

Belief the armistice was near, and other factors unknown to the men who
had put their hearts, souls, sweat, and blood into the outpost's defense,
weighed heavily in the decision. To give up voluntarily what so many had
given their lives to defend seemed incomprehensible, an almost impossible
mission to perform. Yet, there were many who breathed a sigh of relief.
They questioned the continued loss of life to hold Pork Chop. But the time
had passed to argue the point either way. Planning went ahead for a daylight withdrawal.

The Ruse

Planning for withdrawal from Pork Chop began the night of 10–11 July,
when Eighth Army declined to approve General Trudeau's plan to launch
a battalion counterattack on Old Baldy and the Chinese again committed
a battalion or more in another counterattack to reassert control of the hill.
While it was clear the Chinese absorbed terrible losses in the five-day
struggle for Pork Chop, and their 67th Division was shattered by relentless
assaults and brutal fighting, the 7th Infantry Division had taken heavy
casualties as well.

The 17th Regiment bore the brunt of the enemy assault. Able Company,
manning the hill when the assault began the night of 6 July, was the first of
eight of the regiment's nine rifle companies, plus a machine-gun platoon
from How Company, to fight in defense of Pork Chop. Elements of the regiment's remaining two heavy weapons companies, D and M, supported the
hill's defense. The 32d Regiment committed five rifle companies, Easy and
Fox of the 2d Battalion, and Item, King, and Love of the 3d Battalion. The
entire 32d Regiment had been pulled off the right flank (east) sector of the

7th Division's MLR, replaced by I Corps' reserve—the 14th Regimental Combat Team from the 25th Division.

Every single field artillery battalion in the division, plus several other supporting battalions, had poured an almost incomprehensible number of rounds onto the outpost and the enemy's approach routes to the hill—plus counterbattery, countermortar fire, and extensive shelling of enemy assembly areas. Pork Chop's trenches and bunkers, so painstakingly rebuilt after the April battle, with every intent to hold firm, had again been reduced to a shambles. Few defense networks built under fire, as Pork Chop's were, could ever withstand the relentless, round-the-clock battering by artillery and mortars from both sides. Pork Chop's defenses, no matter how well built and strengthened, were no exception.

Air strikes on the enemy MLR supply and communication routes beginning 9 July failed to dent the Communists' determination to secure complete control of Pork Chop Hill.

Now came the question: How best to withdraw from the outpost without additional heavy casualties? Withdrawal is one of the most difficult maneuvers on any battlefield. Withdrawal from Pork Chop would be difficult enough after five days of bitter fighting and heavy losses. If an aggressive enemy discovers a withdrawal is in progress, and can muster the energy, strength, and forces to immediately pursue, a withdrawal can quickly turn into a rout and even heavier losses. Pulling off the hill necessitated careful planning to avoid both.

Gen. Maxwell Taylor recommended a night withdrawal, but left the decision to the commanders in the field. General Trudeau, his staff and commanders devised a plan that worked to near perfection.

Trudeau issued the order to withdraw from Pork Chop Hill at 11:45 A.M. on 11 July. The commander, 2d Battalion of the 32d Regiment, who went forward to the outpost, was to organize and execute the evacuation of all friendly personnel. Movement of all tactical units subsequent to return to the MLR was to be coordinated by Colonel Van Way, commander of the 32d Infantry. Fire support during the withdrawal was to be coordinated, controlled, and adjusted from Hill 347 by the commander of the 1st Battalion, 32d Infantry.

To better coordinate fire support from Hill 347, Lt. Col. Rocky Read, the 1st Battalion of the 17th's commander agreed to send his battalion executive officer, Maj. Billy E. Fritts, to assist in coordinating fire support.

Fritts, in fact, volunteered. He was the officer who shouldered the responsibility for rebuilding Pork beginning in May, not only to bring together the manpower and skills needed to do the job, but to maintain continuity in the project and ensure the entire layout of the hill's defenses was tactically sound. Fritts, who had spent many hours on the hill during its rebuilding, was thus intimately familiar with both the outpost's trenches and bunkers, as well as the outlying terrain and enemy approaches to the hill. With the support of forward observers and good communications, he was well suited to bring to bear, at the right time and in the right places, the division's heavy supporting firepower.

The division augmented communications facilities between the outpost, checkpoint, Hill 347, and Hill 200. The 1st Battalion of the 17th's operations officer, Capt. Stephen J. Patrick, designated commander of the checkpoint, was given the mission of coordinating the movement of all APCs to and from the outpost. Additionally, he would ensure all men returning from the outpost were immediately evacuated to assigned areas in the rear of the MLR.

Tanks from the 73d Tank Battalion were emplaced along the road to the outpost to deliver 90-mm tank gunfire against snipers attempting to hamper operations. Four T-18 APCs were to be employed concurrently to permit rapid evacuation of the outpost.[24]

The entire plan, complete with heavy concentrations of artillery and mortar fire, direct, devastating fire from tank guns, and T-18s to conceal and protect their occupants, was intended to sow doubt in the minds of the enemy and feign the appearance of preparations for a massive counterattack. The ruse worked to perfection, aided by planned events which followed later in the day and on 12 July.

. When the evacuation began, defenders occupied two portions of the Chop. King of the 32d occupied the west sector adjacent to the APC landing, and Item and Love Companies of the 32d held the east sector. At 12:35 P.M., while heavy supporting fires began hitting enemy positions, primarily in the area of the Rat's Nest, messages went to Lieutenant Colonel Taylor in the left sector and the Love Company commander in the right sector, advising them of the decision to abandon the outpost. Orders followed to immediately evacuate all wounded, first from the left sector and then from the right. Lieutenant Colonel Taylor would return to the MLR and supervise the withdrawal of the rest of his units when the last of the

Maj. Charles E. Undercoffer, executive officer, 73d Tank Battalion, directs covering fire from an M-46 Patton tank against enemy positions as 7th Division units withdraw from Pork Chop, 11 July 1953.
Courtesy of National Archives

wounded were evacuated. Taylor, just rescued from a caved-in bunker, chose to ignore the order, saying he would remain on Pork Chop until he ensured all his men were either off the outpost or in the process of leaving.

The plan was to evacuate remaining effective troops and the dead following the evacuation of wounded. Troops holding the right sector were to man covering positions while those on the left evacuated. An officer in each sector was ordered to be the last man to depart that portion of the outpost.[25]

Three Surprises for the Enemy

While events proceeded apace to evacuate Pork Chop Hill, the 7th Infantry Division planned two additional surprises for the men of the CCF's battered 67th Division, certain to be reaching for their hard won prize beginning the night of 11 July after they learned the outpost was abandoned.

Quad .50-caliber machine guns and crew from the 15th AAA (SP) Battalion on an M-16 half-track. Note the crew commander standing on the hood of the M-16 with a phone in his left hand and a raised signal flag in his right, relaying targeting information to the crew from a controller at the command post. *Courtesy of Robert M. Euwer*

First Lt. David Bills, the battalion supply officer in the 13th Engineers, had been in Seoul, working as the special effects technical director filming the not-yet-finished movie *Cease Fire*. Bills, an acknowledged explosives and demolition expert, regarded the movie project as fun and interesting—different. The work was somewhat hazardous at times, though tame when measured against life near or on the MLR—or an outpost forward of the MLR. On the morning of 11 July he returned to the 13th Engineers' supply yard to obtain additional explosives and equipment for the film project. While there, he received word the battalion commander, Lt. Col. Earl Icke, wanted to see him.

The 7th Division's "chief engineer," General Trudeau, wanted the 13th Engineers to mine and booby-trap Pork Chop—every section of the hill they could reach. The engineers' mission was to be the first of two missions to ensure Pork Chop Hill would be totally unusable by the Chinese, a worthless prize. After the engineers finished their work, the second mission to seal the destruction of Pork Chop was for artillery and tactical aircraft.

When Bills reported to Icke, he received quite a talk Bills later considered an exceptionally effective "sales pitch." The battalion commander recounted Bills's experience and reputation as a solid engineering officer and demolition expert, and then told him he was "invited" on a mission, a "volunteer" mission. He was to collect nineteen more volunteers, proceed

to Pork Chop Hill, and mine and booby-trap the outpost's remaining fortifications, late that afternoon. The hill was being evacuated. Normally, the
mission would have been given to Bulldozer Able, Capt. Jim Brettell's Able
Company, but Bills rightly surmised that Able Company had already taken
excessive casualties in building the Bailey Bridge on 7–8 July. Of course,
Bills volunteered—"Yes, Sir!"—and promptly drove to the company area
to round up the nineteen volunteers.

When he arrived he learned the company first sergeant had already
held a formation to accept, or select, the nineteen soldiers, including three
NCOs: Sgt. John D. Devin, Sgt. James L. Halter, and Sgt. Anthony F.
Novak. Bills gave the nineteen a brief description of the mission, ordered
them to load on two trucks and report to the battalion's S-4 area—supply
area—for training and issue of supplies.

From approximately 11:30 A.M. to 12:30 P.M. Bills conducted a class on
the various explosive devices the engineers would take with them. He particularly explained the use of pull (trip wire) actuated fuses and pressure
actuated fuses for booby traps. He demonstrated how to attach a #8 blasting cap to a fuse using regular pliers because regularly issued nonsparking
crimpers were not normally available.

He discussed the use of M-2 tetratol blocks and one-pound TNT blocks
mainly because they were fitted with blasting cap wells. The M-2 blocks were
issued in a canvas bag holding eight two-and-a-half-pound blocks. Each
man received one twenty-pound bag and one empty bag to carry fuses, pliers, and a flashlight. The bags had shoulder straps so each man could also
carry his personal weapon with free hands.

Bills issued blasting caps to the senior NCOs in 30-cap wooden boxes,
and carried an eight-cap box for his use. All these supplies were assembled
by soldiers in battalion supply while he trained the demolitions team for the
afternoon's mission. The supplies included two cases of TNT, each holding
fifty one-pound blocks. After these preparations, the detail climbed aboard
the two trucks, and Bills settled himself into a jeep. With the jeep in the
lead, at 1:00 P.M., the small convoy departed the 13th Engineers' area for
Pork Chop Hill and made its way to the checkpoint behind Hill 200. Shortly
after they arrived at the checkpoint, 1st Lt. Thor Sundt, a 1952 West Point
graduate, and Second Lieutenant Gordon, both from B Company, 13th
Engineers, joined them. Both men had prior knowledge of Pork Chop's
trench and bunker network because B Company routinely supported the 32d
Regiment, which had participated in rebuilding the hill's defenses in April.

At the checkpoint, they were also joined by Capt. James Brettell, the 13th's Able Company commander, whose men had been heavily involved in rebuilding Pork Chop's defenses. Brettell, who would ride out to Pork Chop on an APC with them, then return, began orienting them on the outpost's layout. As a result, they organized into two groups to expedite the setting of charges and evacuation of the hill. One group setting charges, led by David Bills, would enter the covered main trench, which ran beneath the crest of the hill and past the company CP. The second group of ten explosives experts would enter the trench network leading into the platoon CP on the east shoulder of the hill. Sergeant Halter would lead them.

The engineers' preparations continued while Pork Chop's wounded were being evacuated through the checkpoint on APCs. Before David Bills's demolition and mining group boarded an APC to begin what some considered a suicide mission, the first of the hill's defenders, and Pork Chop's dead, began returning to the checkpoint on APCs.[26]

Repairing the Lifeline One Last Time

In the meantime, early the same afternoon, another 13th Engineer Able Company officer, Lt. Richard White, who had been heavily involved in building the Bailey Bridge on 7–8 July, received word of a road repair job needing prompt attention. He was told the access road to Pork Chop was badly scarred by deep potholes, the products of heavy rains and APC traffic over the five-day period. When the rains first began, the potholes were small, inconsequential, but became progressively larger and deeper as the heavy tracked vehicles splashed more and more mud out of the ever enlarging gouges in the road surface.

Though the rain had eased off the last two days, the road was becoming increasingly hazardous and rough to traverse with new tracked vehicles already showing wear and tear—proving operational tests during combat had exposed needed modifications of the T-18s. While maintenance crews inventively scrambled to maintain and repair the new vehicles, and keep them in commission in harsh operating conditions, the engineers had improvised an ingeniously simple solution to repair and maintain a road frequently threatened with heavy rain, APC traffic, artillery and mortar fire.

The solution was to fill sand bags with rocks, load them on a dump truck, take them to the checkpoint, and load them on APCs when needed. At the checkpoint on 11 July, Richard White let himself down through the open T-18 APC commander's hatch, and with his head out, above the hatch, started the ride toward Pork Chop's evacuation landing. KSCs were in the troop compartment ready to drop bags of rocks when White called for them. The driver kept the vehicle's rear doors open and White observed the road for potholes needing fill.

As they approached a location needing repair, he pulled himself up and lay across the top of the vehicle so he could see the road and shout instructions to the driver and KSCs. When the vehicle approached a pothole, he shouted at the driver to slow down, or sometimes stop and back up, to ensure they dropped the bags of rocks in exactly the right positions to fill the potholes. In this manner they worked slowly toward the APC landing, smoothing out the rough road, all the while watching artillery and mortar rounds explode nearby as the enemy tried vainly to score a direct hit. At one point in the road repair trip, approaching the trench leading to the platoon CP on the hill's east shoulder, White heard enemy burp gun rounds stitching the side of the armored vehicle, which reminded him how fortunate they were to be in a T-18—and how vulnerable he was lying on top of the vehicle giving commands to the crew.

When White and the rest of the men on the APC finally arrived at the evacuation landing he learned for the first time, from a lieutenant manning the outpost, the defenders had been ordered to withdraw from Pork Chop. The evacuation of wounded was complete as planned by 3:00 P.M., and the withdrawal of remaining soldiers and the dead began immediately thereafter.[27]

The first surprise for the enemy was from the 7th Infantry Division, the second from the 13th Engineers, both later that night. The third, a surprise more devastating than the second, was to be 12 July.

Extraordinary Heroism on Hill 347

At noon on 10 July, as part of planning to form a 32d Regimental Combat Team for a battalion counterattack the next day, forward observers met in a field in the 48th Field Artillery Battalion area. They were assigned to various infantry companies and afterward departed for the companies to which they were assigned—except for Lt. Ronald K. Freedman. He and his FO crew remained behind. The next morning he was told he would be the regimental FO for the counterattack. He and his FO crew were never made aware the planned counterattack had been canceled.

Ron Freedman, an FO assigned to C Battery of the 48th, was from Newton Center, Massachusetts, and an OCS graduate. He arrived in Korea in January, and first served as a platoon leader in an AAA Automatic Weapon company at Osan Air Base until he requested reassignment as an FO. He came to the 48th in May.

On 11 July at about 10:00 A.M., Freedman was taken by jeep to a motor park behind Hill 347, where, for the first time, he met 1st Lt. Raymond N. Barry from the town of Hollis, Oklahoma. Barry, a 1950 West Point graduate, had recently commanded B Battery of the 48th but was now artillery liaison officer with the 32d Infantry. Lt. Col. Joseph S. Kimmitt, a native of Montana, commanded the 48th, a 105-mm howitzer battalion in direct support of the 32d, and had selected Barry to coordinate and control supporting fires from the 48th and three other battalions for the counterattack. Kimmitt was an aggressive, hard-charging artillery commander who always worked closely with the infantry.

When Barry met Freedman behind Hill 347, he explained they would be calling in and adjusting multiple fire missions concurrently from both direct-support and general-support artillery. They went by jeep to the top of the hill. On the way, Barry stressed the importance of selecting a good observation post. They chose OP 13. There were two windows—apertures—in the OP, one facing almost due north, with a clear view of Pork Chop and most of the enemy approaches to the hill. The other faced more northeast, toward Hill 200, with a view of both 200 and Pork Chop.

When they arrived in the OP, Major Fritts, the executive officer of 1st Battalion, 17th Infantry, had already occupied the position facing more toward the northeast and Hill 200. Fritts had been a dedicated, nonstop soldier throughout the battle. Because of his in-depth knowledge of the hill's trench and bunker layout, the terrain surrounding the outpost, and tactical considerations in constructing Pork Chop's defenses, which he was responsible for rebuilding after the April battle, he was literally, tirelessly, all over the area behind the MLR briefing and advising battalion and company commanders and their staffs who were about to send or lead their rifle companies onto the outpost. In the last two days before 11 July, he delivered similar advice and assistance to 32d Regiment commanders and their staffs, who were relatively less familiar with the Chop and its defensive network.

In the bunker with Fritts, Freedman, and Barry were Maj. Paul A. Baltes, 73d Tank Battalion; Maj. Richard R. Hallock, 32d Infantry Regiment; and Cpl. Robert A. Henne, a radio chief from headquarters company, 17th Regiment. Hallock was working with Fritts at the same northeast facing aperture. The FOs were connected by field phone to the Fire Direction Center and FO controllers at the base of Hill 347. The liaison officers were twins, Clark and Alan Adickes. Except for Majors Fritts, Baltes, and Hallock, none knew at the time that they were executing "a carefully devised supporting fire plan [to keep] enemy interference to a minimum" while the withdrawal from Pork Chop proceeded.[28] The fire plan included coordinating, controlling, and adjusting both direct fires from tank guns, recoilless rifles, and AAA weapons and indirect fires by artillery and mortars.

When Freedman and Barry first arrived in OP 13, artillery and mortar firing was random, less frequent, jumping from one target to another, primarily incoming on Hill 347 and outgoing on the front side of Pork Chop. Freedman began calling in fire missions by phone at about 11:00 A.M.

As the afternoon wore on, it became more and more apparent that there would be no counterattack on Pork Chop, but the controllers urged the FOs to continue calling in fire missions, with particular attention to the Rat's Nest. There were also indications the Chinese were mounting another attack. Through his binoculars, Barry observed hundreds of Chinese soldiers boldly making their way toward Pork Chop in broad daylight. As outgoing artillery fire continued to fall on the Rat's Nest, the intensity of both incoming and outgoing gradually increased. To Freedman, the situation seemed acceptable, though the incoming was getting stronger.

The only hitch was incoming apparently knocked out phone lines to the Fire Direction Center, and the FOs had to shift to the backup communication mode, radio, to call in requests. Frequent and continued use of radio presented Chinese intelligence units greater opportunity to home in on the broadcasts and triangulate more precisely on the OP's Hill 347 location.

At approximately 2:30 P.M., Freedman, who had been calling in fire missions by phone, called in his first firing request on the radio. The answer came back, "Unknown station, please say again." The response meant he did not have the current call sign, which changed periodically on a schedule which was classified. He had forgotten the scheduled call-sign change.

Chastened, he called the FO controllers on their radio net, and they told him his correct call sign was "Gallivant Charlie 595." While the insistence on good radio discipline seemed incongruous and irritating, the change in call signs was a security procedure intended to reduce successful enemy intervention and insertion of erroneous mission information in the fire control radio net.

One of the Adickes twins called and asked about the intensity of incoming on Pork Chop. The Chop remained relatively quiet except for mortar rounds mostly on the western slopes, but Ron's response to the question drew a chewing out. He answered, saying, "It's light over there, but we are experiencing about thirty rounds per minute." The chewing out resulted because the controllers said he "divulged information and the enemy had probably tapped the phone lines."

About 3:30 Freedman, peering through binoculars, noted an APC traveling up the access road to Pork Chop, then returning shortly. What he and everyone in the OP did not know was the wounded on Pork Chop had already been evacuated, and the evacuation of remaining effectives and the dead was in progress.

Incoming on Hill 347 was now heavy, extremely heavy. The din was almost deafening. More than once the men in OP 13 were knocked off their feet by the force of near-misses by large-caliber artillery rounds. Billy Fritts took wood splinters thrown in his face from a round that struck the parapet below the aperture where he was standing. To better hear radio communications and avoid shrapnel wounds, Freedmen was ducking below the aperture's lower edge at the sound of incoming. The enemy had taken the crest of Hill 347 under close observation and were pouring in precision fire, intent on destroying its OPs. Men familiar with artillery and mortar barrages knew they were playing "Russian Roulette" by remaining in place, calling in fire missions. It was a matter of time until their bunker would be hit. Most continued, but a few, unnerved by the pounding, decided it prudent to evacuate the position and take cover down the back slope—and left the bunker. Remaining at their posts, Fritts, Freedman, and Barry continued adjusting fire with deadly effect on enemy troops approaching Pork Chop.

At approximately 3:50, the CP immediately behind OP 13 took a direct hit, and five minutes later dust, flying debris, and darkness engulfed the interior of OP 13. A direct hit. Corporal Henne awoke moments later.

Dust still filled the air. The first man he saw as the dust began to settle was Maj. Billy Fritts, his body sprawled on the bunker floor, leaning against the wall. The exploding enemy artillery round had decapitated him.

When Ron Freedman awoke he was lying face down on a pile of dirt previously not there. A number of logs in the bunker were burning. He could not move his legs. He remembered saying, "Jesus, I don't think I'm dead." Then he heard groaning behind him, toward his right side. He raised his head, turning as far as he could to his right, and saw Barry had fallen on his back, across the back of Ron's legs. Barry was critically wounded, temporarily blinded, and bleeding profusely from the neck and face.

Still stunned and in shock, Freedman remembered his first aid training, and wiggled from beneath Barry to help him. But what to do? Barry was bleeding heavily, but Freedman realized he could not possibly put a tourniquet around his neck. Barry tried to talk, but was not able. When Freedman spoke to him all he could hear from Barry were muffled gurgles. Barry would surely bleed to death if Freedman did not get help quickly. Freedman pulled away from him, and said, "Hang on! I'll be right back. I'm going for the medics."

He ran outside and screamed, "Medics! OP one three!" No one came. They were still under fire and Freedman thought no one could hear him. He turned right and ran down the access road, then turned left and followed the trench line, still yelling for the medics. Incoming continued. The trench turned right, right again, and right again, back out onto the road leading back up the hill to the OP. He went back to the OP and went inside. He saw Major Fritts's body, but none of the other men who had been in the bunker, except Ray Barry. Three medics were working on Barry. They had heard Ron Freedman yelling for them.

When the medics gave Barry all the help they could, they called for an APC to evacuate him to the battalion aid station at the base of Hill 347. Now that the bombardment had subsided, Ron Freedman realized he could not use his left leg. A log had struck his knee when the bunker collapsed.

A colonel appeared at the bunker and asked if Ron would man the position overnight, and he at first said yes. But no one else was around, and he would have to remain there alone. Instead, he went with Barry as the medics carried both to the vehicle on stretchers, and rode the APC to the battalion aid station. Barry was lapsing in and out of consciousness, and light rain was falling. En route a damaged jeep temporarily blocked the APC's way—until it was pushed over the side of the hill.

Lieutenant Colonel Kimmitt was at the infantry battalion CP when the personnel carrier brought Ray Barry and Ron Freedman to the nearby battalion aid station. Kimmitt had been told the OP on 347 had been hit by incoming, went into the battalion aid station, and saw his former battery commander, Barry, on a table, obviously critically wounded and near death. Freedman was sitting in a chair near Barry's head. A few minutes earlier, the 7th Division G-2, General Trudeau's senior intelligence staff officer, had arrived at the nearby battalion CP, having been flown there by helicopter. Kimmitt, seeing the severity of Barry's wounds, went immediately to the helicopter and told the waiting pilot to fly the wounded officer to the MASH. The chopper was specially equipped, as were all the division light helicopters, to carry two litter patients, outboard on each side, in emergency evacuations.

At first the pilot balked, and told Kimmitt the helicopter belonged to the division G-2. With a few choice, sharp words Kimmitt said he did not give a damn who it belonged to, the pilot would fly Barry to a MASH, right now. When Kimmitt told the battalion surgeon who examined Barry he had a helicopter to evacuate him, the surgeon's words were less than encouraging. "He won't make it to the MASH. He's lost too much blood." Barry, who continued to lapse in and out of consciousness, heard the surgeon's words. The chopper, with Barry aboard, left immediately. Freedman was close to the bunker wall, with his back toward the sandbags. A Major Jones walked by, and Ron told him Major Fritts was dead. Jones immediately started to cry and walked away. Shortly afterward, Freedman went by ambulance to the regimental medical clearing station.

As soon as Barry arrived at the MASH, they placed him on the X-ray table. He was still wearing his demolished flak vest. Shrapnel had ripped open his face and jaw and destroyed his palate. As he lay there, hurriedly being prepared for surgery and massive blood transfusions, he lost hope after a well-meaning chaplain came by and said the Lord's Prayer over him.

But a minute later, another man, perhaps a chaplain of another faith, came over and whispered in Barry's ear, "Listen, Son, we have some of the finest doctors in the world here. If you'll just help them with your will to live, they'll pull you through." When he heard those words, Barry felt an indescribable flow of strength surge through his entire body and mind, and he thought to himself, I'm going to make it. And he did.

At the regimental medical clearing station, Ron Freedman lay on a stretcher until a corpsman came around, and Freedman asked him where information was gathered to send telegrams to families notifying them of wounds. "I do that," said the medic, whereupon Freedman promptly got up from the stretcher, hobbled out of the tent, and thumbed a ride back to C Battery. He did not want his family worried for what he knew to be a minor injury.

Later, in C Battery of the 48th, he began documenting Barry's duty performance the afternoon of 11 July, submitting him for a Silver Star. For forty-four years Freedman thought Barry had died. If Barry received the Silver Star, he probably received it posthumously. But Barry gradually recovered, received the award while still in the hospital, and eventually returned to active duty.

In 1997, after learning Barry was a retired colonel living in Colorado, Freedman contacted him and they exchanged recollections of their Korean War experiences. A few years later, Barry recommended to the Department of the Army that Freedman, the man who had helped save his life, be officially recognized and decorated for his courageous actions under fire in 1953. With the help of Freedman's Florida congressman, Freedman received a Silver Star forty-seven years after that fateful day.[29]

Maj. Billy E. Fritts, 1st Battalion, 17th Infantry Regiment, was posthumously awarded the nation's second highest decoration for extraordinary heroism, the Distinguished Service Cross. The men in OP 13, by their courage and sense of duty toward the soldiers fighting on Pork Chop Hill that day, prevented numerous casualties. The fire they brought down on the Chinese kept the enemy at bay, undoubtedly caused numerous casualties, and avoided pursuit of the withdrawing force. By staying at their posts and calling in fire missions while disregarding the increasing danger to themselves, they helped sow uncertainty and hesitation in the minds of enemy commanders. As American intelligence intercepts would show in the coming twenty-four hours, the ruse had indeed worked to perfection. The Chinese became convinced the 7th Infantry Division was reinforcing Pork Chop, preparing to launch another major counterattack. The withdrawal operation was complete late the evening of 11 July without the loss of a single additional soldier during the pullback from Pork Chop Hill.[30]

As events would prove, the success of the ruse did not come easy. King, Item, and Love Companies and the 13th Engineers learned firsthand just how tense, difficult, and dangerous the withdrawal would be.

The Second Surprise

Approximately 4:00 P.M., as Ron Freedman and medics in the wrecked OP 13 on Hill 347 were working frantically to save Ray Barry's life, Capt. Jim Brettell, Lt. David Bills, Lt. Thor Sundt, and Lieutenant Gordon, plus nineteen enlisted men, were continuing their planning for the mining and booby trapping of the Chop. At 5:30 they boarded a T-18 for the trip from the checkpoint to Pork Chop. On the ride to the Chop, Jim Brettell continued filling in the engineers on details of the hill's layout. A tough, now-experienced, grizzled, veteran combat engineer, in his mind he harbored some not too optimistic thoughts. He feared he would never see these 13th Engineer soldiers again. This well could be a suicide mission.

At the first stop, Sergeant Halter and his demolition team exited the vehicle and moved into the trench network on the east shoulder of Pork Chop, still held by members of Item and Love Companies, 32d Regiment. Onto the APC came infantrymen leaving the hill. When the APC doors opened the second time, David Bills's group unloaded and took cover in the tunnel-like entrance to the main trench. Bills contacted an NCO in the 32d who agreed to take him on a reconnaissance of the area under King Company's control.

Before David Bills and the NCO left the tunnel entrance, Bills agreed to have his men help load casualties on and in the APC. The dead, stacked not far from the trench entrance, were loaded both inside and on top of the T-18, for the return trip, while Bills and his K Company guide made their way through the trenches and bunkers.

The two proceeded to a partially collapsed trench section which was exposed to the upper slope, and stopped short of the open area. The guide advised firing their weapons up slope as they passed through the section. That morning sniper fire caused a head wound casualty. The NCO fired off a half clip from his carbine, and David Bills fired two rounds from his Colt 38 pistol as they moved rapidly through the collapsed section of trench.

Approximately fifty yards ahead they turned left for another ten yards, then right for two more. The NCO told Bills this was as far as he would go. There were two unexploded Chinese "potato masher" hand grenades on the trench floor in front of them. Bills saw the strings were pulled which activated the fuses to cause the grenades to detonate, but the two explosive devices obviously malfunctioned.

Given the short time available for the engineers to do their job, David Bills asked his guide to backtrack and pass on to his NCOs, to spread their soldiers up and down the trench and begin work, but not to arm any of the explosives until Bills withdrew to each of them in turn.

There was an abandoned BAR on the left leg of the trench near the Chinese grenades. Bills placed two M-2 blocks behind a vertical support timber and armed the booby trap with a pull fuse wire to the butt plate of the BAR. Returning to the long stretch of trench about ten yards back, he found the wood lid from an ammunition box. He dug a narrow trench large enough for a single M-2 block with a pressure fuse. After pulling the arming and safety pins, he placed the lid over the assembly and concealed it by covering the lid with loose dirt. He thought the disguise looked natural, even in the darkening evening twilight. Thereafter, David Bills backed out, stopping to check each soldier's work, watching them stretch their trip wires and pull safety pins to arm their M-2 explosives. The soldiers used only pull fuses because they were speedier and safer to install.

On returning to the entrance of the main trench, David Bills's group assembled, ready to depart. But there was not an APC waiting, so they took cover, hoping they were not forgotten. Bills noticed one of their full cases of TNT nearby. He had brought some chemical fuses in his canvas bag. They were activated by crushing an acid-filled glass vial, which initiated corrosion of a copper wire holding back a firing pin. Ambient temperature affected speed of corrosion. Bills selected one color coded for about sixteen hours at seventy degrees Fahrenheit.

With help he removed the wood lid from the case of one-pound blocks, took out several, placed a fused block in the middle, and concealed it under the other blocks. After replacing the lid, he and another soldier moved the case within view of the entrance. They hoped some Chinese soldier would carry it back to his commanding officer!

An APC finally arrived at approximately 7:00 P.M. As David Bills and his men loaded up, he walked into a confrontation with a King Company lieu-

Number of APCs in Operation and Miles Traveled, *6–11 July 1953*

Type	6th	7th	8th	9th	10th	11th	Average per Day
T-18	4	4	6	6	7	9	6
M-39	7	7	9	9	10	12	9
Miles	143	110	134	112	108	168	129.16

Note: Each day is a twenty-four hour period, 12:01 A.M. to 12:00 P.M.

tenant, who had been told he was to be the last man to leave the west sector of the hill. Pointing his 45 Colt automatic pistol in Bills's face the officer demanded to know if there were any more of his men left on the outpost. After assuring him that these engineer soldiers were the last to leave the premises, and asking him to holster his weapon, Bills climbed aboard for the trip off the Chop.

On arriving at the checkpoint, David Bills waited to see if the rest of his men returned from the east sector of the hill. Love Company of the 32d and the 13th's engineer soldiers would be the last to leave the hill, since the withdrawal plan required Company L to cover King and Item Companies' pullback. Bills would not have long to wait.

Sergeant Halter and his group set their charges rapidly. The first sight that greeted them when they left the APC to begin their work was the dead stacked next to the access road, outside the trench which led them into the east trench and bunker network. The trench forked left and right at the crest of the hill. To the left it was dark and Pfc. Sigifredo "Fred" Ortiz did not have a flashlight. To the right, there was light, but when he walked the downward slope, the trench seemed a quagmire of mud—and blood. In the main bunker which had been the Able of the 17th's 2d Platoon CP, they found supplies, weapons, cases of grenades, wounded, and more dead. They helped load the wounded and dead, placing the dead on top of the APC. With the last of Love Company, they boarded their APC. They took fire from the enemy as they boarded, and Sergeant Halter returned fire with his and Fred Ortiz's rifles as they prepared to close the doors for the last trip to the checkpoint.

At 7:20 P.M. the evening of 11 July 1953, the last APC, with its load of dead and wounded, Love Company survivors, and eleven soldiers from the 13th Engineer Battalion arrived at the checkpoint. David Bills, the 13th's supply officer, took a head count of the soldiers who had made the trip to

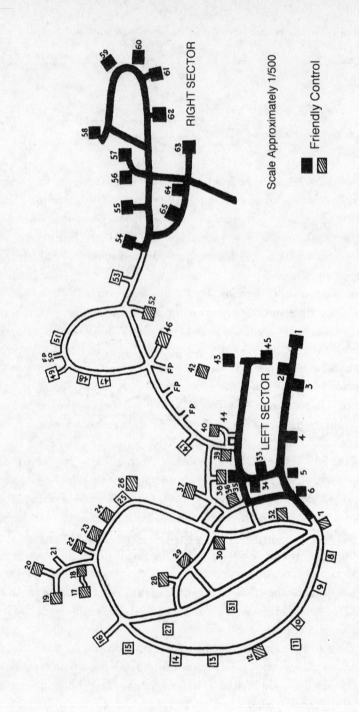

RIGHT SECTOR

LEFT SECTOR

Scale Approximately 1/500

■ Friendly Control

The Pork Chop trench and bunker system and friendly disposition at start of withdrawal, 5:30 P.M. on 11 July 1953.

the Chop nearly two hours earlier. All twenty-two were present. Then he watched them leave for the Company D area.

A short time later, the 13th's commander, Lieutenant Colonel Icke, found David Bills and Bills recalled he had never seen a happier more relieved man. He insisted Bills return with him to division headquarters so the two of them could personally report the success of the mission to General Trudeau. Once there David Bills asked Icke to let him stay in the jeep, because Bills was soaked with sweat and dirt. After Icke's report the two men returned to the 13th's headquarters approximately 8:30. David Bills washed, ate and slept. He was dog tired. The day had been long and hectic.

Pork Chop Hill stood dark and abandoned, waiting for the next assault. If an assault ever came, the skirmishers would be Chinese, and they would find no response to their advance to take full control of the prize they had so bitterly fought to take and hold. A response would come, but not on 11 July—except for enemy soldiers who had the misfortune to trigger the deadly devices left behind by the 13th Engineers. The next morning Bills loaded his jeep and trailer with explosives, sandbags, communication wire, and electric blasting caps—and headed back to Seoul to resume work on the movie production *Cease Fire*.[31]

The Third Surprise

Among the last men to leave the hill late in the afternoon of 11 July was Able Company of the 17th's Cpl. Dale W. Cain, who had been beside Lt. Dick Shea in the three-day period just prior to the battle, had stayed at his post as a radio operator, and fought with a carbine and grenades through five terrible days. When Able Company was relieved and left the hill on 8 July, Dale had been almost totally isolated in his bunker, separated from the rest of the company. He came back to Able Company and Pork Chop from the battalion CP just days prior to the battle.[32] Because of heavy turnover in personnel in Able Company after he was wounded in April, and his return to duty on the outpost during the company's heightened state of alert, few knew him as a veteran member of the company when he returned. Those who did either did not survive, had been wounded and evacuated, or were unaware of his whereabouts and circumstance. But

Cain miraculously survived. He knew he was fortunate. He was among the hundreds of men who fought and lived to remember the hell that was the Chop in July 1953.

Casualties in the last battle for Pork Chop Hill were heavy. In the 17th Infantry Regiment, at the end of July, three officers were reported killed and eight missing in action, with an additional twenty-one officers evacuated as battle casualties—wounded. Among the officers reported missing were Lt. Richard T. Shea, Jr., and Lt. Richard G. Inman. Thirty-four enlisted men were reported killed and 132 missing, with 590 evacuated, wounded in action.[33] The 17th's losses in killed, wounded, and missing were equivalent to one entire, fully manned infantry battalion—four companies.

The losses in the 32d Infantry were less severe. A total of 18 were reported killed in action, 304 wounded, with 41 missing—half a battalion.[34] In the month of July, KATUSAs, the South Koreans augmenting American units, lost 15 killed in action, 129 wounded, and 17 missing in action, nearly all the result of the battle for Pork Chop.

The UN counted 517 Chinese dead and another 128 wounded. Estimates were 1,494 dead and 3,912 wounded.[35] While the totals approximating 2,011 dead and 4,040 wounded cannot be verified, the estimates are most likely conservative.

Among American wounded moved to a Norwegian MASH to the rear of the MLR was a severely wounded Lt. MacPherson Conner. On the morning of 11 July, Mac received a visitor. General Trudeau, the 7th Infantry Division commander, told him the 7th had been hit by two Chinese divisions, and the decision had been made to pull off Pork Chop. The outpost would be obliterated by artillery and airpower, and made unusable by the Chinese.[36]

Trudeau had been at the commanders' conference that morning and knew what was coming. The exploding demolition charges left on Pork Chop by the engineers were the beginning. A brief pause followed. Then came the artillery.

The American withdrawal was skillfully done, albeit painful and emotional for the men given the mission, as well as those who watched. The Chinese eventually recognized the pullback was in progress, and moved to fill the void, intending to firmly occupy their hard won terrain. As they moved to secure the vacated positions the next day, eight battalions and two batteries of artillery opened fire at a prearranged time, and the systematic ravaging of the outpost began. Among the hundreds of projectiles falling on the hill were VT fused rounds, which exploded above the ground and shredded everything beneath and around them with shrapnel. The rest of the artillery fire missions were "destruction missions," intended to destroy the last remaining vestiges of the trench and bunker system built in the months following the April battle. Big guns and howitzers dug deep craters and smashed what remained of the defense network, collapsing trenches, splintering the supports for overhead cover, and caving in bunkers. The barrage continued relentlessly, lifting occasionally while UN aircraft added more fury with tons of bombs.

At noon on 12 July, while Captain Brettell and many other 7th Division officers were having lunch with General Trudeau, Pork Chop's crest was rocked and shattered by a huge explosion. David Bills's delayed fuse had worked.[37]

On Pork Chop the night of 11 July, and most of the next day, the Chinese encountered what David Hughes and the men of K Company, 7th Cavalry had met on Hill 339 nearly two years earlier, when 339 seemed so easy to take: an artillery barrage. But this was far worse, a holocaust. The carnage the remaining Chinese soldiers endured 11 and 12 July ended the last battle for Pork Chop Hill.

Artillery fired in the final battle was staggering and far surpassed the total rounds expended in April's forty-eight-hour struggle for the outpost. While more artillery rounds would be fired in support of the U.S. 3d Infantry Division in the period 13–20 July, the volume of fire poured onto, above, near, and on the approaches to the one-company outpost named Pork Chop Hill is probably unmatched in military history. The Chinese fired 71,826 rounds of mixed artillery and mortar onto the hill, its lines of communication and supply, and the MLR immediately behind it, plus an additional 1,066 mortar rounds and 843 artillery. Into rear areas, on CPs and firing positions, they struck with 475 more artillery rounds.

Six battalions of field artillery, including one ROK battalion, provided support to the men defending and counterattacking Pork Chop. They reported firing 104,176 rounds in the period 7–12 July. Two battalions in I Corps, plus other heavy artillery batteries located in the 7th Division rear area, fired another 11,587 rounds, for a total of 115,763. Of the total, 26,239 rounds were from the heavies, 155-mm guns and howitzers, 8-inch and 240-mm.

Ammunition Expended in Pork Chop Action, 7–12 July 1953

	NUMBER OF MISSIONS						
Type of Mission	48FA	49FA	57FA	187FA	69FA	31FA	Total Missions
Defensive Fires	27	90	13	—	27	64	221
Counter Mortar	373	266	139	307	39	52	1,176
Counter Battery	38	21	2	—	3	106	170
Enemy in Open	40	64	39	11	7	30	191
Machine Guns	—	3	—	—	—	—	3
Direct Fire Weapons	—	11	—	—	3	1	15
Active Mortar	—	5	8	—	—	—	13
Armored Vehicles	6	5	—	—	1	18	30
Harassing and Interdicting	10	11	6	4	25	9	65
Flak Suppression	38	19	23	3	1	—	84
Marking for Air Strikes	—	7	4	—	—	—	11
Destruction Missions	6	—	—	9	1	14	30
Cover for Troops	—	22	6	—	—	11	39
Assembly Areas and Approach Routes	39	14	9	11	—	18	91
Illumination	—	17	—	—	—	—	17
Registration	—	7	11	—	3	1	22
Totals	577	562	260	345	110	324	2,178

Abbreviations

FA and FA Bn	Field Artillery Battalion
CM	Counter Mortar
CBtry	Counter Battery
Arty	Artillery
SP	Self-Propelled
AAA	Antiaircraft Artillery
AW	Automatic Weapon
Def Fires	Defensive Fires
How	Howitzer

[1]Out of 104,176 rounds expended, 15,239 were 155-mm How rounds.
34.91 percent expended on CM
10.05 percent expended on enemy troop areas
25.05 percent expended on def fires
3.08 percent expended on CBtry

Type of Mission	48FA	49FA	57FA	187FA	69FA	31FA	Total Rounds
Defensive Fires	5,175	13,532	3,359	—	80	4,232	26,378
Counter Mortar	11,985	7,750	6,027	7,216	707	2,683	36,368
Counter Battery	458	403	38	—	19	2,301	3,219
Enemy in Open	1,875	2,925	2,387	425	52	3,016	10,680
Machine Guns	—	18	—	—	—	—	18
Direct Fire Weapons	213	221	—	—	18	115	567
Active Mortar	—	5	8	—	—	—	13
Armored Vehicles	6	5	—	—	1	18	30
Harassing and Interdicting	10	11	6	4	25	9	65
Flak Suppression	38	19	23	3	1	—	84
Marking for Air Strikes	—	7	4	—	—	—	11
Destruction Missions	6	—	—	9	1	14	30
Cover for Troops	—	22	6	—	—	11	39
Assembly Areas and Approach Routes	39	14	9	11	—	18	91
Illumination	—	17	—	—	—	—	17
Registration	—	7	11	—	3	1	22
Totals	19,805	24,956	11,878	7,668	907	12,418	77,632

	CBtry	Def Fires
The 623d FA Bn (155-mm How—I Corps Arty) fired	4,283	564
The 999th FA Bn (155-mm How [SP]—I Corps Arty) fired	4,134	2,606
Total	8,417	3,170

Including the 8,417 rounds shown here, I Corps Arty fired 25,247 rounds.

CMR Plots	449
Counter Fire Plots	284
Shell Reports	594
Total Incoming Arty in Friendly Rear Areas	475

15th AAA AW (SP) Rounds Expended, 7–12 July 1953

.50 cal.	500,644
40 mm	3,924

The 15th AAA (AW) Battalion fired an additional 3,924 rounds of 40-mm and 500,644 rounds of .50-caliber ammunition.[38] The totals exclude an enormous unreported volume of mortar rounds, numbered in the tens of thousands, plus recoilless rifles, and 90- and 76-mm tank guns. While UN casualties were heavy, the punishing rain of steel on the Communists undoubtedly prevented hundreds more UN casualties, and in combination with an unyielding defense of the hill by American and ROK soldiers and the Americans' KATUSA allies, broke the back of any Chinese ambitions to penetrate the MLR.

Temporary Quiet in the 7th Division Sector

The morning of 12 July, Dale Cain and six other Able Company soldiers assembled in a formation on a hillside in the 1st Battalion area south of Pork Chop. The day before, when Pork Chop was evacuated, Cain had been taken off the hill on an APC and then transported further, via a two-and-a-half-ton truck, to the rear area. Captain Roberts was at the morning formation and asked if the seven soldiers would like to talk with a chaplain. Cain did not learn until years later that Able Company had been relieved from Pork Chop on 8 July.[39]

The night of 13 July the Communists launched a major assault on the central front. The Chinese threw six divisions into the attack, three against the ROK Capitol Division, nearly shattering it. Centered on the ROK divisions east of the 7th Infantry sector, the Chinese advanced in the Kumsong area. For six days the Eighth Army battled to stabilize the sector the enemy breached. On 19 July, Gen. Mark Clark, commander, Far Eastern Command, called Gen. Maxwell Taylor in Seoul and instructed him to inform President Rhee that an armistice agreement seemed "near at hand" in Panmunjom. Taylor reported back to Clark by phone later in the day. He had informed Rhee, who expressed no reaction to the message.[40]

By 20 July the Chinese offensive ran out of steam due to powerful counterattacks and heavy casualties, and the Eighth Army straightened the line. The Communist offensive operations in June and July 1953 had sparked the heaviest fighting of the war since April and May 1951. The bitter fighting was costly to both sides, and added to the already frightful toll of the final two months of the war.[41]

The night of 23–24 July the Chinese launched reinforced company-sized attacks on outposts Westview and Dale in the 7th Division's 31st Infantry sector. The attacks, which resulted in fierce fighting, were surprising and costly to both sides. On outpost Dale the 3d Battalion of the 31st's Item Company lost two killed in action and eight wounded, while King Company lost two killed and ten wounded. Defenders counted twenty enemy dead between Dale and Westview, and estimated another twenty-five killed in front of the outpost, with fifty more wounded.

The 3d Battalion's King and Love Companies suffered grievously on Westview that night, beginning barely seventy-four hours prior to the negotiated cease-fire. The 2d Platoon of King Company lost nineteen men killed and twenty-five wounded, 3d Platoon eleven wounded, and 2d Platoon of Love Company suffered two killed and twelve wounded. The outpost's defenders had been caught by surprise, still deploying their outguards when the enemy attacked. Westview defenders counted thirty-five enemy dead, estimated another seventy-five killed and one hundred wounded. The 3d Battalion's M Company, the heavy weapons company, lost four killed, four wounded, and two missing.

In addition to the losses in the rifle companies, the 31st suffered two killed and fourteen more wounded in other units in the month of July. Seven wounded occurred during the Dale and Westview fights, two each in the headquarters and tank companies, and three in the medical company. Seven wounded and two killed were in the 2d Battalion's rifle companies. Thus, to the terrible losses taken by the 17th and 32d Regiments during the battle for Pork Chop, the 31st Infantry added thirty killed in action, seventy-four wounded, and two missing.[42]

On 26 July, General Clark called General Taylor again. This time he asked the Eighth Army commander to inform President Rhee the armistice would be signed at 10:00 A.M. the next day, 27 July, and Clark would be arriving in Seoul late the afternoon of the twenty-sixth.[43]

The end was near.

13

AFTERMATH

IN INDIANA, IOWA, NEW JERSEY, AND VIRGINIA, WHILE THE FINAL BATTLE for Pork Chop raged, the wives and families of Lt. Dick Shea and Lt. Dick Inman, Able and Baker Companies of the 17th, anxiously watched and listened to news broadcasts and read of the Chinese Army's powerful offensive in the west-central sector of the Korean front. Before news stories appeared on television and in the newspapers, confirming the Chinese attack, Barbara Inman had a deeply disturbing dream. She saw Dick in a train station buying a ticket home. When he got on the train, he discovered it was not going home. She waked screaming and crying, which brought her mother rushing to console her.[1]

The comforting flow of letters from both men ceased. Early in the third week of July, the parents of both were informed by the Department of the Army that their sons were missing in action. Dick Shea's parents immediately phoned Joyce's home in New Milford, New Jersey. Her dad answered and heard the news brought in the brief, sad telegram the Sheas received. He then turned to Joyce to deliver what none of them had ever wished to hear.

Dick Inman's parents assumed Barbara had been notified and expected a phone call. Like Joyce Shea, she had not been told. On the second day, after the Inmans had heard nothing from Barbara, Becky Inman, Dick's mother, phoned her. The rest of the Inman family, hopeful, yet deeply worried, left the house and walked into their backyard, not wanting to hear the conversation. They heard Becky's anguished reaction when she learned Barbara had not been notified of Dick's missing in action status.[2]

Barbara was at home with her parents for the summer months, in Fort Madison, Iowa.[3] Her haunting dream had become a real-life nightmare. Now began the heartrending ordeal of two families, and two soldiers' wives, waiting, wondering, hoping, not knowing, praying their sons and husbands would return from the chaos and confusion of a war the entire nation hoped was nearing an end.

The Sounds of Silence

In April, General Trudeau had written in his first 7th Division Command Report: "With respect to abandonment of major outposts, a consideration is its probable psychological effect upon the enemy's estimate of the situation. I believe he would interpret such a withdrawal as a confession of weakness and an invitation to assault essential MLR positions."

His remarks concentrated on the enemy's reaction to abandonment of major outposts such as Old Baldy and Pork Chop, and did not mention the reaction among men of the 7th Division. The American soldiers' reactions ranged from collective sighs of relief to anger and bitter frustration. Though Trudeau's words were never seen by Lt. Robert M. Euwer in the 15th AAA Battalion, Bob Euwer, like others who had been on the line, reacted angrily to the withdrawal in his 15 July letter home to his wife, Barbara. Three days earlier, the CCF had launched its furious assault on ROK divisions on the central front:

> Today—today it is raining, mud growing thicker—situation getting worse. We've already lost Pork Chop—the papers, radio say we withdrew— yeah, we withdrew with a bayonet in our back—tell me when its tactical to withdraw when you've thrown three regiments in the battle (3000 men per reg—total 9000 men). The 17th Regiment—known as the Buffalo

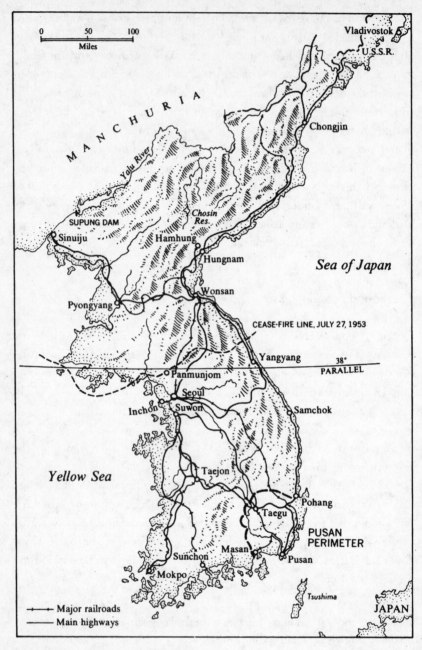

The final front line, 27 July 1953.
From E. B. Potter, ed., Sea Power: A Naval History *(Annapolis, Md.: Naval Institute Press, 1981), 364.*

Regiment—never been beaten before—beaten so bad they say they put the remainders in a 2½ ton truck and went back to the rear to recuperate and reorganize.

Things got so bad they had to bring two full regiments in for reinforcement from the 25th and 2d Divisions in reserve. They tried on Old Baldy also—real bloody—very unsuccessful—now we'll just try to hold what we got. To our right 70,000 Chinese are attacking—the largest force of Chinese committed in the war. Just think, old Joe has that bunker that was blown on top of me on Pork Chop now. Things sure change quickly.[4]

Less than two weeks later, on 27 July 1953, all along the front of the tortured, divided peninsula in northeast Asia, the guns of Korea fell silent. At 10:00 A.M., in a grim, cold final meeting of the two truce negotiating teams, the armistice was signed, to take effect twelve hours later. The signing took seven minutes.

The killing mercifully ceased, blessed relief for the infantrymen who, in the war's last months, suffered the brunt of its frustrating daily grind, and survived. The "half-war," the "yo-yo war," the brutal trench war, was over. For the American citizenry's half who were not personally touched by the Korean War, life went on as before.

In the 7th Infantry Division sector, reactions to the truce varied widely: disbelief, uncertainty, caution, elation, a sense of freedom, and the inexpressible feeling a heavy, grinding pall had been lifted from the shoulders of every soldier in the division, particularly the men on the line. Many wounded who had survived the ordeal of Pork Chop Hill were in hospitals, in Korea, Japan, and the United States. Many with minor wounds, and those who escaped the bullets, explosives, and shrapnel of those five hellish days, had returned to duty, some back on the line. Their feelings and reactions to the truce reflected their release from the deadly vise-grip of war.

Cpl. Doug Halbert from the Clearing Company of the 7th Medical Battalion was well to the rear of the MLR at 10:00 P.M. He had heard the distant, ceaseless pounding of artillery from both sides in the two-hour period before the cease-fire. Then it became quiet. He stood gazing north where the fighting had been. The quiet was surreal. Shortly after the cease-fire he saw flares being dropped all along the MLR, by low flying aircraft, just south and parallel to the truce line.[5]

Henry Baker, Charlie Company of the 17th, was on outpost duty on Yoke the night the armistice took effect. As wristwatches told men the agreed time of 10:00 P.M. had arrived, Henry suddenly heard whistles, horns, and shouts coming from the direction of the Chinese positions. They were similar to the sounds he had heard all too frequently in the months before—the sounds of an onrushing enemy assault wave. He and the other men manning Yoke's forward bunkers tensed, and cocked their weapons, ready to fire. The field phone rang in his bunker. "Hold your fire," said the caller's voice.

The next morning, Charlie Company soldiers cautiously came out of their bunkers into the morning sunlight, leaving their rifles resting in the firing apertures, pointed toward the enemy across the valley in front of outpost Yoke. To this day, Henry Baker expresses the deep emotions engendered by his experiences on the company-sized outpost in front of Hill 200, three weeks prior to the truce: "I've never left Pork Chop Hill."[6]

Fox of the 17's Art Lowe, on Hill 347 when the truce took effect, was struck by the eerie silence which followed. The next morning he stood on the forward side of the large hill's crest and gazed across the valley—still not accustomed to the absence of gunfire and great danger.[7]

On 347 the same evening, gazing at the occasionally flare lit night was Sgt. Bob Schaefer, operations sergeant in the S-3 section, 2d Battalion of the 17th. The three to four days prior to the truce, he had been working nearly nonstop, with little sleep. The pace was always brisk and wearing in the S-3 section, which twenty-four hours daily was immersed in planning and controlling the battalion's day-to-day combat operations and training, including all their rifle companies' patrols sent out in front of the MLR and OPLR. Patrols never let up, right on through the time the truce took effect. Fatigue kept Schaefer from absorbing the full impact of the moment.[8]

Lt. Ken Swift, the assistant operations officer in the 2d Battalion of the 17th, aware the cease-fire hour was coming, decided to return to George Company to be among the men in the platoon he had led during the fierce April battle for Pork Chop. A few mortar rounds were still falling along the front as the hour approached. Then all quiet. The next morning, he left the safety of the trenches and bunkers and walked about, gazing across "no man's land" at Chinese soldiers on the ridge lines facing them. To Ken, it appeared the Chinese were reacting in the same manner, walking around, gazing at their adversaries.[9]

The morning of 27 July, Lt. Ron Freedman, 48th Field Artillery, had been told to relieve another forward observer, Willy Dixon, on Hill 200, where the 32d Regiment was now manning the MLR, its men warily scanning the south slopes of Pork Chop Hill. Ron was packing his "war bag" preparing to leave for duty on Hill 200 when the battery executive officer walked in and told him the war would be over at 10:00 that night. When the hour arrived, Ron and a group of observers drove a jeep to the crest of 200 "to see and hear the quiet." Searchlights had been turned off, adding darkness to the pervading quiet. Ron and others lit cigarettes, talked quietly, and gazed into the darkness, which an occasional flare briefly lifted.[10]

Lt. Bob Euwer was scheduled for liaison officer duty in the 15th AAA Battalion headquarters the night of 27 July. When word arrived the truce would be signed that morning, his duty was canceled. There would be no more coordinated fire missions. Instead, at 7:30 P.M. he went to an outdoor movie titled *Apache War Smoke*. Artillery continued in the distance, while the film played. At 9:45 P.M. artillery fire began tapering off. The last artillery round fired in the 7th Division was saved for General Trudeau, who pulled the weapon's lanyard and retrieved the shell casing to take home as a souvenir.

The next morning Bob went to high ground on the MLR, where he could have a direct view of Hasakkol, the ridge due north of Pork Chop. There were numerous Chinese moving about the ridge. On top of Old Baldy the Chinese unfurled a large red flag. Music blared from their loudspeakers, as one Chinese soldier beat a drum. A group danced around the flag, a woman among them. On another hill the Chinese raised enormous banners with English words spelling out big red letters on a white background, "May You Go Home Early" and "Long Live Peace."

Chinese were yelling from Old Baldy to GIs on Westview, a startlingly short distance away—and they were yelling back. GIs from outpost Dale went down in the valley and talked with some of their enemies of yesterday, who gave them whiskey to drink. GIs were bathing in the creeks, and an American officer from Dale brought a Chinese officer up to the outpost.

Bob and other men could see numerous caves and tunnels they had never before seen, and standing and moving about on Pork Chop's crest were unusually large Chinese soldiers, perhaps as tall as six feet, five inches. Mongolians, Bob and his friends concluded. During the battle for the Chop, Americans had seen soldiers they believed were Mongolians.[11]

On 28 July 1953, the morning after the truce, a still-cautious soldier keeps his helmet on while he stares across the valley from Hill 200 to a completely shattered Pork Chop Hill and Chinese soldiers beginning to emerge on its crest. *Courtesy of Time-Pix*

Medic Jim Leal, attached to King Company, 17th Regiment, was in the eastern sector of the line, on outpost Ice Cream Cone. He was with three squads from one platoon, with their fourth squad back on the MLR. Jim did not sleep all night. Early in the evening, the Chinese were periodically firing direct-fire weapons past the outpost, hitting the MLR. One round did hit the outpost, a direct hit on a bunker housing one of Jim's friends. He instinctively jumped to his feet and ran to see if there were casualties. When he returned, the platoon leader, a lieutenant, was waiting. "Did you go check it out?" he asked. "Yes, Sir, I already did. Everyone's OK." The silence was eerie after 10:00 P.M., only the sound of flares popping occasionally.

Most men did not trust the Chinese to keep their word, and the platoon leader was no exception. All line companies had been instructed to man their listening posts and send out patrols that night. Prior to the cease-fire, the lieutenant asked for a patrol to go out approximately 150 yards and "just lay down and wait." A sergeant known for his zealous aggressiveness took two men out with him. A soldier and friend Jim knew volunteered to go along. Jim, knowing the sergeant's reputation, asked his friend, "Why in hell are you going with him?" His answer did not make sense to Jim, and sure enough they went well beyond 150 yards. Quiet prevailed the rest of the night, and all three returned safely.[12]

Lt. David Bills, 13th Engineers, was in Seoul 27 July, still working as special effects technical director on the movie *Cease Fire*. The schedule for filming had been moving right along since David returned from his mining and booby-trap mission to Pork Chop late the afternoon of 11 July. Ironically, on 27 July, the film crew completed the last ground-combat scene—a fitting day to call an end to *Cease Fire* battle sequences.[13]

A medic attached to Baker Company, 17th Regiment, William J. "Buster" Duncan, who had survived those first two harrowing nights on Pork Chop Hill, and had mixed feelings, including anger, about the 7th Division's pulling off the hill on 11 July, was back on outpost Arsenal when the truce went into effect. He wondered why all those men had to die on Pork Chop. The morning after the cease-fire, he scanned Chinese-held T-Bone and saw a huge banner raised by their soldiers. The words on the banner did not register in his memory. The war was over.[14]

Sgt. James N. Butcher, Fox of the 17th's field first sergeant, had fought in the April battle, but his company commander in July told him to stay in the rear when Fox went forward on APCs for their 9 July counterattack on the Chop. He vividly recalls the night and morning after the truce:

That night, battalion headquarters issued orders that all line companies were to deploy listening posts in front of our positions and to run reconnaissance patrols into "no man's land" as usual. However, we were ordered not to carry loaded weapons to prevent accidental fire fights that would violate the agreed cease fire.

At company level, however, these instructions got slightly modified, and troops were directed to carry a magazine in their weapons, but no rounds in the chambers of their weapons. We did not trust the situation enough to send unarmed patrols into the valley. Instructions specified that we could fire only if we were directly fired upon by the enemy. There was to be no firing of weapons after 10:00 P.M., accidental or otherwise. . . .

The cease fire began in earnest at 10:00 P.M. There was no more firing from either side. I believe that we, Americans and Chinese alike, all had our fill of war.

All along the line that night there was total silence. The night sky was bathed in natural summer moonlight. This was the most incredible silence experienced in all my life. Not an exploding round was heard— only the light wind rustling through the barbed wire entanglements and old tin cans in front of our positions. We marveled at the deadening silence as we walked nonchalantly around our positions, now unconcerned as to whether "Ole Joe" was going to test our resolve in some way during the night.

Absolutely nothing happened.

The night eased by. We were ordered to pull our watch as always, but we didn't mind being awake that night. No one felt like sleeping. The excitement of the dead silence was too much. The evening passed without incident. The war was really over. . . .

When dawn broke on the morning of July 28, 1953, I awoke feeling numb from sleeping on the hard, makeshift commo-wire bunk in the command post.

The grimy faces in the trench showed we were still awed by the silence of the guns—Korea really had become the land of the morning calm. This day was indeed different: There were no shells, no machine gun fire, no cries for "medic."

Upon leaving the bunker I climbed up on the ridge line and scanned the Chinese-held hill in the distance with my binoculars. I was expecting to see the usual barren hills devoid of vegetation and absent of human life. I was astounded by the sight across the valley floor. Instead of bleak, naked hills, there were thousands of Chinese soldiers stretching from their forward caves and trenches all the way back to their rear echelon areas.

The Chinese soldiers were standing a few feet apart, passing supplies and equipment backward in an endless assembly line, like robots. We watched for a long time, marveling over the immense number of enemy soldiers that were now visible. Had we known the extent of their forces, had we known the locations from which these men moved out their guns, we would not have been so complacent.

The truce agreement called for withdrawal by both sides sufficient to open up a three-mile-wide DMZ within seventy-two hours. Every division on the line was pulling back toward prepared positions, from which an active defense could be conducted should the enemy change his mind and resume fighting.

James Butcher continued his recollections of the withdrawal from battlegrounds where so many had bled and died for nearly twenty months:

> Our own movements toward the rear were less spectacular. We awkwardly made our way down the hill, burdened with weapons, ammunition and personal items. At the bottom were our waiting trucks.
>
> We left land mines and booby traps in front of the coiled barbed wire, spent cartridges, worn-out clothing, old blankets, empty ammunition tins, a leaky five gallon water can, miles of wire bunks and a calendar with the date July 28, 1953 circled. Along with the intentionally discarded items of war were some things left by accident, such as one soldier's picture of his girlfriend. Everything that was not taken was doomed to remain as it was left, for decades.
>
> Some guys wrote notes that they left tied to bunker posts for posterity. Some of the notes were simple statements that "So-and-so slept here!" Others—whether bluntly aggressive or more philosophical—expressed what the writer thought about the enemy, and almost always were punctuated with four-letter words.[15]

Lt. Raymond Clark, the H Company machine-gun platoon leader who was evacuated from Pork Chop on an open-topped M-39 APC on 10 July, wrote of his last glimpse of the hills on which so many fell:

Infantrymen of the 7th Division prepare to abandon MLR positions and move south while the Chinese pull back toward the north, 28 July 1953.
Courtesy of National Archives and Robert M. Euwer.

All fortifications in the [DMZ] were removed or destroyed. No combat troops were allowed in the Zone, only unarmed workers clearing the area. Company H was tapped to conduct the first patrol of the new line across the division front. We received clean fatigues and blue scarves, washed our jeeps, oiled our helmet liners, and went on patrol with unloaded weapons.

A week after the armistice . . . section leader Staff Sergeant Honn, an unnamed KATUSA, and I drove a jeep into the restricted area to see it one last time. We went to the rear of Hill 347 where the H Company CP had been, hid the jeep, and hiked to the top of the hill. All the bunkers and barbed wire of the large fortified complex were gone, sand bags opened and dumped. Already, the trenches were filling with dirt from heavy rains. On the forward slope of Hill 347 we stood and looked out over the valley. Old Baldy, Chink Baldy and Pork Chop Hill looked peaceful on that clear, sunny summer day. We met no one else on Hill 347 but could see enemy work parties in front of Pork Chop. On Old Baldy there was a long white cloth or wood sign printed in Chinese characters which [the South Korean] translated as, "Liberated by the Chinese People's Army." I took a few photos before we departed from the hill. A couple of weeks later I left the 7th Division and have never revisited that area.[16]

From two separate locations well north of the DMZ, two American soldiers would soon be taken south to Panmunjom by the Chinese, and released during Operation Big Switch, the final exchange of POWs. Pvts. Harvey Jordan and George Sakasegawa, both from Able Company of the 17th Regiment, had been held in two different locations since their capture on Pork Chop Hill the morning of 7 July.

For a time in their odyssey following their capture, the two men had been together, along with Cpl. William Helliean, a black medic from Baker Company, but were eventually separated. Both were surprised by the treatment they received at the hands of the Chinese. They expected far worse.

George Sakasegawa, the American of Japanese ancestry, who, as a boy, was interned with his parents and hundreds of other Nisei in a camp in Poston, Arizona, during World War II, might have expected not too kind treatment by the Chinese. The Chinese might reasonably harbor bitter memories of the brutal Japanese assault and occupation of China beginning in the 1930s, well before and extending through World War II. Apparently, such was not the case. Instead, Sakasegawa witnessed harsh treatment of an American of Korean ancestry, last name Park, from Hawaii. The Chinese accused Park of being a traitor, and with the intent of producing a confession, pushed bamboo shoots underneath his fingernails as part of the physical torture given the soldier.

As for the wounds George Sakasegawa received, the Chinese treated and bandaged them but never changed the bandages. Maggots got into the wounds.

Perhaps the worst experience Sakasegawa had was the strafing of their camp by an American F-80 jet fighter-bomber. Before the day of the incident, one of the prisoners evaded guards, crawled on top of one of the buildings in the compound, and painted an American flag on the roof. The pilot obviously did not realize he was attacking a POW camp holding Americans. Sadly, the POW who painted the flag on the building at considerable risk to himself was grievously wounded in the knee by a .50-caliber bullet fired from the aircraft's machine guns.

The Chinese permitted both George Sakasegawa and Harvey Jordan to keep their personal belongings, except for fingernail clippers. For example, Sakasegawa was allowed to keep his Omega watch, and the Chinese held his script—money—in safe keeping until they tried to return it to him when he was to be repatriated. The soon-to-be-repatriated POWs did not want the script. They considered it worthless.

The Chinese let Harvey Jordan keep his money, the small New Testament his grandmother had given him before he left for Korea, and the picture of his wife, Jean. The latter two keepsakes were crucial in lifting Harvey's spirits during his month and a half of captivity with permanently disabling wounds. He was taken to see a movie by a guard, though it was a propaganda film about the glories of the harvest, Chinese Communist style.

Twice during captivity the Chinese operated on Harvey Jordan's right arm, after fluoroscope examinations by a man he presumed was a doctor. Ether was the anesthesia used two days in succession. The operations and subsequent treatment, including treatment in U.S. Army and veterans' hospitals when Jordan was repatriated, did not correct the damage to his right arm, a wound that has hampered him his entire life. Upon observing the Chinese medics at work on his arm, he decided he would not divulge to them shrapnel had damaged his right eye. He did not want the Chinese to attempt surgery on his eye.

An older Chinese man, whom Jordan gauged to be in his fifties, befriended him while he was held in the prison camp. He showed the American soldier photos of his family, and Jordan showed him the picture of his wife Jean. The two would-be enemies smoked cigarettes, and though neither understood the other's language, they communicated through their own versions of sign language.

It was from the older Chinese captor that Harvey learned the war was over. The language used was simple. The elder man pointed the forefinger of one hand as though it was a gun, while making a noise simulating the firing of a gun. He then put both arms in front of his body, his hands and fingers extended, palms down, and moved them back and forth, side to side, while shaking his head no.

On 23 August, Harvey Jordan and George Sakasegawa passed through "Freedom Village." The war was over for the two men from Able of the 17th. They were on their way home. William Helliean, the black medic in Baker Company, came home as well.[17]

But the war wasn't over for all Americans. Not for the Inmans and Sheas, not for Joyce and Barbara, and the wives and families of 5,178 missing in action. Not for the families, friends, and loved ones of the 54,246 dead—33,624 of them killed in action—or the 103,248 wounded. For the families of the dead, missing, maimed, and deeply scarred, the war's torment had just begun. And for survivors of Pork Chop's final battle, and their families, substantially different casualty figures emerged.

Time and reality dramatically altered the initial July 1953 reports of Pork Chop's killed, wounded, and missing in action. As the years passed, it became clear the preponderance of the missing did not survive the fury of the battle for Pork Chop. Only 9 of the 172 reported missing in action in the 17th and 32d Infantry Regiments were captured by the enemy and returned during Operation Big Switch. The remainder initially declared missing were later declared killed in action, or simply declared dead— their whereabouts never determined and their remains never found.

Notable examples of those declared killed in action, their remains never recovered, are Lt. Richard G. Inman, platoon leader, 2d Platoon, Baker of the 17th; and Cpl. Dan D. Schoonover, squad leader, 1st Platoon, Able Company, 13th Engineer Battalion. Though there were witnesses to the death of M.Sgt. Howard C. Hovey, field first sergeant in Able Company, 1st Battalion of the 17th Infantry Regiment, his remains were also never recovered.

The 1,099 killed, wounded, and missing Americans first reported as casualties in the last battle for Pork Chop Hill now total 1,159. Instead of the 72 killed in action initially reported, 243 were killed in action or died of wounds, or as POWs, without their remains ever having been recovered. There were 916 wounded, a number of whom were severely wounded and later died of their wounds. The totals exclude KATUSA casualties suffered those five days.[18] Their numbers added significantly to the totals.

Missing in Action

As soon as Joyce Shea collected herself following the phone call from Dick's father early the third week in July, she called the office of the Army's adjutant general, from which the telegram had come to Dick's home in Portsmouth. She hoped to learn more. Perhaps additional information had come in saying Dick had been found alive. There was none. There were similar reactions by Dick Inman's mother and father in Vincennes, Indiana, and his wife Barbara in Fort Madison, Iowa.

Then, Joyce Shea and Barbara Inman received virtually identical letters within two to three days after the telephone calls. Only the names and dates were different:

> 17 JULY 1953
>
> Dear Mrs. Shea:
>
> I regret that I must inform you that your husband, Second Lieutenant Richard T. Shea, Jr., has been reported missing in action in Korea since 8 July 1953. The report states his position was attacked by opposing forces at the time he became missing in action. Telegraphic notification was made to Mr. and Mrs. Richard T. Shea, Sr., parents, designated by your husband as the persons to be notified in case of emergency.
>
> I know that added distress is caused by failure to receive more information or details. Therefore, I wish to assure you that at any time additional information is received it will be transmitted to you without delay.
>
> The term "missing in action" is used only to indicate that the whereabouts or status of an individual is not immediately known. It is not intended to convey the impression that the case is closed. I wish to emphasize that every effort is exerted continuously to clear up status of our personnel, although under battle conditions this is a difficult task as you must readily realize. Experience has shown that a number of persons reported missing in action are subsequently reported as returned to duty or being hospitalized for injuries. . . .

Permit me to extend to you my heartfelt sympathy during this period of uncertainty.

Sincerely yours,

W. M. E. BERGIN

Major General, USA

The Adjutant General of the Army

However Joyce and Barbara felt about the telegrams and letters, both remained hopeful, even optimistic their husbands would be found alive and return home safely. But not knowing was excruciating. Each in her own way began determined efforts to learn more. Joyce wrote the 17th Regiment chaplain Dick had mentioned in his letters home. She wrote Lou Davis, Dick's West Point classmate, close friend and track teammate; other friends and West Point classmates, anyone who might remotely have knowledge of his whereabouts and the circumstances surrounding his status as missing in action.

She daily listened to the news and read the names of American prisoners being released by the North Koreans and Chinese. The prospect of learning the worst didn't restrain her. She, like Barbara, was certain her Richard would be back. He, too, had so much promise, so many reasons to live. Their lives together couldn't possibly be so short, and end this way. And there was the child she carried. Dick Shea must see their first born, expected in late August.

IN THE absence of any additional information about Dick Inman, his parents, George and Becky Inman, and his wife Barbara pursued answers through other avenues. Telephone calls and letters from friends of his parents went to Congressman William "Bill" G. Bray of Indiana's 7th District, which included Vincennes. On 15 August, Mr. Admiral R. Weathers wrote Congressman Bray, asking for help. Weathers had learned the congressman was leaving on a trip to Korea in September:

The Inmans are close friends of ours, and their son has been a very close friend of our son for years. . . .

It would certainly be appreciated if you could learn any information regarding the circumstances, and if there is a possibility he was captured.

I thought perhaps you could go through channels before your

departure for Korea next month, and if nothing comes through, to follow up when you are over there.

Barbara formulated her own way of finding out what might have happened to Dick. Instead of continuing to teach school, she joined the Red Cross during the summer, entered training at Fort Hood, Texas, and asked to be sent to Korea. There she intended to conduct her own search for answers, and the whereabouts of the young husband she loved so deeply, and who now seemed to have vanished from the face of the earth. She clung desperately to hope.

JOYCE SHEA was five months pregnant when Dick left for Korea in late April. On 26 August 1953, she gave birth to Richard Thomas Shea III. Her joy was tinged with sadness. A week after she returned home from the hospital, a letter arrived from Korea. It was from Dick's battalion commander, Lt. Col. Rocky Read. She opened it, anxious for good news she was certain must come. The handwriting was broad-stroked, heavy, flowing, and filled with emotion.

KOREA
AUGUST 31, 1953

Dear Mrs. Shea,

I hope that I am not reopening old wounds but I would like to write to you about Dick. I was his Battalion Commander on Pork Chop and can give you some factual information which you may not have.

In the early attacks by the Chinese he led to my personal knowledge five counterattacks. In one of these he received a slight wound on the cheek. He gave me much valuable information all during the action. On the 8th of July I personally stopped him from exposing himself in a trench near my CP. At this time I received orders that the remainder of my battalion would be relieved and replaced by a new unit. There were about 25 A Company men in the right sector. Dick's job was to keep these men together and to leave the hill with them. I personally covered his run to this action with rifle fire—he made it safely. Shortly thereafter the new unit attacked—my people were being withdrawn. One of the platoons of the new unit suffered casualties among its officers and non commissioned officers. Dick saw their confusion and carefully turned the remaining men of "A" Company over to another man, reorganized the troops from the other unit and personally led them in an attack in which he was killed. The battle continued and the ground was taken and retaken many times. Dick's action was beyond the call of duty in many respects. First, he took command of other troops than his own, he could have evacuated himself, or he could have simply held the disorganized men under cover. As you know any action other than the action he took would not have been characteristic of him. His action saved lives because the people he took were lost without his leadership.

He was clearly the most outstanding officer of his grade I have served with. He was recommended for the Medal of Honor because we his comrades know he earned it and we loved him.

He used to kid me about being too old to keep up with him—my father was track coach at VMI for 30 years and I ran (poorly). I am from Lexington, Virginia and he did say that Virginians should stick together and not let the *wall* Korea builds separate them. At 33, not 23, it was a job keeping up with him. I have two sons and I hope that someday they will show the same sense of honor and duty that your husband displayed.

He was much more to me than a young rifle platoon leader. His life will be a constant inspiration to me and I shall be a better man for having known him.

My heart is too full to say more and I'm sorry I can't express what I feel.

May God bless you.

BM Read
Lt Colonel
Infantry
17th Inf Regiment

Lieutenant Colonel Read's letter was shattering, devastating. Joyce wept, heartbroken and sick with grief. After she regained her composure, she again called the Adjutant General's office in Washington, and told them she had received a letter saying Dick had been killed. They told her he was still missing in action. There had been no confirmation he had been killed. After her call there was no follow-up letter from the adjutant general's office.

She wrote Lieutenant Colonel Read while Barbara and the Inman family continued their search for answers. The days and months would slip by without a letter from Dick Shea's battalion commander. Two men were still missing in action. Sadness, grief, hope, questions with no answers, and interminable waiting settled in the homes of two families and two wives, as in thousands more. Throughout the early fall of 1953, Barbara Inman and Joyce Shea suffered through the agony of not knowing the fates of their husbands.

Meanwhile Dick Inman's parents tried to find answers through other sources. Aside from A. R. Weathers's 15 August letter to Congressman Bray, Howard Greenlee, publisher of the *Vincennes Sun Commercial*, contacted Bray as well, anticipating the Congressman's visit to Korea. Greenlee asked him to seek answers to Dick Inman's status. Might he still be alive?

On Tuesday, 6 October, Congressman Bray responded to the *Sun Commercial* publisher. The letter, which Bray mailed that afternoon, brought devastating news, ending dreams for the future, for Barbara and Dick, and for the Inman family:

HONG KONG, B.C.C.
OCTOBER 6, 1953

Dear Howard:

I am writing this letter in Hong Kong but will mail it this afternoon in Manila. While in Korea I went to the Headquarters of the 7th Division and talked to one officer and three of the men who were with Lt. Inman. I am also including statements made by these men. My conversations included more than is included in these statements, and in my opinion there is no doubt but that Inman was killed. The Commanding General is already making attempts to recover the body. Lt. Inman was most courageous as was plain from my conversations with those who were with him. As soon as I get any additional information I will notify you. . . .

Will be seeing you in November.

Sincerely,

William G. Bray

Enclosures:

Four sworn statements

One diagram

Now began the unwelcome finality of grievous loss, and a void never filled.

The officer Congressman Bray talked with on his trip to Korea was Lt. David R. Willcox, 2d Platoon, A Company, 17th Infantry Regiment. The three soldiers were Pfc. Irwin Greenberg, Cpl. Harm Tipton, and Pfc. Clarence Mouser, men who returned from Dick Inman's ambush patrol. Dick's actions led them to safety on Pork Chop Hill, and new leases on life that terrible night of 6–7 July 1953. Each had written sworn statements and signed them 27 September. On 15 October the telegram from the Army's Adjutant General arrived at the Inman home in Vincennes, confirming Dick Inman was killed in action.

For the Inmans, Sheas, Riemanns, and Kipps, like thousands more who had lost loved ones in the war, that Christmas couldn't possibly be the same as in years past. Christmas at the Riemann family home in New Milford, New Jersey, bore an air of melancholy, as did the holidays for the Shea family in Portsmouth, Virginia, the Inmans in Vincennes, Indiana, and the Kipps in Fort Madison, Iowa.

In Indiana and Iowa many questions lingered, though uncertainty vanished about whether Dick Inman was alive. The vague outlines of how and why he died were in the statements included in the letter Congressman Bray wrote in Hong Kong. However, uncertainty remained as to whether Dick Inman's body would ever be recovered and returned home for burial.

In New Jersey and Virginia there were tenuous shreds of hope while waiting continued for further communications from the adjutant general about Dick Shea. But no letters arrived for Joyce, not by the first of the year. Then, in January she received a visitor from Able Company of the 17th Regiment.

David Willcox came to see her at her parents' home in New Milford. Richard Thomas Shea III was not yet five months old. Joyce still hoped Dick would come home despite the shattering news Lieutenant Colonel Read's August letter brought her.

David had a sad duty to perform. He couldn't provide Joyce new hope, only one more piece of information toward the finality Barbara Inman and Dick Inman's mother and father endured in October. The good things that happened to A Company's 2d Platoon, and the man David Willcox knew Dick Shea to be, fueled in David a powerful obligation and courage to perform the duty of bringing more sad news to Joyce.

He was on the hill with Dick Shea. The two had had frequent contact with one another before the battle. Though not close, fast friends, they had worked together, trained together, planned together, shared the same dangers, fought the same fights when A Company was on the line, and had developed a growing respect for each other.

All the men in Willcox's platoon had survived those first three days of fighting though all but a few were wounded. Dick Shea hadn't. He wasn't among the 2d Platoon men who came off the hill when Charlie Company relieved them on 9 July, nor was he among the George Company soldiers who were relieved on 10 July, or men like Dale Cain, who came off the hill on 11 July, when the last of the Americans and ROK soldiers were evacuated from Pork Chop.

David Willcox did not see Dick Shea fall, was not near and could not see his last personal battle. None who came off the hill, and were close to him in the final moments, survived to tell what they had seen. Yet until the Army verified Dick's death, David could not tell Joyce Shea with absolute certainty Dick had not survived, though in David's mind he was convinced. He could tell her, however, that a work party which had braved a heavily mined Pork Chop Hill, in the DMZ, had found a shallow grave on 12 November. The grave contained the remains of several men. Facts and circumstances known about her husband's final moments suggested one of those found was Dick. She would be told if comparisons of remains with records verified the remains were his. There really wasn't any hope.[19]

The work party David Willcox described to Joyce was similar to the one Sgt. Danny L. Peters from Charlie Company participated in 28 October, four months after the last battle for Pork Chop. Dan fought on the hill during the counterattack that relieved Willcox's 2d Platoon. All twenty men chosen for the work party had fought in the battle for the Chop.

Early that October morning Peters and the other nineteen men were issued DMZ passes, transported unarmed to a checkpoint in the northern half of the DMZ, searched by Chinese soldiers, divided into two- and three-man teams accompanied by an armed Chinese soldier, and rode in trucks with the Chinese to Pork Chop. They recovered the remains of fourteen or fifteen American soldiers in the western sector, the left flank of the hill. Among those found was a soldier Dan Peters had known. The Chinese had found the partly buried bodies and invited the Americans to come retrieve them.[20]

Dan's difficult experience was far better than that of Bob Wilson from Easy Company of the 17th, shortly after the 27 July truce. His company commander's jeep driver, he was asked to go to Seoul, to graves registration, with one officer and three other men from Easy, to attempt identifying remains from among nearly one hundred bodies of American soldiers brought off the hill. Though he had been fortunate to remain at the checkpoint behind Hill 200 during the final battle for Pork Chop, and escaped additional wounds, his slow walk through the four graves registration tents was a sad reminder of the horrors of battle in the final months of the Korean War. Not one man could he identify. To this day he carries the painful memory of the duty he was given.[21]

After telling Joyce the shattering news, David Willcox talked with her, telling her about men's reactions in war, their personal responses to the dangers, chaos, and fears that swirl around them. Each man reacts differently, some with towering calm, courage, decisiveness, selflessness, and inspiration under the most extreme conditions. Others are overwhelmed with self-consuming, self-destructive fear, sometimes fleeing, throwing down their weapons, cowering, whimpering, attempting to hide from the grotesque, abject horror they find themselves in—and thus greatly increase the risks to fellow soldiers. Dick Shea was the former, a tower of strength and inspiration.[22]

Joyce was once more numbed by the news David Willcox brought, and remembered few of his words about men's reactions in the extremes of war. The news was simply too stunning. It seemed each time she talked with or received letters from men who had known Dick or had information about when last he was seen alive, Dick was killed again. But not in her heart, not in her dearest wish, or her dreams. The desperate hopes and stinging setbacks were almost too much to bear. Yet she clung to the notion he would be found alive in spite of David Willcox's difficult visit and Lieutenant Colonel Read's August letter, received days after Joyce and Dick's son was born.[23]

Condolences continued to come in to the Inmans and Barbara, through Christmas and on into January. An unusual and touching letter and package arrived in the Inman home in Vincennes at the end of February. The return address on the envelope was the director of athletics at the University of Pennsylvania:

FEBRUARY 23, 1954

Dear Mr. and Mrs. Inman:

Some time ago your good friend, Frank M. Dobson of Carlisle, Indiana, informed me of the tragic death of your son Richard in Korea, and he mentioned certain circumstances of Richard's death that involved the loss of the Penn Relays watch.

We are very proud of our Relay Carnival and very proud your fine son participated in it in 1952 while a cadet at the United States Military Academy.

If you will accept from me on behalf of the University of Pennsylvania a watch identical to that which was awarded your son in 1952, I would consider it a great compliment to the University of Pennsylvania. I send this in the hope that you will place it with other mementos of your son's outstanding military and athletic career.

My sincerest sympathies go out to both of you at your loss of such a fine son.

Sincerely yours,

Jeremiah Ford II

The final answer came to Joyce Shea just prior to Easter 1954, in another letter from the adjutant general's office:

21 APRIL 1954

Dear Mrs. Shea:

I am writing you concerning your husband, First Lieutenant Richard T. Shea, Jr., 0 66 428, Infantry, who was reported missing in action in Korea on 8 July 1953.

Information has now been received that your husband was killed in action in Korea on 8 July 1953. The records of this office are being amended accordingly.

The Office of the Quartermaster General, Washington 25, D.C., is responsible for furnishing information on recovery, identification and disposition of remains of our dead. It is customary for that Office to communicate promptly with the next of kin upon receipt of definite information from the overseas command. . . .

I know the sorrow this message brings to you and it is my hope that in time the knowledge of your husband's sacrifice for his country may be of sustaining comfort to you.

My heartfelt sympathy is with you in the great loss you have sustained.

Sincerely yours,

JOHN A. KLEIN

Major General, US

Acting the Adjutant General

A few days later a second letter came from Col. John D. Martz, Jr., in the Office of the Quartermaster General. He gave more detailed information about the recovery and identification of Dick's body, telling Joyce he was not yet certain when his remains would return to the United States. Martz would notify her by telegram and asked that she inform him where she wished her husband's remains interred.

Then came a second letter from Lieutenant Colonel Read. When he wrote Joyce this time, he had been reassigned as the executive officer of the 17th Infantry Regiment. Once more, in heavy, broad strokes of the pen, his words spoke of deep personal anguish and regret for all Joyce had been through since Dick had been declared missing in action.

KOREA

EASTER 1954

Dear Mrs. Shea,

In all my life I have never been more crushed and saddened by the turn of events which caused you so much pain. I hope and pray that Higher Headquarters has given you the information which you dreadfully needed. I have been given permission to write so I am sure that you have been notified.

I know that explanations are difficult if not impossible to understand but I shall give you all of the information I was able to uncover. The hardest thing was not being able to write.

Please don't think ill of the system because in many cases it averts a situation such as yours. First, after receipt of your letter I personally went to every higher headquarters in Korea and begged that information be expedited on Dick. When a casualty occurs, frequently Department of the Army will rightfully hold on the report to relatives until all available witnesses are questioned and sometimes these are in the hospital or unable to speak at that time. Then if witness statements conflict and are not considered conclusive additional checks are made. This is necessary because many times a man may see a friend hit and report him killed. Actually, the man may be in a state of shock and recover or become a prisoner. In some cases witnesses give an oral report to a unit leader and subsequently the witnesses are killed or badly wounded. Their hearsay evidence cannot always be considered conclusive. Both of the above things happened in Dick's case. One of the wounded witnesses is in this status now. Lt. David Willcox. He was not a witness to Dick's actual death but saw him after the action. As you probably know Dick was fighting in a particularly vicious sector where many men were hit, bunkers were collapsed and totally destroyed, and in some cases the whole trench and bunker pattern was wholly unrecognizable to people counter-attacking only a matter of hours later. We brought back all our dead and wounded who could be found even though we were under attack at the time our unit was replaced by another battalion. After waiting the prescribed 45 days as regulations prescribe the regimental Commander Col. Ben Harris and I were informed through personnel channels that Dick's status had been established as killed in action. Obviously, I already knew this from being out there but the letters Col. Harris and I wrote to you were later stopped at higher headquarters for more conclusive evidence. Dick was listed as missing.

I know how you must have felt. I was in despair. Neither I nor my regimental C.O. was notified of the change until your letter arrived which indicated that my [August] letter had been sent on to you but his had been stopped. No criticism implied. People in higher headquarters had thousands of reports pouring in from Eighth Army in the last Chinese pushes. In the vast majority of cases considerate and efficient handling of letters and reports was the rule. Dept. of the Army notified me through channels of your letter and I was told not to write again until the official notification came through. That is why I haven't written. God knows the sleepless and tortured nights have been long for me and I know they must have been dreadful for you. I am still afraid that this is a poor expression of my feelings. As a man who has been in the Pacific three times in ten years and in two wars I can only say that Dick was the finest leader I ever saw in action, and his actions will inspire many men who are left. . . .

I hope that in future years you will allow me to keep in touch with you and your youngster. This is not a stereotyped letter or offer—I am available for any help you may ever need of any type. My heart rides on this pen and I can only say I pray for a full and happy Easter to one whom I know has the same courage and character that her husband so gallantly displayed.

As ever,

BM Read

Lt. Colonel, Infantry

(ex)C.O. 1st Bn, 17th Inf.

Dick Shea was buried in Portsmouth, Virginia, the first week in June 1954, two years after his graduation from West Point, and their marriage. At Joyce's request, Bob Shea, Dick's brother, escorted his body home for burial when it arrived in the States. Joyce's mother and father, Dick's family, and many friends attended the funeral. She remembers, "Sometimes, when we do all the required moves at a time of sadness, because we have to, it's like walking through a maze. You cannot believe this is reality, but it is."

One month later, on 6 July 1954, in the auditorium of the First Christian Church in Vincennes, Indiana, Col. Frederick B. Mann, commanding officer of the Indiana Military District for the U.S. Army, posthumously awarded the Silver Star "for gallantry in action" to Richard George Inman, pinning the award on Barbara's blouse in a brief, moving ceremony. The date marked the first anniversary of the Chinese assault on Pork Chop Hill, and Dick's sacrifice for the men in his patrol. The Inman family, and some friends, were at the ceremony, as were Barbara's parents.

LT. RICHARD T. Shea, Jr., West Point class of 1952, posthumous winner of the Medal of Honor, rests in Olive Branch Cemetery, not far from his boyhood home near Portsmouth, Virginia, half a world away from Pork Chop Hill. On a sunny day in May 1955, at Fort Myer, Virginia, the Secretary of the Army presented the nation's highest decoration to Dick Shea's widow, Joyce Riemann Shea. Dick Shea had "distinguished himself by conspicuous gallantry and indomitable courage above and beyond the call of duty in action against the enemy near Sokkogae, Korea, from 6 to 8 July 1953."

In her arms she held their son, Richard T. Shea III, born a month and a half after Dick Shea was killed in action. Young Richard cried during the first part of the thirty-five-minute ceremony, until the band began to play, and the 3d Infantry Regiment, the Old Guard, passed in review. Joyce, accompanied by Dick Shea's mother and two brothers, S.Sgt. Robert Shea and William Shea, maintained her composure throughout the ceremony. She remarked she was proud to receive the award and knew someday their son would be equally proud of his father.

On a simple bronze plaque in West Point's Cullum Hall are found the names of Military Academy graduates who have won the Congressional Medal of Honor. Dick Shea is one of two graduates who received the award for their incomparable acts of courage and heroism during the Korean War.

On Saturday, 10 May 1958, at a brigade full-dress review on the Plain at West Point, the Army Athletic Association presented a plaque to the Corps of Cadets, renaming the academy's track stadium in memory of Dick Shea. Shea Stadium overlooks the track where he ran and won nearly every race he entered, and set records that stood for years.

At Virginia Tech, where Dick Shea was a seventeen-year-old enlisted man late in World War II, his name can be found engraved on the Cenotaph above the school's Chapel, among 6 other Virginia Tech recipients of the Medal of Honor—and among the names of 411 Virginia Tech dead on the pylons of its war memorial.

Dick Shea's widow, Joyce, eventually married Theodore Himka, an engineering manager in Boeing Aircraft Company. They are a close, loving family, which, until 2002, included three sons and their families. The entire family respectfully and devotedly protect the memory of a man that none ever knew, save Joyce. Their son, Richard Thomas Shea III, was proud of his father as Joyce had said he would be, but sadly, with no warning of trouble, he died of a heart attack on 22 January 2002, at the age of forty-eight.

In 1973, men from Dick Shea's West Point class of 1952 dedicated a memorial plaque in Dick Shea's name. The plaque is on a wall at Youngsan Army Garrison, in Seoul, Korea, not far from the headquarters of the ROK-US Combined Forces Command and the Republic of Korea Ministry of National Defense.

The 7th Infantry Division, which suffered grievous losses on Pork Chop Hill, has named its outstanding junior officer award in memory of Lt. Richard Thomas Shea, Jr.

The class of 1952 held its fiftieth reunion at West Point, during the academy's bicentennial celebration in 2002. Dick Shea's classmates elected, as their fiftieth reunion gift to West Point, to tear down and completely rebuild a larger, modernized Shea Stadium, using private donations. The stadium overlooks a refurbished, updated track and field where Dick Shea ran to glory half a century earlier.

At the north end of the stadium, affixed to the outer wall, are three plaques: the original Shea Stadium dedication plaque; the gift of a Medal of Honor plaque from the academy's class of 1939; and a 2002, Bicentennial dedication plaque containing a bronze relief of Dick Shea and the Medal of Honor medallion. On the field at the north end of the stadium is a Class of 1952 Memorial Plaza, which includes a flag staff at its center, to fly the national colors. The wall of the Memorial Plaza is inscribed with the names of twenty-nine men in the class who were killed in action in Korea and Vietnam, or who died in accidents during military operations. Among the names are Dick Inman and Dick Shea, who died on Pork Chop Hill during those fateful five days in July 1953.

Also inscribed on the wall is the academy's motto, "Duty Honor Country"; the cadet honor code, "A cadet will not lie, cheat or steal, nor tolerate those who do"; and Gen. Douglas MacArthur's words, spoken in 1922, when MacArthur was the academy superintendent, "Upon the fields of friendly strife are sown the seeds that, upon other fields, on other days, will bear the fruits of victory." Joyce Himka and Mary Jo Vermillion, Dick Inman's oldest sister, attended the class of 1952 reunion and the dedication ceremony for the new Shea Stadium.[24]

Nineteen-year-old Cpl. Dan Schoonover still sleeps where he fell. The young soldier from A Company, 13th Combat Engineer Battalion, posthumously received the Medal of Honor for his valor and sacrifice on Pork Chop Hill. Dan was the youngest of four boys, and all his brothers had entered the service when he went off to war. It was partly to be with his older brother, Pat, who had enlisted in the Army, that Dan enlisted and arrived in Korea in late 1952.

His mother, Mrs. George A. Hess, received a brief telegram from the Department of the Army on 17 July 1953, notifying her he had been killed in action on 10 July. He died having elected to stay on Pork Chop after the surviving men of the 17th's George Company were withdrawn a day earlier. In 1982, his remarried mother, Peggy Schroeder, reminisced about her son who never came home. "He was doing what he wanted to do," she said. She told of talking with one of Dan's comrades. "He said he asked

Capt. James A. Brettell (*left*) and Sen. Frank Church of Idaho participate in the 1957 dedication of Schoonover Barracks at Fort Belvoir, Virginia, in memory of Cpl. Dan D. Schoonover.

Danny to go down the hill with him [on 9 July]. Danny told him, 'Some of these other men are married and have families. I'll stay.'"

Dan's former company commander, Capt. Jim Brettell, was instrumental in naming a five-hundred-man barracks at Fort Belvoir, Virginia, the home of the Army's Corps of Engineers, for Dan Schoonover. On the Wall of the Missing on the island of Oahu, Hawaii, is inscribed Dan's name. On 24 September 1973, in the Field of Honor II in Boise, Idaho's Morris Hill/Pioneer Cemetery, Dan's family placed a bronze memorial plaque bearing his name.[25]

Lt. Richard G. Inman, the classmate, Army football player, and track teammate of Dick Shea who died on Pork Chop Hill late the night of 6 July 1953, less than two days prior to the loss of Dick Shea, like Dan Schoonover, still sleeps where he fell. Barbara, who had joined the Red Cross after Dick was declared missing, in hopes she could be sent to Korea to find him still living, later was transferred to Africa where she continued her work in the Red Cross. In Tangiers, Africa, she married three years after Dick Inman's death. She remained happily married to John Colby and was residing in Bridgewater, Massachusetts, when she died on 1 February 1999.

Dick Inman is survived by two sisters and a brother. Mary Jo Inman Vermillion lives with her daughter in Vincennes, Indiana, where Dick grew up. His brother, Robert, is retired and lives in Sun City Center, Florida. His youngest sister, Bonnie Ruth Wright, about whom Dick penned a loving poem, resides with her family in Keil, Wisconsin.

In February 1998, a year before Barbara Colby died, she and Mary Jo Vermillion received telephone calls from the Department of the Army, seeking information and DNA tests of Mary Jo, the first of a series of steps toward attempting to locate and recover the remains of a fallen soldier.

For Barbara Colby, the telephone calls from the Department of the Army stirred bittersweet memories of a love long past, and a young soldier who is yet to come home.

The entire Inman family, and their descendants, hold fast to their loving memories of Dick Inman, his zest for life, and his sacrifice.[26]

Hundreds of men who fought the last battle for Pork Chop Hill are living, many active in fraternal and professional military associations such as the 17th, 31st, 32d Infantry Regiment, the 13th Engineers, and 7th Infantry Division Associations. Recently, reunion activities have grown in number and attendance. During reunions the men renew their acquaintances and close wartime friendships, remember the battles and their harrowing experiences, recount the stories of courage and devotion they witnessed, and reaffirm their dedication to those who didn't return from the Korean War. Many, late in life, driven by poignant, aching memories, have begun active searches for long lost comrades, unsure if the men who became separated from them during those chaotic five days survived the war and the passage of years.

Similarly, thousands of searches are being initiated by surviving family members and descendants of those who didn't return from the war. The searches to learn of the lives and fates, the last few moments or hours of loved ones, are spurred in part by the same, poignant motivations of their loved ones' comrades in arms, and the explosive growth in America's telecommunications industry—the Internet.

Valor and Irony

When Lieutenant Bob Euwer wrote his wife on 15 July 1953, he began his letter with a comments about two soldiers in his AAA platoon:

> My Dearest Barbara,
>   Hi honey,
>   I just finished writing up a story for one of my crews—in order that they may be rightly decorated. They had a terrific round for round dual with a Chinese direct fire weapon. Two men were hurt but not critically. My men stuck to their gun even though they received two direct hits and continued to throw fire out until they had destroyed the enemy crew and weapon. It certainly was an act of courage that can not be overlooked.[27]

The men of Pork Chop Hill lived and died the words courage, bravery, heroism, sacrifice, and valor. Though the men who survived those five days are quick to say the purpose of their sacrifice was not for recognition or medals, the Medals of Honor bestowed posthumously on Richard Thomas Shea, Jr., and Dan Dwayne Schoonover led a list of hundreds of decorations for valor—Distinguished Service Crosses, Silver Stars, and Bronze Star Medals for Valor—given the men who fought to hold the outpost. Ten received the Distinguished Service Cross, the nation's second highest decoration for valor: 1st Lt. Thomas J. Barnes, K Company, 17th Infantry Regiment, posthumously; 2d Lt. Samuel E. Daniel, E Company, 17th Infantry; Maj. Billy E. Fritts, executive officer, 1st Battalion, 17th Infantry, posthumously; M.Sgt. Howard C. Hovey, A Company, 17th Infantry, posthumously; 1st Lt. William E. McDonald, 57th Field Artillery Battalion, posthumously; Maj. Joseph E. Noble, Jr., commander, 2d Battalion, 17th Infantry; Sgt. Robert Northcutt, G Company, 17th Infantry; Lt. Col. Beverly M. Read, commander, 1st Battalion, 17th Infantry; Lt. Col. Royal R. Taylor, commander, 3d Battalion, 32d Infantry; and 2d Lt. Steven H. Wood, F Company, 17th Infantry. Pvt. Robert E. Miller, Cpl. Charles Brooks, and Lt. David R. Willcox, all in A Company, 17th Infantry, received Silver Stars, as did Sgt. Anton Cicak, B Company.

Maj. Gen. Arthur G. Trudeau received a second Silver Star, based upon his personal assessment of the situation on Pork Chop Hill the afternoon of 7 July, an award which provoked comment, rumors, and controversy. Years later he encountered probing questions during his oral history interview at the Army's Military History Institute in Carlisle Barracks, Pennsylvania.

Col. Calvin J. Landau conducted the interview of then-retired Lt. Gen. Arthur G. Trudeau. Colonel Landau read aloud from an article in the 15 September 1953 issue of the *Bayonet*, the 7th Infantry Division newspaper:

Feeling that he could not gain adequate knowledge of the situation from second-hand reports, General Trudeau traded his star-studded steel helmet for that worn by his driver, Sergeant First Class Albert F. Clampert of Leavenworth, Kansas, and led the regimental commander and the counterattacking battalion reconnaissance party to the contested outpost. LTC Beverly M. Read, commanding officer of the 1st Battalion, 17th Infantry, Buffalo Regiment, whose men had held Pork Chop for two days, met the General there when he arrived. "About noon when General Trudeau arrived at the outpost we were under heavy artillery, mortar and small arms fire," said Colonel Read. "He moved across open ground under direct fire from enemy snipers located about 50 yards from the main entrance to the position we had."

Colonel Landau continued, "I know this is embarrassing to you for me to read it, but it did bring you a second Silver Star, and I think for the record it certainly should be in [this interview]. Do you recall that day?"

General Trudeau replied,

I certainly do, you don't forget days like that. No, the situation was tight, we had heavy losses up there. I had to decide what to do, when to replace the units. This was the early part of the attack, and it probably might have been the first or second day of the attack—I've forgotten. I decided that I really needed firsthand information of the situation. I had been through those bunkers. I watched the building of them for two months. We were using KSC labor, and they had really been built as well as you can. Nothing can withstand heavy artillery fire, of course, for any long period of time. I was going to make certain changes there, and I wanted to find out for myself, and some of my people said, "You don't belong out there," and all of that, but I felt I needed to know. So I went.[28]

Ironically, the policy General Trudeau advocated and practiced, decorating men "on the spot," probably kept H Company's Lt. Raymond Clark from receiving a Silver Star. A day or two after the Chinese took control of Pork Chop, Major Noble, Clark's battalion commander, sent word for the lieutenant to report to him—promptly. When Clark presented himself to Noble, the major began to chew him out. Clark had no idea what he had done wrong. Then Noble grinned and told him he was now a first lieutenant instead of a second lieutenant, and that General Trudeau was coming to the company motor pool to present decorations to some of the men in H Company. Clark should be there.

When the division commander arrived, he presented Bronze Stars for Valor, including one to Clark. Trudeau, who was not authorized to approve the award of Silver Stars, did not know, and probably never knew, that recommendations for Silver Stars for Clark and some of the men in his platoon were being prepared in H Company. When Clark's nominating document went forward from company, to battalion, to regiment, and then division, it was returned: "General Trudeau has already awarded Lieutenant Clark a Bronze Star for Valor, for the same action." An attempt was made to explain to the staff officer processing the nomination, and try again. "I'm sure the General knew what he was doing," was the reply.[29] The second answer apparently discouraged any further attempts by Clark's company commander.

There were hundreds more who gave their all in far more heroic acts on Pork Chop, again and again. Sometimes their final acts were performed alone, without benefit of witnesses. Infantry battles' casualty rates of 40 to 60 percent and more have cruel ways of denying recognition to deserving men. Acts of self-sacrifice and heroism all too often go unreported because there are no surviving witnesses, or the witnesses do not take the initiative to ensure the men they have seen perform valorous acts are recognized. In some cases soldiers do not know those they see performing magnificent deeds of courage, and, because of chaotic and dangerous circumstances, are unable to learn their names or units.

The wounded and dead streaming off Pork Chop Hill those five days included an inordinately high percentage of officers and NCOs. Many from among the wounded, including witnesses to valor and the men who would ordinarily take the initiative to reward valor, were scattered to hospitals in Korea, Japan, and the United States. Then the war ended days later. A large number never returned to their units—and, for a variety of reasons, did not reconnect with the units they were in or the men they fought beside.

The New Totalitarians

During the Korean War, for the first time in the bloodiest century in human history, eighteen nations under the banner of the United Nations banded together, along with the Republic of Korea, to stand against the new totalitarians, the communist dictators of the twentieth century, in the first major war within the forty-year span of the cold war. All but a few of the eighteen were Western democracies.

There had been no republic and no democracy in the Korean peninsula's history until after World War II. The nations who sent combat forces fought for many reasons, some not so idealistic. No matter the reasons each entered the fight, they saved a fledgling democracy, however imperfect it was, made democracy possible in the southern half of an ancient land that had a history of emperors, warlords, and dynasties, and nearly a half century of brutal Japanese occupation.

The call to duty for the American soldier in Korea was abrupt. For the second time in nine years, our nation was not prepared for war, was surprised, and paid a terrible price. As Gen. Douglas MacArthur would write years later, "The Korean War meant entry into action 'as is.' No time out for recruiting rallies or to build up and get ready. It was move in—and shoot." Fought during the potentially cataclysmic cold war, the war placed ugly demands and stark choices before UN forces and American soldiers, sailors, marines, and airmen. It was unbelievably difficult and painful for professionals in the armed forces who knew, through the bitter experiences of World War II, that once war is joined, the best and quickest way to end it is with overwhelming, combat-ready forces, well planned, prepared, and applied—on the offensive, swiftly, vigorously, and violently if necessary—to keep loss of life to a minimum.

But Korea wasn't that kind of war. Instead, the UN forces suffered twenty months of intractable trench warfare, and far more bleeding by both sides. At the end of the long period of fight-fight, talk-talk, places like Pork Chop Hill became metaphors for the entire war. Stalemate and frustration.

Yet in spite of it all, the sacrifices made have brought the gifts of democracy and freedom to the Republic of Korea, and protected those same hard won gifts for the United States, and all Western democracies—enormous gains by any measure. The Republic of Korea is today a free nation, a vibrant, thriving nation whose democratic form of government and free market economy have become one of the great success stories of Asia and the twentieth century. Its democracy is growing, maturing, and progressively freeing the enormous creative energies of its people.

To the north is the Democratic People's Republic of Korea, a reclusive, isolated, and still-belligerent holdover of Stalinist and Maoist Communism, and the cold war. It remains a closed culture, one of the most secretive nations in the modern world.

The tightly controlled state economy is near collapse, staggering under the weight of a spartan, repressive, militaristic government, that recently divulged it had a nuclear weapons program based on enriched uranium—thus violating a 1994 accord in which it agreed to halt nuclear weapons development. Its people are suffering the consequences of belligerent, armed-to-the-teeth isolation, which has brought increasing malnutrition and slow starvation for many, as resources are diverted to maintain a huge war making capability. Only under threat of total economic collapse has the North Korean government relented and permitted international aid organizations to render humanitarian assistance to its people.

To the south, along each side of the DMZ, North and South Korea maintain armies totaling nearly one million men each, in defensive positions, always vigilant and wary of one another. Their two armies are backed by air and naval power. They remain in an uneasy truce, frequently punctuated with strident hostility, shooting incidents, and periods of sharply increased tensions.

Since the armistice was signed on 27 July 1953, the United States has maintained ground, air, and naval forces in or near the Republic of Korea to help ensure peace, freedom, and democracy for the Republic of Korea, as well as the security of the island nation of Japan, now a strong ally and bulwark of democracy in northeast Asia and the Western World. The United States Army's 2d Infantry Division, which entered the fight in the

Pusan Perimeter during the summer of 1950 is located not far south of the DMZ, in the Chorwon Valley. The 2d Division is a trip wire and deterrent, ready to join in battle once more should the North Korean regime launch an invasion of the Republic of Korea.

In November 1997, an agreement was reached to begin talks between South and North Korea, the United States, and the People's Republic of China, in Geneva, Switzerland, aimed at reaching a comprehensive peace agreement finally ending the Korean War. To date, there has been no resolution of fundamental differences.

In 2002, prior to the public revelation of North Korea's violation of its agreement to end its nuclear weapons program the President of the United States described North Korea, Iraq, and Iran as three nations constituting an "axis of evil" in the world.

In the DMZ between South and North Korea, a deeply scarred place called Pork Chop Hill still stands, mournful, silent, an outpost without soldiers at the ready, its trenches and bunkers long vanished. Nearby in the same no-man's-land are other silent sentinels: Hill 347, Hill 200, Westview, Dale, Snook, Uncle, Arsenal, Erie, Old Baldy, and Ice Cream Cone.

In the DMZ there are no villages, towns, or cities. No busy thoroughfares. Rich greenery and a growing, thriving, 155-mile-long, three-mile-wide wildlife sanctuary cloak and enrich the hills with natural beauty, and hide Pork Chop's deep scars. Nature's mantle, and the hidden guns of nearly a million men on each side of the widened line, are the keepers of hallowed ground, a truce, unwavering vigilance, and peace.

On 30 June 1950, the day that President Harry S. Truman authorized the introduction of American ground forces into Korea, he approved the sending of the first seventeen American advisers to French Indochina.

In 1953, France asked the Eisenhower administration for U.S. help in fighting a rebellion in the former French colony. The request was approved. On 6 May 1954, a C-119 cargo aircraft in the Central Intelligence Agency–owned airline, Civil Air Transport (CAT), was hit by ground fire during a last-ditch resupply mission over Dien Bien Phu and crashed near the village of Ban Sot in Laos, killing its American pilots. The next day, Ho Chi Minh's Viet-Minh revolutionary forces overran the last French strong points at Dien Bien Phu, ending a siege that had captured the world's headlines for three months.

James McGovern, the aircraft commander, had been a member of Maj. Gen. Claire Chennault's World War II, 14th Air Force "Tiger Shark" squadron, and was credited with four Japanese airplanes shot down and five destroyed on the ground during the war. The copilot was Wallace Buford, a former C-119 pilot during the Korean War. The U.S. response to the French request was to be another step in the growing commitment which eventually deepened into American involvement in the Vietnam War.

For the next quarter-century after American troops entered the Korean War on 25 June 1950, nuclear weaponry dominated U.S. military strategy. As a result, Gen. Maxwell D. Taylor, the Eighth Army's last wartime commander and later chairman of the Joint Chiefs of Staff during the Vietnam War, recalled, "There was no thoroughgoing analysis ever made of the lessons to be learned from Korea, and later policy-makers proceeded to repeat many of the same mistakes."[30]

NOTES

Chapter 1. THE FIRST HALF

1. David R. Hughes, "Report . . . from Korea." *Pointer*, 2 November 1951, 5.
2. David Halberstam, *The Fifties* (New York: Fawcett Columbine, 1993), 70–71.
3. Ibid.
4. Clay Blair, *The Forgotten War* (New York: Doubleday, 1987), 157.
5. Ibid., 156–57.
6. Ibid., 167.
7. Ibid.
8. Ibid., 168.
9. Ibid., 172.
10. Ibid., 168–70.
11. Department of Military Art and Engineering, *Operations in Korea* (West Point, N.Y.: United States Military Academy, 1955), 17.
12. Ibid.
13. Ibid., 18.
14. Ibid., 21.
15. Ibid., 29.
16. Ibid., 21–22.
17. Blair, *Forgotten War*, 380–85; Department of Military Art and Engineering, *Operations in Korea*, Map No. 7.
18. Department of Military Art and Engineering, *Operations in Korea*, 24.
19. Ibid.
20. The description of the destruction of Task Force Faith in Blair, *Forgotten War*, 514–19.
21. Department of Military Art and Engineering, *Operations in Korea*, 25–26.
22. The description of General Matthew Ridgway's turnaround of the Eighth Army in Blair, *Forgotten War*, 570–85.
23. Blair, *Forgotten War*, 808.
24. Department of Military Art and Engineering, *Operations in Korea*, 43.
25. Ibid., 43–44.
26. Ibid., 44.
27. Blair, *Forgotten War*, 586; Department of Military Art and Engineering, *Operations in Korea*, 44.
28. Hughes to Flynn, March 1952.
29. Marshall, *Pork Chop Hill*, 44 (map).
30. The name for Hill 347 described by M.Sgt. Monroe McKenzie in a sworn statement accompanying "Recommendation for Decoration for Heroism" (Distinguished

Service Cross) and accompanying depositions and citation, for Lt. David Ralph Hughes, 11 January 1952.

31. Hughes to Flynn, March 1952; "Recommendation for Decoration for Heroism," for David Ralph Hughes.

32. Hughes to Flynn, March 1952.

33. Blair, *Forgotten War*, 949.

34. Hughes, interview with author; Hughes to Flynn, March 1952.

Chapter 2. TO HOLD THE HILLS

1. Blair, *Forgotten War*, 946.

2. Ibid., 947.

3. Ibid., 951.

4. Ibid., 955.

5. Ibid., 957.

6. Ibid., 958–59.

7. Ibid., 959.

8. Ibid., 959–60.

9. Ibid., 960.

10. Ibid.

11. Ibid.

12. Ibid.

13. Ibid., 960–61.

14. Ibid., 961.

15. Ibid.

16. Ibid., 962.

17. Ibid.

18. Ibid., 962.

19. Ibid.

20. Ibid., 962–63.

21. Article 118 of the Geneva Convention of 1949, which the United States had signed but not yet ratified, but abided by and intended to ratify, stated, "Prisoners of war shall be repatriated without delay after cessation of hostilities." The "without delay" language had been incorporated into the article because the Soviet Union had retained thousands of German and Japanese POWs in slave-labor camps after the conclusion of World War II. That some POWs might not want to return to the country of origin had not been anticipated, and no provision had been made in the convention for that contingency. Ibid.; ibid., 963.

22. Ibid.

23. Ibid.

24. Ibid., 964.

25. Ibid.

26. Owing to inaccurate records and other factors, neither side actually had accurate figures on the other's POWs. Secretly, however, the UN did not believe the Communists were withholding 88,000 names. On 27 October, Ridgway had cabled the

JCS that he estimated the Communists held an "estimated maximum" of "about 28,000 ROKs" and 6,000 non-ROKs. Ibid.

27. Ibid., 965.

28. Ibid.

29. Ibid.

30. Ibid.

31. Ibid., 966.

32. Ibid.

33. Ibid., 966–67.

34. Ibid., 967.

35. Bill McWilliams, *A Return to Glory: The Untold Story of Honor, Dishonor, and Triumph at the United States Military Academy, 1950–53* (Lynchburg, Va.: Warwick House Publishing, 2000), 577–82.

36. Blair, *Forgotten War*, 967–68.

37. Ibid., 968.

38. Ibid.

39. Ibid.

40. Ibid., 969.

41. Ibid.

42. Ibid.

43. Ibid., 969–70.

44. Of the many generals' sons serving in the Korean War, Don Faith and James A. Van Fleet Jr. were the only ones killed in action. A battalion commander in the 32d Infantry Regiment, 7th Division, Lt. Col. Don Faith was killed during the destruction of Task Force Faith, east of the Chosin Reservoir in December 1950 and posthumously received the Medal of Honor. Capt. James A. Van Fleet was piloting a B-26 bomber on his fourth combat mission, a night mission over North Korea, on 4 April 1952, when the aircraft went down and was never found. First declared missing in action, he was declared dead a year later. Gen. Hap Gay's son, Hobart R. Jr., was killed in an aircraft accident in August 1952, after completing 105 FEAF bombing missions. Richard Gruenther, son of Gen. Alfred Gruenther, was severely wounded in northeastern Korea. Gen. Mark Clark's son William, who rose to become the executive officer of the 9th Infantry Regiment, was wounded three times. The last time, in October 1951, on Heartbreak Ridge, he was wounded so severely that he was ultimately forced to retire. The sons of George Stewart, the assistant division commander, 2d Division, and Eighth Army engineer Pat Strong were wounded and physically disabled, necessitating medical evacuation. Paul F. Braim, *The Will to Win: The Life of General James A. Van Fleet* (Annapolis: Naval Institute Press, 2001), 295; Blair, *Forgotten War*, 970.

45. Ibid.

46. Ibid.

47. Ibid., 971.

48. Ibid.

49. Ibid., 971.

50. Ibid.

51. Ibid.

52. Headquarters Eighth Army, "Letter of Instruction Number One," Seoul, Korea, 1 March 1953.

53. Command Report, 7th Infantry Division, May 1953, 1.

54. Ibid.

55. Ibid., 2.

56. Excerpt from a pamphlet titled *Notes for the Course in the History of Military Art* (United States Military Academy, 1953).

57. Command Report, 7th Infantry Division, March 1953, 1.

58. Ibid., 3.

59. Ibid., 2.

60. Ibid., 2–3.

61. Ibid., 2.

62. Ibid., 3.

63. Ibid., 3–8.

64. Ibid., 4.

65. Ibid., 5.

66. Ibid., 6.

67. Ibid., 7.

68. Ibid., 4–5.

69. Ibid., 5–6.

Chapter 3. THE FALL OF OLD BALDY

1. Command Report, 7th Infantry Division, March 1953, 14.

2. Ibid.

3. Command Report, 7th Infantry Division, March 1953, 1 and 26; Command Report, 31st Infantry Regiment, March 1953, 4.

4. Command Report, 7th Infantry Division, March 1953, 9; *2002 Register of Graduates and Former Cadets, United States Military Academy* (West Point, N.Y.: Association of Graduates, USMA).

5. Command Report, 7th Infantry Division, March 1953, 9, 25.

6. Ibid., 9–10 and 22.

7. Ibid., 22.

8. Ibid.

9. Ibid., 29.

10. Ibid.

11. Ronald K. Freedman, interview with author.

12. Command Report, 7th Infantry Division, March 1953, 23.

13. Ibid., 25 and 37.

14. Ibid., 37–38.

15. Ibid.

16. Ibid., 38–39.

17. Ibid., 10, 38–39.

18. Ibid., 45.

19. Ibid., 39–40.

20. Intelligence debriefing statement by 2d Lt. Albert DeLaGarza following his release during "Little Switch," 25 April 1953.

21. Command Report, 7th Infantry Division, March 1953, 40.

22. Ibid.

23. Ibid., 42.

24. Ibid.

25. Ibid.

26. Ibid., 43.

27. Ibid.

28. Ibid., 43–44.

29. *Houston Post,* 25 March 1953; Command Report, 7th Infantry Division, March 1953, 43–44.

30. Command Report, 7th Infantry Division, March 1953, 44.

31. Ibid., 10.

32. Ibid., 46.

33. Ibid.

34. Ibid.

35. Ibid.

36. Ibid., 47.

37. "Americans in Bunker Call Down Artillery Fire on Own Heads," *Houston Post,* 26 March 1953; Robert M. Euwer, *No Longer Forgotten, The Korean War and Its Memorial* (Baltimore: Gateway Press, 1995), 26 and 81; Command Report, 7th Infantry Division, May 1953, 86.

38. Command Report, 7th Infantry Division, May 1953, 50.

39. Ibid.

40. Ibid.

41. Marshall, *Pork Chop Hill,* 47.

42. Command Report, 7th Infantry Division, March 1953, 51.

43. Ibid.

44. Ibid.

45. Ibid.

46. Ibid.

47. Ibid., 52.

48. Ibid.

49. Ibid.

50. Ibid., 53.

51. Ibid.

52. Blair, *Forgotten War,* 971–72.

53. Ibid., 971.

54. Ibid.

55. Command Report, 7th Infantry Division, April 1953, 5.

56. Ibid., 26.

57. Ibid., 8.

58. Ibid., 9.

59. Ibid.

60. Ibid., 50.

61. Ibid.

62. Ibid., 8.

63. Marshall, *Pork Chop Hill,* 53.

64. Ibid., 115–16.

65. Command Report, 7th Infantry Division, April 1953, 18.

Chapter 4. UPPING THE ANTE

1. Command Report, 7th Infantry Division, April 1953, 10.

2. Marshall, *Pork Chop Hill,* 31.

3. Command Report, 7th Infantry Division, April 1953, 14.

4. Ibid., 15.

5. Marshall, *Pork Chop Hill,* 114.

6. Command Report, 7th Infantry Division, April 1953, 42.

7. Command Report, 7th Infantry Division, April 1953; Command Report, 31st Infantry Regiment, April 1953, 2.

8. Command Report, 7th Infantry Division, April 1953, 18 and 42.

9. Ibid., 42.

10. Ibid., 43; Marshall, *Pork Chop Hill,* 117–18.

11. Command Report, 7th Infantry Division, April 1953, 43.

12. Ibid.; Marshall, *Pork Chop Hill,* 125.

13. Ibid.

14. Command Report, 31st Infantry Regiment, April 1953, 12.

15. Ibid., 13.

16. Marshall, *Pork Chop Hill,* 130.

17. Ibid.

18. Command Report, 31st Infantry Regiment, April 1953, 13.

19. Ibid.

20. Ibid., 14; Marshall, *Pork Chop Hill,* 103–13.

21. Command Report, 31st Infantry Regiment, April 1953, 14.

22. Ibid; Marshall, *Pork Chop Hill,* 143.

23. Ibid.

24. Ibid.

25. Command Report, 31st Infantry Regiment, April 1953, 14–15; Marshall, *Pork Chop Hill,* 143–44.

26. Marshall, *Pork Chop Hill,* 156–59.

27. Ibid., 151.

28. Command Report, 31st Infantry Regiment, April 1953, 15; Command Report, 17th Infantry Regiment, April 1953, 17–19; Marshall, *Pork Chop Hill,* 159; Walter B. Russell, Jr., interview with author.

29. Command Report, 31st Infantry Regiment, April 1953, 15; Command Report, 17th Infantry Regiment, April 1953, 17–19; Russell interview.

30. Command Report, 31st Infantry Regiment, April 1953, 15; Command Report, 17th Infantry Regiment, April 1953, 17–19; Russell interview.

31. Marshall, *Pork Chop Hill,* 160–64.

32. Ibid., 164.

33. Ibid., 164–66.

34. Ibid., 166.

35. Ibid., 185.

36. Ibid.

37. Command Report, 17th Infantry Regiment, April 1953, 18.

38. Command Report, 31st Infantry Regiment, April 1953, 16; Command Report, 17th Infantry Regiment, April 1953, 18; Marshall, *Pork Chop Hill*, 192.

39. Joseph E. Gonsalves, *Battle at the 38th Parallel: Surviving the Peace Talks at Panmunjom* (Central Point, Oreg.: Hellgate Press, 2001), 171.

40. Marshall, *Pork Chop Hill*, 193–94.

41. Ibid., 188–91.

42. Ibid., 188–91.

43. Gonsalves, *Battle at the 38th Parallel*, 162–63.

44. Marshall, *Pork Chop Hill*, 191–95; Command Report, 7th Infantry Division, April 1953, 47–48; James N. Butcher, "From Softball Field to Gates of Hell, Fox Company on Pork Chop," *Buffalo Bugle*, March 2000, p. 24; "New Assault at Pork Chop Beaten," *Houston Post*, 18 April 1953; Command Report, Eighth Army, May 1953, 86.

45. Marshall, *Pork Chop Hill*, 191–95; Command Report, 7th Infantry Division, April 1953, 47–48.

46. Former corporal Dale Cain's written responses to author's interview questions, 10 February 2002.

47. Gonsalves, *Battle at the 38th Parallel*, 172.

48. Command Report, 7th Infantry Division, April 1953, 18–19.

49. Marshall, *Pork Chop Hill*, 18.

50. Ibid., 196.

Chapter 5. REBUILDING

1. Blair, *Forgotten War*, 972.

2. Intelligence debriefing statement by 2d Lt. Albert DeLaGarza.

3. Command Report, 7th Infantry Division, March 1953, 65.

4. Ibid.

5. Ibid., 66.

6. Ibid., 66–71.

7. Joseph K. Bratton, "With the 13th Engineers, 7th Infantry Division," *Army Engineers*, June 1997, 36; James A. Brettell, interview with author.

8. Brettell interview.

9. Richard W. White, interview with author.

10. Command Report, 7th Infantry Division, April 1953, 61–62.

11. White interview.

12. James R. Goudy, interview with author.

13. Brettell interview.

14. Gonsalves, *Battle at the 38th Parallel*, 42.

15. Ibid., 21.

16. Joseph S. Kimmitt, interview with author; Robert J. Schaefer, interview with author.

17. Robert M. Euwer, written narrative provided to author.

18. Gonsalves, *Battle at the 38th Parallel,* 200–1.

19. Ibid., 26–33.

20. Euwer, *No Longer Forgotten,* 117–18.

21. Goudy interview.

22. Command Report, 17th Infantry Regiment, May 1953, 3; deposition by Lieutenant Colonel Beverly M. Read, in the nomination of Major Billy F. Fritts for the Distinguished Service Cross.

23. Brettell interview.

24. Brettell interview; Goudy interview; White interview; "With the 13th Engineers, 7th Infantry Division," 38.

25. White interview.

26. Ibid.

27. Goudy interview.

28. Anton Cicak, author's interview.

29. Blair, *Forgotten War,* 972.

30. Joyce E. Shea Himka, interview with author; Mary Jo Inman Vermillion, interview with author; Barbara Inman Colby, interview with author.

Chapter 6. CALM BEFORE THE STORM

1. Command Report, 7th Infantry Division, May 1953, 2–4.

2. Ibid., 3.

3. Ibid., 5.

4. Ibid., 10.

5. Command Report, 17th Infantry Regiment, May 1953, 2; Command Report, 7th Infantry Division, May 1953, 10 and 13.

6. Command Report, 7th Infantry Division, May 1953, 10.

7. Gonsalves, *Battle at the 38th Parallel,* 166.

8. William R. Kintner, "Pork Chop," *Army Combat Forces Journal,* March 1955, 41.

9. Blair, *Forgotten War,* 972–73.

10. Command Report, 7th Infantry Division, May 1953, 11.

11. Marshall, *Pork Chop Hill,* 233–36.

12. 1 February 1953 newspaper clipping of unknown origin, provided to the author by Juan Raigoza.

13. Juan Raigoza, interview with author.

14. Kimmitt interview.

15. Command Report, 7th Infantry Division, March 1953, 33–34.

16. Command Report, 7th Infantry Division, May 1953, 11.

17. Ibid., 11–12.

18. Command Report, 7th Infantry Division, May 1953, 3.

19. Marshall, *Pork Chop Hill,* 233–49; Command Report, 7th Infantry Division, May 1953, 12–13.

20. "Report on Chinese Attack Against Ethiopian Positions on Outpost Yoke, 20 May 1953," 32d Infantry Regiment Battle Records Board, 3–4.

21. Command Report, 17th Infantry Regiment, May 1953, 2.

22. Kathryn Wise, "Colonel Beverly M. Read '41 Retires as Editor of the VMI Alumni Review," *VMI Alumni Review,* Fall 1986, 7–8.

23. Blair, *Forgotten War,* 973.

24. David L. Bills, interview with author.

25. Letter courtesy of Mary Jo Inman Vermillion.

26. William J. Duncan, interview with author.

27. Command Report, Eighth Army, May 1953, 54.

28. Ibid., June 1953, 23.

29. Ibid., 19.

30. Command Report, 7th Infantry Division, May 1953, 18.

31. Ibid., 7 and 16.

32. Euwer, *No Longer Forgotten,* 129–30.

33. Command Report, 7th Infantry Division, May 1953, 16.

34. Command Report, 17th Infantry Regiment, May 1953, 5–6.

35. Russell interview.

36. Senior Officers Debriefing Program, "Conversations Between Lieutenant General Arthur Gilbert Trudeau and Colonel Calvin J. Landau," U.S. Army Military History Research Collection, vol. 2, Carlisle Barracks Pennsylvania, 29.

37. Command Report, 7th Infantry Division, July 1953, Enclosure 6, 1–2.

38. Brettell interview; *Idaho Statesman,* 30 May 1982.

39. *Idaho Statesman,* 30 May 1982.

Chapter 7. SIGNS OF TROUBLE

1. Command Report, Eighth Army, May 1953, 1–2.

2. Ibid., 2 and 49–50.

3. Ibid., 2–3.

4. Command Report, 17th Infantry Regiment, June 1953, 3.

5. Ibid., 9.

6. Ibid.

7. Blair, *Forgotten War,* 973.

8. Richard G. Inman to his parents (courtesy of Mary Jo Vermillion).

9. Blair, *Forgotten War,* 973.

10. Command Report, 17th Infantry Regiment, June 1953, 2.

11. Richard T. Shea Jr. to Joyce E. Shea, courtesy of Joyce E. Himka.

12. Command Report, 7th Infantry Division, June 1953, 9–10.

13. Command Report, Eighth Army, June 1953, 1.

14. Richard T. Shea Jr. to Joyce E. Shea (courtesy of Joyce E. Himka).

15. Command Report, Eighth Army, June 1953, 2; Blair, *Forgotten War,* 974.

16. Command Report, Eighth Army, June 1953, 2.

17. Command Report, 7th Infantry Regiment, June 1953, 2; Blair, *Forgotten War*, 974.

18. Ibid., 974.

19. Ibid.

20. Richard T. Shea, Jr., to Joyce E. Shea (courtesy of Joyce E. Himka).

21. Richard G. Inman to his parents (courtesy of Mary Jo Vermillion).

22. Command Report, 17th Infantry Regiment, June 1953, 2.

23. Richard T. Shea, Jr., to Joyce E. Shea (courtesy of Joyce E. Himka); Barbara K. Inman to Richard G. Inman's parents (courtesy of Mary Jo Vermillion).

24. Command Report, Eighth Army, June 1953, 4–8.

25. Ibid., 13.

26. Command Report, 7th Infantry Division, June 1953, 6.

Chapter 8. THE BEGINNING

1. Letter courtesy of Mary Jo Vermillion.

2. Letter courtesy of Mary Jo Vermillion.

3. Richard G. Inman's poem, "My Toys," courtesy of Mary Jo Vermillion.

4. Command Report, 7th Infantry Division, June 1953, 2.

5. William J. Ryan, interview with author.

6. 7th Infantry Division Battle Records Board, " 'C' Company Raid on Enemy Positions on Finger Running Between Pork Chop and Hassakol on 4 July 1953," 1–7, and map sketch; Harold H. Hackett, interview with author; Henry Baker, interview with author.

7. Depositions given by Harm J. Tipton, Irwin Greenberg, Clarence H. Mouser, and David R. Willcox, 27 September 1953; David R. Willcox, interview with author; Cicak interview.

8. Robert E. Miller, interview with author; Dale W. Cain, Jr., interview with author.

9. Sworn statements from Harm J. Tipton, Irwin Greenberg, Clarence H. Mouser, and David R. Willcox, 27 September 1953; Duncan interview; Cicak interview.

10. Harvey D. Jordan, author's interview.

11. Cain interview; Miller interview; Herbert C. Hollander, interview with author.

12. Emmett D. Gladwell, interview with author.

13. Ibid.

14. Robert L. Wilson, interview with author.

15. Lee H. Johnson, interview with author.

16. Paul Anderson, interview with author.

17. Johnson interview.

18. Henry Bakker, author's interview.

19. Anderson interview.

20. Gladwell interview.

21. Wilson interview.

22. Miller interview.

23. Cain interview.

24. Jordan interview.

25. George Sakasegawa, interview with author.

26. Charles W. Brooks, interview with author.

27. John A. Coulter II, "Richard Thomas Shea," unpublished manuscript, chap. 6, p. 48.

28. Deposition by Clarence R. Mouser, 27 September 1953.

29. Brettell interview; White interview.

30. Command Report, 7th Infantry Division, July 1953, Sketch No. 1.

31. Kintner, "Pork Chop," 41.

32. Jordan interview.

33. Sakasegawa interview.

34. Kintner, "Pork Chop," 41–42.

35. Willcox interview.

36. Brooks interview.

37. Willcox interview; Richard Baker, interview with author; depositions by George H. Cunningham, Jesse Foster, Jr., and William R. Garman, 10 September 1953.

38. Depositions by Clarence R. Mouser, Harm J. Tipton, Irwin Greenberg, and David R. Willcox, 27 September 1953; Willcox interview.

39. Deposition by Irwin Greenberg, 27 September 1953.

40. "Action on Outpost Pork Chop, 6–11 July"; Command Report, 7th Infantry Division, July 1953, 4.

41. Ibid.

42. Ibid.

43. Willcox interview.

44. Unpublished recollections of Richard D. Hovey.

45. Citation for the award of the Distinguished Service Cross to Howard C. Hovey.

46. Duncan interview.

47. "Action on Outpost Pork Chop, 6–11 July," 4; Cicak interview.

48. Cicak interview.

49. Ibid.

50. "Action on Outpost Pork Chop, 6–11 July," 4.

Chapter 9. HOLDING TIGHT

1. "Action on Outpost Pork Chop, 6–11 July," 4–5.

2. Ibid., 5.

3. Cicak interview.

4. Kintner, "Pork Chop," 42.

5. Cicak interview.

6. MacPherson Conner, interview with author.

7. Ibid.; "Action on Outpost Pork Chop," 6.

8. "Action on Outpost Pork Chop," 6.

9. Conner interview; ibid., 5–6.

10. Kintner, "Pork Chop," 42; "Action on Outpost Pork Chop," 5–6.

11. "Action on Outpost Pork Chop," 6.

12. Citation accompanying award of the Medal of Honor to Richard T. Shea, Jr.

13. Conner interview; Jackie L. McWhirter, interview with author.

14. Conner interview; citation accompanying the award of the Medal of Honor to Richard T. Shea, Jr.

15. Kintner, "Pork Chop," 42.

16. Brooks interview; Miller interview.

17. Jordan interview; Sakasegawa interview.

18. "Action on Outpost Pork Chop," 6.

19. Ibid., 6; Schaefer interview.

20. Kenneth Swift, interview with author.

21. Kintner, "Pork Chop," 42; Senior Officers Debriefing Program, "Conversations," 33–34.

22. Kintner, "Pork Chop," 42.

23. James E. McKenzie, interview with author; McWhirter interview.

24. Cicak interview; Duncan interview.

25. Brettell interview; Goudy interview; White interview; James A. Brettell, "Engineer Support for Pork Chop Hill," *Army Engineer,* January 1996, 20–22; James A. Brettell, text of talk given to the Association of the 13th Engineers at their reunion, 7–10 October 1998.

26. "Action on Pork Chop," Command Report, 7th Infantry Division, July 1953, 8.

27. Cicak interview.

28. Henry Baker interview; Raldo D. Horman, interview with author.

29. Kintner, "Pork Chop," 42; Cicak interview.

30. "Action on Pork Chop," 8; Kintner, "Pork Chop," 42.

31. Kintner, "Pork Chop," 42; Emory Ballengee, interview with author.

32. Ballengee interview.

33. Cicak interview.

34. Kintner, "Pork Chop," 43; "Action on Pork Chop," 7.

35. Citation accompanying award of the Bronze Star for Heroic Achievement, 16 September 1953.

36. Citation accompanying award of the Bronze Star for Heroic Achievement, 23 September 1953.

37. McKenzie interview.

38. McWhirter interview.

39. Kintner, "Pork Chop," 43; "Action on Pork Chop," 7.

40. Ballengee interview.

41. Kintner, "Pork Chop," 43.

42. White interview; Goudy interview.

Chapter 10. BATTALION COUNTERATTACK

1. "Action on Pork Chop," 9–10.

2. Kintner, "Pork Chop," 43.

3. Headquarters Eighth Army, "Letter of Instruction Number One"; Gonsalves, *Battle for the 38th Parallel*, 183.

4. Conner interview.

5. Command Report, 7th Infantry Division, July 1953, 10.

6. Ibid.

7. Miller interview.

8. Lieutenant Colonel Read to Joyce E. Shea, 24 August 1953.

9. McKenzie interview.

10. Conner interview.

11. John W. Phillips, "A Reminiscence," 1–4.

12. Robert Northcutt, unpublished written recollections.

13. "Action on Pork Chop," 10–11.

14. Wilson interview.

15. Robert Northcutt, unpublished written recollections; Robert Northcutt, interview with author.

16. Ibid.; Phillips, "Reminiscence," 5–6.

17. Phillips, "Reminiscence," 5–9.

18. Northcutt interview.

19. Kintner, "Pork Chop," 43–44; Northcutt interview.

20. Northcutt interview; citation accompanying the award of the Distinguished Service Cross to Robert Northcutt.

21. Northcutt interview.

22. Citation accompanying the award of the Medal of Honor to Corporal Dan D. Schoonover.

23. Citation for award of the Medal of Honor to Richard T. Shea, Jr.; Lieutenant Colonel Read to Joyce E. Shea; Willcox interview.

24. Eugene Urban, interview with author.

25. Paul Serchia, interview with author; Arthur Lowe, interview with author; "Recommendation for Decoration for Heroism" (Distinguished Service Cross) and accompanying depositions and citation, for Lt. Steven M. Wood, 23 August 1953.

26. Kintner, "Pork Chop," 45; "Action on Pork Chop," 10.

27. "Action on Pork Chop," 10–11.

28. Phillips, "Reminiscence," 9.

29. Wilson interview; Cordell Hadley, interview with author; "Recommendation for Award for Heroism" (Distinguished Service Cross) and accompanying depositions and citation, for Lt. Samuel E. Daniel, 30 July 1953.

30. Command Report, 7th Infantry Division, July 1953, 11.

31. Ibid., 11–12; Kintner, "Pork Chop," 44.

Chapter 11. THREE COMPANIES AND A PLATOON

1. Earl C. Acuff, interview with author.

2. Northcutt interview; Kintner, "Pork Chop," 44–45; Command Report, 7th Infantry Division, July 1953, 12–13; citation accompanying the award of the Distinguished Service Cross to Corporal Robert Northcutt.

3. Kintner, "Pork Chop," 44; Conner interview.

4. Kintner, "Pork Chop," 45; Command Report, 7th Infantry Division, July 1953, 13.

5. Urban interview.

6. Raymond N. Clark, interview with author; written recollections of Raymond N. Clark, contained in *Korea: The Longest War,* by Dale W. Cain, Jr. (Seoul, Korea: Ministry of Patriots and Veterans Affairs, 1997), 83–95.

7. Clark interview; Danny L. Peters, interview with author; Danny L. Peters, exchange of correspondence with author; Kintner, "Pork Chop," 45; Command Report, 7th Infantry Division, July 1953, 14.

8. Oral Grimmett, interview with author.

9. Henry Baker interview.

10. Command Report, 7th Infantry Division, July 1953, 14.

11. James Leal, interview with author.

12. Willcox interview; McKenzie interview.

13. Willcox interview; Richard Baker interview; depositions from Cpl. William R. Garman, Pfc. Jesse Foster, Jr., and Pfc. George H. Cunningham, 10 November 1953.

14. White interview; Clark recollections in Cain, *Longest War,* 83–95.

15. Raymond N. Clark's recollections, Command Report, 7th Infantry Division, July 1953, 15.

16. Kintner, "Pork Chop," 45; Command Report, 7th Infantry Division, July 1953, 15.

17. Clark recollections in Cain, *Longest War,* 83–95; Command Report, 7th Infantry Division, July 1953, 15–16.

18. Blair, *Forgotten War,* 975.

19. Command Report, Eighth Army, July 1953, 1–2.

20. Trudeau's oral history, 30.

21. Ibid.

22. Ibid., 30–31.

Chapter 12. FINAL DECISIONS AND SURPRISES

1. Kintner, "Pork Chop," 45.

2. Louis Salovich, interview with author.

3. Kintner, "Pork Chop," 45.

4. Clark's recollections in Cain, *Longest War.*

5. Richard A. Baughman, interview with author.

6. Clark's recollections in Cain, *Longest War.*

7. Baughman interview.

8. Leal interview.

9. Clark interview.

10. Schaefer interview; Wilson interview; John Phillips's written recollections.

11. Command Report, 7th Infantry Division, 17.

12. John Dean, "Boisean Recalls Death of Her Son on Pork Chop Hill," *Idaho Statesman,* 30 May 1982; citation accompanying the posthumous award of the Medal of Honor to Dan D. Schoonover.

13. Sworn statement by Reginald G. Watkins, Nomination for the Distinguished Service Cross for Royal R. Taylor, 30 July 1953.

14. Command Report, 7th Infantry Division, 17.

15. Sworn statement by Reginald G. Watkins.

16. Salovich interview.

17. Command Report, 7th Infantry Division, 17–18.

18. Citation accompanying the award of the Silver Star to Thomas M. Armour, October 1953.

19. Citation accompanying the award of the Bronze Star for Valor to Rother Temple, 16 October 1953.

20. Citation for the award of the Bronze Star for Valor to James W. Lee, 24 September 1953.

21. Sworn statement by Reginald G. Watkins; sworn statement by Obel H. Wells, attached to Nomination for the Distinguished Service Cross for Royal R. Taylor, 27 July 1953.

22. Sworn statement by Robert W. Lewis, attached to Nomination for the Distinguished Service Cross for Royal R. Taylor, 27 July 1953.

23. Command Report, 7th Infantry Division, 18–19.

24. Trudeau's oral history; Command Report, 7th Infantry Division, 19.

25. Command Report, 7th Infantry Division, 19–20.

26. David L. Bills, "Pork Chop—the Final Hours," draft article for 13th Combat Engineers Association newsletter, n.d.

27. Bills interview; White interview; Brettell interview; written recollections by David Bills, Richard W. White, and James A. Brettell.

28. Kintner, "Pork Chop," 45.

29. Freedman, Barry, and Kimmitt, written recollections and interviews with author; nomination and award of the Distinguished Service Cross (Posthumously) to Major Billy E. Fritts, 1 October 1953.

30. "Action on Pork Chop," 20.

31. Bills interview; Brettell interview; written recollections by David L. Bills and James A. Brettell.

32. Cain interview.

33. Command Report, 17th Infantry Regiment, 2.

34. Command Report, 32d Infantry Regiment, July 1953, 4.

35. "Action on Pork Chop," 21.

36. Conner interview.

37. Brettell interview.

38. "Artillery After Action Report," Command Report, 7th Infantry Division, 1–3 and Enclosure 1.

39. Cain interview.

40. Command Report, Eighth Army, July 1953, 2.

41. Ibid., 45–46.

42. "After Action Report Involving Outpost Dale," Command Report, 31st Infantry Regiment, July 1953; "After Action Report Involving Outpost Westview," Command Report, 31st Infantry Regiment, July 1953.

43. Command Report, Eighth Army, July 1953.

Chapter 13. AFTERMATH

1. Colby interview; Himka interview; Vermillion interview.
2. Robert E. Inman, "They Call Me Bob: An Anecdotal Biography of Robert E. Inman," unpublished manuscript.
3. Colby interview.
4. Letter courtesy of Robert M. Euwer.
5. Douglas Halbert, unpublished written recollections of armistice, 27 July 1953.
6. Henry Baker interview.
7. Lowe interview.
8. Schaefer interview.
9. Swift interview.
10. Freedman interview.
11. Robert M. Euwer, unpublished written recollections.
12. Leal interview.
13. Bills interview.
14. Duncan interview.
15. James N. Butcher, "Return of Morning Calm," *Stars and Stripes,* 18 June 2000, 44–45.
16. Raymond Clark, written recollections.
17. Jordan interview; Sakasegawa interview; U.S. Army Korean War Casualty File, National Archives Center for Electronic Records, 10 July 2002.
18. U.S. Army Korean War Casualty File, National Archives Center for Electronic Records, 10 July 2002; "War in Korea—Major U.S. Unit Combat Casualties in Korea," *VFW,* June/July 1993, 34.
19. Himka interview; Vermillion interview; Willcox interview. Letters courtesy of Joyce Shea Himka and Mary Jo Vermillion.
20. Peters interview.
21. Wilson interview.
22. Willcox interview.
23. Himka interview.
24. Himka interview; Vermillion interview; Willcox interview; family keepsakes provided by Joyce Shea Himka and Mary Jo Inman Vermillion; letters courtesy of Joyce Shea Himka and Mary Jo Vermillion.
25. Dean, "Boisean Recalls Death"; Brettell interview.
26. Vermillion interview; Colby interview.
27. Letter courtesy of Robert M. Euwer.
28. "Conversations Between Lieutenant General Arthur Gilbert Trudeau and Colonel Calvin J. Landau," U.S. Army Military History Research Collection, vol 2, Carlisle Barracks, Pennsylvania, 33–34.
29. Clark interview.
30. Harry G. Summers, "Korea, Then and Now: Why U.S. Involvement Matters," *Stars and Stripes,* 18 June 2000, 46; Richard Pyle, "Remains of Soldier Sought after 48 Years," *Las Vegas Review-Journal,* 24 November 2002, 39A–40A.

BIBLIOGRAPHY

Interviews with the Author

All interviews by telephone unless otherwise noted.

Acuff, Earl C. 23 September 2002.

Anderson, Paul. 25 April 2002.

Baker, Henry. 25 April 2002.

Baker, Richard. 26 August 2002.

Bakker, Henry. 13 May 2002.

Ballengee, Emory E. 9 February 2002.

Barry, Raymond N. 27 May 2002.

Baughman, Richard A. 30 September 2002.

Bills, David L. 17 July 2002.

Brettell, James A. 23 and 29 May 2002.

Brooks, Charles W. 16 March 1999.

Butcher, James N.

Cain, Dale W., Sr. 13 February 1999; 26 July, Las Vegas, Nevada.

Cicak, Anton. 31 July 2002.

Clark, Raymond N. 30 September 2002.

Colby, Barbara Kipp (Inman). 28 February and 8 July 2002.

Conner, MacPherson. 13 February and 7 April 1998.

Duncan, William J. 25 July 2002.

Euwer, Robert M. 23 January 2002.

Freedman, Ronald K. 21 May 2002.

Gladwell, Emmett D. 29 January 1999.

Goudy, James R. 26 June 2002.

Grimmett, Oral. 29 January 2002.

Hackett, Harold H. 7 September 2002.

Hadley, Cordell. 30 October 2001.

Himka, Joyce E. (Shea). All interviews by correspondence.

Hollander, Herbert C. 30 July 2002.

Horman, Raldo. 23 October 2002.

Hovey, Richard D.

Hughes, David R. 21 May and 29 June 1997.

Johnson, Lee H. 15 January 1999.

Jordan, Harvey D. 7 August 2002.

Kimmitt, Joseph S. 26 June 2002.

Leal, James R. 10 August, 25 and 27 October 2001.

Lowe, Arthur. 26 May 2002.

McKenzie, James E. 10 December 1998.

McWhirter, Jackie L. 23 October 2001.

Miller, Miles. 21 February 2002, Las Vegas, Nevada.

Miller, Robert E. 25 February 1999 and 29 July 2002.

Northcutt, Robert. 16 March 1999.

Peters, Danny L. 1999.

Phillips, John W.

Raigoza, Juan. 18 July 2002.

Roemer, William R. 21 August 2002.

Russell, Walter B., Jr. 13 May 2002.

Ryan, William J. 15 March 1996.

Sakasegawa, George. 4 September 2002.

Salovich, Louis. 21 February 2002.

Schaefer, Robert J. 24 June 2002.

Serchia, Paul. 23 April 2002.

Swift, Kenneth. 20 April 2002.

Urban, Eugene. 24 October 2002.

Vermillion, Mary Jo. 27 February, 2 and 12 March 1998.

White, Richard W. 16 August 2002.

Willcox, David R. 9 and 11 November 1998, 20 January 1999.

Wilson, Robert L. 19 August 2002.

Books

Blair, Clay. *The Forgotten War.* New York: Doubleday, 1987.

Braim, Paul F. *The Will to Win: The Life of General James A. Van Fleet.* Annapolis: Naval Institute Press, 2001.

Cain, Dale W., Jr. *Korea: The Longest War.* Seoul, Korea: Ministry of Patriots and Veterans Affairs, 1997.

Department of Military Art and Engineering. *Operations in Korea.* West Point, N.Y.: United States Military Academy, 1955.

Euwer, Robert M. *No Longer Forgotten: The Korean War and Its Memorial.* Baltimore: Gateway Press, 1995.

Gonsalves, Joseph E. *Battle at the 38th Parallel: Surviving the Peace Talks at Panmunjom*. Central Point, Oreg.: Hellgate Press, 2001.

Halberstam, David. *The Fifties*. New York: Fawcett Columbine, 1993.

Knox, Donald. *The Korean War: Uncertain Victory*. San Diego: Harcourt Brace Jovanovich, 1988.

MacArthur, Douglas. *Reminiscences*. New York: McGraw-Hill, 1964.

Marshall, S. L. A. *Pork Chop Hill*. Nashville: Battery Press, 1986.

McWilliams, Bill. *A Return to Glory: The Untold Story of Honor, Dishonor, and Triumph at the United States Military Academy, 1950–53*. Lynchburg, Va.: Warwick House Publishing, 2000.

1952 Howitzer. West Point, N.Y.: Class of 1952, United States Corps of Cadets.

Sobieski, Anthony J. *Fire Mission: The Story of the 213th Field Artillery Battalion in Korea 1951–1954*. Philadelphia: Privately published, 2000.

2002 Register of Graduates and Former Cadets, United States Military Academy. West Point, N.Y.: Association of Graduates, USMA.

Articles

Bills, David L. "Pork Chop—the final hours." Draft article for 13th Combat Engineers Association newsletter, n.d.

Bratton, Joseph K. "With the 13th Engineers, 7th Infantry Division." *Army Engineer*, June 1997.

Brettell, James A. "Engineer Support for Pork Chop Hill." *Army Engineer*, January 1996.

Butcher, James N. "From Softball Field to Gates of Hell, Fox Company on Pork Chop." *Buffalo Bugle*, March 2000, p. 24.

Hughes, David R. "Report . . . from Korea." *Pointer*, 2 November 1951.

Kintner, William R. "Pork Chop." *Army Combat Forces Journal*, March 1955.

Love, J. B. "Remember the Price They Paid." *Assembly*, March/April 1997.

Summers, Harry G. "Korea, Then and Now: Why U.S. Involvement Matters." *Stars and Stripes*, 18 June 2000, 46.

"War in Korea—Major U.S. Unit Combat Casualties in Korea." *VFW*, June/July 1993, 34.

Wise, Kathryn. "Colonel Beverly M. Read '41 Retires as Editor of the VMI Alumni Review." *VMI Alumni Review*, Fall 1986.

Magazines and Newspapers

Argosy. December 1953.

Assembly. October 1951, January 1954, October 1954, July 1955, Winter 1959.

Houston Post. 26 March, 18 April 1953.

Idaho Statesman. 30 May 1982.

Las Vegas Review-Journal. 24 November 2002.

New York Times. 6–11, 13, and 27–28 July 1953.

Vincennes-Sun Commercial. 8 March 1953, 7 July 1954.

Unpublished Sources

7th Infantry Division Battle Records Board. " 'C' Company Raid on Enemy Positions on Finger Running Between Pork Chop and Hasakkol on 4 July 1953."

"After Action Report Involving Outpost Westview." 31st Infantry Regiment Command Report, July 1953.

Bills, David L., LTC USA (Ret.). "Pork Chop Hill—the Final Hours." Manuscript draft. N.d.

Brettell, James A. Text of talk given to the Association of the 13th Engineers at their reunion, 7–10 October 1998.

"Bridge to Pork Chop Hill." Manuscript. Capt. James A. Brettell, Commander, Company A, 13th Engineer Battalion. N.d.

Citation accompanying Bronze Star for Heroic Achievement awarded to Hugh D. Porterfield, 16 September 1953.

Citation accompanying Bronze Star for Heroic Achievement awarded to Robert L. Pothoof, 23 September 1953.

Citation accompanying Bronze Star for Valor awarded to James W. Lee, 24 September 1953.

Citation accompanying Bronze Star for Valor awarded to Rother Temple, 16 October 1953.

Citation accompanying Congressional Medal of Honor awarded posthumously to Dan D. Schoonover, January 1955.

Citation accompanying Congressional Medal of Honor awarded posthumously to Richard Thomas Shea, Jr., given to Joyce Riemann Shea, May 1954.

Citation accompanying Distinguished Service Cross awarded posthumously to Howard C. Hovey, given to Mrs. Evelyn S. Hovey.

Citation accompanying Distinguished Service Cross awarded to Robert Northcutt.

Citation accompanying Silver Star awarded posthumously to Richard George Inman, given to Barbara Kipp (Inman) Colby, 6 July 1954.

Citation accompanying Silver Star awarded to Thomas M. Armour, October 1953.

Command Report. 7th Infantry Division. March 1953, April 1953, May 1953, June 1953, July 1953.

Command Report. 17th Infantry Regiment. March 1953, April 1953, May 1953, June 1953, July 1953.

Command Report. 31st Infantry Regiment. March 1953, April 1953, July 1953.

Command Report. 32nd Infantry Regiment. March 1953, June 1953, July 1953.

Command Report. Eighth Army. May 1953, June 1953, July 1953.

Coulter, John A., II. "Richard Thomas Shea." Unpublished manuscript. Chap. 6, p. 48.

Deposition by George H. Cunningham, attached to nomination for award of the Silver Star to David R. Willcox, 10 September 1953.

Deposition by Jesse Foster, Jr., attached to nomination for award of the Silver Star to David R. Willcox, 10 September 1953.

Deposition by William R. Garman, attached to nomination for award of the Silver Star to David R. Willcox, 10 September 1953. William R. Garman.

Deposition given by Clarence H. Mouser to Congressman William Bray of Indiana, 27 September 1953. Courtesy of Mary Jo Inman Vermillion.

Deposition given by David R. Willcox to Congressman William Bray of Indiana, 27 September 1953. Courtesy of Mary Jo Inman Vermillion.

Deposition given by Harm J. Tipton to Congressman William Bray of Indiana, 27 September 1953. Courtesy of Mary Jo Inman Vermillion.

Deposition given by Irwin Greenberg to Congressman William Bray of Indiana, 27 September 1953. Courtesy of Mary Jo Inman Vermillion.

Halbert, Douglas. Unpublished recollections of the armistice. 27 July 1953.

Headquarters Eighth Army. "Letter of Instruction Number One." Seoul, Korea, 1 March 1953.

Hovey, Richard D. Written recollections of Howard C. Hovey, by his son.

Inman, Richard G. Personal papers, correspondence, and poem. Courtesy of Mary Jo Inman Vermillion.

Inman, Robert E. "They Call Me Bob: An Anecdotal Biography of Robert E. Inman." Unpublished manuscript.

Intelligence debriefing statement by 2d Lt. Albert DeLaGarza following his release during "Little Switch," 25 April 1953.

Nomination of Major Billy E. Fritts for the Distinguished Service Cross, 11 August 1953. Notes for the Course in the History of Military Art. United States Military Academy, 1953.

Phillips, John W. "A Reminiscence." Unpublished written recollections.

"Recommendation for Award for Heroism" (Distinguished Service Cross) and accompanying depositions and citation. For Lt. Samuel E. Daniel, 30 July 1953.

"Recommendation for Award for Heroism" (Distinguished Service Cross) and accompanying depositions and citation. For Maj. Billy E. Fritts, 30 July 1953.

"Recommendation for Decoration for Heroism" (Distinguished Service Cross) and accompanying depositions and citation. For Lt. Col. Royal R. Taylor, 9 October 1953.

"Recommendation for Decoration for Heroism" (Distinguished Service Cross) and accompanying depositions and citation. For Lt. David Ralph Hughes, United States Army, 7th Cavalry Regiment, 11 January 1952.

"Recommendation for Decoration for Heroism" (Distinguished Service Cross) and accompanying depositions and citation. For Lt. Steven M. Wood, 23 August 1953.

"Report on Chinese Attack Against Ethiopian Positions on Outpost Yoke, 20 May 1953." 32d Infantry Regiment Battle Records Board.

Senior Officers Debriefing Program. "Conversations Between Lieutenant General Arthur Gilbert Trudeau and Colonel Calvin J. Landau." U.S. Army Military History Research Collection, vol 2. Carlisle Barracks, Pennsylvania.

Letters

Euwer, Robert M., to his wife, Barbara. 15 July 1953. Courtesy of Robert M. Euwer.

Himka, Joyce Riemann (Shea), to the author. 6, 11 March 1998.

Hollander, Herbert C., to Louis M. Davis. 6 November 1953.

Hughes, David R., to Capt. John R. Flynn. March 1952.

Inman, Barbara K., to Mr. and Mrs. Inman. 30 June, 2 July 1953. Courtesy of Mary Jo Inman Vermillion.

Inman, Richard G., to Mr. and Mrs. Inman. 27 May, 4 June, 25 June, 2 July 1953. Courtesy of Mary Jo Inman Vermillion.

Read, Lt. Col. Beverly M., to Joyce Riemann Shea. 31 August 1953, Easter 1954. Courtesy of Joyce (Shea) Himka.

Shea, Richard T., Jr., to Joyce Riemann Shea. 9, 14, 23, 29 June 1953. Courtesy of Joyce (Shea) Himka.

Vermillion, Mary Jo Inman, to the author. 6, 17 March 1998.

INDEX

access road, 130; maintenance and repair, 139; threatened by monsoon flooding, 295; monsoon and battle effects on, 279; repaired for last time, 403–4

active defense, 51–52; Trudeau's comments on, 128–29; Trudeau on improvements in ground organization, 130–32; vigorous patrolling during May, 167

Acuff, Earl C., 120, 187

Adams, Paul D., 51

Adickes, Alan, 406

Adickes, Clark, 406

aerial observation by Allied forces, 162

Affere, Arage, 177

Aleu, Addis, 184

Allied/UN combat operations, 279

Allison, William J., 242, 268–72

Almond, Edward M., 19

ambushes by Chinese and North Koreans, 141

ambush patrol, 243, 247

Anderson, Harvey "Andy," 96, 80

Anderson, Paul, 250, 251

armistice signing, 421

armored personnel carriers (APCs): during April battle, 102; Provisional Armored Personnel Carrier Platoon established, 196; Trudeau brings T-18 to 7th Division, 198–200; APCs during July battle, 279; becomes weapons platform, 285; increasing use during battle, 350

Armour, Thomas M., 392

artillery: evolution of variable timed fuse "on position," 78–80; Chinese Communist Forces' (CCF) barrages during March battle, 79; Allied supporting rounds during April battle, 121–24; CCF harassment and interdiction rounds, 141; Allied and CCF patterns of artillery support during July battle, 278–79; devastating effects of fire,

348–49; rates of fire, 356, 389; fire direction center, 406; radio discipline and security, 406–7; "Russian Roulette," 407; destruction missions against Pork Chop, 416–17; Allied supporting rounds during July battle, 417–20

Asfaw, Zeneke, 177–87

Assfaw, Andargue, 172

Atkins, George, 99

attacker–defender circumstances, intermingled and stalemated, 348–49, 350–52

awards and decorations, 134

Ayela, Bezabib, 180, 181

Bailey Bridge: built by 13th Engineers, 295–99; enemy observes construction from Old Baldy, 297; construction, 309–12

Baker, Henry, 239–42, 300–302, 371–72, 426

Baker, Richard, 259, 375

Bakker, Henry, 250–51

Balduzzi, James J., 240, 369

Ballengee, Emory, 303–5, 308

Baltes, Paul A., 406

BAR (Browning automatic rifle), 272

Baron, John L., 113–15

Barr, David G., 10, 21

Barry, Raymond N., 405–10

battle fatigue, 286, 291

Baughman, Richard A., 385–86

Beacher, Richard G., 370

Bechtel, Homer F., 99

Bergin, William E., 436–37

Bills, David L.: does special effects in film *Cease Fire,* 189; "volunteers" for and plans demolition mission, 401–3; describes explosives used in demolition, 402; leads demolition mission, 411–15; recollections of truce, 429

Bixler, Thomas M., 388

body armor, 153–54

Bratton, Joseph K., 138, 152, 297

Bray, William "Bill" G., 437–38, 440, 441

Brettell, James A.: background and assignment to Korea, 136–38; helps rebuild Pork Chop after April battle, 152; orders company to assemble dressed for battle, 295; "Bouncing Betty" mine incident, 297–98; demolition mission to Pork Chop, 411; helps get barracks named for Dan Schoonover, 450

Bridges, William H., 106

Briggs, Ellis O., 212

Brinson's Finger, 271, 302, 377

Brobst, Robert G., 324, 388

"Brockway" trucks, 299

Brooks, Charles W., 252, 286, 287

Browning automatic rifle (BAR), 272

Brubaker, Lloyd W., 242

Buford, Wallace, 458

"bug out," 5, 253, 388

bunker warfare, 55

Butcher, James N., 116–17, 429–31

Cain, Dale W.: goes to war at sixteen, 119; on Pork Chop in April, 119–20; observations of Lieutenant Shea, 244–45; radio net comes alive during CCF assault, 252; among last to leave Pork Chop, 415–16

casualties, Allied: on arrival in Pusan Perimeter, 9–10; 5th and 8th Cavalry Regiments, near Unsan, DPRK, 15; 1st Cavalry Division in Operation Commando, 30; UN casualties during first five months of truce negotiations, 37; U.S. casualties in final eighteen months of war, 39; at beginning of election year 1952, 45; during fighting in the Iron Triangle, October 1952, 47; Colombians on Old Baldy, 75; G Company, 17th Regiment, in April battle, 105; K Company, 31st Regiment, in April battle, 105, 146; E Company, 17th Regiment, in April battle, 147; enlisted men and officers, 147–48; Puerto Ricans in E Company, 17th Regiment, 150; 7th Division, June 1953, 224; C Company, 17th Regiment, in raid on Rat's Nest, 241; A and B Companies, 17th Regiment, 6–7 July, 266; wounded and dead in July battle, 280–81, 416, 435–36; in 31st Regiment, 23–24 July, 421; on outposts Dale and Westview 23–24 July, 421

casualties, Chinese Communist Forces (CCF) and North Korean People's Army (NKPA): prisoners, mid-September 1950, 11; list of POWs held by Allies 18 December 1951, 41; during fighting in the Iron Triangle, October 1952, 54; CCF during March assault on Pork Chop, 78; CCF at end of April battle, 121; estimated CCF casualties in failed 8 May assault, 165; CCF counted by Asfaw, "Incredible Patrol" leader, 186; CCF counted in Battle Records Board review of 20 May battle for Yoke, 187; U.S. Eighth Army end-June estimate of CCF casualties during limited-objective offensive, 222; at end of July battle, 416; on outposts Dale and Westview, 23–24 July, 421

Cease Fire, 189, 429

Chandler, George B., 345

Chinese Communist Forces' defensive positions, 87–88

Chinese Communist Forces' offensive operations: attempted battalion assault on Pork Chop, 6–7 March, 62; signs of, in early March, 66; assault on Pork Chop, 23 March, 76; assault on Pork Chop, 16 April, 93–94; attempted assault on Pork Chop, 8 May, 164–65; powerful offensive, 25 May, 167; limited-objective attacks beginning 11 May, 202; assaults on Yoke and Uncle, 4 June, 204; assault on Pork Chop, 6 July, 251–66; infantry and night operations in July battle, 278–79; MLR penetration at Pork Chop and Arrowhead, 314–15; preparing for final paroxysm, 381; major assault on central front, 420

Chinese intervention: indicators verify Chinese presence, 13; fighting tactics, 14; CCF intervention escalates, 15; MacArthur describes situation, 16; Allied forces fight withdrawal southward, 18

to assist France in Indochina in 1953, 457

Ess, Harry: reconnoiters Pork Chop, 289–90.

Ethiopian Battalion: attached to 7th Infantry Division, 56; the "Incredible Patrol," 167–90; soldiers' skill on trails, 175; training for 3d Battalion, 7th Division, 176; uses Capt. Juan Raigoza's artillery targeting scheme, 180–86; replaces 3d Battalion, 32d Regiment on MLR, 341

Euwer, Robert M.: forward observer, Hill 200, during March battle, 79; during April battle, 80; recalls experience with black officer, 150–51; writes 15 July letter to his wife, 423–25; recollections of truce, 427; writes home 15 July about decorations his soldiers deserved, 452

evacuation of wounded and dead, 350–52

Faith, Don, 17, 18
Far East Air Force (FEAF), 166–67
Fehrenbach, T. R., 5
Felger, Allen Craig: forward observer on Pork Chop during March battle, 78–80; awarded Distinguished Service Cross, 79

Fire Direction Center (FDC), 321, 406
1st Cavalry Division, 25–30
1st Marine Division: comes ashore at Inchon, 10; crosses the Han River, 19 September 1950, 11; evacuation at Hungnam, 19

flares, effects of, on night vision and fighting, 349

"Flash Fire": definition and description, 81; "Flash Pork Chop," 264, 269

Ford, Jerimiah, II, 444
Forton, James, 115–16
Foster, George E., 17–18
Foster, Jesse, Jr., 260, 375
Freedman, Ronald K.: forward observer on Hill 347, 405–10; wounded, walked out of aid station, 408–11; recollections of truce, 427

Fritts, Billy E.: assigned to rebuild Pork Chop, 152; coordinates fire support for withdrawal from Pork Chop, 399; uncommon valor on Hill 347, 404–7; detailed knowledge of Pork Chop

defenses and terrain, 405; death of, 408; posthumously awarded Distinguished Service Cross, 410

Garman, William R., 260
Gay, Hobart R. "Hap": commander, 1st Cavalry Division, 7; as Patton's chief of staff, 7–8; attempts to rescue 8th Cavalry Regiment, 15

Gebreheyot, Gebrasadik, 173
Gladwell, Emmett "Johnny," 251
Gonsalves, Joseph E.: former member, Company E, 17th Regiment, 148; on U.S. Army integration in Korea, 148–50

"go to ground," 253, 311
Goudy, James R.: platoon sergeant, 2d Platoon, Company A, 13th Engineer Battalion, 143; improves Pork Chop access road for night dashes to evacuation landing, 143–44; "Bouncing Betty" mine incident, 297–98; role in building Bailey Bridge, 311

Greenberg, Irwin: in assault element of ambush patrol, 6 July, 242; attempts to retrieve Dick Inman's body, 263; hears American soldier yelling, "Take cover! VTs going to come in!" 264

Greenlee, Howard, 440
Grimmet, Oral, 241, 370
Guthrie, Frank, 336
Gutner, Robert C., 73

Hackett, Harold H., 239–40
Hadley, Cordell, 343, 344–45
Haikawa, Donald, 345
Halbert, Doug, 425
Hallock, Richard R., 406
Halter, James L., 402, 413
Hardick, William L., 62
Harold, Thomas L., 30
Harris, Benjamin T.: asks Trudeau to release division reserve, Company E, 32d Regiment, 275; orders reserve units and provisional companies reconstituted, 288; orders Noble to prepare counterattack, 299

Harrison, William K., Jr.: replaces Joy as chief UN negotiator, 47; delivers letter of apology to Communist truce negotiators, 213

Harrold, Thomas U., 93

Long, Houston, 154
Lonning, Stanley N., 396
Lowe, Arthur R. "Buzz," 335, 338, 426

MacArthur, Douglas: visits Walker at
Taegu, 27 July, 8; strategic surprise at
Inchon, 10; explains intelligence fail-
ure and CCF's surprise intervention,
13; relieved of command, 22; "On
fields of friendly strife," 449; Korean
War "meant move in and shoot," 455
Malenkov, Georgi M., 50
Maliszewski, George M., 77, 97
Mann, Frederick B., 447
Marshall, Arthur A., 99
Marshall, S. L. A.: describes "Incredible
Patrol," 177–87; blunt criticism of
ambush patrols, 248
Martz, John D., Jr., 444–45
McAllister, Edward B., 324
McGovern, James, 458
McKenzie, James M.: as medic during
Rat's Nest raid, 241; supports Com-
pany A, 17th Regiment, 292; helps
wounded soldier, 292–93; crosses
access road to aid 2d Platoon, Com-
pany A, 318; in Bunker 64 tending
wounded, 373; remembers dead
stacked like cord wood, 374
McWhirter, Jackie L., 292, 307
medics, 292
Michaelis, John H. "Iron Mike," 6
military policy, 51–52
Miller, Robert E.: as rifleman, 1st Platoon,
Company A, 17th Regiment, 245;
Shea's recollections of, 245–46; "All
hell's broken loose," 251; loses right
leg to grenade, 286; left behind with
grenades, 287; wounded, rescued, and
evacuated, 317–18
Misgina, Kassa, 181
Mobile Army Surgical Hospital (MASH),
281
mortar counterbattery radar, 235
Moulte, Awilachen, 181
Mouser, Clarence H., 262
MSQ-10 radar, 235
Noble, Joseph E., Jr.: reconnoiters Pork
Chop, 289–90; plans for battalion
counterattack, 314–15; unable to con-
trol defensive units, 364–65; notes

units lack cohesion, 378; evacuation
plan, 9 July, 378
Northcutt, Robert: as squad leader and
machine gunner, Company G, 2d Battalion, 17th Regiment, 325, 331–32;
wounded by mortar fragments, 332;
receives Distinguished Service Cross,
355
North Korean Peoples Army (NKPA): *In
Min Gun,* 5; routed after Inchon landing, 11; loses 135,000 prisoners, 11–12
Novak, Anthony F., 402

Old Baldy: signs of impending CCF
attack on, 66, 68; 31st Regiment prepares to defend, 67; Kern inspects
Colombian Battalion's defensive positions, 68; Company B relieved by
Company C, Colombia Battalion, 69;
Company B, 31st Infantry, reinforces,
72; Outpost Westview's role in defending, 72–73; tanks from 73d Tank Battalion help defend, 73; counterattacks
by 1st Battalion, 32d Infantry, 73–74;
plans for counterattack after 25 March
withdrawal, 74–76; Taylor decides not
to retake, 75; strategic effects of losing, 75–76, 88–89; described by S. L.
A. Marshall, 87–88; causes increasingly serious trouble for Pork Chop,
88–89; plans for diversionary attack
on, 381–82
Operation Big Switch, 433
Operation Commando, 30
Operation Everready, 214
Operation Little Switch, 84, 125
Operation Smack, 92
Ortiz, Sigifredo, 413
outguard elements, 64–65
Outpost Alligator Jaws, 86
Outpost Arrowhead, 259, 313
Outpost Arsenal, 80
Outpost Dale: signs of impending CCF
assault on, 86; defense and counterat-
tack on, 17 April, 96–97; CCF attacks,
10 June, 208–9; CCF assaults, 23–24
July, 421
Outpost Snook, 168
Outpost Uncle, assaults on: 19–20 May,
178–87; 4 June, 204
Outpost Upper Alligator Jaw, 82–83

Korean peninsula, 210–11; historical animosity toward invaders, 211; anger over signs of impending DPRK attack, 211; agrees to stop obstructing armistice, 380; armistice signing, 421

Ridgway, Matthew B.: replaces commanders, 20; selected to replace Walker, 20; ready for offensive, 25 January 1951, 21; replaces MacArthur in Japan, 22; advocates unrelenting military pressure during truce negotiations, 23; replaces Eisenhower at NATO, 46

Robertson, Walter, 212

Robinson, Roscoe, Jr., 69–70

Robison, Bryant W., 321

Rosa-Cordero, Marcellino, 150

Ruiz-Novoa, Alberto, 67

Russell, Walter B., Jr.: commander, Company G, 2d Battalion, 17th Regiment, 100; draws his pistol on one of his soldiers, 102; takes command of Pork Chop defense, 102; "throughout the [April] battle for Pork Chop we never saw one field grade officer on the outpost," 198

Ryan, William J., 230–31

Sakasegawa, George: as BAR man, Company A, 17th Regiment, during CCF assault, 252, 258; wounded, 259; captured, 287–88; as prisoner of Chinese, 433–34

Salovich, Louis, 383, 390–92

Schaefer, Robert J., 426

Schoonover, Dan D.: background, 200–1; 30 May 1953 letter to his mother, 201; attached to Company G for counterattack, 325, 331; "I'll stay . . . some are married and have families," 388; still sleeps where he fell, 449–50

Schroeder, Peggy (Mrs. George Hess), Dan Schoonover's mother, 449

searches for lost comrades and family members, 451

searchlights, 118, 427

Seoul: falls to U.S. forces 26 September, 11; changes hands for third time, 4 January 1951, 20; demonstrations in, 203

Serchia, Paul, 335–40; carries flame thrower, 336; wounded, 339–40

17th Infantry Regiment: defends east sector of division during March battle with three battalions on line, 80; relieved of responsibility for Eirie and Arsenal defense, continues defending Pork Chop, 217

7th Infantry Division: comes ashore at Inchon, 10; joins pursuit of crumbling NKPA, 11; joins 1st Cavalry Division, 26 September, 11; tragedy at Chosin Reservoir, 17; history prior to Pork Chop battles, 52–54; principal tactical activity through 22 March 1953, 55; life on stalemated front, 55–56; strength as of 15 March 1953, 55–56; casualties increasing, 56; shortage of officers, 56; rear-area security on stabilized front, 58–59; history since landing at Inchon, 59; defends with two regiments on line, 61; front reorganized in May into three regiments on line, 162–63; May command report, 192–96

Shea, Bob (Richard's brother), 447

Shea, Joyce Elaine Riemann (Himka): expecting baby when Richard left for Korea, 160; notified by phone Richard missing in action, 422; notified by letter Richard missing in action, 436–37; Richard T. Shea III born, 438; visited by David R. Willcox, 441–42; attends West Point class of 1952 reunion for Shea Stadium dedication, 449; receives letter verifying Richard T. Shea, Jr., killed in action, 444

Shea, Richard T., Jr.: married after graduating from West Point, 160; departs for Korea, 159–60; strengthens Company A's fortifications, 209; writes letter to Joyce 9 June, 207–8; writes letter to Joyce 14 June, 209–10; names Company A's officers, 210; describes Company A's weapons platoon, 214; writes letter to Joyce 22 June, 214–15; writes letter to Joyce 29 June, 218–22; bright, shining light, 281–82; organizes twenty George Company soldiers for counterattack, 334; death of, 335; missing in action, 422; posthumous Medal of Honor and other posthumous recognition, 447–49

Shelgren, Frederick "Fritz," 336

Shivishe, Ayelow, 180–82

overrun, 270; decides to go to Pork
Chop, 288, 290–91; on "doing a George
Patton," 291; asks Clarke to commit
reserve regiment, 378; plans diversionary counterattack on Old Baldy,
380–81; planning and rationale for
withdrawal from Pork Chop, 397–98;
concerned Pork Chop would be obliterated by artillery and airpower, 416;
on psychological effect of abandoning
major outposts, 423; fires last 7th Division artillery round before truce, 427;
explains his Silver Star to Landau, 453

Trudeau, Paul R., 230–31

Truman, Harry S.: attention to cold War
divided, 4; Korean War as a strategic
diversion, 4; key cabinet decisions during first five days, 7; declares national
emergency, December 1950, 19; fears
truce negotiations will break down, 22;
advocates voluntary POW repatriation,
40, 44; administration under attack in
1952, 45–46; authorizes first seventeen
advisors to French Indochina, 457

Tully, James R., 98

24th Infantry Division, 12

Urban, Eugene, 336

U.S. Army in Korea, 4–7. *See also* specific
companies, units

U.S. Eighth Army: four divisions badly
understrength, 6, 7; first into the
ground war, 7; intelligence assessments
May 1953, 202; resumes combat
patrols, 218; intelligence assessments,
June 1953, 222; command report
expresses rationale for aggressive CCF
operations in July, 381. *See also*
specific companies, units

U.S. Military Academy class of 1950, 2

Van Fleet, James A.: replaces Ridgway as
field commander, April 1951, 22; seeks
Ridgway's guidance, 22; resumes
offensive when truce negotiations
break off in August 1951, 23; uses
Ridgway's aggressive, methodical
approach to win battles, 24; launches
Operation Commando, 25; concerned
about Eighth Army's combat readiness
during truce negotiations, 34; plan to

retake Kaesong thwarted by strafing
incident in "neutral zone," 34; incurs
Ridgway's and Truman's displeasure
over restrictions on offensive operations after Communists accept truce
line on 27 November 1951, 36–37

Van Way, George L.: commander, 32d
Regiment, 62; relieves 3d Battalion,
32d Regiment, from MLR and replaces
with Ethiopian Battalion, 341

variable time fused artillery (VT): 7th
Division infantry and artillery procedure, 79–80; "VT on position" on Pork
Chop, 6–7 July, 264; VT wounds APC
driver, 302

Vermillion, Mary Jo (Richard G. Inman's
sister): attends West Point class of 1952
reunion for Shea Stadium dedication,
449; Department of Army requests
DNA tests of, 451

VT. *See* variable time fused artillery

Waite, Nathaniel, 237

Walker, Walton H. ("Johnnie"): commander, Eighth U.S. Army, 7; concedes
holding actions north and west of
Naktong River might not succeed, 8;
MacArthur and Almond visit at Taegu,
27 July, 8; gives "stand or die" talk
to division commanders, 29 July, 9;
shrinking Pusan Perimeter easier
to defend, 9; death in jeep accident,
23 December 1950, 20

Wallis, Hal, 189

Watkins, Reginald G.: temporarily takes
command of Pork Chop's defense,
389; briefs Taylor then ordered off
Pork Chop to supervise resupply and
evacuation, 394

Watson, Raymond A., 150

weather, effects of: on combat operations,
144–45; on firing mortars, 321

Weathers, Admiral R., 437

Webb, William, 235

Wells, Obel H., 394–95

White, Richard W.: platoon leader, 3d
Platoon, Company A, 13th Engineer
Battalion, 139; solves the problem of
KSCs riding on top of T-18s, 139–40;
grades Pork Chop access road at
night, 141–42; his 3d Platoon provides

White, Richard W. *(continued)*
security during building of Bailey
Bridge, 298; helps Dietz build bridge,
309; nearly drowns in stream, 310;
helps wounded KATUSA on security
detail, 310–11; repairs access road for
last time, 403–4
White, William L., 298
Willcox, David R.,: assigned operational
control of Company B ambush patrol,
243; calls ambush patrol and outguards back into 2d Platoon, 254; two
platoons rush Willcox's sector, 255;
Company A loses contact with him,
259; makes rounds to check positions,
259; gets open back wound, 260; all
communication with company CP is
lost, 265; prepares to relieve 2d Platoon, 318–20; "hell in a small place,"

374–75; the Lord's Prayer, 375; meets
with Bray, 441; visits Joyce Shea,
441–43
Wilson, Charles E., 84
Wilson, Robert L.: background, 249;
directed by to stay behind at checkpoint during July battle, 326
Wood, Steven H., 338–40
wounded and dead, evacuation of, 350–52
Wright, Bonnie Ruth (Inman), Richard G.
Inman's sister, 451

X Corps: advance stopped by nine Chinese divisions, 16; divides into two
enclaves for evacuation, 19

Yung, Lee Kil, 240

Zegaig, George, 338

ABOUT THE AUTHOR

The author was born in Brownsville, Texas, raised in small towns in Texas, New Mexico, and Colorado, and received an appointment to the United States Military Academy at West Point, N.Y., through competitive examinations in Colorado's third congressional district. He graduated with a bachelor of science degree, and during a career of service in the Air Force, earned a masters of science in business administration from the George Washington University while attending the Air Command and Staff College at Maxwell Air Force Base, Alabama. He later attended the U.S. Army War College in Carlisle Barracks, Pennsylvania, where he completed ten months of senior management training, equivalent to a master's degree in public administration.

His Air Force service included assignments as a flight and classroom instructor in undergraduate pilot training and fighter training, a seven-month combat tour in Vietnam, where he flew 128 missions, and a United States Air Force Academy air officer commanding and flight instructor for cadets training in light aircraft. Later he served in the Republic of Korea, and at the Air Force Tactical Fighter Weapons Center in Las Vegas, Nevada. After leaving the Air Force he worked for more than eight years in various management positions in industry.

He has broad experience in interviewing, investigative research, management system evaluation and improvement, process improvement, and auditing work in both the public and private sectors. While serving in operational and management positions he conducted investigations and published reports on contentious and sensitive management, civil service, and military personnel issues and participated, in various capacities, in investigating and reporting causes of fourteen major USAF aircraft accidents. He has also negotiated government employee–union contracts, resolved trade union disputes and personnel complaints, worked with state and local governments as a major installation commander, and led and completed numerous management system analyses, evaluations, and audits.

His writing includes an eleven-hundred page Korean War history and true story, *A Return to Glory: The Untold Story of Honor, Dishonor, and Triumph at the United States Military Academy, 1950–53*, as well as articles, columns, and letters published in California and Texas newspapers, *VFW Magazine*, base and company newspapers, a variety of Air Force safety publications, and fraternal and professional organization newsletters.

He and his wife, Ronnie, married the day after he graduated from the Military Academy and live in Las Vegas. They have three grown children, who reside with their families in Boise, Idaho.